DATE DUE

Revolutionary France 1770–1880

FRANÇOIS FURET

Translated by
Antonia Nevill

BLACKWELL
Oxford UK & Cambridge USA

Copyright © Hachette, 1988
English translation copyright © Basil Blackwell, 1992

The right of François Furet to be identified as author of this work has been asserted in accordance with the Copyright, Designs and Patents Act 1988.

First published 1988

English translation first published 1992
Reprinted 1993
First published in paperback 1995

Blackwell Publishers Ltd
108 Cowley Road
Oxford OX4 1JF
UK

Blackwell Publishers Inc.
238 Main Street
Cambridge, Massachusetts 02142
USA

British Library Cataloguing in Publication Data

A CIP catalogue record for this book is available from the British Library.

Library of Congress Cataloging-in-Publication Data

Furet, François, 1927–
  [Révolution. English]
  Revolutionary France 1770–1880 / François Furet; translated by Antonia Nevill.
     p.   cm. — (History of France)
  Includes bibliographical references.
  Translation of: La Révolution.
  ISBN 0–631–17029–4 (hbk) — ISBN 0–631–19808–3 (pbk)
  1. France—History—Revolution, 1789–1799.   2. France—History—19th century.   3. France—History—Revolution, 1789–1799—Influence.   I. Series.
  DC148.F8713   1992
  944.04—dc20
                                                                91-47098
                                                                CIP

Typeset in 10½ on 12 pt Plantin by Best-Set Typesetter Ltd., Hong Kong
Printed in Great Britain by T. J. Press Ltd., Padstow, Cornwall.

This book is printed on acid-free paper.

Contents

List of Illustrations

The French Revolution is such an extraordinary event that it must serve as the starting-point for any systematic consideration of the affairs of our own times. Everything of importance which takes place in France is a direct consequence of this fundamental event, which has profoundly altered the conditions of life in our country.

Ernest Renan, 'Constitutional Monarchy in France', *Revue des Deux Mondes*, 1 November 1869.

The translator gratefully acknowledges the expert guidance on historical terminology and the invaluable textual clarifications given by Professor Norman Hampson.

Foreword

The French Revolution began in 1789, but there is no clear date for its end. It has no American-style definitive close like the 1787 constitution, which became the sacred ark of the nation. Nor does it claim to live on indefinitely, in Soviet fashion, but it falls somewhere between the two extremes. Like the American Revolution, and at almost the same epoch, its desire was to found, within the law, a body politic of free and equal individuals; but the French Revolution was continually revising the terms of the undertaking, deferring its final outcome or success, and so reproducing *ad infinitum* the fear that it had been dispossessed.

One can trace a short-term history of its course, stopping at the fall of Robespierre or the arrival of Bonaparte. The method I have chosen in this book is, by contrast, to write an extended version, spread over the hundred years and more between Turgot and Gambetta. The central theme is that only the victory of republicans over monarchists in 1876–7 provided modern France with a regime that established in lasting form the full range of the principles of 1789 ensuring not only civic equality but also political liberty. Thus I have attempted to encompass and depict the first century of democracy in France.

This falls into two great cycles, widely commented upon in the nineteenth century. The first covers the French Revolution (in the narrow sense), from the *ancien régime* to the Napoleonic Empire. It comprises the successive forms of public authority which made up the catalogue of French political struggles: the Bourbon dynasty, the constitutional monarchy, the Jacobin dictatorship, the parliamentary Republic, Bonapartism. The last managed to implant the revolutionary heritage in a centralized administrative state, and thus to 'close' the Revolution.

In 1814, however, the Empire, vanquished by a European coalition, inaugurated a second chain of events through which the first began anew, in fresh circumstances, but still haunted by the memory of what had happened before. Not only did *ancien régime* and Revolution again confront each other, but equally opposed were the traditional sources of conflict born of the Revolution itself: 1789 and 1793, the Rights of Man and Jacobinism, liberty and equality, representative government and Bonapartism.

The restored Bourbons fell in 1830 because it was thought they aimed to bring back the *ancien régime*. The July monarchy foundered in 1848 in its attempt to restrict the vote for the benefit of the few. The Second Republic for a brief moment regained the democratic brotherhood of the Festival of the Federation, but had to crush a popular rising in June 1848 before leaving the two royalist traditions to fight it out with Bonaparte's nephew.

Even that sequence of French history which had been thought unique, linked to an incomparable man and exceptional times – the Empire – reappeared for twenty years, without war, heroes, military glory, victorious generals, merely through the power of memory. The defeat of 1870 brought a new Parisian revolution, followed by a final attempt to restore the Bourbons. This was a dual failure which opened the way to the lasting victory of the French Revolution, in a republican version which finally won the acceptance of the country.

However, between the two cycles of this long period lies an essential difference. At the end of the eighteenth century, the Revolution smashed the entire structure of the *ancien régime*. In the nineteenth century, the prefects survived the revolutions. The country's administrative constitution, dating from the Consulate, stood throughout the whole era like an inviolable monument. Thus, in its own way, the centralized state ensured the continuity of public authority and national unity; but at the same time it constantly intensified post-revolutionary civil struggles over the 1789 heritage. Being the vital centre of the nation, it had only to seize control to become the master of society. Paradoxically, the points on which the French were in agreement only inflamed their differences; the conservative in them was also the revolutionary, bound by a common conception of the state. This is exactly what we learn from de Tocqueville, when he remarks that Napoleon 'by constructing this powerful hierarchy . . . suddenly made revolutions easier for us, yet at the same time less destructive'.[1]

By establishing the state, through universal suffrage in the name of the equality of its citizens, the republicans of the 1870s managed to entrench the law on a lasting basis in the sovereignty of the people. Thus they at last completed the task begun in 1789.

---

[1] Alexis de Tocqueville, *L'Ancien Régime et la Révolution*, *Oeuvres complètes*, part II, vol. 2, p. 274, note.

PART I

The French Revolution

I

The *Ancien Régime*

The French revolutionaries gave a name to what they had abolished. They christened it the *ancien régime*. In doing so they were defining not so much what they had suppressed, but more what they wanted to create – a complete break with the past, which was to be cast into the shadows of barbarism. Of the past itself, its nature and its history, the revolutionaries said scarcely more than the imprecatory phrase they used to decribe it, a phrase which was coined very early, at the end of the summer of 1789: the Abbé Sieyès, in his noted January pamphlet of the same year, had already made a sweeping condemnation of that 'night', as opposed to the day which was just dawning.

The notion of a past entirely corrupted by usurpation and irrationality was surely one of the paths by which his pamphlet, *Qu'est-ce que le Tiers Etat?* (What is the Third Estate?) penetrated public opinion so rapidly and so deeply. So the historian studying the history of France in the second half of the eighteenth century, some decades before the Revolution, can find a way in by means of this question about the term *ancien régime*: what did the men of 1789 understand by it? What sort of past did they have in mind, to damn it so utterly? That regime which they believed they were extirpating – how long had it lasted and who had begun it? The enigmatic strangeness of the French *tabula rasa*, which so disconcerted and angered the British whig parliamentarian, Edmund Burke, in 1790, can still serve as an introduction to the later years of eighteenth-century France.

As of old, the king of France was an absolute monarch. The adjective means that he enjoyed the *summa potestas* defined by Jean Bodin: he was not subject to the laws, since he was their originator. Supreme power, which may be exercised by the people (democracy), or by the few (aristocracy), in France had found its supreme upholder in the monarchy since the very dawn of the nation. The king was the fountainhead of all public authority, all magistracy, all legislation. His *dignitas* that is to say, both his office and his function, was immortal, received on the death of his predecessor and transmitted to his successor, transcending the mortal nature of his private person. For that lifelong possession of the highest authority in the land he was accountable to God alone, the true source of all human law. Thus behind the power of kings, however absolute, lay the essential constraint of an even greater power – infinitely great – beside which even monarchs were as nothing. This of itself entailed the obligation to behave as a Christian sovereign.

The respect for divine law, however, was not the only law to which the king of France had to submit, for all that he was absolute monarch and not bound by any human law. Over the centuries something had developed which it is perhaps too much to call a constitution, or even a body of doctrine, yet which appears in retrospect as a set of custom-based principles, untouchable and inalienable: primogeniture, the Catholic faith of the sovereign, respect for the liberty and property of his subjects, the integrity of the royal domain. Above the law, yet subject to law, the king of France was no tyrant: the French monarchy, a state based on law, must not be confused with despotism, which is the unfettered power of a master. Nevertheless, despotism was monarchy's temptation, as Montesquieu explained; to degenerate, it needed only to ignore the established body of laws.

Did this traditional concept change in the eighteenth century, at the zenith of state power? Not basically. Under Louis XIV it had noticeably shifted towards deification of the king himself. Starting from the idea of the divine origin of his power, the *Grand Roi* had instigated, or allowed to be formed about his person, a cult which was at the heart of court civilization at Versailles. Many other elements entered into it, besides the old monarchic doctrine, and the attribution of divinity to the king soon became a factor in the enfeeblement of royalty, as would be seen in his successors; unlike their illustrious ancestor, neither Louis XV nor Louis XVI was able to bear the weight of a burden which had become inseparable from their private persons.

From being the means of ceremonial acclamation, the court under their reigns became a battlefield for malicious cliques, spurred on by the atmosphere of the times. However, the idea of a king as the sole repository of sovereignty, in keeping with ancient tradition, and the concept of a monarchy both absolute and enshrined in custom, in the view of the king and his lawyers had undeniably survived absolutist exaggeration.

Evidence of this lies in Louis XV's famous text, declaimed in 1766 before the parlement of Paris, condemning the aspirations of the kingdom's judicial high courts to monitor or even have a share in royal authority:

To attempt to establish such pernicious innovations as principles is to affront the magistrature, to betray its interests and to ignore the true, fundamental laws of the state, as if it were permissible to disregard the fact that in my person alone lies that sovereign power whose very nature is the spirit of counsel, justice and reason. From me alone the courts receive their existence and authority. The fullness of this

Hyacinthe Rigaud Louis XV in coronation robes, *Musée Versailles, Paris.*
(Photo: Lauros-Giraudon)

authority, which they exercise in my name only, remains permanently vested in me, and its use can never be turned against me. Legislative power is mine alone, without subordination or division. It is by my sole authority that the officers of my courts effect, not the creation of the law, but its registration, promulgation and execution, and that they have the right of remonstrance, as is the duty of good and faithful counsellors. Public order in its entirety emanates from me. I am its supreme guardian. My people are one with me, and the rights and interests of the nation – which some dare to make into a body separate from the monarch – are of necessity united with my own and rest entirely in my hands.

This speech was composed by the king's counsellors to be read out solemnly at that famous session known as the 'Flagellation', but who among Louis XV's predecessors would not have claimed it for his own?

However, the nature of royalty changed more rapidly than its image. Dominated by wars, always short of money, the monarchy, while taking care to keep a tight hold on the reins, continued to spread an administrative network throughout the country in order to mobilize men and wealth more effectively. Gradually it placed alongside the pyramid of feudal vassalages from which it had derived its first principle the authority of a sovereign set at the heart of a more or less centralized administration capped by a council of ministers. The core of this system, progressively built up from the end of the fifteenth century, was constituted by levying direct taxation, organized by the Controller-General of Finance with the help of administrators appointed for the task, each within his own *généralité* – the *intendants*. Originally vested with a sort of judicial high office, the king had become the head of a government; lord of lords, he was also chief of a burgeoning bureaucracy.

The two roles, far from being incompatible, were superimposed; but the second was characteristic of absolutism and gained its classic image in the seventeenth century: Colbert, Louis XIV's Controller-General, is its most illustrious symbol. The leading specialist on this subject, Michel Antoine,[1] places the transition from the judicial state to the financial state in 1661, at the beginning of the personal reign of Louis XIV. At the precise moment when the king formed the focal point of his vast personal theatre, known as the court, he simultaneously became the most elevated person in the huge, abstract machinery of administration. He still reigned over his kingdom as possessor of the immortal *dignitas* which had surrounded his ancestors, but now as head of the state as well. The second part of his office overlapped the first the more easily because absolutism, in making a cult of royalty, tended to weaken its traditional image, while it firmly established the institution in the fulfilment of its modern functions.

However, the chief innovation of this development lay in its effects on society. On the one hand, it certainly tended towards the levelling off of an aristocratic world inherited from feudal times. For the top civil servants of the monarchy, symbolized by Colbert, had been constantly irritated by the

---

[1] M. Antoine, *Le Conseil du roi sous le règne de Louis XIV*.

obstacles raised against royal administration by privileges on all sides; the reasoning behind their action aimed at uniting the nation into so many individuals all bound by the same laws, the same regulations and the same taxes.

It was not enough that the monarchy had gradually deprived the aristocracy of its political rights, nibbled away at its judicial powers, rendered useless that protective function which had characterized the feudal period; it was not enough that it had reduced the greatest families in the kingdom to begging for a glance from the king at Versailles: it had to exercise over all the bodies and orders in the realm, starting with the nobility, a standardizing process which in this case was inseparable from the formation of the nation. On the other hand, at the very time when it was seeking uniformity, the administrative monarchy multiplied the obstacles to it; here lay what is without doubt its chief contradiction.

In fact, the kings of France did not build and extend their power over a passive society; on the contrary, they had to negotiate each increase in it – for example, the famous 'extraordinary' taxes, so called because they were new – with a social world organized on the aristocratic principle, in orders and bodies arranged in hierarchies. Holding entirely new offices, assuming an unprecedented role, the king also remained the highest lord on the feudal pyramid, in accordance with tradition.

His need for money was immense. To obtain the means of carrying on the interminable war for supremacy waged against the Habsburgs, the Bourbons – and before them the Valois – had raised money from all possible sources. They had gradually set up a centralized administration to levy the *taille* (a direct tax on commoners), and soon afterwards a poll tax, to try to increase the kingdom's wealth; they had leased out to the Farmers General a host of indirect taxes. But taxation was not enough to meet requirement. The monarchy also made money from the privileges and 'liberties' (the two words have the same sense) of various social bodies.

Privilege consisted of the particular rights of certain bodies in relation to society as a whole; tax exemption for the bourgeois of a town, rules of co-optation of a guild, exemptions from common law conferred by tenure of an office, advantages attached to noble rank – the sources were numerous. If some were lost in the mists of antiquity, the majority were not so old; the monarchic state had generally renegotiated the form of ancient privileges, or invented and constantly remodelled the terms of recent 'liberties'.

The mechanism was simple. Driven by the pressing need for money, the monarchy raised loans through one or more of the bodies in the realm: the order of clergy, the city government of Paris or the Company of the King's Secretaries. If the body in question did not have all the necessary money available, it had to raise it by pledging its assets, which consisted chiefly of the market value of the exclusive advantages which it enjoyed, defined by the office held by each of its members. In return, the king again guaranteed those privileges, if need be extending them, even if, ten or twenty years later, the principle was once more threatened so that the king could procure a fresh supply of money through a renegotiation of the advantages granted. The whole of the society of orders (which could also be termed aristocratic society) thus played the role of a vast bank for the government, in the absence of a state bank (only the English had had one since the beginning of the eighteenth century); but because of this it underwent a profound transformation.

The monarchy had thus sold off a portion of public power, included in a good number of those offices – for example, those involving the exercise of justice. The institution itself was old, but hereditary ownership of public offices dated only from the seventeenth century, and from then on the sales of those posts had proliferated, in step with the king's need for money, starting from the Thirty Years War. The most elevated, and therefore the most expensive, of them gave access to the nobility within one or two generations, on terms which varied according to the price.

Thus, alongside the *intendant*, an appointed and dismissible functionary, the kings had built up a body of state servants who owned their own offices. This was a double-edged sword, for though the massive sale of offices allowed the acquisition of the beneficiaries' cash – chiefly that of wealthy commoners – and simultaneously bound to the destiny of the state a new and powerful group of office-holders, dominated by the parlements, it also presented a twofold disadvantage.

First, all these officials enjoyed the independence conferred by ownership, even if from time to time they had to renegotiate the price with the king; since they were not dismissible, they could, should the day come, resist the king – mainly with the help of the right of remonstrance used by the parlements when required to register a royal edict which did not meet with their approval. Second, and more important, on another plane, ennoblement for money introduced into aristocratic society a principle which was as foreign to it as the admission into the nobility, at the will of the king, of senior civil servants of the administrative state: if nobility depended on the hazards of fortune or the will of the King, what was it and what would become of it?

There is no better record of that question bedevilling the inner core of the second order of the kingdom than the memoirs of the Duc de Saint-Simon. French nobility had ceased to be a sort of English-style gentry, with access from below for newcomers by custom, provided they had acquired a seigniory. On the one hand, its members had to cross a legal frontier, held by the administrative monarchy, if they were to be accepted. On the other, they were thereafter subject to the rule of *dérogeance* (losing rank and title), which excluded them from the majority of professions. In short, the nobility was a body defined by the state, which kept a register of its members, and by a set of privileges, both honorific and actual – of which the former were no less coveted, since they conferred the right of entry to the theatre of social distinctions.

The administrative monarchy was therefore an unstable compromise

between the construction of a modern state and an aristocratic society
remodelled by that state. On the one hand, it continued slyly to subvert
the traditional social fabric by levelling its ranks under general submission
to a sole authority, and breaking up the hierarchies of birth and tradition,
which were by then reduced to the mere enjoyment of exemptions or
honours. On the other hand, it separated the orders of society into castes
by converting them into cash, weighing each privilege at its highest price,
and creating out of an *esprit de corps* a passion for separateness.

At the summit of the edifice, the monarchy alone decreed who was noble
and who was not: every candidate had to forget his origins, abandon all
commercial or industrial activity, in order to be simply a privileged person
– designated as such on the separate registers of fiscal administration –
before he could hope one day to gain for his family the attention of the
king's genealogists.

This evolution was probably essential in the formation of what could be
termed 'national spirit': even after the Revolution and equality, Bonaparte
would use as one of the mainsprings of his dominance what he, anticipating Stendhal, would call the 'vanity' of the French. The example had
come from the *ancien régime* nobility, who were defined by what separated
them from the body of society, taking as their very essence what 1789
would turn into the principle of their exclusion. To understand how the
French monarchy had uprooted the nation's nobility before the Revolution
drove them out, one should read the admirable ninth chapter of Book II of
de Tocqueville's *L'Ancien Régime*, which is perhaps the most profound
chapter in that profound book: it contains virtually everything.

The eighteenth century had aggravated the tensions of this mixed system
of absolute monarchy and aristocratic society. The death of Louis XIV in
1715, after an interminable reign, had restored independence to society.
The Regent had encouraged the movement. None of the Great King's
successors was in a position to control even the court, let alone Paris.
Everything conspired to enfeeble them: intellectual activity, the growth
of wealth, the emergence of public opinion. However, the old French
monarchy, simultaneously very ancient and very new, that of the Valois
and that of the Bourbons, remained for a long time the centre of a
matchless civilization.

It was no longer what it had been in the preceding century, the precarious means of mobilizing national resources to wage an almost permanent war against the Habsburgs; it inherited the progress accomplished
under Louis XIV, not the constraints which the latter had demanded
or accepted. Its offices were run by a small army of civil servants and
technicians, often trained, from the start of the second half of the century,
in special schools created for the purpose – for example, the schools of civil
and mining engineering.

At the same time, specific sets of administrative regulations had been
developed, through the concept of privilege applied to the state and its
servants – a significant reversal which extended the particular scope of

individual rights to the whole of the machinery of state, emancipating the king's officials in the name of public interest. Administrative affairs received their own rules, sanctioned by their own jurisdictions, crowned by the king's Council. The modern state was being formed.

With the spirit of the century assisting, it could devote more care and money to the great tasks of the new age – town building, public health, agricultural and commercial development, market unification, education. Henceforth, the *intendant* was well and truly in command, outranking the traditional authorities and with a finger in every pie. He was at the centre of a vast effort for knowledge and administrative reform, proliferating economic and demographic enquiries, rationalizing his actions with the help of the first social statistics on a national scale in French history. He wrested from the clergy and the nobility almost all their remaining functions in local supervision; even elementary education, that old private hunting-ground of the Church, came increasingly under his thumb, and threatened to develop in a way which disturbed many of the *philosophes*, who were concerned at the thought of seeing rural labours abandoned by all these future educated Frenchmen. Far from being reactionary, or imprisoned by self-interest, the monarchic state in the eighteenth century was one of the foremost agents of change and progress – a permanent building-ground for 'enlightened' reform.

THE NOBILITY

At the same time, however, the state remained bound to the social compromise carefully developed over the preceding centuries, and was rendered the more powerless to affect the society of orders because by its actions it was completely destroying the spirit of that society. The latter was falling apart under the joint pressure of economic improvement, the increasing number of individual initiatives and aspirations and the spread of culture. Money and merit were coming up against 'birth'; in their path they found the state, guaranteeing privileges.

By ennoblement, by selling off the most coveted positions, that state continued to integrate into the second order of the realm the commoners who had served it best – above all, those who had made the most money, often in its service (for example in financial posts) – but by doing so it dangerously exposed its authority. In fact, the 'old' nobility (not only that of the Middle Ages, which was relatively rare, but also that dating from the sixteenth and seventeenth centuries), often less wealthy than the recently ennobled, felt a great sense of resentment and insisted on elevating true distinction to the celebrated four quarterings (that is, four generations of nobility), which would define true 'blue blood'.

As for the new nobles, they behaved like all newcomers in this kind of system: hardly had they squeezed through the narrow gate when their first thought was to close it behind them, since a proliferation of beneficiaries would devalue what they had just acquired. Thence sprang that French mania for rank, which resounded from top to bottom of society and doubtless gave rise, by reaction, to the surge of revolutionary egalitarianism. Under the *ancien régime*, the state became inseparable from this nexus of passions and personal interests, since it was the power which distributed rank and title, and far too parsimoniously, for an expanding society. All it succeeded in doing was to alienate 'its' nobility, without ever having the means to organize a ruling class in the English manner.

Everything points to this crisis in the eighteenth-century French nobility, though not in the sense in which it is usually understood. For the nobles were not a group – or a class – in decline. Nobility had never been so brilliant; never had civilization been so 'aristocratic' as in the time of the Enlightenment, and specially marked at this point by the adaptation of fine court manners to the conversation of the salons. Established on vast land ownership (though infinitely less extensive than that of the English gentry), often associated with huge trading concerns and owning interests in the management of the king's finances, the rich nobility embodied the prosperity of the era.

But the nobility as an order of society never managed to adjust its relations with the state. With the wane of its traditional powers, it had lost the essence of its *raison d'être*, and never succeeded in redefining its political vocation within the framework of the administrative monarchy. At the death of Louis XIV, three potential destinies lay before it: to become a 'Polish' nobility, hostile to the state, nostalgic for its old rights of jurisdiction, ready for the reconquest of a golden age; a 'Prussian' nobility, associated with an enlightened despotism, a class of dedicated administrative or military service linked to immense land ownership, the backbone of the national state; or, finally, an 'English' nobility, controlling the House of Lords, but together with the Commons making a constitutional monarchy – a parliamentary aristocracy of a much wider political class to which money provided open access.

However, French nobles had espoused none of those alternatives; the state had not offered them the opportunity. The first was hopeless, a backward-looking dream of a lost identity; in France it had nurtured a certain nobiliary anarchism, never a policy. The second was scarcely compatible with a rich and developed civil society, a nobility owning only a quarter of the land and made up of officials who owned their own offices. It is significant that this course had often been advocated by poor minor nobles – the very ones in whose favour the monarchy had designed preferential treatment in the army, with the opening of special military schools (1776).

One has only to look at the outcry raised in 1781 by the Marquis de Ségur's ordinance reserving officer grade in certain regiments for young nobles with four quarterings to realize the unsuitability of a 'Prussian' solution to the French situation. As for the 'English' answer, it was quite simply incompatible with the very principle of absolute monarchy, since it

Joseph Siffrein Duplessis Jacques Necker, *1791, Musée Versailles, Paris.*
(*Photo: Lauros-Giraudon*)

presupposed a sharing of sovereignty. Moreover, in the parlements for example, where the idea was to some extent developed, there existed also an ardent defence of French-style aristocratic society, based on privilege. An English kind of nobility supposed at least the end of tax exemptions; that was a minimum requirement for the constitution of a dominant class based on wealth, and the condition for that landowners' monarchy which was desired in such different quarters – two very different financial administrators, Turgot and Necker, for once in accord.

There lay the origins of the social and political crisis of eighteenth-century France, giving rise to a part of the French Revolution and its prolongation into the nineteenth century. Neither the French king nor the nobility put forward a policy which might unite state and ruling society around a minimum consensus: because of that, royal action oscillated between despotism and capitulation. Chiefly on the crucial question of taxation, which aroused the interests and passions of all: each man's place in society, and each man's conception of that place were simultaneously at stake. But if the state was unable to point the way, because of the host of ties by which it had bound itself to corporate society, the nobles were equally impotent, since they had lost their identity together with their social autonomy. They had but one principle left to reunify them: to defend their privileges in the name of a collective personality whose secret they had lost and whose memory or legend they had no other way of reviving.

Thus Louis XIV had been able to control the process of promotion and unification of elites within a society divided into orders, and had turned it into one of the foundations for building the state. Louis XV had no longer managed to do so, and Louis XVI even less. They were constantly torn between the demands of the administrative state and their solidarity with aristocratic society. Not only did they carry that loyalty in their blood, as descendants of the most illustrious family in French nobility, which had reigned over the kingdom for so many centuries; they had also mingled it with something more modern, related to both sentiment and necessity – for aristocratic society, since the end of the sixteenth century, had largely been the work of the Bourbons. It was they who had built the modern state on the sale of offices, privileges, status and rank; how could their descendants go back on the word of their predecessors? In any case, how could they materially do without privileges, which formed the resources of their kingdom? That was what Chancellor Maupeou had gambled on in his attempted reform in 1771, in the last years of Louis XV: could the King, in the name of the state's authority, go back on what he had guaranteed?

Thus the kings of France passed their time in yielding now to some, now to others, wavering between the clans and cliques of the court, the *philosophes* and the *dévots*, the Jansenists and the Jesuits, the physiocrats and the mercantilists. They tried successive policies, but never followed them through; they upheld Machault, then Choiseul, Maupeou then Turgot. Each time, the action of the state aroused hostility from one or other part of the ruling groups, without ever welding them together, either in favour of an enlightened despotism *à la* Maupeou, or of a liberal reformism *à la* Turgot. These eighteenth-century elites were at the same time close to the government, yet in revolt against it. In reality, they settled their internal differences to the detriment of absolutism.

Even the crisis of 1789 would be powerless to rebuild their unity, save in the imagination of Third Estate ideologists: neither the outbreak of the Revolution, through what historians call the 'aristocratic revolt', nor the revolutionary behaviour of several noble members of the Constituent Assembly, nor the work itself of the Assembly is intelligible without reference to the crisis between the monarchy and the nobility in the eighteenth century. If the French Revolution – like all revolutions – met with such poorly co-ordinated resistance at its start, it was because the political *ancien régime* had died before it was struck down. It had died of isolation and because it could no longer find any political support within 'its' nobility, although the latter was more than ever at the centre of its vision of society.

THE ENLIGHTENMENT

If that is how things were in the government of the kingdom, what can be said of the intellectual sphere? The society which the monarchy had fragmented was united by the culture of the century: public opinion was burgeoning in the twilight of the court and in the birth of a formidable power – which would last until universal suffrage was achieved – the omnipotence of Paris. The nobles of both Versailles and the capital read the same books as the cultured bourgeoisie, discussed Descartes and Newton, wept over the misfortunes of Prévost's Manon Lescaut, enjoyed Voltaires *Lettres philosophiques*, d'Alembert's *Encyclopédie* or Rousseau's *Nouvelle Héloïse*.

The monarchy, the orders, the guilds, had separated the elites by isolating them in rival strongholds. In contrast, ideas gave them a meeting-point, with special privileged place: the salons, academies, Freemasons' lodges, societies, cafés and theatres had woven an enlightened community which combined breeding, wealth and talent, and whose kings were the writers. An unstable and seductive combination of intelligence and rank, wit and snobbery, this world was capable of criticizing everything, including and not least itself; it was unwittingly presiding over a tremendous reshaping of ideas and values.

As if by chance, the ennobled nobility, in the legal profession and particularly in finance, played a vital part. They threw a bridge between the world from which they had come and the one in which they had arrived; an additional testimony to the strategic importance of that grave-yard area of society, groping – with that slightly masochistic irony born of a dual awareness of its strangeness and its success – for something which resembled neither of those worlds.

The new intellectual realm was the workshop where the notion of *ancien régime* would be forged, although it did not employ that term before the Revolution. What characterized it in the political field, quite apart from its philosophical and literary brilliance, was in fact the scale and the forceful-ness of the condemnation it brought to bear on contemporary life – including the Church and religion. There was a violently anticlerical and anti-Catholic side to the philosophy of the French Enlightenment which had no equivalent in European thought.

Take, for example, Voltaire and Hume: of the two, Voltaire was probably not the more irreligious, as he was a deist and at least regarded
religion as indispensable to the social order. But though Hume discredited
rational proofs of God's existence, including that of First Cause, so dear to
Voltaire, there was in his philosophical discourse none of the antireligious
aggressiveness to be found in the sage of Ferney. Hume lived at peace with
the diversity of Protestant churches, whereas the Frenchman made war on
the Catholic Church.

France had had her religious wars, but no victorious Reformation. On
the contrary, absolutism had extirpated Calvinism by brute force: the Edict
of Nantes had given toleration to Protestants for nearly a century; its
revocation in 1685 consecrated the king in his role of protector of the
Catholic Church, and the Church as indissolubly bound to the king. The
French movement of the Enlightenment has been little studied in the light
of its debt to that very recent past. Nevertheless, in a France brought back
to Catholicism by religious intolerance and royal power, the Church and
the absolute monarchy together had formed an almost natural target for the
attacks of a 'philosophy' which was all the more radical for not being built,
as in England, on the foundation of a previous religious revolution.

Moreover, that independent religious revolution had still sought an
identity, within Catholicism this time, in the form of Jansenism: a new
emphasis on the miracle of divine Grace in a world given over to sin. But
the Jansenism of solitary recluses engaged in meditation on Grace had
probably contributed to the isolation of the Church in old French society;
it had been too insistent on the difficulty of the asceticism which was
indispensable to the sinner wishing to receive the sacraments, and too
sharply condemned so many ministers of religion, Jesuits first and foremost. Also, the Jansenist movement itself in the eighteenth century had
been taken up and made subordinate to politics. It had become Gallican
and *parlementaire*, the banner which united lowly folk and great judges
against the Church, and often against the king, in the name of the rights of
the nation.

The transformation of this French-style belated Protestantism into a
movement for national liberties says a great deal about the secularization of
the public mentality. In the sixteenth century, politics had been completely
enveloped in religion; in the eighteenth, even currents of opinion with a
religious origin were absorbed by the debate on the state, in opposition to
the absolutism of the king and his ally, the Church. It is certainly true that
the Revolution, at the end of the century, did not deliberately seek conflict
with the Catholic Church; but many elements of the century's culture had
borne it in that direction, and it had taken that path as if naturally,
without, however, having decided to do so or weighed the consequences.

Together with the Church, the other great culprit was the absolute
monarchy, which was incapable of appearing before the court of reason.
Not the monarchy per se, because nobody could imagine a republic in a
large country, but that particular monarchy, encumbered with 'gothic'

prejudices, the distributor of arbitrary privileges, reigning over a kingdom filled with vestiges of feudalism. It mattered little that France was in reality the least feudal country in Europe, as a result of the very activities of the administrative state, and that it was also the country where criticism of the state by reason was the most systematic: suddenly the remains of feudalism – for example, seigniorial rights, or the last serfs in the kingdom – were perceived as all the more oppressive precisely because they were residual.

Features which came after feudalism – privileges bestowed by the king in return for the loan of money, the corporate structure of society, a nobility largely uprooted from the land and defined by the state, for instance – were included in the overall condemnation of that historical monster; not only a 'feudal monarchy' (already it was difficult to think of these two aspects in conjunction), but on top of that an 'administrative despotism'. The incoherent character of the definition at least has the merit of highlighting the nature of the accusation.

Royalty, which was too modern for what it had preserved and refashioned of the traditional, and too traditional for what it already had in the way of modern administration, tended to turn itself into the scapegoat for an increasingly independent society, which was nevertheless still bound hand and foot to the government, deprived of political rights and representation, trying to work out its autonomy in terms of government by reason.

That royalty reaffirmed its familiar image, or its mystery – the incarnation of the nation by the king. In 1766, for example, in the famous 'Flagellation' sitting cited earlier, Louis XV had appeared before the parlement in order to bring discredit on what was already being termed 'opinion': he let it be understood that public discussion had no place except within the body of the monarchy, which he represented in his person, alone having the power to create unity from the patchwork of private privileges.

In actual fact, the monarchy had lost its authority over opinion: it no longer obtained consent for its actions, or imposed its arbitration on the burning questions of the hour – the struggle of Jansenists and parlements with the Church, fiscal reform, and disputes about the grain trade. Paris, especially, produced an ever-increasing number of pamphlets and debates, dominated by the writers, orchestrated by the salons and cafés. The centralization effected by the royal administration had its bureaucratic heart at Versailles, near to the king, but had also turned Paris into the only arena of public discussion.

For want of a representational system implanted in the provinces, opposition to the Versailles bureaucracy became centralized in nearby Paris; by not associating the elites of the city with the government of the kingdom, it transformed the literary life of the capital into a forum for the reform of the state. Moreover, the Crown followed the trend; it too bought defenders, paid writers, financed pamphlets and argued its cause before the new tribunal.

From the middle of the century, and even more so in the last years of
Louis XV's reign, the most important term was 'opinion'. The semantic
derivation of this word is significant. Starting from the classic definition
given in the *Encyclopédie* (Latin *opinio* (Greek *doxa*) as opposed to true
knowledge), ten or twenty years later the noun came to designate something very different: a counterbalance to despotism, developed by men of
letters. 'Opinion' was more generally produced by the activity of society,
its development, its growing wealth, its *lumières* – a constant theme in
fin-de-siècle France, to be systematically developed on the other side of the
Channel by Scottish economists and philosophers.

It constituted a public tribunal, in contrast with the secrecy of the king;
it was universal, in contrast with the particularism of 'feudal' laws; and
objective, in contrast with monarchic arbitrariness: in short, a court of
appeal of reason, judging all matters of state, in the name of public interest
alone. It was a means of getting away from a society of orders and guilds
without falling into the disarray of private interests and factions. Well
before the Revolution, this idea transferred the features of royal sovereignty to a new authority, also unique, which was an exact copy of the
monarchic idea: on the ruins of feudal monarchy, it had only to build a
monarchy of reason. It was in this transfer that a revolution took place.

PROJECTS FOR REFORM

Nevertheless, in the last four years of his life, between 1770 and 1774,
Louis XV, at the age of sixty, engaged in the decisive battle of his reign,
and probably of the last monarchic century. He wanted to crush the
parlements, regain the initiative and his authority, and rebuild the unity of
the nation around the throne. The campaign began in January 1771,
through Maupeou – a theorist of royal authority. The son of a chancellor
who had presided over the Parlement of Paris, president himself until
1768, the new chancellor had the clear-sightedness and relentless determination of all who have changed sides. This learned and hard-working
little man's office became his driving passion. In order to crush attempts
by the parlements to monitor royal power on the pretext of the right
of remonstrance, Maupeou forbade them to have any contact with one
another, or to go on strike. The result was a refusal to register new laws,
lits de justice, fresh remonstrances.

In January 1771 came a trial of strength: 130 Parisian representatives
were exiled, and the entire legal profession went on strike. Maupeou
retaliated in February with a general reorganization of the judiciary
system: five upper councils were thenceforth given the task of dealing with
all civil and criminal matters in the immense jurisdiction of the parlement
of Paris, the parlement being confined to its right of registration and
remonstrance. Above all – and these were major innovations – the sale of
official and judicial posts was abolished. New magistrates, appointed for

life by the king, would be paid by the Crown. Not without some difficulty, Maupeou found and installed his new judges and his new chambers.

It was more than a reform. It was a social revolution: it involved the expropriation of an order of society which for some centuries had been accustomed to passing on the family office from father to son. In this sense, the entire nobility was attacked, and with it the whole of corporate society.

It retaliated not only in support of its own interests and in selfish isolation. On the contrary, it enveloped the defence of its possessions in the defence of the liberties of the realm. On 18 February the Cour des Aides expressed this perfectly in the remonstrances drawn up by its first president, Malesherbes:

Our silence would make the whole nation accuse us of betrayal and cowardice. All we are asking for today is the rights of that nation . . . At present, the courts are the sole protectors of the weak and unfortunate; the Estates-General, and in the greater part of the country the Provincial Estates, have long since ceased to exist; all bodies except the courts are reduced to dumb and passive obedience. No private person in the provinces would dare to lay himself open to the vengeance of a commandant, of a ministerial agent, and even less, of one of your Majesty's ministers.

And the final touch: 'Sire, interrogate the nation itself, since it is the only thing that may gain your Majesty's ear.'

This fine speech was historic. The demands of the parlements widened into a national appeal. Of course, resort to the Estates-General was still a resort to tradition. But tradition here included the future in the past, the reformism of the *philosophes* in the society of intermediary bodies: a man like Malesherbes saw no contradiction in that, because restoration of the past was seen as a necessary condition for the future. This profound product of the collective consciousness explains, just as much as royal irregularities, the popularity of parlements. Despite Voltaire, who continued his lampoon war against them – and in company with the *parti dévot*! – public opinion saw the recent conquerors of the Jesuits as its indispensable defenders. Petty officials united behind important office-holders, the *basoche* (petty officers of the court) behind the magistrates, all the corps of local and provincial autonomous groups behind the most solidly entrenched privileges. Against the arbitrary rule of one person alone, democracy was mobilized behind oligarchy, the people behind the nobility: this was the century's tradition and political dynamic.

The king had only one way (ever the same) of dispersing this increasingly powerful trend: to take the initiative in reform, especially of financial and tax administration. This he could do the more easily since, in the years 1770–4, the Crown had liberated itself from the lawcourts by breaking up the parlements, and theoretically had a free hand.

The Controller of Finance was a former clerical counsellor to the parlement, the Abbé Terray. Without any particular doctrine, but quick and intelligent, he belonged to that breed of empirical financiers who mistrusted abstract innovation and took refuge in budgetary balance. His management was both effective and unpopular, financially sound and politically deplorable. On taking office in 1769, he found a budgetary deficit of 100 million, a debt due for payment of over 400 million livres, and all the 1770 revenues earmarked in advance, without a sou in the coffers. When he left office in 1774, the budgetary deficit had dropped from 100 to thirty million, and the state's debts were reduced to twenty million. But these are the historian's figures and not those of his contemporaries.

For Terray's creation of supplementary revenues had borrowed from the most classic methods: on the one hand, fleecing the state's creditors; on the other, increased taxation, chiefly indirect. He cut down pensions, reduced State annuities, suspended certain payments such as the *billets des fermes* owed to the Crown's creditors. There were also new consumer taxes. A further move was the extension of the second *vingtième*, a 5 per cent tax on income, justified by this clear comment: 'We do not doubt that our subjects . . . will bear these charges with the zeal which they have shown on so many occasions, and we count on it all the more since the price of goods – one of the causes of the increase in our expenditure – has at the same time improved returns on land to a proportion in excess of the increase in taxation.'

The undeniable technical success of Terray's management – which was measurable by the growing success of royal borrowing – certainly helped the monarchy to gain time. But in the longer term it was accompanied by a double political failure. Firstly, it aroused against the king and his minister not only the world of capitalist speculators, but also all the *rentiers* (people who lived on annuities). Most of all, and more profoundly, it revealed the narrow confines of monarchic reformism; Terray was looking for better productivity from taxation, but without being able to proceed to a general review of fiscal assessment, an idea which had occurred to him as it had to others.

In short, the traditional character of the financial recovery effected in 1771–4 enables one to make a precise analysis of the last and greatest of Louis XV's ministries: the regime created no reformist counterbalance, launched no fiscal counteroffensive such as might split up the anti-absolutist coalition which the war against the parlements had established. In the terminology of the time, it was less a matter of an attempt at enlightened despotism, than despotism plain and simple. The ageing Louis XV had not turned into Voltaire's king; he tried in vain to resuscitate Louis XIV.

In his last years, that meant solitude. When he died on 10 May 1774, he was so damned in public opinion that he had to be buried at night as if in great haste. Paris had not prayed for the king's salvation. It is at this moment that Jules Michelet fixes the death of the monarchy in France.

Son of the Dauphin who had died in 1765, himself born in 1754, Louis XVI was not yet twenty when he inherited the awesome succession of his

Joseph Siffrein Duplessis Louis XVI in coronation robes, *Musée Carnavalet, Paris.*
(*Photo: Lauros-Giraudon*)

grandfather. He could not talk with the ministers who had seen Louis XV during his last illness and might therefore contaminate him. He had to make a very quick decision between the two clans of the court. On the one side, the *parti dévot*, who wanted to pursue Maupeou's policies, the definitive crushing of the parlements, Jansenism and the *philosophes*. Mesdames, Louis XV's daughters and the King's aunts, felt strengthened by the precipitate departure of his mistress, Madame du Barry, and the Church took advantage of a rediscovered morality. But against them was the entire *parti Choiseuliste*: Louis XV's former minister, disgraced in 1770, had been restlessly waiting at his estate at Chanteloup for over four years, backed by a network of noble and *parlementaire* friends, his popularity still intact, and finally with the reliable support of the new queen of France, whose marriage Choiseul had arranged.

Nevertheless, the queen remained cautious, and the king had chosen not to make a choice. Louis XVI recalled a former Secretary of State for the Navy, who had been out of favour for a quarter of a century and was thus a stranger to recent struggles: the Comte de Maurepas, who took the title of Minister of State. He would become much more. For in this old man of seventy-three, who had waited so long in exile, there was much suppressed ambition, a great deal of *savoir-faire* and intellect, and that sensual love of power which was the crowning point of his existence so late in life. Installed in lodgings close to the king, Maurepas governed the first years of the reign.

The Duc d'Aiguillon was the first of the old ministers to go, irredeemably compromised by Madame du Barry's friendship: the Comte de Vergennes, who owed everything to Maurepas, succeeded him in Foreign Affairs. The following month, there was a secondary rearrangement: Turgot, *intendant* of the Limousin, was well recommended to Maurepas and appointed to the Navy. But the great problem was that of the parlements and the management of finances, the areas of Maupeou and Terray. It was settled on 24 August by the departure of the two ministers. Louis XVI gave the Seals to Miromesnil, and transferred Turgot to the post of Controller-General.

It is the second name which has made the first ministry of Louis XVI's reign famous. That is only fair, for one can say with Edgar Faure that 'the general control of finance was Monsieur Turgot's final cause.'[2] The son of a dynasty of office-holders, at first destined for the Church, he was almost obsessed with serving the state; in his time as *conseiller* (counsellor) to the parlement, as *maître des requêtes* (counsel to the Conseil d'Etat), then as *intendant* of the Limousin, he had but one passion – the public good. This passion had its source in his very strong intellectual convictions: Turgot was a philosopher in the service of the state. This exception to the rule which, in the eighteenth century, separated practitioners of politics and specialists in ideas, was a rare and fragile moment when, after Maupeou

[2] Edgar Faure, *La Disgrâce de Turgot*.

and on a quite different plane, the *ancien régime*'s other last chance was at stake – a monarchy that was both liberal and rational.

The heart of Turgot's philosophy belonged to the physiocratic school, of which he was one of the outstanding intellects. He held that there was a natural order of society, intelligible through reason, which it was consequently the duty and wisdom of governments to actualize: this was a way of thinking diametrically opposed to the idea so often nurtured among *parlementaire* opposition that, somewhere in the mists of time, there might be a royal 'constitution' containing all the original rights of the nation *visà-vis* the king. Turgot recognized no authority other than reason, which was the sole foundation for a true social order. Society would thereby be completely liberated from its past, with the idea of tradition emptied of all meaning, while the state, in contrast, would have the task of personifying that reason, which was simultaneously the public interest.

Royal absolutism for him was absolute only in the sense that its function was to institute the natural order: productive agriculture, booming land revenues managed by the owners, and all sectors of the economy stimulated through free trade. The old notion of 'fundamental laws' was turned from its original sense to mean the exact opposite: it no longer referred to history and tradition, but to reason, property and the rights of propertyowners. By replacing the idea of privilege with that of ownership, physiocratic thinking in general, and Turgot in particular, introduced the protection of liberties into universal modern language.

The text which expresses this most clearly is the famous *Mémoire sur les municipalités* (Memorandum on the municipalities), written during the years of Turgot's ministry, under his authority, by his adviser and friend Du Pont de Nemours, who was also a staunch supporter of physiocracy. We know from Condorcet, who was also in the inner circle of the new Controller-General and a fierce supporter of his ministry, that Du Pont gave shape to an old idea of Turgot's, both fiscal and political. In order to transform the assessment and collection of taxes, and to assist the development of agricultural productivity and of the economy, it was necessary to set up a system of assemblies representing property-owning society, which would be given the task of carefully working out reforms, overseeing their implementation and replacing, at least partially, the King's *intendants*.

Turgot, who was more a disciple of Vincent de Gournay and *laissez-faire* than of the physiocratic sect in its strict sense, had never favoured the idea of 'legal despotism', according to which good monarchic power could not be shared since it was supposed to be the means of revealing reason. On the contrary, he had visualized a pyramid of elected assemblies, from the parochial *municipalité* to the 'general *municipalité*' of the kingdom, by way of two intermediate stages. In this four-tier arrangement, described by Du Pont, where each body delegates to the higher level, the electors are property-owners on a pro rata basis of the value of their property: the 'free citizen' fulfils the criterion of wealth which grants full suffrage, while the 'fractional' citizen must join a group of others to obtain the same electoral unit of power. There are therefore only a few members in these assemblies, which is a condition of their rational operation: theirs would be the task, each at its own level, of fiscal reform and administration. Turgot envisaged, for a future of which he would not be in control, one single general contribution for all incomes; but Du Pont's memorandum did not go quite so far, and was limited to a proposed reform of the *taille*, intended to make things easier for the farmers, hitting only the landowners, in order to increase crop productivity.

The most original aspect of the project identifies the representation of society and its administration with the ownership of property. Turgot's monarchy according to reason was also a monarchy of co-ownership between the king and all possessors of property. Within this concept, over and above a precise diagnosis of the crisis between state and society which was sounding the death knell of the *ancien régime*, lay a very modern line of thinking: it was a matter of representing the interests of society and not, as with Rousseau for example, the political will of those involved.

The parlements – those courts of justice peopled by judges who had purchased nobility together with their office – could not be the guardians of those interests, because they had their privileges to defend; therefore it was necessary to conceive completely new structures. The plan helps us to understand how the idea of the *tabula rasa*, which would have such a brilliant revolutionary career, emerged naturally from the *ancien régime*, which produced it.

In short, those interests which must be represented generate social unity, by the mediation of reason: a different concept from that of Adam Smith's 'invisible hand', although the problem is posed in comparable terms. The French version of liberal society did not include that miracle of final equilibrium which creates order out of disorder. It presupposed that all the participants, especially the state, were subject to a constraint which lay outside and above society – that of reason – and which would avert anarchy from a community defined in terms of individual interests. Du Pont's *municipalités* dealt in their own way with a question which would obsess Condorcet: on what conditions could a rational decision be obtained from an assembly? From its very origins, French thinking about representation guarded itself against the fear of social breakdown by having recourse to reason and science: an oscillation which would continually haunt and characterize it for a century, right up to the time of Guizot and Jules Ferry.

Here we have, then, ready to get down to work, the first and last team of *philosophes* peaceably preparing an assault on the *ancien régime*, with the shaky support of a young king. If the ideas were revolutionary, the means of implementing them were not. Condorcet, in the shadow of the Controller-General, began his apprenticeship in the world and work of politics, where he would never truly be at ease. Philosophy had finally encountered the state.

The promotion of 24 August 1774 immediately revealed the limitations of this economic and political experiment. The new Keeper of the Seals, Miromesnil, former first president of the parlement of Rouen – one of the most turbulent in the kingdom – had refused since 1771 to sit in the 'Maupeou parlement'. The dismissal of the chancellor had, moreover, aroused such enthusiasm in Paris that the consequences were almost inevitable: two months later, the parlements were reconvened, hereditary rights and the sale of offices restored. The 'guarantees' demanded in return by the young king – such as the prohibition of collective resignations and the interruption of justice – were so shaky that they immediately became the subject of complaints by the *avocat général* (government law officer), Séguier, at the registration session for the edicts of recall.

Turgot had taken no direct part in the decision, but he had given his agreement. Was this a tactical manoevre towards the young sovereign and Maurepas, who wanted to please public opinion? Was it the influence of his friend Malesherbes? At all events, the new Controller had always had his reservations about 'legal despotism' as described by his physiocrat friends, being imbued with the feeling that one should woo opinion in order to educate it rather than put obstacles in its way. In reality, as Condorcet had warned him, he had just given a hand to those who would be his most formidable adversaries. Did he foresee this? It is not certain. At least he could reflect that the popularity of the new ministry gave him a free hand in the immediate future.

In the financial area, nothing was urgent. Taking over from Terray, inheriting a management which was both efficient and unpopular, formed the best possible accession. Wisely, Turgot shelved his old project, ripened while he was *intendant* of Limoges, of improving the assessment for levying the *taille*. He handled the court with equal care; the only 'cutbacks' he operated on state expenditure were aimed at the costs of tax collection and the exorbitant profits of tax farmers.

This slowness, however, was not entirely tactical. Turgot was more of an economist than a financier. He believed less in budgetary techniques than in increased production. As a good physiocrat, he linked tax surpluses to the enrichment of the kingdom, which itself depended on the priority given to grain policy. He had made this clear in 1770 in his *Lettres sur la liberté du commerce des grains* (Letters on the freedom of the grain trade): annual fluctuations in the quantity and price of grain could be reduced only by free trade. The resulting rise in the average price would be slow and gradual, and would create more jobs and better wages; the broad trend of physiocratic prosperity would replace the violent cyclical contractions which periodically bred poverty and famine.

An initial liberal experiment had been attempted in 1763–4. Under the influence of the current situation and the economists, internal free trade and, to a certain extent, exports of corn, had been authorized. But the continuous increase in prices which had fed the euphoria of the landowners and the *laissez-faire* of the liberals had grown to such proportions that it had offered the sticklers for regulation their revenge. It was in the name of the wretched populace, in 1770–1, during the peak of a cyclical price rise, that Terray had returned to banning exports and to the traditional policy of corn provision by the state in order to stabilize prices. To this end he had re-established not the old policy governing the movement of goods between provinces, but complex market regulation.

Turgot suppressed that regulation by his edict of September 1774, the fine preamble to which is a long piece of liberal pedagogy, resuming the argument of his *Lettres*. Voltaire comments in a letter to d'Alembert: 'I have just read M. Turgot's masterpiece. What new heavens and new earths, it would seem!' But already general reaction was far from unanimous, and some words from Nicolas Baudeau, the physiocratic abbé, concerning this preamble throw light on forthcoming events: 'The two extremes of the people did not heed him, namely, those of the court and the leading townsmen and those of the populace. For a long time I have noticed a strong conformity of propensities and opinions between these two extremes.' The court – any step towards a liberal economy threatened the world of acquired rights. Leading townsmen – the representatives were hostile to the innovations of economists and *philosophes* alike. Lastly, the 'populace' lived in age-old terror of dear bread, which was imputed not to the nature of things but to the maliciousness of men.

The drama took shape in the following spring, with the exhaustion of the previous year's harvest. From eleven sous for four livres in weight, the price during the summer and winter, bread went up to fourteen sous; cheaper than at Terray's 'peak' period, but relatively dearer in that stocks had been exhausted by previous high prices. In the second fortnight of April 1775, a sort of generalized rioting developed around Paris, culminating in the capital itself at the beginning of May.

This episode, known as the Flour War, indicated, in the less impoverished France of the eighteenth century, the lasting nature of old popular emotions aroused during the gap between the exhaustion of stocks and the new harvest. Contemporaries in favour of Turgot believed some aristocratic or clerical conspiracy was at the bottom of it, though we have no proof of this other than a convergence of hostile intent towards the minister. Historians today insist that it was the 1775 forerunner of the rural revolts of July–August 1789: such comparison underlines the sameness of popular mentality and reaction in the face of high prices and poverty.

There was the same kind of anarchistic rumour-mongering, the same spontaneous demands for state price-fixing and protection, the same train of violence and looting of markets and bakeries. On 5 May at Brie-Comte-Robert, to quote from the report of the tax inspector Dufresne, 400 people 'who appeared to be artisans from the villages around Paris' formed a mob outside his house; about forty got inside and demanded 'in furious tones' that he give them corn at twelve livres 'like at Choisy-le-Roi'. They added that 'if they were to be hanged they would suffer less than by dying slowly of starvation'.

Upheld by the king, Turgot gained the upper hand from early May, but his liberal experiment was ultimately brought into discredit. The parlement of Paris solemnly condemned his policy. At Versailles, the intrigues of the cliques resumed against the Controller: chiefly the Choiseulists, who had the important backing of the queen, unhappy about the appointment of Malesherbes to the king's household during the summer of 1775. Necker made history by publishing *La Législation et le commerce des grains* (Legislation and the Grain Trade), a counter-offensive in favour of economic controls. A whole society of monopolies and privileges united in opposition to liberal innovation.

Turgot, feeling himself threatened, chose a solution which worsened the situation; such audacity, or tactical imprudence, has nurtured the thesis that he was a doctrinaire minister, heedless of reality. In January 1776, he persuaded the king to sign a series of six edicts, which actually comprised two important reforms: of the *corvée*, which was replaced by a money tax on landowners; and of the trade guilds, which were purely and simply abolished.

The edicts appeared less daunting for what they contained than for what they foreshadowed. Turgot was suspected of wanting to do away with the traditional organization of the kingdom. It was feared that the end of the *corvée* might mean the end of seigneurial society: the disappearance of the guilds prefigured the confusion over 'rank' and 'status'. A whole range of society united against that prospect: clergy, nobility, magistracy and the organized sectors of traditional urban life – *basoche*, master craftsmen and merchants. Erstwhile enemies made a holy alliance, magistrature and clergy, Choiseulists and the *parti dévot*, financiers and the petty nobility.

On the opposite side, how much weight did Voltaire or Condorcet carry, the *philosophes* and the economists? The truth is that Turgot's reforms affected noble society enough to rouse it against him, and not enough to separate important strata of the bourgeoisie from it. They revealed the political deadlock of that society of propertied voters so desired by the physiocrats, and showed the resistance of civil society as well as the strength of the nobles' counter-offensive. From top to bottom, aristocratic society united around the same defensive reflex, admirably defined by an expression of Trudaine: they were not 'sure if they would wake the next morning to the same status'.

Nevertheless, the edicts got through, after a long battle in the parlement. But Turgot had been isolated in the ministry and at court. Everyone was against him: Maurepas, the queen, the king's brothers, his aunts, his kinsman the Prince de Condé. Malesherbes hesitated, and wanted to resign. Louis XVI yielded to the general wave of feeling and dismissed Turgot on 12 May 1776. In August, the guilds were re-established in new forms, and the *corvée* made subject to possible redemption by parishes.

Thus, after the downfall of the triumvirate's neo-absolutist attempt, came the failure of the philosophical and reforming monarchy. In six years, the two paths of state arbitration had been explored in vain. At the end of this double shipwreck there remained an ever more anti-absolutist public opinion and a monarchy which was falling apart.

LOUIS XVI

The King who mounted the throne in 1774 was the third son of the Dauphin, son of Louis XV.[3] His father had married Maria Theresa of Spain, who died in childbirth at the age of twenty, and whose death had left him inconsolable. He had been very quickly remarried to Marie-Josèphe of Saxony; even if he did not love her, he at least gave her a number of children: a first daughter, who died very young; then Louis-Joseph, Duc de Bourgogne, born 1751; Marie-Joseph, Duc d'Aquitaine, in 1753 (died the next year); then, in 1754, the child who would be Louis XVI, receiving the title of Duc de Berry.

His birth was followed by that of two brothers who would also reign, but over post-revolutionary France, between 1814 and 1830: Louis-Stanislas, Comte de Provence, born in 1755, and Charles Philippe, Comte d'Artois, in 1757. Lastly, two daughters brought the list to a close, Marie-Adélaïde Clotilde, in 1759, then Elisabeth Philippine Marie-Hélène, in 1764 – the Madame Elisabeth who would share her brother's captivity in the Temple prison. In this enormous family, which did not escape the curse of high infant mortality, the Duc de Berry became heir to the throne because of the death of his older brother, the Duc de Bourgogne, in 1761 at the age of ten. His father, the Dauphin, died in 1765. The future Louis XVI thus knew his destiny at the age of eleven; he would be king of France.

This hereditary devolution wrought by God's hand broke what God's hand seemed to have prepared: death had struck the child whom everything had destined for the throne, to the advantage of one who showed only ordinary aptitudes. Where Bourgogne had been lively, charming, adulated, precociously authoritarian and genetically a king, Berry was withdrawn, solitary, graceless. The grief of his parents and grandfather – papa-Roi, as he called him – brought no extra affection his way; it was the turn of his young brothers, Provence and Artois, to be the favourites. In short, Louis XVI was the unpopular member of the family.

That was a psychological misfortune which probably added its effects to his paternal heritage, and which distanced him from his grandfather and similarly from the task of kingship. For his father, the Dauphin, had been kept apart all his life from a political role or even apprenticeship. In fact, under Louis XV, the royal family had transposed a drama from bourgeois repertory to the court of France. On the one hand, the king and his mistress, Madame de Pompadour, who reigned at Versailles and even, if her enemies were to be believed, over the kingdom's politics: she was the protectress of the *philosophe* party, of Choiseul and the Austrian alliance. On the other, the queen, Marie Leczynska, ill and ageing, but drawing

---

[3] Here I am using part of an article on Louis XVI in Furet and Ozouf, *Critical Dictionary*.

strength from the outraged loyalty of her children, guardians of morality
and religion.

The Dauphin had sided with his mother: he was the symbol and hope of
the *parti dévot*, the Jesuits' man, a bitter adversary of Choiseul and the
Austrian policy. This plump, almost obese, man, intellectually lazy, with
the typically Bourbon combination of sensuality and devoutness, was
carefully kept away from matters of the realm by Louis XV. He never
forgot the respect he owed his father; but he was a living reproach and a
potential rival. He died too soon – nine years before his father – to be able
to reign. However, he had taken great care over the education of his
children to prepare them for their future role, as if he had realized that the
throne of France was going to 'jump' a generation.

When he died, in 1766, the Duc de la Vauguyon, governor to the
Children of France, took charge of the new Dauphin without in any way
modifying his programme of studies. It was a serious programme, with an
industrious pupil, but perhaps neither deserves the excessive praise which
whitewashing historiography has sought to shower on them. There were
few innovations in the subject matter: the basis of the lessons and 'discussions' drawn up for the instruction of the future king remained a
mixture of religion, morality and humanities, to which the shade of
Fénelon lent an unreal quality and the ponderousness of the pedagogue-
duke a touch of grandiloquence.

As far as the pupil is concerned, his work manifests a docile and un-
imaginative way of thinking, reflecting only what he was being taught. His
style, sometimes elegant, is more interesting than his thoughts, which are
always banal; in these pastorals on paternal monarchy, superficial commentaries on Fénelon's *Télémaque* or the *Politique tirée de l'Ecriture sainte*
by Bossuet the future king learned neither to conduct a reasoned argument
nor to govern a State.

The great event – and the greatest failure – of his youth was his
marriage, negotiated in 1768 under the influence of the Choiseul party,
to an Austrian princess: the youngest daughter of Maria-Theresa, the
Archduchess Marie-Antoinette. The union was celebrated in 1770; the
Dauphin was sixteen, his bride fifteen. For seven years, until the summer
of 1777, he would not manage to consummate the marriage. For seven
years, the Court of Versailles, Paris, the entire kingdom and foreign
courts, according to circumstance, would make this fiasco into a state
problem or an object of mockery – the one not excluding the other.
When he became king (1774), Louis XVI was the butt of this European
vaudeville.

He was not impotent, properly speaking, like his brother Provence, but
incapable of ejaculation – and, in any event, he was little inclined towards
love and women. One can imagine that this anomaly would have intrigued
his libidinous grandfather, quite apart from the harm it was doing to the
future of the kingdom. There may well have entered into it a justifiable
repudiation of his cynical and blasé grandfather, with his weakness for

Madame du Barry, and a sort of loyalty to his paternal heritage: through Louis XVI, the Bourbons would end in virtue, but without capitalizing on it, since that virtue had begun by being ludicrous. It appears that, in the end, a chat with his brother-in-law Joseph, who came to France incognito in 1777, freed Louis from his inhibition. In August, court correspondence mentioned the event, and the queen's pregnancy confirmed it the following year. The future emperor of Austria – perhaps with the help of a small operation (it is not certain) – settled the affair privately, but without being able to obliterate all traces of it in public opinion or in the royal couple themselves.

Thus, the still adolescent man who came to the throne on 10 May 1774, on the death of his grandfather, had already had long experience of loneliness, which the exercise of power would intensify. That was what gave his personality that 'indecipherable' quality remarked upon by his contemporaries, which Marie-Antoinette also wondered about in her letters to her mother.

When he became king of France at twenty, Louis XVI was a rather gauche young man, already tending to portliness, with a full face, Bourbon nose and a short-sighted gaze which was not without a certain gentleness. Michelet stresses the Germanic heredity (through his mother, daughter of the Elector of Saxony) of this heavy, slow, thick-blooded prince, who ate and drank too much. But it is equally easy to trace these traits back to his father, the Dauphin, son of Louis XV and Marie Leczynska.

The dominant motif of contemporary accounts of the young king, apart from his lack of grace, was his difficulty in communicating, and even in reacting. With no conversation, no distinction, he had good sense but was short on wit: the best document in this regard is the diary he kept of his daily activities, in which are noted, together with his hunts, his meals and his meetings, and family events. This list never discloses the slightest emotion, the smallest personal comment: it reveals a soul without any strong vibrations, a mind numbed by habit.

By contrast, what a lot of physical exercise! Louis XVI spent on hunting – which was his passion – the energy he saved in his contacts with men or his relations with his wife. He watched with meticulous care over the upkeep of forests and animals, knew the men and dogs of the hunting teams, and devoted long hours, often several times a week, to staghunting, a typically Bourbon pastime from which he would emerge exhausted but happy, with the evening in which to listen to discussions of the afternoon's exploits.

Another practice which was characteristic of his solitary and rather arid nature was manual work, tinkering about, locksmithing: above his apartment, Louis XVI had a little forge set up where, with a modest talent, he made locks and keys. From there he could ascend a further storey to reach his belvedere and watch through a telescope all that was happening in the gardens of Versailles. On some days he took the opportunity to wander through the attics of the château, chasing stray cats.

It is easy to see how historians have been able to turn this really very average man into a hero, an incompetent, a martyr or a culprit: this honourable king, with his simple nature, ill adapted for the role he had to assume and the history which awaited him, can equally well inspire emotion at the unfairness of fate or an indictment against his lack of foresight as a sovereign. Where personal qualities were concerned, Louis XVI was not the ideal monarch to personify the twilight of royalty in the history of France; he was too serious, too faithful to his duties, too thrifty, too chaste and, in his final hour, too courageous. But through his visceral attachment to tradition, the adolescent who had spent his youth clinging to his aunts' apron-strings and in the shadow of the *parti dévot*, would be the man of a monarchy which was no longer suited to him or the era.

Michelet grasped this well and truly, seeing in that royalty in God's image the supreme ill of the *ancien régime*. He recognized that Louis XVI was its poor, final symbol – too scrupulous, too domestic, too 'national' as well (because of the war against England, and American independence). He had, in fact, to pay the price for his grandfather's sins, for the harem of the Parc-aux-Cerfs and the alliance with Austria. For Michelet, the drama of the French monarchy had been played out under Louis XV. When his grandson mounted the throne, it was too late; the monarchy was already dead.

That profound intuition explains where Louis XVI's real failure lay: less in his day-to-day politics, at home or abroad, which did have some great moments, than in his powerlessness to resuscitate on any lasting basis the great moribund body of old royalty as it used to be. The new king received the consecration of his coronation at Reims in 1775, like his predecessors, but thereafter the only legitimate consecration would be by public opinion. For a brief while he obtained this by virtue of his youth, his good will, the reinstatement of the parlements, and Turgot; but all too soon he let this popularity be swept up into the unpopularity of the queen and the court.

MARIE-ANTOINETTE

The queen was an archduchess of Austria, daughter of the Empress Maria Theresa, married to the Dauphin after lengthy diplomatic manoeuvres by Choiseul. On her mother's orders, she was accompanied by the ambassador, Mercy-Argenteau, doubling as mentor and spy, who had been given the task of ensuring that the Austrian capital invested in the French marriage bore profitable fruit; but she did not succeed for very long in the difficult role assigned to her. She could find nobody to lean on at the court: hostile to Madame du Barry, Louis XV's last official mistress, she therefore became close to the *parti dévot* and the king's daughters, who would have liked to put an end to their father's misconduct; but she was Austrian, thus in the Choiseul camp, and found herself the very symbol of a policy which had been rejected, together with the minister, in 1770; its adversaries were in power, including, within the royal family, the aunts of the king and her own husband, the future king.

With little education, as badly prepared as could be for the role of Austrian 'antenna' at Versailles, which her mother would have liked to see her play, she had to live through those long early years with the court speculating every morning on what had happened – or rather, what had *not* happened – in her bed; gossip travelled swiftly from Versailles to Paris, and she was soon credited with lovers (of both sexes), since her husband seemed to be so inadequate. When children finally appeared (first a daughter, the future Madame Royale, in 1778, a Dauphin in 1781, another son in 1785 and a daughter the next year), the damage was already done: the image of the Austrian Messalina had been fixed by Parisian lampoons. On her side, there was a certain flightiness, due to her temperament; she was a poorly educated princess, disliked, lacking understanding of events or men. But the world of Versailles offered this rootless foreign queen, who enjoyed no support, a virtually impossible role.

Her personality harboured an incurable impassivity, a lack of concern for advice and circumstances which made her behaviour difficult to fathom. The ambassador Mercy-Argenteau complained about it to Maria Theresa, to excuse himself for his failure to manipulate the young queen. Later the Comte de Mirabeau and Antoine Barnave had the same experience. They knew or guessed that Marie-Antoinette had the stronger character of the royal couple, but they came up against her secret. In her hour of tragedy, which she faced courageously, having matured in her loneliness, she was just the same as she had always been, rather indifferent to the outside world.

In contrast with Paris, at the time of Marie-Antoinette's arrival the court already presented the almost perfect image of what would a little later be termed the *ancien régime*. Absolutism had invented Versailles where, far from Paris and the people, Louis XIV had set up his undivided government, the instrument of an untrammelled authority. In addition, that government had surrounded itself with a parasitic aristocracy, dancing around the king the sycophantic ballet of the courtiers, half vice, half servility.

From being a means of taming the nobles, under Louis XIV, the court under Louis XVI had become the symbol of their dominance. The king no longer reigned over them – he obeyed them: in this telescoping of absolute monarchy and aristocracy was forged the overall rejection of what was no longer, in actual fact, either absolute monarchy or aristocracy, but something born of the decadence of the two principles and still surviving on their complicity, at the expense of the people.

Louis XVI contributed to this image concocted by the Parisian satirists through his lack of inclination for important matters and that slightly affected kind of spinelessness which was the most obvious trait in his make-up. But the king was always careful about the image of his calling, never compromised tradition and, by his serious-mindedness and personal virtue, would even be able to revive for both his person and his office a respect that the old Louis XV had not left intact. Now that novelty – a chaste Bourbon – itself became a butt: the faithful king was impotent; the virtuous sovereign had married a shameless hussy.

Yet he still maintained at least the façade of the court, and sheltered his shaky relationship with the world behind observance of etiquette, the ultimate legacy of tradition. His rash Austrian queen, on the other hand, elbowed aside this last rampart and revealed the rack and ruin behind the walls. She wanted, and obtained, private apartments; created a little court within the court, where she amused herself with selected friends, destroying the nature of the monarchy's public image offered at Versailles, and exposing only the aristocratic coteries. Public opinion deeply resented such dereliction of the duties and trappings of the reign: Marie-Antoinette presented a trebly vulnerable target – queen, foreigner and woman. The King's mistresses had been lampooned. The queen's lovers were even more detested. By making its object female, opinion's frustration changed into hatred. This was the hidden curse of Marie-Antoinette's life. Turning reality upside down, opinion condemned the queen for pleasures in which she had not indulged.

A scandal of the time gives some measure of Marie-Antoinette's unpopularity. The Cardinal de Rohan, bishop of Strasbourg, a luxury-loving *grand seigneur* who combined extreme ambition with extreme frivolity, longed to regain the favour of the queen, whom he had offended by his life-style and his *mots*. He made contact with a gang of adventurers who painted him a vivid picture of secret dealings at Court, and held out the prospect of a reconciliation: he handed over 150,000 livres to them, and they undertook to arrange a rendezvous, in a Versailles grove, with a 'queen' – in reality an accomplice – who promised him pardon. That was not all: he then had to buy, on behalf of a queen who was mad about diamonds, a necklace worth nearly two million livres – originally intended for Madame du Barry – which had become too dear even for the queen of France.

The plot was unmasked in the summer of 1785 when the jewellers vainly demanded the first payment. By then the necklace was out of reach, in London. The affair threw a lurid light on court life. The queen had tangled with crooks, including the alchemist Cagliostro; Rohan was the dupe, and won the sympathy of the public; handed over to the parlement, he was cleared of responsibility. The queen had sunk so low in public opinion that he was judged not guilty in having believed her to be promiscuous or (even worse) mercenary. Paris acclaimed him. The kingdom thought like the cardinal. When majesty ceases to be majestic, there can no longer be such a thing as *lèse-majesté*.

The verdict of public opinion gradually discredited everyone at court: the king's two brothers, the Comte de Provence, the underhand intriguer, and the Comte d'Artois, the queen's friend; his cousin the Duc d'Orléans, another shifty figure, biding his time at the Palais Royal;

the aristocracy, savouring the last happy days of what Talleyrand later called *la douceur de vivre*. To free itself from the external constraints of good conduct and piety, the court had effectively become a daily miracle of wit and pleasure. But it was rousing the entire town population against it. Jealous of a world from which it was excluded, enemy of a luxury which discredited its spirit of thrift, the bourgeois town – the laboratory of democracy, hard work and talent – threw its repressions and its hopes into the battle. The court, where nobles ruled, must be ruinous, reactionary and debauched, and reason, progress and morality must be mobilized against it.

THE FINANCIAL CRISIS

The last two charges of the indictment were more than justifiable. But what about the first? The collapse of public finance gave it a particular resonance. In reality, the court absorbed only 6 per cent of the Treasury's revenues – a relatively low percentage. Moreover, in its anathema, opinion constantly confused two kinds of expenditure: one relating to splendour and festival, and the other to official position. Financially, the second was the larger: not everything in it could be cut down – the king's household troops, for example, who drew their pay from the Versailles budget, could hardly be cut back after the 1775 reforms. But spectacular examples of waste abounded, so permanent was the confusion at Versailles between pensions and gifts, remuneration for public office, the speculative resale of the benefits of office, all kinds of financial devices. Finally, among Marie-Antoinette's entourage, the arbitrary nature of favour was more and more glaringly obvious. Madame de Lamballe, who already received 170,000 livres as superintendent of the queen's household, procured 600,000 livres on domains in Lorraine, plus 54,000 livres for her brother. Madame de Polignac and her family, other well-known protégés of the queen, were registered for a pension of 700,000 livres.

Had he attacked court wastefulness, Louis XVI would not have saved his finances, but he might perhaps have salvaged even more – the monarchy itself. His weakness in the face of the court was symbolic of the abdication of the monarchy before the aristocracy.

This erosion of royal power, marked by the nobles' victory at court, was not so rapid that it prevented Louis XVI from harvesting the last fruits of the century's progress, and of a better management of wealth and men. There are other examples of a power in decline and an enduring administration.

Since Choiseul, France had been preparing its revenge for defeat in the Seven Years War (1756–63). In 1775 – in the midst of the Turgot affair – the king summoned back to the War Ministry an old retired *condottiere*, the Comte de Saint-Germain, who in the space of two years 'Prussianized' the French military system, with efficient assistance from officialdom. He pruned the overmanned and over-costly corps, such as the king's household troops, whose expenses were the highest; he reduced the militias to the benefit of the regular army, whose numbers were doubled. Under the direction of Gribeauval, the French artillery became the best in Europe; on the advice of the Comte de Guibert, the light infantry updated military tactics: such were the two great debts that the Revolution owed to the *ancien régime*.

Finally, Saint-Germain attacked the sale of military posts. All his life he had pleaded the cause of the poor nobility; he was a man of Prussian-style military nobility, a specialist in the field of arms. As he could not redeem all posts at one stroke, he decided that they should lose one quarter of their value each time one was vacated, so that the financial value would be written off within four generations.

After Saint-Germain, Ségur pursued the work of technical renovation. He maintained its social inspiration, making further cutbacks by the 1781 regulation which reserved certain military ranks for sons who possessed at least four quarterings. But it was done rather grudgingly, for he declared to the Council: 'It would be better to tackle the unreasonable prejudice which is the ruin of the nobility by allowing it no other activity than the practice of arms.' While the attack on the sale of office pleased the poor nobles, who were rich in title alone and did not want to see its value diminished, the edict pertaining to the four quarterings united all the ancient nobility. It was in essence directed against the ennobled, since within the second order it disqualified all nobility after the middle of Louis XIV's reign.

This is significant evidence of the mechanism of aristocratic distinctions constantly in operation in old society, by which, among those who had held them for a long time, new privileges arrived to compensate for the risk of an upsurge in the number of titles, brought about by the financial needs of the monarchy. That mechanism, which split the second order into castes, created even more malcontents within the Third Estate than among the recently ennobled: by continually pushing farther back the barrier guarding the way to the highest social status, it made the way still less accessible to those who had not passed through the preliminary stages.

What the Third Estate bourgeois rightly took to be aristocratic arrogance frequently had its source in conflict between the nobles themselves. The 'feudal' *grand seigneur*, who despised the ennobled financier (though he might often marry his daughter), gave the tone to what Mirabeau called 'a torrent of contempt', the psychological mainspring of old French society. Adopted in order to reconstruct a military nobility, this edict aroused the Third Estate against 'reaction'. There was no state reform which could be compatible with the reinforcing of inequality, even if the intention was to replace parasitism and privilege with service to the state.

Under the long ministry of Vergennes (1774–87), a wise and methodical diplomat, the effort towards overseas recovery which had been made since Choiseul's time finally paid off: its aim at that time was revenge against Britain. At the same time, Vergennes did not abdicate from the European scene, where the partition of Poland had caused French influence to lose ground; he refused to help the Austrian ally in its German ambitions, and maintained a balance between the houses of Brandenburg and Habsburg. But the American conflict provided the opportunity for the great design against England.

In the conflict which developed in 1773–6, when American desire for autonomy had garbed itself in the Declaration of Independence (1776), French opinion had good reasons for taking sides: patriotism and philosophy, combined to form a new passion. An American office set up near Versailles enrolled volunteers with illustrious names – the Marquis de La Fayette, the Vicomte de Noailles, Ségur. In a strong position because of the family pact, Vergennes sought the support of Spain, then hesitated. At the beginning of 1778, he decided to sign a treaty of alliance with the new United States: this quickly led to war, in which Spain joined the following year.

While the naval war was going on, with great feats on both sides, and Admiral Suffren in the Indies was avenging the defeats of the Seven Years War, the decisive action took place in America itself: the relief army sent from Versailles to the American colonists, commanded by the Comte de Rochambeau, joined de Grasse's fleet and Washington's troops to obtain the capitulation of the British expeditionary force at Yorktown, in Chesapeake Bay (1781). The peace treaty was signed at Versailles at the beginning of 1783. France gained nothing from it but the freedom to fortify Dunkirk, plus Saint-Pierre and Miquelon, Tobago and the Senegal trading posts. But it had taken its revenge on Britain and erased the shame of the Treaty of Paris in 1763.

Nevertheless, the dynamic of weak governments is such that even their victories are turned into losses. The American war not only multiplied in the kingdom the numbers of admirers of the 1776 Declaration, soon to be known as 'patriots'; it had also cost, over five years, more than a thousand million livres and had aggravated the chronic malady of the country – its finances. It was a chronic disease, because no cure was possible, and one which became more and more serious as the urgency and impossibility of relief became more obvious. Public expenditure continued to grow in line with the obligations of the state. Under Antoine de Sartine, the reorganization of the Navy was swallowing up sums of money which swelled every year. Servicing the public debt became an ever heavier burden.

After Turgot, and some months of traditionalist reaction, it was Necker's turn. The monarchy stepped up its forms of therapy: after the liberal economist came the banker and economic planner. The choice, however, did not result from doctrinal alternatives. In reality, it marked a crucial watershed in the monarchy's policy: resort to pure financial technique and confidence in banks took the place of vague impulses towards fiscal reform. It was doubly a sign of the times, characteristic of the slackening hold of the government and the growing strength of banking capitalism. Not that Louis XVI's ancestors had never resorted to it, but *they* had not actually installed it in the post of Controller-General.

To be more precise, since he was not only a banker, but also Swiss and

Protestant, Necker did not receive the traditional title: first, he was Director of the Treasury, under the nominal supervision of an ousted Controller, and in the following year he became Director-General of Finance with sole authority. This only emphasized the technical limits of his powers: Necker had no right of entry to the king's Council, where the important decisions were made, notably about peace or war. He would not be able, as with Terray against Choiseul, or Turgot against Vergennes, to oppose war and its train of expenses: he was given the task of paying them off painlessly. To hark back to a classic distinction under the *ancien régime*, his advent marked the abdication of finance in the face of banking.

The great officers of the royal finances – known as *financiers* – were at the end of their wits and their resources; Terray's bankruptcies had ended by dealing a blow to the old system of borrowing against lifetime annuities. Now it was the turn of the banks, and of a private capitalist – without office and without country, but with a keen awareness of public opinion, and excellent at raising loans. After him, the great officers – Joly de Fleury, d'Ormesson, Calonne – remained trapped by these techniques.

It was a sign of the times that the abdications of the old monarchy in the face of money was greeted with joy by public opinion: mistrust of the government and the prestige of money joined hands. Moreover, there was Necker himself, eager to please, manipulated by family propaganda, naturalized by success and opinion. This banker was also a thinker, who would leave behind an important work, written mostly after this period, in leisure time left to him by political failure. But when he first came to power, it was not so much his thoughts that were fêted in Paris as his success and his image: that kind of overwhelming public approval was a very modern phenomenon.

Turgot had also received a similar welcome, but he had been one of the insiders naturally destined for the Control-General. Necker, though, having made a fortune in brilliant speculations on the Indies Company, had neither office nor even status, in a society where everything *was* office and status, and, apart from money, had but one other imponderable asset: the favour of public opinion.

On that he had built his road to power. Madame Necker's Fridays were one of the high spots of Paris, when the master of the house spent his money paying homage to sensibility and virtue in political and literary conversations. An *Éloge de Colbert*, a polemic against Turgot's *laissez-faire*, had further reassured traditional economists: Necker did not intend to abandon the poor to the cruelties of the market. In short, the Swiss banker was perhaps less revolutionary than the liberal *intendant*. Furthermore, at the court there was less to fear from a man whose best interests would be served if his past were forgotten, and who could reveal modern monetary secrets to the monarchy. Parisian *rentiers* living on their private means rejoiced as if they were the ones being put into power. That was why public opinion hailed a genius, where Maurepas had seen nothing but a banker.

His management would be rather in the form of administrative modernization. Orchestrated by fashionable philanthropic propaganda, the basic reforms of this saviour-minister mainly affected the running of the state's financial machinery: a reduction in the costs of tax collection, the termination of a certain number of useless offices, dismantling of the Tax Farm, attempts to improve public accountancy and, finally, in another sphere, the abolition of serfdom in the king's domains. Yet, for fear of the parlements and the clergy, this Protestant made not a single gesture on behalf of his fellow Protestants. For fear of the nobility's reactions, this commoner proposed no tax reforms. His most important idea in truly political affairs was once more to present to the king the concept of political representation.

He was unaware of the memorandum prepared by Du Pont for Turgot, but his project had no need of precise antecedents because it was so much in tune with the mood of the times. He had set out its principles in a confidential document to the king published in 1791: to entrust provincial fiscal and economic management to assemblies of property-holders, made up half from the Third Estate, a quarter from the nobility and a quarter from the clergy, voting by head. Necker preserved the distinction between the orders (doubling the representation of the Third, it is true), whereas Turgot (or Du Pont) had given consideration to property-owners only. He also abandoned the elective principle.

Four of these assemblies were created in 1779–80: one in Berry, the next in the Dauphiné, the third in Haute-Guyenne and the fourth in Moulins. The first members were appointed by the king, and thereafter co-opted their colleagues. Even this timid attempt, however, immediately ran into strong opposition: courtiers, *intendants*, parlements were all worried about these new powers; the institutions functioned only in Berry and Haute-Guyenne. This episode revealed once again the monarchy's inability to give the enlightened classes any organized means of being party to the administration of the kingdom.

Because he could not forge ahead with a policy of reforms, the banker Necker was administering a deficit and paying for the American war by way of royal lotteries and ever more costly loans. His main expedient was to increase state-guaranteed life annuities – manna for the bank, which specialized increasingly in the investment of public securities, thus foreshadowing one of its major later roles under the Restoration and the July monarchy. Not only did Necker obtain life annuity loans without making any distinction in interest rates according to the age ranges of the lenders, but he also left to the *rentiers* the choice of subjects on whose lives the interest would run.

It was a chance for lenders to think up almost endless variations on speculative schemes; the best-known was perfected by the Genevan banks, which gathered local capital together around thirty girls of tender age, selected on the best medical expertise for their optimal chances of survival. The figure of thirty met the need to find the lowest starting number on which to base the calculation of probabilities – the Dutch went as far as eighty.

Each of these young girls, surrounded by vigilant and single-minded solicitude on the part of everyone of importance in Geneva, concealed a fortune in each heartbeat. The town went into mourning at the early demise of one Pernette Elisabeth Martin, at the age of eight, on 16 July 1788, as she took with her a capital of over two million livres in life income. But that catastrophe was the exception, and the progress of the demographic forecast ensured the fortunes of the lenders and their banking intermediaries. It was the symptom of an entirely new mentality: the old tax expedients of the monarchy were being turned to the triumph of movable asset capitalism.

In total, between 1776 and 1781, 530 million in loans of all kinds fed the Treasury and financed a war which was all the more popular because it was painless. Money continued to flow in, and the resale of annuities enriched Parisian speculation. Even if the state was seriously compromising its future, Necker retained his popularity. In 1781, to counter-attack court intrigues to find his successor, he published the *Compte rendu*, a statement of accounts which concealed the expenditure of the extraordinary budget and revealed an apparent surplus revenue of ten million livres.

After three years of war and no new taxes, that was truly financial wizardry! But though this little book enjoyed immense public favour, it created conflict at court. The parlement drew up remonstrances on the provincial assemblies, the king's ministers were jealous, and the old *financiers* absolutely clear-sighted: the real deficit lay in the region of eighty million. Necker wanted to get the support of public opinion. He asked for the title of Minister of State, and also for general application of the system of provincial assemblies. On the king's refusal, he fell in May 1781.

His successors, Joly de Fleury and d'Ormesson, made mediocre, almost timid, use of the ordinary routine. Increases in taxes on consumer goods, a third *vingtième*, sales of offices, and, above all, massive borrowing: more than 400 million livres in two and a half years. When d'Ormesson came to grief against the Farm, suppressing its lease three years ahead of term in 1783, the fashionable Vaudreuil and Polignac coteries had their candidate, Calonne, accepted.

Calonne deserves better than association with those names; better, too, than his posthumous reputation. He is greater than the image of dishonest liquidator in which revolutionary historiography has imprisoned him. On many points he had ideas well in advance of his time: his plan rested chiefly on the modern concept that state expenditure should be favourable to the circulation of money, create purchasing power, 'initiate' an economic revival in order to boost the pool of tax revenue.

This interpretation of Calonne in a Keynesian light in fact rehabilitates part of his administration. The new Controller-General masterminded an entire economic policy: public works, fitting out of ports, a road network, various encouragements to industrial and commercial enterprises, the creation of a new Indies Company. He spent money in order to invest. He paid out in order to inspire confidence: annuity arrears (arrears on interest due) were honoured at term. To siphon speculative money towards the Treasury, he put an end to speculation in shares in the Discount Bank and on the import of Spanish piastres.

In the short term, however, this policy could live only on credit: on his installation as Controller, Calonne had found, out of 600 million livres in annual revenue, 176 million committed in advance, 250 million absorbed by debt service and 390 million in accounts in arrears to be settled. He borrowed money on all sides, even more and at a higher rate than his predecessors: 650 million in three and a half years. Necker had a good opportunity in 1784, in his *Administration des finances*, to explain to public opinion – which believed in his *Compte rendu* of 1781 – the mechanism of bankruptcy. For he was touching a sensitive spot: he was denouncing the last of the great court *financiers* to bourgeois *rentiers*, to an entire Parisian democracy for whom he, Necker, was the ideal man.

On this point, the hatred of the Jacobins – or, conversely, the friendship of the Polignacs – had not mistaken its object. Calonne's ministry belonged to the last fine days of the aristocracy. A true son of the times, the descendant of a long line of eminent lawyers, former king's *intendant* in Lille, he was the man of the *grands seigneurs*.

Historians have for too long paid too much attention to the polemics of the era and the little cliques of intriguers and speculators who hovered around Calonne anticipating with their pocket-books the decisions of the state. But the essence lies elsewhere, often concealed in the mystery of princely book-keeping, royal gifts and court speculation: one would need to reconstruct the entire circuit of the money borrowed by Calonne to understand how these years were without doubt the most dazzling in court civilization. Versailles fêted a magician who handed out money right and left – another financial wizard like John Law, in an even shakier world.

In 1785 the king spent 137 million in the cash settlement of debts to unnamed beneficiaries. During that time, he wrote off several princely bankruptcies: that of the Comte d'Artois, the second in six years: those of two great families, the Guéménées and Soubises. The 'enrichissez-vous' of Calonne was not that of the bourgeois king; he was addressing court society, princely and noble houses and, for the time being, the *financiers* in their service. It was neither a surreptitiously revolutionary attempt, nor an international banking conspiracy; it was the last great effort to restore *ancien régime* society in all its glory and splendour.

Sinking borrowed money into the parasitic round of court life proved eventually to be the downfall of this aristocratic sleight-of-hand: never had it been more apparent that the social and political structures of the *ancien régime* were compromising economic and financial stability. In a kingdom where, ultimately, everything depended on agricultural wealth and taxes levied on land, court nobles and the King – in short, the state – were increasingly living beyond their means; that was what the townspeople and the *rentiers* quite rightly perceived in their hatred of Calonne.

It is therefore true that the last great *financier* of the monarchy had helped to crystallize anti-aristocratic feeling, and had certainly brought forward by several years the moment of decisive choice. During the summer of 1786, the deficit was running at over 100 million livres, there were 250 million of debt in arrears outstanding, and half the income of the year ahead was spent in advance. Loyal to the only world he could imagine, which he loved, Calonne unearthed the greatest plan for saving the *ancien régime* that the century had produced: that of the physiocrats.

On 20 August 1786 he presented to the king his *Précis d'un plan d'amélioration des finances* (Outline of a plan to improve finances), built round the idea of fiscal reform. It comprised the replacement of the *vingtièmes* by a tax levied on all lands, without exception, and proportional to income. This was the 'territorial subsidy', which would be paid in kind; the physiocratic tax system had found a new follower. Calonne moreover advocated the reduction of the *taille*, the simplification of the *gabelle* (salt tax) and gradual cancellation of state debts by the transfer of royal domains. A second series of measures aimed at unifying the national market by freeing the grain trade, and the total abolition of internal Customs.

Finally, as with Turgot and Necker, the plan was crowned by a pyramid of consultative assemblies which were to give all property-owners a part in the government of the kingdom: they would have to be elected by suffrage based on property qualification (*censitaire*), without reference to the traditional orders of society. Calonne was thus closer to the *municipalités* of Du Pont's memorandum than to Necker's assemblies. Du Pont, as always, was still lurking in the wings. Never, even under Turgot, had such a vast and daring reorganization been proposed to Louis XVI. The king allowed himself to be convinced. In any case, he hardly had a choice any more, because he refused the bankruptcy which some of the privileged were seeking, in total indifference to the fate of the bourgeois *rentiers*.

But Calonne knew that there was no chance of getting such projects accepted by the parlement of Paris. He suggested to the king a procedure used in the past by Henri IV and Louis XIII: the meeting of an assembly of notables, appointed by the Crown, whose docility could be more easily relied upon. Despite Vergennes's misgivings, this plan pleased the king. As usual, execution was slow, while Calonne survived only by expedients. On 29 December 1786, at the end of a royal Council, Louis XVI announced his intention of 'assembling people of various conditions and the most qualified in my state, in order to inform them of my views on the relief of my peoples, the ordering of my finances and the reform of various abuses.'

He thought he was merely defining a procedure. In fact, he was setting in motion a system.

2

The Revolution of 1789: 1787–1791

With the convening of the notables, the French monarchy had entered into the machinery of consultation: a strong government, a definite policy might have found support in that. But a weak and indecisive government risked exposing its isolation and hastening its own downfall; a single breach in the wall and a rout would ensue. Calonne's little artifice thus unleashed one of the most gigantic crashes in history. It inaugurated an acceleration of events in which the historian can with hindsight read the preface to a revolution.

It all started with the nobility. For those notables were nobles. When one considers how many of them were bishops, *parlementaires* and ennobled members of the Third Estate, noble privilege and the tradition of rank entirely dominated this small assembly, suddenly vested with a role that was too great for it: to represent the nation to the king. How strange was the spectacle of a Controller-General assembling the largest shareholders of a company in order to ask them to do away with the profits. But Calonne had overestimated the indulgence of his audience. Coaxed by Parisian opinion, the assembly of notables found it all the easier to refuse to submit, since Calonne's proposals effectively threatened tradition.

By opposing a single and proportional tax, they were protecting their own interests and at the same time gratifying public opinion. They had only to follow this trend to unite, in an anti-absolutist outburst, with the general feeling of nearby Paris, still hankering after the good Necker, and to make a scapegoat of the man who had sought their backing. In this manoeuvre, which backfired on him, Calonne became the personification of the deficit and a wasteful financial system. The shortfall of 113 million livres, to which he had admitted, was ascribed to his mismanagement alone. In April the King yielded to the notables and replaced Calonne with one of the most vehement among them – Marie-Antoinette's candidate, Loménie de Brienne, archbishop of Toulouse.

An intelligent and ambitious prelate, the archbishop began by giving with open hands. He took liberal measures, such as recognizing the civil status of Protestants, which annoyed the clergy. He persuaded Louis XVI to accept a fundamental reform of the state: just before its demise, the *ancien régime* professed to renounce one of its constituent principles, administrative centralization.

Brienne had inherited the idea of provincial assemblies from Calonne: set up in the *généralités* of the *pays d'élection* (areas in which provincial assemblies ceded their right to approve taxation) these assemblies, composed of the three orders (with a doubled Third Estate), would move in beside the *intendants* and would be called upon to replace them gradually in the country's administration. The king appointed half the members within each of the three orders: co-optation provided the remainder.

About twenty of these assemblies began to operate at the end of the year, leaving 'intermediary commissions' between the plenary sessions to keep an eye on grain, side by side with the *intendant* who, in theory at least, was largely relieved of his office. Thus a revolution had occurred before the Revolution, effected by the monarchy which, by renouncing its nature, was making way for society. Versailles no longer controlled very much, least of all the pace of change. The time of reforms from above had passed, to the benefit of public opinion, which paid heed to the demagogy of the parlements, the regional high courts.

It was necessary to get back to the heart of the problem: how to raise money. In certain periods of history there is a sort of inevitability attached to office: Brienne was forced to resume the idea of a land tax, to which he added an increased stamp charge. He aroused anew the hostility of his erstwhile colleagues, who declared themselves without mandate to vote on these projects; this was an implicit reference to another assembly which *would* have received such a mandate. So the Estates-General came about through the nobles' grand plan to regain control of the state. Everyone – reformist, conservative, bourgeois, aristocrat - rushed to welcome it in the name of anti-absolutism. Louis XVI, who had never understood how to divide and rule, was now up against the moment of liberal unanimity, or, one might as well say, of the parlements.

A sort of gradual widening of the campaign developed: the notables having been dispatched, the parliamentary relay transmitted the new watchword from the court to the Hôtel de Ville (town hall of Paris), and from Paris to the provinces. For some months the large towns in the realm regained their traditional spokesmen. In July 1787, after the dismissal of the notables, the parlement of Paris demanded an Estates-General, affirming it to be the only body with the power to agree to new taxes: that was why, in August, it rejected the financial part of Brienne's programme. Conflict, *lit de justice*, exile, recall: the classic scenario lasted barely a summer. In October, there was no longer any question of reform, but simply of borrowing: the reinstated parlement made registration conditional upon the convening of the Estates-General.

Enfeebled government made a last effort and imposed the loan. To the

Duc d'Orléans, who objected that this was illegal, Louis XVI retaliated with what he had always been taught: 'It is legal because I wish it.' He exiled his cousin and, at the very last, in May 1788, accepted a series of edicts from his Keeper of the Seals, Lamoignon, 'decapitating' the parlements: it was the story of Maupeou all over again. Taking the initiative, the magistrates had just reaffirmed the 'fundamental laws of the realm', voting on taxes by the Estates-General, the right of registration, and the liberties and rights of individuals and corporate bodies. The royal army surrounded the Paris parlement, which yielded only to force, after thirty hours of warnings.

The year 1788 thus saw the culmination of the old struggle which had begun after Louis XIV's death, between absolutist administration and *parlementaire* resistance. But it soon revealed to what extent the inequality of political forces had grown since Louis XVI's accession. Between a solitary and discredited monarchy, with nothing to offer but vague inclinations, and the great liberating watchword of the Estates-General, uniting all ambitions, public feeling did not hesitate.

The provincial towns were even more vociferous than Paris. High court magistrates flew to the aid of Parisian colleagues, enveloped in the same popular fervour. French clergy and local nobility were no less ardent in their battle for 'liberties', during this short year when no one could yet gauge the chasm which could separate the plural from the singular in such a word. In fact, the provinces in which the first two orders of the realm possessed the strongest political positions were the most relentless in combating the king's and Lamoignon's edicts. They were the ones who had Provincial Estates, or remembered when they had had them, and who now asked for their restitution: the eighteenth century briefly blossomed for the nobility for an instant before it vanished.

Unrest reached all towns with a parlement. Risings were especially violent in places where the conflict between the courts and the Crown was most long-standing, and where it had smouldered throughout the century: in Béarn, Brittany and the Dauphiné. In Rennes, where the nobility immediately declared its solidarity with the parlement, gentlemen, barristers and students held a combined demonstration on 9 May; the next day, the king's representatives were stoned by the crowd and forced to take refuge in the governor's palace. In Grenoble, the protesting parlement was exiled by the Duc de Clermont-Tonnerre, commanding the province. On the day fixed for the departure of the magistrates, 7 June, the tocsin was sounded, summoning a town already filled with people: it was market day. All the folk from the surrounding mountains came down to lend a hand. Clermont-Tonnerre's soldiers were pelted with tiles hurled from the rooftops. The revolt was so violent that the king's representative capitulated and allowed the parlement to be reinstated.

But it had also given rise to a revolutionary institution: a 'central committee', dominated by barristers like Jean-Joseph Mounier and Barnave, which on its own authority, at the end of July, convoked the

Provincial Estates. In the big château of the rich merchant, Claude Périer, where the three orders met together, the assembly of Vizille heralded a new era: contrary to what was happening in Pau or Rennes, the men of the Third Estate had the numbers and the authority: they did not confine themselves to demanding the restoration of old provincial franchises, but drew the nobles with them to the national level: in response to Mounier, they in fact voted that 'the three orders of the province shall not grant taxes, by free gift or otherwise, until their representatives have discussed the matter in the Estates-General of the realm.' Parlements and personal privileges were immediately superseded. A national will was taking shape behind anti-absolutist unanimity.

Louis XVI himself could do nothing but yield to the torrent; on 8 August, the Estates-General was convened for 1 May 1789. Not before time, because on 15 August state payments were suspended. The 24th saw the dismissal of Brienne. Necker had become the providential, or rather, inevitable man; his name alone deferred bankruptcy and set Lamoigon's efforts at naught. The wave of popularity which carried him back to power was far too strong to be controlled; nothing mattered any more in France except the imminent meeting of the Estates-General.

At that precise moment, the end of the summer of 1788, history unveiled its real significance to clear-sighted contemporaries, rather as, at the theatre, when the scenery shifts a little and discloses what is going on behind the façade. But what really *was* going on? The nobility and parlements refused to alter anything whatsoever in the traditional method of designation and voting of the Estates: one third of the representatives for each order, and voting by order, which automatically conferred the majority on the privileged. Now the Third Estate advanced the example of Vizille, where its representation had been doubled, and the orders held a common meeting; this was an admission that it wanted the means of dominating the common assembly, since it expected – with good reason – some backing from among the nobility and the lower clergy.

Besides, it had already received a certain amount: the 'national party' – the term 'patriot' also was already in use – which organized the campaign for the 'doubling' of Third Estate representation brought together a number of liberal aristocrats and enlightened bourgeois. The collective wave of hope was so strong that it transported many imaginations beyond social confines, towards a reconciled nation of 25 million citizens. Though the notables of the Third Estate, in towns throughout the kingdom, formed the nucleus of this vast movement of opinion, co-ordinated at the summit by a Committee of Thirty, they did not hold the monopoly: the culture of the century and a growing recognition of merit, which had been spreading for a long time, brought many instances of individual support from above.

The increased number of provincial academies, clubs and Freemasons' societies had foreshadowed the new world in which 'ranks' would henceforth fraternize. Thus, alongside Jacques-Pierre Brissot, Mounier or

Barnave, or the young *Parlementaire* Adrien Du Port, several heirs to the greatest names in the kingdom signified their support in advance for the end of privileges: La Fayette, hero of the war in America; Bishop Talleyrand, just appointed to Autun; the Duc de La Rochefoucauld, inimical to the morals of the court; his cousin Liancourt, the philanthropic agronomist; the Duc d'Aiguillon, one of the richest landowners in France.

All the same, some of these liberal *grands seigneurs* retained a sense of distance and conceived their action as an indispensable adaptation of the aristocracy to the new times: everything must change so that everything could stay the same. The Third Estate revolution would spontaneously feel itself closer to renegades like the Abbé Sieyès or the Comte de Mirabeau, elected on its own lists.

At the end of 1788, it put forward the quintessential revolutionary idea: going beyond liberal unanimity, it demanded equality. The fight against absolutism was already won – and had been for far longer than contemporaries imagined. It then discovered an essential element which had remained buried, undisclosed, like humiliation: the hatred born of a society of orders and a 'racism' of birth, exacerbated by the separation into the castes of the various ranks of society. Aristocratic society at the end of the eighteenth century, corrupt in its principle, suddenly revealed the psychological and political ravages provoked by the obsessive fear of differentiation: *bourgeois honour impugned had become equality*. History was already being accelerated in this cut-and-dried equation. It had made compromise between the enlightened classes very difficult; on the contrary, all parts of the Third Estate shared a common hatred of the aristocracy. That is evident from just one example: the Abbé Sieyès had become the man of the moment.

SIEYÈS

We must linger a little over the name of Sieyès – the best symbol of the French Revolution. Jacques Bainville observes that Sieyès punctuated the frenzied advance of the French Revolution with three utterances. At the beginning of 1789: 'What is the Third Estate? Everything. What has it been up to now in the political order? Nothing.' After 1793: 'I survived.' In the autumn of 1799: 'I seek a sword.' He was not the greatest man of action of the French Revolution; he was, however, its most profound political thinker. He gave it an initial impetus, in the winter of 1788–9, with three successive pamphlets: *Essai sur les privilèges* (Essay on privileges), *Vues sur les moyens d'exécution dont les représentants de la France pourront disposer en 1789* (Views on the means of action available to representatives of France in 1789), and lastly, *Qu'est-ce que le Tiers État?* (What is the Third Estate?), the most celebrated, which made his name renowned in the space of a few weeks.

They all appeared over two months, between November 1788 and

January 1789, at the time when Louis XVI and Necker were taking their decisions on methods of convening and assembling the Estates, in the throes of political crisis. Few books have acted with as much force on major events as these three occasional pamphlets, written in haste but with extraordinary power, in which a priest who had not been too badly treated by the *ancien régime* developed a philosophy of revolution in the name of the Third Estate.

Sieyès was a priest. Born in Fréjus into a modest bourgeois family which was hard put to it to establish its five children, he followed the usual ecclesiastical channels, without any special vocation but as an intellectually gifted child. Taken under the wing of the Jesuits, those great unearthers of talent, and then by the Congréganistes de la Doctrine Chrétienne, he was in Paris in 1765 at the small seminary of Saint-Sulpice – the large one was for young noblemen training to become bishops – where his teachers found nothing to remark on, apart from his 'sly' nature, but his insatiable appetite for books.

Ordained a priest in 1772, he had read everything about the philosophy of the Enlightenment, both French and English. The notes he made during those long years of study, preserved in the National Archives, show evidence of an unlimited intellectual appetite, somewhat undisciplined, ranging from literature to metaphysics, art and music, with an especial passion for philosophy and political economy; Locke and the physiocrats were the writers whom he constantly read, reread, discussed, challenged, questioned.

In 1775 he wrote a *Lettre aux économistes sur leur système de politique et de morale* (Letter to the physiocrats on their political and moral system), which he did not publish. Everything in the mechanism of different societies interested the young Sieyès: money, banking, labour, trade, production, property, sovereignty, citizenship – everything, with the exception of history. The basis of his thinking was political, in the widest sense of the word, and conformed to the dominant trend of French Englightenment philosophy: it was a question of thinking of society in accordance with reason, whereas it offered only the spectacle of unreason. From an early age Sieyès was fanatical about public happiness.

The potent and simplifying genius of this young priest could find no outlet in the world of the *ancien régime*. First of all, he needed protectors in order to get himself a post, to find a sinecure and help his family. A letter of 1773 to his father – he was twenty-five years old – at the time when he had just missed a coveted benefice, is very revealing both of him and of the old society: 'If it had gone well, I would have been somebody, instead of which I am nothing. Never mind, I cannot complain yet, because my course is not yet run. I will either make my way in life or perish.' He found that life in the train of an aristocratic bishop, first of Tréguier, then of Chartres, Jean-Baptiste Joseph de Lubersac, a *philosophe* like himself, and also like him an administrative priest. So the Abbé Sieyès was established, soon provided with a benefice, then becoming a canon of Chartres in 1783, and finally Vicar General, the bishop's closest assistant and already a minor personality in the Church of France.

He had a fine status, but his real life lay elsewhere: not in religion (there is not the slightest evidence that he was ever interested in that) nor yet in his private life (everything indicates that he did not have one), but in his books and the intellectual life of the century, which he was continually debating, pen in hand, for his own satisfaction. When history's hour struck, this priest had published nothing but had written a great deal; he had lived nothing but meditated on everything: the *philosophes* Helvétius and Condillac, Rousseau, Turgot, the physiocrats, Hume, Adam Smith.

A contemporary, the Swiss Étienne Dumont, a friend of Mirabeau and one of the sharpest observers of the political world of 1789, has left the best pages yet on the subject of Sieyès, as witness this note, indispensable for anyone wanting to understand the nature of his intellect and the secret of his oracular behaviour in 1789–90: 'One day, having dined at M. de Talleyrand's, we went for a long walk in the Tuileries; the Abbé Sieyès was more communicative, more talkative than usual; in a burst of familiarity and openness, having talked to me about several of his works, his studies, his manuscripts, he spoke this striking sentence: "Politics is a science which I believe I have mastered."' Here was the rare coincidence of a man who had been unable to set down his ideas now finding a theatre where they could be enacted.

When he published his first pamphlet in November 1788, it was clear that this deviser of systems, the abstract intellectual, ideal prey for the great critics of 1789, from Burke to Taine, was also driven by a tremendous passion. The *Essai sur les privilèges* effectively set the tone for what was to be the motivating force of the Revolution several months before it broke out: hatred of the aristocracy. It is a short work of about twenty pages, violent, categorical, taut as an arrow winging to its target and piercing old society in its vital spot – privilege.

What is it, what else can it be, this privilege, if not the ultimate corruption of the concept of law, since it forms categories of individuals who are strangers to what makes the community? Sieyès at once establishes democratic universalism as the natural law of society, the only one which conforms with reason. Privilege removes its beneficiary from the public sphere of the state in order to define him by particular interests which keep him apart from it by placing him outside citizenship. It also brings in its wake antisocial psychological effects: the feeling of belonging to another race, the passion for domination, exaggerated self-esteem, etc.

Unlike Rousseau, Sieyès was not against modern society; if he occasionally speaks with Rousseau's accents, it is to denounce the moral corruption of aristocratic society alone. In that society, where privilege abounds, there is but one culprit, the very incarnation of evil: the nobility. The nobles have the monopoly of honour, the great driving force of every society; they cannot support their lofty position without money, the other great social reward; but, deprived by their very privilege of legal means of earning wealth, they live only as court parasites, estranged from the nation as a whole, their sole industry being a kind of high-class mendicancy.

Sieyès, who had taken such a long time to write anything other than notes on his reading, had reached the age of forty before circumstances drove him to publish his first twenty pages. But what pages they were! The nobility stands condemned there before the tribunal of reason, cast out from the nation, together with the court turned into the scapegoat of the movement of opinion in favour of the regeneration of the kingdom. The solitary abbé had guessed what was to happen, and suddenly took a hand in shaping events. His pamphlet even suggested what one year later would be called the *'ancien régime'* – that imaginary breaking point which consigned preceding centuries to nothingness: 'A time will come when our outraged offspring will be astounded to read our history, and will give that most inconceivable insanity the names it deserves.'

Sieyès's second pamphlet, *Vues sur les moyens d'exécution dont les représentants de la France pourront disposer en 1789* deals with the matter of the Estates-General from the angle of their necessary transformation into a 'National Assembly', vested with constituent sovereignty. The abbé was aware of the classic objection made to a republic, that is, a people's government, in a large country: the nation can no longer be assembled to allow it to discuss and vote on laws, as was done in the ancient city.

He got round this by way of a theory of representation, by which he extended to the political field the idea of division of labour elaborated by one of his favourite authors, Adam Smith. It was a question of 'selecting from the mass of citizens different classes of representatives who as a whole form, in their person and their kind of work, what we call the *public establishment*'. This 'establishment' is set up in accordance with a 'proxy' given by society to its mandatories, whether they be executive agents or legislators. In all cases, these mandatories do not therefore represent mere fractions of the social body (their electorate, for example) but the entire nation.

Moreover, the process of delegation of legislative power must not be handed on too far down the line, so that it can stay close to its source: 'Every legislature continually needs to be refreshed by the democratic spirit; it must therefore not be placed too far distant from the original initiators. Representation is there for those being represented; so the general will must not be lost, by passing through a number of intermediaries, in a disastrous aristocratism.' Thus Sieyès laid down the foundations of a theory of representative government, one torn from the start between the inalienable nature of the nation's rights and the delegated sovereignty of its representatives. Even before it had taken place, the Revolution had pinpointed what would be one of its greatest problems.

Shortly afterwards, in January 1789, *Qu'est-ce que le Tiers Etat?* resumed the argument of the *Essai sur les privilèges*, enlarging on it and being more specific. It is a longer, more complex pamphlet, simultaneously more theoretical and more practical, a treatise and a battlecry, a mixture which accurately presages the spirit of the Revolution. On a philosophical plane, the beginning of the text shows the extent of Sieyès's debt to the physiocrats and English political economy: society is approached from the viewpoint of the economic activity of its members, and as the place where the progress of civilization operates by the production of wealth. From all the useful classes that contribute to it by their labour, nobility is by definition excluded, since it cannot exercise a private profession; as for the public services which it is supposed to undertake, these could be more usefully carried out by men of the Third Estate. For it is absurd to place at the head of the state people who are defined by what separates them from the public good, these 'strangers in our very midst', says Sieyès, a 'caste':

That is the right word. It denotes a class of men who, without function and without usefulness, enjoy personal privileges merely by the fact of their existence . . . The noble caste has usurped all the good positions; it has turned them into a kind of hereditary possession and therefore exploits them, not in the spirit of social law, but for its private profit.

By this device, Sieyès extends the accusation to the monarchy, which is guilty of being the slave of that parasitic aristocracy: it is not the king who reigns, it is the court. The complementary nature of the nobility and the king, which Montesquieu had seen as a balancing act favouring the liberty of individuals, becomes for the abbé the combined domination of private interests over those of the nation: a forceful argument, with a promising future in that it shifts condemnation from the social to the political, including the old royalty in the curse hurled at the nobility. The court was there, close at hand, buzzing with intrigues and loaded with wealth, a very exclusive party for the privileged, perfectly illustrating the evil denounced by the prosecutor for the people. Monarchic centralization had produced both Versailles and Paris, *the* court and *the* town, as if to present two perfectly opposed embodiments – of privilege and public opinion.

What sort of society could be rebuilt upon this excommunication of the nobility, upon the ruins of that absurd regime? One dictated by reason, or science, which is its other name. Sieyès challenged every lesson drawn from the nation's past, and every example from abroad. Reading him, one realizes how revolutionary reason had been constructed, like an abstract deduction drawn from absolute and universal principles: as has been seen, he rejected any adjustment of the existing order, which stood condemned in its entirety; he denied the worth of any example in the English constitution, although acknowledging that it had a character 'astounding for the time when it was established'. But a century after 1688, the French were benefiting from the progress of the Enlightenment: 'Do not let us be discouraged if we find nothing in history to suit our situation. The true science of the state of society does not go back very far.' What he meant was that he had just founded it! A little later Mirabeau called him 'Mahomet'.

All those individuals, or the ensemble of those classes of individuals, engaged in the production of social wealth or in public service form a political community which Sieyès calls a *nation*: a cardinal word, one of the strongest in revolutionary vocabulary, but also one of the most enigmatic, because it reprocesses the 'flesh' of all the history constituted by the kings to form the basis of what is being born – the unique legitimacy of the community. The 'laws of the nation' in the face of royal 'despotism' had been a current theme of *parlementaire* opposition, by which jurists referred to the kingdom's customary 'constitution', buried in the mists of antiquity. For Sieyès, the nation means the community formed by the association of individuals who decide to live freely under a common law, forged by their representatives. It is the constituent will, the social contract itself in its founding act; the nobility has no part in it, since nobles escape the universality of the law and have their own private assemblies.

It was towards this founding act that the next Estates-General could and must proceed; the people already enjoyed a certain civil emancipation, through the progress of what the Scottish philosophers had called 'commercial society'. Now it had to constitute itself into a political society in order ultimately to form a nation. Only the Third Estate could do this, because it alone constituted in advance the body of those associated with the common enterprise.

It was nothing, yet it was everything: that was the famous phrase in which Sieyès gave a radically new meaning to the old institution of the Estates-General, and showed the future representatives of the Third Estate where their duty lay, as sole guardians of the national will. It was not enough that the numbers of members of the commons should be doubled or that voting should be by head: the privileged, for as long as they were defined by privilege, were not representable. The Third Estate must meet separately: 'It will not join with the nobility and the clergy, and will not vote with them either by order or by head . . . It will be said that the Third Estate by itself cannot form the Estates-General: it will make up a National Assembly.'

The argument of this celebrated book is such that it can be read at two levels. Sieyès presents a complex theory of the formation of the body politic starting from individuals in civil society; he combines a classically liberal starting-point, the multiplicity of private interests typifying modern man, with the construction – almost an obsession – of a unitarian general will, which is inalienably possessed by the nation, delegated to and subsequently exercised by its representatives.

But the triumph of the pamphlet lies less in this learned reflection than in what it offers, with brilliant simplicity, to anti-aristocratic passion. Public opinion is burying the years of contempt under a rediscovered equality, which has once more become the natural principle of every society. It excludes nobles from the nation. It celebrates the death of the court and its courtiers, the end of noble arrogance, and its own deliverance from social humiliation. *Qu'est-ce que le Tiers État?* offers us the French

Revolution's biggest secret, which will form its deepest motivating force –
hatred of the nobility: as well as being a thinker, the abbé was a resentful
man, settling old scores with the old society. In resolving his lifetime's
quarrel with the well-born, he had touched the fiercest passion of public
opinion, which found a voice in him.

Now, the king was seeking advice from that very opinion, though he
believed he was still addressing the orders of the realm. This misunderstanding deserves some comment.

PREPARATIONS FOR THE ESTATES-GENERAL

The institution of the Estates-General had belonged to the tradition of the
French monarchy since the end of the Middle Ages; it had often been used
by kings of France between the fourteenth and sixteenth centuries.[1] Its
purpose was to assemble round the monarch, when he so desired, the
'representation' of the kingdom, intended to assist him with its opinions
and advice. 'Representation' must be understood in the old sense of the
word – one of the most interesting in both ancient and modern politics –
which goes back to the very nature of old society. The individual had no
existence other than by membership and solidarity with units such as the
family, the community, the corporate body, the order – defined by rights
which were both collective and personal, since they were group privileges
shared by each of the members. The social universe was thus formed by a
pyramid of corporate bodies which had received their position and their
titles from history and the king of France, according to a hierarchy in
keeping with the natural order of the world.

The 'representation' of this universe to the king worked quite naturally
from the bottom upwards: the upper level 'represented' the lower which,
by its position, it incorporated and whose identity it took over. The king of
France, at the summit of the pyramid, subsumed and embodied the
ensemble of corporate bodies constituting the nation, to fashion from them
one sole body of which he was the head; his consultation with the 'Estates'
had as its only objective to set the seal on the unity-identity of society and
its government. In the framework of this concept of the social aspect, the
process of 'representation' was not intended to develop a common political
will arising from the interests or wills of individuals, but rather to express
and transmit from the bottom upwards, and right to the very top, the
requests (by definition homogeneous) of the corporate bodies of the realm.
That is why it was linked to the 'imperative mandate', by which every
community delegated to the higher level representatives who were not

---

[1] In the following pages I summarize an article which I wrote for a collection entitled *The
Political Culture of the Old Regime*, vol. 2 of K. M. Baker (ed.), *The French Revolution and
the Creation of Modern Political Culture*.

entrusted with the task of 'representing' them in the modern sense of the word, but simply with being the faithful spokesmen of their wishes.

The rules of convocation had never acquired a fixed form. Electoral methods, right to vote, the number of constituencies and deputies – nothing more. If a systematic history of the Estates-General were to be made, it would offer an excellent illustration of the characteristic incapability of the *ancien régime* – in spite or because of its incessant legislative activity – to formulate fixed rules regarding public law and official institutions (a theme dear to de Tocqueville, who saw in it one of the origins of the Revolution's *tabula rasa*).

When, in July 1788, the decision was taken to convene the Estates-General to consult it on ways of resolving the crisis the kingdom was going through, no body of doctrine or statutory documents existed to help the royal administration define the rules of the electoral game. Moreover, that consultation procedure had fallen into disuse, at the wish of the kings, since the first half of the seventeenth century. If, for want of a doctrine, the King's jurists wished to find a legal precedent, they had to turn back to the Estates-General of 1614. The last sitting was already nearly 200 years old: there were no archives, not even an oral record. The victim of its own practices, absolute monarchy no longer possessed either heritage or tradition which would allow it to consult public opinion in indisputable form.

Therefore, by decree of the king's Council on 5 July 1788, the king asked his subjects to send to the court 'memoranda, information and clarifications' on the conduct of the Estates. He appealed chiefly to the learned societies, by the device of a tribute to the academies, which prompted ironic comment from de Tocqueville, who was surprised that such a topic had been submitted to them. But during those last years of the eighteenth century the problem of the vote and political representation – in the modern sense this time – had really become a philosophical question, discussed by the savants, as can be seen in the works of Condorcet, for example. Though tradition was silent, confused, too distant or too faint, philosophy could answer in its place, at the behest of the monarchy itself.

With the hindsight of two centuries of democratic practice, no government in the world today would engage, with this kind of innocence, in a problem with such far-reaching consequences as the methods of organizing a ballot. But that experience was precisely what the French monarchy lacked. It trusted in the new spirit, which was already prevailing, to return to an ancient institution with very few rules. Not that matters really had such clear-cut simplicity, because many political intrigues interfered with regulatory decisions: the royal entourage tried to settle old scores with the privileged, who were guilty of unleashing the revolt, while Necker, at least the most popular if not the most influential minister, cautiously explored the route towards an English-style monarchy. But in the two key texts of 27 December 1788 and 24 January 1789, as well as in all the documents relating to the organization of the impending Estates-General, the general management of thoughts and decision was certainly influenced by that dialogue of the new spirit with a lost tradition, which it permeated throughout without obliterating it.

On 6 November 1788, when Louis XVI met the assembly of notables to get their advice on the matter, Necker, opening the session, underlined the changes which had taken place since 1614, and put forward the idea of 'equity' of representation: that meant not only the doubling of the Third Estate, but also proportionality between the numbers of those represented and their representatives. The two proposals were justified by the recent transformations in the economy and in society. The implementation of the first would have the greatest bearing on the subsequent sequence of events, after the fusion of the deputies of all three orders into the National Assembly in June.

Intellectually speaking, however, the second idea is the more revolutionary. In fact, even if it seemed for the moment limited only to the Third Estate elections, it was inseparable from the modern idea of representation: in trying to set up a stable connection between every representative and the number of his electors, it came back to the concept of individuals possessing equal rights in the formation of political power and of a 'national' assembly. From what one can read of the deliberations of the notables, who were nobles, it is less surprising to find them on the whole hostile to the doubling of the Third Estate and innovations, than to see them devote so much comment to the idea of a necessary proportionality between the population of a constituency and the number of its deputies.

There are many quotations on this theme to be extracted from the records of a meeting which assembled the greatest noble names in the French monarchy. The importance attached to argument in opposition to its final decisions on the doubling of the Third Estate and proportionality between represented and representatives reveals how little assured the majority of those 'notables' were about the imprescriptibility of their rights. Furthermore, when it came to discussing methods of voting within the Third Estate, this assembly of the privileged came out in favour of universal suffrage, by a very large majority, without making any distinction between the right to elect and to be elected – whereas that distinction would be characteristic of revolutionary legislation.

Now at last, Necker's report of 27 December 1788 on the preparation of electoral regulation could allow the spirit of the times a major role. Recalled to power by opinion rather than by royalty, the philosopher-administrator finally had the chance to implement his ideas on the need to let elected assemblies participate in government, representing the wants of society. But the Protestant banker, mindful of his failure in 1781, also knew better than anyone that he would have to mollify the nobility and the 'grands', handling their amour-propre even more delicately than their vested interests, as he had shrewdly noted in *L'Administration des finances* ('In France, distinctions of status form the keenest subject of interest; obviously, no one objects to the pecuniary advantages to be gained, but it is the tactful handling of ideas of superiority which satisfies the most active feeling.') From that stemmed the contradictory nature of his text, midway between tradition and innovation. Not in the sense that a political compromise would be effected within each of the points under discussion: certain questions were treated according to the spirit of innovation, others left to tradition – or, rather, to the prevailing understanding of tradition. Two spirits are in contention for the minister's document, but they are simply superimposed, with no attempt made to reconcile them.

They are both stated successively at the beginning of the report: the first rests on the precedent of 1614, the second on public opinion, which in so far as principles were concerned, was the minister's overriding reference, since it led him to make the fundamental recommendation of proportioning the number of Third Estate deputies to the size of the population represented:

There is only one opinion in the kingdom on the necessity to adjust, as far as possible, the number of deputies from each *bailliage* [bailiwick] to the size of its population, and since it is possible in 1788 to establish this proportion on the basis of certain knowledge, it would obviously be unreasonable to abandon these measures of enlightened justice merely to follow in servile fashion the example of 1614.

These few lines said it all, through the indirect praise for the statistical efforts of the *intendants* and their staff: drawing its unanimity from knowledge and justice, public opinion was paramount, while at the same time there was a kind of modern political representation, based on both the equal rights of individuals and technico-administrative rationality. Noteworthy also is the rejection of a 'servile' imitation of the 1614 precedent. Through the intermediary of its minister, the monarchy itself set reason and justice against tradition.

The recommendation for doubling the Third Estate was made, starting from an exposition of the order's motives. On that point – the most hotly discussed in the current national debate – Necker first prudently presented the list of supporters for each of the two arguments. But this double enumeration revealed the incomparable superiority in influence and numbers of the innovators, because when all was said and done, besides a minority of notables and nobles, they comprised 'the public wish of that vast portion of your subjects known as the Third Estate'. Lastly, for good measure, the minister invoked 'the deep murmur of the whole of Europe, which generally favours all ideas of common equity'. This was a way of introducing into the weighing-up of royal decision the key argument of the irreversibility of history – with whose future in the nineteenth century we are all familiar.

History versus tradition: through this contrast one can measure to what extent the French monarchy itself – contrary to what Burke would write – had stopped referring to a traditionalist vision of the kingdom's constitution, seemingly to open the way to reform, but in reality to a subversion of its spirit and history. Into the necessity for changes acknowledged by the minister came not so much a concern for institutional renovation as a feeling of inevitable evolution.

However, while the December document contained this major shift in the idea of representation to the benefit of the Third Estate, in the name of the progress of civilization, it insisted more than ever on the separation of the orders in the consultation which was about to start and the meeting which must follow: a point which, theoretically, cancelled out the doubling of the Third Estate, since the orders would sit separately; then, whatever the number of deputies for each entity, the two privileged orders would be in a position to dominate the third.

In this connection, it is interesting that the separation of the orders should be recommended in a far more radical fashion than in the sixteenth century or in 1614, when the bailiwick assemblies had frequently mingled the nobility and the Third Estate. So that at the very moment when it was laying claim, at least implicitly, to a democratic conception of the vote within the Third, the royal government was on the other hand reinforcing its aristocratic character, falling back on its own tradition.

That central contradiction is to be found throughout the regulatory arrangements organizing the elections, as set out in the bill of 24 January. On the one hand, apart from the watertight separation of the orders, the regulations hark back to tradition, insisting on the idea of an assembly intended purely to advise the king, stipulating that in towns inhabitants should meet in corps and trade guilds, increasing the number of particular cases and exemptions in the name of acquired privileges. Above all, it preserved the traditional procedure of the *cahier de doléances*, or list of grievances, which was supposed to present the unanimous wishes of each community: a procedure inseparable from the concept of the imperative mandate, and incompatible with any public electoral competition according to the modern plan.

On the other hand, however, the text of 24 January – similarly prepared by Necker – made an appeal to the spirit of the age, to the development of mentalities, underlining the need to make the representation of bailiwicks more or less proportional to their population, and set itself the objective of 'an assembly representative of the entire nation'. All the regulations carefully worked out in the January bill and those which followed bore witness to the will to institute, as fully as possible, a 'fixed' principle, and to organize consultation with all the people of the realm, by transforming into a voter every adult Frenchman enrolled on the tax registers. As Michelet clearly saw, the French people – with the peasantry to the fore – were for the first time about to make their massive entry into a political ballot in the spring of 1789.

Over and above everything else, no distinction had been drawn between the right to elect and the right to be elected: every individual with access to electoral assemblies – that is, any Frenchman of age – automatically acquired the right to present himself for the votes of his fellow citizens. If one considers as a whole this dawning of political equality and the adjustment of the number of seats to the population of the bailiwicks, Louis XVI's electoral regulation – in regard to the Third Estate alone – was comparable to a modern district poll, slightly complicated by the different levels of election, from the parish to the *chef-lieu* (administrative centre) of the bailiwick.

Thus, in the organization of a consultation of its own devising, the French monarchy had combined the spirit of tradition and the spirit of geometry, a respect for precedent and democratic innovation. There is no reason for surprise that it should contrive, here and there, to remain faithful to its past: the structure of the society of orders was part of the very nature of the monarchic system. On the contrary, it is surprising that it should combine at one and the same time three consultations, which were distinguished from one another more carefully than ever and corresponding, with the three orders of the realm, with the general implementation of modern democratic principles, as if partial conformity to the traditional vision of government and society were meant only to imbue the conflict between aristocracy and democracy with its already revolutionary purity.

Historical truth invites us to attribute more innocence to the actors in this prologue. For what confers exceptional transparency on this sort of interregnum between the *ancien régime* and the Revolution is not the autonomy and the will of the government of the kingdom: on the contrary, its impact derives from the fact that the old monarchy was for the last time lending its presence to the ambiguities of society and the spirit of the era. It resolved upon the meeting of the Estates-General unaware that, though the *ancien régime* had a very long past, the monarchy had never had any tradition of representation – or even a real tradition at all – in the sense of the English constitution.

Incapable of building an institution on this void, it yielded to the two alternatives offered by its history and its current position: aristocracy and democracy. At the very moment when it was making distinctions within the nobility itself and separating it from the nation, it gave the Third Estate the means of embodying and uniting that nation. Not only did it bequeath democracy to the Revolution but, before expiring, offered it the means of forming itself into a national body politic against the aristocracy.

THE CRISIS OF 1788–1789

An element which, in itself, owed everything to chance added its measure of disorder to the situation. The political crisis was accelerated by one of the biggest economic and social storms of the century; the heavens also were revolutionary. It had all begun with the bad harvest; the storms and floods of 1787, then the drought, and lastly the hail of 13 July 1788, which ravaged western France – everything had conspired against the harvest, which was catastrophic.

Urban industry lacked rural outlets and laid off workers; the ability of business to resist was weakened even more by a Franco-British trade treaty in 1786 which, by reducing import tariffs on British products in France, had increased its vulnerability. This was true mainly of the textile trade, a great industry of the period and the unsurpassable domain of British progress; at the start of 1789, there were 12,000 out of work in Abbeville and 20,000 in Lyon. *Intendants* disclosed the increase in begging and vagrancy. A traditional signal of social crisis and alarm, an explosion of prices further cut back incomes already hit by unemployment; in Paris, at the end of spring, bread cost four sous a livre, where the precarious balance of the popular budget reached its top limit at about three sous.

Violence erupted everywhere; in the countryside, where the small peasant could no longer manage to feed his family from his crops, let alone pay his lord and the king; in the towns, where the lower classes were demanding work and a fixed price for bread. At the end of the 1788–9 winter, which had been so severe, trouble broke out from Provence to Burgundy, from Brittany to Alsace; peasants and workers raided grain stores, stopped the transport of grain, threatened lords who claimed their dues, and *intendants* who symbolized taxation. In Paris, in April, a crowd of poor wretches looted the big Réveillon wallpaper factory and were then massacred by troops.

In this great anarchistic movement, when authority melted away, the traditional elements of the *ancien régime*'s corn riots are recognizable. But its novelty lay in a sort of unanimous direction of the movement, born of the contemporary political situation. It did not matter that the urban masses' demands for regulation were contradictory to the *philosophes*' *laissez-faire*: that was a problem the future would pose, not the present. For the moment, the crisis united the entire Third Estate against seigneurial privilege, against tax assessment, and for a profound reform of traditional political society.

Food riots coincided with the political effervescence of the clubs and enlightened societies, the mutterings in the suburbs with the revolutionary speeches of the Palais Royal. In short, the uprising of the poverty-stricken provided revolutionary consciousness with the strength of numbers and a feeling of urgency. Throughout the entire period of elections to the Estates-General, the tone of the thousands of brochures and pamphlets addressed to the French had noticeably heightened: Sieyès had set the keynote.

The *cahiers de doléances*, drawn up according to custom by local assemblies of the three orders, presented a more delicately shaded picture. It is true that neither the wretched peasant nor the unemployed craftsman could express themselves directly, since they were unable to write and were almost as incapable of speaking in public. They probably had little in the way of spokesmen at these parish or guild assemblies, which met in the village or local district church. The old practice of the imperative mandate which underlay that of the *cahier* presupposed the unanimous agreement of the electorate on the missions given to representatives. That is what makes the ensemble of this multitude of documents, which emerged from the greatest public consultation in modern French history, difficult to interpret and probably misleading: under the umbrella of the people as a whole, it was really the lawyers who were expressing themselves; they had most often presided over the assemblies and drawn up the grievances.

Within the Third Estate, the existence of several electoral strata had also acted as a filter for the demands. The revolutionary radicalism of *Qu'est-ce que le Tiers État?* was not to be found in the *cahiers*, although it was acclaimed by a vast reading public. That divergence forewarns the historian against simplification and allows him to grasp, even if crudely, the existence of several kinds of public opinion. In Paris, revolution was already widely expected, but the French *en masse* still expected the reforms they considered essential to come from the king.

It is true that the reforms demanded constituted a formidable programme of change. Almost all the orders – the clergy less vehemently than the other two – called for the end of 'despotism' and for a controlled monarchy. The Estates-General had become quite a different matter from a mere financial resort. It had been given the task of 'regenerating' the kingdom through a liberal and decentralizing constitution, ensuring forever the natural rights of individuals as conceived by the philosophy of the century: individual liberty, property, intellectual and religious tolerance, compulsory voting on taxation by periodic meetings. The king, once freed from the evil influences of his entourage, remained the supreme guarantor of this new social happiness. The *cahiers* of the nobles were as reformatory on this point as those of the bourgeois.

Beyond this kind of national unanimity – which was already a revolution in itself – appeared the multiple social conflicts of ancient France: that society of 'status' and 'rank' was supremely one of particularisms. Many of the *cahiers*, for example, set rich and poor peasants at odds over the sharing of common pastures, shopkeepers and guild masters over freedom to work, bishops and priests over the democratization of the Church, nobility and clergy over the freedom of the press.

But the essential distinction was the one which separated the privileged orders from the rest of the nation. For the Third Estate was not only in favour of voting by head, which would establish its political supremacy, or of fiscal equality, to which the majority of the nobles' *cahiers* had in the end assented. It was also demanding full equality of rights, the admission of all to public office and military rank, the abolition of seigneurial dues, with or without compensation: in short, the end of the society of orders. Since it was no longer simply a matter of a new state government, but of a new civil law, the holders of privileges dug their heels in against this additional revolution for equality: most of their *cahiers* indicate this very clearly.

The revolt of the parlements, the resignation of the government and the

convening of the Estates had thus already determined two major modifications. Little by little they had transferred public authority to the coming
assembly, by the very fact of the unanimity which had been revealed
regarding a liberal reform of the monarchy. At the same time, however,
the methods of convocation and the electoral campaign had disclosed the
deep and secret wound afflicting society: inequality of birth, which
separated the Third Estate from the privileged orders. Already, any transformation of the monarchy, if it were to be accepted, would of necessity be
accompanied by a total upheaval of aristocratic society: that was the price
paid by absolutism for its systematic manipulation of status and rank.

The development is even more obvious if one moves from the *cahiers*,
which are the visible part of the 1789 poll, to the election of the deputies,
which is the hidden part. In effect, since electoral procedures had for the
most part broken the traditional structures of the kingdom, and since no
opposing debate of programmes or ideas had been foreseen before the
vote of the different assemblies, the Third Estate deputies who emerged
victorious from the interminable consultations were elected less by the
people than by the intrigues and compromises preceding the vote. The
victors were all declared enemies of the aristocracy, carefully selected from
among the Third Estate, with a few rare exceptions like the Abbé Sieyès or
the Comte de Mirabeau, who had broken their ties with their respective
orders.

THE THIRD ESTATE

At the beginning of the twentieth century, Augustin Cochin's great contribution was to grasp this aspect of the 1789 elections, and to show their
mechanisms by way of the Breton and Burgundian examples. In Burgundy,
for instance, in the autumn of 1788 everything revolved around a small
committee at Dijon, which worked out the 'Patriot' platform: doubling of
the Third Estate, voting by head, and also exclusion of the ennobled and
seigneurs' agents from commoners' assemblies – a significant and fundamental precaution against the risk of aristocratic contamination of the will
of the Third Estate.

From this starting-point, the Patriot committee infiltrated all established
bodies. First of all, the barristers, who had almost been won over in
advance, then the minor members of the legal profession, doctors, guilds,
finally the town hall, through the intermediary of one of the sheriffs and
under pressure from 'zealous citizens': in the end, the document concocted
in a small committee had become the unanimous wish of Dijon's Third
Estate. From there, under the usurped authority of Dijon's municipal
officers, the *corps de ville*, it reached other neighbouring towns, where a
similar outflanking of constituted authorities by barristers and laywers took
place. The *intendant*, Amelot, Necker's protégé, who was an adversary of
the parlements, looked favourably on these events. In December, the
nobles organized themselves around what had such a short time ago been

Dijon's *philosophe* and *parlementaire* party. This time they intended to resist the egalitarian exaggeration of their erstwhile allies, the barristers, but they were excluded from the Patriot camp, which held sway over the *cahiers* and the elections.

Most of the history of the 1789 ballot has still to be written. It was long concealed by examination of the *cahiers* only, which often masked the truth. A whole network of propaganda and manipulation had an almost obvious but still little-known hand in it. The historian can pick out certain leading figures, such as the Committee of Thirty, which included many great names of the morrow – Mirabeau, Du Port, Talleyrand, La Fayette – or the small committee which formed around the Duc d'Orléans, with Sieyès and Choderlos de Laclos, but details of intrigues and their results are unknown.

For want of procedures and institutions, the dawning egalitarian democracy developed by way of circuits of enlightened opinion which characterized the century: clubs, Freemasons' lodges, groups of thinkers. There was more deliberate and concerted action towards the incipient revolution than history has recorded, yet no one imagined – or could imagine – the unprecedented nature of what was happening. For the *ancien régime* still appeared to be in place, and the king of France, as in the past, was banking on regaining his authority through the very division of his subjects. But it was only a matter of time. The deputies to the Estates arrived in Paris at the end of April. The opening session was planned for 5 May at Versailles.

Now, between May and August 1789, the entire *ancien régime* came to grief. In three months, the space of a season, in the most extraordinary summer in French history, nothing was left standing of what the centuries and the kings had constituted. The French had turned their rejection of the national past into the principle of the Revolution. A philosophical idea had become incarnate in the history of a people.

It all began with the deputies, who from the start refused to bow before the king. On the day when the Estates met in the hall of the Hôtel des Menus Plaisirs, the main problem was whether to vote by head or by order. Louis XVI reiterated his choice through the protocol of the reception of the deputies, which scrupulously respected the traditional distinctions: at the opening session, he furthermore indicated his wish to limit the competence of the Estates to examination of the financial problems alone.

But he did not have the means to effect this policy. Faced with some 600 deputies of the Third Estate, he could not count on support from all the members of the two privileged assemblies. Among the clergy, where internal strife had been lively, there were only forty-six bishops out of 300 deputies, and many country priests were being attracted by their Third Estate neighbours. One third of the nobility group had been won over to liberal ideas, and was dominated by the reputation of the *parlementaire* Du Port and the American prestige of La Fayette.

On the contrary, the Third Estate's large number of deputies was remarkable for its social and political homogeneity: no peasants, artisans or workmen, but a group of bourgeois, educated and earnest, unanimous in the desire to transform both state and society. The lawyers, who were the most numerous, were not conscious of any distinction between themselves and the merchants and shopkeepers; the local celebrities from the French provinces, whose shining hour had truly arrived, were not intimidated by Paris. The Bretons, Jean Denis Lanjuinais and René Le Chapelier; Jacques Thouret and François Buzot from Normandy; the Dauphinois, Barnave; Rabaut Saint-Etienne from Nîmes and Maximilien Robespierre from Artois were there on equal terms with Sylvain Bailly, the Parisian Academician.

Under the anonymous greyness of costume and origin was concealed the strongest collective will ever to have moved an assembly. The sole concession it made to the aristocratic times – but that, too, was a clever move – was to leave the limelight to two turncoats from the privileged orders: the Abbé Sieyès, elected at the last moment by the Paris Third Estate, and the Comte de Mirabeau, spurned by his order but welcomed by the Third Estate of Aix-en-Provence – the thinker and the artist of the Revolution.

The former we have already met, at the moment when he threw down the gauntlet to the *ancien régime* at the end of the preceding year. The latter, also just turned forty, was equally desirous of settling many an old score with the state of society. However, while the abbé was a studious man who had long cultivated a sort of cold rage against old society, Mirabeau had suffered its injustices from the inside, through the various troubles of his life. Born into a well-known family of Provençal nobility, the son of the famous physiocrat Marquis who was passionately interested in agronomy and political economy, his childhood and adolescence read like a chronicle of the *ancien régime* in which his battles with his father were punctuated by exiles, *lettres de cachet* and jail.

He had a volcanic nature: in early youth he deserted his regiment, ran up debts, compromised women – including his own wife – slept with his sister, fought his rivals. His father took more and more legal actions and prohibitions against him, and on several occasions had him imprisoned. The two men wore themselves out arguing family disputes in court.

Mirabeau emerged from this extraordinary and wretched life about 1780, earning his living by writing: despite his great name, he took on little jobs amid the numerous band who lived on the small change of the Enlightenment, as if that were the inevitable path towards the great roles to come. France was a literary country. Great works and great ideas received a warm welcome from a vast public, and were served by an army of fluent writers with a nose for the market. The old Marquis de Mirabeau, his father, had been a literary man and a crank; he himself acted like all the ambitious young commoners of his age and could imagine only one way to fame:

writing. What were the others doing at the same period – Barnave and Brissot, Camille Desmoulins and Antoine Saint-Just? Since literature had assumed a political function, it also found itself the antechamber to politics.

While he waited, Mirabeau sold his pen – and that of others – without much delicacy in his methods: he had never had any, and never would. In the last years of the *ancien régime*, this impoverished aristocrat wrote for the powerful men of the day, published in favour of Calonne against Necker, for the speculator Isaac Panchaud against his rivals, a series of dissertations often written by others – notably by his associate Etienne Clavière of Geneva, and by the young Brissot, another literary adventurer of lesser rank. Even his friend Chamfort had worked for him for a short while.

Mirabeau had failed at everything: with 1789, everything would smile on him. This disorganized, erratic, unfaithful, venal man grabbed at the opportunity of his life: to be elected deputy of the Aix-en-Provence Third Estate to the Estates-General, to offer his torrents of words to the new nation. Rejected by his own kind, the most despised son of the old nobility had all he needed to become the most brilliant figure in the revolutionary assembly. His talent for oratory, his quick-wittedness, his anger against the past, his temperament – none of which had so far found a use. But he had something else, more deeply concealed, which made him an exceptional person among all those Third Estate legal men.

One would look in vain, among the men of the Revolution, for a similar blend of high birth and unconventionality. Many of the leaders of 1789 would prove to be nobles – La Fayette, the Lameths, Talleyrand – but a liberal noble is not a noble who has lost his class. Quite the opposite: the spirit of liberty is a possession generously available to both bourgeoisie and aristocracy. As for the bohemian element, heaven knows it was well represented in the French Revolution; but in 1789 its time had not yet come: when it did, in 1792, noble birth had become a curse. On the other hand, in the spring of 1789 France was still groping amid the chaos of events for the constitution of an English-style political class, mingling liberal nobility with enlightened bourgeoisie. This fusion, which went back over several centuries of English history, now had to be taken on all at once by the old kingdom, by way of democracy and amid popular tumult. Who could act as its guarantor before the new-born 'nation'? Who was both democratic and aristocratic enough to make the France of yesterday bow before the Revolution? Mirabeau was the only noble sufficiently *déclassé*, and the only *déclassé* noble enough to link the past with this advent.

From that providential cross-breeding of status, like a great musician he would draw superb sounds. The Revolution showed him where his genius lay, providing him with a stage and a job. The assembly which met at Versailles in May 1789 included a number of intelligent and capable men who had made a name for themselves in their various callings, and some who already had a brilliant career. To that earnest community he brought flair, inventiveness and imagination. He produced the decisive words of the epoch. He would have been its leading light had he not dragged in his wake rumours of scandal and money troubles – his *ancien régime* legacy. Nevertheless, he would at least be its voice, and very frequently. This voluminous writer, this amateur, this tempestuous man discovered the strange power of incarnating the Revolution and threw all his formidable energy into it: he was one of the leaders of the great debates in those early months.

THE ESTATES-GENERAL

As from 6 May the Third Estate rechristened itself the 'Commons' (Communes), as if the new name washed it clean of old humiliation. Thus, in a single movement, it held firm against the king. For more than a month it refused to undertake the verification of credentials apart from the other two orders; because through sheer numbers it held sway over the great hall, it chose to wait and let its social weight exercise its attraction. That long month of May 1789 was one of passive revolt. Far from wearing out the commoner-deputies, it welded them together into one soul: on 10 June, at Sieyès's appeal, the Third Estate invited the other two chambers to join it in a communal verification of the credentials of 'all the representatives of the nation'. The roll-call began on 12 June; the next day, the first signs of weakening appeared within the clergy, and three priests from Bas Poitou, by joining the Commons, gave the signal for a support which increased in the following days. Strengthened by this clerical backing, the assembly on 17 June, at Sieyès's urging, declared itself the 'National Assembly'.

It had taken a long time debating this formula, in the consciousness that it was taking a decisive step. Mounier, already cautious and already unaware of what was going on among his colleagues, had argued for a definition which would open the door to a compromise with the privileged orders: 'a legitimate assembly of the representatives of the major part of the nation in the absence of the minor part'. Mirabeau had proposed that the meeting of the Third Estate should be formed of 'representatives of the French people'. But the word 'people' concealed a partial and inferior implication – that of the Roman *plebs* – whereas the term 'National Assembly' had no ambiguity.

By the use of this name alone, the Third Estate relegated to the past the whole of the society of orders, and created a new power, independent of the king. The next day, it assigned itself the vote on taxation and placed the state's creditors 'under the guard of the honour and uprightness of the French nation'. This was a clever way of telling the Parisian bourgeois, who were so near at hand, that if bankruptcy was a royal custom, then the protection of property-owning *rentier* democracy was a revolutionary innovation. Truly a different sovereignty had just been baptized: the Revolution had been born.

The Third Estate's daring move divided the other camp, but hardened the remainder. The mass of the clerical deputies swung towards the National Assembly; a third of the nobles also voted for 'union'. But in the hour of danger, the majority of bishops and nobles rediscovered their natural protector in the figure of Louis XVI. They hurried to Marly, where the king had withdrawn in his sorrow after the death of his eldest son; they preached resistance to him. At the same time, but from a different stand-point, Necker felt that the king must resume the initiative. He put forward the idea of a royal sitting of the Estates, at which the king would simply say what he would and would not accept.

But who was to define what was acceptable? Who would write the royal speech? In the meantime, on the pretext of making the necessary arrangements for this sitting, the large hall of the Menus Plaisirs was closed, and so the deputies of the 'National Assembly' found the doors shut on 20 June. They therefore took themselves off to a large building nearby, the Tennis Court, which they immortalized by their famous oath 'never to separate, and to meet wherever circumstances demand, until the constitution of the kingdom is established and affirmed on solid foundations'. At all events, the reply was given in anticipation of any potential threats from authority.

But what did the king want? For once in his life – the first and the last time – he expressed it clearly on 23 June, in the two declarations which were read out for him. Necker had prepared the first version, but his enemies, upheld by Marie-Antoinette and Artois, had the last word on the final text. On this occasion, Necker did not come. This royal testament granted approval of taxation and loans by the Estates, liberty for the individual and the press, and administrative decentralization; it expressed the wish that the privileged should accept fiscal equality. But it said nothing about equal eligibility to any office for all men, and did not envisage voting by head except in regard to certain limited problems, refusing it explicitly for anything connected with future Estates-General. Lastly, it expressly upheld the hierarchies of aristocratic society. In short, the monarchy acknowledged the liberal demands, but denied equality of rights: it accepted only the reforms which had the assent of the nobles. The threat of the barristers had for once united bureaucracy and the dukes; but only around the death-bed of the old monarchy.

As soon as the king had departed, followed by the deputies from the nobility and the prelates, the young Marquis de Dreux-Brézé, grand master of ceremonies, addressed the men of the Third Estate, who remained there motionless and silent: 'Gentlemen, you know the king's intent.' In the following minutes, the Revolution found three Roman phrases to express the new era. Bailly: 'The assembled nation cannot take orders.' Sieyès: 'You are today what you were yesterday.' Mirabeau: 'We shall not leave our places save at bayonet point.' The National Assembly decided to persist with the preceding resolutions and decreed the inviolability of its members.

Jacques Louis David The Tennis Court Oath of 20 June 1789, *Musée Carnavalet, Paris.*
(Photo: Lauros-Giraudon)

Had Louis XVI the means of imposing his policy in those decisive days? He did not even try. From then on, the resistance of the privileged was broken down by successive defections. On 27 June the King himself accepted the *fait accompli* by inviting 'his faithful clergy and his faithful nobles' to join with the Third Estate. In the evening, Paris was illuminated. The National Assembly had become a constituent body.

Two powers now had a presence; one entirely new, which had suddenly emerged from the Estates-General, the other bequeathed by the centuries: the Assembly and the king. What did this coexistence mean in actual fact? Absolute monarchy was dead, and the aristocratic monarchy outlind on 23 June was stillborn. Could a monarchy and a National Assembly live together? On what conditions? With this completely unprecedented constitutional matter, the first question in the immediate future was one of the authorities charged with public order. In principle, they were still entirely on the king's side, but that was in appearance only.

What did Louis XVI want, in those supremely important weeks? That was one of the questions on which the future would depend, and was already being asked in all its fullness. The historian, however, can merely provide probable answers: the to-ing and fro-ing of decisions and counter-decisions going on at court have left no trace. On 23 June Necker had been defeated by his adversaries, supporters of the confrontation with the Third

Estate barristers; there is no cause to doubt his evidence, which an examination of the speeches confirms.

Between the end of June and 10 July everything points to the fact that Versailles was looking for revenge, and Louis XVI allowed the development of a policy of military concentration around Paris. Was it against the Assembly or against Paris? The clearest outcome of this common threat, on minds which were in any case ready to brandish it, was to unite the fears of both the Parisian mob and the deputies at Versailles.

REVOLUTIONARY VIOLENCE

Paris was the scene of daily excitement, a permanent meeting-place. From the economic viewpoint, nothing was conducive to calm: bread had never been so dear, there were large numbers of unemployed, whose ranks were swollen by a population which rural poverty had recently driven to the capital. Shopkeepers and *rentiers*, the backbone of the urban populace, grew alarmed about the value of their credit on the royal Treasury: when Necker lost ground at Versailles, they too felt threatened. But neither the hardships of life nor worries about private interests can explain the general unrest, which was of a political nature. The Estates-General, the proclamation of the National Assembly, the Tennis Court oath and the victory of the Third Estate had crystallized revolutionary public opinion in Paris, both popular and bourgeois, which was fed by the constant coming and going to Versailles.

That opinion had its centre at the Palais Royal, where 'patriots' of all allegiances converged to listen to orators and agitators. Paris was at last having its revenge on Versailles, where it had its bridgehead, and had already been victorious at court. The news which came through at the beginning of July, and the arrival of the troops both gave signs of a noble counter-offensive, referred to as an 'aristocratic conspiracy' since the spring. With a feeling of having to vanquish a formidable enemy lurking in the shadows, the Parisian revolution was on its feet for several weeks before taking action.

Now royal authority was foundering over the discipline of the soldiers: coaxed by the Parisian bourgeois, unhappy with the harshness of their officers, and won over by an awakening public spirit, their hearts were with Paris. On 30 June a huge crowd opened the gates of the Abbey at Saint-Germain-des-Prés for a number of soldiers who had been imprisoned for indiscipline. It was in this climate that the troops summoned as reinforcements started to arrive: the atmosphere of the Palais Royal won many regiments, even foreigners. It needed just one spark for the blaze to ignite.

It came on 11 July. Even before all the troops summoned were present, the king exiled Necker and dismissed his liberal ministers. The new ministry, formed behind the scenes several weeks before, and whose

Campion The Taking of the Bastille, *Musée Rothschild, Paris.*
(Photo: Lauros-Giraudon)

moving spirit was Breteuil, was a declaration of counter-revolution; but the dismissal of Necker by itself said it all to public opinion, which immediately interpreted this as a doubly unlucky omen: of bankruptcy and counter-revolution.

Reaction was instant. On the afternoon of 12 July Paris rebelled; soldiers of the Garde Française (the palace guards) joined the rioters, who soon controlled the city. The Baron de Besenval, in command of Paris in the king's name, fell back to the Champ de Mars, from which he would not budge: on 13 July the wave of people broke down the tolls, hated symbols of the Farm General's tax collecting activities, and looted the gunsmiths' shops. A new power emerged from the shadows, which had been prepared by the notables of the electoral districts in the spring: this 'permanent Committee', whose first measure was to organize a volunteer militia, wanted both to encourage and to control the insurrection. During the night of 13–14 July all Paris – illuminated by order of the Committee – could hear the first patrols of the new social order on the move. The National Guard was born.

At dawn on 14 July the mob gained control of the Hôtel des Invalides, where it found 32,000 muskets; it was also with the intention of looking for arms that the crowd then thought of the Bastille. This remarkable collective intuition had another, quite different, motive: there was no better symbol of the enemy than the legendary prison which, with its eight large towers, blocked the entry to the faubourg Saint-Antoine. The end of this monstrous urban, political and human anachronism must by its very nature mark the advent of liberty.

The Bastille surrendered in mid-afternoon, after a bloody outburst of shooting, and faced with the cannon captured at the Invalides. The victors – all traditional people, shopkeepers, *rentiers*, artisans, journeymen – then inaugurated the bloodbath which would always be part of all the great revolutionary episodes. The governor, the Marquis de Launay, dragged along the quays to the Hôtel de Ville, was killed in the Place de Grève; the chief municipal magistrate, the *Prévôt des Marchands*, Flesselles, suffered the same fate. Their decapitated heads, stuck on pikes, were paraded all the way to the Palais Royal.

The fall of the fortress, which no one at the time considered to be the decisive event it later became, did not quell the rising: a week later, on 22 July, Joseph Foulon de Doué, one of the men in Breteuil's ministry, was hanged by the people in front of the Hôtel de Ville, together with his son-in-law, Bertier de Sauvigny, *intendant* of Paris, accused of 'having young corn cut' in order to starve the poor; the obsession with corn continued to be the principal cause of accusation and popular terrorism against the men of 'ministerial despotism'.

But it was really on 14 July that the decisive battle was played out: for Louis XVI, having taken the resolve on 11 July, had effectively abdicated on 14 July. At Versailles, the court plied him with contradictory advice: going against the Comte d'Artois, who was already counselling him to take refuge in Metz under the protection of loyal troops, he resigned himself to remaining, or in other words, to giving in.

On 15 July he announced to the Assembly the recall of Necker and the dismissal of the troops; on 17 July he went to Paris in the afternoon and acknowledged the new authorities born of the insurrection, Bailly and La Fayette, respectively mayor and commander of the National Guard. Popular welcome, at first very reserved, warmed up only at the Hôtel de Ville, when Louis put the red and blue municipal cockade in his hat – the cockade which would produce the revolutionary flag when La Fayette added to it the white of old France. In short, the crowds acclaimed the king's capitulation as well as his presence.

The victory in Paris brought in its wake that of the towns; everywhere the kingdom's bourgeoisie seized and channelled the torrent of urban emotions. As if naturally, they relieved *intendants* without powers and governors without troops, making general the Parisian example of the National Guard. It was the revenge of the communes against monarchic centralization, the end of those *corps de ville* in the hands of the monarchy. But the victory of liberty over despotism was not the same as that of the old franchises of aristocratic society. It had taken place in the name of new principles, and was accompanied by a very keen consciousness of the national unity enveloping those principles: suddenly ties of revolutionary brotherhood were woven between town and town, and 'federations' were set up, after the old Latin word. The idea of nation was inseparable from local democracy, which was its condition and guarantee.

The urban revolution joyfully celebrated its triumph. The sporadic outbursts of popular violence which marked this immense transference of power did not yet trouble the clear conscience of the bourgeois. The king appeared to have yielded. While the Bourse greeted regained confidence by resuming trading, the nobles were starting to leave. The court set the example. Those courtiers who had foreseen nothing had long since lost the habit of acting in concert and fighting.

A first wave of several thousands of departures took place in July–August. The Comte d'Artois, the Prince de Condé, the Duc d'Enghien, Breteuil, the Contis, the Polignacs, gave the signal the day after July 14. All the great names of the court abandoned the king and queen in their misfortune: they blamed them for a weakness which they themselves had helped to create and from which they had amply profited. They would continue, from the other side of the Rhine, to discredit both the monarchy and the nobility in the eyes of the new France. It was a role of which they had held the secret since the death of Louis XIV.

But neither the king nor the court had yet drained the cup to the bitter dregs. For the subversion of the traditional order was so general that, after the deputies' revolt and at the same time as the municipal uprising, it revealed a third revolution, emerging from the social depths of the kingdom: it brought to the Parisian Revolution, which had sided with the deputies against Louis XVI, the anarchic support of the vast peasant class. Everything had happened in Paris, and the *journée* of insurrection on 14 July had been the start of the long and exclusive dominance – which would last for a century – of the capital over French public life. But just for once – and it would not occur again – the country areas, instead of merely following, had also risen up with the same intent.

In the spring, the electoral situation had aroused in peasant hearts a hope as vehement as the despair born of the crisis: the injustice of seigneurial dues and the royal tax was a general complaint in the *cahiers*. At the same time, poverty was driving on to the roads and around the hamlets hundreds of vagrants, who aggravated the chronic insecurity of the countryside. Fear of brigands, harking back to the mists of antiquity, seemed more than ever to prowl round villages living in terror. Everywhere, rumour's mysterious voice murmured to the peasant that, come rain or shine, apocalypse or blessed event, it was a decisive moment.

Violence erupted in the second fortnight of July, and sometimes very clearly took the form of social warfare: in the *bocage* (farm enclosures) of Normandy, in Hainaut, in Alsace, in Franche-Comté and the valley of the Saône, armed peasants attacked châteaux and abbeys; in collective celebration they came there to burn the old deeds of their serfdom, as if the destruction of seigneurial archives would deliver them once and for all from the tithe and the field rent. But in the rest of the kingdom, the

peasant revolts took a more complex turn: Georges Lefebvre has reconstructed the paths taken by what was called the Great Fear.

The news of the taking of the Bastille was slow to reach the villages,
and assumed en route end-of-the-world proportions which increasingly
provoked reflexes of panic and defensiveness. It was also harvest time, a
major period of rural life, and destructive brigands were therefore all the
more to be feared. Peasant imagination and rumour, fascinated by echoes
of urban propaganda, saw them as the mercenaries of the enemies of the
people and of that aristocratic conspiracy with another face: foreign
invasion. In Limousin, it was supposed to be the Comte d'Artois coming
from Bordeaux with an army of 16,000 men. To the east, the fear was of
Germans; in the Dauphiné, of Savoyards; in Brittany, of the English.
From village to village the false news spread, grew fat on exaggeration and
tyrannized the countryside. The peasants kept watch and armed themselves as best they could. One can thus follow, from day to day and from
village to village, the route and ramification of the 'Fears': it was the
simultaneously panic-stricken and threatening form assumed by the former
jacqueries (peasant risings) in the hour of the French Revolution.

THE END OF PRIVILEGE

At Versailles, the deputies were surprised to discover the social frailty
of a civilization which had shone so brilliantly during the Enlightenment.
Bourgeois or nobles, they were all, to a greater or lesser degree, property-
owners in one way or another: seigneurial rights were a possession, too,
and it so happened that some commoners enjoyed them if they had
purchased a seigniory. But to re-establish order in the name of property
would shatter the unity of the Patriot group; the new bourgeois militias
would join with the royal mercenaries against the country folk, to the
greater advantage of the king. The other idea was to satisfy the peasants in
order to bind them to the revolutionary nation, but that would have to be
done more widely and more swiftly than had been planned; fiscal equality
would not be enough, nor the abandonment of what remained in France of
ancient serfdom. The entire regime of seigneurial and ecclesiastical dues
was brought into question.

After tending for a moment towards repression, the majority of the
Assembly realized its political impossibility and plunged headlong into
another strategy. On the night of 3–4 August about a hundred deputies
gathered together in a Versailles café by the 'Breton Club' (forerunner of
the Jacobins) decided to take the initiative on the inevitable reforms. In the
evening of 4 August the nobles gave the signal: through the voices of a
younger son of a poor family, the Vicomte de Noailles, and one of the
richest lords in the land, the Duc d'Aiguillon, the peasant uprising made
itself heard by the deputies. The philanthropic tone of that famous sitting

was imparted by those nobles who were sacrificing such ancient feudal titles on the national altar; gone was the oppression of the peasants, gone the 'gothic' distinctions, gone the divisive privileges.

Enthusiasm for civic equality, however, did not rule out a certain amount of calculation. Aiguillon concluded in favour of the need for fiscal equality, straightforward abolition of *corvées* and serfdoms, as well as the redemption of other feudal dues at interest of 'one denier to thirty'. This fairly low rate (3.3 per cent) clearly indicates that the great lord had been careful to set the highest value on the capital to be redeemed. It was a matter of converting the old seigneurial due into a sound bourgeois contract: the nobles saved the essential part, and the propertied men of the Third Estate had everything to gain from the equalizing of noble land and commoners' land. The tithe alone was abolished without compensation: in terms of revenue, the clergy were the principal losers on 4 August.

Abandoning the feudal principle was such an important step that the Assembly was gripped by a kind of magic of transformation: they vied with one another to be first at the tribune to renounce the privileges of the old world, amid general applause. The most famous parliamentary night in French history thus ended the sale of offices and instituted equality of eligibility for jobs, the abandonment of all provincial or local privileges and the triumph of the 'national' spirit. The old parlements, already forgotten, so quickly overtaken, suffered the common fate. The feudal regime was obliterated. At three in the morning, in order to associate him in due solemnity with the birth of the new world, the Assembly proclaimed Louis XVI 'restorer of French liberty', a phrase which indicated that there was still something in the nation's past worthy of being 'restored'.

The debates continued until 11 August, so that the exalted votes of the great night could be drawn up in right and due form. The final decree, written by Du Port, declared that 'the National Assembly completely destroys the feudal regime.' It established the end of personal privileges, the admission of all to any employment, free and equal justice for all, the abolition of any remaining serfdom and the suppression of the tithe, which laid such a burden on peasants' crops. By contrast, the majority of seigneurial dues and judiciary offices were declared redeemable: the Assembly had wanted to save all properties by integrating them into the new law.

In fact, the elimination of what the men of 4 August termed the feudal regime would take place more slowly than the decrees of 11 August would lead one to suppose. The laws were actually completed in 1790 and 1791 by several supplementary decrees. The redemption of suppressed judiciary offices was a long process, taking several years. In the rural areas, the redemption of seigneurial dues was too burdensome for the peasants, and there were sporadic outbreaks of unrest, in Quercy for instance. Finally abolition without compensation was voted in July 1793. Nevertheless, despite the wariness and long-windedness, there was something in the Assembly's and its contemporaries' perception of 4 August which, for the historian, remains fundamentally true: the notion of a break with the old society and the foundation of a new one.

The peasant felt himself victorious over the seigneur. The bourgeois had broken aristocratic privilege. What the deputies had termed feudal comprised an extraordinary variety of properties and rights, because they had included features which were really feudal legacies – such as the vestiges of mortmain (tenure in perpetuity), the residue of seigneurial justice, or the dues paid by the tenant to his lord – and elements which had nothing to do with feudalism – such as the ecclesiastical levy of the tithe – or which came after the feudal era, like the sale of offices. Basically, what the text of 11 August called the destruction of the feudal regime was the annihilation of the aristocratic society which absolute monarchy had patched together on the ruins of feudal society. What disappeared in August 1789 – and for ever – was a society of corporate bodies defined by shared privilege.

What came into being was a modern society of individuals, in its most radical conception, since everything which might come between the public sphere and each actor on the stage of social life was not only suppressed, but also roundly condemned. The Revolution rediscovered an idea put forward by Sieyès at the end of *Qu'est-ce que de Tiers État?* Within the modern individual there are two legitimate sides: the private one, which keeps him apart from others in enjoyment of himself, his family and his private interests, and that of the citizen, which he shares with all other citizens and which, in aggregate, forms public sovereignty. But the third side, that of the social individual who tends to create inter-social coalitions on the basis of particular interests, must be ruthlessly excluded from the state. Hatred of aristocratic society had led the men of the French Revolution to ban associations, in the name of radical individualism: two years later, Le Chapelier's law against trade unions and employers' associations would solemnly confirm this.

CONSTITUTIONAL DEBATE

Thus the laws of 11 August did not only, or especially, establish that property-owning society dreamed of by the monarchy's enlightened reformers in the eighteenth century. Nevertheless such a definition is not completely erroneous: provided 'property-owner' is not confused with 'capitalist' – France was an agrarian country at that time – it may well be said that the night of 4 August, by making all equal before the law, instituted the universal nature of the property contract: not a new economic society, but a new legal society. Quite simply, the nature of the decrees had another significance.

By the ban which they imposed, going beyond privilege, on all associations between private individuals, they excluded from the formation of sovereignty interests which any contracting individuals might have in common in civil society and might wish to see guaranteed or defended within the state. If, in order to have a legitimate existence, the public sphere must undergo such a radical denial of the interests at stake in modern society, that did not make the problem of its constitution and its authority any simpler: how was the divergence between social man and the citizen to be dealt with?

That was the chief question of the summer for the Constituent Assembly; by destroying the 'feudal' regime, it had redefined the French people as individuals who were free and equal in the eyes of the law. It then had to constitute them as such in a corporate political body. Two debates were crucial in this respect. The first concerned the Declaration of the Rights of Man, the principle of which had been accepted before 14 July. But the discussion, punctuated by so many spectacular events, lasted until the end of August. It was long, complex, contradictory, and passed through the filter of numerous preparatory drafts of the final text, which was agreed on 26 August.

The American Declaration of Independence in 1776 was present in all minds, but so was the chasm which separated the situation of the old kingdom from that of the American ex-colonies, peopled by minor land-owners with democratic customs, who from the start had cultivated the spirit of equality, unhampered by external enemies or a feudal or aristocratic heritage. As in the American example, the French declaration had to have as its aim the foundation of the new social contract within natural law, in keeping with the century's philosophy, and the solemn enumeration of the imprescriptible rights possessed by each contracting party, which entry into society guaranteed him.

In France however, those rights had not been in harmony beforehand with the social state: on the contrary, they would be proclaimed after a violent break with the national past, and against the corruption of an old society which had for so long trampled on the mere idea of a contract. This aroused many fears among the more moderate members of the revolutionary camp: Mounier, for example, was afraid of the anarchy which might spring from the contrast between the proclamation of theoretical rights possessed equally by all individuals and the actual social situation of those individuals – poverty, inequality, class distinctions. From that arose the compensatory demand for a declaration of the citizen's duties in order to underline his obligation at the same time as his liberty.

These debates, well known for their abstract quality, show evidence that the deputies recognized quite clearly the scope of the problem they were tackling. They had just declared the complete emancipation of the individual: what then would become of the social bond? Many among them wanted to affirm its equally fundamental nature. That discussion was the grand début of a famous *topos* of modern political philosophy. The idea that affirmation of the subjective rights of individuals as a foundation of the contract carried the risk of social breakdown has haunted European political thought ever since Burke, from conservatives to socialists; it was already fully present in the July and August debates of 1789 in the

Constituent Assembly, chiefly among those who were beginning to be called *Monarchiens*, but also outside.

However, it was the Patriots who easily won the day, and a simple Declaration of the Rights of Man, a preamble to the coming Constitution, was adopted on 26 August. It was a noble and well written text, often close to the American model. The essence was expressed in a very few sentences, leaving the way open to debate on their interpretation. Firstly, what had been done on 4 August: 'Men are born free and live free and with equal rights.' What rights? Liberty, property, safety and resistance to oppression, with all that derives therefrom: civil and fiscal equality, individual liberty, the admissibility of everyone for all employment, *habeas corpus*, non-retroactive laws, guarantee of property.

What most clearly differentiated the French declaration from the American text concerned the coupling of these natural rights with written law. In the American example, those rights were perceived as having preceded society and also being in harmony with its development; moreover, they had been inscribed in its past by the jurisprudential tradition of English Common Law. In the France of 1789, however, emphasis was placed on a certain political voluntarism: the law, produced by the sovereign nation, was established as the supreme guarantee of rights.

Article IV: Liberty consists in being able to do anything as long as it harms no one else. Thus the exercise of each man's natural rights has no limits other than those which ensure that other members of society may enjoy the same rights. These limits can be determined only by the law.

Article XVI: Any society in which guaranteed rights are not assured, or the separation of powers not determined, cannot be said to have a constitution.

So it was society's responsibility, through the intermediary of the law, to ensure the rights of individuals; that law which was constantly referred to in the articles of the declaration as the 'expression of the general will'. The dominant inspiration of the Constituent Assembly was centred on the law: its immediate highlights were the idea of 'general will', intended to define the extent and the exercise of rights, and the refusal to recognize any authority other than that of the sovereign.

Now, this 'sovereign', which was henceforth the people, or the nation, needed to be given a form, to be constituted: for a variety of reasons, that was an extraordinarily difficult problem. France was a modern nation, too vast for its citizens to be summoned together in a public square to vote on laws. It was also a very ancient nation, whose heritage included a hereditary king, at the head of what one of the deputies called 'the gothic colossus of our ancient constitution'. In three months, all of the complete sovereignty which he had held, over a kingdom represented in his person, had entirely disappeared. In its place was a society composed of free and equal individuals, on the one hand; on the other, a people who had reappropriated sovereignty: how was that to be organized? Ever since

Declaration of the Rights of Man and the Citizen, 1789, *Musée de la Ville de Paris, Musée Carnavalet, Paris.*
(Photo: Lauros-Giraudon)

Hobbes, philosophers of the Social contract had been puzzling over this problem, but it was now being posed for the first time in the existence of one of the oldest European monarchies.

To understand how the men of the Revolution tackled it, let us turn to the beginning of the great constitutional discussion at the end of August and start of September: having made the Declaration of Rights, they now had to organize the new public authorities by way of a real constitution. This could not be a shaky monument made up of ancient customs and haphazard revisions, like the *ancien régime* monarchy, but an ensemble of institutions based on the new principles, which were those of reason.

That definition already left outside the Patriot camp a small minority of former revolutionaries who, in fact, had been anxious since June about the way things were going and about the violence in July: among them were Mounier from Grenoble, Malouet, a naval *intendant* and liberal nobles like Lally-Tollendal and Clermont-Tonnerre. What united these *Monarchiens*, as they came to be called, was the desire to 'put an end to the Revolution' – a theme which was beginning its long career in French politics; there were, too, some fundamental convictions which drew them nearer to Necker and isolated them from the majority of the Assembly.

They were against the revolutionary *tabula rasa*, hostile to the reconstruction of a political society on the basis of will or reason. They believed that the extraordinary summer could be turned into no more than a fertile incident if it led to the reform, in a liberal, English sense, of what they called 'monarchic government', the heritage of the national past. Their vision was a joint sovereignty of the king and two chambers, breaking with absolutism but uniting with what a monarchy loyal to its origins ought to become.

A political and intellectual chasm thus separated the *Monarchiens* from what had, since June, been the overriding spirit of the Revolution. They were men who stood for continuity and the adjustment of institutions: this was the nearest that French political tradition came to Burke, and gives some idea of their political isolation in 1789. They battled in vain for a bicameral system, without realizing that, for an assembly which had struggled so hard to join three Estates into one alone, it was hopeless to try to recommend a return to a division between an upper and a lower chamber. The spectre of aristocracy would still stalk the Constituent Assembly without any need of them, but it had marked them out in advance as losers.

The same debate at the beginning of September, in which they were crushed, concerned another, more central, matter: the question of the royal veto and its right over the legislative authority, and therefore of the nature and attribution of sovereignty. On this subject, the Patriot orators were unanimous in excluding the king from either originating or holding sovereignty. The monarchy was merely a government which had just been constituted by the act of the Assembly itself, which had reinvented it by voting, without regard for its history. The prerogative of full and entire sovereignty thus belonged to the Assembly, which had been delegated by the nation to create a constitution; afterwards, once the authorities had been constituted, it would be embodied by the legislative power, of which the king, as head of the executive power, would merely be the secular arm.

Reading the debates, one is struck by the obsession with legitimacy which runs through them, the stress laid on the absolute transfer of sovereignty and the indivisible, ontologically unitarian nature of that sovereignty. Pastor Rabaut Saint-Etienne, the Third Estate deputy from Nîmes, spoke on behalf of all when he said: 'The sovereign is a single and simple entity, since it is all men collectively, without any exception: therefore legislative power is one single and simple entity: and if the sovereign cannot be divided, neither can legislative power.' Elsewhere, on the same day (4 September), like many others, he spoke of the 'general will'.

In these rather rustic phrases, which retain nothing of the complexity of Rousseau's concept, the words of the *Contrat social* nevertheless permitted the naming of the new realities, while concealing what they were unwittingly borrowing from the past: the indivisible and limitless nature of sovereignty was an absolutist inheritance which the 'general will' transposed in terms of the autonomy of individuals producing a collective autonomy.

From that democratic chemistry, which went straight from the individual to the universal, Rousseau had excluded representation as incompatible with the very principle of will. The Constituent Assembly, on the other hand, combined a certain naïveté about the mechanisms of representation with such a unitarian conception of the sovereign. Here again, the most systematic theory was advanced by Sieyès who, as we have seen, thought of this political representation, which was essential within bodies as vast and complex as modern nations, by analogy with the division of labour within the economy: the 'representatives' were appointed to legislative activity, acting by proxy for society, elected by virtue of their particular capacities by their constituencies, but holding their mandate from the entire nation, and thus collectively sovereign.

The Patriots in the Assembly did not espouse all the arguments of this complicated theory; but the common feeling was certainly to give the vote to those citizens who were enlightened and capable of autonomy, so as to make will and reason coincide, and together to resolve all the problems posed by Rousseau and the physiocrats. The general will of the Constituent Assembly went no farther than the sovereignty of a body which was supposed to concentrate in its bosom both free individual wills and the evidence of reason.

The eventual attribution to the king – despite Sieyès's advice – of a suspensive veto on the Assembly's decrees during two legislative sessions did not modify the general economy of the new constitution. For it was not a matter of a government constituted as a counterweight, American fashion, within a shared sovereignty; the king's provisional veto was conceived as a simple possibility of appeal to the nation, a right given to the head of the executive to verify that representatives were faithful to the general will.

It changed nothing in the nature of the constitutional system being set up, where the Assembly was sovereign and the king exercised only a

secondary power which it delegated to him, as the president of a republic
calling itself a monarchy. The consequences of this daunting ambiguity
would dominate French political history from the summer of 1789 right up
to the second half of the twentieth century, when the problem was settled
by the 1958 Constitution, modified in 1962.

MONARCHY, CHURCH AND REVOLUTION

These consequences became obvious at once, at the end of September
1789, and confirmed the 'republican' interpretation of the laws already
voted. Louis XVI was reluctant to give his sanction to the decrees of 11
August, to the Declaration of the Rights of Man and to the first constitutional measures. He tried to use subterfuge, while the Assembly
regarded all these votes as so many shares in constituent power, outside
royal sanction. As at the beginning of July, he opened up a political crisis
from a position of weakness.

The outcome was all the more to be expected since unrest had hardly
ceased in Paris, sustained by municipal elections and the revolutionary
incitement of the newspapers, and it increased rapidly in September,
nourished by the debate on the veto and the food crisis. For though the
1789 harvest was good, it had not yet been threshed and interim provision
had not been made. The disturbances of the summer made the circulation
of grain and the provisioning of markets more difficult than ever.
Unemployment was brutally aggravated by the emigration of many
aristocratic families, who dismissed their servants and threw out of work
their suppliers among the Parisian craftsmen. Money went to ground while
waiting for better days: the failure of the two Necker loans in August had
revived the fears of bourgeois *rentiers*.

When, at the end of September, the Flanders regiment summoned by
the king arrived at Versailles, all Paris felt a renewed threat of counter-
revolution, and was already talking of the possibility of the king's fleeing to
Metz. In this emergency, the entire Patriot party, united by the summer's
events – Versailles deputies, National Guard, Parisian democracy – prepared
for a new day of action to force the king to draw back. La Fayette and
Bailly, who could not have been unaware of it, and who remained the legal
resort in that urban anarchy, made no objection. Mirabeau, who was
already in favour of a strong royal government, was not in the habit of
going against the tide; moreover, having got the measure of Louis XVI,
it is probable that he supported the Duc d'Orléans's intrigues for the
succession, in the hope of reconciling monarchy and popularity.

In this dangerous situation, amid so many menaces, Louis XVI and
Marie-Antoinette provided the rioters with a cause. On 1 October the
officers of the king's bodyguard had invited the officers from the Flanders
regiment to dine in the beautiful opera theatre at Versailles. At the end of
the banquet, at which many toasts to the health of the king and the royal

family had been drunk, the king and queen, appeared in their *loge* with the Dauphin in his mother's arms. An immense acclamation accompanied them back to their apartments, where the tricolour cockade was trampled underfoot. The insult aroused fury in Paris: the next Sunday, 4 October, the Palais Royal crowd demanded a march on Versailles. The king was to be brought back to Paris.

Was it in order to isolate him from the accursed court? or so that if Paris regained its king, food and work might also return? The French Revolution was beginning its tempestuous relationship with urban poverty. The revolutionary lower classes continued to confuse the grain issue with politics; on 5 October a long column, mostly of women, formed at the Hôtel de Ville and started out for Versailles. Shortly afterwards, the 15,000 National Guards forced La Fayette to follow them. It was raining on that autumn Monday, which was the king's last day at Versailles. Having returned in haste from the hunt, Louis XVI gave in, after contemplating flight: he promised the women to have Paris reprovisioned, and the Assembly that he would sign the August decrees. But the arrival of the second Parisian procession as night was falling gave the crisis a second impetus: two commissioners of the Commune, who were escorting La Fayette, demanded that the king should return.

Everything was postponed until the next day; but the people, who had camped on the *Place d'Armes* finally invaded the château early in the morning. La Fayette, having rushed to protect the royal family, had no choice but to sanction the people's victory: from the balcony of the marble courtyard, where he appeared with a silent and distressed Louis XVI, he made promises and calmed things down. Louis XVI himself announced his departure for Paris: as in July, it was the king's defeat which won him the people's acclaim.

The huge procession of men and women moved off at the beginning of the afternoon. Following the National Guards, bearing loaves impaled on their bayonets, and the armed women and disarmed soldiers of the king, came the royal carriage, as heavy as a hearse, with the deputies and the victorious crowd in its wake. The people had imposed the tricolour emblem, together with the other symbols of their revolt: they were bringing back 'the baker, the baker's wife and the baker's lad'. At nightfall, after stopping by the Hôtel de Ville, Louis XVI arrived at the Tuileries, a prisoner in his own capital. A second wave of émigrés promptly fled the country.

By leaving Versailles, the monarchy was obeying the force of circumstance: exactly one month after the deputies had placed it under the yoke of the new sovereign, it was brought back to Paris under their supervision. Those two October days, as decisive as 14 July, marked the end of the sunlike solitude in which Louis XIV had revealed his royal omnipotence to his subjects, the people. All at once, they destroyed in actual fact the little that had remained of that power; in the streets they demonstrated the unlimited strength of the people's sovereignty, decreed by the Assembly. In Paris, the vast, melancholy Tuileries, where the royal couple were installed, had been more or less abandoned since the young Louis XV had left it in 1722 to go to Versailles: since then it had given shelter to a succession of 'squatters' including the Opera and the Comédie Française for a while. The royal pair, together with a small Court, were as if in exile in Paris.

To finish with this year of 1789, and even to go a little farther, something has to be said on the Revolution's relationships with the Catholic Church and the traditional religion of the French, through which the Revolution added a major element to the unprecedented break it introduced into national history.

That break, however, had not been brought about deliberately. It is certainly true that the French philosophy of the Enlightenment was anti-clerical in spirit, sometimes antireligious, and that in the act of inaugurating its reign, democratic civilization substituted the rights of man for a world regulated according to divine order. On another level, the clergy had been the first order in the kingdom, and the Church the greatest partner of absolute monarchy. But if, for that reason, it was inevitably wounded in the destruction of the *ancien régime*, the Catholic religion as such was not threatened by the revolutionary majority of the Constituent Assembly.

Republican historians of the nineteenth century, such as Michelet or Edgar Quinet, frequently remarked quite rightly on this point (to deplore it, however) that the 1789 Revolution did not intend to substitute a new religion for the old. Its ambition was limited to the radical rebuilding of the body politic on universal principles. In that it included, at least formally, features which gave it similarity to a religious movement; but the Assembly had never taken the step which would have placed the revolutionary concept in competition or contradiction with the Catholic faith. Although it had quickly given rise to a crisis with incalculable consequences between revolution and Catholicism, it was by way of a political logic of struggle against the *ancien régime*. By uprooting the Catholic Church from society, depriving it of its stability and possessions, it had violently separated French democracy from Catholic tradition. Here began a conflict which was fundamental yet circumstantial, from which France is barely emerging two hundred years later.

Its origins can be pinpointed as far back as the summer of 1789, since the Catholic Church had the most to lose through the reforms of summer and autumn. It received the first blow on 4 August, as the owner of 'feudal' dues, but it had to be reimbursed for these, according to common law. A far more swingeing blow, in the days that followed, was the suppression of tithes, this time with no indemnity. That exception had shocked Sieyès – the personification of equality before the law – but Mirabeau had justified it as making up for the public nature of the services rendered by the Church: if the tithe was too dear a tax for what it served to finance (education, welfare), the nation had the right to make use of the revenues for itself.

There was worse to come. The Church was also going to have to pay off the deficit which had given rise to the meeting of the Estates-General. On 2 November 1789 on the proposal of Talleyrand, Bishop of Autun, the Assembly placed 'at the disposal of the nation' the wealth of the clergy, to be used to repay the national debt. There again, the explanation of the motives was drawn from the idea of public service: the Church should not be considered as a true property-owner, but merely as the steward of its wealth, which was intended to allow it to fill offices which were themselves revocable. In any case, this type of confiscation was not unheard of in Europe's history, since the English crown and German princes had practised it under the banner of Protestantism, and Joseph II, Louis XVI's brother-in-law, had given a more recent example of it in Austria in the name of enlightened despotism. In the French instance, the men of 1789, who were not especially anticlerical, and were in no way antireligious as a whole, killed two birds with one stone: they resolved the problem of the public debt by dispossessing one of the privileged orders of the *ancien régime*.

That was without counting a third gain – the most important of all: by selling the Church's possessions to the public, by lot, they firmly bound a large proportion of the French people to the Revolution, by way of their new acquisitions. In a first stage (December 1789), the Constituent Assembly authorized the Treasury to issue 400 million notes (*assignats*) bearing 5 per cent interest, and with preferential entitlement in the purchase of ecclesiastical properties, which had become '*biens nationaux*'. This first issue would be used to discharge the most urgent of the state's debts. But the Assembly took a further step in autumn 1790: the debt had become worse because of the undertaking given in August to repay the capital of suppressed offices; the old taxes were no longer coming in, the new ones not yet, and the political situation offered nothing sure enough to discourage speculation.

In September, just after the dismissal of Necker, whose reputation had ebbed away during the past year, the assignat became paper money, with no interest, as legal tender, despite all the expert voices which were raised (Talleyrand, Condorcet, Du Pont de Nemours) to warn against its rapid depreciation in the face of metal coin. It would be the Revolution's great financial instrument, but also its political weapon: 'Assignats', said the Abbé de Montesquiou, 'will form the link between all private interests and the general interest. Their adversaries will themselves become property-owners and citizens by means of the Revolution and for the Revolution.' Thus the Revolution had provided itself with a tremendous political instrument to involve both bourgeois and peasants in its future, by the same act through which it ran the risk of ultimately alienating a large part of the Catholic population.

In the matter of relationships with the Church, the deputies had been drawn since the end of 1789 into a logic whose constraints they had certainly not foreseen. If the Church were merely a corporation under the jurisdiction of civil power, what was to be said and done about the corporate bodies existing within it, such as the monastic orders? The Assembly's Ecclesiastical Committee had a bill passed in February 1790 stipulating that the law no longer recognized monastic vows and authorizing freedom to leave monasteries for those who wished to do so. During the discussion, the bishop of Nancy wanted to obtain the Assembly's recognition that Catholicism was the national religion: the motion was rejected.

There still remained the question of who would take over the administration of the Church's property and possessions which had been 'placed at the disposal of the nation': this was a tense debate, rough at times – notably when the Assembly again refused to declare Catholicism the national religion – which concluded with the transfer of the property to the new departmental and district administrations. It was the moment of truth, which split the apparent unanimity of the autumn.

At that time, the mass of clergy and the faithful had espoused the Patriots' cause. Neither the suppression of the tithe nor the vote of 2 November had deeply affected the general enthusiasm, or yet called into question the relations between Church and state. The clergy had remained loyal to the national role it had played in the previous spring, at the time of the meeting of the orders. Moreover, it had gained something from the Revolution: during the beginning of 1790, when passions were running high, the Assembly had allocated to the Catholic religion a maintenance budget which, for the majority of priests, meant an improvement. The high dignitaries themselves, Boisgelin, archbishop of Aix, and Champion de Cicé, archbishop of Bordeaux, whose duties were more administrative than pastoral, had experienced less difficulty in entering into negotiations with the state because the entire *ancien régime* had well prepared them for it; although they lacked enthusiasm for the new principles, they had at least rediscovered in them, now transferred to the people, the temporal sovereignty they had been accustomed to acknowledge in the king.

It is true that for the jurists of the Third Estate this Gallican spirit was underlined by the memory of the parlements' battles against the papal bull *Unigenitus* of 1713 and by the Jansenist tradition. Hostility towards Rome and any papal intervention was very widespread among them, as was the will not to accept any authority of appeal against the Assembly's decrees: the sovereignty of the people was no more able to compromise in the matter of its omnipotence than that of the kings. But though the Catholic Church had been accustomed to this subordination to temporal power, it was still dependent on Rome in spiritual matters.

Thus the political ground which was common to the Revolution and the Church of France – the predominance of national sovereignty over Rome – could also give rise to a conflict of principles concerning the domain of the Catholic faith and the authority of the pope on the subject. The legal non-existence of monastic vows had offered a foretaste of this in February. Although French kings had frequently made laws on the religious orders during the eighteenth century, they had not destroyed their principle: with the Assembly's vote, was it or was it not a matter of unacceptable encroachment on the spiritual by the temporal?

Two additional elements, of a different kind but both of major import- ance, added their weight of uncertainty to the risks the Assembly was taking on the path which was gradually leading it towards legislative innovations regarding the Catholic Church. The first was that a section of public opinion was beginning to be disturbed by the blows struck at religious tradition, for instance in the Cévennes, where the Catholic popu- lation faced strong Protestant minorities and the Revolution reawakened old memories of the Wars of Religion. July 1789 had been celebrated on all sides, but since November the spectre of religious confrontation had been on the prowl, and that could offer the first piece of popular support for the vanquished aristocracy.

The rejection of Dom Gerle's motion, on 13 April – Dom Gerle was the monk, 'ardent Patriot, but nonetheless a good Catholic' (Michelet) who had wanted to have Catholicism declared the national religion – sparked off trouble at Nîmes and the surrounding area. A strong Protestant bourgeoisie, cautious but also firm, was confronted by a Catholic crowd, stirred up by demagogues; they might well have rearisen from the sixteenth century.

The other element, of course, was the attitude of the pope. Born into the aristocracy, a narrow-minded priest and ostentatious pontiff, Pius VI well embodied the Roman tradition, and that implies how far distant the Revolution was from his mental universe. He did not even have to wait for the night of 4 August (when he lost the *annates*, those dues levied by Rome on the occasion of the presentation of certain benefices) in order to feel hostile to the new spirit. But in 1789 events in France provoked revolutionary disturbances among his subjects in Avignon and, to a lesser degree, in the Comtat Venaissin: the Holy See was attacked not only through the Church of France but also within its estates. On 29 March 1790, on the advice of the French ambassador – the old Cardinal de Bernis, disloyal to his mandate – the pope condemned the principles of the Declaration of the Rights of Man in secret consistory. The conflict was as yet only latent.

In Paris, it was not perceived as imminent, or even certain. Neither the men of the Assembly's Ecclesiastical Committee, who at the end of 1789 were considering the reorganization of the Church of France, nor yet the prelates of that Church, who were not totally dedicated to the Roman Curia, had any presentiment of an out-and-out conflict. Historians have restored to that period of history what, for its contemporaries, had been unforeseen and unexpected. The Civil Constitution of the Clergy was not the work of anticlericals out to destroy the Catholic Church. Nor had it rudely aroused the French episcopate to a state of holy indignation. Although it marked the point at which the Revolution and the Church went their separate ways to become merciless adversaries, the men of spring 1790 were not yet aware of it. Through its decree, the Constituent

Assembly had gradually been brought into this conflict, without ever having desired its consequences.

From that, perhaps, comes the fact that the parliamentary debate from which the Civil Constitution would emerge – from the end of May to mid-July 1790 – frequently seems rather a disappointment to historians; it did not match up to the high stakes it was dealing with, which the future would reveal. 'The discussion was neither powerful nor profound', wrote Michelet, who extracted from it only one important thought – that of the Jansenist Armand Camus, one of the leaders in the debate: 'We are a national convention; assuredly we have the power to change religion; however, we shall not do so.'

In that moment of time which the Paris deputy allows us to glimpse, Michelet dreamed of the religion of the Revolution which, according to him, could then have seized its opportunity but failed to do so. He read into that claim – withdrawn almost as soon as it was put forward – the spiritual timidity of the Assembly which, like the kings, was obsessed only with its own sovereignty. In fact, though long and painstaking, the discussions on the bill which would produce the Civil Constitution of the Clergy evinced a drying up of ideas when faced with the immense question of the relations between the new principles and the old religion; they were discussions between politicians, jurists, quibblers over procedure; between an exhausted, subservient, almost secularized Catholicism and a Revolution huddled over its brand-new power, which had been conceived, however, on the absolutist model.

The bill comprised four headings. The first substituted new electoral districts for the Church's old constituencies, worked out on the recent division of France into eighty-three *départements*. There would therefore be only eighty-three bishoprics instead of 130, plus ten metropolitan *arrondissements*. Overall appointments of clergy were rationalized and simplified by the suppression of all traditional titles and offices – prebends, canonries, abbacies, chapters, etc. Episcopal authority was henceforth collective, each bishop having to be assisted by a permanent council of curates compulsorily associated with the exercise of his jurisdiction.

Article 5 of section I disengaged the Church from any submission to foreign bishops or metropolitans, that is to say, in the last resort, from Rome. Section II, still more innovatory, substituted election for the customary canonical formulae for the nomination of ecclesiastical incumbents. All electors could take part in the vote, which was equally necessary for bishops and priests. Paid by the state, bishops and priests must undergo the obligation of an oath of loyalty to the constitution. Section III fixed the remuneration of members of the clergy, reducing it noticeably. Section IV insisted on their residence, under the control of the municipalities.

The religious order was thus brought into line with the civil order, the edifice of the Church structured on that of the state, founded on a constitutional sovereignty deriving its legitimacy from election by the people, its links with the papacy were severed; now it depended entirely on temporal government.

Faced with a reform of this scope, the opposition, led by Boisgelin de Cucé, argued the incompetence of the state in matters spiritual. A law touching on such fundamental Christian traditions as the authority of bishops or the choice of priests must also be approved by a national council of the Church of France or by the head of the universal Church. The retort came next day from Jean Baptiste Treilhard, the Paris deputy. It extended to Church organization the curse which the Revolution had laid on the *ancien régime*, condemning it as a tissue of disorders and abuses which could be judged only by civil government: he immediately let it be clearly understood that what was going to cost the Church so dear, in this debate, was not religion itself, but its close involvement in the old order, its collusion with the power of yesteryear. In any case, who had defended the spirit of that religion better than the men of the Ecclesiastical Committee since, by the election of priests, they wanted to restore it to rules which were closer to its origins? There was therefore no reason at all to question the absolute right of the sovereign over ecclesiastical discipline: the constant tradition of the monarchy had vouched for it.

The discussion of the articles, which began on 1 June 1790, was interminable, grim and interspersed with other bills and debates which had also been planned for the agenda. However, the Ecclesiastical Committee finally managed to get the essence of its plan voted in mid-June. The whole was adopted on 12 July.

Although it overturned its entire organization, the law was not unacceptable to a Church which French kings had accustomed to the rough supremacy of political power. In any case, not so long before, its Austrian namesake had been subjected by Joseph II to reforms of comparable brutality. The majority of bishops had shown some reservations on the Civil Constitution, but the main body of the clergy seemed willing to accept. Nearly all the prelates, moreover, were playing a waiting game, uncertain about the ultimate incompatibility of reform with canon law; meanwhile they were not over-anxious to fuel the suspicions of aristocracy that their names aroused. On the advice of the bishops, with Champion de Cicé at their head, Louis XIV, more hesitant than ever, signed the decree.

But it was still necessary to obtain the support of Rome and, more importantly, once the effect of surprise had worn off, the firm and deep-rooted adherence of Catholic opinion. The Civil Constitution of the Clergy would not withstand the test of time.

PROGRESS OF THE REVOLUTION

Those nobles hostile to the new era had emigrated, were emigrating or keeping a very low profile. The abdication or dispersal of the different social groups composing the nobility is a quite surprising and relatively little known phenomenon. Doubtless it had its roots far back in national history, in the humiliation accepted under Louis XIV, the political abasement and the acceptance of sycophancy; and then, in the time of the Enlightenment, in provincial isolation or the irresponsibility of salon or court life. A great era for the nobility as regards the brilliance of the art of living, the eighteenth century had at the same time multiplied the proofs of the nobles' political incapacity: emigration was their ultimate penalty.

There is additional evidence of the way the nobles were dispersed: in the Constituent Assembly, a nobility that supported the Revolution was constructing the new France in company with the commoners of the old Third Estate. In the Patriot camp, two La Rochefoucaulds, a Montmorency, a Talleyrand-Périgord and La Fayette, at the summit of his popularity, heading the National Guard, or in other words, Paris. Among his rivals of the 'triumvirate', contesting his authority, were a member of the 'old nobility', Alexandre de Lameth, and the former *parlementaire* Du Port, side by side with Barnave, the non-noble barrister from Grenoble. Lastly, there was Mirabeau, superior to all by virtue of his genius, but for that very reason and for what was known about his past, suspected by all.

During 1790 something began to evoke an 'English-style' fusion between the revolutionary great nobility, which had maintained its social prestige, and the bourgeois revolution. The Festival of Federation, which celebrated the 'national' spirit as opposed to the vanished 'feudalism', was the outstanding testimony. It was the year of a very temporary – although they were unaware of it – reign of an Enlightened society which had been formed by the entire cultural evolution of the century, in which liberal nobles and successful bourgeois could share ideas. Salons, clubs and newspapers were the marvellously new means of spreading and discussing the great topics debated by the age, which had finally become reality. Even the Friends of the Constitution, established in December 1789 in the former Jacobin monastery and soon known as the Jacobin Club, took care to keep the poor at a distance by imposing a hefty subscription: here was a France of notables and property-owners replacing that of the seigneurs.

Was this the France that innumerable reformers of 'abuses', *philosophes* and physiocrats had so tirelessly mapped out? Was this the France that provincial academies' learned societies and Freemasons' lodges had tirelessly – and somewhat more timidly – argued about? Yes, certainly, to some extent: the idea of a property-owners' monarchy was older than the Revolution. But the way in which it had finally come to pass, in the abstractness of principles and a social storm, enveloped its birth in the ephemeral on both the monarchic and the property-owning side.

What had been most spectacular and profound about the event was related to the universality of its message, which had made it resemble a new religion. The 1789 Revolution had wanted to rebuild society and the body politic on the idea that the essence of man, and therefore common to all men, was liberty. It has emancipated the individual from the age-old bondage of dependence, simultaneously destroyed the power of divine right and aristocratic domination, rethought society on the basis of the rights of each contracting party, and the body politic on the free consent of the electorate, by means of representation.

It had in fact combined two inspirational sources: liberal individualism on the one hand, according to which the constituent element of the social pact is the free activity of men in the pursuit of their interests and their happiness; on the other, a very unitarian conception of the sovereignty of the people, through the idea of the nation or 'general will'. Those two sources had been violently separated by French philosophical tradition, since Rousseau's *Contrat social* can be read as a criticism of the first by the second. But the men of 1789 made a fragile synthesis of them, using the concept of reason, which allows one to pick out in each individual the share which he can contribute to collective sovereignty, and which, moreover, is educable; if man's universality was not yet quite ready for the exercise of all political rights, at least it might be in the future.

In the Constituent Assembly's debates and the laws it passed, one may thus endlessly follow that tension between the universal principles on which it prided itself and their adjustment to the current situation of the old kingdom, which was a product of its 'gothic' past. The idea of '*ancien régime*' explained what it could not yet do; that of 'revolution', by contrast, meant being torn away from that accursed past by the advent of rational legislation. The new rights of the French had been stated negatively on 4 August, by the destruction of 'feudal' law, and positively, on 26 August, by the Declaration: now it remained to define them in statutory law.

The universality of civil laws encompassed all Frenchmen without exception. The Constituent Assembly had wavered a little before the question of Alsatian Jews, who were less 'assimilated' than the Bordeaux Sephardim and were the victims of a strong local anti-Semitism, which had its spokesmen in the Assembly. To begin with, in integrated the second group into civil equality before the first group, which it emancipated 'in extremis' in September 1791, during the last days of its session. Even the 'Mosaic religion', that cement of Alsatian ghettos which seemed so strange to this old Catholic country, was in the eyes of the law no more than a private affair of individuals, to be absorbed into the legal equality of citizens, which was a constituent of national unity.

Classic ground for this tension between philosophical abstractions and political realities was the redivision of national territory. The Assembly wanted to give a rational basis to both the representation and the administration of the old kingdom. The session of 4 August had done away with the tangle of 'feudal' electoral districts. At the end of September 1789, Thouret, for the Constitution Committee, had proposed his geometric plan for eighty-one *départements*, composed of absolutely regular squares. As each representative of the people held his mandate not from his personal electorate but from the entire nation, the best equivalent of this wholeness of the nation was to have each part of it exactly equal to all the others.

To that logic, history, geography and economy opposed theirs: the reality of national space, composed of such differing populations, traditions and activities. Mirabeau countered the committee's idea with one of demographic equality, and Barnave invoked the weight of customs and 'usages'. A debate started in those days to which, by letter and by delegation, communities from the heartlands of France would contribute in the name of their preferences, customs and ambitions. The final division of the territory emerged from a compromise between rationalism and empiricism, the spirit of unity and that of local government. The new France was divided into *départements* of comparable size, mapped out by deputies in accordance with reason and history, and baptized by their natural elements, such as rivers and mountains; each of them was sub-divided into districts, cantons and communes. All were provided with elected administrations.

Elected by whom? Political citizenship is a complex affair. Its regulation by the Assembly explains how 1789 also belonged to the bourgeois order, even if the ideas which had inspired the Revolution burst right through that reality to which so many historians have tried to reduce them. The Constituent Assembly had decreed equality, but it had also learned from the century's books that aptitude for government and public life was born of independence and education, and therefore from property and affluence. Hence arose a complex stratification of political rights according to tax thresholds, which contributed again to social inequality.

The precautions taken against the poorest acted both ways, as much against the aristocrats as against the multitude, who would both be equally capable of trying to exploit their ignorance. Another indication of the time: domestics, who were particularly numerous in the service of noble families, were excluded from the right to vote on the grounds that they were not independent citizens. Nevertheless, right at the bottom of the pyramid, there were still more than four million 'active citizens' – an enormous, audacious figure when contrasted with the 200,000 electors in Louis-Philippe's France, fifty years later.

Above them came the second-degree electors, then those who were eligible, who formed the new framework of the country. Theirs was the new, elected administration – municipality, district, *département* – liberated from the detested and centralizing *intendant*; theirs was the new justice, independent of the government; theirs was the new army, the National Guard, which had sprung from the events of 1789 and was guardian of the new order. Enlightened society was a revolution of occupations.

Another aspect of bourgeois ascendancy was the freeing of economic interests. The Assembly abolished monopolies, regulations, industrial and commercial privileges. It instituted the freedom of internal trade and also, in 1791, eliminated the democracy of corporate interests by Le Chapelier's law – which extended to the labour contract the equality of individuals before the law. No one had any thought of defending the right of employees to form a coalition; that would have been to recreate the corporations and trade guilds.

In the countryside the new liberal orthodoxy, learned from François Quesnay, Gournav and Adam Smith, clashed with the old community system, the psychological and economic importance of which for the small peasant has been demonstrated by Georges Lefebvre. The big farmer beloved by the physiocrats had for a long time been demanding the opening up of markets and prices, the end of village constraints, freedom to rotate crops, the right to enclose fields and meadows and the end of collective grazing: rural capitalism was the condition of better productivity. In the end, the Assembly compromised. On the one hand, it instituted freedom of prices and, on the other, authorized that of crops, for the benefit of the needy and poverty-stricken. Similarly, Enlightenment France gave way to popular France over international free trade: despite the good harvest of 1790, it prohibited the export of corm: the old fear of famine still ruled people's minds.

Nevertheless, the important measure which welded the French peasantry to the philosophy of the Enlightenment was the sale of the Church's possessions: the municipalities' action of putting them up for sale by auction in small lots which might go as low as 500 livres, with ample facilities for deferred payment, put the seal on what Michelet called 'the wedding of the peasant and the Revolution'. With the exception of regions such as a good part of the west (with the Vendée to the forefront, of course), it also marked the alliance of the rural world with the bourgeoisie, which derived the greatest profit from the sale of the *biens nationaux*.

All the beneficiaries, both large and small, werc henceforth united, equally irreconcilable to the *ancient régime*. The break of 1789, which was so potent in national imagination, had another equally deep-rooted foundation in the private interests of innumerable families. Up until at least the middle of the nineteenth century, the question of *biens nationaux* would form one of the centres of gravity in French politics. It also played an essential, though less spectacular, role in the country's economic history: by multiplying peasant ownership, which crowned and accelerated a movement that had been going on for several centuries, the Revolution consolidated a pre-capitalist rural France – history thumbing its nose at the creation, at the same moment, of 'bourgeois' economic institutions.

However, the ordinary people of France, both peasant and bourgeois, who had celebrated the first anniversary of 14 July in apparent unanimity, split in 1790 over the religious question.

The Church and the king had accepted the Civil Constitution only subject to approval by a spiritual authority. The Assembly had rejected a national synod. There remained the pope, who was grappling with the matter of Avignon, a papal fief which was demanding unity with the France of 1789 and, both on principle and in the current circumstances, was little inclined to moderate his condemnation of the Revolution by making a fine distinction between the spiritual and the temporal. From prudence, both because of Avignon and in order not to expose the French bishops too soon, he did not condemn the Civil Constitution until 10 March 1791; but his opposition was known as early as May 1790, and widely used, chiefly through the self-interested channel of the tireless Bernis.

In any case, Catholic France was stirring ahead of its priests, mobilized by intolerance and intrigue, alarmed by all the novelties regarding Protestants and Jews, and annoyed that the Assembly should have refused to concede to the old religion a 'national' status which would have allowed it to retain a sort of privilege. The tradition of intolerance had resumed where it was strongest, in the towns of the Midi where Catholics and Protestants confronted one another: Nîmes, Uzès, Montauban. In Nîmes, in the middle of June, during the Assembly's discussion on the Civil Constitution of the Clergy, civil war raged for several days, to the great detriment of the Catholic forces, who were beaten and massacred.

At the end of the summer, the situation hardened everywhere. The Civil Constitution had been published in the *départements*, and was benefiting from the sometimes aggressive support of the new administrations elected in the spring. Popular clubs and societies were agitating for the immediate application of the law. On the other side, Catholic opinion was increasingly hostile. The bishops who were members of the Assembly broke their silence and on 30 October published, under the title *Exposition des principes sur la Constitution civile du clergé* (Exposition of principles on the Civil Constitution of the Clergy), a formal refutation of the law passed in July. Faced with this situation, where violence was still the exception but calm was precarious, the Assembly chose to go ahead: a decree of 27 November allowed practising priests two months in which to take the oath of the Constitution, and consequently of the Civil Constitution of the Clergy which had been included in it. This proved to be both the signal and the start of the schism.

One third of the Assembly's ecclesiastical members agreed to take the oath in January 1791. Only seven bishops, three of them without dioceses, took the oath. But the Assembly no longer counted: it was the country that mattered. Almost everywhere, the publication of the 27 November decree, followed by the ceremony of the oath in January 1791, gave rise to troubles on both sides, for and against the Civil Constitution. These disturbances were all the more serious when parts of the populace upheld or even anticipated refusals to take the oath.

In Paris, of course, it was the opposite: organized popular pressure was brought to bear on priests who wavered or jibbed, to force them to take the plunge. On the Sunday planned for the swearing of the oath, a huge crowd invaded Saint-Sulpice and threatened the recalcitrant curé, who managed to escape, to cries of 'Swear or swing'. But in Alsace, in the Massif Central – notably in the Catholic highlands of the Velay and Rouergue – and in the west – especially in what would become in 1793 the 'military Vendée', the region of the armed insurrection – the crowds forcibly opposed the ceremony of the oath: quite often it was the local authorities, the mayors and municipal officers, who had to give in.

These cases of resistance proved so strong and so widespread that the Constituent Assembly had to make concessions: having chosen intransigence on 4 January 1791, it climbed down on 21 January, authorizing refractory priests to remain in their parishes until replaced (and in all cases guaranteeing them a small pension). On 7 May it voted the decree known as the '*tolérance*' decree, giving the force of law to a measure taken in April by the directory of the Paris *département*, according to which refractory priests could celebrate mass in 'constitutional' churches.

This measure 'froze' the situation rather than sought to find a remedy for it. It simply took note of the political and religious impasse to which the Constitution had brought the Revolution. Indeed, at the beginning of the summer, the pope's hostility to the Act had become obvious to all, and the position of the 'public ecclesiastical officers' was unambiguous: the refractory priests had been replaced, or were on the point of being. But they stayed on in the villages or suburban districts, and the Assembly, in its desire for stability, finally had to accept the existence of two Churches, of which only one complied with the law. The Constituent Assembly wanted to put an end to the Revolution: it had provided counter-revolution with its officers and troops.

The numerous efforts of the past quarter-century to find social or socio-economic causes for rural counter-revolution have yielded only negative or very tenuous conclusions. The regions and social groups which rose up in 1793 against the Revolution were not, in 1789, any more favourable to the *ancien régime* than the rest: the *cahiers de doléances* of the future insurgent areas or of the parishes in the 'military Vendée' were as hostile to feudal rights as the other texts drawn up in the name of French rural communities.

It is hardly possible, either, to attribute the peasant counter-revolution – where it can be observed with hindsight starting from the events of 1793 – to a particular antagonism between town and country, bourgeois and rustics. For however spectacular that antagonism seemed to be during the war in the Vendeé, it was fairly general and took vastly different forms: the peasants of Quercy, for instance, well after 4 August 1789, continued the struggle for their own claims for abolition of seigneurial dues without compensation, defying the authority of the new urban administrations; but Quercy did not rebel against the dictatorship of Paris and the towns in 1793. It was more to the north, in Lozère, that an uprising began at that time. Furthermore, the antagonism between town and country might well have been more political than social, had not the cultural arrogance of the new gentlemen of the *chefs-lieux* in regard to the country regions proved more unbearable in practice than the seigneur's paternalistic extortions.

In the interpretation of the factors contributing to the counter-revolution, it does not seem that the religious element can be reduced to another level of reality. What is clear, on the other hand, is that this religious element was immediately transformed into a political problem, in that first the absolute monarchy, then the Revolution, had turned the Catholic Church into a body which was subordinate to the state. The crisis of the oath revived, in a more acute and infinitely more massive form, episodes from the history of relations between the old monarchy of the seventeenth century and the Jansenist clergy, such as the proposal to make them sign *billets de confession* renouncing their Calvinist doctrines. In 1791 the entire Catholic Church had to pay the price for its pact with the absolutist state: Jansenist revenge, in the name of Gallicanism, had only accentuated its political subordination. Henceforth, all its priests were obliged to choose between Rome and Paris, the Church's universality and French citizenship, inner conviction and the authority of the state. And behind the priests, or with them, the Catholic country's millions of faithful understood and espoused that dilemma, which was inextricably religious and political.

If one wants to understand the depth of the conflict which started on this dual level in 1790–1, one has only to consider how long it was destined to last: the map showing religious practice in mid-twentieth-century France – which, incidentally, is the least inaccurate approximation to that of the political right wing – is also very similar to that of the refractory priests of 1791. This bears witness to the fact that the national crisis begun by the Civil Constitution continued to dominate the nineteenth and a large part of the twentieth century in France.

The Revolution had struggled against the Catholic Church without breaking with Catholicism. Too close to the Jansenist and Gallican legacy to conceive of a secularized democratic state, it was also too far removed from it to imagine the start of a new Protestantism. Quinet was the most profound commentator on that impasse from which, without any deliberate intent, would arise an antireligious revolutionary culture still imbued with the spirit of a worn-out Catholicism.

Until the clerical schism, counter-revolutionary emigration had scarcely found an echo in France. The Comte d'Artois's little court at Turin, where Calonne had taken up service and gained promotion, had begun its long career of plots and counter-plots, but it tried in vain to revive the war of the Languedoc Catholics against the sons of the Calvinist *Camisards* of the Cévennes. Before mid-1790, the *ancien régime* had no popular banner. The religious affair provided them with one.

In Paris, it reactivated debates on the king, 14 July and the October days. The Assembly, since then, had organized its own royalty. It was sovereign itself, since Louis XVI was subordinate to it. He was no longer anything but the nation's first servitor, bound by the oath of fidelity to the constitution. The holder of a provisional veto, which was more theoretical than actual, he remained without authority over the majority of his officers, who were elected. He retained control over his ministers, but they were regarded with suspicion by the Assembly, where the real power lay.

There he was, subjected to the surveillance of the National Guard, which in turn was closely watched by Parisian activists, at Jean-Paul Marat's command. The days of action in July and October 1789 henceforth acted as models of revolutionary political behaviour: the king represented the heart of the plot, and the people the arm which broke the plot. A powerful image which, in the name of the people, superimposed on the legal sovereignty of the Assembly the organized or brute force of the sovereignty of the people, plain and simple.

It is too often forgotten that the Assembly itself had to hold its sittings under a hail of vituperation from the galleries, where every day there were crowds of readers of Marat's *L'Ami du peuple*, and vociferous extremists. As a way of compensating for the deputies' monopolizing of the general will, the people themselves were supposed in this way to keep an eye on the deliberations of their representatives: that was the double pathology of modern 'representation', the inconveniences of which mounted up rather than neutralized one another. In actual fact, the authority of the 'nation' tended to be exercised by two oligarchies: that of the representatives and that of the Parisian activists.

In this France without an executive, this constitutional monarchy without a constitutional king, a revolutionary dialectic was a quite natural response to royal resistance; that was the role of Paris, where three powers held sway – the municipality, the National Guard and the *sections*, or administrative divisions. The first two, elected or recruited on the basis of property qualification, were in the hands of the Assembly's patriots, La Fayette and Bailly. But the forty-eight *sections*, which in 1790 succeeded the sixty districts, played a more popular and autonomous role: through their primary assemblies, through their committees which enjoyed police powers, through their petitions, their addresses, their decrees, they were popular sovereignty in the flesh.

The unrest over corn had subsided with the good harvests of 1789 and the following years; revolutionary vigilance roused the *sections* against Marie-Antoinette, the 'Austrian bitch' who was hatching her intrigues in the secrecy of the Tuileries. In the winter of 1789–90 a violent conflict had set the Cordeliers district, presided over by Georges Jacques Danton, against the legal jurisdiction of the Châtelet of Paris, which wanted Marat arrested for his incendiary articles. The Assembly legislated under the constant pressure of this demagogy, which declared itself the guardian of the new legitimacy: that was already the revolutionary tradition.

In 1791, at the same time as the political climate worsened, urban anticlericalism made its appearance: one would have to look for the roots of this phenomenon, which antedated the Revolution, in the crises of Parisian Jansenism in 1720 and 1730. The democratic movement got under way through the creation of popular clubs and fraternal societies where, by candlelight, men joined together in the public reading of truly 'patriotic' leaflets. Marat and Danton ran the Cordeliers, on the left bank, and many local societies federated in 1791 around a central committee.

The revolutionary forces, which were critical of the Assembly's moderation thus made ready for their coming role by organizing the *sections* and the street mobs. But in order to be in the right, to win, they needed royal treason, just as the Assembly would have need of the royal word in order to contain Parisian extremism and revolutionary passion. But what if Paris and the king were in accord – even if from opposite directions – against the Assembly?

While its commissions, filled with earnest and competent men, accomplished an immense amount of legislative work, the Assembly, already in a doubly precarious position, had furthermore been continually split by the jealousies of its leaders – none of whom had been able to gain the upper hand. Mirabeau, the thundering orator of 1789, the bourgeois Assembly's *déclassé* aristocrat, was soon suspect in the eyes of Parisian democrats; it was not long before he was in the king's pay, vainly advising him to accept the new rules of play, and he wore out his genius in a double game of politics, dying in the spring of 1791. It was the same story for La Fayette – though he was less venal and less of a genius: the commander of the National Guard did not have the ear of the royal household, who could not forgive him for the October days, and on the other side Marat continually denounced him to the Patriots.

The 'triumvirate' (of Barnave, Du Port and Alexandre de Lameth) was under suspicion. The 1791 colonial debate showed that clearly. In the West Indies, the treasure-house of eighteenth-century France, news of the Revolution had exploded the fragile social balance between colonists, free mulattos and black slaves. The former wanted to take advantage of the opportunity to free themselves from the metropolitan 'Exclusive' rule and trade freely with all countries. But they had no intention of giving up any part of their local and racial proponderance, at a time when the mulattos were pleading the 1789 principles in order to claim political rights. Jean Jaurès has admirably recounted and interpreted those long debates in which the Lameths and Barnave supported the colonists, and Robespierre the mulattos.

Backed by Parisian societies – one of which was called Friends of the Blacks – the mulattos' cause finished in triumph. No one in the Assembly had really posed the problem of slavery; but the political dividing-line which had been established went beyond the mulattos, because it was a matter of the application of democratic universalism defined by the Revolution. It showed that, after Mounier, after Mirabeau, it was the turn of Barnave, Du Port and Lameth to do battle with the extremism of Parisian societies and the little group acting as their spokesmen in the Assembly. In truth, was Paris overstepping the mark, or was the triumvirate retreating? The very nature of the revolutionary imbalance explains that both were true: in this triangular debate, fear of Parisian excess brought successive waves of quite a few Patriot deputies closer to the king's cause. Speaking to the Assembly, Du Port stated quite clearly: 'The Revolution is over. It must be settled and protected by combating excesses. We must restrain equality, reduce liberty and settle opinion. The government must be strong, firm and stable' (17 May 1791).

A DEMOCRATIC MONARCHY?

After the *Monarchiens*, this was the second version of the need to 'terminate the Revolution'. But like their predecessors in 1789, the triumvirs of 1791, in order to achieve it, needed royal authority which was both strong and frankly committed to their side – that authority which they had destroyed two years earlier. It had resisted them then; it was no more favourable to them because it had been broken. A secret letter exists from Louis XVI to his cousin the king of Spain, written in October 1789, in which the phantom king of the Tuileries protests against all the edicts which had been wrung from him since July.

Between 1790 and 1791 there was Mirabeau's admirable secret correspondence with the court, the great man's extraordinary monologue to a king who paid for the advice of the genius without even being able to understand it. The deputy from Aix argued that the Revolution had carried away the *ancien régime* with no hope of return, but that it was not by any means incompatible with a renewed monarchy: the existence of a society composed of equal individuals, as opposed to the former corporate society (Richelieu would have liked the idea, writes Mirabeau, looking for illustrious sponsors), was actually favourable to a strong royal government. Mirabeau had never felt at ease with the idea of a virtually absolute sovereignty attributed in actual fact to representation; he had always denounced the danger of its handing over the will of the nation to a parliamentary oligarchy. Against a slide in that direction, the presence of a strong king was a guarantee: in any case, was he not the personification of national history, coming from the mists of antiquity, uniting the past and the present, and giving modern democracy the firm anchorage of tradition? Mirabeau was Chateaubriand thirty years in advance: it was just a question of 'nationalizing' the monarchy.

The monarchy, on the contrary, chose to offer the spectacle of its separation from the nation. Louis XVI's reply to the policy proposed by Mirabeau, who died in April, was attempted flight in June. It would not be fair to ascribe sole responsibility to the king for the failed dialogue and the untried policy: we have seen that the spirit of the Revolution left hardly any room for even a partial retrocession of public authority.

The circumstances of spring 1791 were less accommodating than ever: in April, Louis XVI had been prevented by the crowd from leaving the Tuileries to perform his Easter duties at Saint-Cloud and to receive communion from the hands of a priest of his choice. In the mind of the king, who was deeply Christian, the religious schism added impiety to all the other reasons he had for hating the Revolution. Captive in Paris, a stranger in the midst of a people who no longer recognized him, the king had wanted to flee, leaving in the Tuileries a solemn declaration of his hostility towards the Revolution. He was counting on the French undergoing a change of heart once he was out of the country; in reality, he made his own contribution to the death of the monarchy in public opinion.

Perhaps nothing speaks such volumes on revolutionary France as the tocsin at Varennes, that mobilization of a remote little village on the arrival of the strange carriage – and the silent crowds on the return trip, watching bare-headed over the convoy: Louis XVI started to die on 21 June 1791. He was not yet a hostage, but he was already little more than a stake in the game. For his flight tore away the veil of that false constitutional monarchy and once more confronted the Patriot party with the whole problem of the Revolution's future.

The watchword 'republic' was launched by small enlightened circles gathered around the Marquis de Condorcet and Jacques-Pierre Brissot. Robespierre mistrusted a republic which might lead to oligarchy. Together with the Assembly's left, and the popular societies and clubs, he contented himself with demanding the trial and punishment of the king: he made himself spokesman for the punitive reaction of the people faced with this proof of an 'aristocratic conspiracy'. The king was no longer sacred, but the fact was that he was guilty; the father of the nation had become its executioner.

How, then, was the Revolution to be 'settled'? The moderate Patriots of the Assembly tried desperately, though at the price of a fiction which would cost them dear in the future: La Fayette, Bailly and the 'triumvirs' persuaded the deputies to vote on a version according to which the king had been 'abducted'; dominated by fear of renewed revolutionary fervour, they pleaded the constitutional law, the king's inviolability, respect for what had been voted. Barnave acted with the most intelligence, explaining that the choice must by definition remain independent of the qualities of the monarch:

Either the constitution you have created is wrong, or he whom the chance of birth has given you for king, and whom the law cannot touch, must not, by his individual actions or his personal faculties, be important to the stability and soundness of the government . . . I will say to those who are holding forth so furiously against the one who has sinned: Would you be at his feet if you were satisfied with him? (15 July 1791)

The argument had its vulnerable side, however, since it acknowledged Louis XVI's faults as transformed into buttresses of the law. Paris was more sensitive about the flight than about the constitution. A vast campaign of petitions for the King's punishment climaxed in a central demonstration at the Champ de Mars on 17 July. One year after the great misleading festival of national unanimity, and on the very spot where he had been acclaimed, La Fayette gave the National Guard the order to shoot into the crowd. This was an important date. For the first time, the authorities who had emerged from the Revolution did what they had not dared to do against the peasants in August 1789, or against Paris in October: they turned against the 'people', on the side of the king. They had booked their places on the morrow's scaffold.

They were temporarily the victors, but at the cost of a new and serious split among the Patriots. Deserting the Jacobins' club, the moderates installed themselves in the Feuillants' monastery, whether they were followed by nearly all the deputies, while Robespierre went out of his way to keep the affiliated provincial societies true to the Jacobins – they would prove a formidable instrument for the future.

For the time being, the Feuillants seemed to be triumphant: they had some Parisian agitators arrested, maintained order in the streets and voted for several cautious alterations to the constitution. The property qualification for electoral purposes was raised, the eligibility rating was decreased. The Civil Constitution of the Clergy lost its character of constitutional law, so that it was not unassailable.

But the crucial vote for the future had been obtained by Robespierre one month before the flight to Varennes: the deputy from Arras, who had already seized control of the court of public morality, had had members of the Constituent Assembly decreed ineligible for the next Assembly. It was a decision which it was diffult to fight, on pain of passing for a self-interested Patriot, and which pleased a good number of tired deputies who were keen to return home; yet it was a demagogic decree, since it instituted a second revolutionary *tabula rasa*, more limited, it is true, than that of 1789, but nevertheless affecting all the parliamentary personnel who had had two and a half years of experience in the political arena. The constitution was deprived in advance of the support of those who had formed it.

Robespierre began his dual career of moralist and tactician. The ineligibility of the Constituents allowed him to marginalize experienced adversaries, like the chief Feuillants, and at the same time to give additional weight to the militants of the Parisian Revolution, who alone would keep the advantage of length of service: since he paid court assiduously to the clubs, his own influence would thereby be reinforced, including his influence over the brand-new deputies.

On 14 September 1791 Louix XVI – as in February 1790 – solemnly swore an oath of loyalty to a revised Constitution which he accepted no more sincerely than before, and the Constituent Assembly proudly proclaimed before parting: 'The end of the Revolution has arrived.' But its words were firmer than its convictions. In reality, it was bequeathing to the new men of the coming Assembly, in addition to its lasting achievements, the ephemera it had reconstructed.

The historian who seeks to understand why can begin from the extraordinary ease with which, on 4 August, the fate of old society had been sealed and civil equality inaugurated, in order to contrast the violence and uncertainties of political reconstruction. In fact, what had been accomplished in the civil sphere in 1789 was irrevocable, at the same time as, in the political sphere, there was an end to the absolutism of divine right, which was swept away with the whole of the *ancien régime*. On the other hand, the Revolution came up against the reconstruction of public authority: no one could believe, in the summer following the Varennes expedition, that this *de facto* republic, accompanied by a former absolute sovereign, instituted by the constitution, could be destined for an easy future.

Edgar Quinet put forward an interpretation of this contrast: the 'difficulties' – as he called them – of the Revolution were not in the civil order, where 1789 simply accomplished, or crowned, so to speak, the work of centuries. 'Not a voice was raised', he writes regarding 4 August, 'to retain civil inequality. There was the unanimity imposed by necessity. Men took stock of the ruin, rather than brought it about.'[2] The civil Revolution was thus almost a natural product of the *ancien régime*, a simple updating of history, conceded as a necessity even by the privileged, an invention of the time; the political Revolution, being devised by men, was infinitely more difficult precisely because its object was the free participation of citizens in the new sovereignty.

The strong point of Quinet's theory is that it allows one to consider the two faces of the same event: one looking towards the past, the other turned to the future; one showing its determination, the other revealing its chancy nature, in both the exact and the popular sense of the word. Basically, when the Thermidorian successors of Robespierre, some years later, contrasted the *good* results of the Revolution with its *bad* development, they would say more or less the same thing in other words: what had been necessary in 1789 did not extend to what had followed.

Nevertheless, neither type of reality – civil or political – nor the two successive stages of the Revolution can be separated by such fine distinctions. History does not present, in order, first a civil society which was immediately revealed to itself, in July–August 1789, in its modern true form of free and equal individuals, then a state reconstituted with great difficulty, at the cost of a flood of events which began only in that year and would prove uncontrollable. On the contrary, we have seen that in 1789 everything had been put in place together in the name of the same universal principles, and that this ambition for radical construction from scratch was the dominant feature of the six extraordinary months of spring and summer, in both the civil and political spheres.

Society, and that society's government, were replaced together. By placing the rights of man as the foundation of the social contract, the men of 1789 had no difficulty in instituting civil equality, since they repaid in capital most of the possessions connected with the previous aristocratic social state. The movement of ideas and passions did the rest. But radical philosophical individualism, which could not be divorced from the uprooting of orders and corporate bodies, made the construction of the new body politic infinitely more difficult.

How, in fact, was it possible to envisage sovereignty, starting from a society of individuals, and how could its representation be formed?

---

[2] Edgar Quinet, *La Révolution*.

Imagining it presented no problem: there was a single, all-powerful, inalienable general will. But as for its organization, in this ancient, vast, populous nation-state . . . It was necessary to pass via the idea of delegating the sovereignty through the representation of individuals, even if it meant in theory leaving the nation entitled to regain its rights at any time – rights which could not be alienated once and for all.

The year 1789 had caused the appearance, on the one hand, of *homo democraticus* in his modern purity, free in all things not forbidden by law, equal to any single one of his fellow men; and on the other, a new sovereign power constituted from that basis, forming a general will as absolute and autonomous as all the individual wills from which it proceeded. The Revolution had avoided the risk of the atomization of individuals in society by reinventing a sovereignty as indivisible and inalienable as that of the former king, but even more powerful since it had nothing – not even God – above it: henceforth it issued from the people, or from the nation, where it remained latent until the moment of the constituent contract.

But once 'constituted', in and by the National Assembly in May–June 1789, it had instituted representation: a major institution, under which the law was not agreed directly by each citizen, as in Rousseau, but through the mediation of representatives. These were not elected by the universality of citizens, but chosen by the more enlightened, in accordance with a double fiscal selection. Certainly, the electorate envisaged by the 1791 constitution was incredibly vast for the era; none the less, it rested on a distinction between civil rights, which were universal, and political rights, which were not: to that democratic man who was the central representation of the Revolution it added a contradictory element, at the sensitive spot. It was not by chance that Robespierre built his reputation as defender of the people on criticism of the *censitaire* electoral system.

In the new institutions bequeathed by the Constituent Assembly, there was therefore a dominating spirit of 'pure democracy': Burke had made no mistake when he wrote using these terms in 1790. He had thus designated the revolutionary *tabula rasa*, the universalist abstractness of the Rights of Man, equality, the destruction of aristocratic bodies, the turning of royal sovereignty to the benefit of the people. But the Assembly had preserved the king in a republican constitution, and had placed the universality of rights alongside representative government chosen only by a class of citizens. The royal problem would outlast it, although that had been decided in advance by the subordinate role given to the former sovereign in 1789.

For a time it would be a thorn in the flesh of the revolutionary movement. In depth, however, it was the tension between the idea of democracy and the extent of inequality retained by the Constituent Assembly in the new body politic which formed the mainspring of the Revolution. Anti-aristocratic feeling could just as easily become anti-bourgeois: it could be transferred all the more easily from breeding to vested interests, and even property, since it had the more vigorously embraced the abstract idea of equality. By the same movement, it could the better ignore representative government because the concept of a general will and a sovereign people inevitably evoked direct democracy. At all events, battle lines were being drawn up; on the other side, the religious quarrel had provided possible popular support for nostalgia for the *ancien régime*, and an entire 'Feuillant' bourgeoisie was beginning to worry about the consequences of 1789.

The Constituent Assembly had destroyed corporate society and instituted civil equality in the old kingdom. It had not settled the question of its government. The problem was to last for a hundred years.

3

The Jacobin Republic: 1791–1794

Between 1787 and the autumn of 1791 the unprecedented fluctuations of the French upheaval were due entirely to internal reasons: the legacies of aristocratic society and absolutism, the power vacuum, the king's resistance, the intellectual and political daring of the deputies of the Third Estate, Parisian and national agitation. The welcome given by Europe to 1789 – enthusiastic among intellectuals and the public of the Enlightenment, somewhat lukewarm in royal courts – had not turned the Revolution towards Europe. Furthermore, the 'Internationale' of the kings and the great had in the end managed to endure the fall of French aristocracy and the woes of Louis XVI without too much distress: they had made no move, despite appeals from the émigrés. For the sovereigns of continental Europe were counting on gaining territorial advantages from the disorder they saw in France: Austria and Prussia in Poland, and Russia in the Turkish empire. As for Britain, it was simply rejoicing in the enfeeblement of its rival.

Several events – consequences of what was taking place within the country – had contrived to upset this spirit of coexistence which, though disapproving, was peaceable and cautious. Between 1789 and 1791 the word 'patriotism' meant first and foremost attachment to the new France, even if those proclaiming it went on to celebrate the progress of the great principles of 1789 beyond French borders. As if hesitantly, and taking pains to avoid any conflict, the Constituent Assembly had been led gradually to proclaim a new international law extending the liberty of citizens to other nations.

To the German princes holding possessions in Alsace, who were demanding their feudal dues, maintaining that they were not subject to French laws, the Assembly replied, while offering them compensation as it had to the landowning seigneurs, that Alsace was French not by right of conquest, in accordance with the Treaty of Westphalia, but by its voluntary membership of the great 'Federation' of provinces of 1789–90.

In the old papal territory of Avignon, it had waited until September 1791, right at the end of its mandate, to declare an annexation that had been ratified beforehand by the population who had been demanding it for two years: it was the clash with the pope over the Civil Constitution of the Clergy which led the deputies to confirm the right of peoples to self-determination.

This was a formidable threat to international order and dynastic Europe, but it was still only implicit. Although they worked hard at it, the émigrés alone would not be able to open the road leading to war between the Revolution and Europe. In the end, it was the king who unwittingly showed the way, and quickly became its symbol and its chief stake. He was constantly writing to his cousin, the king of Spain, and to his 'brother' in Vienna, to whom he imparted his plans for flight. If the Parisian press, with Marat in the forefront, so frequently denounced those plans, of which it really knew nothing, and the *sections* mounted guard around the Tuileries – as in war one guesses at enemy movements – it was because of a presentiment that in Louis XVI they held a hostage against the European monarchies.

In fact, the people immediately saw his attempted escape in June 1791 as a prelude to invasion; the arrest of the king at Varennes and his return under guard seemed a victory over the foreigner. The Patriots were already at war before the kings gave any serious thought to coming to the assistance of their cousin in France: after Varennes, the Emperor Leopold and the king of Prussia limited themselves to signing the declaration of Pillnitz, which made any intervention subject to a general agreement of the European sovereigns. But if the Parisian clubs were mistaken about the diplomatic reality, they correctly read the wishes of the royal couple. They knew instinctively what the European chancelleries had not yet been able to grasp: when war came, it would be a war between two ideas. Louis XVI knew this too: the shared secret established a kind of complicity, an ardent wish held in common, but in opposite directions.

In the march towards war, therefore, there was no technical calculation or territorial ambition on the French side; none of that Machiavellian and princely rationality, those diplomatic or military calculations which typified war under the *ancien régime*; no evaluation of chances and risks. In this period France's strength lay in the century's demographic growth, the impetus given to society by the Revolution, and good technical reforms carried out in the military field by the *ancien régime*'s last ministers.

At the same time, however, the army was disorganized by the emigration of numerous officers and the subversion of discipline by democratic ideas; the volunteers levied after Varennes were still low in number. But this mixed balance sheet misses the essential point, which is that war with Europe would constitute the new form and intensification of the revolutionary explosion with all its contradictions.

Sieyès and the men of the Revolution had conceived the nation from the starting-point of the expulsion of the aristocracy, who were outside the community. When they drew, within the social body, a dividing-line which had hitherto separated Frenchmen only from foreigners and potential enemies, they replaced the traditional membership of all in the nation-state built by kings with a definition of the new nation, which was both wider-ranging yet more restricted: wider-ranging because it was rooted in democratic universality; more restricted because it cut into the historic community, from which the privileged were now excluded.

This idea, which was the fount of revolutionary hatred for the aristocracy and the secret of its violence, would find a sort of natural confirmation in war. Already the émigrés had occupied the place beyond the frontiers marked out for them in advance by *Qu'est-ce que le Tiers État?*: they were the perfect embodiment of the nobility according to the revolutionaries, even before they began to fight alongside the enemies of the nation. Armed conflict would thus superimpose internal and external enemies, civil and foreign war, aristocracy and treason, democracy and patriotism, around the same images, feelings and values. In this set of identifications the historian can discover much of the secret which made war so popular with the Revolution, and made it such a powerful instrument of political acceleration.

For centuries, under the kings, the nation had been formed in an antagonistic relationship with neighbouring dynasties and territories, at the cost of long wars and shared dangers. The French were not a new community, like the young American republic, whose citizens faced no external threat and were united in the desire to live in peaceful happiness. Like other European peoples, and perhaps *par excellence* among them, the French were accustomed to define themselves in relation to an enemy, to close ranks in the hour of invasion and to respond to the sovereign's appeal when 'public safety' was in jeopardy.

It was not so long since the ageing Louis XIV had appealed to the entire nation for its aid. Now that assortment of memories, habits and emotions could be mobilized against the monarchy which had been, for so many centuries, both their catalyst and beneficiary. The Third Estate had only had to brandish them against the aristocracy to bring down the king as well. By placing Louis XVI in the émigrés' camp, war would finish what 1789 had begun: it would strip the monarchy of its share in French history. The Republic, already implicit in institutions, would be inscribed in people's minds.

How could Louis XVI possibly understand this process, and thus avoid becoming its unwilling accomplice? He contented himself with playing his usual part in the symphony of escalation. After Varennes, the royal couple had hoped for war as their last chance for restoration. They imagined France as enfeebled, torn apart by the Revolution and incapable of resisting the professional armies of their cousins and brothers-in-law. In fact they strengthened the forces of the Revolution, offering the latter exclusive rights to their ancestral heritage transformed by 1789 – the nation. This enigmatic and all-powerful word effected the devolution of the collective patrimony from the monarchy to revolutionary democracy. It had defined the citizens' sovereignty; now it would feed their patriotism against the treason of the aristocrats and the king.

The concepts of democracy and nation, which had come together in 1789, forged around the war which began in 1792 a body of very strong feelings, welding together classes and the Revolution itself in a common passion. The philosophy of the Enlightenment, so cosmopolitan and European, had won over only a limited public, aristocratic and bourgeois, and almost entirely urban. Here, in its most democratic form, it was penetrating the mass of the people in both town and country through an unexpected channel: national sentiment. It was thereby simplified and radicalized to a point where very soon the Europe of the Enlightenment no longer recognized 'its' philosophy.

But what did that matter to the French revolutionaries? They gave the peasants and *sansculottes* leaving for the frontiers the chance to democratize glory – that caress of life which for so long had been reserved for the nobility – and to win in their turn a marshal's baton. By the precocious synthesis – destined for such a great future – which it effected between intellectual messianism and national feeling, the Revolution had integrated the masses with the state, and created to its own profit the modern sentiment of collectively belonging. In this sense, the French experience turned that of enlightened despotism upside down: democratic nationalism had taken up, against all the kings of Europe, the universal message of philosophy.

From then on, the Revolution's objectives received a new dimension, and its rhythm added acceleration, which its partisans hoped for and counted on: there was no foreseeable end to the war with Europe. Natural frontiers? Albert Sorel's brilliant and systematic book[1] seeks to portray them as the French goal in the conflict: the Girondins had said so, and Danton, and also Jean François Reubell, under the Directory. But Brissot, in a letter to Joseph Servan, also spoke of 'setting fire to the whole of Europe'. And the Montagnard Pierre Chaumette expressed even more vividly the almost emotional excesses of the revolutionary crusade: 'The land which separates Paris from Petersburg will soon be Gallicized, municipalized, Jacobinized.'

In fact, the revolutionary war had no definite aim because it sprang from deep within the Revolution itself, and could only end with it. That is why even French victories could at best result only in truces; to look for peace was as suspect as being defeated – both were betrayals of revolutionary patriotism. This is a measure of the extraordinary power of internal instability the war would have in all its phases – defeats and victories. It would bring three groups in succession to that ephemeral power conferred by a dominant role in the Revolution: the Girondins, the Montagnards and the Thermidorians. It would provide the backdrop for two successive types

[1] Albert Sorel, *L'Europe et la Révolution française*.

of republican regimes, on either side of 9 Thermidor 1794: dictatorship by the Terror, also called 'revolutionary government', and the Thermidorian republic, which would survive only by repeated coups d'état from start to finish.

Since the flight to Varennes and the Declaration of Pillnitz in August 1791 (an acceptance by the Austrian and Prussian Sovereigns that the safety of Louis XVI was a matter of concern to them), the French Revolution had clearly become a European question. Louis XVI had set the example by fleeing towards the frontier, towards the Germany of the princes and his brother-in-law the Austrian emperor, where the majority of French émigrés had already gathered on the banks of the Rhine. The Legislative Assembly, which succeeded the Constituent in Paris, immediately turned its attention towards these groups of 'ci-devants' who had left the country uttering threats to return on the morrow as the king's avengers.

The Assembly was made up of men who were new to parliamentary office, which is not to say new to revolutionary politics, since nearly all of them came from various administrative bodies elected in 1790 and 1791, chiefly from the districts and *départements*. The primary assemblies had for the most part voted in June, before Varennes, and the major electors had elected the deputies, in each *département*'s main town, in the summer during the crisis brought on between Feuillants and Jacobins by the king's flight.

The two clubs, which had been rivals since the split in July 1791, could both claim their share of the new deputies, 250 to 300 Feuillants, 140 Jacobins. These figures have only a relative significance: revolutionary events, by definition, could not obey the laws of a parliamentary arithmetic. Even more than the Constituent, the Legislative Assembly would have to sit under pressure from the people in the galleries, in a constant uproar, and amid the exaggerations of popular newspapers and societies. The Jacobin Club, kept going by Robespierre in the summer of 1791, brought together the most advanced Patriot leaders and formed the federating element of the movement. The Revolution would slip rapidly towards the government of minorities.

The most illustrious figure in this Legislative Assembly was Condorect, who had just managed to get elected in Paris, where the Feuillants had controlled most of the electoral choices: he was one of the few republicans of July 1791, at the time when Barnave and his friends had rescued Louis XVI, and was ahead of the Revolution before becoming too late for it. Apart from him, the newly elected members were not nationally known: minor provincial notables, they were mostly young, and were a less homogeneous group than the 1789 Third Estate.

For example, there was Brissot, a future Girondin leader, and already a kind of authority in the Parisian clubs, where he had been one of the destroyers of the Feuillants, notably Barnave. The son of a Chartres caterer, he had not succeeded, under the *ancien régime*, in his many enterprises. He had gone bankrupt in the bookselling business (hence a short spell of imprisonment), before becoming a hired article writer, dealing with topical subjects. He had Mirabeau's unconventionality, without Mirabeau's genius, and was the embodiment of the kind of political personnel through whom the Revolution would map out its course in 1792 and 1793. The men of 1789 had for, good reason, had no experience in such matters. He had what he had learned in revolutionary activism since 1789: ultra-patriotic rhetoric, superimposed on a politico-literary culture, the whole enveloped in daring oratory, a vigour born of confidence, a sort of ice-cold fever, which made him one of the Assembly's leaders in October, when he spoke against the emigration.

In fact, the spirit of revolutionary overstatement dominated the first debates; it led the deputies to take up the royal challenge on its own ground: war with Europe. In November, decrees against the émigrés, who were summoned to return, and an ultimatum to the German princelings – the Electors of Trier and Mainz – ordered them to break up the gatherings which had formed on their territory. That was the start of the conflict.

THE FALL OF THE MONARCHY

The royal family had painted things as black as possible. They had tried everything to get La Fayette beaten in the municipal elections and thus to place the Jacobin Jérôme Pétion in command in Paris. They wanted war, which they could not envisage as victorious. That was a secret calculation, since it could not be admitted, yet it was public because it was so obvious. In this encounter between the Revolution's suspicious mind and the secretive mysteries of royal policy lay a tragic complicity which led to war as if to a test of truth.

However, the kind of unanimity in the revolutionary camp was less clear than the wishes of the royal couple. Fresh claimants to the role of princely advisers, pushing their men into the ministries, the Feuillants, with a few intelligent exceptions (including Barnave), encouraged bellicosity: La Fayette was counting on getting command of an army, and the entire group hoped that a short and limited war would bring internal stability, through the power it would give to the generals. But these inaccurate calculations were secondary.

The main fact of the matter was that war was popular, advocated by the Assembly's left and waved like a flag in the faces of the Jacobins. The reasoning behind Brissot's great speeches is well known: on the one hand, to destroy Koblenz, the home of the émigrés, would mean putting an end to Louis XVI's double game and forcing him to choose; on the other, the war against the kings was won in advance, since the French army would be welcomed as liberator of the peoples. The increasingly isolated resistance of Robespierre in the Jacobin minority group is equally well known.

For once, the Incorruptible not only cut himself off from the revolutionary camp but also took a stand against excess and the relentless pursuit of the same policy. With his genius for mistrust, he had seen right through the objective complicity which the political situation had started between Louis XVI and the Brissotins. The king desired war because it would bring him allies who were much more powerful than the Revolution; Brissot sought it as a road to power; he had uttered this extraordinary phrase, which reveals all: 'We have a need for great betrayals.'

Robespierre had understood this language: it was also his own; but he turned it against his rivals. Betrayal, in fact, was already their crime if their wishes matched those of the king. In those great debates in December 1791 and January 1792 the two principal actors played opposite roles. Robespierre clear-sightedly denounced the perils of military messianism ('no one likes armed missionaries') and the danger that a conquering general might take away French liberty. Brissot, for his part, had sensed that war with Europe would speed up revolutionary radicalism; he was unaware that he would be the big loser in the venture.

Brissot played the role of sorcerer's apprentice. Revolutionary opinion backed him. What has been little studied yet deserves attention, is the social echo awakened by the talk of national messianism in revolutionary France – how the patriotism of 1789, fed by the violent split with the aristocracy, was transformed into the missionary zeal of 1792. It is easy to see what brings the two together, but the second stage is so immense and vague that it is difficult to imagine today how the French at the end of the eighteenth century could use it both as a slogan and as a political and military programme. Swept along by Brissot and his friends, the Legislative Assembly's greatest original act was to make this transformation clear and to give the unstable blend of the national and the universal an obviousness which even now seems a creation of the recent past. Every Frenchman can still, two hundred years later, recognize the similarity of present attitudes to those of 1792.

Louis XVI yielded to the tide the more willingly because he had already given his agreement, though for opposite reasons. In the spring he set up a 'Brissotin' ministry, losing what little autonomy remained to him as regards the Assembly, in the hope of regaining everything. The accession of Francis II of Austria, who was also determined on war, led in the same direction. On 20 April 1792, on the king's proposal, an almost unanimous Assembly (with seven dissentients) voted to declare war on the 'king of Bohemia and Hungary' (who was also emperor of Austria). That was a major decision, which would have consequences quite opposite to the intentions of those who had taken it: war would be the undoing of Louis XVI. It would break Brissot and his friends. It would bring Robespierre to power, before leading him to the scaffold, like the two others.

From that date on, Parisian and more generally urban popular riots would find a new catalyst – defeat. Not that the previous ones had disappeared: on the contrary, the inevitable depreciation of the assignat (it had already fallen to 60 per cent of its nominal value) and the rise in prices renewed outcries against the dearness of goods. The 'aristocratic conspiracy' was blamed more sharply than ever. But what better proof of treason could there be than defeat? If the revolutionary army retreated before the enemy, it was because the king, the nobles, the generals and the rich were betraying the nation: so it was necessary to punish in order to conquer, as it was necessary to punish in order to eat.

By radicalizing the popular militants' latent Manichaeanism and investing it with the aura of public safety, war gave a fearful impulsion to the terrorist idea, which was an extreme form of revolutionary political involvement. The ambiguous behaviour of La Fayette, who did not discount the idea of using his army to help the Feuillants, awoke the Parisians' worst fears: it was proof of the 'aristocratic conspiracy' and its infiltration into the heart of the Revolution itself. One of the great figures of 1789, the former idolized head of the National Guard, was nothing but a counter-revolutionary! Thus the Revolution progressed, leaving men and epochs crushed in its wake.

The bad news of the first engagements near Lille again triggered the already classic mechanism: mobilization of the *sections*, clubs and popular societies, denouncing the 'Austrian Committee' of the Tuileries. There was anxiety in the Assembly, which voted to call up 20,000 National Guards for the defence of Paris, at the same time making a decree against refractory priests, which was vetoed by Louis XVI, who moreover sacked his Girondin ministers in order to recall the Feuillants. In contrast with 1791, but as in 1789, it would be the street mobs who would deliver judgement: it was a sign of the times. The 'repression' of July 1791 had merely been an isolated episode.

On the first occasion, on 20 June 1792, the revolt which gained control of the Tuileries did not manage to break the king's resistance. The initiative had not come from the Brissotin group, or from the Jacobins or from Robespierre, playing his waiting game and still loyal to his post-Varennes position – the whole constitution and nothing but the constitution. The *journée* was organized by local agitators in the working-class suburbs to the east and south-east of Paris, Saint-Antoine and Saint-Marceau. The crowd of sansculottes (breeches with silk hose had become the sartorial symbol of aristocrats) forced the Assembly to receive its petitioners, then invaded the nearby palace, where Louis XVI, wedged into an embrasure, had to drink to the health of the people. But he would not give in about either the ministry or the decrees.

The failure of 20 June turned to success seven weeks later, on 10 August 1792, with the help of the revolutionary provinces. The distinctive nature of this decisive period lay in the contribution to a Parisian *journée* made, for the first time, by provincial *fédérés* (soldiers of the National Guard) chiefly from Marseille. The tenth of August thus marked the crowning achievement of an entire patriotic stirring against betrayal: France was threatened with invasion (the Prussians had entered the war in July on Austria's side) and the Assembly had declared *la patrie en danger* (the country in danger).

Against this background, demands for a Republic returned and developed, put forward by the Parisian *sections* and upheld by the Jacobins. The great Parisian club, at the centre of a national network, had since the preceding summer abandoned any reference to constitutional law in its struggle against the Feuillants. In July, it recommended the election of a new Constituent Assembly, that is to say, a Convention, and therefore a second Revolution. Robespierre backed the movement behind the scenes, before giving it its full direction on 29 July, in a great speech in which he dropped his position of 'defender of the constitution' (the title of a newspaper he had published at the start of the Legislative Assembly).

Those fiery weeks of summer 1792 set the seal on the alliance between the Parisian popular movement and the great bourgeois club where Robespierre was not yet absolutely dominant, but was becoming the principal authority: he built a bridge between democratic escalation of the principles of 1789 and sansculotte extremism, and at the same time between the past and the future. There are no written traces of the Jacobins' participation in the insurrection of 10 August, though such participation seems likely, by means of a clandestine directory: too many club militants made their mark on the day for there not to have been any consultation beforehand, and after the fall of the Tuileries, Jacobins were to be found in the command positions.

As always, the 'day' had benefited from an involuntary contribution from the foe: that was the Duke of Brunswick's manifesto, as commander of the enemy troops, enjoining the French not to harm their king. The text became known in Paris during the first days of August, and the uprising made ready in broad daylight while the authorities remained powerless. The *fédérés* played their part, but the Parisian *sections*, invaded by 'passive' citizens – a sign of the times – provided the main impetus.

In the early hours of 10 August an insurrectionist Commune (government of Paris) was formed by deputies of the *sections*, and the legal municipality was eliminated. Two columns of very large numbers of demonstrators marched on the royal palace, one on the right bank, coming from the suburb of Saint-Antoine, the other on the left bank and from Saint-Marceau, swollen by men from Marseille and Brest. Louis XVI and his family took refuge in the Assembly, just before the Tuileries were taken by storm by the rioters, at the cost of a fusillade from the Swiss troops whose duty it was to defend them.

Royalty, the stake in the battle, could not survive the victory of the people: the Assembly, surrounded and invaded by the victors of the day, had no other choice than to suspend Louis XVI and substitute a provisional Executive Council for what was no longer anything more than the phantom power of past centuries. In accordance with what the Parisian *sections*, together with Robespierre and the Jacobins, had demanded at the end of July, it convoked a new Constituent Assembly, the Convention, which was to be elected by universal suffrage.

The day of action thus tore out the last of the monarchy only by debasing the Assembly. The Brissotins had vacillated, trapped between the logic of their own policy and fear of an insurrection taking place without them – therefore against them; they were obliged to defend the throne without really wanting to, since in the denunciation of royal treason which the Parisian mob used as a sort of battle-standard, Brissot, Pierre Vergniaud and Armand Gensonné (soon to be called the Girondins) had set an example several months ahead of the time.

On the eve of the decisive uprising, they had not dared to accuse La Fayette. The latter, however, had appeared in the Assembly on 28 June, indignant – almost threatening – about the *journée* of 20 June. On 7 August the Commission known as the 'Twenty-one', elected by the Assembly to serve as a deputy executive, and presided over by Condorcet, had voted for his indictment, but on the following day, the Assembly had refused to pursue it, Brissot's and Vergniaud's friends voting with the Feuillants. La Fayette went to Luxemburg and fell into the hands of the Austrians on 19 August; the shadow of his 'treachery' extended not only to the Feuillants but also to the Girondins.

The deputies finally suspended Louis XVI only under threat of arms. The street crowds that had saved the Constituent Assembly three years before, condemned the Legislative. In July and October 1789, the poor of Paris had come to the aid of the National Assembly: not that this motive, or pretext, is enough to define the two insurrectionary *journées*, the second even less than the first; but in the end, 14 July had probably rendered irrevocable and put out of reach of a royal counteroffensive the title 'National Assembly' adopted by the deputies of the Third Estate. After 6 October 1789, forcibly brought back to Paris, Louis XVI had had to accept the Declaration of Rights, just as he had to acquiesce in the measures of 4 August and the lowering of his role before the sovereignty embodied in the representatives of the people. In both cases, the intervention of direct democracy – insurrection in the name of the sovereign people – had occurred in the sense of support for national representation: different, even heterogeneous, the two 'wills' had remained parallel.

By contrast, 10 August 1792 went further than the Assembly and forced its hand. It was not a matter of helping representatives to resist the king, or even to put paid to royal betrayal; it was a matter of taking to the streets to proclaim the end of royalty, and therefore of the Constitution and the Legislative Assembly. Direct democracy intervened *against* the representatives.

In this respect, the *journée* of 10 August demonstrated the fragility, in revolutionary opinion, to say nothing of any other, of the political concept envisaged by the Constituent Assembly: the power of representatives is sovereign, although it is only secondary (constituted) in relation to the constituent will, which is the prerogative of the nation. Consequently, national representation is both omnipotent and fragile: fragile *because* it is omnipotent. Since it belongs entirely in a single, indivisible body of deputies, with no external ties, it is also entirely dependent on its sole possessor: the people. They have the constant, indefinite power to re-possess it. The tenth of August illustrates this primitive scene of democracy. The Feuillants had wanted to bring the Revolution to a close. On the contrary, it had to be recommenced, to be taken back to its origins, in accordance with its spirit.

What changed on that day, even more than the political form of the regime – it has been seen that the constitutional monarchy of the Constituent Assembly was broadly republican – was the core of its nature: after 10 August the Revolution tended to disappear as a means of instituting a new order through the law; it existed increasingly as an end in itself. The Republic designated the way in which the revolutionary militants expressed their search for a political government with the same identity as its constituent element – the people. The Revolution became the theatre for the dilemma of democratic representation explored by Rousseau. Sieyès thought he had resolved it, but history had rediscovered it: in a large country, direct democracy in the style of classical antiquity was impossible, and without it, how was it possible to avoid usurpation of the sovereignty of the people by the deputies?

This political transformation by no means concealed, as Albert Mathiez has written, a social revolution: in this regard, the summer of 1789 is still the fundamental episode of French contemporary history. But it is true that the guiding forces of the Revolution had changed. Ex-nobles had become rare, notables with an *ancien régime* career less numerous, and the dominant tone was set by fairly unknown men of letters like Brissot, Marat and Desmoulins.

It would be wrong, however, to think of all the principal actors in the period just beginning as marginal or embittered. It is a useful explanation, but only in small doses. Neither Vergniaud nor Robespierre had exactly failed in their lives before 1789, to say nothing of Condorcet, who had been a member of the Academy of Sciences at the age of twenty-five. The truth is that the personnel of the 'second' Revolution comprised not only fewer nobles, but also fewer bourgeois examples than that of 1789, which it nevertheless resembled by virtue of the large number of men from the bar and the legal fraternity, and because it was dominated by a daunting involvement in political extremism, which formed the prevailing climate. Demagogues excelled – Marat, for instance.

In short, the factor these men had in common, for the most part, was not to have played a star role in 1789. They were not so much sons of the *ancien régime* as of the revolutionary years, having done their training in administrations and clubs. Since then, they had been biding their time, schooled in the particular discipline of revolutionary language and less distanced from the people than their predecessors. They had learned

Nicolas Henry Jeaurat de Bertry Revolutionary Allegory, *1794, Musée de la Ville de Paris, Musée Carnavalet, Paris.*
(*Photo: Lauros-Giraudon*)

respect for property in the century's books, but needed to form an alliance with the 'lowly' in order to win and exercise power, or what remained of it. That was also what would divide them.

The period following 10 August and preceding the meeting of the Convention (21 September) was marked by a duality of power: Paris and the Assembly. The legal government of the Legislative Assembly, which had only a month more to run, was counterbalanced by the urban dictatorship of an insurrectionist Commune which had emerged from 10 August. The Parisian *sectionnaire* movement of local revolutionary committees had found its spokesman, and its constant pressure forced the Assembly to back a policy foreshadowing the Terror. The *sections'* surveillance committees increased the number of searches, corn requisitions and arrests of suspects; the Assembly appointed an Executive Council of six members to replace the imprisoned king, set up a special tribunal and worsened the penalties against non-juring priests.

On the Executive Council, which the Girondins had hoped to control through their three former ministers, Clavière, Servan and Jean-Marie Roland, the chief personage was Danton, because he was the link with the Commune – the real power in the summer. Like Robespierre, snatched away from the bar by 1789, he was one of the conspicuous men in Parisian activism, based in the Cordelier Club, which had a stronger working-class membership than the Jacobins. From 1790, his role was as leader of the Parisian *sections* petitioning the Constituent Assembly against the king's ministers. The following year, after Varennes, he was one of the chief agitators for the suspension of the sovereign. His role on 10 August has been the subject of celebrated controversy among historians. According to Alphonse Aulard, he did almost everything; according to Albert Mathiez, almost nothing. Nevertheless, he was among those who profited greatly from that day, and was the symbolic figure of 1792.

Feature for feature, he was the complete opposite of Robespierre, although not yet politically separated from him: in style, temperament and type of talent. Danton was what is called a 'natural', an instinctive orator, the antithesis of the studious, retiring Robespierre the 'Incorruptible'. But he lacked continuity in his planning, and that impressive economy of means to be used for a project, which characterized Robespierrist strategy. He was erratic, a pleasure-lover, familiar with money worries and the value of private happiness; in short, as has often been said, a popular version of Mirabeau, to whom he was much inferior in intelligence. His demagogic talent found ample scope in the circumstances of summer 1792. Danton personified both the *patrie en danger* and the first version of the Terror.

Not eveything depended on circumstance, however, in the revolutionary thrust of August–September. The longer-term legislative work was similarly speeded up by the situation: the secularization of the clergy, the institution of divorce, and new concessions to the peasantry. Émigrés' properties were put up for sale in small lots, and compulsory redemption of seigneurial dues disappeared, except on production of the original deed.

Portrait of Maximilien Robespierre, *Musée Carnavalet, Paris.*
(Photo: Lauros-Giraudon)

Thus 10 August 1792 completed the great measures of 1789 and hastened seigneurial dispossession: that was one of the Parisian revolution's trump cards with regard to the rural world. The dying Assembly had allowed the Terror to be set up in Paris, under the iron rule of the insurrectionist Commune. But in those terrible circumstances it still pursued its legislative work, by which it instituted a new civic society maintaining the spirit of 1789, a contrast destined to be perpetuated with the Convention.

However, neither the Assembly nor the Executive Council, nor even Danton, who was the outstanding voice of the summer, managed to channel – let alone control – insurrectionist pressure which, on the contrary, was magnified by the bad news from the fronts (the fall of Longwy and Verdun). The organized massacres perpetrated in the Paris prisons between 2 and 5 September bear tragic witness to the chain of images dominating terrorist ideology: defeat, betrayal, punishment. But by their savagery – between 1,000 and 1,500 victims, mostly common law prisoners – they also reveal to what extent these bloody excesses had risen since the spring. Danton, the Minister of Justice, had kept quiet; the Girondins were paralysed with fear: Robespierre had already accused Brissot of treason. In the Commune, a complete style of rhetoric had developed to justify the event. The struggles of men and groups to gain power henceforth borrowed the language of terror from the *sections*.

Portrait of Danton, *Musée de la Ville de Paris, Musée Carnavalet, Paris.*
(Photo: Lauros-Giraudon)

On the very day when the Convention was constituted (20 September), victory at Valmy saved France from invasion: this was both a political and a psychological triumph, because the army of volunteers had held fast in the face of the best soldiers of the era, but from a military point of view it was only half a victory, followed by negotiations whereby General Dumouriez allowed the Prussians to go peacefully back to their winter quarters. The famous artillery duel had therefore settled nothing in the long term, and 10 August had been followed by a flood of diplomatic breaks with Europe.

The Convention, which met on 21 September, had thus been elected in conditions which had nothing to do with a free ballot in peaceable circumstances, as seen in modern democracies. It was the advent of universal suffrage in French history, but only militant revolutionaries dared to make an appearance in the assemblies. Everyone demanded Louis XVI's dethronement. The decisive ballot took place at departmental level, in the assembly of electors of the *chef-lieu*, among supporters of what had happened on 10 August. In Paris and several of the *départements*, election took place in the Jacobin Club, in public and out loud.

The Convention had therefore been elected by a small minority of the population, but those who were the most determined. That explains the ambiguity of the word 'popular' when it is applied to this period: 'popular' the French Revolution was certainly *not* in the sense of participation by the people in public affairs. Michelet stressed this, to contrast the period with 1789: the end of 1792 marked the beginning of the withdrawal of public opinion, when the people 'went home';[2] fear had commenced its reign. But if the word 'popular' is taken to mean that revolutionary policy was formed under pressure from the sansculotte movement and organized minorities, and received an egalitarian impetus from them, then yes, the Revolution had well and truly entered its 'popular' age.

However, the Convention – 749 members strong – was a bourgeois assembly. It comprised nearly half the deputies who had sat in the Constituent or the Legislative Assemblies, the same weight of lawyers and barristers, the inimitable style of the epoch which the years had intensified. All these men had three or four years of political battles behind them but, in that era, experience was exactly the opposite of practice in these matters. There was a marked and increasing separation between intellectual and actual politics.

By recommencing the Revolution, the *Conventionnels* escalated the spirit of 1789. For the moment, they had a tendency to decide their voting in the light of the most recent events: that period from 10 August to 20 September when the Paris Commune, born of insurrection, had overridden a Legislative Assembly which was doomed from the outset. The Girondins did not form an organized group in the modern sense of a party, nor did the Montagnards. But Brissot and his friends, Vergniaud, Buzot, Roland and Jean Louis Carra, formed a focus of opinion (more than reluctant when faced with the consequences of 10 August), while the Paris deputies often came from the headquarters of the insurrectionist Commune: Robespierre, Collot d'Herbois, Billaud-Varenne, Camille Desmoulins, Danton. Events yet to come, and firstly the king's trial, would crystallize these two antagonistic groups on one or other side of the divide which already separated Robespierre from Brissot, or Roland from Danton.

At the time it met, the mass of the Convention contained men who had not taken sides: they were referred to as the *Plaine* (or *Marais*). It would be a misinterpretation to infer from those contemporary names an idea of centre politicians, accustomed to the safe subtleties of parliamentary compromise. The Conventionnels of the Marais were men of the 10 August Revolution, 'patriots' of the revolutionary war, bitter adversaries of the *ancien régime* – including the monarchy. Certainly, they were still bourgeois supporters of freedom of contracts and trade, and counted property among the foundations of the social order; but that did not make them any the less deputies engaged in irrevocable conflict with old France and the Europe of the kings. They included the indestructible Sieyès, faithful to his post, slightly less to the fore than in 1789 but constant in his hatred of the aristocracy.

---

[2] Jules Michelet, *Histoire de la Révolution française*, book IX, ch. 1.

THE EXECUTION OF LOUIS XVI

After its inauguration on 20 September, the Convention met on the 21st. It marked its advent by two significant votes; one to its left, the other to its right. It was simultaneously decreed that the future constitution would be submitted to the people, and that 'all territorial properties, both personal and industrial, shall be maintained in perpetuity.' But above all, in an atmosphere which harked back to the night of 4 August, it declared unanimously that royalty in France was abolished: the other part of the *ancien régime*, the monarchy after feudalism, was buried amid the same enthusiasm.

The word 'republic' had not been uttered, as if the Assembly were hesitating on the brink of the first precipice to be tackled: a republic, likened at the time to direct democracy (as can be seen in the Sieyès of 1789), was a regime belonging to antiquity, possible in city-states but incompatible with the vast populations and huge territories brought together in modern monarchies. However, the Convention took the plunge the next day. It accompanied its decision with a major consequence of a symbolic nature: the advent of the Republic would also be the date of the first day of Year I of liberty. The year 1789 was cast back into the *ancien régime*! To a member (Dr Salle) who indeed proposed Year IV, instead of Year I, to place the event in continuity with 1789, Marc-David Lasource replied: 'It is ridiculous to date it Year IV of liberty; for, under the constitution, the people had no true liberty . . . No, gentlemen, we have been free only since we have no longer had a king.' His words were greeted with applause.

What was to be done with the king? The Commune had placed him with his family in the keep of the Temple, in the heart of Paris, but it was for the Convention to decide the fate of this person who had no precedent in French history – a deposed king. The Convention had wrested from the Commune the papers seized in the Tuileries, and appointed a Commission to examine them. It had begun to discuss the conditions of the monarch's trial when, 20 November, the accidental discovery of a secret cupboard which had been contrived in one of the Tuileries walls delivered to the Commissioners part of the king's confidential correspondence – mainly with his Austrian in-laws.

If it was not enough to prove treason in the strictest sense, this correspondence nevertheless formed a dossier about counter-revolution which allowed the king's duplicity to be established on documentary evidence: Mirabeau's letters, in revolutionary opinion, dishonoured the greatest man of 1789 while at the same time bearing witness to *ancien régime* corruption at work in the failed regeneration of that celebrated year. Such contamination revived a crucial question: which Louis XVI was to be tried? When it destroyed the *ancien régime*, the Revolution had preserved the king; it had reinvented and rechristened him, turning him into the nation's first servant, in the terms of the 1791 constitution. It was that king who had been suspended on 10 August, and deposed on 21 September, and who therefore had to be tried; but he had also personified the *ancien régime*, which his ancestors had embodied for so many centuries.

Of those two images superimposed in one man, the Convention retained only one: that of the constitutional king, established by the Act finally voted in September 1791. The court's task was not made any easier thereby, since the constitution had guaranteed inviolability to the king, as to the deputies. Moreover, Barnave and the Feuillants had used the argument in July 1791 to save Louis from deposition after Varennes. The law had provided for only three possibilities of this guarantee being called into question: if the king left the kingdom, placed himself at the head of a foreign army or refused to take the constitutional oath.

In November 1792, none of these was demonstrable from the documents in the dossier, although every deputy was personally convinced that Louis XVI had toyed with all these plans: he had been caught just in time at Varennes, and the letter of the law put Louis XVI out of reach, although he was guilty in the eyes of all. From that arose the predicament in which the Convention found itself during the whole discussion on inviolability in November and December.

That predicament also expressed a scrupulous regard for legality which was enough to place the king's trial outside the revolutionary institution of the Terror, which came afterwards. The Conventionnels had in mind the English precedent of 1649, when an improvised court of deputies appointed by Cromwell had brought a botched action against a Charles I who was very sure of his law. They, on the other hand, represented national sovereignty, and intended to judge Louis XVI according to the law which both they and he had shared in common: that of the constitution.

In fact, they could not do so. Firstly, because the obstacle posed by inviolability was impossible to remove legally as things stood. Then, above all, because the legitimacy – or the crime – of Louis XVI had its roots far beyond that date of 1791, and called into question infinitely more than an argument about constitutional law. The fact remains that parliamentary debate during the last two months of 1792 – as Jaurès, one of the few great commentators on the debate, has noted – went deeply into those fundamental questions. One may think, in company with an American philosopher,[3] that the Convention wanted to cover with a 'maximum of legality' a decision which could not find its source in the Constitution. That was a sign that it had not yet reached the stage when it identified law with power.

For all the orators, the image of the *ancien régime* king was never far away; even for those pleading the 1791 text as jurists (for and against inviolability). All the force of Saint-Just's speech, on 13 November, went into showing its radical incompatibility with revolutionary citizenship. The young deputy from the Aisne, author in 1791 of a fairly moderate little

[3] Michel Walzer (ed.), *Regicide and Revolution: Speeches at the Trial of Louis XVI*.

book, had chosen to make his entry into the Convention as an extremist: he brought the sovereignty of the nation face to face with that of the king, legitimacy with usurpation; he declaimed against the nullity of the 1791 contract, denied the existence of any legal relationship between a king and a people – and therefore even the possibility of a trial: Louis XVI was a criminal simply because he had been king and, as such, should be killed, not tried.

Robespierre, a little later (December 3), adopted the same tone in building a more political argument, holding that the respect for judicial formalities displayed by the Convention implied doubt about what the people had done on 10 August: if the king could be brought to trial and therefore presumed innocent by a court, could the hypothesis be made that the Revolution was guilty? That was a formidable trick question, elaborated by his Machiavellian mind which always steered a middle course between principles and objectives; it was addressed to the Paris activists, and pointed out to them their new enemies in the Assembly.

The Convention's debate, however, remained centred on the interpretation of the 1791 constitution and inviolability. To try the *ancien régime* king would go against the principle of non-retroactive laws. Jean Mailhe, the *rapporteur* presenting the recommendations of the Legislation Committee, had said very early on all that could be said against inviolability: the latter ceased to apply when acts were committed outside legal functions; Louis had now become an ordinary citizen, and thus liable to prosecution. Furthermore, if he had committed none of the three crimes for which inviolability could be suspended, he had frequently, as king, put himself in breach of the law, immediately coming within the scope of laws which targeted corrupt officials.

Today's historians, reading this long legal quibble over a dead constitution, are astounded by its strangeness: the deputies argued over the king's inviolability, while Louis XVI languished in prison. Nevertheless, if the situation, rather than the law, indicated the fatal outcome of the discussion, it is very important to understand the Convention's interrogation of itself and the Revolution, on the brink of events which would carry away part of its authority.

The king was declared able to be brought to trial on 3 December, and the Convention transformed itself into a court of justice, deeming itself the only tribunal equal to this national act. Then the trial proper began, the king making two appearances, on 11 and 26 December, the day after Christmas. These were unhappy debates, in which the former monarch – deprived of his royal majesty, lacklustre, tragic because so out of his element – retreated with his lawyers into a narrow system of defence, incapable of pleading the cause of the French monarchy and even of personifying its memory.

The indictment's reference to the 1791 constitution effaced everything that had happened before. After that date, Louis XVI, whom the judges addressed as Capet, his family name, just like any other citizen, sheltered behind his ministers, or took refuge in his poor memory, or yet again denied everything – even the evidence, such as the documents signed by him. The secret of this sad farewell lies not only in his political mediocrity, his taciturn nature or his solitariness; above all, it was due to the fact that he was being interrogated in a world quite foreign to him. The king of England, Charles I, had outclassed his judges in 1649; but he had been on his own ground; he had brandished the English Constitution, by virtue of which he was king, to demand of Cromwell's judges by what right they judged him.

In the France of 1792 the situation was reversed. The ex-king did not have in common with his judges a royal constitution which he could use against them. The Revolution had created the one of 1791; how could he defend what he was, on the basis of that Act which already made him entirely dependent on it, and by which he had given his support before-hand to the curse laid on the *ancien régime*? Louis XVI kept silent because he had nothing to say in answer to the questions he was being asked; his shared history with France had ceased earlier. His counsel, Raymond de Sèze, François Tronchet and old Malesherbes, would plead such a meagre case that Jaurès – an unlikely defender of the old monarchy – rewrote their script: one of the most moving passages in the admirable *Histoire socialiste de la Révolution française* is the imaginary speech for the defence, in which the writer, who belonged to so different a tradition, renders homage to the fallen king.

The monarchy was dead, but the Girondin deputies wanted to save the king, to spare him from being sentenced to death, or at least from having the sentence carried out. The outlines of the group in the Convention become more clearly discernible around this common desire. Brissot, Vergniaud and their friends, after being the chief instigators of the war with Europe, and enemies of the court, had become moderates – a change of front found throughout the course of the Revolution among those in command, but which, for them, had happened very quickly, between July and November. Not that they had become royalists, as their adversaries would inevitably maintain. But they feared Paris and Parisian revolu-tionary extremism. Memories of the summer were one of their obsessions: the dictatorship of the insurrectionist Commune, the prison massacres – which had gone unpunished and were therefore excused – and the passion of the crowds that continued to intervene in the Assembly's debates.

All those second-generation provincial bourgeois, such as Vergniaud, Buzot, Gensonné and Guadet, had dreamed about revolutionary France more than they had actually known it. Rather like their oracle, Madame Roland – a sensitive and earnest woman, but enclosed in a literary re-lationship with the times she was living through – they lacked any real political strength: detested by the right, hated by the left, caught between two lines of fire, retreating from what they had undertaken. Those who had been the great apostles of the war to free the peoples now feared that the king's death might bring in its wake a rupture with Britain and Spain.

But that was a secondary argument, which derived from their parliamentary conflict with the men who had backed the Commune in the summer, Robespierre and Marat to the fore.

They had manoeuvred in vain to delay the trial. The idea which brought them together in December was to submit the Convention's judgement to the primary assemblies, thus to the people: this idea was apparently irrefutable, since it drew directly on the core of revolutionary argument, going from the representatives back to the nation which had constituted them. The first great parliamentary battle between Girondins and Montagnards took place with each side reversing its expected stance: Vergniaud based the appeal to the people on a criticism of representation, and Bertrand Barère, speaking against an appeal to the people, extolled the sovereignty of the Convention. The conflict of principles exposed the uncertainty of ideas, but chiefly the political stakes.

The weakness of Girondin argument lay in the fact that it left its supporters open to the accusation of royalism. The *appelants* (they would keep this name) were those deputies who appealed for help from the *départements* against Paris in order to save the king's head; their desire was less to consult the people than to rally moderatism against the victors of 10 August. Against them, Barère, the son of a notary from Tarbes, who was not a true-blue Montagnard, gained the ear of the Assembly by his decisive speech at the beginning of January: he described the circumstances, demonstrated the lack of realism of a national consultation, the risks of civil war and the equivocal nature of Girondin intentions. Finally he argued for the Convention's responsibility: you must not, he said to his colleagues, 'throw back on the sovereign the task the sovereign has given you to perform.'

Voting was by name, a defeat for the clemency camp, since every man had publicly to mark out his place for the morrow. Three questions were put: first that of guilt; then whether there should be an appeal to the people; and finally that of sentence. The Montagnards gained a new advantage, since the first vote, which was almost unanimous, would weigh on the other two. An appeal to the people was then rejected by 424 votes to 287; death was decided upon by a small majority. But because forty-six deputies wanted to suspend capital punishment, with various demands for a reprieve, the Convention voted a fourth time on a reprieve, which was rejected by 380 votes to 310.

Louis XVI was executed on the morning of 21 January 1793, in the Place de la Révolution (today Place de la Concorde). He had been a poor defendant; he died with simple and majestic courage: 'His royal and Christian upbringing, which had not provided him with the wherewithal for a political defence, had taught him how to die. This he did as a very Christian King, thus transforming regicide into deicide, as Ballanche saw so clearly.'[4] A great throng of people attended his execution; but, contrary

---

[4] Mona Ozouf, 'Procès du roi', in *Critical Dictionary*.

to that of Charles I in seventeenth-century England, his death prompted no visible movement of opinion in the weeks that followed. The peasants of the Vendée, who rose up in March, did not take up arms in the name of the guillotined king.

The important, and still mysterious, question is whether the Revolution, in bringing Louis XVI to the scaffold, cut the thread of a living royalty, or put an end to an institution which, in public opinion, was already dead. A view of French public life in the nineteenth century would incline one towards the second hypothesis: as opposed to the English revolution, the French Revolution killed not only the king of France, but royalty itself. In this sense, even if the Conventionnels had only transformed into a national tragedy what the last century of absolutism had already marked out as inevitable, they had at least accomplished their aim: to strip royalty from the nation's future. By executing the king, they had severed France's last ties with her past, and made the rupture with the *ancien régime* complete. Michelet, giving the republican regicide its deepest meaning, wrote:

It was necessary to *expose to the light* that ridiculous mystery which barbaric humanity had for so long turned into a religion, the *mystery of royal incarnation*, that bizarre fiction which imagines the wisdom of a great people concentrated in an imbecile . . . Royalty had to be dragged into the daylight, exposed before and behind, opened up, so that the inside of this worm-eaten idol could be clearly seen, full of insects and worms, giving the lie to its beautiful gilded head.[5]

Michelet, however, would have preferred, once the demonstration by public trial had been carried out, that Louis XVI should not be executed, for fear that his punishment should transform him into a martyr and revive the monarchy. By contrast, in deciding on his execution, the Conventionnels had intended to prevent for ever the return to the throne of any of his family, to strike out the institution of royalty from the pages of the future; and they had put their lives on the line. All who had voted for the king's death had been fully aware of it: there could be no royal restoration in France which would not turn them into criminals. They had burnt their boats. So had the Revolution.

CIVIL WAR

After Valmy and the retreat of the Austro-Prussian armies, the French had advanced beyond the frontiers: in Savoy, to Nice, on the left bank of the Rhine. General Dumouriez, who owed his new career to the Girondins, occupied Belgium following the victory of Jemappes: pieces of territory which, in wars of yesteryear, could have been used as bargaining points in an advantageous negotiation. But the Convention remained true to the

[5] Michelet, *La Révolution*, book IX, ch. 7.

spirit of the new times when it annexed Savoy, by voting for 'brotherhood and help for all peoples who wish to enjoy liberty', by introducing into the conquered countries French principles and legislation, together with the assignat and compulsory taxation. The king's death radicalized the conflict, as the Girondins had at first keenly desired, and then feared: spring 1793 witnessed the entry into the war of Britain, the pope, Spain and German and Italian princes.

However badly organized it may have been, that immense coalition soon caused the spectre of defeat and the threat of invasion to reappear, renewing in 1793 the situation of the preceding year, which had been the backdrop to 10 August. The Prussians reconquered the left bank of the Rhine; beaten in Belgium, Dumouriez plunged into political intrigues and ended by going over to the Austrians, as had La Fayette a year before. The latter had dishonoured his Feuillant friends, the former discredited his Girondin protectors. But the war brought to the rising revolutionary wave even more massive proof of the internal betrayal and secret corruption which were ceaselessly at work within the body politic of the Republic: the insurrection in the Vendée.

The revolt began in March as a rejection of conscription. To reinforce the Republic's military numbers, the Convention had voted in February for a levy of 300,000 men, to be chosen at random among the unmarried men of each commune. The arrival of recruiting officers, which brought to mind the monarchy's procedures, gave rise almost everywhere in French rural areas to resistance and even signs of sedition, which was swiftly put down. But matters took a particularly grave turn to the south of the lower course of the Loire, in the Mauges and the farmlands of the Vendée.

During the first few days of March, at Cholet, a large textile township at the junction of the two regions, young people from the surrounding communes, peasants and weavers together, invaded the town and killed the commander of the National Guard there, a Patriot manufacturer. A week later, the violence spread to the western fringe of the farmlands, into the Breton marshes: hundreds of Patriots were massacred there. To the north, near the Loire, a large band of peasants took possession of Saint-Florent-le-Vieil, under the leadership of a carter, Cathelineau, and a gamekeeper, Stofflet.

On 19 March a small republican army of 3,000 men, which had left La Rochelle to go to Nantes, scattered at Pont-Charrault in the Vendée, under the attack of a rural band. Rioting had turned into insurrection. This covered a four-sided area which it was impossible to demarcate in administrative terms: it straddled the *généralités* of Poitiers and Tours – according to the *ancien régime* classification; or the *départements* of Maine-et-Loire, Loire-Inférieure, Vendée and Deux-Sèvres – according to the 1790 redistribution. The heart of the movement lay in the Mauges and the *bocage*, a vast area about one hundred kilometres square, with Cholet at its centre. The periphery of this zone, chiefly to the west, in the Breton marshes, between Montaigu and the sea, would never be completely controlled by the insurgents, but would be endlessly torn between the two camps, depending on the luck of the battle.

The 'Vendée militaire' which, for the space of a few months, would totally evade Parisian authority, in 1789 had not been a region in moral secession from the rest of the nation: at least, there are no noticeable traces of it in the parishes' *cahiers de doléances*, which were quite 'normally' hostile to seigneurial rights, and reasonably reformist in matters of justice or taxation. It was therefore not the fall of the *ancien régime* which roused the populace against the Revolution, but the setting up of the new one: the unprecedented mapping of districts and *départements*, the administrative dictatorship in towns and villages and, above all, the affair of the clergy's oath to the constitution, which presented clandestine resistance with the banner, the faith and the additional backing of the refractory priests.

In August 1792 there had already been the beginning of a revolt, quickly repressed. But in 1793 it was not the January regicide which unleashed the rising: it was the return of forced conscription. This is further proof of the fact that, though the people of the Vendée inscribed 'God and the King' on their flags, they were endowing those inevitable symbols of their tradition with something other than simple regret for an *ancien régime* whose death they had witnessed without any feelings of grief.

The Convention, viewing a rising of the people againt the people's Revolution, could only read into it a new aspect – perhaps the most serious – of the 'aristocratic conspiracy' to restore the old world on the ruins of the Republic. On 19 March it voted an initial decree instituting capital punishment within twenty-four hours for anyone taken carrying arms or wearing the white cockade. In its own way, it too provided the insurrection with a banner. The die had been cast in the space of two weeks.

Thus, by force of circumstance, the war in the Vendée became part of the merciless conflict between revolution and counter-revolution. In Paris, the Convention had no other way of analysing the situation: the idea of a vast conspiracy intended to destroy the Republic simultaneously from within and without united the Montagnards with the militants of the *sections*, and cemented their alliance. On the opposite side, the old nobility saw this uprising as an unexpected windfall. Cut off since 1789 by the inglorious emigration of its best-known names, it now regained the opportunity – with a providentially counter-revolutionary part of the populace – to wage war on the Revolution from elsewhere than abroad. Everything conspired to endow this uprising with a fearful echo of the civil war between the *ancien régime* and the Revolution.

However, in 1789 there had been nothing to foretell the call to action of the Vendéen peasants. What appeared in their recent history was rather a growing political hostility to the upheavals inflicted on their daily lives by the Constituent Assembly's reforms: the creation of *départements* and districts, new taxes, the massive purchase of '*biens nationaux*' by the town-dwelling bourgeois. To those upheavals much was contributed by equally new administrations, organized and staffed by bourgeois readers of

Voltaire and the *Encyclopédie*, large purchasers of Church estates, who flaunted an air of conclusive superiority regarding the backwardness of rural areas. In many of the western *départements*, the age-old antagonism between town and country assumed an unprecedented vigour when there were clashes between the interventionism of brand-new administrative authorities and rural communities jealous of their autonomy and little inclined to innovation.

Beginning with the Civil Constitution, the burning question was the religious issue. The March 1793 insurrection was preceded by a series of local incidents arising from the obligation to take the oath and the division of the Church into two inimical sets of clergy. Everything points to the fact that the mainspring of the Vendéen revolt was religious, and not social or simply political: just as the nobles appeared as latecomers on the scene, royalism came only second, in the wake of the call to God and the Catholic tradition. Lastly, the insurrection's military heroism – when there was any, because the Vendéen army was also subject to panics – was fed by religious fanaticism and the promise of paradise. That collective attachment to the old faith and the old Church, which were seen as inextricably threatened by the Revolution, exceeded the limits of conflict between town and countryside. It explains why the royal and Catholic army also included artisans from the towns, not to mention notables, both great and humble.

To get things in perspective, one must abandon the 'republican' obsession, inherited from the Enlightenment and so much in evidence in Michelet, about manipulation of half-civilized peasants by refractory priests. The Vendéen people must be given back their faith and their traditional forms of worship, with which revolutionary reorganization – so swiftly perceived as antireligious – had crossed swords. It is a little-known, still mysterious, and perhaps unknowable story, probably because there are so few sources of information.

The Counter-Reformation had given the population of the Mauges and the Vendéen *bocage* a religious tradition which was both clerical and popular, centred around frequent and regular devotions, supervised by a Church with large numbers of priests. That tradition, which was doubtless not so ancient or 'feudal' as they believed, but which they were so little prepared to understand, the bourgeois revolutionary administrations in the towns regarded as mere superstition, obscurantism and brutishness: they were disciples of the *philosophes*, not of Catholic reconquest. The war in the Vendée arose from the head-on clash of those two worlds, which knew nothing of each other, set in motion by the Revolution and, in the space of a few years, revealed to each other in a difference which war turned into radical antagonism.

The patriotic unity of the Federations in the summer of 1789, and the great national brotherhood of 14 July of the following year had therefore not survived the Revolution. The Revolution of 1789 had been able to exclude the aristocracy from the nation because the monarchy itself, over the preceding centuries, had prepared the ground for that uprooting; 1793 was able to separate part of the French peasantry from the national body politic only at the price of liquidating a conspiracy, which led to the mass terror.

In this sense, the Vendée revealed at the deepest level the dual nature of what had been attempted since 1789: the Revolution had founded the modern nation on the universality of citizens, but at the same time had torn history and society to pieces. That was why the rural uprising of March 1793 threatened it more profoundly than the situation abroad, however bad that might be. It was also why the Convention could find no other way of overcoming or even thinking about it than by putting it purely and simply in the same category as the enemy: a new and lethal version of *Qu'est-ce que le Tiers État?*

FALL OF THE GIRONDINS

Now this national crisis in spring 1793 found the Revolution once again without a real government, torn between the generals, the Executive Council and the Convention. The latter was itself divided between a Gironde and a Montagne which grew daily more antagonistic, and was subjected to pressure from the Parisian sansculottes who had allies on the spot, such as Marat. Quite independently of men, the very situation manufactured remedies which aggravated it, and added viciousness and resonance to the slogans in the *sections*: Girondin treason, public safety, terror, price-fixing, requisitioning.

In the same way that religion and politics could not be dissociated in the Vendée, in Paris the social question could not be separated from the revolutionary activism of the *sections*. The Montagne armed itself with it and the Convention followed suit, voting the assignats to be legal tender, imposing price controls (the *Maximum*) for grain, dispatching representatives with full powers to the armies, setting up a revolutionary Tribunal and a new executive authority, elected by the Convention, the Committee of Public Safety. To start with, in April, it elected to the Committee only deputies who were not too involved in the row between Gironde and Montagne, and who desired unity, men like Barère and Danton.

It was the Girondins, however, who unwisely engaged in an internal battle for power, by seeking to mobilize the *départements* against the Parisian authorities. They had been unable to get Marat condemned by the revolutionary Tribunal. They succeeded in having a commission elected to inquire into the Commune's activities, and in placing under warrant for arrest two chiefs of the 'popular' party, Jacques Hébert and Jean Varlet. In Lyon local supporters of the Girondins seized control of the town by force from the Montagnard municipality on 29 May and were soon joined by the remaining royalists: another civil war was starting.

Robespierre would doubtless have liked to rally a majority in the Convention to eliminate the Girondin deputies: thus national sovereignty would have remained master of its fate, by a sort of self-purging of the parliament of the Revolution. But events took another turn, more in keeping with what was already revolutionary tradition: two Parisian *journées* decided the Girondins' fate, organized like the others by local ringleaders, launched by the *sections* and an insurgents' committee formed on 30 May, which met in the bishop's palace.

Neither the Convention, where Robespierre remained cautious, nor the Jacobins, who hesitated, nor the Paris Commune where Hébert, who had been freed, tried to instil moderation, gave any encouragement to this movement. Moreover, on 31 May the Paris *sections* wavered between the bishop's palace committee and the authorities constituted after 10 August. Nevertheless, the news was bad: Lyon in the hands of a revolt, the Vendée on the offensive, France wide open to foreign armies.

On 31 May the sansculotte agitators already had enough followers to surround the Convention and present their demands: the arrest of those Girondins most hostile to Paris, a tax on the rich, the creation of an army of revolutionary militants to punish suspects, the right of suffrage for sansculottes only. The Convention voted only for the suppression of the Girondin commission of inquiry on Paris. But everything started up again two days later, on Sunday 2 June, and this time in earnest.

The *sections* had mobilized large numbers of people around the Tuileries, where the Convention had been meeting since 10 May. The day had been methodically planned, but no one knew by whom. Had the leaders of the Montagne taken a hand in it? There is no evidence. The sansculottes had brought with them the National Guard, under the charge of François Hanriot, one of their men, a former toll clerk turned captain, a loudmouth from the Mouffetard quarter who had just recently been promoted to general-in-command by the new insurgents from the bishop's palace.

One hundred and fifty cannon barred the exit from the Convention, where one of Danton's friends, Hérault de Séchelles, was presiding over the gloomy sitting. The deputies – apart from about thirty Montagnards, Robespierrists and Maratists – tried to leave: Hanriot demanded that the guilty should be handed over. There was a tremendous scene, where for the first time there appeared, in razor-sharp clarity, the confrontation between national representation and direct democracy personified in the brute force of the poorer classes and their guns.

Did the representatives yield to force or to the people who had constituted them? To both at once: if they had no other choice for the moment than to yield before Hanriot's artillery, their legitimacy was too frail and too recent to give the necessary weight to a feeling of obedience to the law. Born of 10 August, which had shattered the 1791 constitution, what could be more legitimate for the representatives than the people who had carried them into power? With greater internal strength, Hérault and the Conventionnels might perhaps have broken the blockade of cannon; but they went back into the meeting hall to obey Hanriot's ultimatum and hand over, by acclamation, twenty-nine Girondin deputies into custody.

That was therefore the end of the Girondins politically, and the prelude to their end plain and simple. It was also an important date in the history of the Revolution: the Montagne had paid for its victory with a popular coup d'état against the national representatives. This feature had already existed in the *journée* of 10 August, which had dismissed both king and Legislative Assembly. But it had been concealed by the overthrow of the monarchy, which had really brought to term the Revolution's victory over the *ancien régime*.

The taking of the Tuileries had obscured the violence done to the Assembly: recommencing what 1789 had not been able to carry through to the finish, it had cloaked itself in the legitimacy of the Revolution and the need for its intensification. But less than a year later, on 2 June 1793, there was no longer a king to be conquered. The Convention itself, elected by universal suffrage, had to lower its flag in the face of the Parisian *sections* and their cannon. It was the national representatives who had been vanquished, those who had been entrusted with the task of forming the Republic's new constitution and who had just begun debating it.

The Revolution could no longer come to an end within the law. Cut off despite itself from part of its members, the Convention was now merely a rump parliament sharing its sovereignty with the street mobs. Public Safety, the Terror, speeches about civic virtue might well, for the moment, cast a veil over this public anarchy, but the day of 2 June would nevertheless extend its disastrous shadow over the concept of national representation. Edgar Quinet saw it as the sansculotte version of Napoleon's coup d'état of 18 Brumaire.

REVOLUTIONARY GOVERNMENT

The men of June 1793 could not see so far. The French Revolution had once more torn itself apart, in the most spectacular fashion, at the moment when it faced the gravest situation in its history. There was a link between the two sets of circumstances: national territory was being invaded on all fronts – to the north, on the Rhine, in the Alpine valleys and the Mediterranean south – and civil war had spread. After 2 June the Norman and Breton *départements* had formed a federation against Paris under the Girondin banner. Bordeaux expelled the Convention's representatives. Lyon gradually went over to overt royalism, which had also won towns in the south-east, in August opening the port of Toulon to the English. Refractory priests were busier than ever sowing the counter-revolutionary message, and further 'rural Vendées' were hatching in the Catholic lands of the old kingdom, alongside villages and towns held by the Patriots: in the whole of the heart of the west, in Lozère, on the borders of the Margeride and the Rouergue.

I shall illustrate the danger incurred by the Revolution with an example borrowed yet again from the region where the depth of the civil and military crisis found particular expression – the Vendée. Though the

Girondin revolt was limited, caught in a pincer movement from right and left, the counter-revolution, for its part, was waging a veritable war. The peasants, who had adopted as leaders nobles who had withdrawn to the country, like d'Elbée or Lescure, but also Cathelineau, the Pin-et-Mauges carter, and Stofflet, the Maulévrier gamekeeper, had finally organized a 'royal and Catholic army' which formed the main body of their forces.

Operating on the borders of Poitou and Anjou (while Charette de la Contrie carried on the war on his side more to the west, in the Vendéen marshes), this army, at its best, numbered 40,000 soldiers; it controlled the Mauges and the *bocage* in April 1793: villages and towns, lacking republican garrisons, had fallen without resistance. To the west, Les Sables d'Olonne fought back, but in the east, even the towns were conquered: Bressuire, Parthenay, Thouars and Saumur on 9 June, when the town royalists gave the peasants a helping hand.

From there, the chief rebels decided to go and take Nantes, that rich metropolis of the west, and there to open up the republic to the English and the émigrés. The town, defended every inch of the way, remained in Patriot hands. But the rural uprising maintained its mastery over a vast quadrilateral, on occasion beating Republican columns of troops which were even more disorganized than their own. The threat hanging over the Revolution and Paris lasted the entire summer.

In these circumstances, revolutionary opinion restored extraordinary force to one of national history's old ideas, the classic resort of the monarchy – public safety. Kings had frequently made use of it in justification of 'extraordinary' measures – both military and fiscal; the men of 1793 enlarged the scope of the royal 'extraordinary' to turn public safety into a regime which suspended constitutional laws and was entirely directed towards the rebuilding of a strong central government which would be obeyed unquestioningly. Public need was placed above the law, and the state's arbitrariness accepted in the name of its efficacy.

The contrast was all the keener with the Convention's original mission, and even with the bills debated and voted on by the Assembly. For prior to 2 June Condorcet had proposed a plan for a constitution intended to avoid popular insurrections like that of 10 August by giving the people themselves, in their primary assemblies, control over the laws and the appointment of the executive. After 2 June the Montagnards had not dared completely to go back on that democratic utopia. On 24 June they too had voted their constitution, with a new Declaration of Rights which differed little from the previous one (though citizens' equality, the guarantee of rights by society and the indivisibility of power received additional emphasis). The role of primary assemblies in the development of the law was limited but maintained.

As soon as it was voted, however, this somewhat slapdash text had its application suspended until peace was restored: nevertheless, the Montagnard constitution of June 1793, which had never even begun to be implemented, would be an essential reference point for nineteenth-century republican tradition, as if it had been the sacred ark of the Convention. At the beginning of the Third Republic, Aulard still placed it at the heart of Montagnard conceptions. Nothing speaks more eloquently of the lasting nature, in French history, of that separation between political ideas and realities created by the Revolution.

So, in June 1793 the principles were safe but suspended; the nation's government would be arranged by other means: the dictatorship of Public Safety, which was set up in the summer.

There existed therefore a *de facto* regime, the nature of which was defined from the start by forces rather than by institutions: the Assembly, purged on 2 June, and thenceforth dominated by the Montagnards, provisionally shared power with the Parisian sansculottes. During the summer of 1793, the Parisian *sections'* movement reached its apogee at the same time as the national crisis, and not by chance. Its victory on 2 June caused it to play a temporarily decisive role in the situation: it could not do without the mediation of the Montagnards in the Convention, but neither could the Montagnard deputies, who were indebted to it for the Girondin expulsion, afford to ignore its demands.

Today the revolutionary government no longer appears as the most 'advanced' point of the Revolution, but rather as the arbitrator of an alliance combining deputies of the Plaine and the urban lower classes: those who were called the sansculottes. If modern historiography has preserved the name given to them at the time, it is not for want of seeking another denomination more in keeping with the collective dignity of a class; but this negative sartorial designation still gives the best definition of the mixed character of that population. Poverty-stricken – their numbers swollen by rural immigration into Paris since the 1789 crisis – factory workers, those who worked at home, journeymen, but also artisans, shopkeepers or 'ex-bourgeois of Paris' from the *ancien régime*, sansculottes are better defined by a political state of mind than by economic status. They often invoked Rousseau because they liked direct democracy, but they had not really gone deeply into the concepts of the *Contrat social*. They also doubtless drew on the old Christian millenarism: the cruel yet exhilarating times they were living in represented the advent of brotherhood.

An age-old religious sensitivity had been invested – or perhaps inverted – in a return to its sources and the image of a 'sansculotte Jesus': in opposition to the Church, which had betrayed its mission, it nurtured a new eschatology, secularized by the cult of the Revolution's saints and martyrs. One can also detect the psychological signs of the more recent past: the red bonnet, the pike in hand, the use of '*tu*', virtue – the sansculotte personified the reverse of aristocratic society. He was the very embodiment of equality. His enemies? the enemies of equality and that poor and virtuous community he dreamed of: not only nobles and the rich, but also the powerful, whom it was essential to keep constantly under the threat of the guillotine, that 'scythe of equality'.

The passion for punishment and terror, nourished by a deep desire for revenge and the overturning of society, thus complemented direct democracy as practised in the *sections*, which the sansculottes wanted to extend to the Convention by permanent control of the deputies: not through the old idea of the imperative mandate, but by making elected members subject to removal.

In the social and economic field, there was the same belief in interventionism and supervision, the latter inherited from the *ancien régime*, and diametrically opposed to the principles of bourgeois liberalism which were shared by the whole Convention: the government must hold prices (in the inflationist storm of the assignat), keep an eye on stocks of provisions, and give to the destitute what it took from the rich. Urban unrest was still defined by the egalitarian distribution of hardship, not by the solidarity of producers.

In 1792–3, there was even the traditional character of the revolutionary *curé*, the priest who was a friend to the poor and faithful to Jesus against the Church – the figure who passes through the history of European popular revolts: this was Jacques Roux, an unfrocked priest from the Gravilliers *section* of Paris, leader of the extreme revolutionary *Enragés*. The sansculotte movement was inextricably anti-liberal and extremist; the bourgeois in the Convention, with the Montagnards to the fore, were all *laissez-faire, laissez-passer* men in economic matters. At their side, the Parisian revolution had set up the first great collective actors in what would later be called the 'social question'.

During 1793 – mainly up till the semi-failure of the demonstration of 5 September (see p. 133) and the end of the permanent session of the *sections'* assemblies – those popular demands would be taken into account by the Montagnards, to whom the revolutionary government would owe a number of its features. Links existed between the *sectionnaire* movement and the central institutions: firstly, Marat, whose newspaper had affected and mobilized the public since 1789, making endless appeals for vigilance, suspicion and violence. He was assassinated in July, but he left plenty of emulators and even rivals to take over from him. Collot d'Herbois and Billaud-Varenne were the members of the Committee of Public Safety who were closest to Parisian ultra-revolutionary 'maximalism'. In the Paris Commune and in the Ministry of War, the sansculottes were there in force, protected by personalities like Hébert or Jean Pache, the mayor of Paris, who vied with the leaders of the Enragés, Jacques Roux and Varlet, for an extremist following.

But although the Montagnard group was sensitive to the pressure from the streets and from its own 'left', and though it brought in the Terror and planned economy, it also needed to retain the support of the Convention which, without daring to say too much, was already blaming it for giving in on 2 June. In control of the Jacobins, and soon of the Committee of Public Safety, it had no intention of yielding entirely to the demands of the streets; it drew its strength from its position of temporary arbiter.

The Constituent Assembly had legislated through its commissions. The Convention governed by means of its committees. Two of them were of essential importance: Public Safety and General Security. The second, which had formidable police powers, is less well known than the first, which was the true executive authority and was armed with immense prerogatives. It dated from April, but its composition was thoroughly reshuffled during the summer: Danton resigned from it on 10 July, and Robespierre joined it on 27 July.

This exchange recalls the long-lasting argument which, in French historiography, has divided partisans of Danton and of Robespierre, notably Aulard and Mathiez, at the beginning of the century. In so far as the two men had real value as symbols, in July 1793 it was certainly less a matter of moral opposition between corruption and integrity than of a conflict between two policies; Georges Lefebvre has clarified that point very convincingly.[6] The elements which make Danton's venality more than likely have been put forward without, however, showing the services he had rendered the counter-revolution in exchange.

Of more importance was his policy during spring 1793, when he dominated the brand-new committee: the most moderate of the Montagnards secretly explored the possibility of a compromise peace, doubtless prepared to exchange the queen for European recognition of the French Revolution. But he came up against the military situation, which was unfavourable to the French armies, and he was equally unable to break the internal machinery of the revolutionary war. His resignation from the committee marked the failure of his policy.

Paradoxically, it was Robespierre who, because he possessed great influence over public opinion and the knack of adapting to circumstances, had become the key man of a messianic war he had originally opposed. He was certainly, at the beginning, the key figure of the great Committee of Public Safety, although he did not yet dominate it as he would some months later: he brought to it his conviction that only an alliance between the bourgeoisie and the people could save the Revolution, together with the image of living embodiment of the great principles which he had so cleverly built up for himself since the Constituent Assembly.

Flanked by his supporters, Georges Couthon and Saint-Just, he was the necessary 'bridge' between Paris and the Convention. As a consummate parliamentary tactician, he conveyed this fact to the Convention: the committee was renewable each month. But the Robespierrist group was not enough to define the committee, which was always managed collegially, despite the specific nature of the tasks of each director: the division of its members into 'politicians' and 'technicians' was a Thermidorian invention, intended to lay the corpses of the Terror at the door of the Robespierrists alone.

Many things, however, set the twelve committee members at logger-

---

[6] Georges Lefebvre, 'Sur Danton', *Annales Historiques de la Révolution française* (1932).

heads; Barère was more a man of the Convention than of the committee, and was a link with the Plaine. Robert Lindet had qualms about the Terror which, by contrast, was the outstanding theme of Collot d'Herbois and Billaud-Varenne, latecomers to the committee, forced on it by the sansculottes in September; unlike Robespierre and his friends, Lazare Carnot had given his support only provisionally and for reasons of state to a policy of concessions to the people. But the situation which united them in the summer of 1793 was stronger than those differences of opinion; the break-up of the Montagnard group, which would lead to the dictatorship of the Robespierrist group alone (April–July 1794), occurred only after the relative re-establishment of the situation at home and abroad, in the autumn and winter of 1793–4.

The dictatorship of the Convention and the committees, simultaneously supported and controlled by the Parisian *sections*, representing the sovereign people in permanent session, lasted from June to September. It governed through a network of institutions set up haphazardly since spring: in March, the revolutionary Tribunal and representatives on mission in the *départements*; followed the next month by the Convention's representatives to the armies, also armed with unlimited powers; enforced acceptance of the assignat as the sole legal tender in May, price controls for grain and the forced loan of a billion livres from the rich.

The summer saw sansculotte disturbances reach a peak, under a double banner: price-fixing and terror. In the name of the wretched poverty of the people, the leaders of the *Enragés*, Jacques Roux at their head, called for a planned economy from a Convention with no liking for the idea. But the revolutionary logic of the mobilization of resources by national dictatorship was infinitely more powerful than economic doctrine: if Robespierre and the committee managed to make Jacques Roux retreat, it was by adopting part of his programme. In August, a series of decrees gave the authorities virtually discretionary powers over the production and circulation of grain, accompanied by ferocious punishments for fraud, with the inevitable reward promised to informers. 'Granaries of plenty' were prepared, to stock corn requisitioned by the authorities in each district. On 23 August the decree on the *levée en masse* turned able-bodied civilians into soldiers, and multiplied the number of mouths to be fed by the state. It was a mixture of national lyricism and social utopia.

The Parisian disturbances did not stop; they were inspired by the threats hanging over the nation and by their earlier successes. On 5 September Paris tried to recreate 2 June. Armed *sections* again encircled the Convention to demand the setting up of an internal revolutionary army, the arrest of suspects and a purge of the committees. The Revolution was a theatre where the tune of the sovereign people was endlessly replayed in the streets.

It was probably the key day in the formation of the revolutionary government: the Convention yielded, but kept control of events. It put the Terror on the agenda on 5 September, on the 6th elected Collot d'Herbois and Billaud-Varenne to the Committee of Public Safety, on the 9th created the revolutionary army, on the 11th decreed the Maximum for grain and fodder (and general controls for prices and wages on the 29th), on the 14th reorganized the revolutionary Tribunal, on the 17th voted the law on suspects, and on the 20th gave the local revolutionary committees the task of drawing up lists of them. But at the same time, it had the chiefs of the *Enragés*, Jacques Roux and Varlet, arrested: once it had endorsed their programme, it had removed the source of their strength.

The 'revolutionary government' was thus born of a gradual but rapid institutionalization by the Convention of the main demands of the *sectionnaire* movement. It was written into the logic of Montagnard policy, which had needed the sansculottes in order to break the Girondins in the spring, and wanted to retain them as allies without in any way handing over to them the essentials of government. That was what allowed it, through the Convention's deliberations, to maintain a connection, albeit truncated, with the inherent legitimacy of the Revolution, after giving their due – in the name of direct democracy – to the many *de facto* powers which dominated the Paris streets. Saint-Just made that balance of forces the subject of a decree on 10 October, although his rhetoric did not mitigate its legal flimsiness, even if Article 1 of the decree assigned it a closing date: 'The provisional government of France is revolutionary until there is peace.'

The ensemble of institutions, measures and procedures which constituted it was codified in a slightly later decree of 14 Frimaire (4 December), which in an overall Act set the seal on what had been the gradual development of a centralized dictatorship founded on the Terror. The debate, introduced by Billaud-Varenne, lasted eleven hours, and had as its aim the simplification and tightening-up of the system's 'intermediate mechanisms'. In the centre was the Convention, whose secular arm was the Committee of Public Safety, vested with immense powers: it interpreted the Convention's decrees and settled their methods of application; under its immediate authority it had all state bodies and all civil servants (even the ministers would disappear in April 1794); it directed military and diplomatic activity, appointed generals and members of other committees, subject to ratification by the Convention. It held responsibility for conducting war, public order and the provisioning of the population. The Commune of Paris, famous sansculotte bastion, was neutralized by coming under its control.

THE TERROR

In order to govern, the committee relied in the provinces on the districts (departmental authorities, suspected of federalism, were short-circuited), municipalities and revolutionary committees, which were given the task of applying public safety measures. Its direct spokesmen with these local authorities, apart from representatives on mission, were a body of 'national agents' chosen locally by a 'purging ballot' (which meant by local activists) and vested with authority by the Convention.

Technically, authority was less centralized than it appeared on paper: just like former absolutism, the government of the Revolution came up against the slowness of communications and the inertia of habits and mentalities. In order to overcome this, it relied, on the one hand, on fear of the guillotine and, on the other, on a huge propaganda effort ranging from the introduction of the revolutionary calendar to systematic coverage of the territory by the Montagnard press, in which the Jacobin Club played an important role through its hundreds of branches. Revolutionary government was inseparable from ideological orthodoxy, which forbade plurality of opinions.

In other words, it ruled through fear, making the threat of death hang over all servants of the state and citizens alike. At the summit of the apparatus of the Terror sat the Committee of General Security, the state's second organ, consisting of twelve members elected each month by the Convention, and vested with security, surveillance and police functions, over civil and military authorities as well. It employed a large staff, headed the gradually constituted network of local revolutionary committees, and applied the law on suspects by sifting through the thousands of local denunciations and arrests which it then had to try.

The dossiers to be investigated and the people to be sent for trial were passed to the revolutionary Tribunal: reorganized in September, this displayed considerable and expeditious activity from October onwards. In the *départements*, the situation was more varied. When there had been civil confrontations, the representatives on mission had superimposed *ad hoc* legal commissions on the ordinary criminal courts, in order to direct repression against the Revolution's adversaries: in Lyon, Marseille, Nîmes, Toulouse and in all the west. The revolutionary government had therefore generally suspended the rights of man in the name of reasons of state.

Finally, it exercised full power over the economy. That prerogative remained rather theoretical in financial matters, in that the administration set up by the Constituent Assembly, largely staffed by *ancien régime* specialists, did not undergo any great changes: throughout the period it came under the control of Pierre Joseph Cambon, president of the Finance Committee of the Convention. But in the economic field, properly speaking, where it was occupied by the old regal obsession with feeding the population – and chiefly those in Paris, in order to avoid an uprising – the Committee of Public Safety had installed a completely new administration, headed by the subsistence commission (22 October). Directed by three Patriots, this body, armed with the law of the general Maximum, had the task of regulating production, transport and consumption.

Under its jurisdiction it had sectors as varied as foreign purchases, internal requisitions, price control, the provisioning of Paris and the armies, not to mention the progress of agricultural production, forests, mines, etc. Divided into three large departments, and employing about 500 people, the subsistence commission revived the statistical and regulatory spirit of the former Control-General. But despite the Terror, despite the hunt for 'hoarders', the state's enterprise of directing the national economy by means of requisitions and controls ran headlong nearly everywhere into a general spread of fraud through all classes of the population.

The revolutionary government, by resuming the state's centralizing and regulatory tradition, which had been briefly interrupted by the Constituent Assembly, was the source of a great increase in the number of adminis-trative jobs from which revolutionary personnel benefited. Whereas records show only 670 posts in the ministries in 1791 (a number com-parable to that of the last years of the *ancien régime*), there were 3,000 at the beginning of 1794 and nearly 5,000 at the end of the year (for the fall of Robespierre did not reverse the trend).

When they were not in the armies, the sansculottes staffed police offices or those concerned with war or subsistence. At the very time when Robespierre and Saint-Just were accusing these same 'bureaux' (the term, as it is accepted today, was spreading at that period) of being just so many screens between the committees and the people, the representatives and their mandate, by their action they increased the bureaux's influence, role and number. The revolutionary government's political rhetoric thus collided with its sociological truth.

That rhetoric, however, is crucial to an understanding of the motivating forces and passions linking this period with the history of the Revolution in general. The regime of Year II in effect constituted the application – paradoxical, but full and complete – of what was perhaps the French Revolution's supreme principle: the absolute and indivisible sovereignty of a single Assembly, deemed to represent the general will stemming from universal suffrage. It is a paradoxical application, because the Convention after 2 June was not the Convention of universal suffrage, and the 'revo-lutionary government, was a political concept cobbled together under pressure from supporters of direct democracy.

Yet, it was a full and complete application in so far as the Convention was the sole centre of government and the Committee of Public Safety, the true organ of the dictatorship, was not an executive power distinct from it, but merely one of its committees – a part of itself and therefore sharing the same identity. It was not by chance that Billaud-Varenne, in his intro-ductory report of 28 Brumaire (16 November), had criticized as criminal the Constituent Assembly's organization of an executive power distinct from itself.

Thus, at the moment when the Revolution seemed farthest away from its early aim of founding society on the universality of the law, it was also most faithful to its concept of sovereignty: which shows that 1789 and 1793 may be contrasted or linked, as the case may be. In Year II, the power of the people finally rested on a pyramid of identities: the people were in the Convention, which was in the Committee of Public Safety, which would soon repose in Robespierre. The Terror and virtue, each in its own sector, had the task of making this stream of abstractions hold together.

The 'revolutionary government's' most elaborate 'theory' was probably the report presented by Robespierre to the Convention on 5 Nivôse Year II (25 December 1793) on behalf of the Committee of Public Safety. An unprecedented form of government, which the 'political writers' had consequently neither anticipated nor studied, it contrasted with constitutional government in that it obeyed 'less uniform and less rigorous rules' – which was a way of saying that it was outside the law. Nevertheless it was a kind of prelude, since its aim was to 'institute' the nation against its enemies on whom it waged a war of liberty: 'The objective of constitutional government is to preserve the Republic: that of revolutionary government is to establish it.'

What did 'establish' mean? First of all, to preserve its existence not only against the enemy without, but also against the 'factions' within: Robespierre held the old idea that the greatest risk encountered by the sovereignty of the people was of being usurped by groups pursuing private interests. That justified the beginning, in the winter of 1793–4 of the struggle against the *Indulgents*, who wished to end the Terror, and the Hébertists, who aimed to extend it. What was to draw the line between the people and the factions, good and evil? 'Love of one's homeland and of the truth'. In the last resort, it was therefore a moral criterion which dominated political life, and if the French people recognized themselves in the Convention, it was less according to the law than the 'character' of the action taken by the Assembly.

What permitted the temporary suspension of the law, and for example the rights of man, was therefore something even beyond public safety – the loftier need to establish society on the virtue of the citizens. The Revolution had inherited from the *ancien régime* corrupt men who had distorted the nature of its very actions; before ruling by the law, it had to regenerate each actor in the new social contract. What, for Rousseau, constituted the transition from man to citizen – a difficult, perhaps almost impossible passage – had become the Revolution's goal, through the radical action of the revolutionary government.

Behind the politico-philosophical façade of the revolutionary government, local stories of the period underline the total diversity of situations, according to circumstance and also the dictatorship's available communication network. Civil war was latent, or overt, only in the west and south-east: elsewhere, there were villages where the Revolution had meant only the abolition of feudal rights, the end of the *taille* and conscription. Revolutionary authority took various forms, and the Convention's directives were modified by the nature of local people's societies and district administrations: the rule of acting minorities was far from uniform.

Furthermore, deputies sent as 'representatives on mission' by the Committee of Public Safety, armed with full powers, reacted according to both local situations and their own temperaments: Lindet pacified the

Girondin west in July without a single death sentence; in Lyon, some months later, Collot d'Herbois and Joseph Fouché relied on frequent summary executions by shooting because the guillotine was not working swiftly enough. The same thing occurred in the economic sphere, where the bureaucratic utopia instituted by the Convention's decrees created a steep decline in good citizenship, immediately feeding the guillotine, wherever it passed, accompanied by the 'revolutionary army'.

The reason why the improvised administrative and political system of summer 1793 left a legendary trace in the Republican tradition, was because revolutionary France had loosened its mortal stranglehold at the beginning of autumn, and the gloomy start of the epoch could be covered over by the poetry of national vigour, itself enveloped in universality. Indeed, by force of circumstance, the Revolution had now carried its glory to the frontiers. It had not yet overturned the rules of conventional strategy and, like its enemies, retained the old superstition about siege warfare and line formation; but it had a new army, amalgamated with the old, under the undisputed authority of the civil government, and the Convention kept an eye on developments through its representatives to the armies.

Victory or death: the terrible rule did not belong only to the Terror, but also to patriotism. It had allowed renewal of command and promotion to young generals like Hoche and Jourdan: the nation's war belonged to the children of the people, as the kings' wars had to the aristocrats. At the beginning of September the Anglo-Hanoverian army was beaten at Hondschoote, which liberated Dunkirk from enemy pressure. In October the battle of Wattignies freed Maubeuge from the Austrian army. The Sardinian army was driven out of Savoy, and the Spanish withdrew across the Pyrenees. In the autumn, on the eve of withdrawal to winter quarters, the situation at the fronts was thus redressed.

At the same time, the areas of civil war were reduced, but at a very high cost, in no way related to the need for public safety. The Revolution no longer struck at foreigners, but at those Frenchmen who had defied it, or simply those suspected of doing so: an unlimited category which merely indicated government by fear. The Terror was being installed, no longer a spontaneous reaction of the masses, as in the September 1792 massacres, but a judicial and administrative institution set up by the Convention and the committees. The central repressive apparatus had been in place since March, because the revolutionary Tribunal had been created at that time. But the activity of this Tribunal had been restricted until September, even though its character was already in evidence, by allowing judges to choose only between acquittal and the guillotine.

The sharp rise in the number of the Terror's victims began in October: precisely at the moment when the situation was improving. The phenomenon was very clear in Paris: almost 200 guillotined at the end of 1793. Not only did these include Marie-Antoinette and the ex-Duc d'Orléans, who had in vain called himself Philippe-Egalité, but also the groups defeated by the Revolution: the Girondins who had been arrested or under suspicion since spring, notably Brissot and Vergniaud, plus the remainder of the Feuillants, Bailly and Barnave. The guillotine simultaneously wiped out the *ancien régime* and the first years of the Revolution.

The Terror operated from preference in towns and zones which had risen against the Republic, coming after victory, as a sort of punishment-cum-obliteration of the insurrection. The Girondins had taken control of Lyon on 29 May, at the very time when they were about to be eliminated in Paris. It was a town of merchants and silk workers, where Jacobinism had taken on the aspect of a class war between the poor silk workers and the merchants. From the Girondins, the town had gone over to the royalists, who had reigned there all summer; but it was retaken by the Convention's troops on 9 October. Like so many others, it was 'dechristened' and given a new name, becoming Ville Affranchie, symbolically torn from its accursed past and destined by a Convention decree to partial destruction, limited to the 'houses of the rich'. In November, Collot d'Herbois and Fouché commenced massive repression. The great mansions on the banks of the Saône began to be destroyed. Several thousand suspects were guillotined, shot or collectively gunned down in order to speed things up. The Terror lasted until March 1794.

The history of the revolutionary Terror in the Vendée followed the same reasoning and chronology. This also was a matter of putting down an insurrection – the most serious that the Revolution had had to confront. As in Lyon, repression not only followed victory, but was going full blast several months after victory. Indeed, the Vendéen revolt began in March 1793, and news of its triumphs filled the spring and the beginning of autumn. But, starting from mid-October, it ebbed when the peasant army was crushed at Cholet, and passed to the north of the Loire in the hope of joining up with an English fleet at Granville, before what remained of it was wiped out in December in the battles of Le Mans and Savenay. The revolutionary Terror – which must be distinguished from the atrocities and massacres committed in the heat of battle – raged between February and April 1794.

If the war had been merciless on both sides, what began afterwards was of a different nature: it was mass repression organized from above, on the orders of the Convention, with intent to destroy not only the rebels but also the population, farms, crops, villages – everything which had formed the home ground of the 'brigands'. The guillotine could not cope with such a task: in December, the Convention's representative, Jean-Baptiste Carrier, resorted to collective drownings in the Loire. Starting from January, there came into action a decree brought by Barère to the Convention on 1 August, ordering the 'destruction of the Vendée': the Republican troops were divided into several columns, each entrusted with a particular itinerary, with the explicit mission of burning every dwelling and exterminating the population, including women and children. This appalling operation lasted until May 1794, and its sinister balance should be added to war casualties proper: the 'military Vendée' territory lost 20 per cent of its housing and a large percentage of its population.

Numerical estimates of human losses remain a subject for argument. It is impossible to calculate them with even a modicum of precision: on the one hand, no specific sources exist, and the historian must resort to comparisons between earlier and later censuses, which are hypothetical. On the other hand, these documents do not enable one to make a distinction between three types of death: those killed in the war (on both sides), those who died as a result of terrorist repression (sentenced by a court or simply massacred), and finally the decline in the birthrate and increase in mortality following the war years. So it is not possible to put forward a precise evaluation of the Terror's victims in the Vendée; but taking into account both the victims of Carrier's repression in Nantes and those of General Turreau's fiendish columns, the number is in the order of several tens of thousands, perhaps more than one hundred thousand.

Thus the Terror struck out blindly during the last months of 1793 and the first few of 1794, after the dramatic situation of the summer had been put to rights and after the worst times of pressure on the Convention by the Parisian *sections*. It also formed part of the deputies' political culture, as all the parliamentary debates bear witness so prolifically. For it would be wrong to think of it as simply the product of sansculottes' pressure or the bloody excesses of certain representatives on mission. In reality, it was inseparable from the revolutionary universe, of which it had constituted one of the potentialities from the very beginning.

As early as 1789, the French Revolution could envisage resistance – real or imaginary – only as a gigantic and permanent conspiracy, which it must ceaselessly crush, by means of a people constituted as a single body, in the name of its indivisible sovereignty. Its political repertoire had never given the slightest opening to legal expressions of disagreement, let alone conflict: the people had appropriated the absolutist heritage and taken the place of the king. As a result, there was only one way to think of them in their regained legitimacy, and that was to imagine them as one, and as independent of the private interests characterizing each of their individual members.

Conspiracy was the other face of that vision, a counter-revolution that was concealed and evil, in contrast with the people who were public and good, and nearly as powerful as they, for it had to be overcome again and again. For Sieyès, the aristocracy – that wrong side of the nation – had still been defined legally by its hereditary privileges. The category had since gradually extended to all those conquered by the Revolution, who were stigmatized by their conquerors: the Feuillants were aristocrats, and after them, the Girondins.

The Terror was a regime where men in power designated those who were to be excluded in order to purify the body of the nation. The Vendéen peasants had had their turn. Danton awaited his. This analysis does not imply that there was no difference between 1789 and 1793. The circumstances were not comparable, and naturally played their part. But the political culture which could lead to the Terror was present in the French Revolution right from the summer of 1789.

However, it had not had the whole-hearted support of all the Montagnards, since at the start it had been a sansculotte demand, passed on by the Jacobin Club and by the left of the Montagnards and the committees. This would later allow Michelet, for example, to approve of Public Safety, but not the Terror, the Montagnards but not the Jacobins, Carnot but not Robespierre. That distinction was too biased to be truly in keeping with the facts, as has been seen: no voice was raised against the Terror when this was placed on the Convention's agenda on 5 September 1793, or with regard to any of the great terrorist decrees of the autumn. With the improvement of the situation, at the end of the year fresh conflicts began within the Revolution, in which it was at stake. The Parisian *sections* no longer played a central role; that was now assumed by the Paris Commune and the Cordelier Club, and above all by the Jacobins and the Convention.

After September, Parisian extremism had found a new outlet in the person of Jacques Hébert, who had made a speciality of gathering together round his newspaper, *Le Père Duchesne*, those customers left stranded by the demise of Marat's *L'Ami du peuple*. He was a less spontaneous, less genuine spokesman for the militant people than the leading *Enragés* in the summer, but more influential and better placed; the campaign he launched in November over the policy of the committees did not directly concern the Terror, but dechristianization. Representatives on mission, like Fouché in Nevers, were briskly taking the guillotine into the town centres, carrying out a campaign of extirpating the Catholic form of worship, which was tainted no longer only as a Church but as a faith, by the curse levelled at the *ancien régime*. The Paris Commune had also taken a part in it, by antireligious masquerades and then by closing churches. A whole popular and urban anticlericalism, the origins of which were less clear than its future, temporarily found a substitute cult in the Revolution.

The majority of the Convention, which had voted for the Republican calendar, was antireligious. But, being more realistic than the dechristianizers, it saw in Hébertist exaggeration an additional and gratuitous motive for civil dissension. Robespierre, moreover, detested atheism – that legacy from aristocracy and the rich – which was why, at that period, he moved closer to a more moderate group among the Montagnards who wanted to halt the machinery of the Terror, and to which some credit could be restored by the improvement in the situation. It was the moment of a very temporary alliance with the man who sought to personify that turning-point, Danton.

The Committee of Public Safety therefore allowed an anti-Hébertist offensive to develop, brilliantly orchestrated by Camille Desmoulins's *Le Vieux Cordelier*, which appeared in December; going beyond dechristianization, this aimed at the Terror itself. Perhaps Danton also remained loyal to his dream of a compromise with Europe; in this area, the Committee of Public Safety was more cautious than the Girondins. Robespierre himself, in his November and December speeches, introduced distinctions between the nations which had formed a coalition against the Revolution.

That policy, however, which at least was Danton's, could not be professed in public. In the France of 1793 the quest for peace clashed head on not only with the Paris *sections* but with all the recently promoted revolutionary personnel, who were bound to the Terror and to war. Furthermore, Danton was compromised through certain of his friends, who were suspected of corrupt practices in the liquidation of the former Indies Company.

In January 1794 Robespierre backed off, abandoning Danton, and developed the 'centrist' theme of the 'two factions' threatening the Revolution. In order to break the Hébertist offensive which developed at the end of the winter, originating from the Cordeliers, he urged the Committee to strike first at the extremists, Hébert and his friends; in exchange, he left Danton and Desmoulins to the Committee of General Security. Cleverly amalgamated with the corrupt deputies, they were guillotined less than two weeks after their adversaries, at the beginning of April. Hesitantly, the Convention had ended up by following Robespierre's line.

Now it was the hour of the Committee of Public Safety's absolute dictatorship, which the Parisian activists no longer disputed. For the tumbril which had carried Hébertists to the guillotine had reduced revolutionary Paris to silence. Thenceforward the Commune obeyed, societies and clubs held their tongues or disappeared, and Saint-Just would remark, with his gift for a phrase, 'The Revolution is frozen.' The Convention was the prisoner of the Terror, which had just struck at national representatives; it obeyed the Committee of Public Safety, whose members it had elected and re-elected.

In the bosom of the Committee, the winter's internal events and the two purges of the Hébertists and the Dantonists had definitively closed the book on a collegial executive: Robespierre was, in fact, the head of the Republic's government. In those times, that meant infinitely more than a phrase borrowed from constitutional vocabulary. In this personal dictatorship, the old revolutionary dilemma of 'representation' of the sovereign people found an unprecedented solution: the source of Robespierrist power lay both in the Convention and in the sovereignty of the people. It can be better expressed in monarchic vocabulary, provided 'revolution' replaces 'kingdom': the Incorruptible had ended up by personifying the Revolution.

ROBESPIERRE

It was an immense, though fleeting, victory. It was enough to isolate Robespierre from the politicians of the epoch and make him a figure apart, which he remains to this day. As Michelet understood so well, the French Revolution had not had any really great men, a Cromwell or a Washington: since 1789, it had involved many actors, but swept them along in its wake, and not one of them was capable of taming its fearsome advance. It was the event which was 'great', without precedent and without equal: it had cast into the void all those who had come forward in succession to put an end to it, *Monarchiens* and Feuillants, Girondins and Dantonists.

If, however, the historian wants to single out certain men among that cohort caught up in the tide of events, he can cite Sieyès and Mirabeau, and add Robespierre, but not Danton. Sieyès, because he had the presentiment about the Revolution, formed its philosophy and anticipated its features and passions; but never did he take the leading role, even in 1789. Mirabeau had been the most brilliant of the Constituents, before becoming secretly the most lucid commentator of his time; but he had had to retire into the wings because he could not even dominate the Assembly, let alone Paris. As for Danton, who had lent his great voice to *la patrie en danger*, but who also, in the Ministry of Justice, had covered up the massacres of September 1792, he was too erratic a politician to give true consistency to a more moderate version of Montagnard politics. If he enjoyed frequent popularity among nineteenth-century Republican authors, it was just because he seemed to offer a less bloody image than Robespierre, owing to the last months of his life. But at no time did he play a role comparable to that of his famous rival. Robespierre's greatness in the French Revolution – tragic, but unique – was to have gradually assumed power and, for a few months, exercised it.

He is not an easy man to portray, for he had no private life. His existence prior to the Revolution remains rather mysterious simply because it was so commonplace: Maximilien Robespierre appears in Arras as a barrister who has done pretty well, living amid his sister and aunts and spoilt, as his sister would say in her memoirs, 'by a host of little attentions of which only women are capable'. Without deep feeling, holding only the ideas of his era, protected by the women of the family, with a steady clientele, a member of the local academy, he is the exact opposite of Mirabeau, and the counterpart of Sieyès: during his *ancien régime* life he showed no sign of what would turn him into the Revolution's greatest spokesman.

His case is even more mysterious since, although he had published nothing, the abbé had at least written a great deal for himself: all those notes on so many subjects and authors which bear witness to a split personality and to his revolutionary turn of mind prior to the revolutionary years. There is nothing remotely like this in the pre-1788 Robespierre: a smooth, almost empty, existence; a professional life developing along classic lines; the ideas of the Enlightenment tinged with *fin-de-siècle* moralism – just like almost everyone else in his profession, generation and social circle.

With the Third Estate elections in Arras, a new person was born. In one sense he remained entirely true to himself: he would stay a deputy, an austere, self-controlled politician, rather stiff and starchy in both his attire and his tone, and ever chaste. Much feminine jealousy would surround him, but only over who would keep house for him: that was the domestic side of his existence, when he had to choose between his sister and the carpenter Duplay, his landlord, who had daughters. Like the Arras barrister, the Robespierre of the Revolution put no energy into private intercourse with his fellow men. But the new times revealed that he possessed a formidable power of identification with the public good. Maximilien Robespierre, lacking any other private existence than that which he had received willy-nilly, had found himself truly at home among the principles of the French Revolution. From the emptiness of his private life he derived the strength of his political action.

That was the first of his secrets, which Mirabeau had summed up in the witticism: 'He will go far, because he believes everything he says.' Mirabeau was in a good position to grasp this, since he lived several lives, spoke at least two tongues – one to the king and the other to the Assembly – did not say everything he believed and did not believe everything he said. For Robespierre, the political ideas and the principles which he constantly invoked were deeply rooted in universal morality, itself based on the existence of a 'Supreme Being'. He had a kind of circular conception of politics by which action legitimized itself as good solely from the fact that it could be deduced from principles which it had to translate into reality. His reasoning never emerged from a world where a kind of transparency had to exist between history and morality: a patently absurd supposition, but extremely potent in revolutionary France, which had inscribed it on its banner. That was Robespierre's 'Rousseauism', far more than his admiration for the *Contrat social*, to which his politics referred only by opportunism. The deputy from Arras endlessly extolled virtue: a quality which was no longer simply the civic selflessness of antiquity, but which constantly mingled with that heritage the subjective feeling of modern morality. Robespierre shared the same sensitivity with the France that had raved over *La Nouvelle Héloïse*.

The influence over opinion, which he gradually acquired with the Jacobins and in Parisian societies between 1789 and 1792, he drew from the inevitable tension between those rights proclaimed as belonging equally to all and the true state of society. His words tirelessly returned to that flaw, a component of democracy itself, with a vigour and consistency of thought which no doubt could assail, because the principles of 1789 had been finally decreed only so that they should be applied. In the Constituent Assembly, for example, one of his favourite topics had been criticism of the *censitaire* electoral system (based on property-owning qualification): not only were the French split into three categories (those who voted, those who could be second-stage electors, and those who were eligible); but in the end, one had to be rich to be elected by the people. Jean-Jacques, his beloved Jean-Jacques, could not have been!

This deputy, with his tendency towards the abstract, who identified so completely with the idea of man's universality, also possessed immense talent as a tactician. That was Robespierre's second, and probably principal, secret; at all events the less known. For the first immediately strikes anyone who reads his speeches, and was not linked to a great intellectual originality: the Arras deputy was not a true thinker. On the other hand, if viewed from the aspect of the conquest of power, he was a great strategist and a profound politician.

In his public life during those years, his moralistic turn of mind had instilled in him a veritable obsession with suspicion, through which he encountered the distinctive spirit of revolutionary democracy; thence he obtained unlimited scope for manoeuvres, punctuated with insinuations or accusations according to circumstance, but always used with consummate art to weaken his adversary before destroying him. Robespierre ceaselessly mapped out his route to power by continually denouncing power.

During the Constituent Assembly, filled with men not so new to the game as he, he was not a candidate for anything, yet he gradually played an increasingly central role – becoming the personification of principles in the Assembly and the Jacobin Club, and weaving his web in the heart of the political scene too. It was he who in May 1791 moved the vote on the ineligibility of deputies for the new Assembly, by which means at a single stroke he cleared future ground, for his own advantage, in the name of civic virtue.

Varennes happened, and the crisis following the enforced return of the king, during which he played a masterly game. He kept himself apart from the republican campaign, careful not to place himself outside constitutional law; but against the Feuillants he supported the clubs and popular societies demanding the punishment of Louis XVI. He took no part in the *journée* of 17 July 1791 on the Champ de Mars, during which the National Guard fired on the people. But he made great capital, on his own account, of hostility to Feuillant repression, and in 1791 made it the banner of the Jacobins who remained loyal to the old club when Barnave and his friends had left it.

This sequence of events is of value as an example. Robespierre was not a leader of *journées*: he did not participate on 20 June or 10 August 1792 or 2 June 1793. He had a studious temperament, and gifts of strategy. Popular for the doctrinal purity of his speeches, he drew on this capital by a subtle mixture of daring and caution: he accompanied the Parisian revolutionary movement, uniting it and giving it direction.

That doctrinal purity was bound to be fictitious, even though he had the art of preserving an illusion of it, doubtless within his own heart of hearts as well, because of his obsession with morality: for instance, this 'Rousseauist' took a succession of inconsistent stands on the question of representation. In 1792, he remained true for a long time to his position as inflexible defender of the constitution, and thus of the Assembly's inviolability; then, on 29 July, following the *sections* and widening their audience, he argued in a great speech to the Jacobins for the deposition of the king and the election of a Convention by universal suffrage.

The same thing occurred on 2 June 1793: he had taken no part in the sansculotte movement, and there is no evidence that he had encouraged it secretly; but he stayed inside the Assembly when most of his colleagues went out to try to break the encircling ranks of Hanriot's cannon, and he was one of those who benefited most from the anti-parliamentary coup d'état which eliminated his Girondin foes. Immediately afterwards, he became once again the herald of national representation, the man of the Convention, elected and returned by it to the Committee of Public Safety. His power came from the representatives of the people, but also from the people themselves. Such was the strange chemistry which allowed the two features of his talent to combine and lets us understand the secrets of his dominance. His ideological mastery offers a means of reconciling the two democratic legitimacies.

The idea of 'revolutionary government' was the field in which he excelled, for it freed him from all reference to the formalities of the law, leaving only principles and men on their own. The Revolution would at last come into power through him, but it no longer had any other end but itself: it was that gap that he pathetically tried to fill by talking of the absolute necessity for the regeneration of individuals through virtue, which was the condition of a Republic of true citizens. In 1794, however, this national pedagogy was effected by the Terror, a regime with no fixed laws, defined by a moral mission – to separate the 'good' from the 'bad'. That is why the Incorruptible's enemies had so often been mistaken when they credited him with a particularly repressive nature. Many of his proconsuls and his future conquerors tragically outdid him in that respect: Collot, Fouché, Carrier, for example. For him, the bloodiness was abstract, like the political system: the guillotine was fed by his moral preachings.

When he finally attained sole power, surrounded by his faithful supporters, with Saint-Just and Couthon in the forefront, two batches had gone to the scaffold: the Hébertists and the Dantonists. But the first carried off with Hébert the remainder of the *sectionnaire* movement, thus putting him at the mercy of the Convention, still trembling for having abandoned Danton. So the revolutionary government attained its dictatorial fullness of authority at the moment when its Parisian bases disappeared: at the same time the Committee of Public Safety had crushed the extremists of the guillotine and threatened Danton's fate to anyone seeking a policy of clemency. It no longer directed anything but a vast terrorist bureaucracy, which governed by arrests and fear.

One year after the creation of the revolutionary Tribunal, spring 1794 was the period when the Terror became institutionalized as an administration. A decree of 27 Germinal (16 April), introduced by Saint-Just, had centralized revolutionary justice in Paris. Then came the terrible law of 22 Prairial (10 June). Its novelty lay in the redefinition of the mission and the expeditious all-powerfulness of that fearsome court. Article 4 of the law stated that 'the Tribunal is instituted to punish the enemies of the people', a definition which heralded somewhat more than summary procedures. The Act suppressed investigation, at the same time allowing indictment to be based on a simple accusation; it denied the accused the assistance of a lawyer, and did away with the point of an open hearing by also authorizing judges not to hear witnesses. The draft of the bill is in Couthon's hand; Robespierre, who presided over the Convention on 22 Prairial, came into the debate to back his lieutenant against some deputies who were disturbed by the nature of the law: 'We shall defy the treacherous insinuations by which some would ascribe excessive severity to those measures which the public interest prescribes. Such severity is to be feared only by conspirators, only by the enemies of liberty.'

In fact, the two Acts of Germinal and Prairial sum up the mechanism of that bureaucratized Terror. The increase in executions in Paris, which may be seen from the monthly figures of those guillotined in spring 1794, arose partly because repression was now centralized in the capital. But it came about also because the revolutionary Tribunal hardly pronounced anything but the death sentence any longer: nearly 1,500 executions in seven weeks, between the law of Prairial and the fall of Robespierre, on 9 Thermidor (27 July). Parisian prisons were overcrowded: they harboured more than 8,000 'suspects' at the start of Thermidor. Historians generally apply the term 'Great Terror' to this period of revolutionary repression.

Almost at the moment when he had put the law of Prairial to the vote, two days beforehand (8 June), Robespierre had presided over a ceremony of a very different nature, the Festival of the Supreme Being, anticipated in his great Floréal text, with the magnificent title: 'On the relationships between religious and moral ideas and Republican principles, and on national festivals'. On that morning, processions from the forty-eight *sections* converged on the Tuileries, men and boys on the right with their branches of oak, women and girls on the left with their bouquets of roses and their baskets. At noon, the Convention made an appearance, looking magnificent in the costume which Jacques-Louis David, the great pageant-master, had determined in such detail that, of the three coloured feathers adorning the hat, one learns that the red one 'must be the tallest'.

Facing the Convention's stand stood an arrogant statue, Atheism, emerging from an enigmatic group in which ambition, discord, selfishness and false simplicity were supposed to be recognizable. The star of this first act was Robespierre, president of the Convention since 16 Prairial (4 June), who appeared with a torch in his hand. The main attraction was the setting fire to the group, which disclosed Wisdom, with a slightly blackened nose. Robespierre's speech revealed the meaning of the scene: by burning Atheism, man could be rescued from the desolating Hébertist creed (that death leaves nothing but 'separated molecules') and returned to the belief that it is possible to 'link this transitory life to God himself and to immortality'. 'Man, whoever you are', concluded Robespierre, 'you may still conceive great ideas about yourself.'

After this, the Convention moved off, flanked by the *sections* – twenty-four in front and twenty-four behind – and itself surrounding a sort of chariot of the national heritage, laden with 'produce of French territory'.

Draped in red, it was pulled by oxen with gilded horns towards the festival's second venue, the Champ de Mars, where a 'mountain' awaited it, dotted with 'accidents of nature', grottoes, boulders, brambles, and crowned with the tree of liberty. The Convention took its place on high, musicians half-way up, mothers to the left, and old men and adolescents to the right. The different groups, each in turn, intoned a verse of the hymn dedicated by Marie-Joseph Chénier to the Supreme Being. The last one, sung in unison by all those assembled on the 'mountain' announced the final scene: the adolescents brandished their sabres, the old blessed them and the young girls threw their flowers to the Supreme Being. However, the last cry of the participants was not addressed to him after the final artillery salvo: the fête, like so many others, ended with a cry of 'Long live the Republic.'

On this famous day, which took place all over France, historians have formed differing judgements which frequently tie in with their feelings about Robespierre. Some have seen no more in it than an additional means of crowd manipulation in the hands of the master, while others view it as an initiative dictated by his deep convictions. As the Incorruptible's personality precisely combined these two kinds of reality, the two inter-pretations are not incompatible. There is no reason to doubt Robespierre's sincerity, since he had always hated atheism as a destroyer of morality, loathed the *Encyclopédistes* and extolled Rousseau; even in his condem-nation of the dechristianizers in November 1793, there was more than mere political concern to handle the traditional faith of the people care-fully. In him, however, this fundamental feeling is as hard as the rest to distinguish from political strategy. Through this Festival of the Supreme Being, he was also trying to terminate the Revolution in his own way and to his own advantage – in the utopia of a social harmony in tune with nature.

The event produced something more enigmatic than its instigator had intended: the crowds who attended, dressed in their Sunday best, taking an active part and in very large numbers. Accounts agree on this point, which is hard to comprehend, since the Terror was going full swing and the dread machine had been still for only a day. Was the public at the fête simply because of the lovely June day, or was it too, in imagination, laying the first stone in the building of the future? After all, the spectacle presented was that of the religion of the century, and those who had read a little knew its repertoire in advance. If they could add a thought to exorcize the present, the idea of an end and a fresh beginning, the *journée* had truly found its public. Charles Nodier, who gave an admirable account of the festival, wrote that 'to appreciate it, one must take the trouble to go back to that time. Nothing was left. Here, therefore, was the cornerstone of a nascent society.'[7]

---

[7] Charles Nodier, 'Recherches sur l'éloquence révolutionnaire', part II, 'La Montagne', in *Souvenirs de la Révolution et de l'Empire*.

In any case, the illusion did not last very long – the bloody law of Prairial followed in a couple of days. Nor did the festival have a favourable effect on the Conventionnels, who had seen in it only its political, and even personal, aspect. The Supreme Being did not have the same hold over them as the Committee of Public Safety. War and fear remained the political and psychological mainsprings of the revolutionary dictatorship. War, at that time, was beginning to loosen its stranglehold.

Carnot had laid the plan of campaign at the moment when operations recommenced: the idea was to take the offensive on the northern frontier, by the co-ordinated action of three armies – those of Flanders, the Ardennes and the Moselle. In the end Saint-Just imposed a strategy which caused the principal effort to fall on the Sambre, at the centre of the front, where the Duke of Coburg was putting on the pressure. Sole command of the armies of the Ardennes and Moselle was entrusted to Jourdan. The Sambre et Meuse army hammered the Austrians at Fleurus on 26 June: it was a victory which opened Belgium to the French. On 10 July they got through to Brussels where Pichegru, commanding in Flanders, linked up with Jourdan.

Revolutionary expansion began, but victory abroad was a defeat at home for Robespierre and the Robespierrists. For if France was victorious, why the guillotine and why the dictatorship? That question was asked only within the revolutionary system of reasoning but, for that very reason, touched the right spot: if the Terror was detested by public opinion, as was demonstrated by the enormous collective relief at Robespierre's downfall, it could be overturned only by the Convention, which had given it life before becoming imprisoned by it.

There was no other power left standing which could confront Robespierre: the generals were under close supervision and the army had not yet entered politics. Within the country, fear prevented any public demonstration of opposition. Because of this, the *journée* of 9 Thermidor (27 July) which, in the days that followed, met with such spectacular assent, established the victory of a parliamentary conspiracy hatched amid intrigues of which, in the nature of things, no trace has been preserved.

Two active nuclei may be discerned, very different from each other in all respects. Firstly, the former extreme left of the committees and the Convention, which had kept silent since the execution of the Hébertists: Collot d'Herbois and Billaud-Varenne on the Committee of Public Safety; André Amar and Marc Guillaume Vadier, on the Committee of General Security, who had been keen 'dechristianizers'; and ex-terrorists on mission like Fouché, Louis Fréron, Jean Tallien or Paul Barras. Scenting a change, they wanted to maintain the initiative. They had seen the Festival of the Supreme Being as nothing more than a dictatorial masquerade; the Terror frightened the terrorists too, many of whom had been less incorruptible than the tyrant they wanted to bring down. At the other end of the spectrum were the moderates of the Committee of Public Safety: Lindet, who had refused to sign the order to arrest Danton, and Carnot, at loggerheads with Saint-Just over the conduct of the war. Then there were the former Dantonists, Louis Legendre, Thuriot de la Rozière.

Who was the conductor of this orchestra? Probably no one. The essence of the matter is that when these two oppositions united, they became a majority in the Convention; the famous Plaine, which had followed Montagnard policy since the king's trial and 2 June 1793, turned against the Robespierrist dictatorship, which was its ultimate expression. Everyone wanted some breathing space to ward off the fear that stalked abroad – in short, to enjoy life. Fleurus had struck the hour of a return to liberty. Thus passed the month of July 1794 in the Convention.

Nobody had any inkling of what Robespierre had sensed, or what he planned to do. Since the beginning of July he had been very distracted, very silent, in both the Assembly and the committee. On 8 Thermidor (July 26), from the rostrum of the Convention he denounced his adversaries, without naming them, and called for 'unity in the government'. Intimidation hovered over everyone. The reply came next day. The men of the extreme left played the leading roles: Billaud-Varenne, who attacked, and Collot-d'Herbois, who presided. Robespierre and his friends were not allowed to speak, and their indictment was decreed. In the same movement, the Conventionnels, who knew the score, relieved Hanriot of his command of the National Guard.

The last scene was played out in Paris, at the Hôtel de Ville, during the night of 9–10 Thermidor (27–8 July). The Paris Commune, loyal to the man who had inspired it, had released the arrested deputies in the evening and mobilized two or three thousand militants. The Convention outlawed the Robespierrist groups and its liberators. That was the crucial moment. But decisiveness had deserted the insurgents, and the Convention had mobilized, under the command of Barras, National Guards from the rich quarters of Paris, making a reappearance in the history of the Revolution. They recaptured the prisoners in the middle of the night and made a round-up of Jacobins in Paris. Robespierre shot himself in the jaw with a pistol, without managing to kill himself. He was guillotined the next day with his chief companions, Saint-Just, Couthon and nineteen others; two cartloads followed on the next day, and the one after that.

4

The Thermidorian Republic: 1794–1799

In the Convention's proclamation to the French people, read by the omnipresent Barère on 10 Thermidor (28 July 1794), celebrating the downfall of the new 'conspirators', there is a sentence which makes no sense and yet says everything: 'On 31 May the people had their revolution; on 9 Thermidor the National Convention had its own; liberty acclaimed both equally.'

What, therefore, had happened between 31 May and 2 June 1793? A violent take-over by the armed Parisian *sections* against the Convention, forcing the national representatives to rid themselves of twenty-nine Girondin deputies. The 9 Thermidor, on the other hand, was a victory for the Assembly over the Parisian street mobs, the first since July 1791. A double victory even, since the deputies has overthrown Robespierre and subsequently enforced their decision against the Commune and the remainder of the sansculottes.

The *journées* of spring 1793 and 9 Thermidor (1794) had in common a resort to violence: in both cases a group of deputies was arrested, then guillotined. However, they reveal a break in the history of the Revolution, since on 9 Thermidor the Convention had imposed its law, while on 31 May–2 June it had capitulated. It is this break that Barère's proclamation is trying to conceal, by spreading the common benediction of liberty like a veil over two contrasting events.

Nevertheless he was telling the Convention the psychological truth of the time. For those men who had decreed the arrest of Robespierre on 9 Thermidor were the ones who had elected him and returned him each month to the Committee of Public Safety since July 1793. They were the same men who, shortly before, had allowed the days of 31 May–2 June to occur, had abandoned to a Terror imposed by the Parisian *sections* their Girondin colleagues, elected by the people like themselves. Certain among them had done so from revolutionary fanaticism, but the majority from a sort of bowing to the inevitable: the parliamentary coalition of 9

Thermidor had brought together the extreme terrorist left and a crowd of deputies whose desire was to put an end to the Terror; Carnot numbered among the latter. Moreover the situation of the first group was complex, because even pronounced ex-terrorists like Tallien, proconsul of the Bordeaux scaffold, wanted to end the Terror.

At all events, by whatever routes they had followed, fanaticism or cowardice, the Thermidorian Conventionnels had had the same history and shared the same memories. They had founded the Republic; they had voted for the death of the king; they had excluded the Girondins and set up the revolutionary government; they had abandoned Danton to the guillotine and had finally sent Robespierre there as well. Quite a dramatic journey in less than two years; the country was rid of the enemy and victory was on the horizon. That served as a pardonable excuse, but provided no explanation for the deadly struggles in which they had confronted one another. If Robespierre, who had denounced so many conspiracies, was himself a 'conspirator', and the most dangerous of all, if he was merely the last of an interminable list to which he had already added a host of momentarily famous names, how could the Revolution make any sense?

Barère's wording offered no explanation; it was purely incantatory. The interest lies in its indication of the question present in the minds of Robespierre's conquerors: they could not begin the Revolution once again, starting from 9 Thermidor, reinvent a Year I by destroying the pages they had just written, as they had done on 21 September 1792. They had to shoulder that history, and allocate the parts to be remembered and those to be forgotten: a sign that the revolutionary concept had at last begun to lose whatever utopian content it had had since its formation.

They had a muddled, chaotic, contradictory and bloody history, but they were convinced they were its sons. They had put Robespierre to death, but they had not overthrown the Revolution, quite the contrary; that was the kind of speech which recurred endlessly during the days and weeks following 9 and 10 Thermidor. How in fact could they indulge in this repudiation of their past when they had all played an essential role as legislators, either since 1789, like Sieyès or Boissy d'Anglas, or since 10 August, like Fouché or Barras? Their lives were their sole link with that recent past. They had successively destroyed the old society and the old monarchy, they had cast down the aristocracy, and most of them had voted for the death of Louis XVI, while yet others had been pitiless agents of the Terror: among Robespierre's victors were, for instance, Carrier and Collot d'Herbois, and Barère, who had had the terrible decree of extermination in the Vendée voted in August 1793.

They shared different solidarities with the different ages of the Revolution; but their interests bound them to it as to a unique and liberating event. Many had purchased *biens nationaux*; all were uncompromising over the destruction of privileges and the creation of a society of civil equality. The Revolution had seen various governments follow one another, but its assemblies had never stopped legislating in the spirit of 4 August 1789: liberty of individuals and contracts, equal rights of succession, the institution of divorce, the suppression of compulsory compensation for seigneurial dues, etc.

Of that upheaval, the Conventionnels were both the latest authors and the heirs. They cherished it. They were the new breed of owners, freed from all seigneurial, 'gothic' servitude on what they owned or had acquired. The return of aristocratic society was unacceptable in their eyes. The Thermidorians brought back and would give lasting life to that new race of political men that the Feuillants had managed to personify for one summer alone – conservative revolutionaries. The Revolution was leaving the shores of utopia to discover the strength of personal interests.

Reality reimposed itself. All these men – who were not so very old – felt as if they were survivors. They had just lived through some terrible years, subjected to the tensions of overwork, exacerbated emotions and the threat of the guillotine. They were so enclosed in that world of terrorist politics that it took them several days after 9 Thermidor to comprehend what they had done. But they were soon informed by a public opinion which was being reborn as if by magic, sending them delegations and beginning once more to express itself in public nearly everywhere in the towns: Robespierre's fall swiftly signalled the opening up of prisons, the end of arbitary arrests and the tyranny of surveillance committees, the cessation of the guillotine.

Within a few weeks, 9 Thermidor restored to its former self a French society which had been alienated in the bloody and fictitious political unity of the revolutionary government. But it also roused or rekindled against the Terror feelings and passions which hardly distinguished 1793 from 1789, and thereby called into question the Revolution as such. The latter relied on a variety of new political and social interests, which continued to feed hatred of the aristocracy and the *ancien régime*; but the Republic had replaced liberty with the Terror. The Thermidorians were caught up in this contradictory legacy. They too had to 'terminate' the Revolution, to root it definitively, no longer in a regenerated citizenry, but in society and the law, as in 1789–91; at the same time exorcizing, no less definitively, the tragic memories it had left in national opinion.

If the fall of the dictator marked the end of the Terror, it did not signal the end of the Revolution; it merely opened up the possibility, should the Convention finally manage to give the Republic a constitution. However, the return to liberty revealed the spectacle of a country more divided than it had ever been since 1790, for the Terror and the end of the Terror had brought to a head the civil struggles born of the conflict over religion; Thermidor began an era of score-settling in towns and villages while the state remained impotent.

Abroad the émigrés still embodied the threat of counter-revolution, with the two brothers of the martyred king, Provence and Artois; they had in no way considered Robespierre's end as the end of the Revolution. Lastly, the

war was still going on. By the summer of 1794 it had begun to be a
victorious war, but had not changed its character: it remained a mixture
of military domination, economic looting and social emancipation. In
conquered territories the French armies abolished seigneurial rights and
the tithe, but they lived off the inhabitants. When things went badly, the
war had been the pretext for dictatorship. When it went well, it remained
indivisible from the Revolution in that it was invested with the same
national consciousness, surrounding the figure of the new France with a
halo of universality.

If revolutionary patriotism had stopped rallying the street mobs, it
lost none of its immense force by being channelled towards military
glory. But it made the war difficult to check, as it was also – though for
opposite reasons – on the counter-revolutionary side. Neither Danton nor
Robespierre had dared openly to seek an end to it. It was a legacy from
the Girondins, which they had passed on to the Thermidorians. The
Plaine, that majority of the Convention dominated since its inception and
successively by the Girondins and the Montagnards, at last found its true
political place and autonomy with Thermidor. Its time had come. The war
of the Revolution belonged to it.

Revolutionary history too rarely stresses that continuity from one side of
9 Thermidor to the other. Broadly speaking, the same parliamentary
majority had successively supported – or rather, given free rein to – the
Girondins, the Montagnards, and then the Thermidorians during the
Convention, later perpetuating itself, as we shall see, in the leadership of
the Directory. These Conventionnels of the Plaine, neither Girondins nor
Montagnards, of whom Sieyès once again provides an excellent example,
personify a fundamental loyalty through so many vicissitudes; they wanted
to build a great Republic, without nobles and without a king, to stand
against monarchic Europe. They had paid a high price for it with the
Terror. They had put an end to that, but were not prepared to buy
peace at the cost of compromising their ideas or denying their past. If
peace meant the return of the Bourbons and the old order, rather even
than the law they would prefer to have the revolutionary war, which kept
them in power in the name of the principles of 1789.

To understand this, it is enough to observe the care taken by the
men governing France between Robespierre's downfall and the advent
of Bonaparte (1794–9) to keep power in the hands of the regicides; the
votes of January 1793 denoted the demarcation line between the sure
and the unsure, between those who could not betray the Revolution
because they would be risking their lives, and the others who could,
because they were not risking everything. After the Convention, from
autumn 1795, the group of Conventionnels who had voted for the death of
the king continued to govern the Directory, often in defiance of the
constitution. In that sense, they were faithful to the Girondin promises in
all their original ambivalence; the war of liberation was also a war of
conquest.

Robespierre's victors held two additional trump cards over the Girondins and the Montagnards – they arrived after the Terror and they were victorious. They could thus substitute messianism abroad for activism at home, and free their oligarchic rule from the extremism of the mobs. But by carrying on and extending beyond the frontiers a war which they could not arrest, they would create – like Brissot, Danton or Robespierre – the conditions of their downfall. It was additional proof that this war had become consubstantial with the Revolution, almost its second nature. By halting it, the Revolution would be repudiating itself; but by pursuing the war, it would also open the way to its conqueror.

This described the political situation dominating those Thermidorians, who came to be known as the *Perpétuels* (Perpetuals) under the Directory, and whose symbolic figure is Barras. Squeezed in between Year II and Bonaparte, they do not enjoy a good press in French history; they do not contribute anything to the chronicle of national glories. Compared with the heroes of the Committee of Public Safety and the legendary genius of Napoleon, they present a picture of corrupt intermediaries clinging on to power with no scruples about their methods. The left disliked the world they made, one dominated by pleasure and self-interest, and the conservatives were content to settle for that password of 18 Brumaire: Bonaparte has put an end to corruption and disorder.

However, when one analyses those regicide representatives, those former servants of the revolutionary government, those generals risen from the ranks, those men grown rich in the business of war and the state, they present no less interesting a picture than that of the preceding regime: not the reign of public-spiritedness but, on a quite different level, government by a political class still defending a threatened Revolution while it is already the offspring of a Revolution which has succeeded. The historian can thus compare the Republic of self-interest with that of virtue, and try to understand why the one did no better than the other in establishing itself.

The Conventionnels who had overthrown Robespierre took several weeks, even months, to draw their conclusions from the event of 9 Thermidor. The 'revolutionary government' was at cruising speed, the war continued, the Republic had no other organized government. Moreover, any blunt challenging of the past raised only too clearly the question of the Convention's responsibility, over which the deputies were deeply divided. There were too many ex-terrorist *exagérés* (extremists) among them – Collot d'Herbois, Vadier, Billaud-Varenne, Fouché, Tallien etc. – to make the problem easy to formulate, even if some like Tallien, whose mistress 9 Thermidor had saved from the scaffold, went to the other extreme. Anyway the main body of the Convention remained cautious, following the example of the most moderate member of the old Committee of Public Safety, Lindet, who advised: 'Let us not reproach ourselves for either our misfortunes or our mistakes!'

Nevertheless the parliamentary debates of the period make very exciting reading, in which one can trace the birth of the first interpretations of the terrorist dictatorship: the Robespierrist 'conspiracy' against the Revolution, Robespierre's monarchic ambitions, the excuse of circumstances (destined for a long future), the oppression of the Assembly by the 'tyrant' and his accomplices. In a report written by Courtois in January 1795, commenting on the inventory of papers found in the conspirator's home in the carpenter Duplay's house, there is even the germ of a philosophic idea; the former dictator's confusion of public happiness with private pleasures, and his attempt to force individuals into egalitarian austerity.

If this debate rumbled on within the Convention almost in spite of itself, the reason was not an obsession with old memories but because public opinion imposed it. Totally repressed by force since 2 June 1793 and the setting up of the dictatorship, it had burst out after Robespierre's fall in a sort of immense collective relief in which the strength and vitality of French urban society reappeared, as spectacularly as in the last years of the *ancien régime* and the first of the Revolution.

As always, Paris led the way, mingling politics with the liberating of morals. It was as if opinion were living the anti-Robespierrist reasoning which Courtois would present in January 1795, before it had actually been formulated: the dictatorship had preached austerity, the summer of 9 Thermidor wedded rediscovered freedom with pleasure. The salons began to reopen, fashion and conversation to reign once more, and the growing number of balls held in August and September were like so many political allegories: it was the summer of the opening of prisons and the dismantling of the revolutionary dictatorship.

A new press accompanied the movement, and even the mobs went wild with anti-Robespierrism. The Thermidorian 'reaction' found its sansculottes in little bands of young people from the smart districts, the dandified *muscadins*, who specialized in anti-Jacobinism and operated on behalf of Tallien and his friends. This movement of opinion, which was so spectacular that it gave rise to innumerable accounts of it, was not yet royalist, but in its way it evidenced the relative isolation of the Convention, an old power worn out by a too difficult past and now without support from the left, discredited on the right, and yet still the only government, since it had gathered to its bosom the prerogatives of the committees through the intermediary of its commissions.

Nevertheless the Convention manoeuvred wisely. It yielded to the tide, but slowly. It had to let go of those of its members most compromised under the Terror, but purges were kept to a minimum: Carrier, the man of the Nantes drownings, was condemned and executed in the autumn; then, in the winter, Barère, Collot d'Herbois, Billaud-Varenne and Vadier were charged. But the right of the Convention, led by penitent former Montagnards, such as Tallien and Fréron, raised another ghost from the past: what about the Girondins whom violence had excluded from the Assembly? That was a far-reaching question, as one orator said, because quite simply it cast doubt on the validity of the laws voted since 2 June 1793.

Here again, the Convention made a realistic decision. There were three categories of Girondins: the principal leaders, arrested in June and guillotined in October 1793; twenty-one deputies who had taken flight on 31 May and had been outlawed, and seventy-one other ex-Conventionnels, imprisoned for having signed a protest against the coup d'état of 2 June. The reinstatement of the last two groups – the third first (as it had not been 'outlawed') and then the second, in March 1795 – has been admirably commented upon by Mona Ozouf.[1]

This painful rehabilitation once again brought face to face the Convention and its past, the Revolution and its law: the collective capitulation before Hanriot's cannon on 2 June 1793 was a constant source of remorse for the Convention and re-emerged in a bitter debate between left and right, to such an extent that, on 18 Ventôse (8 March 1795), to conclude the discussion, Sieyès deemed it necessary to add a postscript intended for the deputies who were to be reinstated:

It seems to me that, in a kind of preamble to the decree or, if you prefer, a letter from the president, a few words should be added to let it be known that if, since 9 Thermidor, we have appeared to waver in recalling our colleagues, it was due to considerations which they would themselves wish to respect. We have not wanted to deny their powers; that would have been to wish to destroy our own; we have not repulsed them – we did not have the right; but in reciprocal trust, you in their republican virtues, they in our legislative wisdom, we have presumed that they have voluntarily consented to that prolongation of their honourable exile until common opinion, more enlightened, more just, should itself have determined the time when it was permitted to announce and effect their return, with all the advantages that this measure must have for the nation.

Excuse, advice, warning, of which those returning took good note: in their name, Louvet de Couvray soon replied: 'Let us draw an impenetrable curtain over the past. May it conceal from history, if possible, the errors to which the Convention and the entire French people have been party.'

Easier said than done; the Conventionnels were far from being off the hook. The revolution in the faubourgs came knocking at their gate one last time in spring 1795, set in motion as before by the exposure of the illusions of equality. It had been stunned by Robespierre's ovethrow, and the remainder of its leaders had momentarily been caught up in the wave of Thermidorian opinion: dyed-in-the-wool sansculottes like Varlet or François Babeuf in the summer of 1794 had joined in the chorus of malediction against the 'tyrant'. While gradually dismantling the revolutionary government, the Convention had also returned to its long-held convictions in economic matters; between October and December 1794 it had restored freedom of trading and prices. In fact the relaxation of

---

[1] Mona Ozouf, 'Thermidor ou le travail de l'oubli', in *L'Ecole de la France*.

government control over the economy had begun earlier, in the spring, with the fall of the Hébertists and the disbanding of the revolutionary army at the end of March; shortage reigned in Paris, and Robespierre had taken advantage of the elimination of Hébert to cheat a little over the general Maximum. In fact, the economy was profoundly disorganized by the consequences of the Revolution: money went into hiding, taxes were not coming in, there was the need to feed vast armies, and the country as a whole was converting fraud into a new industry.

The end of the Terror brought with it a return to *laissez-faire*, but the most immediate effect of the abolition of the general Maximum in December 1794 was a terrible burst of inflation; goods certainly reappeared a little in the markets, but at astronomical prices well out of reach of the majority of buyers. The scapegoat was soon trotted out; it had existed for centuries – the state. From December onwards, the crowds no longer blamed regulations or requisitioning, but bourgeois selfishness, taking advantage of unrestricted prices and wages.

FACING THE FUTURE

The beginning of spring 1795 saw the rebirth of a classic situation, but in a very different context from that of 1792 and 1793. The Convention had executed Robespierre, who had executed Hébert. Parisian powers had died twice; in putting an end to the Terror, the Assembly had brought back to itself the public authority of the Revolution. The few remaining Montagnards in its bosom, ready to side with an insurrection in order to relaunch the mechanism of 1793, were insignificant: the Thermidorian bourgeois were afraid of their past; they wanted to end the Revolution, not start it again.

Because of this, the two great Parisian *journées* in the spring – their failure assured in advance by the new balance of power – assumed an unprecedented character, although the combatants were the same as before: it was less a battle for power-sharing than a social war. The poor against the rich. Later on, the Conventionnel René Levasseur, deputy of the Sarthe, would write in his memoirs: 'One saw Paris divided into two nations: on the one hand, the people; on the other, the bourgeoisie.' The two great antagonists were named for the coming century. Before it had definitively vanquished the *ancien régime* and the aristocracy, the bourgeoisie was already standing alongside the accused in the court of revolutionary equality.

The first of these two *journées*, 12 Germinal (1 April 1795), was a copy, in a minor key, of 31 May 1793. The mobilization points were classic: the faubourg Saint-Antoine, the central and eastern *sections* of Paris. The 1793 constitution (the second, that of the Montagnards), a rather fetishist reference – since it was the first, Condorcet's, which contained most direct democracy – began its long career in the extreme republican left.

The armed mob also demanded bread. It invaded the Tuileries and the Convention, where it had petitions read out for several hours, while the majority of deputies made themselves scarce. At the end of the day, battalions of the National Guard from the west of Paris evacuated the old royal palace without incident. It was a victory for the Convention, which took advantage of it to vote for the deportation to Guiana of Collot d'Herbois, Billaud-Varenne, Barère and Vadier. Barère escaped from prison, Vadier hid; the other two started the history of the penal colony of Cayenne.

Some weeks later, on 1 Pairial (20 May), events took a tragic turn. It was the same crowd, roused against the Convention by the same hunger, the same memories, shouting the same slogans, better armed than in April, men and women together. The same scenario, as well, in keeping with tradition: in the middle of the day, the insurgents from the suburbs and the eastern *sections* marched on the Convention; they overran the buildings, killing Jean Féraud, a representative who tried to intervene. His head was presented on a pike to the president of the session, Boissy d'Anglas, but only a handful of deputies supported the rising. It remained without objectives and without leaders, entirely caught up in interminable discussions and petitions, while the Convention, with the strength of experience, succeeded – not without difficulty, and late into the night – in getting the National Guard battalions to intervene on its behalf.

Strictly speaking, the victory was less military than political, 'which shows in retrospect', as Denis Richet has observed, 'how much influence was wielded in Year II by bourgeois, Montagnard or Hébertist leadership'.[2] That was the moment when the Convention exorcized its past in deeds, after spending so long debating about it: in the days which followed, it arrested and condemned the remaining Jacobins and Montagnards in Paris (including those within its own bosom), 'purged' the *sections* and sent an army of 20,000 carefully picked volunteers to remove the cannon and arms from the faubourg Saint-Antoine. The greatest twentieth-century historian of the Jacobins in the Revolution casts a melancholy eye on this moment: 'This date should mark the end of the Revolution: its mainspring had been broken.'[3]

Lacking that 'mainspring', had the Convention placed itself at the mercy of the right and the bands of *muscadins*, through whom there inevitably advanced the idea of a royal restoration? The deputies of the old Plaine might well fear so at this period, because they were already caught between two stools, too bourgeois for the faubourg Saint-Antoine, but too revolutionary for Bourbon supporters. In February, they had agreed to give their authority to an armistice in the Vendée, by which the remaining guerillas of Stofflet and Charette 'recognized' the Republic. But the said

[2] François Furet and Denis Richet, *La Révolution française*, ch. 8: 'Thermidor ou l'impossible oubli'.

[3] Georges Lefebvre, *La Révolution française*, book IV, ch. 3, 'La réaction thermidorienne et les traités de 1795'.

Republic had pledged itself to accept refractory worship and not to levy soldiers or taxes among the insurgents for ten years.

During this era, while egalitarian extremism was being reborn in Paris, the violence of anti-Jacobin revenge took hold of the country – called by historians the White Terror. It was also characterized by almost savage outbursts of violence and a trail of massacres in towns and villages, chiefly in the south-east, in those places where confrontation between partisans and adversaries of the Revolution had been so strong since 1790: for example, in Nîmes, Tarascon, Aix and Marseille. The hunting season for Jacobins was open: a reversal of the situation of 1793, revenge taken against the surveillance committees of the period and their militants. In this sense the two Terrors were truly opposite and comparable, and the blood spilt gives some idea of the extraordinary social violence which runs through the years of the Revolution.

However, there is something misleading in the comparison. The White Terror was never institutional; it had no courts and no administration; it was never sanctioned by instruments of justice or law. In this regard, it was nearer to the massacres of September 1792 (it also invaded the prisons) than to the Terror set up by the revolutionary government. Furthermore, the Convention reacted rather like the public authorities (or what stood for them) in 1792: it just let things happen. For it was more obsessed by past than by present violence. In 1795, as we have seen, the faubourg Saint-Antoine was again the focus of its fears.

Could it, would it, take the risk of favouring the return of the royalist idea in post-Thermidor France? The question arose principally after the anti-Jacobin repression of Prairial (see p. 159). But what had become of the royalist idea in 1795? Recent history presented at least two versions of it: that of pre-1789 and that of 1791. The first took up again with absolutism and the *ancien régime*; the second might correspond with a development of what had been missed by Mirabeau, La Fayette and the Feuillants between 1789 and 1791. The first rejected the entire Revolution out of hand, including 1789 and civil equality. It was largely held by the émigrés, who had assumed the role cut out for the nobility by Sieyès. It made war on revolutionary France in the army of the princes. Louis XVI's two brothers, Provence and Artois, were its chief figures, each with his little court – the former in Verona, the latter in England.

As for the other royalism, it was still only a vague project, though none the less powerful, in bourgeois opinion: precedents were not lacking, from *Monarchiens* to Feuillants. They had failed, but at a time when the revolutionary tide was rising. On the ebb tide, they could benefit from the discredit into which the Jacobin Republic had fallen, gain the support of disappointed Girondins or repentant Montagnards. If a republican regime were truly impossible in a big country, as the wisdom of the century had predicted before the Terror confirmed it, what else was left but a king wedded to civil equality? But the idea did not receive influential support among the émigrés, where a hierarchy of seniority had been established among the counter-revolutionaries: those who had left in 1789 disliked those who had joined them later.

Moderate royalism had no king: Louis XVI's young son had died in the Temple prison on 8 June 1795, and Provence lost no time in proclaiming himself Louis XVIII. Thus in the months of spring 1795, the problem that 1789 had not been able to resolve took shape again: a restored monarchy might perhaps, this time, take advantage of the weariness of the country, but it would have to meet it half-way. Louis XVI's brother and his circle were not willing to do so. A royal proclamation signed at Verona placed on the agenda for their return the punishment of the regicides and the re-establishment of the orders of society.

Moreover, in June, the British – Pitt had hesitated – financed and transported émigré troops to the Breton shores; the plan was to link up the two extremes of the counter-revolution, émigrés and insurrectionary royalist *chouans*, nobles and peasants, to turn them into a civil war army against the Convention. But the expedition only managed in the end to isolate 4,000 *chouans* and a few hundred émigrés in English uniforms on the peninsula of Quiberon. Hoche surrounded them like mice in a trap on 21 July. The military commanders – in whose ranks Tallien resumed service – had the 748 émigrés shot as traitors. The Thermidorian regicides continued to show no sentiment towards the counter-revolution. They were fighting on two fronts, against the residue of Jacobinism and against the aristocracy in association with the Europe of the kings. They spoke most about the first battle, because it penetrated their lives and their memories. But it was the second which continued to be the main front, as all their history would show.

They launched themselves into a daring foreign policy which linked up again with the Girondin dream of 1792, but changed its character. The French were victorious. They had been in the act of conquering Belgium when the Convention had overthrown Robespierre; in the autumn, the Sambre et Meuse army was advancing in Prussian territory towards the Rhine, and in January 1795, making use of the ice to cross the rivers, General Pichegru had mastered Holland. France and the Revolution therefore faced a new situation: spread out as far as Amsterdam, occupying the left bank of the Rhine, while Holland had capitulated and Prussia, totally engrossed in its rivalry with Austria and Russia over the new partition of Poland, was ready to make a separate peace in the west.

What did the Convention and its committees want? Opinion desired peace, even a partial one, but what would be its political and territorial conditions? One could imagine a prudent policy of gains limited intentionally so that they could be accomplished more easily. A man like Carnot at the time personified that old realism of the kings of France: the Meuse could provide a good frontier. But the Revolution had dreamed dreams which were too grand for those careful calculations of a hereditary prince. At the moment when it was losing its internal fire, it had all the greater need to invest its loyalty to itself in other issues.

As usual, Sieyès, who had been at war with the nobles since 1789, showed his colours by putting forward a policy of 'natural frontiers'. Together with many other Thermidorians, like the Alsatian Reubell, he made himself one of the principal advocates of that policy. But because it incorporated in the new France (liberated from aristocracy and kings) the entire left bank of the Rhine, from Strasbourg to its mouth, the formula clothed in geographical terms the French Revolution's European ascendancy. It was Girondin messianism rewritten in Thermidorian language: a revolutionary heritage composed of ideas and interests, uniting the nation around its conquests and its glory, since it was unable to unite it in a civil consensus on the years it had just lived through.

Therefore, the two advantageous treaties obtained by the Convention in 1795 – one with Prussia, which ceded its share of the left bank of the Rhine, the other with Spain, which evacuated French Catalonia – reveal only the division of external enemies, or the temporary withdrawal of the less determined. In matters of foreign policy, the most significant event of the year was the transformation of Holland into the Batavian Republic, soon bound to its big French 'sister' by the hard reality of an economic and political protectorate: forced to relinquish some territory, obliged to provide for the upkeep of an army, to pay a huge indemnity and to submit to the pillage of its works of art. Belgium was purely and simply 'reunited' with the French Republic a little later. The Thermidorians thus inaugurated a foreign policy destined for far-reaching repercussion which they could not gauge, any more than could the Girondins; they would, however, have control over its development for somewhat longer.

THE CONSTITUTION OF 1795

Finally they had to face up to the great day of reckoning at home. The Convention had been elected in September 1792 to set up a constitution, after the people had taken the Tuileries and overthrown the king. It had voted for one which was immediately invalidated by the sansculottes; then another, which was straight away suspended. Now was the time for the third, the good one – or, if the adjective seems excessive considering the short life of that document, at least the one which would determine the features of the Republic's government until the coup d'état of Brumaire (November 1799).

It was voted on 22 August, having been the subject of a long and gripping discussion. All the fundamental problems debated in the decisive months of 1789, between June and October, resurface in it. In this way, the historian has the unexpected chance of seeing a second run of the film, in its emended version, and of being able to measure the weight of events on consciences. Amongst the principals, certain actors have not changed. Boissy d'Anglas, *rapporteur* of the Constitution of Year III, had in 1789 been the deputy to the Estates-General for the seneschalship of Annonay, and had won renown in June of that year by backing the designation of 'National Assembly' for the meeting of the Third Estate. During Louis XVI's trial, he had voted for an appeal to the people, detention and reprieve.

Sieyès, however, was a regicide: on 2 and 18 Thermidor (20 July and 5 August 1795) he gave two of his greatest constitutional speeches. Unable to have all his recommendations put to the vote, he refused to have anything to do with the final bill, as with the first constitution after the summer of 1789. But his interventions in summer 1795, perhaps too philosophical for the occasion, remain essential for anyone wanting to understand the questions raised.

The third great name in the debate was Daunou, the deputy from the Pas-de-Calais, an ex-Oratorian, in favour of the Civil Constitution of the Clergy. He had proposed the trial of the king by a special High Court, before voting for his imprisonment and banishment. He was one of the seventy-three deputies arrested for protesting against 2 June 1793, and among the first to be reinstated in December 1794. He typified the dominant political tone: very hostile to the Terror, very closely bound to the Revolution, which now needed to be implanted in the law and in men's minds. It was up to legislation and philosophy to signpost the new road which had been opened in 1789 and lost in 1793.

The Revolution retraced its steps. It reopened the discussion about the Declaration of Rights, the sovereignty of the people, representation. It sought to write a document which would render impossible any return to the revolutionary government, which it branded 'anarchy', the lawless regime, and finally to bring 1789 to an end by a Republic governed by reason and property-ownership. The new declaration, like the two preceding ones, was included in the constitution. It contained the supremacy of the law, which was an expression of the general will of the people, as the guarantee of rights. But the right of 'resisting oppression' (1789) or of 'insurrection' (1793) had disappeared, to prevent any challenge to what had been instituted according to law.

Equality was still within the rights of man, together with liberty, safety and property, but it retrieved its 1789 status, defined by the same rights for every citizen before the law: there was no more reference, as in 1793, to the right to work, aid or education. Finally, the 1795 declaration contained a second addendum entitled 'Duties': it was the very one that the Constitutent Assembly had refused the *Monarchiens* in July–August 1789. It laid down, together with the obligations of legislators, those of the citizens, namely, obedience to the laws, productive labour and service to the *patrie*. It was all aimed at avoiding the tension between the unlimited nature of rights and the necessity for social order based on the law: since 1789, the internal revolutionary dynamic had found its source in that gap, which the Conventionnels could not fill but which they tried to narrow.

Another great question was the sovereignty of the people. The deputies were by now well aware that a much more oppressive government than the old absolute monarchy could reign in its name. Between 1792 and 1794 they had discovered the fearsome and literally boundless power concealed within the democratic idea of sovereignty: had it not attempted, under Robespierre, to engulf citizens' private lives, even their thoughts?

Comparison between the old absolute power of the kings and the Robespierrist dictatorship cropped up constantly in political discussion after 9 Thermidor. It gave Sieyès the opportunity, in his speech of 2 Thermidor (1795), for an explanation which has lost none of its historic value:

This expression [the sovereignty of the people] has loomed so large in imaginations only because French minds, still filled with superstitions about royalty, felt duty-bound to imbue it with the entire heritage of pompous attributes and absolute powers which gave the usurped sovereignties their glitter; we have even seen the public mind, in its immense liberality, become angry that it could not endow it still further; men seemed to think, with a sort of patriotic pride, that if the sovereignty of great kings is so powerful, so terrible, then the sovereignty of a great people should be something else again. For myself, I maintain that, as men become enlightened and distance themselves from the times when they believed they had knowledge, but in reality had only the desire, the concept of sovereignty will return to its rightful confines for, once again, the sovereignty of the people is not limitless, and many honoured and lauded systems – including the one to which we believe we still have the greatest obligations – will come to appear as mere monastic conceptions, poor blueprints for the '*rétotale*' rather than the '*république*', and equally disastrous for liberty and ruinous for both the public and the private.

Thus, according to the former Vicar-General of Chartres, the Revolution's mistake lay in having transferred the power of the king to the people. The only way to rectify that error was to entrust to them only the amount of power necessary for the existence of a nation of free and equal individuals, defined first and foremost by what belonged only to each one of them. Here began a long liberal tradition of reflection on the concept of sovereignty, to be found in Benjamin Constant, Madame de Staël, Royer-Collard and Guizot.

For the moment, one of Sieyès's ideas for limiting sovereignty was to have a *jurie constitutionnaire*, a special body which would have the task of judging complaints against any attack made on the constitution: this was the first appearance in French history of the notion of a jurisdiction superior to the legislative power, since it would exercise control over the constitutionality of laws and administrative regulations. With Sieyès, this was not born of a reflection on Montesquieu or on the necessary balance of powers. On the contrary, the *jurie constitutionnaire* was only one of the 'representative' authorities of society, armed with the special *procuration* to watch over the constitution, alongside several other *juries*, endowed with other *procurations*: Sieyès never considered the organization of public power in terms of weight and counterweight, American fashion, but – good French rationalist that he was – as a clockwork mechanism.

As in 1789, The Assembly adopted the spirit rather than the letter of his advice. To limit sovereignty by dividing it, while at the same time founding the Republic on the enlightened 'representation' of the people, charged with delegating its executive power to a college: such were the aims of the majority of deputies. The new constitution comprised two assemblies vested with legislative power: an innovation in revolutionary history, because since 1789 the two-chamber system had been tainted with 'aristocracy'. But it was now only a matter of dividing up the tasks: the Five Hundred, with a minimum age of thirty, discussed and voted on resolutions which the 'Ancients' (250 deputies aged at least forty) transformed into laws, or not, as the case might be.

Sieyès's constitutional jurisdiction had disappeared, not understood by his contemporaries: the sovereignty of the people was represented by two assemblies, but remained without total control. In the end, the deputies sought to moderate, rather than limit, it by specifying electoral rights, as in 1791. Voting continued to be two-tiered. All Frenchmen enrolled on the tax lists voted, but could elect only well-to-do electors (the rating conditions varied according to the size of the townships): this is where the *propriétaires* had such an advantage in national representation.

Executive power was in keeping with what might be expected in a republic: elected and collegial, therefore relatively weak – five Directors, chiefs of the Executive, and ministers chosen by the Ancients from a list of fifty names put forward by the Five Hundred. The assemblies were replaceable by a third and the Directory by a fifth each year. Executive power in the hands of the Directory was extensive, almost by nature in the France of 1795: war, diplomacy, police, administration.

The limiting factor was the existence of a college of five Directors, plus the rebirth of the elective principle for departmental and municipal administrations, which were nevertheless placed under the control of agents of the central government. But the most acute constitutional problem facing the Constitution of Year III concerned the relations between the legislature and the executive. The assemblies made and voted on laws, elected Directors but did not control their actions, except that they could indict them. Powers were separate, and how their co-operation was to be organized had not been precisely established.

As soon as it had completed the constitution, the Convention moved on to another debate, entitled in the *Moniteur*, the official journal of the time, 'Discussion on the means of ending the Revolution.' The question implicit in this already classic wording had been put clearly by Baudin, deputy for the Ardennes and a member of the Constitution Committee, on 1 Fructidor (18 August): it was less the end of the Revolution than its continuity that was in question.

The withdrawal of the Constituent Assembly is enough to teach you that, if an untried constitution is set in motion, a totally new legislature is an infallible means of overturning it . . . The Legislative Assembly, bound to uphold the monarchy as it had pledged with such ceremony, perhaps itself contributed to its rapid under-mining, and did not believe it was acting disloyally by saving the country. You should fear lest the establishment of the Republic encounter the same hazards, if you risk putting it to the same test, and that after so many jolts and wrenches and convulsions, liberty may succumb in a new revolution which you would have made possible by an act of weakness.

What was he trying to say, through this appeal to memories? This: the Convention had to do the opposite of what the Constituent Assembly had done, and keep control over what was to follow. By leaving the people to elect freely the two assemblies whose formation it had just decided upon, it was running the risk of a royalist majority which would imperil revolutionary ideas and interests. His speech was understood, because it was followed on 5 Fructidor (22 August) by a vote for a decree on the 'formation of a new legislative body'. Article II, section i, stipulates: 'All members presently active in the Convention are re-eligible. Electoral assemblies may not take fewer than two-thirds of them to form the legislative body.'

That was the famous law of the Two-Thirds, followed shortly after by a supplementary safety clause: if the quota was not observed, the re-elected Conventionnels would co-opt their former colleagues. In May 1791 Robespierre had had the ineligibility of the Constituents voted in order to give forward impetus to the Revolution. In August 1795 the Convention perpetuated itself in order to preserve it. It paid a heavy price, for in doing so it inflicted a congenital weakness on the institutions it had just developed, and destroyed what had been at the very heart of its plan – a Republic founded on law. The entire history of the Directory had already been cast: all that was missing was the victorious general who would, as if by chance, make his appearance in the political crisis instigated by the cynical decision of the Perpetuals.

The decree went down badly with an urban opinion that had 'gone royalist,' and for which the Convention remained associated with the Terror. All the elements of French bourgeois life that had been reborn since the summer of 1794 – the new salons, the new newspapers, the new gentlemen and the beautiful ladies dressed in Roman fashion – had impatiently awaited the departure of those Public Safety veterans who should have taken the bad memories away with them. Now here were those same discredited men about to fill the new institutions, in the name of their worst habits, nullifying in advance the feeling of the country. Through them the Revolution would pursue its dictatorship. As Robespierre had suspended his constitution to make his power absolute, they had decided to abolish in actual fact the elective principle they had just sanctioned.

However, confronted with the moderates' anger (echoed by a minority on the right) the Convention had the logic of the situation on its side. Revolutionary France had a foreign war on its hands, and was increasingly detested by the émigrés and men of the *ancien régime*; the country was in a state of bankruptcy and unpopularity, which still carried the risk of re-igniting the sparks of the great *journées* of earlier days. The Perpetuals were the product of these circumstances, according the sovereignty of the people only the share which the situation allowed: that was a completely empirical strategy, which made such a sharp contrast with the abstractions of revolu-tionary government, and which would win for that very reason. The Convention and its committees had the power, and made use of it. They managed to get all the *départements* to accept the new constitution and the decrees of the two-thirds.

In Paris, on 13 Vendémiaire (5 October), they crushed a rising of the moderate *sections* of the west, led by the privileged youth. These last had rather played the role of sorcerer's apprentice in trying to repeat, to the advantage of the right, the great scenes of crowd-rousing against the Assembly. It was a scenario that the deputies of the former Plaine knew better. They even knew it by heart. And the *muscadins* were easier to bring down than the sansculottes. The Convention had entrusted the affair to Barras who, in order to crush moderate Paris, had recruited a young unemployed general, a former Robespierrist, who was trailing along in his entourage: Napoleon Bonaparte. All the same, there were 20,000 insurgents on the streets, but the cannon were in the Convention's camp and decided the matter without further ado near the church of Saint-Roch.

At the time when it dispersed at the end of October, the Convention was therefore more than ever the incarnation of the Revolution and its power; so that no one should remain unaware of it, on 3 Brumaire (25 October), at its penultimate sitting, it passed a law which reaffirmed and extended the curse laid on the aristocracy since 1789, because it forbade relatives of émigrés to hold public office. Not that the émigrés at that time were all nobles – far from it. But the idea of emigration was inseparable from that of aristocracy, and the Revolution continued its mission, extended to Europe. It was under this banner that the Thermidorian bourgeois put the finishing touch to their work by a last law of exception, before installing themselves in the Directory in the places they had reserved for themselves in advance.

The elections would therefore bring back 500 Conventionnels out of 750 deputies divided into two chambers. As many of these veterans had been chosen by several constituencies, their numbers were short and their old and new colleagues had to co-opt about a hundred more. So there were three categories of deputies: the elected Conventionnels, the co-opted Conventionnels and a final third, the most moderate, freely chosen by the electoral assemblies. Lots were drawn among the over-forties to pick the 250 who would form the 'Ancients'. This personnel was still perforce dominated by the majority of the old Thermidorian Convention, amongst whom the great names still appeared: Sieyès, Carnot, Treilhard, Jean-Jacques de Cambacérès, Barras.

They were not all former members of the Plaine who had once given the support of their votes to the Montagnard dictatorship; there were also reinstated ex-Girondins, like Louvet and Daunou, who were more deeply attached to the Republic than to their bad memories of post-2 June 1793. The right was composed mainly of the newly elected, but also included some former members. It was even more different in its loyalties, because it contained men of the old Feuillant group, Barbé-Marbois, Tronson-Ducoudray, Du Pont de Nemours – a lot of royalists without a king; and there were some supporters of the royal cause, like Henry-Larivière, an outlawed ex-Girondin, reinstated with the last group in March 1795, but not at all keen to 'draw a veil over the past', and a bitter adversary of the Republic.

The chief concern was the election of the Directory. It was prepared in a series of secret meetings of the Five Hundred, intended to pass on to the Ancients a broad list made up in such a way that the five desired names would impose themselves by virtue of their renown. They were – in order of votes received – five Conventionnels, La Révellière-Lépeaux, Reubell, Sieyès, Charles Letourneur and Barras. All regicides, save Reubell, who had been on mission to the Mainz army at the time of the king's trial. Sieyès declined, pleading his lack of enthusiasm for the office, and also aggrieved that his plan for the constitution had not been accepted. The Ancients replaced him with Carnot, another great name of the Revolution, another regicide, who had succeeded in personifying the glory of the Committee of Public Safety without its crimes.

In this team which had emerged from 1793, only La Révellière-Lépeaux was a former Girondin, proscribed by the Terror but still Girondin, that is to say, anticlerical and annexationist. Barras and Reubell were ex-terrorists who had little regard for means but were uncompromising over the revolutionary heritage. Barras, an ex-Vicomte, had saved the Convention on 13 Vendémiaire. He was a corrupt but energetic sensualist, the strong member of the team, protector of all the surviving Jacobin personnel in the administration, and watchdog over royalist intrigues. Letourneur, a captain in the Engineers, was an understudy for Carnot, the moderate member of this first Directory; the man who had sat with Robespierre and Saint-Just on the Grand Committee surely did not welcome the idea of the return of the kings, but above all he feared social disorder.

The Directors shared responsibilities: the Interior went to Barras, War to Carnot, Diplomacy and Finance to Reubell, Public Education to La Révellière-Lépeaux and the Navy to Letourneur. They appointed ministers, who were no longer anything but top civil servants, to head their administrations. The Republic was in place. It soon gave itself another ministry, also supervised by Barras – that of Police. There was certainly a need for it: barely established, it was already a discredited regime. The contrast which would be its undoing, between the glory of France abroad and the contempt in which the government was held at home, existed from the moment it took its first steps.

CONSTANT

One can better understand the reasons if one listens to a young Swiss who had just arrived in Paris, in the middle of 1795, in the train of Madame de Staël, with whom he was in love: Benjamin Constant. He was a child prodigy of Enlightenment Europe, who had studied classical antiquity, history and philosophy in the best universities of the era, in Germany and Edinburgh. He was twenty-eight years old. Here he was at last in Paris, the centre of universal history since 1789. There was no sharper observer of the political situation.

He had begun by writing an article against the decree of the two-thirds, before rallying to its support shortly afterwards: his life would offer other examples of that kind of about-face, but like those which followed, this can be explained by reasons which are not all circumstantial. For the young Swiss was a supporter of Year III of the Republic, yet at the same time aware of the threats hanging over it. He had absolutely no attachment to the aristocracy, for whom he had fewer regrets – if possible – than his famous friend, Necker's daughter Germaine de Staël.

His entire thinking, even ahead of his ambitions and interests, drew him to support the new world born in 1789. But from his vast range of studies he had also retained the classic impossibility of establishing a Republican government in a large country: modern nation-states were too immense for the people to vote on laws, as they had in Athens. In Thermidorian France, facts seemed to have endorsed that politico-philosophical dilemma, since the 1792 Republic had been unable to apply its own constitution, and had degenerated into a terrorist dictatorship. In doing so, it had added an element of emotive revulsion to what had hitherto been merely the philosophical acknowledgement of a contradiction. Benjamin Constant did not truly belong to the Thermidorians, because he had not shared their past, having lived outside France until 1795; but this young man would be their profoundest thinker.

In April 1796 he published a pamphlet entitled *De la force du gouvernement actuel et de la nécessité de s'y rallier* (On the strength of the present government and the need to support it). A significant title, which meant the opposite of what it proclaimed, at least in its first part: the government was weak, therefore it needed support. In fact, Constant was attempting to reply to the wave of reaction which had shown itself on 13 Vendémiaire and continued to accompany the first steps of the new regime. He had buckled down to a daunting, almost impossible, task: to establish the Republic in public opinion, in order to root it firmly in the law, two years after the Terror and several months after the decrees of the two-thirds.

The heart of the argument lies in making the French Revolution a part of historical necessity. Constant refutes Burke, who had become the source from which all counter-revolutionary thought drew its nourishment, and at the same time transforms the problem of the causes of 1789. The break with the *ancien régime* did not represent a sudden eruption of the 'natural rights' of individuals, or their rediscovery in a society corrupted by 'gothic' institutions. It demonstrated the operation of a historic reason which had been at work from the very beginning – the concept of equality. 'The origin of the social state is a great enigma, but its progress is simple and uniform . . . Emerging from the impenetrable cloud which covers its birth, we see humankind go forward towards equality over the ruins of institutions of all kinds. There has been no going back on any step taken in this direction.'[4] Thus, the end of the *ancien régime*, foretold by Enlightenment philosophy, wipes out what he calls the system of 'heredity', in which the destiny of individuals is written in their birth: it inaugurates modern equality, whereby everyone receives his due according to his merit, by virtue of a law which is common to all and in accordance with reason.

There was therefore no sense in opposing an inevitable history, as the counter-revolutionaries were doing, and being all the more harmful because they were anachronistic. The Revolution was modern France, born of a general shift in public opinion, and firmly implanted in new ways and new interests: assent was not only wise, it was inseparable from public peace, which the French so ardently desired. It alone could rebuild a united opinion around the principles of 1789. However, that was to suppose that the problem of the Terror had been settled, which it certainly was not. How could the renascent Republic in Year III be separated from its first two years, when all the efforts of reactionaries and neo-Jacobins were working in the opposite direction? The former cast the Revolution as an indivisible whole, entirely to be damned; the Terror providentially revealed the true nature of the event while forming its very heart: it was a thesis which Joseph de Maistre argued in the next year (1797) in his *Considérations sur la France*.

On the other hand, as has been seen, the 1793 constitution was beginning to be the subject of a special cult: among those nostalgic for Year II, the term in reality covered the entire revolutionary programme, equality of poor and rich, the Maximum, the guillotine, dictatorship. In order to conquer the émigré and royalist right, Constant had not only to emphasize the historic necessity for the Revolution, but at the same time to sever the Republic from its revolutionary origins. That was the condition for the institution of the law and the rallying of public opinion. He was the first to grapple with a problem which all nineteenth-century liberals would encounter, whether monarchists or republicans. There is no other modern political heritage in France but that of the Revolution; that heritage includes a portion which is not compatible with liberty, and which it is not possible to 'forget', because 1793 also has its heirs.

In Constant's language, used by his contemporaries as well, the Revolution was a good thing, but its development had been uncertain, chaotic,

---

[4] *De la force du gouvernement actuel de la France et de la nécessité de s'y rallier*, p. 96.

sometimes detestable, because the revolutionary Terror duplicated the arbitrary nature of absolute power and caused the reappearance of an *ancien régime* characteristic. Constant endlessly explored the reasons for that contradiction between a necessary event and its mysterious course, even if he was unable to explain its nature. He would devote two further pamphlets to the subject in 1797. He could see the role played by the heritage of the past and the counter-revolution, but clear-sightedly refused to explain the Revolution's crimes only by reference to those of the *ancien régime*. He was the first to point out that the scaffold had most often followed Jacobin victory, instead of being its prerequisite. Finally, he put forward an explanation by anachronism. Revolutions were intended to reconcile the institutions of a people with its 'ideas', when the former lagged behind the latter; but the dictatorship of Year II had gone beyond the said 'ideas', threatening property; that was why it had provoked a sort of backlash movement of political 'reactions' which might well bring back the Revolution short of its principles, and serve the enemies of 1789 without really meaning to.

That explained the fragility of the regime of Year III, demonstrated by the decree of the two-thirds. For Constant, the young Republic was haunted by the spectre of arbitrary rule. The *ancien régime* had been subject to the whim of the king, revolutionary dictatorship had been lawless; and very soon, if 'reaction' triumphed, it would put the finishing touch to this tragic sequence: 'Those who seek to overthrow the Republic are strangely taken in by words. They have seen what a terrible and dire event a revolution is, and conclude that what they call a counter-revolution would be a happy one. They do not realize that this counter-revolution would itself be only a new revolution.'[5]

In order to break out of the fatal sequence, there was but one remedy; to rally general feeling behind the Republic of Year III, to entrench the principles of 1789 in a peaceable, durable political regime, which would be accepted, that is to say in both public opinion and the law. Benjamin Constant had not yet completely developed his theory of 'representative government', which he was nevertheless already hailing as the great modern invention; but he was the first to map out the republicans' and liberals' questionnaire on the Revolution. And he had put his finger on the nub of the French political problem, which would last for a hundred years: restoration of the monarchy brings back the *ancien régime*, but the Republic is indivisble from dictatorship in French history and French memories.

BABEUF

The French formed a nation of bourgeois, peasants and landowners. But not entirely. Almost at the very moment when Constant's first booklet made its appearance in April 1796, the Directory dramatically eliminated a

[5] *De la force du gouvernement*, p. 21.

communist conspiracy aiming to set up an egalitarian dictatorship in France. This chronological quasi-coincidence speaks volumes about the extraordinary segmentation of political traditions all harking back to the Revolution, and the precocity of their development on the very heels of that Revolution: 1789, 1793 – they were only yesterday; Robespierre's death had not reached its second anniversary when the revolutionary adventure found its heirs not only divided but enemies. Constant tried to justify the Revolution, Babeuf wanted to start it again.

The concept had as its background the spectacle of poverty, rendered even more cruel by the blatant luxury of the few. The parvenus of the Revolution, the Thermidorians, were also frequently made wealthy by it. The nobles had gone, or were in hiding; the court was nothing more than a distant memory. The bourgeois dominated Parisian society, where *biens nationaux* and public bankruptcy had offered the opportunity for profitable speculation, adding its effects to more traditional forms of profiteering – augmented by circumstances – such as army supplies and state markets. The *financiers* of the *ancien régime* had found their heirs.

This bourgeoisie had been liberated from aristocratic arrogance since 1789, but it had been separated from the people since 1792. The terms aristocracy, bourgeoisie, people, must be taken both in their very general social acceptance and as political categories defining extremely strong class feeling, inherited from the *ancien régime* and intensified by the Revolution. Post-revolutionary society unwittingly combined equality, which had remained its banner against the nobles, with the aristocratic heritage, turned against the people. To put it into an imprecise but clear nineteenth-century vocabulary, the *ancien régime* and the Revolution had cut the middle class off from both the upper and the lower classes.

The economic and financial situation constituted a permanent incitement to the resentment of the poor and intensified memories of Year II. The Directory had inherited a financial mess, and continued to honour settlements with increasingly devalued assignats. A feeble government, lacking credit in the country as a whole, or even among the wealthy, in March it botched an operation for financial stabilization, which ended up in the squandering of two billion of *biens nationaux*, sold for a song to the joyful speculators. Moreover, it had very bad luck: the harvests of 1794 and 1795 were poor, and the icy winter of 1795–6 was the hardest of all in the revolutionary years. Parisian police reports of the time, which were already adopting the modern practice of keeping note for the government of movements of opinion, all speak of the bad state of mind; one of them, on 2 January 1796, reports that the 'societies of patriots' coming into being again 'are made up only of terrorists and revived Jacobins whose influence and pernicious maxims are a threat'.

It was in that context that the Conspiracy of Equals was formed by Babeuf. For a time it lacked any great importance since it did not really threaten the government. Nor is it certain that its principal hero deserves, for the profundity of his writings, the attention he has received in the twentieth century. However, that very attention, notably on the part of communist historiography, indicates Babeuf's egalitarianism was more than a failed conspiracy: it was the basis of a tradition whereby the French Revolution entered the extreme left in the nineteenth and twentieth centuries.

An ex-militant sansculotte who in 1793 had passed into the revolutionary administration, participating for some months after 9 Thermidor in anti-Robespierrist reaction, Babeuf had soon returned to egalitarian extremism and had been imprisoned in February 1795 for 'incitement to rebellion, murder and the dissolution of national representation'. It was in prison – first in Paris at the Plessis, then in Arras, where he was transferred – that the nucleus of the future Conspiracy of Equals was formed, with the ex- and neo-terrorists that he met there: Germain, Bodson, Debon and Filippo Buonarroti. The last, a descendant of a great Pisan family, an intellectual nurtured on the philosophy of the Enlightenment and a loyal Robespierrist who became a naturalized Frenchman in 1793 – also the future historiographer of Babouvism – was able to play an important role in the doctrinal redevelopment of the group. At all events, when he emerged from prison in October (after the Vendémiaire royalist uprising, amnesty was granted to all Republicans) Babeuf, now transformed into *Gracchus* Babeuf, was the man whose new Roman forename evoked the sharing out of lands and the egalitarian distribution of wealth. That was the new banner of his newspaper and his activities.

In the terrible winter of 1795–6, Babeuf's group came across a group nostalgic for 1793, ex-Hébertists, ex-Maratists, ex-Robespierrists, brought together by the general misfortune of the times and seeking a popular platform against the newly established Directory. They all regrouped around the former Conventionnel Amar, famous for his role in the Committee of General Security, and met in clubs, the most active of which, the Panthéon, was gradually radicalized under the influence of Germain, Buonarroti and Darthe, one of the most extreme terrorists of the heroic epoch. From the fusion of these groups and men would emerge, in the autumn of 1796, the idea of the need for clandestine and direct action as a substitute for popular apathy.

After the Directory had had the Panthéon Club closed in February, the conspirators in their turn formed a 'secret Directory of Public Safety', consisting of seven members. Participating were communists like Babeuf and the amiable publicist, Sylvain Maréchal, who had strayed into this tragic sheepfold; he was the author of the *Manifeste des Égaux*. On the side of the neo-Robespierrists dating from the great epoch were such as Félix le Peletier, brother of the Montagnard Conventionnel assassinated in 1793, a rich banker who had possibly sponsored the team; finally Buonarroti, who exactly personified the transition from Robespierrism to Babouvism. This 'Secret Directory' put its agents in place for the day of action: one per *arrondissement* and, in the army, one per unit of troops. In the provinces it relied on the support of a certain number of nostalgic Conventionnels. It

Louis Lejeune Battle of the Bridge at Lodi, 10 May 1796, *Musée Versailles, Paris. (Photo: Photographie Bulloz)*

adopted as its banner and its programme the 1793 constitution, the return to the sovereignty of the people. The rest was known only to a small circle of conspirators.

But the other Directory – the real one – was well informed. Barras knew a little of what was being plotted through his informers and the relationships he had kept up with former friends. He took no action, fearing, since Vendémiaire, the royalists more than the sansculottes, who had been crushed in Germinal and Prairial. He was also a 'wait and see' specialist. Carnot, by contrast, knew every detail of the conspiracy, thanks to one of the conspirators, whose treachery he had bought. The former member of the Committee of Public Safety almost obsessively exorcized his own past through his combat against the Equals. Backed by Letourneur and La Révellière, while Reubell did nothing, he became the figurehead of the Directory against the terrorists and 'Levellers'. Through him, certain bourgeois members of Year III tried to turn the Babeuf affair into something of a bogey.

The conspirators were picked up by the police on 21 Floréal (10 May 1796). Of this new tumbril-load public opinion knew only the names of the old Conventionnels, Jean-Baptiste Drouet (the man of Varennes), Robert Lindet, Vadier, Amar. It saw this episode as the fall of a new terrorist faction, the final spasm of Jacobinism. Less famous, the 'Equals', strictly speaking, were masked by memories of 1793. Nevertheless, at the trial in Vendôme the following year, of the sixty-five accused who had decided to deny the conspiracy despite the evidence, only Babeuf and Darthe were sentenced to death and executed; seven, including Buonarroti, were sentenced to deportation; all the others were acquitted: from this judgement one may infer the solidarity of the ex-Conventionnel circle.

The affair had not therefore been very serious; first and foremost, it gave Carnot the chance to organize the first 'red peril' in modern history, which would know plenty of others. But it was important chiefly for the ideas it left. Buonarroti would make a book about them, published at the end of the Restoration: through this 'Constitution of Equals', the most egalitarian version of the Revolution would transform the great memories of 1793 into visions of the future.

The heart of the conspiracy was the concept of equality, glorified as the aim of the Revolution, since it was the law of nature and man's prime need and *therefore* – that was the crucial word – society's ultimate goal.

The French Revolution had seen the target, but had not been able to reach it. The historic development of the reasons for this failure is to be found in Buonarroti's book, but the idea was implicit everywhere in the texts of 1795, and served as a link between Babouvists and neo-Robespierrists: the Revolution had been taken over in its early stages by the aristocrats, whom Buonarroti likened to supporters of English political economy and self-centred individualism. But the 1793 constitution (the second, after the defeat of the Girondins) and Robespierre's revolutionary government had restored power to the people and to equality. Alas, not for long, since 9 Thermidor brought back their adversaries. Babouvism had thus formed the early ground for a Robespierrist historiography of the Revolution destined for a bright future, critical of both 1789 and Thermidor. But in Year IV, if one listens to the *Manifeste des Égaux* again, it was more a matter of an agenda: 'The French Revolution is merely the forerunner of another bigger, much more solemn, revolution, which will be the last.'

What revolution was meant? What could make equality 'real'? The suppression of private ownership? In this regard, Babeuf's contribution seems to have been decisive, in so far as his pre-1789 correspondence already bears witness to his interest in a general plan for social reorganization founded on the equal distribution of possessions. The leader of the 'Equals' was not a great thinker, and all his life remained more of an ideologist than a philosopher. He was an innocent and sentimental autodidact, an admirer of Rousseau and the Abbé Mably, advancing the idea of splitting up large farms for the benefit of the poorest people, commenting passionately, in his letters of 1787, on a work on the means of stamping out pauperism. His *Cadastre perpétuel* (Perpetual Land Register), which appeared in 1789, revolved around the same question. During the revolutionary years, Babeuf finally put forward not the idea of 'agrarian law', which suggested an egalitarian distribution of lands among individuals, but a community of land, which would rule out all private ownership, and an equal sharing out of its produce among all citizens who would be equally conscripted to work on it. Such sharing agrarian communism was not unknown in the store-house of eighteenth-century literary utopias, but in Babouvism it presented the new characteristic of constituting a revolutionary programme. It undeniably marked the entry of communism into public life.

The last distinctive feature of the conspiracy concerned its conception of politics; it owed more to Jacobinism than to Enlightenment philosophy. In 1794–5 Babeuf and his friends had adopted, as a unifying slogan, the watchword of a return to the 1793 Montagnard constitution. They praised its practice of direct democracy (by referring laws to primary assemblies), although they secretly criticized it for guaranteeing the right of ownership. But behind this exaltation of the one and indivisible will of the people lay, as with the Jacobins and perhaps even more so, the justification of dictatorship: that of the only true interpreters of that sovereign will, the purest revolutionaries – the Equals.

Like the Jacobins, Babeuf exaggerated the power of political action to change society and to maintain its strictly egalitarian nature when it had done so. According to Buonarroti, the distribution of possessions was to be carried out under the control of magistrates appointed, over a long period, by the members of the 'Secret Directory'. The revolutionary tradition of political voluntarism thus blossomed with the Conspiracy of Equals; in this respect, it is significant that the majority of Babouvist documents eschew the term liberty in favour of the word equality.

What should have followed success by the conspiracy can be seen in its concrete preparation. Babeuf borrowed his idea of political action from Marat and the Hébertists: the people who had been subjugated and deceived (this time by an evil conspiracy of the wealthy) could be freed from their chains only by a clandestine insurrectionist minority, organized along military lines, and determined at all costs to institute, at least temporarily, a dictatorship in the name of, and to the benefit of, the people.

That vision surely reveals the inability of the conspirators, in the circumstances of Year IV, to stir up the resigned mass of the people to recover the atmosphere of the great revolutionary *journées*. But it was infinitely more than this sad reflection of their isolation; it was the ultimate expression of the revolutionary belief that political will could achieve everything. The last wave of Jacobin extremism – and doubtless the only political synthesis of the passion for equality of those time – here elaborated the theory of the revolutionary *coup*, which had no real support in Thermidorian society, but was at least appropriate to the nature of a centralized state: he who conquers the ministries in Paris could be master of the country.

THE DIRECTORY

For the time being, however, in the year 1796, which witnessed the ruthless elimination of the Babouvist conspiracy, the danger for the Perpetuals did not lie on their left. It was precisely where Constant had foreseen it, on their right, in the disaffection and even contempt felt by 'enlightened' opinion for the regime of Year III and its men. Autumn saw the arrival of the first electoral date: one third of the Councils would have to be replaced, and the new Councils would then elect one new Director out of the five. How could they avoid a royalist success, which would open a dangerous breach in the Republican fortress?

Barras and Reubell had moderated the repression of Babouvism because they were the protectors of the revolutionary heritage. They had filled the new administration with former Jacobins, with whom they shared the will to oppose by all possible means a royalist restoration, including one by stealth. In opposition to them, Carnot sniffed the prevailing wind, as in 1793, but this time from the other direction, sensing the conservative trend of bourgeois opinion, like most of the two councils. But the parliamentary right, composed chiefly of deputies who had not sat in the Convention, was demanding more than they were prepared to give. It wanted the abolition of the law of 3 Brumaire (25 October 1795), which prohibited émigrés' relatives from holding public office.

All it obtained was an extension of the ban to the sixty-eight Conventionnels pursued after 9 Thermidor, who had been amnestied after 13 Vendémiaire and once again renegotiated like hostages in the shifting balance of forces: it was a strange decision, which reveals much about the spirit of the era, the influence of symbols and the powerful effect of memories. In order not to have to relinquish them, the old Plaine temporized by extending to terrorists laws of exclusion aimed at émigrés' families.

Neither counter-revolution nor Terror. This combat on two fronts could still be defined only in relation to civil war, and could still express itself only by exceptional laws. Nevertheless, if it allowed the government to continue without lapsing into tyranny, it was firstly because it found backing in private interests; the government was post-revolutionary and bourgeois, wedding politics and money, guaranteeing assets, reassuring the owners of *biens nationaux*, opening careers in the administration and the army. It kept going almost uniquely because it was the embodiment of that social continuity with 1789, and the heart of the country, including the peasantry, was not prepared to re-exchange the Revolution for the *ancien régime*. But it also presented a fragile governmental version of 1789, in the hands of an oligarchy without credit even in the eyes of those citizens it was protecting. In post-1793 France, private interests were very demanding in the matter of political guarantees. It was the Directory's good fortune not to have on its right a royalist opposition which could make this France a more secure offer.

Not that there were no moderate royalists seeking to reconcile the royal family with civil equality. On the contrary, the country was full of them, because it was a question of linking up with 1789 and not with the *ancien régime*, and of rediscovering a *Monarchien* version of royalty which would include the sale of *biens nationaux*, which had been decided upon two months after the defeat of the *Monarchiens*. That, roughly speaking, was the programme of the moderate notables who met together at Clichy in the mansion of Louis XVI's ex-minister, Bertin, under the leadership of General Mathieu Dumas, veteran of the American war, La Fayette's former right-hand man in Paris and Feuillant ex-deputy to the Legislative Assembly.

These men, who formed the right wing of the councils, felt that they were carried by public opinion, by that very numerous class which, in 1790 and 1791, had staffed the administrations of the new *départements* before being eliminated by the 1792 Republic and the 'revolutionary government'. They disliked the Perpetuals, detested Barras, and had hardly more confidence in Carnot, who had sat so long with Robespierre on the Committee of Public Safety. They did not believe, like Constant, that the Thermidorian Republic was capable of restoring concord in a country which was gradually sliding towards a sort of soft anarchy. France was too vast a country, where the roots of royalty were too ancient for any power other than monarchy to be able to bring back order and revive respect for property.

But which monarchy? The drama of these 'constitutional royalists' of Years IV and V, also known as the Clichyens – unlike the 1789 *Monarchiens*, or even the 1791 Feuillants – was that the regime they envisaged would again mean the subversion of institutions; and, supposing this subversion should take place, it would restore to power not a constitutional king, but the family of the martyr-king and his train of émigrés.

Certainly, since 1792, emigration had ceased to be essentially aristocratic; fear and events had driven tens of thousands of Frenchmen of all classes out of the country, especially from *départements* near to frontiers. But, just as for Madame de Staël the only good emigration was the one following 10 August, so for the aristocracy, monarchist loyalty was measured by the earliness of the date of exile, and it continued to mount a close guard around the king's brothers. It surrounded Provence and Artois with little courts more finicky than ever about etiquette, and all the great roles were played out in the minor key, including those of favourites: Madame de Balbi for the former, and Madame de Polastron for the latter.

The most terrible indictment brought against the aristocracy was written by one of the most ardent advocates of the counter-revolution, Joseph de Maistre, who took up his pen just at that time to reply to Constant's pamphlet of spring 1796.

One of the laws of the French Revolution is that émigrés can attack it only for their misfortunes, and are totally excluded from whatever work is being undertaken. From the first wild dreams of the counter-revolution, right up to the ever-appalling Quiberon enterprise, they have never undertaken anything which has succeeded, or even which has not gone against them. Not only do they not succeed, but everything they turn their hand to is stamped with such a mark of impotence and uselessness that opinion has finally become accustomed to looking on them as men who stubbornly persist in defending an outlawed party; that puts them in a disfavour which even their friends notice. And such disfavour will not occasion much surprise among men who believe that the principal cause of the French Revolution lay in the moral degradation of the nobility.[6]

It was all well and good for Maistre to explain in his book that the re-establishment of the monarchy would not be a counter-revolution, an 'opposite revolution', but the 'opposite of a revolution'; the émigrés gathered about the king's brothers would in fact prove Benjamin Constant right. Artois's entourage was even more reactionary than Provence's, and the old *Monarchiens* were indeed starting to provoke, in the circles surrounding the future Louis XVIII, a debate on the nature of monarchic tradition, in which men such as Jacques Mallet du Pan, Malouet, Lally Tollendal and Montlosier acquired some renown.

Nevertheless, since its origins, the restoration project had been marked throughout by a radical hostility to the Revolution: Burke's *Reflections* had been the seminal reference work in this respect. As can be seen in Bonald (who in 1796 published his *Théorie du pouvoir politique et religieux*), counter-revolutionary thought borrowed the criticism of revolutionary

[6] Joseph de Maistre, *Considérations sur la France*, part X, ch. 3.

'abstractness' from the British liberal, but it added to the political heritage
of the ancient Gallican monarchy an unprecedented theocratic vision of
royal government, and at least an implicit criticism of the secularization of
which French kings had made themselves the instruments. For Bonald,
as for Maistre, the whole truth of politics lay in the religious sphere:
this feature gives some measure of the drift of counter-revolutionary
thought, or rather its novelty, in relation to absolutism. Moreover, French
aristocracy had returned to religion, with which in any case common
misfortunes had reunited it, and which additionally offered it a means of
expiating its eighteenth century.

It was thus the bad luck of constitutional royalism, which was putting
down deep roots in moderate opinion at that period, to be without any
constitutional king. The Comte de Provence had assumed the name Louis
XVIII, while abroad, but his actual re-establishment on the throne would
not mean a return to 1789; it would inaugurate a revenge of which the
White Terror had given some idea: a resumption of violence, instead of a
pacification. The Clichyens dreamed in vain of a new Henri IV, capable of
reconciling the nobles' France with the France of those who had bought
biens nationaux. Lacking a liberal prince, they were inevitably led to
place themselves at the mercy of the princes available, who were Louis
XVI's two brothers; this both perverted their plan and also made it more
threatening for the Thermidorians.

In fact, Provence and Artois made great efforts and succeeded in getting
their own men put in charge of the vast opinion campaign organized by the
royalists of the councils in the summer and autumn of 1796 with a view to
winning the next elections. They found support in the remaining counter-
revolutionary rebelliousness in the west: the *chouannerie* in Brittany,
Normandy and around Le Mans, those spasmodic guerrilla wars which
lasted like so many vestiges of the great uprising of the Vendée. But their
principal support remained in the Catholic Church, cleft in two by the oath
of 1791, whose persecution during the revolutionary government had
aggravated the trend hostile to the Revolution. Borne on the wave of
Thermidorian reaction, the Church was – depending on the area – more
than ever at the heart of moderate opinion and counter-revolutionary
hopes. Its unresolved dispute with the Revolution, which Carnot – fortified
by Bonaparte's Italian conquests – had for a while hoped to settle with
Rome, proved insoluble, since it would be necessary to obtain from the
pope, after the event, acceptance of the Civil Constitution of the Clergy.

Besides, the majority of Thermidorian personnel, especially the
Directors, were both anticlerical and anti-Catholic; they were eighteenth-
century-style deists, loathing priests and 'superstition', wanting to give the
Revolution roots not only in education, but also in the civil religion of
décadaire ceremonies, when the feast of the *décadi*, every ten days, was
substituted for Sunday Mass. One of the Directors, the former Girondin
La Révellière-Lépeaux, even wanted to implant a cult of his own devising,
theophilanthropy, which was not very much different from the *décadaire*

meeting, except that authority had no hand in it. It was the religion of Voltaire, rather than of Rousseau, a cold rationalist deism, that had had its images banned (they were covered with veils in the churches), a cult of the Great Architect of the Universe.

When the Directory held its first elections in Germinal (March–April 1797), they revealed the disparity of strength in public opinion between the moderates, whose ranks were swelled by extreme royalists, supported by the Catholic Church, and the anticlerical and republican bourgeoisie who supported the Perpetuals. They also showed the fragility of electoral rights, because in certain *département* capitals the Republicans did not even have access to the second-degree assembly. Nearly all the *départements* had swung to the right, and the Conventionnel majority artificially maintained by the two-thirds disappeared. On 7 Floréal (26 May) fate chose Carnot's friend, Letourneur, to be the one to leave the Directory, where he was replaced by a lacklustre Clichyen, Barthélémy.

Royalists took control of the assemblies, General Pichegru presided over the Five Hundred and Barbé-Marbois over the Ancients. They voted for the abolition of the law of 3 Brumaire Year IV, and several measures alleviating the fate of refractory priests; moreover, émigrés had started to return in small numbers, taking advantage of a process of being struck off the fatal list which made them liable to the death penalty imposed by one of the Convention's laws. Were things leading to a restoration? A large part of the country feared so: first and foremost, those who had acquired *biens nationaux*; next, the army, which had carried the Revolution's flag so high and so far.

The men of the new majority were divided over the nature of this restoration, since the so-called 'white Jacobins' – Pichegru, Imbert-Colomès, Willot – had decided on a coup d'état to bring back Louis XVIII and the émigrés, while the moderate royalists, like Portalis, Mathieu Dumas and Royer-Collard, held fast to the basic tenets of 1789 and to the respect for legal procedures. 'There is no one more dangerous', wrote Mallet de Pan at this period, 'than those who are known in France today as "decent people": were they to fill the legislative body for thousands of years, they would never decide to vote on an effective method of restoration unless they were totally sure in advance that there would be no risk involved.'

In the Directory, Carnot was the chief of those Republicans who had become conservatives, but in losing Letourneur he had lost an ally: Barthélémy did not belong to his political persuasion, and hardly counted anyway. By contrast, the other side of the Executive was ready for a coup d'état to defend the Revolution: Reubell first of all, in March. Colmar's former Third Estate deputy to the Constituent Assembly, who had spent a large part of his Conventionnel mandate as a representative to the armies, brought to the defence of the Republic and the natural frontiers a violent nature and stubbornly held convictions. He was joined by Barras, who had waited for a while and negotiated secretly with the other camp to see what their game was, but who had everything to fear from a return of the Bourbons; Bonaparte's former protector had made contact with the army of Italy and his choice was decided in spring 1797, when one of his friends brought back from Milan the news – passed on by the General-in-Chief – that Pichegru was in the service of Louis XVIII. As for La Révellière-Lépeaux, the theophilanthropist, he was outraged by the measures taken by the councils announcing the return to grace of refractory priests. There was therefore a majority in the Directory which could break the new royalist majority in the councils.

With whom? Where could they get their support? The sansculottes were no longer available and had, in any case, become unacceptable allies in post-Thermidor bourgeois France. Barras still looked after them, on occasion, when they became functionaries of the Republic, police *commissaires*, national agents, administrators. But the republican state was feeble. By this time, the only great popular force in the service of the Republic was the army, which had just covered itself with glory in Italy. Owing to its regimented structure, the army offered the additional, inestimable advantage of being unlikely to take an egalitarian tack, as on 10 August or 2 June. It could come to the aid of republican order without creating disorder. Of the three great military chiefs, Moreau, with the army of the Rhine, was not completely reliable; he did not commit himself to the royalists, but agreed to listen to them. In Italy, Bonaparte was in favour of the Directory's 'triumvirate', but he did not wish to stick his neck out; he was lukewarm about putting his victories at the service of the Paris Lawyers; he would send one of his lieutenants, Augereau.

It was Hoche, at the head of the Sambre et Meuse army, who gave the decisive helping hand by having 9,000 men marched towards Paris in July, on the pretext of a transfer of troops to Brest, destined for an expedition to Ireland. Under this new protection, then, the triumvirs proceeded to hold a ministerial reshuffle on the left, with Hoche going to War and Talleyrand, returned from exile in America, to Foreign Affairs. It was open crisis with the Councils, refereed by Hoche's soldiers. In the night of 17–18 Fructidor (4–5 September 1797) Paris was occupied by the military. Augereau arrested Pichegru and his friends in the councils. Carnot, who was in neither camp, went into hiding before getting out of the country. No one had made a move. On the morning of 18 Fructidor, a great poster proclamation of the Rump-Directory informed the Parisians and the country that a royalist plot had been broken up, and that any individual guilty of wishing to re-establish royalty or the 1793 constitution would be shot without trial.

Those members of the councils who could be assembled sat during that day and the ones that followed, to vote on measures of 'public safety': the invalidation of 'bad' elections, which excluded one third of the legislative body, deportation to Guiana of fifty-three deputies and two Directors, Carnot and Barthélémy, plus several notorious royalists. The Directory, or what was left of it, quashed the elections of administrative authorities and local judiciaries, thenceforth to be at its discretion. The press was muzzled. Lastly, a series of laws hit émigrés and refractory priests once again, rendering them liable to the death sentence or deportation. The law of 3 Brumaire Year IV, only just abolished, was re-established, as if to show that the war against the aristocracy was still the Revolution's ultimate cause.

Like 2 June 1793, 18 Fructidor Year V (5 September 1797) was an anti-parliamentary coup d'état, a purging of the people's representatives in the name of public safety. As on 2 June, the operation was accompanied – though in a minor key – by a revolutionary Terror. The principal difference was that, in the role of secular arm of the Revolution, the sansculottes had been replaced by the army. Barras and Reubell triumphed, but were indebted to the generals. Hoche died suddenly in September, but a little Corsican general, who had already become one of the nation's glories by conquering Italy, could in his turn be looked on as its saviour.

THE RISE OF NAPOLEON

If one considers the destiny that awaited him, Napoleon was born at the right time,[7] twenty years before the Revolution; but not in the right place, a small outlying island, only recently incorporated into France and not at all happy about it. The Bonapartes were an entirely Corsican family, numerous, tribal, grubbing a living from a few vines and olive trees near Ajaccio, whose patriarch had the bright idea of rallying to the support of France and deserting the flag of independence brandished by his friend Paoli. For although the Bonapartes were poor, they were gentlemen, and for that reason could claim the benefit of the royal edicts of 1776, which had provided for the free education of impecunious nobility in the new military schools.

The two eldest, Joseph and Napoleon, obtained these new grants which constituted passports for a career in France, and through which Louis XVI offered the assistance of the old monarchy to the one that would follow. Napoleon studied at Brienne (1779–84), where he received a good education, which Stendhal would deplore later on as too absolutist: 'If he had been brought up in an establishment not run by the state, he would perhaps have studied Hume and Montesquieu; he would perhaps have understood the strength which opinion gives to government.'[8] Perhaps; but at Brienne Napoleon learned French, which he spoke all his life with an Italian accent; history, which filled his imagination as a child of the Mediterranean, and mathematics, at which he was good. In 1784 he was admitted to the Ecole Militaire; in 1785 he was graded forty-second out of

---

[7] This portrait of Bonaparte is an enlarged version of the text written for Furet and Ozouf, *Critical Dictionary*. Cf. also ch. 5, below, pp. 218–19.

[8] Stendhal, *Vie de Napoléon*.

fifty-eight, and taken on as sublieutenant of artillery at La Fère. Ségur's *Mémoires* attribute the following appraisal to his history teacher: 'Corsican by nationality and by temperament, this young man will go far, if circumstances are kind to him.'

The strange part of the story of his early years is that for a long time he continued to be a 'transplant', without any interest in what was going on in France: someone whose life was elsewhere, a poor scholarship student, then an idle soldier, thinking about what he had left behind, his family and his island. He was 'Corsican by temperament', traditionalist, touchy, somewhat shy, with none of that worldly apprenticeship which at the time typified the upper-class Frenchman. No officer could ever have been farther removed from court civilization. 'Corsican by nationality' as well: he went back on his father's choice and rejoined the Paoli clan.

During his garrison life, he spent every leave in Corsica; he seemed to want to confine himself to this tiny theatre. His encounter with France did not take place in 1789, and even that momentous year did not touch him. Little is known of him between the ages of nineteen and twenty-four. Michelet pictures him as a royalist because, according to Bourrienne, one of his Brienne schoolfriends, he exclaimed that Louis XVI should have fired on the rising of 20 June 1792. In reality, nothing linked him to the Revolution's losers, but there is no evidence of any enthusiasm on his part for the victors. He spent a great deal of time in Corsica, as he had before 1789. When the cannon thundered at Valmy in September 1792, he was still waiting for a boat to take him back to his island. But in Ajaccio, his brother Lucien was a leader of the local Jacobins (while the eldest, Joseph, failed in the elections to the Convention).

The family returned to the French side when Paoli considered opening the island to the English: the victorious insurrection of April 1793 broke the Bonapartes' links with their ancestral land, and Napoleon's with his childhood. The Bonaparte tribe, exiled as pro-French, had to leave Ajaccio. The family disembarked at Toulon with all their worldly goods: Madame Letizia, a thrifty and colourful widow who had inherited the patriarchal authority, the girls, who were pretty, and the boys, ambitious and active; the two eldest (Joseph and Napoleon), being familiar with mainland France, were able to cushion the family's feeling of disorientation.

It was in June 1793, after the purging of the Convention under the threat of Hanriot's cannon, in the terrible summer of the Revolution, that the family entered French history, at the moment that would forever mark off true partisans of the Revolution, those who had staked everything on it, from its lukewarm sympathizers. Coming from another world, brought up in another language, the tribe of islanders had nothing in common with the old France, whereas the Republic offered them the opportunity of finding their fortune, with the country in danger, open to any and every talent, where one could be on familiar terms with ministers almost as soon as one had arrived.

A compatriot, Saliceti, a Montagnard deputy to the Convention, dutifully opened some doors for the three oldest, Joseph, Napoleon and Lucien. Through this protection, Napoleon became not only a Montagnard, but also a Robespierrist. Captain of artillery in the army of Italy, given a mission in Avignon in August, he composed a topical pamphlet against the federalists who had brought civil war into the Midi: it was a work lacking in originality, consisting of a conversation between a soldier, a Nîmois, a Marseille shopkeeper and a manufacturer from Montpellier on the federalist revolt in Marseille; in it the soldier has the best part, arguing the cause of public safety. But it was a key document, because it marked the entry of the Corsican artillery captain into revolutionary politics with a Jacobin passport.

What did this young officer find to please him so much in those terrible months? Things that coincided with his temperament, his tastes, his career: a crudeness of manner that suited the brutality of his native island; a government with an antiquity-like energy, the limitless authority of national power; and higher rank open to merit, where a military talent would be honoured if victorious; the promise of equality in a profession where, as a young man, he had met only snobbery and discrimination. By serving the Montagnard dictatorship under the leadership of Saliceti, who was the Convention's representative on mission to the south-east, Napoleon Bonaparte was following both his inclination and his personal interests. In December 1793 it was he who devised the plan for regaining Toulon from the British. Almost immediately afterwards, he was a brigadier, earning enough to support his mother and sisters. The family was nicely settled in the Republic: Lucien had become one of the Jacobin personalities of Saint-Maximin; Napoleon took his young brother, Louis, with him to the army of Italy, to which he was appointed at the beginning of 1794, and waged war on the Austrians; the last brother, Jerome, was still at college.

Then came 9 Thermidor. Temporarily casting aside the young brigadier, who even spent a few weeks in prison, Robespierre's conquerors confirmed his Robespierrist reputation. But the Convention carried on the Revolution in its own way, and the following year gave him the chance to make a spectacular comeback on the *journée* of 13 Vendemiaire (5 October 1795). After Toulon, this was the second central scene of his marriage to revolutionary France: on that day Barras was at the head of an 'extraordinary commission' with full powers to crush a royalist rising in the fashionable districts of Paris. He assembled a small republican army, with Bonaparte commanding part of it, which raked the *muscadin* ranks with cannon fire, in the environs of the church of Saint-Roch. This easy victory had another aspect: the brigadier became one of the close associates of Barras, the great political chief of the regime then coming into being. For Napoleon, the Directory began under the best auspices; he had become one of the personalities of the new Parisian society.

That society was an odd blend of revolutionary *nomenklatura* and the rule of money, a world simultaneously very closed, because it was dominated by shared memories, and very open, because it contained nothing old enough to be truly definite. The modern pact between government and finance had replaced Robespierre's virtuous Republic. It was the time of private interests and pleasures, well personified by Barras, once a Vicomte, a former terrorist, cynical and corrupt, surrounded by a Byzantine court, but gifted with real political talent and keeping a watchful eye on what the Revolution had already won. In this milieu, the Corsican general cut an unusual figure, bony, emaciated, taciturn. An islander who had just come from his native scrubland, with his yellowish face dominated by huge eyes, framed by long hair falling to his shoulders in 'dog's ears'. The salons of the parvenu revolutionaries where the brilliant Madame Tallien reigned smiled a little over this soldier who had inherited nothing of the ways of the world, and did not even appear to want to imitate them.

The story of Napoleon's marriage to Josephine de Beauharnais, some months after Vendémiaire, says everything about what bound him to that society which was so foreign to him. It can be told as comedy. He married a ruined *demi-mondaine* (whom Barras had put in his bed), believing he was joining his destiny with that of a rich heiress of the old aristocracy. For once he hid from his family, because he had roused a storm among them which did not die down until the divorce: not only had he added to the Corsican clan a somewhat faded, wily Parisian woman who was too old for him, but also another family, for this widow had two children. Yet the marriage can also be painted in colours more touching and no less true. It bound together two people whose lives originally had very little chance of crossing; in the great upheaval of Thermidorian mores, Napoleon married for love. The burning passion he felt for Josephine had its source in everything that his wife's name led him to believe about her past; it was fed less by the vulgar ambitiousness of the era than by the way it erased, through the beloved object, his humiliation as a scholarship student at Brienne.

This little Corsican was a stranger to the world of the bourgeoisie, but he shared its most deep-rooted collective feeling – a love-hate for the aristocracy, that passion for French-style equality, an inheritance from the old court in its post-revolutionary guise, which could be appeased only by an acquired, acknowledged, guaranteed, almost obsessive recognition of superiority over the 'equal', the neighbour, the brother. Stendhal called it, as Napoleon did, 'vanity'. Little Bonaparte, who married the widow Beauharnais, was indeed, through her, truly naturalized a Frenchman.

For him, however, that national passion was transfigured by his imagination. At the time, such was his love for Josephine – pathetic, because it was not returned – that it was perpetuated by the dreams it fabricated. In the same way, his ideas of 'success' did not lie in money or power, as it did for the Thermidorian bourgeois. He derived it from political and military history (Alexander, Caesar, Charlemagne) and combined it with his recently acquired ambition – with was still in keeping with those great men of the past – to control the most tremendous event in modern history.

To control the Revolution: he had had numerous precursors – Mirabeau, La Fayette, Barnave, Brissot, Robespierre, Barras; but this rational Mediterranean dreamer had the advantage over them of arriving on the scene young in the later stages of a political drama on which he could impose his own script. Like the rest, he stood for 'equality', but he came from elsewhere; he was better then they, because he wanted to transform revolutionary passion into a means of authority. That idea alone would not have sufficed to take him where he was going, if he had not also contributed the awesome brilliance stemming from his own genius to the glory of the nation.

The army of Italy formed part of Josephine's dowry: at least, Barras suggests as much in his memoirs, but La Révellière-Lépeaux, in his, recalls that Napoleon was the unanimous choice of the Directory. The winter of 1795–6 was ending. Three armies were to advance against the Austrians: in Germany, the Sambre et Meuse under Jourdan, the Rhin et Moselle under Moreau; lastly, starting from Nice, the troops of Italy, placed under Bonaparte on 2 March. Since the short campaign in 1794, he had dreamed about waging war in Italy: it was, after all, in a way his country, his language, and the ideal theatre in which to unite his two homelands in victory. He had submitted his plan a long time before: to separate the Piedmontese from the Austrians by a rapid offensive, then to force the Turin monarchy to make peace and, if possible, an alliance with the French; lastly, to drive the Austrians out of Lombardy.

He did not have the best army, and there have been many descriptions of the barefoot, undisciplined cohorts (45,000 men, nevertheless) which he took under his command. But, with the aid of victory, he straight away demonstrated that plebiscitary quality of authority which was his hallmark: within one month, the little civil war general and protégé of Barras had become a military glory. It must also be said, he left no one else the task of publicizing him: his dispatches, his proclamations, his correspondence with the Directory all reveal an extraordinary talent for getting himself noticed. At twenty-six, this man possessed military genius combined with taste and an intuitive understanding of public opinion: that of the soldiers, as he well understood that they formed his first public, and that of the French, the great driving force of modern political power. The spectacle of a general speaking a language half civic, half praetorian, was entirely new, and one which he had invented; he retained the basic rhetoric in favour of the emancipation of the people, enveloping it in promises of glory and riches.

The first part of the military programme was thus achieved in April: it was the easiest. Bonaparte based his strategy on rapidity of move-ment, concentrated attacks and local numerical superiority. He managed to separate Colli's Piedmontese from Beaulieu's Austrians, and forced Colli to yield by the converging offensive of his generals, Masséna, Augereau and Sérurier. On 28 April King Victor-Amadeus signed the armistice of Cherasco, defeated and worried about the first stirrings of Italian Jacobins for a 'free Italy'. The Austrian army under Beaulieu fell back to the left bank of the Po, leaving on the river at Lodi a rearguard which the French armies beat on 10 May, but without getting through to the main part of the enemy forces. On the 14th Masséna occupied Milan, and on the next day Bonaparte made his triumphal entry. May 1796: one might cite this month, and his provisional installation as General-in-Chief in the Lombard capital, as the turning-point in his life.

The Directory was not yet as weak as in the following year after the royalist elections to the councils: but it no longer had control of the army of Italy. From Paris, Carnot had written to his chief of staff to urge him to abandon pursuit of the Austrians for the time being, in order to make some gains in central Italy: this was a movement Bonaparte favoured, but he attributed a different interpretation to it. Personally he wanted a policy of emancipation in the Italian states; against orders from Paris, he let the Jacobin and patriotic elements go ahead. Furthermore, Carnot had made a move to hand Lombardy over to Kellermann, while Bonaparte was to ransom off central Italy. He received a categorical refusal from the General-in-Chief, in the face of which the Directory gave way.

Was it because the Paris government could not survive financially without Italy's treasures? In fact, it had even greater need of victories and glory. There was an unequal balance between Carnot and Bonaparte. For example, Bonaparte wrote to him on 9 May, shortly before his entry into Milan:

What we have taken from the enemy is incalculable. I shall have twenty paintings by the greatest masters sent to you, from Correggio to Michelangelo. I owe you special thanks for all you are doing for my wife. Look after her: she is a sincere patriot, and I love her to distraction. I hope things are going well, and am sending you twelve or so million to Paris; that should be useful to you for the army of the Rhine.

One cannot fail to see that, behind this outpouring of gifts, power is starting to change hands.

Bonaparte was not yet king of France, but from that May on, he was king of a poor, subjugated, pillaged Italy – reinvented, so to speak, as if the land of ancient Rome and the villas of the Renaissance were part of his heritage. He lived in the palace of Montebello in Milan, more like a sovereign than a general of the Republic, surrounded by a little court, protected by strict etiquette, starting to live in the world of omnipotence. Josephine had come to join him, deceitful as ever, accompanied by one of her lovers. The brothers and sisters had got there before her, trafficking in his victories, thirsty for honours and profit, making money hand over fist: this Balzacian side of his parvenu life would never come to an end.

He just let it happen, and even condoned these sordid little games, provided he was their originator: these were the sidelines of his glory, the prizes offered to those who served him. But he was already in a different world, separated from his most celebrated generals by their acknowledgement of his superiority, holding discussions on an equal footing with the

Directory, and imposing his views on it because of his power over public opinion, receiving France's most esteemed thinkers and men of science: Gaspard Monge and Claude Berthollet were his guests of honour. He already possessed an idea of what life held, together with the certainty that he would achieve it; that his 'destiny' – according to one of his later expressions – 'would not be able to withstand his will' – which may be a definition of modern happiness.

The most interesting part of what he said at Montebello – already reported by numerous attentive witnesses – lies in this confidence:

What I have done so far is nothing. I am only at the beginning of the career that lies before me. Do you suppose that I have triumphed in Italy for the mere aggrandizement of the Directory lawyers, the Carnots, the Barras of this world? What an idea! A republic of thirty million men! With our habits, our vices! How can it be possible? It is a wild dream, with which the French are infatuated, but it will pass like so many before it. They must have glory, the satisfactions of vanity. But as for liberty, they understand nothing about it.

Indeed, in those sentences lies much more than the avowal of an ambition, none the less evident at that time; there is what he learned from the century's literature about the impossibility of a republic in a large country, aggravated by a pessimistic view of Thermidorian society, whose citizens presented quite the reverse image of republican virtue. Enclosed in the selfishness of private interests and pleasures, their abiding passion was vanity: individual vanity, which demanded 'toys' – the tiny differences in status and prestige indispensable to the world of equality; collective vanity, jealous of national glory and the greatness of the new France. Let the government satisfy those interests, and the French would forget about republican liberty. Formulated very early on, this philosophy of government reconciled national passions with the ambitions and character of the General-in-Chief of the army of Italy. It was simple, almost simplistic, and yet magisterial. It was the formula for revolutionary dictatorship, based no longer on virtue but on interests. Bonaparte alone, among the great generals of the Republic, showed such understanding of the motivating forces of national politics.

After holding to ransom all central Italy as far as the Papal States in June and July, he had soldiers who were paid in cash, rich generals, Paris receiving its share and, perforce, leaving him with a free hand. But he still had to conquer the Austrian army, part of which was entrenched in Mantua, north of the Po. He could pursue Beaulieu more to the north towards the Alpine slopes, but since neither Moreau nor Jourdan had succeeded early enough in the breakthrough in Germany planned by Carnot, Napoleon was afraid to start an engagement on his own without numerical superiority. The summer battles therefore took place around Mantua: they were difficult combats, for he had to lift the siege in order to confront several Austrian armies which had descended from the Tyrol.

In the autumn, his situation was not good: Italy was not inexhaustible and the army was showing signs of fatigue after several months of campaigning. Moreover, the Republic was in a difficult pass, for the Sambre et Meuse army, under Jourdan, victorious in July, withdrew across the Rhine in September; and the Rhin et Moselle army, which had reached as far as Munich, also beat a retreat in the autumn. The defeated generals were scarcely more obedient to Carnot than the conqueror of Italy had been; but their failures enhanced the glory of the Proconsul of Milan, who became more and more king of Italy: in October, he got rid of the Directory's *commissaires* and took it upon himself to form a Cispadane Republic, with Modena and the Legations taken from the pope.

Nevertheless throughout the autumn the military situation remained uncertain in the territories around and to the north of Mantua. At Arcola, on 15 November, Bonaparte had to set an example to check panic among the soldiery. He had to take the troops in hand again, and modify their command, while from Paris Carnot sent General Clarke to make a report on the army of Italy, and to explore the possibilities of a compromise with Austria at the cost of leaving Lombardy and the Cispadane Republic. The victory at Rivoli in January 1797 was decisive, with the rout of General Alvinczy's Austrian columns, followed shortly by the capitulation of Mantua on 2 February. After several very difficult months, Bonaparte triumphed, at the very moment when the authorities needed him most in Paris.

It was the period when Barras and Reubell were apprehensively watching the approach of the regime's first electoral date, and fearing that Carnot was ready to compromise with the royalists at home and the Europe of the kings. By contrast, as a good ex-Girondin, the hesitant La Révellière liked the policy of sister republics, and even more, as a good theophilanthropist, the dismemberment of the Papal States. The republican triumvirate in Paris could gain support against the royalists only by the amount of freedom it left to the victorious general. The latter, engrossed in his definitive victory over Austria, indulged himself by not following its instructions to destroy the seat of Catholic unity; once again he contented himself with a ransom.

After Rivoli, it was clear to everyone that he held the Republic's principal command. The makeshift troops he had been leading for a year were reinforced by other contingents coming from the Rhine: the heroic period was over, when his almost superhuman energy, his omnipresence, his capacity for endless activity and his power to intimidate had finally compensated for the improvised nature of his armies. In March 1797 he launched an offensive towards Vienna, across the Alps, with rested and reorganized troops. On the last day of the month, from a position of strength, he proposed an armistice to his adversary, the Austrian Archduke Charles, on the following conditions: either Austria ceded Belgium and Lombardy, acquiring in exchange most of the Veneto (excepting Venice); or it abandoned the Rhineland as well as Belgium, regaining Lombardy, with some Venetian territories. The terms of the choice dictated the reply, which formed the basis of the armistice of Leoben on 18 April. Austria left Belgium and the Milanese region to France, but kept the left bank of the Rhine, and its domain in the Veneto. It was the republic of the Doges which paid the dearest price, for it was conquered, occupied and soon wiped off the map, following a popular rising in Verona against the French troops.

The armistice, laying down the conditions of peace with Austria – the first since 1792 – had been conceived, negotiated and signed by Bonaparte, who thus took over the Republic's foreign policy. In Paris the Directory was in the worst of political situations, just after the elections had brought a royalist majority to the councils. It was therefore less than ever in a position to discuss initiatives and decisions with the conquering general. Carnot and his shadow, Letourneur, were not interested in the left bank of the Rhine: the right of the Parisian Executive had no reason to dislike Leoben. The triumvirate, on the other hand, was in favour of 'natural frontiers', and therefore the Rhine, but they also liked the idea of sister republics, particularly La Révellière; he would gladly have taken all together, Rhineland and Lombardy. In the end, he settled for Lombardy as a consolation for the Rhineland. Anyway, he had no choice, for the idea of an army-aided republican coup d'état was already in the wind.

The Leoben armistice was therefore an important turning-point for revolutionary policy abroad. Initially, because its negotiation had for the first time evaded the civil government, and then, because it designated war aims which went well beyond 'natural frontiers'. Holland had already been transformed by the Thermidorians into a sister Republic, but in essence it could be considered as part of the left bank of the Rhine. With the Po valley came the start of another story: that of French expansion and domination in Europe under the impetus of a genius who had inherited the spirit of the Revolution while at the same time transforming it.

Bonaparte, in effect, refashioned Italy, which was a prey to disturbances on all sides – pro-French, anti-French, Jacobins and Catholics. He took up his quarters again near Milan, this time in the castle of Mombello, and redesigned the map of his second homeland. With Lombardy he formed a Cisalpine Republic, to which in July he gave a French-style constitution, with institutions similar to those of Year III, but where he himself appointed the members of the Directory and the Legislative Council. In the summer, he dispatched Augereau to protect the triumvirs' coup d'état against Carnot and a royalist restoration.

Immediately afterwards, he settled the conditions of peace with Austria, in the spirit of Leoben, to which he added an unprecedented clause: the suppression of the ancient republic of Venice, conquered in May and given to the Habsburgs in exchange for an enlargement of the new Cisalpine Republic. Austria had to accept the cession of the left bank of the Rhine, less the Cologne region, where there were Prussian possessions. The Treaty of Campo Formio on 17 October 1797 introduced a new element to the Leoben stipulation, borrowed from the arbitrary powers of the kings: the suppression of one of Europe's oldest states, the Most Serene Republic, in the same way that Poland, in 1772 and 1793, had been suppressed by the monarchies of central and eastern Europe.

Campo Formio took place after 18 Fructidor in Paris. That month of October, which had brought back the revolutionary Republic and its exceptional measures at home, also set the seal on the triumph of its arms abroad: the Terror and victory; a paradoxical combination, with a division of the roles, Barras in the first and Bonaparte in the second.

DIFFICULTIES OF THE DIRECTORY

There was indeed a Terror: but this was not the Year II, with its surveillance committees and the revolutionary Tribunal. It was the application of the exceptional laws of 19 and 22 Fructidor (5 and 8 September 1797) against returned émigrés and those suspected of royalist conspiracies on the one hand, and refractory priests on the other: six years after the beginnings of the Legislative Assembly, here again were the two great categories of the guilty who had served as fodder for the revolutionary dynamic.

The royalist danger had reawoken hatred for the nobles. There were 160 death sentences in Paris between autumn 1797 and spring 1799. According to La Révellière's memoirs, Sieyès seems to have proposed to the Directory – where two ex-ministers, Merlin de Douai and François de Neufchâteau, had replaced Carnot and Barthélémy – the banishment of all nobility outside the Republic, which would have actualized the expulsion suggested in a passage of *Qu'est-ce que le Tiers État?* But the idea, defended in the Five Hundred by Boulay de la Meurthe in October, was finally reduced to civic exclusion by deprivation of political rights. As the list of those excepted had yet to be drawn up, the law could not be applied.

After the aristocrats came the refractory priests, also the subject of a very vast repressive legislation since 1792, revived in October 1797. The death penalty was replaced by deportation to Guiana. More than a thousand were arrested, of whom 263 left for the penal colony, while the rest remained dumped in the most appalling conditions on the hulks of Ré and Oléron. As usual, repression varied between the regions, local situations and the state of mind of the administrations. But it revived a climate: censored press, domiciliary visits, preventive arrest, where former scenes were re-enacted and vengeance taken. Also as usual, the arbitrariness of the laws increased disobedience to those laws. The France of Catholic loyalty, chiefly the rural west but also the south-east, slipped outside public authority.

In this bourgeois version of the revolutionary Terror, there reappeared two themes from the great epoch, but in a watered-down administrative form: civil religion and the regeneration of the citizen. There is no period in revolutionary history when the administration took a greater hand in the organization of a new cult, with celebrations every *décadi*, and on the anniversaries of the Revolution's principal dates: 21 September (birth of the Republic), 21 January (death of the tyrant), 9 Thermidor (end of the other tyrant) and 18 Fructidor (unmasking of the last royalist conspiracy).

Re-christened 'temples', the churches were used for three forms of worship: the constitutional Catholic Church, caught in the pincer movement between refractory priests and the administrators of the republican religion, theophilanthropy, and the official ceremony of *décadi*, when the citizens and municipal authorities honoured the laws. Only this last had the government seal of approval, and it was just as well to be seen there if one had something to ask for – or perhaps something one would like forgotten.

Thus the Revolutionary calendar had found full use under the Directory; the new era, opened by the Revolution, had a regulated form of worship, overseen by the administration, to liberate citizens from superstition and the tyranny of priests. The idea of reason, rather than virtue, served as a basis for the republican civics to be inculcated: civil religion was closer to Condorcet than to Robespierre. If the citizens were enlightened, and therefore reasonable, they could not desire other than the public good, which was also their own. That gave rise to great emphasis on education, inherited from the first years of the Revolution; schools became the essential means of regenerating citizens, which was indispensable to the foundation of the Republic. The role Robespierre had assigned to the Terror had devolved into the pedagogy of reason.

The most ambitious projects date back to the Convention which, in 1793, had debated the educational plans of Condorcet, then those of the Montagnard Michel Le Peletier, and had even voted in December 1793 for compulsory primary education at the expense of the state. But the practical measures were not taken until after Thermidor, and were put into effect by the Directory. Under the *ancien régime*, education had been dispensed by the Church and was therefore obscurantist; with the Revolution, it became public and secular. The Montagnards had legislated for all the Republic's children, the Thermidorians were chiefly concerned about the children of *propriétaires*.

The fundamental law had been that of 3 Brumaire (25 October 1795), on the eve of the Convention's dispersal, the same day as the vote on the bill against émigrés' families. The primary school was sacrificed; for the teacher once more became an employee of local communities, as before 1789, and nothing was said about compulsory schooling, which had been emphasized in 1793: in actual fact, it was a return to the old system, and many semi-clandestine little schools were reopened under the leadership of a refractory priest who had reappeared as an instructor, rivalling the public teacher maintained by the administration.

The republican efforts of the Thermidorians had been directed at the secondary and higher levels; these terms are still not quite adequate, for the 'central schools' planned by the law of 24 February 1795 to replace the *ancien régime* schools run by religious orders were midway between the two levels, organized in the chief town of each *département*. They were a

somewhat utopian kind of grammar school, with optional courses made up
in three successive sections: firstly, drawing, natural history, ancient and
modern languages; next, the sciences (mathematics, physics, chemistry)
from fourteen to sixteen years of age; beyond that, what the law calls
'general grammar': great literature, history, legislation, taught according to
the science of sensualist psychology, in which the origin of ideas was to be
found by analysing the sensations of individuals, and thus in a study of
their development by means of their environment. All the disciplines were
remodelled so as to form the reason of young citizens through science, in a
spirit that was incredibly revolutionary on the educational plane, without precedent and also without issue; a good many of the century's
propositions were included: secularism, the promotion of the sciences,
encyclopaedic ambition, the supremacy of French over ancient languages,
and the reign of reason.

Above these central schools was a whole network of higher establishments, also created by the Thermidorian Convention, which would enjoy a
longer life: the Conservatory of Applied Arts and Crafts; the School of
Public Services for the army, the navy and highways, which would become
the present-day Ecole Polytechnique; three Schools of Medicine in Paris,
Lyon and Montpellier; the Ecole Normale Supérieure, with the task
of training teachers; the School of Oriental Languages, the Museum of
French Monuments, the Museum, the Observatory. If the Thermidorians
had surrendered part of the Montagnard ambitions for junior schools –
although they were still fighting on that ground too, even if they were
retreating – they had reconstructed on the ruins of universities abolished
together with the trade guilds (even the Académie Française had not
escaped the common law), higher teaching institutions which were freed
from clerical administration and conceived according to the spirit of the
Enlightenment.

At the very summit, they had devised the Institut, to crown this structure of knowledge, enlighten politics and give a central impetus to the
minds of the public: the system already contained the spirit of a 'republic
of teachers', in which opinion had to be carefully formed and informed by
the most learned men in order eventually, with the help of time, to weld
together a body politic of citizens. The Institut had three classes to crown
the ensemble of disciplines – physical sciences and mathematics, literature
and fine arts, and (a great novelty) political and moral sciences.

This was the spiritual powerhouse of the regime, envisaged in the
constitution, like the councils and the Directory, peopled with the great
notables of science and public life: Monge, Berthollet, Lagrange, Chaptal,
Lamarck, Cuvier, Geoffroy Saint-Hilaire, Daunou, Marie-Joseph Chénier,
La Révellière-Lépeaux. Bonaparte, having returned to Paris after Campio
Formio, had himself elected to it at the end of 1797 in place of the
wretched 'Fructidorized' Carnot. The passage of the hero of Italy to a place
among the thinkers was a good investment. France was still a country
which loved literature and ideas.

Heaven knows, the survivors who were running the country had re-discovered the importance of interests, but they hung on to 1789's funda-mental plan to found society on reason, and that characteristic would distinguish their heirs right up to the twentieth century. For the political and intellectual elite of the epoch, that plan had taken the form of what was called 'ideology', which was the reigning doctrine, the last-born of the Enlightenment, and would bring the era to its close. It was an experi-mental rationalism, which eschewed any metaphysical explanation of knowledge, any input by God, or innate ideas, and wanted to found a science of intellectual formation starting from the senses. From that stemmed an ambition to arrive also at a science of morals and behaviour, and the content of 'moral and political sciences'.

Bonaparte was honoured to be the colleague of Dr Cabanis, Destutt de Tracy and Constantin Volney; at the time, he signed his documents 'Bonaparte, General-in-Chief and Member of the Institut National'. In this post-Revolution learned world lay a completely revitalized eighteenth century, its rediscovered encyclopaedic ambition mocked by the brothers Goncourt: 'Not only German, but also Greek, not only Spanish but also Latin, logic *and* rhetoric, geography *and* history, foreign exchange *and* weights and measures, man *and* the decimal system, philosophy *and* grammar, the reason for God, book-keeping, even French. Paris wants to learn all about everything in between two quadrilles.'[9] Learned societies were being reborn, public education was fashionable, the great new institu-tions were surrounded by general respect. The Republic may not have been sheltered from arbitrariness, but it was indivisible from science.

Here, once again, was the French Revolution torn between its uni-versalist ambition and the arbitrariness of its laws. It revered the Institut as the beacon of its historic mission, but it had just purged the councils by an illegal intervention of the army. That second characteristic had struck the Revolution's institutions a crippling blow: the councils' authority was broken by this enforced amputation, and that of the Executive, which had provided the means, had gained nothing from it. Public safety was no longer in danger, and the discredit cast on the politicians extended to the Directors. The relationship between Barras and Bonaparte had been inverted. In the face of the old Conventionnel, dimming his authority amid pleasures and intrigues, it was the young Corsican covered in glory who embodied the Republic. But he went off in the spring of 1798 to make war on the British in Egypt, and French opinion was left alone with its politicians.

At least the Directory took advantage of the respite gained in Fructidor to put forward a certain number of reforms which prepared the settle-ment of the Consulate. The most important was financial. The Minister, Ramel de Nogaret, proposed the great financial law of 9 Vendémiaire (30

[9] Edmond and Jules de Goncourt, *Histoire de la société française pendant le Directoire* (1855), pp. 249–50.

September 1797), seeking to reduce the public debt, which was very
onerous for the Treasury, giving state creditors bonds negotiable against
the possessions of the clergy and émigrés – the inexhaustible capital of the
Revolution; two-thirds of the debts were covered in this way, while the last
third was guaranteed repayable in cash.

But this measure, which was intended to regain the *rentiers'* confidence
after it had been so eroded by the dizzying inflation of the preceding years,
ran into competition with all the other bonds in circulation, which were
also paid by the sale of *biens nationaux*, and this bankruptcy of two-thirds
of the debt did not even ensure the maintenance of a constant value for the
last third, payable in coin of the realm. The resumption of the payment of
annuities in cash did not take place until 1801. Ramel succeeded only in
temporarily reducing the debt. He had also tried to get taxes collected in
an organized manner, but was not able to escape what had been the curse
of the Revolution since 1791: resort to 'extraordinary' measures, selling off
new slices of *biens nationaux*, despoilment of foreign countries, facilities
offered to the speculations of contractors, borrowing.

The return to cash as a means of trading ran up against lack of confidence: money disappeared, and the few banks which reopened served
only a very restricted clientele. The financial situation was as always largely
conditioned by public feeling, which did not believe in the future of the
regime. Why should it? Once acquired, the habit of invalidating annual
elections perpetuated itself like a sort of poisoning of the bloodstream: it
was the surest way to maintain the rule of the old Conventionnels. But in
spring 1798, the royalists, intimidated by the repression that had followed
Fructidor, no longer dared appear at the electoral assemblies.

The electorate in the *départements* had swung towards the Jacobins. For
example, Barère was elected while in hiding in Bordeaux after fleeing from
prison in 1795 in order to avoid the penal colony in Guiana. The Directory
then struck out at the left in the batch of deputies of Year VI: it had the
councils invalidate a number of elections, and confirmed others organized
by irregular assemblies; in short, it operated a sorting-out process among
the elected representatives, without even having the pretext or reason, as it
had in the preceding year, of public safety in the face of a royalist restoration. From its origins, the regime had never been able to respect the results
of a single electoral consultation.

The same thing recurred in the following year, 1799, but in the opposite
direction, on the part of the councils against the Directory: the electors
refused to follow the Executive's recommendations after it had designated
its official candidates, and again the assemblies swung in the neo-Jacobin
direction, neo-Jacobins who were in truth new, looking towards the army
generals rather than the sansculottes of the townships. Even before the
newly elected third sat, the Directory had replaced one of its members:
Reubell, one of the ramparts of the Republic, was destined to be the one to
quit. He was replaced by Sieyès, who had just returned from the Berlin
embassy. Still Sieyès, always Sieyès, this time accepting the post he had

been offered in 1795. There was a new chance – at last – to give the Revolution the good constitution that had eluded it since 1789.

War had resumed, but Bonaparte was in Egypt. It is necessary to make a detour through foreign policy in order to understand all the threads of the revisionist conspiracy of which Sieyès became the centre in spring 1799, before the Corsican general became its beneficiary in the autumn.

After Campo Formio, France had beaten all enemies save Britain. The armies of the Revolution had restored to France's ascendancy in Europe, the secret of which it had lost since the middle of Louis XIV's reign. But at that time, there had been a major difference in the general balance of the states: in the eighteenth century, British ambition had asserted itself, the drive of a formidable maritime, commercial and colonial power, a nation modern and ahead of the others, united around a gigantic city which was becoming the warehouse and economic metropolis of the world. The British had driven the French out of North America and India with the Treaty of Paris (1763), and France had taken a small revenge in the war of American Independence. The war had recommenced at the beginning of 1793 after Louis XVI's execution.

The conflict preserved its former features. The two countries clashed overseas, chiefly in the West Indies, and Britain kept a jealous watch over a European equilibrium which it feared would be destabilized by the French Revolution. French Anglophobia went back a long way, as did English Francophobia: one can easily find a list of examples in a large part of Enlightenment thinking within both countries, to say nothing of public opinion on the subject. But the war that had started in Year I had brought new stakes into play and aggravated hostile feelings. The France of 1789 had pleased quite a few British liberals. In 1793 the radical condemnation made by Burke in 1790 of all the principles of the Revolution had acquired a predictive value; it was shared by almost everyone.

The two greatest national histories in Europe, the two almost immemorial monarchies, built on the same basic elements, were thenceforth separated by two pasts, two traditions, two incompatible regimes. The Revolution destroyed what even the schism between the Anglican Reformation and the Catholic faith had left in common between the two nations. Modern liberty now had two contradictory sources, one British, one French. From the starting-point of the common possession that divided them, the two countries were building the future of the world, but each in its own fashion, and each in its own sphere. Britain invented industry; France, equality.

The two public opinions sensed this mutual strangeness very keenly. At the time of the Constituent Assembly, Britain had become the kingdom where aristocracy reigned through a titled upper chamber and a lower chamber in which seats were acquired by intrigue or money. For the Convention, it was personified by the City of London, homeland of banking and selfish opulence, the exact opposite of Jacobin virtue. The Thermidorians had rediscovered interests, but the Republic's commercial interests, like those of the former monarchy, were precisely the opposite of those of the merchant oligarchy reigning in London. At a time when the French were in Antwerp and Amsterdam, how could Britain think otherwise? Thus the French victories and the peace of Campo Formio had not ended the war: with Britain, they had made it inexpiable. 'Peace with England would seem to me the loss of the Republic', said Reubell at that time.

The British had won the colonial war in the West Indies, that treasure house of French slave trading in the eighteenth century. In 1793, they had taken possession of Martinique, St Lucia, Guadeloupe and Santo Domingo, with the help of colonists hostile to the Revolution. In the last of these isles, the great revolt of black slaves led by Toussaint L'Ouverture drove them out, at first to France's advantage, when the Convention abolished slavery (February 1794), but not for long: the black general finally bought the independence of Haiti by a treaty favourable to British trade (1798). There was one exception: Guadeloupe, where a former merchant marine captain, whose extraordinary adventure has been related by Alejo Carpentier,[10] succeeded in driving out the British and keeping the island in the French domain. In the same years, because Holland had become a French protectorate, Britain had seized the Dutch colonies of Guiana, the Cape and Ceylon.

But how could Britain be vanquished, that island protected by its navy, which was at the heart of European aristocratic intrigue against the Republic? The Directory had on several occasions considered the possibility of invasion. But Hoche's Irish operation at the end of 1796 had failed because of storms, and Bonaparte, assigned the task of examining ways and means a year later on his return from Italy, gave up the idea for want of a good fleet. It was then, in the first few months of 1798, that the idea took shape of going to strike at Britain in Egypt: the strategy was proposed by Talleyrand, and endorsed by the Directory on 5 March. The objectives of the Minister of Foreign Affairs have been the subject of a vast literature, even including his supposed intention to render service to the British by diverting the French ships from the Channel towards the Orient: Talleyrand's reputation was so bad, and his venality so notorious, that even the basest interpretation remained a possibility, though there is no certainty about any of them. The former bishop appears also to have had a plan for carving up the Ottoman empire and for a French colonization of Egypt.

The Directory was wary, since it had little desire, with the Eastern question, to open a conflict not only with the Sultan of Constantinople but also, inevitably, with Russia. It supported only the shorter and limited anti-British version of the project: the aim was to hit the enemy's trade, one of the routes by which its wealth passed between India and London.

Did the Directory also wish to distance Bonaparte, that embarrassing

[10] Alejo Carpentier, *Le Siècle des Lumières* (Paris, Gallimard, 1982).

figure on the Parisian scene, who stood waiting for his great moment, draped in classical simplicity? Possibly. At all events, Bonaparte himself backed the idea of the expedition, and wanted to be given the mission: it would be a good investment of his Italian capital, which his brothers Joseph and Lucien were in any case managing for him in Paris. Moreover, Egypt was part of his imaginary world, at the other side of the Mediterranean, the heart of Greek and Roman antiquity, where he would tread in the footsteps of Alexander and Caesar. The idea combined the theatrical dimension of his nature, his imagination as a gambler doubling his stake in the Orient, and the realism of a calculated internal policy.

I will omit the Egyptian expedition from this account, because it forms a special history on its own, independent of French events, but essential to an understanding of the Eastern question in the nineteenth century. Having arrived at Alexandria on 1 July 1798 with his ships, his soldiers and the battalion of scientists who had embarked with him, Bonaparte stayed more than a year amid his conquests, victorious over the Mameluke warriors, also beating the Sultan's troops which were assembled against him, organizing an 'enlightened' and tolerant protectorate as if, in Cairo, he were in a sort of Islamic Milan. But almost from the beginning, the affair came to nothing, for the British Admiral Nelson had finally found and sunk the French fleet at anchor in Aboukir harbour. The French army's Egyptian contingent was trapped in Egypt and its leader could not bring it back to France. A year later, in August 1799, he left in great secrecy, entrusting his soldiers to one of his generals, Kléber.

During his absence from France, between the middle of spring 1798 and the beginning of autumn 1799, war had begun again between the Revolution and Europe. Even before his departure in March 1798, the Directory had transformed the Swiss cantons into a unitarian republic (except Mulhouse and Geneva, which were annexed to France). At the same time, the French army occupied Rome, whence the pope was exiled to Tuscany. The Directory even imposed on vassal states the vicissitudes of French internal politics. Exporting French political quarrels to Holland, Switzerland and the Cisalpine Republic, it arbitrated between moderate elements and local Jacobins, gave its backing now to its generals and now to its civil agents, dictated constitutions and regimes.

Everywhere, it extracted money both by pillage and by very one-sided economic agreements: treasure seized in Berne had been used to fund the Egyptian expedition. All that remained of the original emancipatory messianism, when the French arrived, was the abolition of the tithe and personal feudal rights. But those measures counted for little compared with military occupation, soldiers living off the country and the systematic looting of local wealth. The years 1798–9 witnessed the birth of a phenomenon which would reach great proportions during the period of Napoleonic expansion: the revolt of occupied nations against French oppression.

The best-known and also the most significant revolt took place in the south of Italy, in the kingdom of Naples. Rome's occupation by

France had given King Ferdinand IV the idea of seizing Benevento and Pontecorvo, old papal enclaves within his possessions. He imprudently launched an attack in November, and at first drove out the French garrison from Rome, where Jacobins and Jews were hounded by the people. But the Directory reacted by declaring war on Ferdinand IV and, for good measure, the King of Piedmont-Sardinia, his reputed accomplice. Joubert occupied Piedmont, which was annexed to France at the beginning of 1799; Championnet retook Rome, and proceeded as far as Naples where, with the help of bourgeois and liberal nobles, he proclaimed a Parthenopean Republic, systematically bled by his army.

The French occupation of the great town, which swarmed with numerous followers of the landowning aristocracy, unleashed a popular uprising under the banner of the king and the faith. The Directory repudiated Championnet and the new sister republic, but the damage had been done: the Italian liberal notables had condoned French looting, but the example of Naples and its *lazzaroni* (criminals) was followed by the peasants of Calabria, creating a new Vendée of the Italian south in rebellion against the Republic of French atheism. Like France in 1793, foreign peasants were also discovering their popular counter-revolution.

At the end of the winter of 1798–9, war resumed between the Directory and Europe, and the French army had to evacuate the extreme south of Italy in order to confront more urgent tasks. Britain had succeeded in reconstituting a coalition. It had easily gained the ear of the Tsar of Russia, Paul I, who was worried about French designs against the Ottoman empire; the king of Naples was another ally for the asking. The plan was to make France withdraw within its 1792 frontiers: Britain was the great financial backer of the undertaking, as it would be until 1814.

There remained to be found an agreement with at least one of the central European powers, Prussia or Austria. At peace with Prussia since the Treaty of Basle in 1795, the Directory would have liked to resume a tradition of the *ancien régime* and make the Hohenzollern dynasty an ally of republican France: sent as ambassador to Berlin in 1798, Sieyès had striven hard to achieve this, but without success. The Prussians had no interest in tying themselves to a French policy of annexation in German territory; but they stayed neutral, closely watching their Austrian rival. At Campo Formio, the Austrian emperor had subordinated his retreat from the left bank of the Rhine to the approval of the Imperial Diet. Negotiations had begun in Rastatt.

Meanwhile, France had occupied Switzerland and Rome and had included the Cologne region in its Rhineland acquisitions. Austria wanted at least Italian compensations, and the guaranteed independence of Tuscany and the kingdom of Naples. The situation slid towards war in the winter of 1798–9, and Jourdan crossed the Rhine in March. Public opinion in Paris had rediscovered the martial accents of the great days; it denounced a new crime of the Europe of the kings in the assassination of two French plenipotentiaries leaving Rastatt in April.

The combats started badly for the Republic. The army of the Danube, under Jourdan, was beaten in Germany at Stokach by the Austrians. In Italy, Scherer and then Moreau also retreated, and abandoned Milan at the end of April. The Russian troops of Suvorov, the first great counter-revolutionary European general, had joined up with the Austrians, and drove the French out of Italy and Switzerland between June and August. It was at this point, when the spectre of public safety was being reborn in Paris, that Bonaparte decided to leave Egypt – precisely during the first days of August, upon reading the news from France announcing that the Rhine frontier was threatened and Italy – his Italy – lost.

The instructions he had received on his departure the preceding year had authorized him in advance to leave his army to his successor; but the conditions of his leaving, since there was no French fleet to bring back his soldiers, gave it the air of a desertion, surrounded as it was with the greatest secrecy. He took with him only Berthier, Murat, Marmont, Lannes and Duroc, plus Monge, Berthollet and the painter Vivant Denon, who had already become the illustrator of his glory. However, he left to Kléber, the new head of his army without a future, his fine letter of 22 August, his Egyptian testament, which combined the concern of a soldier with considerations of universal history:

I have already asked on several occasions for a troupe of actors; I will take special care to send you one. This is very important for the army and as a starting-point for changing the customs of the country. The major post which you will occupy as chief will at last enable you to display those talents which nature has given you. There is an immense interest in what will happen here, and the results for both trade and civilization will be inestimable; this will be the epoch from which all great revolutions will date.

He did not reach France, on the Mediterranean coast, until 9 October 1799. Meanwhile, the military situation had been put right without him. But his return drastically changed the political situation.

In the autumn, indeed, Masséna had repulsed the Austrians and Russians in Switzerland; Suvorov withdrew to his winter quarters. To the north, in Holland, an Anglo-Russian offensive failed in October and the British re-embarked their troops. The Republic had profited more from the political divisions of the coalition than from its own military capacity. It was victorious, but increasingly threatened by its internal weakness.

Sieyès had been with the Directory since May, having returned from his Berlin embassy. The feeling in the air was Jacobin; since the Fructidor coup of 1797, royalism had been under close surveillance; in spring and summer 1799 the military situation reawoke memories of the threatened homeland. If police reports are to be believed, however, Jacobinism was peculiar to the political and military classes, in a somewhat lethargic Paris. In June the councils voted a *levée en masse*, mobilizing five classes of conscripts, and in August a compulsory loan from the rich; meanwhile, in

July, there was a fearsome law on hostages, intended to terrorize internal enemies once more.

The country was in a state of chronic disobedience, and the Republic had hardly any authority left in the west, where royalist insurrections were spreading. Royalist uprisings broke out in the Midi in August. The law of 24 Messidor (12 July 1799) allowed authorities, in *départements* designated by the councils as in a state of unrest, at the proposal of the Directory to take hostages among the relatives of émigrés or *chouans*, and to deport four of them for each assassination of a public official, purchaser of *biens nationaux* or constitutional priest. This law was not really applied, for the country had become tired of the Terror; but it revived a rhetoric, the obsessive fears, the passions which always formed the heart of national politics.

Sieyès had certainly not agreed to take a hand in affairs only so that Year II should live again. He knew better than anyone the dangers of that collection of memories. Six years afterwards, he could also judge their futility. Republican strength no longer lay in the Parisian faubourgs or *sections*, but in the Republic's administration and its army. As in 1789, the point at issue was still to give the state a regulated form, a good constitution, which would be respected by citizens as the public embodiment of reason. What had failed in 1791, 1793 and 1795 could be achieved in 1799. Everything was in its favour: the time which had passed, men's experience, and even the lack of popular involvement in contrast with earlier egalitarian activism. The Revolution had come back into the grasp of its inventor. The former Vicar General of Chartres had made himself master of the Executive, with the complicity of the councils' left, the Corsican deputy in the forefront – Lucien Bonaparte, who would never leave him. The deputies had nullified Treilhard's election to the Directory, then forced La Révellière and Merlin de Douai to resign. The chosen replacements were obscure and republican, two qualities necessary for supporters of a constitutional revision: Louis-Jérôme Gohier, former Minister of Justice under the Convention; Roger Ducos, ex-Conventionnel regicide, and a general without any glory – but Jacobin – Jean François Moulin.

In the Directory, Sieyès therefore had only one rival, Barras, who had been there from the outset, and for that very reason was rather worn out, a quintessential symbol of the discredit into which the regime had fallen. He was therefore in a position of supremacy. He gave responsibility for internal affairs to Cambacérès, also a former Conventionnel. He despised the rhetoric of public safety from the neo-Jacobins on the councils, but he found attentive listeners among the old Plaine of the great revolutionary Assembly, and even among ex-terrorists like Fouché. His following included post-Thermidor centrist republicans, the ideologists of the Institut, Daunou, Boulay de la Meurthe, Marie-Joseph Chénier, Pierre-Louis Roederer, not to mention Talleyrand, who had just left Foreign

Affairs and was sniffing the wind. With victory lending its aid, Sieyès easily crushed a neo-Jacobin offensive in June and July. He found himself the leader of the post-revolutionary Parisian political milieu, the focus of extraordinary esteem, credited with having a constitutional plan which would at last provide the Republic with institutions. A civil saviour, since the military one was in Cairo.

Anyone who wants to get a picture of the ideas circulating in this revisionist environment since the coup d'état of Fructidor Year V (1797), must turn once more to Benjamin Constant and Madame de Staël, who were at the heart of political *Tout-Paris*, although neither had any official post. Constant yearned for one, and indulged in many intrigues to try to achieve that end, but he was both young and Swiss. Since 1797 he had been one of the organizers of the Constitutional Club, created to assemble the Republicans who supported the institutions against the Clichyens. Like Madame de Staël, he had upheld the triumvirs' coup d'état against the royalists: an uncomfortable position for those defenders of the constitution and the laws, but rendered inevitable by their fear of a counter-revolution, which would be a far worse evil. At that time, their idea was to modify the institutions of Year III so that they should retain the principles and interests born of the Revolution, at the same time avoiding the annual swerves, now to the left, now to the right, which arose from elections to the councils.

In autumn 1798 Madame de Staël wrote a lengthy study on the matter, but it was not published: the situation in 1799 was doubtless too uncertain, punctuated as it was by the illegal replacement of three Directors and the neo-Jacobin upsurge, for her not to fear making a blunder. Moreover, the marginal notes with which Benjamin Constant peppered her manuscript continually put her on her guard against the risk of being misunderstood, or of doing herself a disservice. However, this book, which appeared only in 1906, still remains the best evidence of the political questions which were passionately argued by the Thermidorian political milieu in the last year of the Directory. The title is a programme in itself: *Des circonstances actuelles qui peuvent terminer la Révolution et des principes qui doivent fonder la République en France* (Of the present circumstances which could terminate the Revolution and the principles on which the Republic in France must be founded.).

Madame de Staël had two personalities. The more obvious is that of a turbulent, rather vain, very snobbish woman, an 'incorrigible intriguer', says Constant in his journal, unable to bear the idea of not being in on the latest secrets or in the confidence of the powerful, but a faithful friend for all that, tiring herself out in efforts to get one or other of her protégés struck off the list of émigrés, or persuading Barras to nominate Talleyrand for the post of Foreign Affairs: the services she was able to render also gave proof of her power. When she was not at Coppet, where she often went to visit her father, the elderly Necker, who was also constantly writing about French affairs, she held her salon in Paris, or at the Château de Saint-Ouen, a family inheritance. She received the world of politicians, army suppliers, intellectuals and generals that the society of that epoch had become, midway between nineteenth-century *Tout-Paris* and the salons of the eighteenth century.

She did not live in an era when women could aspire to the leading political roles; but she wanted to be in the centre of everything, the Egeria of the Republic and republicans. When Bonaparte had returned from Italy in 1797, she had almost turned him into a cult figure, and had tried to pay court to him, but in vain: the Corsican general disliked women who were mixed up in politics; he feared the indiscreet enthusiasm of this particular woman, and preferred the austere discussions of the Institut to her dinner parties.

Necker's daughter, however, was also a great writer. It was largely through her that in the France of that period there was a revival of the culture of the Enlightenment, a knowledge of German literature, intellectual cosmopolitanism – in the best sense of the term. From her father she had acquired a taste for political philosophy, and her writings at the time owed something to the *Histoire de la Révolution française* written in 1795 by Necker. She lived with Benjamin Constant, the leading philosophical intellect in Paris: in the *Circonstances actuelles* it is impossible to unravel which parts come from him and which from her. One thing is certain, and that is that a whole group of liberal Republicans found their best spokesperson in her.

Though Germaine was republican, and diverged from her father on that point, it was not, as one might suspect, from Jacobin loyalty. On the contrary, she reworked all Constant's examination of the catastrophe represented by the first two years of the Terror, the shadow of opprobrium they had left on the republican concept and the heritage of constitutional instability, the continuance of which had been demonstrated by the coup d'état of Fructidor Year V, followed by the invalidation of many of the 1798 elected members. She was an unhappy 'Fructidorienne', reacting to the military salvage of the Republic, followed by exceptional laws, in the same way that she thought of the Revolution itself: on balance it was good, because the principles of 1789 were those of the Enlightenment; but the means it used were detestable.

In exploring that paradox, which by then had become classic, at the heart of the Thermidorian impasse, she again used some of Constant's arguments, passions bequeathed by *ancien régime* inequality, and above all anachronism: if the Republic had been instituted by the Terror, it had arrived too soon, in a country and a public opinion ill prepared to receive it, much less to endow it with a legal form. 'The Republic has forestalled the Enlightenment; we must hasten the work of time by all true means of public education, and restore institutions and enlightenment to the same level.' But her opus gave yet another reason, destined to receive its most systematic form in Constant's later works; namely, 'the false application of the principle of sovereignty of the people in representative government'.[11]

Madame de Staël here took up the idea put forward by Sieyès in his two speeches of Thermidor Year III (1795), at the time of the discussion on the constitution of Year III: the sovereignty of the people had installed itself in the absolute sovereignty of the king, simultaneously rebuilding under another form what it had claimed to abolish. The only way of preserving liberty among modern people was to break away from that unlimited and indivisible conception of sovereignty which, because it could not hand absolute power to thirty million citizens, entrusted it to 750 deputies:

Pure democracy, through its disadvantages, has great delights, but the only democracy is in the public square in Athens . . . In Europe, where all states are equally civilized, small associations of men have no spirit of emulation, no riches, no fine arts, no great men, and never would any Frenchman agree to give up all he gains in glory and pleasures from his large association, in order to obtain in exchange perfect liberty in a small space, far from the eyes of the world and the enjoyments of wealth.[12]

The contrast between the liberty of the democracies of antiquity and that of the big modern states gives rise in the latter to the need for representative government, the principle of which is neither the proportional nature of representatives in relation to the numbers represented, nor the indivisible omnipotence of the representation; it is the political arrangement which duly puts in charge of the nation those who represent its legitimate interests, therefore its will, shared among several authorities, and limited by those very interests. Madame de Staël rediscovered Sieyès's idea of a *procuration* given by the nation to certain of its citizens whose interests coincide with those of the association, and whose capabilities allow them to carry out this mandate: property-owners, who are also the most enlightened men. Education would gradually open political equality to an ever-increasing number of men.

But what about in 1798, in 1799? The author was not worried about the present, she knew her world: 'During the lifetime of the present Revolutionaries, the Republic will be maintained at all costs, and will not perish. The events of their lives bind them to its existence. The vote for the king's death is, by itself, a stronger tie than all the institutions in the world; but this sort of guarantee is completely revolutionary.'[13] Exactly; but how were they to get away from it? By allowing the elections to the Five Hundred to take place normally, legally, instead of invalidating them, but also by organizing other authorities in a different way, so as to ensure the unity of the whole; Madame de Staël's revision did not seek to set up

---

[11] *Des circonstances actuelles qui peuvent terminer la Révolution, et des principes qui doivent fonder la République en France*, p. 33.
[12] Ibid., pp. 159–60.
[13] Ibid., p. 164.

a counterweight, after the style of Montesquieu; she remained faithful to Sieyès's clockwork mechanism idea, according to which constitutional machinery must produce political reason. That is why she envisaged several of them, according to the diversity of their missions: a Directory with the right of suspensive veto over laws and the right to dissolve the Five Hundred; a Council of Ancients, elected for life, richly pensioned, filled with past and present notabilities of the Revolution, conservatory of the Republic; a *jurie constitutionnaire* – again an idea of Sieyès – entrusted with verifying the constitutionality of the laws. Such were the institutional conditions which she deemed necessary for the establishment of the principles of 1789 within the law.

BRUMAIRE

At the same time, or perhaps a little later, in the summer of 1799, what were the thoughts of the great specialist in constitutions, the oracle that had become the principal personage of the executive power? For several months, between May and November, he was what he had never been, even in 1789, and what he would never be again: in power, sharing all Madame de Staël's politico-constitutional concern, which had been made more urgent by the military situation of summer 1799 and the neo-Jacobin agitation in the Five Hundred. He was the supreme embodiment of the men of the Revolution, and he made full use of that political capital; he had run the whole length of the course, 1789 and the regicide, 9 Thermidor and 18 Fructidor.

His closest supporters were the Thermidorians of the Institut, Daunou, Roederer, Chénier, Boulay de la Meurthe. With the Ancients his authority was considerable; he extended his influence to the Five Hundred, through Lucien Bonaparte, one of the orators of the left, and he also wanted to take under his wing the 1789 veterans and the Fructidor exiles, La Fayette and Carnot. In the army, he had against him the more Jacobin generals, Augereau, Jourdan, Bernadotte, but he had also sounded out Joubert and Moreau for a helping hand, should the need arise.

His aim was still to terminate the Revolution; to close this strange theatre of a Republic which could not even obtain the obedience of its own administration, yet which paraded its flags from Amsterdam to Milan. But how? Sieyès never revealed the constitution that he kept secretly locked in his mind. What little is known of it comes from the notes of Boulay de la Meurthe, one of his closest confidants, and from the remnants used by Bonaparte after Brumaire. The conservative aspect of revolutionary personnel and interests showed quite clearly, in the replacement of free electoral procedures with lists of notabilities from whom the public authority would make its choice, and in the creation of a Senate intended to perpetuate the Conventionnel caste. But it also contained some original devices, such as the Grand Elector, Chief of State with nothing more than the power to arbitrate, while the Executive went to two Consuls, one for external and the other for internal affairs. The concept of this public office had fed the accusation against Sieyès that he intended it for a prince; but it was so much a part of his general constitutional ideas that the imputation may be discounted.

In the France of that era, a coup d'état backed by the army had become sufficiently customary for the plan to come almost naturally into the Director's mind. He still had to find 'the sword', as he called it. He had spoken about it to Joubert, a young Republican general appointed to the army of Italy, which was a promise of glory; but Joubert had been beaten and killed at Novi on 15 August. Sieyès was thinking of Moreau, when Bonaparte disembarked at Fréjus.

Bonaparte's return can be depicted in the colours of a marital spat or in those of a triumph. The former is the private aspect. When the news of his arrival reached Paris on the evening of 13 October, Josephine rushed to take a carriage to go and meet him before he could see his family tribe: she had a number of infidelities for which to ask his pardon. But she took the Burgundy road, whereas Napoleon came back by the Bourbonnais, where he first encountered Joseph and Lucien, who went on interminably about his wife's misconduct. He was the first to arrive in Paris, on the 16th, and two days later there was a great scene with Josephine, who had come in tears, with her two children, to knock at the hero's door; but he already had other ideas in mind.

For the other aspect of his return was its triumphal nature. Between Fréjus and Paris, the country had fêted the general: the magic of Italy more than ever surrounded this conqueror who was returning from Egypt, minus his army, but bringing back in his own person the glory of the nation – a glory which the men of the Directory had forfeited, as they had forfeited public authority, but which already robed him like a king in public opinion. How distant were the times when the Abbé Sieyès had defined the idea of nation by the exclusion of the privileged, by the constituent power of free and equal individuals!

Ten years later, having gone through war, the Terror, the coups d'état, the French were tired of pursuing that ambition which had so often let them down; they were bound to the Revolution by private interests and no longer by ideas; by the greatness of their country and no longer by the sovereignty of the people. From having been the voice of the nation in the face of the king and aristocracy, Sieyès was now nothing more than the representative of an oligarchy of survivors; the royal role, the only great one in French history, had been reallocated by the history of the Revolution and had been out of use since the people as a body had been driven away from it. By a bizarre fate, it fell to the little Corsican noble who had entered so recently, but with such brilliance, into the annals of the nation.

Bonaparte drew almost unanimous acclamation from an exhausted France. On the evening when Paris learned of his return, the theatres

stopped their performances. Along the route, villages were lit up to mark
the passing of his coach. There is an observation made just prior to the
event, bearing witness to the prevalent mood, in the account of a royalist
writer 'Fructidorized' in 1797, Joseph Fiévée, who was then in retirement in Champagne: 'One observation alone reminded me of politics', he
wrote; 'every peasant that I met in the fields, the vineyards or the woods
approached me to ask if there were any news of General Bonaparte, and
why he did not come back to France; never once did anyone enquire about
the Directory.'[14]

Sieyès therefore had no choice. For his coup d'état, the scenario of
which had been ready since summer, the 'sword' could belong only to
Bonaparte. Moreover, the Parisian political milieu itself was caught up in
the new situation. The Five Hundred, where Lucien was playing a leading
role, enthusiastically greeted the news of the return. Paris flocked around
the returned conqueror, scenting the power in the offing. The hero of the
day spent the last two weeks of October receiving, listening and distribut-
ing kindly words to everyone; he knew that he must not be tied to any
party or coterie; that he held the stakes, that he was irreplaceable, whereas
Parisian politicians were unpopular. He wanted to remain what he called
'national'. He mistrusted the ambitions of Sieyès, who in turn mistrusted
his.

Conversations took place at first through other people, chiefly Lucien,
but also Talleyrand, who had to smooth out questions of precedence in the
visits of one to the other: for Sieyès was uncompromising about his
prerogatives as a Director; nor did he possess a courtier's temperament.
Bonaparte also had discussions with Barras, but it was Sieyès who held the
political entourage he needed for the success of a coup d'état. Starting
from 10 Brumaire (November 1), agreement was reached on the scenario
finalized by Sieyès, but Bonaparte had introduced a major modification:
the coup d'état would not be intended to substitute the Convention
envisaged by Sieyès for that of Year III, but to form a government of three
Consuls, charged with drawing up a new Constitution with the help of a
parliamentary commission made up from within the councils.

The *coup* was carried out in two days, 18 and 19 Brumaire (9 and 10
November 1799). On the first day, everything went as planned; on the
second, everything was nearly ruined.

On 18 Brumaire the Ancients, who had been summoned together in the
early hours, voted for the transfer of the councils to Saint-Cloud, on the
pretext of an anarchist plot, and entrusted the execution of the decree to
Bonaparte. Meeting together at eleven o'clock, the Five Hundred, with
Lucien as president, were already very hostile towards Bonaparte, but
agreed to adjourn to Saint-Cloud the next day. Meanwhile, Bonaparte had
arrived at the Tuileries surrounded by troops and a staff of generals; there
Sieyès joined him. The Directory was neutralized: Sieyès and his under-

[14] Joseph Fiévée, *Mémoires*, p. 202.

study, Roger Ducos, were in on the plot; Barras had agreed in the morning to sign a letter of resignation which was handed to him, and to retire to his property of Grosbois. The two others, Gohier and Moulin, were put in the Palais du Luxembourg under military guard.

The ministers, the administration, rallied round, the value of stocks rose, Paris was covered with posters prepared by Roederer giving the watchword: Save the Republic! Moreover, in the morning, in a public altercation carefully planned against Barras's secretary in the Tuileries gardens, Bonaparte had set the tone, with the acclamation of the troops:

In what sort of state did I leave France, and in what sort of state do I find it again? I left you peace and I find war! I left you conquests, and the enemy is crossing our frontiers. I left our arsenals full, and I find not a single weapon! I left you the millions of Italy, and I find spoliatory laws and poverty everywhere!

This speech already contained a few too many 'I's' to have pleased Sieyès.

In the preparations for the next day, the former priest had taken a clearer view than the general. He would have liked to imprison a few dozen of the Jacobin members of the Five Hundred in the afternoon, but Bonaparte insisted on remaining as 'legal' as possible: he wanted to obtain a blank cheque from the two councils. But on 19 Brumaire (10 November) things went badly at Saint-Cloud. Lucien could not control his assembly, which decided to proceed with a solemn oath of loyalty to the institutions of Year III by a roll-call vote. Even the Ancients wavered, and began to negotiate with their Jacobin neighbours on the election of new Directors.

After several hours of idle talk came the arrival of Bonaparte, who was rather out of his depth: he delivered a military harangue, which missed its target. Nevertheless, he wanted to start again with the Five Hundred, whom he had just insulted; he was greeted with cries of 'Outlaw!', jostled and rescued from the deputies by his aides-de-camp. It was Sieyès who gave the practical advice: get the soldier out of here. And it was Lucien, President of the Five Hundred, himself threatened with being outlawed, who on horseback declaimed the decisive address before the troops, whom he asked to drive the 'seditious' members from the assembly. The final act was directed by two generals, Leclerc, Napoleon's brother-in-law, and Murat, his brother-in-law to be: at twilight their grenadiers dispersed the people's representatives.

The Ancients became tractable once more and did what Sieyès asked of them, replacing the Directory with an executive commission of three members – himself, Roger Ducos and Bonaparte, after which they went to dinner. After dinner, however, Lucien wanted a vote from the Five Hundred for his communiqué of the next day. Some one hundred deputies, scattered among the cafés of Saint-Cloud, were rounded up, and this difficult day was brought to a close by candle-light, by a successive vote: the Ancients had had to quash their first vote, so that the second, during the night, could be valid. There were therefore three Consuls, assisted by two legislative commissions representing the Councils; and just in order to remain true to tradition, the victors had excluded sixty-two deputies from the Legislative Body.

Before dawn, everyone went home to a Paris that had stayed quite calm.

5

Napoleon Bonaparte: 1799–1814

THE ATTAINMENT OF POWER

At the time, 18 Brumaire did not have the meaning for its contemporaries which they attributed to it a little later, and which history has permanently fixed: the institution of a despotic regime founded on the authority of one person alone, inaugurating a new period – the last – in the history of the Revolution. The Republic had known so many illegalities since its birth – from Vendémiaire Year IV to Prairial Year VII, by way of Fructidor Year V – that the two days of Brumaire merely meant one more, at least comparable with Fructidor: intervention by the army, expulsion of deputies, annulment of regularly constituted powers. Even a law of proscription against the Jacobins was not omitted. Furthermore, the Republic continued, armed with three Consuls in place of five Directors, stronger than ever in its two great supports: the army, in the person of Bonaparte, and the political framework born of the revolutionary upheaval, represented by Sieyès.

However, one man had grasped the whole picture on 19 Brumaire, apart from Sieyès, who had been eclipsed the day before by the Corsican general and all his praetorians on horseback. That man was Benjamin Constant, who had been in the Director's circle all the summer, but not important enough to be party to the secret; during the morning of 19 Brumaire he in fact wrote to him:

Citizen Director, After the first wave of joy which news of your deliverance inspired in me, I had some other thoughts on the matter which I beg you to read, even if I am attaching too much importance to them: I believe this is a decisive moment for liberty. There is talk of adjourning the councils, but such a measure would seem disastrous to me at this time, since it would be to destroy the only barrier which could be set up against a man whom you associated with yesterday's events but who is thereby only more of a threat to the Republic. His proclamations, in which he speaks only of himself and says that his return has raised hopes that he will put an end to France's ills, have more than ever convinced me that in everything he does he sees nothing but his own elevation. Nevertheless, he has on his side the generals, the soldiers, the aristocratic populace and everyone who enthusiastically embraces the appearance of strength. The Republic has on her side yourself – and certainly that is a great deal – and representation which, good or bad, will always be capable of erecting a barrier to the designs of an individual.[1]

This advice forms a kind of belated echo of Sieyès's own misgivings since Bonaparte's return. It was futile now, because the die had been cast on 19 Brumaire. Today, the historian is struck by the lucidity of their words, and by their blindness. Constant was the first to realize – whereas Mme de Staël, who had just returned from Coppet, greeted the coup d'état with joy – that the days of Brumaire had sounded the knell of what, for him, constituted the Republic: representative government, assemblies, a collegial executive, liberty. It would not prevent him from paying court to Bonaparte in order to obtain at least a post within the new authorities, at the end of the year. He would not be there for long: the impression he had established on 19 Brumaire fixed his opposition to dictatorship for the next fourteen years.

Yet this very intelligent man reveals a great lack of comprehension of the state of the nation. Heaven knows, however, that he had grasped and commented on the extraordinary collective traumatism created in public opinion by the revolutionary years, and the extreme difficulty of recon-stituting, on so many accumulated ruins and antagonistic memories, a body politic freely agreed by the citizens. He had stepped up his flow of writings, before and after Fructidor, to try to convince enlightened opinion to rebuild its unity around a Republic and the principles of 1789. But his was a voice crying in the wilderness.

Among the republicans he was defending, it was the regicides of the Convention who set the tone – those who had relaunched the Terror after Fructidor: an unfortunate way of exorcizing bad memories. As for that France he was speaking of and which he was addressing, it was the France of Parisian society, members of the Institut, deputies to the councils, who shared with him both the philosophy of the Enlightenment and a taste for bourgeois society.

The people with whom he liked best to talk were constitutional royalists, whom he wanted to rally. He knew very little about the depths of the nation. He was a stranger to one of its most powerful passions – national greatness inseparable from glory. When, in his letter of 19 Brumaire to Sieyès, he speaks of the 'aristocratic populace', he is putting his finger on Bonaparte's popularity, but misinterpreting it. For this 'populace', if it is true that it loves the spectacle of strength and arms, is not 'aristocratic', that is to say, counter-revolutionary. It is the arms of the Revolution that it salutes, in the person of the general of Italy and Egypt. Against these, what was the importance of a group of politicians who had clung on to power for so long; and what was the importance of Sieyès, their man?

[1] Letter published in Norman King and Etienne Hofman (eds), 'Les Lettres de Benjamin Constant à Sieyès', *Annales Benjamin Constant*, 3 (1983).

There are two ways of entering that France of 1799, whose state of mind Tocqueville penetrated so brilliantly in the two completed chapters of what would have been his history of the Revolution: firstly, through personal interests, and secondly through national glory. Neither path led to liberty, but both to Bonaparte.

Everyone had suffered from the chaos of events. But, at the end of the road, many people benefited. Peasants and people from the towns had purchased lands and property belonging to the Church and, to a lesser extent, to the émigrés. This was an immense transfer of property, forming the Revolution's bank, with a guarantee that was completely political: it would be nullified by the return of the kings. France today can offer enough abbeys or monastic buildings which at that time were transformed into factories or barns, to give some idea of that huge redistribution of the land and property interests.

The most obvious fortunes in speculation, built up by way of these state sales, were almost hidden by the multiplicity of small deals, or simply of acquired benefits. The inflation which resulted from revolutionary management of public finances had accelerated transfers of ownership. It had also, to a large extent, liberated debtors from their debts and the French from taxes. Lastly, the Revolution had created a very large number of jobs in the public sector, both in the administration and in the army: many posts which, before 1789, had been sold like a formal office, were now open to anyone with ability, and their numbers had increased. The principles of 1789 created a whole democracy of interests, and were therefore now bound to a policy of conserving them.

Was the Republic capable of conserving? Did it know how to? It gave no reassurance on this point to the public. The Thermidorian politicians presented a caricature rather than a picture of beneficiaries of the Revolution. Who would want to be like them? They were too rich, too powerful, too corrupt – in short, too 'bourgeois' – to impart anything but remorse for the immense adventure, whereas the French, on the contrary, wanted to enjoy their new possessions in security, erasing all trace of their recent or questionable origin.

Moreover, the Republican form of the state had allowed the exercise of authority only by the guillotine; since the Terror had ended, the Directory maintained the ascendancy of Robespierre's feeble conquerors, come hell or high water, only by means of a permanent coup d'état. But it had arrived at the end of the road, incapable of truly silencing the two parties threatening the new property-owning France – the Jacobins and the royalists.

It was also incapable of confronting the eternal coalition of European monarchies against the Revolution, as the crisis of summer 1799 had shown. Since 1795, and above all since the Italian victories, France had presented this strange spectacle of a Republic with a weak and divided government, gradually sliding towards internal anarchy, and yet within a few years building a formidable French power outside France: occupying

Belgium, Holland, Italy, Switzerland, the left bank of the Rhine, planting the tricolour flag much farther afield than any king of France had ever done. Public opinion set great store by these victories and conquests, far beyond mere calculation of the gain to be derived from them; much more than because of simple national pride, and on a different plane – the ventures of its armies provided the Revolution with a treasury of good memories to offset the bad ones; they transfigured its image. They had managed to get the Terror excused, and would provide the Republic and its soldiers with a halo.

Military glory – which Constant would soon explain was foreign to modern society, engaged as it was in the productive works of peaceful times – would, on the contrary, in France accompany the birth of democracy. It was gradually transforming its nature. The heroism of the soldier was replacing the civic virtue of the sansculotte. While it opened up swift and unlimited opportunities for advancement on merit, the army at the same time offered a powerful channel for the classical tendencies of the Revolution's passion for equality. In the space of ten years, the ideas of 1789 and hatred of the aristocracy had thus turned into a tremendous national investment. But by looking favourably on this evolution – for want of any other cards to play – the Directorial Republic had also dug its own grave.

As an example which took place a little more than a year before Brumaire there is the festival of 9 Thermidor Year VI (27 July 1798) when the Directory celebrated its birth, as it had each year after 1794. Bonaparte, who had been gone since May, had already gained a foothold in Egypt; yet he alone was the hero of the celebration. In fact, the government had given up the theme of Robespierre's downfall, which smacked too much of civil war; instead, it substituted the triumphal procession of all the looted treasures from Italian churches and palaces.

The comment of Etienne Delécluze, David's young student, in his memoirs was:

This fête which, according to contemporary taste, was given all the appearances of an ancient ceremony, singularly flattered the nation's self-esteem and caused the name of the young Bonaparte – who was just about to make his entry into Cairo – to resound amid still more enthusiasm and gratitude. Scientific and artistic objects, books, manuscripts, antique statues and paintings won by the army of Italy, had been unloaded at Charenton; and during the ten days preceding their entry into Paris, a crowd of the curious had gone along the Seine as far as this village to observe from every angle the packing-cases containing the treasures accumulated by the sword of Bonaparte. Yielding to a generous and peaceable inspiration, the government of the Directory had seized the opportunity to remove from the fête of 9 Thermidor the malevolent political character it had had until then, in order to bring back French hearts, as far as possible, to a spirit of Concord through a common sentiment – national pride.[2]

[2] E. J. Delécluze, *Louis David, son école et son temps*, ch. 7.

There followed an interminable procession of books, minerals, animals and *objets d'art*, divided into four sections so as to give it an encyclopaedic nature, 'an idea which then dominated every speculative intelligence'; each of the four divisions was surrounded by military detachments, members of the Institut and actors from the lyric theatres, who sang hymns of joy to the victorious arms of France. From the Jardin des Plantes to the Champ de Mars, where the Directors stood, there were vast throngs of people: France was simultaneously celebrating her victories and encyclopaedic reason, identifying her conquests with the progress of the human mind, and uniting by her arms temporal order – even territorial order – and spiritual power. The important person missing from this new version of the festival of unity was Bonaparte, since it was his sword which had made it all possible.

Ten years after 1789, the French Revolution had largely become in public opinion that very special something which eluded Constant's analysis: a universalist nationalism, in which the historian can discern its component elements of anti-aristocratic passion and rationalism, transfigured by the idea of the nation's historico-military election. The Directory could no more identify this mixture of sentiments than it could reassure those whose interests were threatened. On both sides there was the implicit demand for a king, but one who was radically different from other kings, since he would be born of the sovereignty of the people and of reason. This was where Napoléon Bonaparte, king of the French Revolution, was born. In 1789, the French had created a Republic, under the name of a monarchy. Ten years later, they created a monarchy, under the name of a Republic.

The matter was not concluded on 19 Brumaire. Bonaparte appeared only in third position on the list of the three Consuls drawn up on that night, coming after Sieyès and Roger Ducos. Unlike the oracle of the revolutionary assemblies, the general did not have his constitution 'in the bag'; he had acted as he would on the battlefield, though less brilliantly, which he would later explain in his phrase: 'One advances and then one has a look round.' That was why the weeks and months which followed were more important than the two days of Brumaire.

Stendhal would write later in his *Vie d'Henri Brulard*, that he had been surprised by news of the coup d'état when in Nemours, on the road leading from his native Grenoble to Paris: 'We learned of it in the evening, and I didn't understand much about it, but I was delighted that young General Bonaparte had made himself king of France.' This snippet says a great deal about the kind of spell this event cast over a large part of French republican tradition in the nineteenth century: it would take the coup d'état of 2 December 1851 to destroy its magic. But Stendhal telescoped several months, between the end of 1799 and the middle of 1800: those during which Bonaparte *was becoming* king of France.

If he lost his head slightly on 19 Brumaire, he played the rest of the game like a great politician, fully aware of the superiority he possessed over his rival, Sieyès. He was not a man to share with others, and he was the only one who could provide a guarantee. Everything took place within the two parliamentary commissions which had survived the Brumaire shipwreck, where he himself, Sieyès and Daunou had the most influence. As days went by, the Parisian political milieu sensed where the strength lay and inclined towards him. Everyone agreed on the need to reinforce the Executive: this was a great innovation, to say the least, in the theory of republican power.

At the head of the Republic, Sieyès would have liked to see a Grand Elector, an arbitrating power charged with the task of designating two Consuls. Did he want the office for himself, finally to become the supreme guardian of the institutions, lavishly maintained by the state, the ultimate incarnation of his doctrine? Had he thought he would swamp his young rival with honours? The first version seems more probable to me. But Bonaparte, helped by Boulay and others, made use of the antagonism between Sieyès and Daunou – each with his own plan – to impose a text which suited him. He kept Sieyès's list of notabilities, which dispensed with true elections, and three assemblies which neutralized one another – Senate, Tribunate, Legislative Body. He put aside the Grand Elector and set up an executive of three Consuls, of whom only the first truly exercised power, with the ability to initiate laws. It was the end of the Republican idea under the name of the Republic.

The electoral system gives a fair indication of the limits of universal suffrage, which the Brumairians had wanted to re-establish in homage to the great principles. In reality, the popular vote was destined only to provide, at all levels in the country, from the commune right up to the Senate, 'lists of notabilities' among which a sorting operation could be effected from above. This procedure had been thought up by Sieyès, in order to avoid the annual hiccups which had dislocated the preceding regime; in fact, it instituted a power which was no longer controlled by the people, even if it continued to call on the spirit of the people: a good definition of enlightened despotism.

At the most, the people would be invited from time to time to ratify an initiative of the authority with a massive 'Yes'. But the doctrine of the new regime, together with the old dream of the Enlightenment, lies in this comment by Cabanis: 'The ignorant classes no longer exercise any influence on either the legislature or the government . . . everything is done for the people and in the name of the people; nothing is done by them, or at their unconsidered dictation.'[3]

One month after Brumaire, before the end of 1799, the constitution of Year VIII thus put Bonaparte into power. Sieyès, who became president of the Senate, received the right to find jobs for his friends. He disappeared under a heap of honours, among the debris of his own ideas, which were

---

[3] P. J. G. Cabanis, *Quelques considérations sur l'organisation sociale en général, et particulièrement sur la nouvelle constitution*, 25 Frimaire Year VIII (16 December 1799).

used in the triumph of his erstwhile associate. As First Consul, Bonaparte chose two colleagues whose names formed a bridge between the present and the two great national memories: Camabacérès, a man of the Revolution, and Charles-François Lebrun, a servant of the *ancien régime*. The first had been a Conventionnel and regicide (but he had voted for a reprieve); the second was a former secretary of Chancellor Maupeou, the last great defender of royal authority against the parlements. Both had the sceptical maturity born of experience, and preferred honours to power. Through them, the two Frances of yesteryear provided the young hero with his retinue.

But this national reconciliation – one of Bonaparte's great ideas – was not a rehabilitation of the past, or even a search for balance between the *ancien régime* and the Revolution. On the contrary, it assumed an acceptance of what had happened since 1789, and the desire to defend revolutionary attainments, both at home and abroad. The First Consul was more keenly aware than anyone, during that first winter when he needed to keep an eye on everything, that his destiny was being decided outside France, on the battlefields where he was awaited by the European coalition which had been repulsed – but not vanquished – in the autumn. For the fundamental contract between Bonaparte and public opinion was the guarantee of revolutionary conquests, and therefore of a victorious peace. The rest – his power, soon to become his regime, internal order, the reconciliation of the French – was subordinate to this suspensive condition: victory. Should this delay or falter, he would be questioned, condemned and as good as lost.

Several months after the coup d'état, Bonaparte was already impatient of any resistance. But having so recently attained supreme power, he still did not control everything, and political society had not yet got the measure or the habitude of his despotism. As witness the incidents which increased over the first few weeks with Madame de Staël and her friends. Benjamin Constant, who had for so long dreamed of being a representative of the people, had in the end been appointed to the Tribunate, the assembly which was supposed to discuss the laws, while the Legislative Body would vote on them. But he realized his ambition just when it no longer meant anything. On 5 January 1800, during one of the first sessions, he affirmed the assembly's independence and its deliberative authority, without which 'there is nothing but servitude and silence – a silence which the whole of Europe would hear.' The First Consul immediately had a violent press attack unleashed against him and Madame de Staël, organised by Fouché, the Minister of Police. It was the first skirmish.

Deep-rooted opinion in the country, exhausted after so many years of revolutionary talk, no longer took any interest in political liberty. Bonaparte's power was based in France on tired consent to servitude, in exchange for the return of order. Bonaparte had had the law of proscription revoked, in order to show clearly that it had belonged to Sieyès. But he had to conquer outside the country. This was the whole story of Marengo, seven months after Brumaire.

The campaign was just right to seize the imagination: the assembling of the army in Burgundy, the crossing of the Alps by the St Bernard and taking the enemy from the rear – the Austrian armies besieging Genoa. Indeed, the French descent into the rich Milanese countryside reawoke the happiness of 1796; but at Marengo, near Alessandria, on 14 June, the decisive clash with the troops of the Austrian General Melas almost turned to a rout. For Bonaparte, in the impeccable lay-out of a strategic design, had committed a tactical error by dispersing his troops in order to 'sound out' his adversary, and with reduced numbers he had encountered the entire Austrian army. At three in the afternoon the French were losing ground, outnumbered, when at the end of the day the arrival of Desaix's corps changed the outcome of the battle.

In Paris news of the defeat had arrived before the final recovery; during several hours, the First Consul vanished from political calculations. Already, while he was with the armies, intrigue and speculation had resumed in all the little Parisian groups, around Daunou, Sieyès and in the salon of Madame de Staël. Possible successors were talked about – ambitious or jealous generals like Moreau and Bernadotte; sober symbols of the Revolution like Carnot; or even those eternal candidates for a constitutional monarchy, personified since 1789 in the Ducs d'Orléans, father and son. Even Joseph, Napoleon's elder brother, had thrust himself forward, while Fouché and Talleyrand, for their part, were working chiefly for themselves.

But lo and behold, rescued by chance – and by Desaix, who lost his life – Bonaparte came straight back to Paris after throwing together a hasty armistice with Melas. He returned on 2 July amid popular jubilation and the nervous silence of the 'politicos'. He had realized that Marengo, far more than Brumaire, had been the true coronation of his power and his regime. This was a coronation which no longer came by divine right, since it was the result of the most one-sided contract that a nation had ever made with its leader, who was forced into a commitment never to be vanquished. It is in this sense that, between Marengo and Waterloo, between the arrival of Desaix and the absence of Grouchy, between fortune and misfortune, there is a difference which is both minute and tremendous: the regime itself was dependent on it. In June 1800, therefore, it was founded. The royalist agent Hyde de Neuville noted at the time that 'Marengo was the baptism of Napoleon's personal power.'

FIRST CONSUL

Then began the happiest period of his life: his marriage with the French Revolution. Republican terminology survived the loss of liberty because it still defined the new France, under the spell of this new sovereign who was her most brilliant son. All that was royal about Bonaparte derived from his being the hero of the Republic. A French Washington, very young and belatedly discovered. The Revolution had exhausted its repertoire, cut off its provisional leaders in the prime of their life, changed those who lived on into mere survivors, and its conquerors into bourgeois. Just at the time when it was closing its theatre it finally found its great man, with his own particular genius: this thirty-year-old Washington did not love liberty and would not finish his days as father of his country. But for several years – until the coronation – he was the master of events and the man who founded the modern state on the heritage of the Revolution.

In order to understand or define him, one can start from what roots him so deeply in French history – this Corsican, Italian, foreigner, this 'Buonaparte' of the Restoration dowagers: his election by the French Revolution, from which he received the strange power not only to embody the new nation – others had had it, such as Mirabeau or Robespierre – but also finally to fulfil it. He had been so acutely aware of it that his writings on St Helena would return almost obsessively to this origin, less in order deliberately to make it into a weapon of posthumous propaganda – which it would nevertheless be – than from a need to recollect those parts of his extraordinary life which might have some explanation.

The 'Citizen Consul', at thirty, was physically at his peak: less sallow than the general of Italy, not yet podgy like the emperor. He lived amid the resonance of his glory and the exhilaration of government work – the two passions of his daily life – even giving up a little of his time to pleasures and amusements: these were the lovely days of Malmaison, recounted by Laure Junot, the future Duchesse d'Abrantès. Bonaparte had not yet acquired a court, and lived surrounded by his aides-de-camp and generals who were his friends, above them all but not separated from them. Josephine had finally realized her exceptional luck, and both of them, by the remarkable nature of their life and love, gave a good representation of the opportunities to be had in the new society; these two 'marginals' of the Revolution, the courtesan from the West Indies and the little Corsican soldier, had ended up by personifying property-owning France. Opinion discovered in the leader it had given itself a style and habits which had all the characteristics of republican simplicity and a civil government. The First Consul had none of the Bourbons' stupid habits: he ate quickly, used to wear the same sort of clothing all the time, liked old hats, and had no wish to waste his time in court ceremony; he hunted little, if at all; he worked and made decisions.

Those images were for his publicity – which he knew very well how to manage – but they also match the truth of the period. Napoleon the Consul mingled the qualities of republican hero and bourgeois king with those despotic and uncontrollable traits which his personality already possessed. He had fully understood the objective conditions which had carried him to power and the civil character of his dictatorship:

I do not govern as a general, but because the nation believes I have the civilian qualities befitting government; if it did not hold that opinion, the government would not survive. I was well aware of what I was doing when, as an army general,

I became a member of the Institut; I was sure of being understood even by the least drummer boy. In the present day, one must not argue about centuries of barbarism. We are thirty million men, united by the Enlightenment, property-ownership and trade. Three or four hundred thousand soldiers are as nothing compared with this great mass.[4]

Enlightenment, property, trade: a definition of the nation which could have been supplied by Necker or Sieyès or Benjamin Constant, and which they had already given, having learnt it from the century's *philosophes*, but without being able to master its potential for instability and civil strife. He also wanted to be its heir and its emblem, the country's guarantor – discovered at long last – and there was a strong bourgeois streak in him which accorded well with this role: unassailable rights of ownership, the idea of marriage and the family, the woman in the home, order in the streets, careers open to anyone with ability.

On the one hand, he endowed all that – which was basically the legacy of 1789 in plain words – with the flamboyant character of his own genius; and on the other, he enveloped it in a sort of Corsican exaggeration, mingling a patriarchal spirit in the birth of modern France. In doing so, he doubly satisfied the national desire. Having just emerged from the epic of the Revolution, the French would not easily have accepted a leader with less national éclat; but exhausted with the Revolutionary repertoire and intent upon their acquisitions, they wanted the strengthening of the guarantees offered to property and law and order.

Both revolutionary and conservative, these rural petits-bourgeois found the Bonaparte of the Civil Code. They spontaneously subscribed to the programme defined in November 1800 in the Council of State: 'We have finished the novel of the Revolution: now we must begin its history, looking only at what is real and possible in the application of its principles, and not what is speculative and hypothetical. If today we followed another path, it would be to philosophize and not to govern.'

A dictatorship of opinion intended to assure the Revolution, the Consulate was also, in Bonaparte's mind, the 'beginning' of its history. The 'novel' of the Revolution had been written by intellectuals who had explored its 'speculative' aspect: he was certainly thinking of Robespierre, and the Republic of virtue, but also to some extent about everyone, from the Constituent Assembly to the Institut, and to Sieyès, for example, his temporary ally of Brumaire, the man of the perfect Constitution.

To begin the real history of the Revolution meant using practical reasoning to deal with the problem which they had approached from the metaphysical standpoint; in short, to found the modern state on experience and reality. This was the other adjunct of the Consulate, by which Bonaparte replaced the model of enlightened despotism through the heritage of post-revolutionary society. An idea which, as far back as 1790, Mirabeau had

[4] 4 May 1802, in the Council of State, in A. C. Thibaudeau, *Mémoires sur le Consulat, 1799 à 1804*, p. 79.

vainly tried to whisper to poor Louis XVI, in his secret correspondence with the court:[5] Why do you jib, he had written in so many words, in the face of the new state of affairs? Instead of bewailing aristocratic society, nobility, parlements and the privileged groups who endlessly hindered your authority, on the contrary, make the most of their disappearance to entrench the monarchy in the new society, by becoming the leader of the nation.

That was a piece of advice that the *ancien régime* king had not accepted or even understood, but one which the new sovereign was well able to put into practice: by temperament he was a thousand times more authoritarian than the former king, and he was governing more than ever a society composed of equal individuals, who were far more helpless than in the past in confrontation with the state. He had the additional advantage over 1790 of a revolutionary tide which had been on the ebb for some years – which, as it receded, revealed with all its strength intact the idea of absolute power, inherited from the kings of France and put to the use of democracy.

The sovereignty of the people had replaced that of the monarch, but it had in no way abdicated from its unlimited extent or its indivisible nature. The consular monarchy thus drew together, to its own advantage, three elements which made it into a stronger power than any other in history. On the one hand, it reigned over isolated men, denied the right to unite into a body, whose equality was guaranteed; on the other, it received its authority from the people, relieved by those same people of fear of God's watchful eye – which had acted as one of the brakes on the power of kings; lastly, it unconsciously drew part of its strength from absolutist tradition. France was still imbued with the very strong feeling that she had broken her ties with the past, and war, émigrés and the king's brothers were there to remind her of it. But the First Consul had fully understood – he said so several times – that his power also partly came from this past and from national habits.

Such were the foundations on which he established his most lasting achievement: the construction of the modern state in France. For the Civil Code, the entire work of juridical unification and legislation, had been started before him, and could have been achieved without him, in a way which would ultimately have been little different. But the new spirit of the state's administrative structures bore his imprint. He drew largely on tradition: Cartesian rationalism imported into the political sphere, enlightened despotism, the long task of centralization carried out by the absolute monarchy, the jurisprudence born of the endless conflicts between the state and the guilds under the *ancien régime*, the trend of customs and minds. He added his mark, both Corsican and military – the mark of one who placed order and authority above all the needs of man, and was so tolerant of his own chief passion: undivided domination.

The administration was the nerve of the state. It had to function on its

---

[5] Mirabeau, *Correspondance avec le comte de Lamarck (1789–1791)*.

own, like a vast framework of men intended to transmit the wishes of
government from the centre as far as the most outlying places, with the
automatism of a living organism:

I had made all my ministries so easy that I had put them within reach of everyone,
as long as they possessed dedication, zeal, energy and capacity for hard work . . .
The organization of the prefectures, their activities and results were admirable and
prodigious. The same impetus was given at the same moment to more than forty
million men; and, with the help of local centres of action, the movement was as
swift at the farthest points as in the very heart.[6]

Thus centralization, while allowing the actualization of the unity and
ubiquity of rational government, excused its agent from everything except
'work' and 'dedication'. All the prefects were 'little emperors' in their
départements, but that power was independent of their merits or their
personal qualities: it was merely the representation in actuality of the
central power.

In vain did Bonaparte periodically resume the argument of 'public
safety', saying that this state dictatorship over the citizens, which virtually
extinguished local life, was due to the war situation; it was difficult to
believe, for these ideas were so imprinted with the marks of his upbringing
and character. For the strong point of the system was also its weak point:
himself. In masterminding the administration, he brought to bear all the
care and attention of his electrifying yet realistic genius. He was capable of
assimilating very different things very rapidly, loving the variety offered by
circumstances to men who govern, knowing the value of detail and the
application of decisions on the spot, intoxicated with the passion for
knowing everything in order to be in command of everything, as if on the
field of battle. He was 'involved in all things', Chateaubriand would write;
'his intellect never rested; he had a sort of perpetual motion of ideas.
Because of his impetuous nature, he advanced by leaps and bounds,
instead of making straightforward and unbroken progress; he threw himself
on the universe and shook it.'[7]

But this activity in itself contained its principle of corruption, and the
ambition for absolute authority implied that authority's debasement into
tyranny; the corruption and debasement were very quickly noticeable in
the First Consul. Nobody could execute his orders swiftly enough, and
nobody ever obeyed him completely. In a country where paying court was
a national tradition, flattery exerted its damage on a personality which
endlessly sought it, aroused it and was very soon intoxicated by it. Hence,
side by side with the famous charming smile, there came that impatience
with contradiction, that violent and sombre eloquence, those rages, that
coarse vulgarity in insults, which Bonaparte used so frequently. Following

[6] Council of State, 1806, in Napoleon, *Pensées politiques et sociales*, ed. A. Dansette (Paris,
Flammarion, 1969), p. 81.
[7] Chateaubriand, *Mémoires d'outre-tombe*, book XXIV, ch. 6.

a very French dialectic, the same man who had deified the abstract sovereignty of the state had made it more fragile by personifying it as if it resided entirely within him. Napoleon was the Louis XIV of the democratic state.

But his possessive passion had never blinded him to the point where he confused private and public. Quite apart from his temperament, the extraordinary nature of his ascent would suffice to explain his tendency to consider everything he had acquired as an inheritance, including the Republic; nevertheless, he was the heir of the Revolution against the *ancien régime*, because the basis of the administrative state which he set up against local authorities was the universality of the law.

Although he increased arbitrary acts, as time went by, and re-established a nobility endowed by the state, the strength of his hold over the nation derived from the fact that he was the delegate of popular sovereignty to make the law and see that it was respected, since it was identical for every citizen. In this sense, he was the last avatar of the crisis of political representation which characterized the French Revolution. He had resolved this crisis by becoming the unique representative, by making a monarchy out of universal suffrage through the screening of lists of notabilities, and out of legislative power through the dispersal of the assemblies' responsibilities. But he himself – and the administration which was merely the extension of his arm – remained the symbols of a new state, founded on the consent of equal citizens and upholding the general interest of the nation.

Through this collective image, he obtained the nation's agreement, re-established order and even effected the reconciliation of those Frenchmen who had been divided by the Revolution: ex-Constituents, ex-Girondins, ex-terrorists and, of course, Thermidorians filled his administration, and provided State councillors, magistrates, prefects, commissioners to the armies, thousands upon thousands of jobs, from top to bottom of the public officialdom. Even the émigrés returned, and many of them rediscovered – enlarged, democratized, but also adorned with incomparable splendour – the two great careers in which their ancestors had proved so illustrious: state service and the army.

As for the position of courtier, they needed no one to teach them. The First Consul despised them, and in talking about them would use the tone of the 1789 Abbé Sieyès: 'I have offered them officer ranks in my army; they didn't want them; I have offered them posts in the administration, and they refused them; but when I opened my antechambers to them, they rushed to get in.' A terrible statement, in which he presented, as he so frequently did, a concentration of absolutist tradition and revolutionary spirit. The French aristocracy had been subdued by the former before being broken by the latter. In the Tuileries salons, gathered round this false prince from Corsica, it had even lost its identity.

Elsewhere, and almost everywhere, in every area which had played a role – no matter how tiny – in France since 1789, what a mad dash there was for employment! The Consulate was an extraordinary job market where, on a national scale, Bonaparte played one of the great roles of the king of France at court: handing out rewards, honours and jobs. He had more than any king had ever had, since he was founding the modern state; he had to provide not only for 'vanity', but also for the needs of a large administration and an immense army. Even more than any past king, he played on the national passion for 'positions'. This democratic trans-figuration of absolutist practices was the Corsican noble's final secret; it reinstated in the nation, in its own fashion, that court heritage which the Revolution had detested and wanted to abolish. It thus provided the hero of modern politics with a reinforcement from the past.

One last trait brought the soldier from Ajaccio close to national tradition: he had absorbed the Catholic religion in his cradle. Not that he was a believer, or that he had a deep relationship with it, but it was a part of his Italian heritage and his French world. Into the conception which he had of it, he introduced Enlightenment utilitarianism – the basis of the culture he had learnt – and political reason pure and simple, unencumbered by the useless passions of the revolutionary years, which led him to reconcile his regime with the age-old beliefs of religion. When he spoke of matters of faith, he introduced into his reflections a typically French bourgeois wisdom, which derived from Voltaire rather than Machiavelli, and which would feed nineteenth-century conservative policy: 'If you remove faith from the people, you are left with nothing but highway robbers.'[8]

Such was Bonaparte, First Consul, son and king of the Revolution; he was the product of an event which the French feared in retrospect but cherished as an inheritance, and because of this wanted to be finally assured of peaceful enjoyment of their lives and possessions. He was the self-made republican dictator, who had given the crown to equality as well as to himself. About this meeting between a man and a nation – so brief, but so dazzling, and one which would take such a long time to forget, since it would last for almost a century – Chateaubriand wrote the most profound comment:

Everyday experience proves that the French turn instinctively towards power: they have no love at all for liberty; equality alone is their idol. Now, equality and despotism have secret links. From both these aspects, Napoleon drew his strength from the hearts of the French, who were militarily inclined towards power, and democratically in love with the idea of equal status. When he ascended the throne, he brought the people to sit there with him; a proletarian king, he humiliated kings and nobles in his antechambers; he levelled out ranks, not by lowering them, but by raising them: to bring them down would have given further encouragement to plebeian envy, raising them was more flattering to their conceit.[9]

---

[8] Council of State, 29 March 1805; A. Marquiset, *Napoléon sténographié au Conseil d'Etat, 1804–1805* (1913), p. 71.

[9] Chateaubriand, *Mémoires d'outre-tombe*, book XXIV, ch. 6.

Marengo had given his brand-new reign a victorious peace, that contradictory dream of public opinion in France. To end the war was an
undertaking of the same order as ending the Revolution: they both needed
the crowning touch. Marengo had not been enough to bring Austria to her
knees; but Moreau's victory at Hohenlinden in December 1800 brought
the Austrian emperor's diplomats to the negotiating table: this was the
peace of Lunéville, signed in February 1801, which extended the losses of
Campo Formio (Belgium, Luxembourg and the left bank of the Rhine) and
confirmed the French protectorate over the Batavian, Swiss and Italian
Republics. The second coalition was completely dismantled. After the
failure of the Anglo-Russian enterprises in Holland, Tsar Paul had changed
sides and approached France, depriving the British government of its last
continental troops.

Paris and London were then obliged to talk by force of circumstance,
despite all reservations. Bonaparte wanted to keep Egypt, and Britain
refused even indirect acceptance of a Franco-Russian alliance. But Egypt
was all the more indefensible since Kléber's death in June 1800. In
London, Pitt had fallen; in Petersburg, the assassination of Tsar Paul
removed some of the British reluctance to negotiate. There remained a
weariness with the war on both sides of the Channel, Britain's social
and economic difficulties and Bonaparte's wish to be the man of peace:
these explain the preliminaries in London in autumn 1801, and the peace
of Amiens (March 1802). England would give back Egypt to Turkey,
Malta to its Knights, the Cape of Good Hope to Holland; France would
evacuate Naples, and the two powers would guarantee the independence of
Portugal and the Ionian Islands. This drawn match, accepted very half-
heartedly by both sides, was greeted as a lasting return to peace; but at the
same time it was felt by French opinion to be the international recognition
of revolutionary legitimacy. If London accepted that the 'great nation'
extended as far as Flanders and the Rhine, it was because Bonapartist
pacification had kept the promises of Year II.

In the same way, the internal power of the First Consul had continued
to consolidate its position in deeds and in the law. After Brumaire, the
new government, by reassuring opinion, had drawn the political teeth of
chouannerie; the military insurrection abated all the more quickly because
the royalist leaders at first banked on the coup d'état for the pretender's
early restoration. When Bonaparte offered them only the option to come
over to his side, they had lost their troops, and the *chouannerie* hatched a
plot. On 24 December 1800, in the rue Saint-Nicaise, while his carriage
was conveying him to the theatre, the First Consul very narrowly escaped
the explosion of a bomb: he used this as a pretext to wipe out the
remainder of a Jacobin opposition which had hardly been a threat, and
shortly afterwards tracked down the real culprits. Two implacable *chouans*
were executed, the others went over to England. In the west, a mixture of
clemency and severity would do the rest.

THE RECONSTRUCTION OF FRANCE

Besides, Bonaparte had at his disposal against the royalist leaders a political weapon which was much more daunting than repression: this was agreement with the Catholic Church. He had inherited a difficult task, for the constitutional Church, organized by Bishop Grégoire, had not succeeded in winning over the majority of the faithful, and the civil cults founded under the Directory – the *décadaire* and theophilanthropic religions – had remained merely cold ceremonies for the notables. The refractory and Roman Church, therefore, in the name of the past, united the religious feelings of the great mass of the peasantry.

Bonaparte approached the problem like a politician; he dropped the great dream of secularizing consciences in order to rally the country around his authority: he did not for a moment believe in the idea of rebuilding a civil religion around the Revolution. In his eyes, that sort of idea belonged to a notable or intellectual, a plan which typified the revolutionary 'novel' he was trying to bring to a close. Even the constitutional Church, which Grégoire had had such diffculty in keeping alive, and which had been the victim of both terrorist dechristianization and the détente of 1795, was sacrificed by Bonaparte without any regret on the altar of reconciliation. According to his view of affairs, he was negotiating with the pope as one sovereign with another, by acknowledging the other's territory, which the Constituent Assembly had wanted to deny: he could not settle the situation of the Church of France without a negotiated agreement with the pope.

To deliver the Catholic people from the clutches of the refractory priests, and therefore also to free them from royalism, he had to go over their heads and reconcile his regime with Rome:

Fifty émigré bishops, paid by England, today guide the French clergy. Their influence must be destroyed; for that, the pope's authority is necessary. He must dismiss them or make them resign. It is said that, as the Catholic religion is followed by the majority of Frenchmen, its practice must be organized. The First Consul appoints fifty bishops, the pope institutes them. They appoint the *curés*, the state gives them a salary. They take the oath. Priests who do not submit are deported. Those who preach against the government are handed over to their superiors for punishment. The pope confirms the sale of the clergy's possessions: he consecrates the Republic. *Salvam fac rem Gallicam* will be sung. The bull has arrived. There are only a few phrases to be altered. They will say that I am a papist; I am nothing at all; in Egypt I was a Mohammedan; here I will be a Catholic, for the good of the people.[10]

In the rough language of the First Consul, these were the terms of the Concordat. With regard to Rome, Bonaparte had made two demands: the acknowledgement of the sale of the Church's possessions, and his right to appoint all bishops, after eliminating the old ones – both refractory and

[10] June 1801, Thibaudeau, *Mémoires*, pp. 152–53.

constitutional – and wiping the past clean at one vast stroke. In short, a guarantee for property acquired since 1789, and a clergy under his thumb: this was a double coup which made him king of the peasants, with God's blessing. The dialogue had been long and difficult; but he had obtained satisfaction in return for the obligation to maintain the new Church, whose bishops would be 'instituted'. On the Catholic side, the compromise with France's new master meant that the Church was founding the bases of the alliance between what the nineteenth century would call the Throne and the Altar. Those who, following the pope's example, chose to give their support, seized the unexpected opportunity to re-establish Catholicism's moral and spiritual authority in the rediscovered harmony with the temporal power.

The agreement roused the anger of refractory priests and counter-revolutionaries; but this was a period when moderate royalist opinion, which had been so agitated against the Directory, accepted the new master as a good substitute for the old vindictive monarchy of the émigrés. Times had changed. Chateaubriand, returned from exile, had just published the *Génie du Christianisme*. Protest, without being really noisy, was more noticeable in Paris, among Republican bourgeois, the people of the Institut. When, at Easter 1802, some weeks after the signing of the peace of Amiens, the capital celebrated with due solemnity Consular France's reunion with the Church of Rome, there were plenty of moans and groans from high-ranking civil and military personnel in the regime – those who had grown old in the struggle against 'superstition'.

The Tribunate had already been purged in March of any possible elements of even virtual 'opposition', by the removal of about twenty of its members, including Benjamin Constant and those ideologists who were high priests of civil religion: Chénier, Cabanis, Ginguené and Daunou. Madame de Staël also hated the Concordat, but for other reasons. Unlike the men of the Institut, but like her father, she believed the Christian religion to be indispensable to modern society; but she had explained at great length in the *Circonstances actuelles* that the state religion associated with the Republic should be Protestantism, which was essential for the lasting foundation of liberty. Bonaparte replied to her later, from St Helena, in a conversation with Las Cases: 'What would I have gained by proclaiming Protestantism? I would have created two great parties in France, whereas I did not want any at all; I would have brought back the fury of the religious wars, whereas the enlightened men of the century, together with my will, had the sole aim of making them vanish completely.'

One of the essential dates of the first 'end' of the Revolution was this peace with the Church, though it did not entirely bury the conflict which had begun in 1789–90, as what followed would show, but at least calmed it down for a while. Bonaparte had not dealt, and had not wanted to deal, with any of the spiritual and moral questions which lay at the heart of the conflict; he had shackled the Church to his success. The Concordat bore the imprint of his realistic genius: an intelligent use of his strong situation,

tempered by a sense of tradition and a bourgeois philosophy of religion. To
this Catholic Church which had been despoiled of its possessions, snatched
from its past by the Revolution, he had restored not its heritage – which
had passed to the new gentlemen in both town and country – but its unity
and status, in exchange for a far tighter subordination than in the times of
the kings of France.

He was dealing with a Church which was no longer the powerful body it
had been under the *ancien régime*, intertwined with aristocratic society by a
thousand ties; he could give himself the public benefit of restoring it
without returning its former powers, as a kind of buttress to his authority.
That was what his old Institut friends had not understood, or perhaps what
they had understood only too well: they saw in it the end of the Republican
spirit, by the re-creation of religious oppression on individual consciences.
As a concession to them, Bonaparte postponed the promulgation of the
Concordat, which he accompanied with a unilateral declaration, 'Gallican'
in tone; but this mini-rebellion of notables, parliamentarians and generals
was a mere nothing compared with public opinion's deep approval of the
double guarantee afforded by the Concordat to property and consciences.

In the Bonapartist reorganization, the dispositions of the Consulate
rested chiefly on the general feeling that a strong government had become
the best instrument for consolidating revolutionary acquisitions. The *rente*
(the rate of return on government stock) had risen again, business had
picked up, the countryside was breathing once more, and the towns were
quiet. It was on the basis of this almost organic calming down that
Bonaparte founded the administrative institutions of contemporary France,
after ten years of tension and violence. There, as in other areas, the various
revolutionary powers had done much of his work for him, without having
ever achieved, after 1789, the minimum social consensus necessary for any
lasting effectiveness.

Naturally, the organization of executive power received all the First
Consul's attention. Beside the government, whose members were appointed
by him and responsible to him, there now existed the Council of State, the
heir to the king's Council of State which had been so important in the
running of the former monarchy. Moreover, its role was similar: to perfect
bills before they were submitted to the Tribunate, whose task was to
discuss them, and to deal at top level with any administrative litigation.
The councillors, to whom junior officials and legal advisers were added
later, were chosen most carefully by Bonaparte, who loved this competent
and discreet top bureaucracy.

The same principle was applied at local level: Bonaparte retained the
départements, increasing the numbers in line with his conquests, heading
each with a prefect, whom he appointed and could dismiss, as on a lower
level the sub-prefect of the *arrondissement*. Alongside them, a general
council for the *département* and an *arrondissement* council enjoyed merely
illusory powers. The prefect was both the representative and the departmental equivalent of the country's new head: he appointed the mayors of

the small communes, while the First Consul directly designated those of the larger ones, so that nothing should be left to chance. Contemporary France was born amid this liquidation of local anarchies which had been inherited from the Revolution, and this posthumous reconciliation of Louis XIV and Robespierre.

The same centralizing and authoritarian spirit presided over the reorganization of other sectors of public life, where Bonaparte proved himself to be both the heir and the liquidator of the Revolution. He retained the hierarchy of courts established by the Constituent Assembly, but suppressed the eligibility of judges and limited the powers of juries to criminal matters. He considerably increased the role and numbers of the police, who under Fouché became one of the essential mechanisms of government.

In matters of finance, the work of the last years of the Directory was consolidated by the care given to the Treasury administration and taxes. The tax system remained based on the Constituent Assembly's three direct taxes, which yielded a fairly low amount, but its typically bourgeois character can be seen in the considerable rise in indirect taxes, which had been very light during the revolutionary decade. In order to combat Britain's economic supremacy, Bonaparte – more of a Colbertist than he thought – also endowed France with financial institutions: the law of 1805 fixed for over a century the gold weight of the 'Germinal franc'; above all, there was the creation of the Banque de France, a private company in the hands of the wealthiest bankers, but responsible for state treasurership.

Education also became a service unified by the state, and received its title in 1808 as the Imperial University. The new regime took no more interest than the Thermidorian Convention or the Directory in primary education, which was left to private initiative, most frequently on the part of the clergy; but it took great care of secondary education – the nursery of the bourgeois elite: the training of future state executives must not be left to chance. The Thermidorian 'central schools', once their pedagogic boldness had been removed, became those mournful secondary schools evoked by Musset in his *Confessions d'un enfant du siècle*, and much akin to the monarchy's Jesuit and Oratory colleges: places where the children were wakened by drumbeats to study the classics. In higher education, the great schools created by the Convention took precedence over the university faculties: this was a specific characteristic of French higher education, dating from the monarchy and persisting right down to the present day.

In short, all those names which are inseparable from national memory – prefects, Banque de France, lycées, *grandes écoles* – which flow from the pens of historians of that epoch, still evoke the France we are living in today, at the end of the twentieth century. The Consulate's weak point was its organization of public authorities, for it depended on the life of one man. The foundation of the modern administrative state was its durable part, since that was the result of a military energy enlightened by understanding of civil history. It had its monument, crowning the legislative work of the Revolution and regulating relations between citizens of the new society in the Code Napoléon or Civil Code, the most important of the great post-Revolutionary legal Acts, which became the very symbol – both within the country and internationally – of France after 1789.

In the text of its promulgation, in 1804, there is a kind of celebration of a centuries-old ambition which has finally been realized, after so very many efforts: 'Roman laws, decrees, general or particular customs, statutes, regulations cease to have the force of general or special law in matters which are the subject of the said laws composing the present Code.' Thus, for all Frenchmen, there was but one Act governing the civil relations which bound them together, one single law for the nation. Here was an old monarchic enterprise, endlessly worked on by the kings' lawyers, constantly called for by the Estates-General, established as an imprescriptible rule by the rationalism of the Enlightenment, worked and reworked by the assemblies of the French Revolution.

The *ancien régime* had never succeeded in building a rational order out of the 'gothic' edifice of its various customs, one which would offer protection against the arbitrary by the uniformity of its measures, and be equally applicable to every citizen. But on this ground, the differing currents of eighteenth-century thought had been almost unanimous in recommending it, from jurisconsults to *philosophes*, from *Encyclopédistes* to physiocrats: Chancellor d'Aguesseau, Voltaire, Linguet and Turgot, all together. There is probably no other domain in which the causal chain linking the Revolution to Enlightenment philosophy and the spirit of the century can be more clearly seen than in that of civil legislation.

Besides, to a large extent, the old monarchy which had so often served the *philosophes* as a scapegoat, had set an example. But, imprisoned by tradition and the financial mechanisms which had tied it inseparably to particularisms and privileges, it had never been able to get to the bottom of the kingdom's juridical diversity; as de Tocqueville explained, the parts it had destroyed only made more odious the parts it had left or was endlessly trying to reconstruct. By overthrowing the corporate or, if you will, 'aristocratic' structure of old society, the 1789 Revolution had flung open the door to the French passion for laws, in which the rationalist universalism which is one of its dominant characteristics finds its finest expression. The new social world comprised only equal individuals, subject to the same laws which fixed their rights and obligations, and which – in case of litigation – the judge had to apply rather than interpret.

The reconstruction of civil legislation had begun at the time of the Constituent Assembly, when a whole series of important debates were devoted to paternal authority, the nature and limitations of the marriage contract, and the freedom to make one's will: even at that period, the dominance was apparent of the spirit of absolute equality of succession among heirs, without the testator's being able to favour any one of them – for fear that privilege for the eldest son might be reconstituted.

The object, written into the Constitution of 1791, was the establishment of a general code of civil law, which the Legislative Assembly inherited. The latter, as has been seen, was very quickly dragged into the slide towards war and the fall of the monarchy; nevertheless, before breaking up, it voted in September 1792 for the secularization of births, marriages and deaths and the institution of divorce. The hardest part of the work had been effected during the revolutionary years by the Convention's Committee for legislation, under the presidency of Cambacérès, the future Consul after 18 Brumaire.

A first project of the Code had been presented by him to the Convention in August 1793, during one of the most dramatic months in the Revolution's history. It bore the mark of the radical spirit of the time, decreeing for example not only equality of succession, but also the admission of recognized natural offspring to rights of inheritance identical with those of legitimate children; paternal power reduced to protective status; marriage and divorce only at the wish of partners who were of age; community of property to be the only matrimonial regulation.

A second bill, again presented by Cambacérès in September 1794 after the fall of Robespierre, put forward the three great principles of the future Code: liberty, property-ownership and the right of contract. The articles proposed did not go back on those of the preceding year. Under the Directory, in June 1796, Cambacérès advanced yet a third plan of the Code, discussion of which was again interrupted by the vicissitudes of the political situation, as if the Revolution, obsessed by problems of its very existence, could not manage to institute itself in civil legislation: these adjournments imposed by circumstance fairly symbolized its course. There had been nothing more unanimous or more definitive in its progress than the decrees of 4–11 August 1789; and in the ten years that followed property-owning individualism did not manage to write its code of statutes.

When Bonaparte got hold of the file, by order of the Consuls on 24 Thermidor (12 August 1800), many of the elements were ready: property, freedom of contract, secularization of births, marriages and deaths, divorce, etc. The new element introduced by the First Consul, apart from the ardour he put into the undertaking, was the search for a politico-legal compromise between revolutionary novelty and ancient customary laws.

The idea was already apparent among the men in charge of drawing up the Code, who would constitute the main working and editing group. The central figure was Portalis, one of the most distinguished barristers in the Aix-en–Provence parlement before 1789, an *ancien régime* jurist who had kept himself apart from the Revolution, and made his appearance only with the constitution of Year III; having returned to public affairs after Brumaire, he was one of the authorities of the Council of State. With him were Tronchet, who had defended Louis XVI, Bigot-Préameneu and Maleville, who had also learnt and practised the civil law of ancient customs and royal decrees.

At last, they were about to start work on realizing the old idea of unifying and setting customary law down in writing. At the same time, their action caused the re-emergence of the spirit of Montesquieu and a tradition of jurisprudence which had largely disappeared from view. But specialists from the revolutionary assemblies were also involved with the preparatory work on the Code, including former Jacobins like Cambacérès and Treilhard. In this way the homoeopathic synthesis which was one of the First Consul's secrets took effect: moderating the French Revolution with a pinch of *ancien régime*.

He had no need to go against his own nature to work out the correct balance. For, although the ultimate aim of his internal policy was to translate the principles of 1789 into laws, the basis of his temperament and upbringing was Corsican, patriarchal, inflexible over paternal authority, woman's subordination, and the primordial nature of the family and good morals. He was too aware of the new realities to refuse divorce, for that would be to reopen the door to Catholic Church authority over society, but he was sufficiently attached to the central value of marriage within the social order to make its dissolution less simple than by the will of the parties concerned. He frequently participated in discussion on the principles and the text, to which he attached extreme importance: the future Code was one of the great instruments of national reconciliation.

As it was promulgated in 1804, it affirmed the unity of a civil law applicable to the entire nation, and the state as the unique source of this law; but it left magistrates a certain latitude in the application of the general maxims, thus reintroducing the idea of jurisprudence into the Revolution's legicentric passion. Besides, the articles were often the result of digesting customary law, to the advantage of Parisian custom, which even before 1789 was the most widespread.

With regard to ownership of property, the drafters hardly had anything but land in view, and it was chiefly a matter of establishing the liquidation of seigneurial property. In these articles, which have so often been read anachronistically as heralding a capitalist economy, a rural France is confirming its rights; a France both bourgeois and peasant, which had emerged from a very long history, and was now liberated from the humiliating, costly and useless yoke of the seigneurs. There was no longer any distinction between lands and properties, which their possessors could enjoy and make use of 'in the most absolute manner'. Fifteen years after the great burgeoning of ideas in 1789, when the new France made its appearance amid the establishment of its interests, a nation of property-owning peasants fixed for ever their rights over the land. At the same time, it confirmed all that had been acquired between 1789 and 1792: a society of individuals, freedom of consciences, contracts and work, and the secularism of the state.

However, between 1789 and the Consulate, political evolution was reflected in a certain number of the articles drafted, which also illustrated the new civil law's slight shift towards conservatism: notably as regards the family. Divorce was retained, but kept within stricter limits. Paternal authority, called into question by the Convention, was reaffirmed; the *patria potestas* inherited from Roman law was restored, but limited to the age of majority and it was no longer permissible to disinherit a child by way of punishment. A natural child lost its right to be a full heir. Adoption remained possible, but that too was limited: the adopting person had to be childless and past the age of marriage.

Women were the principal victims of the Code's legislators, spurred on by the First Consul, who was very 'Mediterranean' in this respect: in his comments, he continualy insisted on the wife's subordination to her husband, which was essential to social order and was a part of the natural weakness of women. The latter were hit by not being allowed any part in the administration of household possessions, rendered dependent in everything concerning administrative or judicial acts, placed under the guardianship of their husbands, to whom they were inferior in rights in cases of both adultery and divorce. The equality of the sexes, proclaimed if not practised by the Convention, was denied by the Code Napoléon.

In the matter of equality of succession, the First Consul's jurists also reinterpreted the unconditional egalitarianism which had linked 1789 and 1793, in order to take into account the diversity of the old France's customs, and to give the head of the family the possibility of favouring an heir. This was an old peasant practice in written law in the French Midi, intended to maintain the continuity of farming businesses. The freedom given to testatory right, as also the coexistence of the dowry and communal estate systems, allowed a clever reconciliation of diverse and incompatible traditions according to the country's regions.

Such was the famous Code – a compromise between the spirit of enlightened despotism and the legacy of the ideas of 1789. The pride of the regime and of Napoleon, this symbol of the new France in Europe and the world was destined to have many imitators. It adjusted the law to the state of minds and morals, thereby rediscovering Montesquieu, whom it reconciled with the dominant rationalism. Basically the First Consul would always make it the monument of his fundamental treaty with the French, whom he understood so well.

The creation of the *Légion d'Honneur* (1802), intended to reward the good servants of the state, did not reinstate inequality; it simply honoured the best in equal competition. The idea of 'national morality', to which the law must be adapted, was so powerful in Napoleon's mind that it explained, a little later (1808), the way in which he treated French Jews, withdrawing from the principles of the Constituent Assembly. In his eyes, the Mosaic particularism of the Askenazim in Alsace was so contrary to French equality and civil unity that he subjected them to special legislation, chiefly in commercial matters, despite recognition by a solemn Assembly – the Grand Sanhedrin – of civil marriage and religious practices controlled by the state, like those of other beliefs.

Like the structures of the administrative state, the Code Napoléon is the Consulate's lasting legacy to modern France. In the two centuries which separate us from it, and most particularly during the course of the nineteenth century, political regimes would change, monarchies, Republics and even another Empire would come and go, but the country would not change its entire foundation, as it had in 1789; it had received its administrative institutions and the decisive features of its law for a long time to come.

The price paid for this national establishment of the principles of 1789 was the disappearance of a representative government, subject to the free choice of the citizens. Bonaparte had invaded the whole political theatre, and occupied it entirely on his own. The democracy of notables, both great and small, which emerged from the Revolution, had rebuilt a *de facto* monarchy, infinitely more powerful and despotic than the old one, since there was no longer any intermediary body to oppose its domination over equal individuals. In these first few years of the nineteenth century, it is easier than at any other time in our history to understand that equality had been the Revolution's ruling passion; and that Bonaparte reigned over France by embodying that alone.

Prisoners of the unforgettable memory of the popular dictatorship of Year II and of the European war, why would the French fear a strong man, if that man was born of their own history? In this sense, despite appearances, there had never been a less military *coup* than Brumaire; there had never been a more civil power than the consular dictatorship of the General-in-Chief of Italy and Egypt, since it was the profound movement of the whole of society which assured him of the conditions for his success and guaranteed for the future his reform of the state.

This national awareness, just as much as personal interests, explains the revolutionary personnel's general support for the Consulate: although the list of émigrés had been declared at an end some months after Brumaire, and Bonaparte had appointed several returned nobles to his administration or given some bishoprics to former refractory prelates, the framework of consular France was secured by men who had served successively and faithfully, like the First Consul himself, the 1791 regime, the dictatorship of the Committee of Public Safety and Robespierre, and Barras's Republic. Where political moralists denounce successive betrayals, here by contrast a fundamental loyalty to the struggle of revolutionary France is revealed.

Only a handful of liberal intellectuals or democratic Jacobins sulked over the Bonaparte of the Consulate; but the men of 1789 and 1793 filled the Council of State: Cambacérès, Roederer, Regnault de Saint-Jean-d'Angély, Boulay de la Meurthe, Antoine Thibaudeau, Treilhard. Bonaparte's ministers: Talleyrand, Carnot, Chaptal and Fouché came from the Constituent Assembly, the Convention, the Committee of Public Safety and the Terror. Since Year II, the army had been, *par excellence*, the body which enjoyed democratic promotion by ability; even the episcopacy, since the Concordat, had been almost completely renewed, as Bonaparte retained only sixteen pre-Revolution prelates.

What was true of the great state careers was probably even more so among the lesser ones, and more clear-cut the line which led the former militant of the Terror to a police commissariat, a sub-prefecture or a minor military rank. The Consulate's great internal strength lay in the fact that careers had been laid open to those with ability, and that Bonaparte was both its symbol and guarantor: it was the paradox of the little Corsican noble who, by the roundabout path of war, had become king of a property-owning France, proud of its state and its army.

TOWARDS THE EMPIRE

Rather than king, he was the precarious sovereign of a political situation, the new Caesar, without legitimacy and without a foreseeable heir, at the mercy of an assassin. He himself said so to his secretary, revealing that stay-at-home facet so surprising in an adventurous man, on that evening in February 1800 when he was moving to the Tuileries, leaving the Luxembourg of the ex-Directors: 'Bourrienne, getting into the Tuileries is not everything; I have to *stay* there.'

Moreover, the legitimate pretender to the throne had been very swift to demand his dues: from his distant Courland, where he had been forced to take refuge, the Comte de Provence had twice urged him to be his General Monk and to prepare the way for his restoration. Bonaparte had taken his time and replied only after Marengo, in September: 'Sir, I have received your letter, and thank you for the courteous things you say. You should not seek to return to France; you would have to walk over one hundred thousand corpses. Sacrifice your interests for the sake of France's peace and happiness. History will take account of your action.' And at the end he added these two sentences, in which can be seen both the habit he had already acquired of speaking as a sovereign, and the unbridgeable gulf which separated him from royalism: 'I am not insensitive to your family misfortunes. I will contribute with pleasure to the pleasantness and tranquillity of your retirement.' In private, as usual he employed a more military turn of phrase: 'The king is in Mitau – let him stay there!'

Brumaire's fundamental pact would therefore not be betrayed; but the first royalist response only narrowly missed the First Consul: that was the bomb explosion in December. However, excluding a royalist restoration was not enough to define the future of the consular regime, which was raising many queries. Before Marengo, a possible replacement had been sought; since then, questions were being asked about a successor. Each group, each clan, busied itself around the sphinx: who was to come after?

Very soon, the ten years promised to him by the Acts of Year VIII had seemed rather absurdly temporary, for a man who was so young and had so quickly become sovereign. The old idea of hereditary power inevitably reappeared under the new incarnation of the state. But what was the solution? Josephine was unable to give him an heir; she knew only that she must oppose the ambitions of the Bonaparte clan – and Joseph and Lucien, her old enemies, who wanted to take all the credit for themselves and be written in at the top of the will. But Lucien unmasked his guns too soon and had to leave the Ministry of the Interior for the embassy in Madrid. Bonaparte was not in too much of a hurry for talk of his succession: at thirty, without children or any hope of having any, why should he go and tie up his future with some ambitious man, creating his own rival? For one person chosen, how many malcontents would he make?

If he had no taste for contemplating his succession, he at least agreed to consolidate his power: less perhaps *vis-à-vis* the royalists, whose hostility he could not hope to break, than in relation to the rival ambitions of his army colleagues, the Bernadottes and the Moreaus. In that political society where his accession to supreme power had provoked among certain of his peers the inevitable 'Why not me?', the life Consulate accorded to him in August 1802 by the vote of three and a half million Frenchmen was an important grip on the future; he added to it the right to designate his successor.

This time, therefore, he was king of the Revolution – and of a Revolution so completely 'ended' that it abandoned even the shadow of an elective system: what was called the constitution of Year X reserved eligibility to a moneyed oligarchy, since the district assemblies, where everyone voted, would be compelled to choose the members of the *département* assembly from among the six hundred most highly taxed notables. This tightly *censitaire* college, elected for life, still only designated candidates to public or representative office, the choice being finally effected by the Senate or the First Consul himself. Thus, the institutional alterations of 1802, completed by the reduction of a somewhat recalcitrant Tribunate and the raising of a docile Senate, revealed the dual desire to create a stable government, to place it at the summit and to bind that government very closely to a property-owning society which had emerged from the Revolution. At bottom, the system was not so far removed from that imagined by Turgot, with his *municipalités*, or Necker, with his provincial assemblies; but in order to work, it would have needed the elimination of both the aristocracy and the king: notables to replace nobles, and a lifetime monarchy substituted for that of the Reims coronation.

It seemed, therefore, that in this lucky year of 1802 the contradictions of the French equation had finally been resolved by political consolidation of a recent society and a huge delegation of powers to the leader it had chosen. Internally, a real balance had been found. Once again, everything would depend on relations with Europe which brought to a climax the national adventure of France, henceforth dominated by yet another mystery, in the person of Bonaparte. It was not enough to end the Revolution on the inside: it still had to be brought to a close externally, which meant both defining its frontiers and getting them accepted by Europe. Was France able to? Did Napoleon want to? Was Europe ready for it? Would Britain give a lasting pledge? So many important questions, to which facts gave a negative reply, for war resumed in 1803. But they still divide historians: as always, it is easier to untangle the elements of Franco-British and Franco-European strife than to formulate a general interpretation of the conflict or to throw light upon the personality of its principal hero.

These elements are well known: Lunéville had brought back and aggravated the problems arising from Campo Formio, and the peace of Amiens (1802) had been signed, on both sides, only as a compromise without any true settlement. At no time, and on neither side, had there been any temptation to bring about a lasting coexistence between the revolutionary 'great nation' and the rest of Europe. Bonaparte made Britain unhappy by his wish to protect French space by customs barriers, and by resuming a colonial policy in Santo Domingo, Louisiana and even in India; he irritated the whole of Europe by developing the Thermidorian policy of sister republics in Holland, Switzerland and Italy: in 1802, he had himself elected President of the new Italian Republic, and kept tight control over the Batavian Republic and the Swiss Confederation.

The reorganization, to his advantage, of the German states, by the ordinance of 1803, foretold the liquidation of the old Germanic Roman Empire and of Habsburg influence. But the *casus belli* of 1803 was the Mediterranean problem: contrary to its undertakings of the preceding year, Britain refused to evacuate Malta; France retaliated by maintaining its garrisons in Naples and the ports of the Papal States. In short, there was a kind of mutual agreement to a break, which took place on 12 May 1803, when Britain recalled its ambassador in Paris. It was the start of the second Napoleonic venture.

But the first, which had brought him from his victories in Italy right to the Tuileries, came to a close only in 1804, since the war continued to determine French internal policy: it was the resumption of the war that influenced the last metamorphosis of Bonaparte's power, by inevitably reviving worries about his succession. Not only did war reawake the image of a leader vulnerable to the hazards of battle, but it also automatically cast doubt – as in 1792, in Year III and on the eve of Brumaire – on the entire revolutionary experience: it was therefore necessary to consolidate both, leader and Revolution, by pursuing the logic of a life Consulate to its very end, that is to say, by hereditary power.

For their part, the enemies of the French Revolution understood this logic, and put it into practice: the European courts still had an eye on Mitau, where Provence had given up none of his legitimate rights; Britain had gathered up Artois and his *chouan* killers who had escaped the 1801 net. In August 1803, it got Georges Cadoudal and his men to cross the Straits of Dover, with the mission of assassinating Bonaparte: British interests and royalist fanaticism had not had much difficulty in thinking up this thrifty way of putting an end to both the war and the Revolution. General Pichegru, deported as a royalist after 18 Fructidor, having escaped from Guiana and taken refuge in England, was brought into the plot; Moreau, the old rival, refused to commit himself to it when he was informed. His silence nevertheless indicated that Bonaparte's assassination was not, in France, merely a royalist idea, and that several republican generals were ready to lend an indulgent ear. But an informer revealed the plot to the police and everyone was put under lock and key in March 1804. Pichegru committed suicide in prison, Moreau was banished; Cadoudal and his accomplices were executed.

During the interrogation, one of the plotters revealed that the signal for the attempt was to have been the presence on French soil of a prince of Bourbon blood. Bonaparte had the ports watched, looking for the Comte d'Artois. But in vain. It was then that Fouché informed him of the presence of the son of the last Condé, the Duc d'Enghien, in the town of Baden, some kilometres from the Rhine; simply on the assumptions of the police, which in any case were imaginary, he had him arrested in a foreign country, brought to Paris, tried and shot forthwith at dawn on 21 March in the ditches of Vincennes. Bonaparte always claimed full and complete responsibility for this crime of state, which had been suggested to him by Fouché and in which others saw the hand of Talleyrand.

Even if he had been afraid, if he had retaliated like a man who has sensed assassins prowling about him, he explained the Duc d'Enghien's execution as a public safety measure, 'quite simply because blood-letting is one of the devices of political medicine'. He never repudiated his comment of 21 March: 'Those people wanted to sow disorder in France and kill the Revolution in my person; I had to defend and avenge it. I showed what it was capable of.' Why should we doubt these reasons of state? They express the same reasoning as that of the assassins: regicide. Fouché's way of thinking, certainly, since 1793, but also Bonaparte's – and now he had his 21 January: he also had shed Bourbon blood, and by resuming on his own account the collective action of the Convention, he had invested his authority with the irreversible sacrament of the Revolution. The likelihood of a compromise between himself and the *ancien régime*, between himself and the Europe of the kings, was weaker than ever.

In fact, Bonaparte was thinking of taking the step from which even Cromwell had recoiled: making himself king. In the spring of 1803, through Talleyrand and the intermediary of Prussia, he had made approaches with the aim of obtaining from the Comte de Provence the renunciation of his rights to the throne. And it was just after the failure – only to be expected – of this exploratory tactic, that he asked the Minister of the Interior to plan the erection of a statue of Charlemagne in the Place Vendôme. He was already striding across the fallen dynasty, to the glory of the one which had preceded it.

The Duc d'Enghien's execution provided the opportunity. Eight days after the Vincennes shooting, there came the Senate's first indication in favour of the right of inheritance, and the Tribunate – by now duly brought to heel – followed suit. The discussion had begun in the Council of State, and the First Consul had not concealed his designs. On 22 Germinal (12 April 1804), in a conversation with Joseph, he confessed that he had 'always intended to end the Revolution by the establishment of the right of inheritance'.[11] This return to the past in order to guarantee the future offered several advantages. For right of inheritance, by fixing the manner of access to supreme authority, did away with a lacuna in the constitution of Year VIII. Although internally it founded a Bonapartist dynasty, this traditional method of transmitting power also weakened the very reasons for external threat, both royalist and terrorist. Yet on the other hand, it abandoned all reference to the Republic and the sovereignty of the people. At the very time when he was farthest from the kings of old Europe, Bonaparte wanted to found his domination on their principle. Therein lay the strangeness of the plan, and of the coronation, by which he distanced himself from the Revolution without drawing any nearer to the kings.

What was more, the problem was not simple from a technical viewpoint. The Consul had no children, or the hope of having any. He was not the eldest son, so there was no sense in instituting a rule of primogeniture; besides, any collateral succession presupposed a common predecessor, who did not exist. Hence arose family warfare with Joseph, his elder brother, to whom Napoleon preferred Louis, one of his three younger brothers, who was married to Josephine's daughter Hortense, through whom the hated Beauharnais yet again appeared among the Bonapartes. In the end, the future sovereign arranged to be given the right to adopt a successor, in default of which Joseph, then Louis, would be able to claim the crown. Lucien had been cast aside because of a marriage disapproved of by Napoleon. The principle of right of inheritance was therefore badly handled from the start, and in the right to choose a successor, Madame de Staël would soon denounce an oriental-style despotism.[12] In the Tribunate, Carnot voted against Curée's motion on the right of inheritance, declaiming against the risk represented by the desire to perpetuate a temporary dictatorship; he recalled the example of Caesar.

To tell the truth, the reactions of political people were mixed. If one takes into account the general climate of flattery which reigned in the Tuileries, they were often unenthusiastic. Miot de Mélito, Councillor of State from 1803 to 1806, whose wife was lady-in-waiting in Joseph's household, gives a melancholy assessment in his memoirs: 'So much blood spilt, so many fortunes destroyed, so many sacrifices . . . will have come to nothing more than giving us a change of master, substituting a family which was unknown ten years ago and was scarcely French at the time when the Revolution began, for a family which had reigned over France for eight centuries!'[13] Even in the heart of the army, feelings were also tormented. Roederer, who had followed the affair very closely, mediating between the First Consul and Joseph, noted in his journal that, among the troops he visited in Metz during June, there were 'feelings of repugnance towards emperorship':

[11] Miot de Mélito, *Mémoires*, vol. 2, p. 176.
[12] Madame de Staël, *Dix années d'exil*, part I, ch. 18.
[13] Miot de Mélito, *Mémoires*, vol. 2, p. 171.

People are humiliated to have gone the full circle of the Revolution just to come back to the same system; or to what is seen as the same system; people are ashamed to disavow what they have done and said against royalty and to forswear the attachment they had professed so strongly and in such good faith under the Republic. Therefore, it is not an aversion to the supreme dignity which torments us; it is the humiliation of admitting the aversion we have shown towards it, of calling it false and hypocritical, or absurd and contemptible, after showing such zest and enthusiasm.[14]

Nevertheless, the matter went forward quickly, since Napoleon wanted it. And on the whole, the Revolution's personnel followed, Roederer at the forefront. The Tribunate had therefore asked at the beginning of May that the title 'Hereditary Emperor of the French' be conferred on him. A new modification of the institutions, proposed by the *senatus consultum* of 18 May 1804, was ratified by an even more massive plebiscite than that of Year VIII, since fewer than ten thousand 'no' votes were counted. This was the last republican homage to what was a fourth dynasty, after the Merovingians, the Carolingians and the Capetians, which belonged to another political world.

THE CORONATION

The proof: the new emperor wanted a coronation. He harboured an idea which is often found even in liberal monarchic literature – Burke or Necker, for example – according to which power must be inseparable from an imposing apparatus of majesty, making a great impression on the people's imagination. The coronation must make a display of this splendour, by which Napoleon abandoned the universe of Washington to try to bring back to life the tradition of the kings: nothing less than to form a link with Charlemagne once more, since the Capetians had been excluded in 1789 from their history with the nation. The emperor himself explained this to Roederer after the stormy meeting of the Brumaire private Council, still in connection with Joseph's rights:

I have raised myself up by my actions, he has stayed at the point where birth placed him. To reign in France, one must be born in grandeur, have been seen from childhood in a palace with guards, or else be a man who is capable of standing out from all the others . . . Right of inheritance, if it is to be successful, must pass to children born in the bosom of greatness.

This gave rise to all that re-establishment of court life which accompanied coronation year, the creation of imperial 'houses', the rebirth of an aristocracy modelled on the old one, with precedences, distinctions

[14] P.-L. Roederer, *Autour de Bonaparte. Journal. Notes intimes et politiques d'un familier des Tuileries* (1909), p. 197.

and a ridiculous determination to rediscover the secrets of the etiquette surrounding kings. As recorded by Pelet de la Lozère:

'An old gentleman, a former page to the King was summoned from the provinces to impart the traditions of Versailles. His arrival in the Tuileries salon was a real event. Except at the theatre, it was a long time since anyone had seen personages from the old court, with their powdered and curled hair, and their frivolous, self-important airs; this gentleman appeared like an oracle who was going to reveal the secrets of past ages and, as they say, rejoin the links with the past. With his help, it was possible to rediscover the laws of ancient etiquette and to compile a volume of them as hefty as that of the Civil Code.'[15]

The coronation ceremony took place in Notre-Dame, on 11 Frimaire Year XIII (2 December 1804). Since the private Council of 3 Floréal (23 April), which had fixed the coronation date for 14 July,[16] and the *senatus consultum* of 28 Floréal (18 May), which fixed the oath to the people during the two years following the emperor's accession, the date and place of the ceremony had changed several times: 14 July, 27 Thermidor (15 August, Napoleon's birthday), 18 Brumaire (9 November); Champ de Mars, church of the Invalides were the dates and places suggested during the six months between the proclamation of the Empire and its celebration. The detailed history of these discussions illustrates very well the meaning which it was desired to attach to the coronation in relation to memories of the Revolution, new democratic legality and the civil authority of the state in the face of the Church of Rome's religious authority. In fact, these discussions intertwined with the diplomatic negotiations which had been opened with the Vatican to persuade the pope to attend the ceremony. At first somewhat reticent, as it wanted guarantees, then favourable, though on very precise conditions, the papal court strewed the negotiations with uncertainties to a point where it unleashed a sort of ultimatum from the French. The result of these laborious discussions would be a very strange, absolutely unique, ceremonial: Napoleon's coronation had no precedent and would have no imitators.

Things went the same way regarding the place. The choice of Notre-Dame was belated. It won the day over the church of Saint-Louis des Invalides, originally proposed by the decree of 21 Messidor (10 July), for practical reasons such as the amount of space available, but also for symbolic reasons, such as its 'more august nature, more suitable for surrounding the ceremony with a sort of divine respect'.[17] But at the start, the idea had been to use the Champ de Mars. Discussed in the Council of State, defended by Regnault de Saint-Jean-d'Angély, this proposal was strongly rejected by the emperor:

[15] Pelet de la Lozère, *Opinions de Napoléon sur divers sujets de politique et d'administration, recueillies par un membre de son Conseil d'État*, p. 69.
[16] Miot de Mélito, *Mémoires*, vol. 2, p. 183.
[17] Pelet de la Lozère, *Opinions*, p. 89.

Jacques Louis David The Coronation of Napoleon I *1806–1807, Musée du Louvre, Paris.* (*Photo: Lauros-Giraudon*)

The Champ de Mars was thought of as a reminder of the Federation, but times have changed: then the people were sovereign, everything had to be done before their eyes: let us be careful not to let them think things are still the same. The people today are represented by legal powers. In any case, I should not like to think that I was seeing the people of Paris, still less the people of France, in twenty or thirty thousand fishwives, or others of that ilk, who would invade the Champ de Mars: they would just be the ignorant and corrupt populace of a large town. The real people, in France, are the presidents of the cantons, and of the electoral colleges; they are the army, in whose ranks are soldiers from every commune in France![18]

As for the setting, planned by the architects Percier and Fontaine, the work inside the cathedral organized space around two centres. On the one hand, the chancel, blocked off by a dais, and on the other, the great imperial throne, at the entry to the nave. This division of the places matched the two parts of the ceremony. The first, essentially religious, which joined the consecration with the crowning according to the pope's wishes, would take place in the cathedral chancel. To the left of the altar, which was reached by eleven steps, the pope's throne was installed. The cardinals took their places on the right. On either side of the chancel were the archbishops, bishops and clergy of Paris. In the middle were the chairs, cushions and prie-dieu for the emperor and his wife, who was playing a leading part in the rite despite the grumbles of the Corsican tribe. The second part of the ceremony, secular and constitutional, would take place at the other end of the church, at the entrance to the great nave. There the grand throne was situated, at the summit of a stairway of twenty-four steps, under a triumphal arch decorated with eagles and hung with red velvet drapery. The Paris cathedral was decked out in the taste of the day, a Greek temple to celebrate the new Alexander.

Apart and opposite to each other, the two spaces were linked, so to speak, by the continuity of the nave, where six thousand invited guests had their places. Starting from the emperor's great throne, on both sides down the steps were ranged ministers, high officials, Councillors of State and presidents of the Legislative Body and the Tribunate. The hierarchy of the Empire in its entirety was seated in descending order of dignity as one approached the altar. Near the great throne, therefore, were senators, legislators, tribunes, members of the Appeal Court, great officers of the Légion d'Honneur, in short, all the constituted authorities, both national and provincial. Raised platforms, to right and left of the throne, were reserved – according to *ancien régime* custom – for high-ranking guests, members of the court and the diplomatic service.

Invited by sealed letter to attend the coronation ('Divine providence and the constitution of the Empire, having placed the imperial dignity in our family...'), the arrival of the guests in the cathedral marked the commencement of the solemn function. But the real start of the ceremony

[18] Ibid.

was tied to the arrival of the pope. According to protocol, Pius VII would have to leave the Tuileries where he was staying in the Pavillon de Flore, at nine in the morning. After being welcomed in rather cavalier fashion by the emperor who, while hunting at Fontainebleau, had feigned a chance meeting, Pius VII continued to be the object of a protocol intended to limit his symbolic importance. It had thus been decided that he would arrive at Notre-Dame ahead of Napoleon. But outside the cathedral, on the Seine side, Percier and Fontaine had erected a wooden gallery, decorated with eagles with spread wings, in order to link the archbishop's palace to the church.

Pius VII would first be received by the archbishop of Paris, then in the great hall of the palace he would don his papal vestments. The first diminution of his splendour: using the pretext of the narrowness of the gallery along which he would have to pass to reach the church, French diplomats had persuaded the pope to give up the use of the *sedia gestatoria* borne by twelve grooms in red damask. Thus Pius VII made his entrance under a white canopy, but on foot. He was preceded by the bishops, wearing their mitres, and arranged by order of their canonical institution by the pope, and not according to the order of their consecration following their appointment by the temporal sovereign, as the emperor would have liked.

Napoleon's arrival was planned to be one hour after that of the pope. But on the appointed day, the wait was much longer – which compounded the Vatican's grievances. Accompanied by Josephine, Napoleon was late in getting to the archbishop's palace, where he donned the coronation robes. This costume, established by decree on 29 Messidor (18 July), was composed of a crimson velvet robe, scattered with golden bees; sprays of olive, laurel and oak were embroidered around the letter N. The long mantle, lined with ermine, was to be the sign of the unique power and extraordinary pre-eminence of the emperor over all the other princes in the family and the great dignitaries of the Empire. Indeed, some weeks before the coronation, Napoleon had ordered that no one but he should wear a long cloak.[19]

Heaven knows how full the cathedral of Paris was that day of princes and dignitaries of the new Empire! Their titles commingled the tradition of the old French monarchy and the grandeur of the Holy Roman Empire. There was a Grand Elector, Joseph; an Arch-Chancellor, Cambacérès; an Arch-Treasurer, Lebrun; also a Constable, Louis; a Grand Admiral, Murat; a Grand Equerry, Armand de Caulaincourt; and a Grand Chamberlain, Talleyrand – not to mention all those Marshals of France, who were most devoted to Republican principles but who bore the title Monseigneur in order to ensure that the imperial divinity had the title Majesty, as Napoleon explained it to Roederer. Nevertheless on that day none of them had the right to wear a long cloak.

[19] Miot de Mélito, *Mémoires*, vol. 2, p. 234.

The allocation of places and roles had of course been the subject of bitter arguments over precedence, whereby the France of Napoleon I reanimated, with a different public, that of Louis XIV. The most violent disputes had brought the women of the family into opposition, the Bonapartes and the Beauharnais. The sisters, Elisa, Pauline and Caroline, were in a permanent rage about the place given to Josephine. They finally agreed to carry the never-ending train (23 metres!) of the empress's cloak only on condition that they should merely 'hold it up', and that they too should have attendants for their own 'train'.

The emperor's crimson mantle, open on the left side, revealed the sword, supported by a white satin scarf embroidered in gold. Napoleon thus made his entrance already wearing the symbols of power. The golden crown of laurel on his head, the sceptre in his right hand and the hand of justice in his left, indicated that he already possessed full sovereignty. This was a remarkable innovation in comparison with the tradition of the royal coronation – from which many ceremonies had been omitted, such as the 'lever du roi', and the old ritual preceding arrival in the church, when the king had to appear clad in a simple tunic and totally divested of the emblems of power. This ritual simplification revealed the desire to expunge all trace of ecclesiastical investiture from the imperial coronation. It also indicated the amount of liberty taken in regard to the historic tradition of the Capetian monarchy.

The visual symbol of the dual historical reference which the Empire had chosen, Clovis and Charlemagne dominated the triumphal arch in which the wooden gallery ended, and which concealed Notre-Dame's portal on the forecourt side. The arch was overhung with the emperor's arms and the figures of the sixteen cohorts of the Légion d'Honneur: a sign that military synthesis joined the founder of a dynasty with the 'philosopher prince, legislator, patriot and conqueror'.

A legacy of the republican interpretation of Mably, Charlemagne lent himself perfectly to the Empire's political plan, offering it an inaugural link. He allowed the new monarchy to be defined by bestowing on it a past which was not the detested *ancien régime*, but a venerable tradition which eighteenth-century philosophy had elaborated. Napoleon had for some time had an eye on this tradition, because he had intended to erect a statue of Charlemagne on the column in the Place Vendôme; in the months preceding the coronation, he had ordered medieval relics of his great predecessor to be collected, and he had gone to meditate on the tomb at Aix-la-Chapelle.

On the day of the coronation, the protocol planned for great splendour to surround the insignia representing the 'honours of Charlemagne'. There was a golden crown, fashioned in accordance with old designs, and held by Kellermann; a sword, carried by Lefebvre; a sceptre, by Pérignon. Napoleon's 'honours', which were entrusted to Bernadotte, Eugène de Beauharnais (Napoleon's stepson) and Berthier, included an object unprecedented in the coronation of former kings: an imperial globe, to evoke

Ingres' portrait of Napoléon, *Musée de l'Armée, Paris.*
(Photo: Roger-Viollet)

the Holy Roman Empire. When the emperor arrived in the cathedral, the Marshals carried the 'honours' to the altar, where they laid them down; then they stood just opposite, where they can still be seen, immortalized in David's painting of the event.

Did the idea of a universal monarchy also enter into this Carolingian kitsch through which Napoleon was showing that he belonged to nobody but himself? At all events, the other dominating feature of the ceremony was the limiting of the role of the Roman pontiff. The emperor had wished him to be present at the coronation, in order to receive the unction at his august hands, but also to have him there at Napoleon's triumph in a subordinate position.

By going to the altar on his own, he did not subject himself to the pope's traditional admonition to the sovereign. In response to the ritual inter-rogation, everything had been cut out of his profession of faith as a Christian sovereign concerning the promise to maintain the Church's possession of goods which it no longer had: this concession was agreed by the Holy Father on condition that he was not obliged to be present at the swearing of the constitutional oath which was to follow the religious ceremony. After the profession of imperial faith ('Profiteor', Napoleon said quite simply) came the prayers, the pope kneeling, his mitre on his head, the emperor and Josephine remaining seated on the small thrones; then the sovereign couple received the triple unction.

At that point the solemn mass began, during which the insignia were blessed – hand of justice, ring and sceptre – and the coronation, properly speaking. Napoleon ascended to the altar, took the crown and placed it on his own head. Then, he took the empress's crown, stood before her and put it on her head; meanwhile the pope recited the prayer used by the archbishop of Reims at the coronation of the kings of France. The suggestion that this was an improvised action (an idea substantiated by Adolphe Thiers and the Comte d'Haussonville in the nineteenth century) is incorrect: Pius VII had agreed to it beforehand on the eve of the ceremony. The Minister of the Interior, Champagny, had impressed upon him that

the emperor also wants to take up the crown in order to avoid any argument between the great dignitaries of the Empire, who would claim to be giving it to him in the name of the people. He thinks that His Holiness blessing the crown and saying a prayer while the emperor places it on his head will be considered an adequate fulfilment of the ancient ceremonial.

Thus crowned, the imperial couple, surrounded by princes, dignitaries, and the grand officers carrying the insignia of the emperor and of Charlemagne, left the chancel for the cathedral entrance, where the great throne was situated. The pope rejoined Napoleon there and enthroned him, using the Reims formula. Then he returned towards the altar, amid *vivats*, and intoned the Te Deum, before the end of the Mass: this was a fundamental detail, and for once a concession from the emperor, for it allowed him to make his departure once the Mass was over and not to be present for the constitutional oath which was to close the ceremony. But beforehand he would have to accept a final infringement of the religious element: the written record of the coronation makes no allusion whatsoever to the communion of the emperor and his wife. In fact, after at first accepting the idea of taking the sacrament, at the last moment Napoleon had insisted on being excused from it: this was an exorbitant demand, which incidentally cancelled the religious value of the unctions, but which Pius VII had had to accept.

The Mass ended, the pope left the cathedral. He removed his vestments in the sacristy, while preparation was made to celebrate the secular part of the inaugural rite. The constitutional oath took place around the great throne. The Grand Almoner brought the gospel to the emperor. The Grand Elector, Prince Joseph, who in the end had yielded to his brother's will, presented to him the president of the Senate (Neufchâteau), the most senior president of the Council of State (Defermon), the president of the Legislative Body (Louis de Fontanes) and the president of the Tribunate (Fabre de l'Aude). They placed the form of oath before the emperor, then lined up to the left of the throne. Napoleon, wearing the crown, his hand raised over the gospel, took the oath while seated. He swore

to maintain the integrity of the Republic's territory, to respect, and cause to be respected, the laws of the Concordat and the freedom of worship, equality of rights, civil and political liberty, the irrevocability of the sales of *biens nationaux*; neither to levy nor to introduce any tax, except in accordance with the law; to maintain the institution of the Légion d'Honneur; to govern with the sole aim of the interests, happiness and glory of the French people.

It was a promise to end the Revolution without betraying its heritage.

Fresh acclamations were followed by an artillery salvo. The clergy came back to the throne with the canopy to conduct the sovereigns to the archbishop's palace once more. Then the emperor's procession, followed by the pope's, went through the streets of Paris. The itinerary led to the Châtelet across the Pont au Change, then to the boulevards and the Place de la Concorde. Michelet, who was six years old, was among the crowd. Fifty years later, in his volumes on *L'Histoire du XIXe siècle*, he recollected having noticed nothing on that day other than a 'mournful and dismal silence'.

THE NEW ORDER

From that point begins a history which cannot be separated from what went before, because the same man fills its entire space; yet it is quite distinct, both at home and abroad. One can understand this watershed, starting from the coronation ceremony, which provides an excellent symbol. Napoleon I was no longer the king for life of the French Republic, as he had been since 1800, but was now hereditary absolute sovereign, surrounded by a court and soon by a new aristocracy. The emperor had a foreign policy which less and less could be defined in terms of revolutionary heritage or even national tradition. In the Carolingian myth lies the mystery of great conquerors and nothing else, so that a large part of that extraordinary life belonged just as much, if not more, to the memory of Europe as to that of France. Everything lasting – or almost everything – that Bonaparte did in national history had been accomplished between 1800 and 1804. Nothing of all his upheaval of frontiers and the country's international situation survived his fall. When he came to grief in 1814, the Bourbons found the same territory belonging to the kingdom that they had left a quarter of a century before.

Let us start the inventory from the inside. Madame de Staël had described the Empire as a despotism which was 'oriental and Carolingian both together', operating a counter-revolution. She meant it firstly in the political sense, to depict the authority's autocratic nature, the generalized police surveillance, the meticulous check kept on opinion and the ever-increasing numbers of 'prisoners of state': after all, liberty was also part of the promises of 1789. But she meant, too, that

Bonaparte conceived the idea of making the counter-revolution work to his own advantage, by preserving nothing new in the state, so to speak, apart from himself. He re-established the throne, the clergy and the nobility: a monarchy, but without legitimacy and without limit; a clergy who preached nothing but despotism; a nobility made up of old and new families, but who had no authority in the state, and served merely as an ornament to the absolute power.[20]

In short, in this return of 'old prejudices', Madame de Staël saw the *ancien régime* being restored by the man who had been the Revolution's most brilliant soldier.

Was she right? No, not entirely. For even amid the Carolingian bric-à-brac of the coronation, the civil ceremony and the swearing of the oath of fidelity to the great conquests of 1789 had survived. The emperor had guaranteed the civil and political liberty of the French; he kept only the first part of the undertaking (in any case, who could have nurtured any illusions about the second?), but , in that part, he abandoned nothing vital. He remained the guarantor of the sold *biens nationaux*, and therefore of the despoilment of clergy and émigrés. He upheld the new civil right of free and equal individuals, recognized and organized minority religions (Protestant and Jewish), codified criminal investigation and criminal law. It is true that he re-established a court and increased pensions, distinctions and emoluments; but since none of these advantages included any legal privileges and were not hereditary, they sanctioned the new meritocracy, which was mostly military, to which they gave the character of public

[20] Madame de Staël, *Considérations sur la Révolution française*, part IV, ch. 11.

service. The dialectic of equality and status wove Napoleonic society together more closely than ever.

In fact, Madame de Staël's criticism is better applied to what the emperor became after 1808, the date of the *senatus consultum* which re-established a true nobility: a nobility of office, which he granted for services rendered, but hereditary, bound up with the great fiefs which he granted in his vassal states, or with *majorats*, domains which were trans-missible to the eldest son. His divorce from Josephine and the Habsburg marriage in 1810 accentuated the evolution towards the aristocratic spirit of the *ancien régime*. The court was increasingly filling up with former nobility. It was at this period that the emperor said to Mathieu Molé: 'Those doctrines which are called the principles of 1789 will always be a threatening weapon to be used by malcontents, the ambitious and ideol-ogists at any time.' Nevertheless, even during the years of his Austrian marriage, even after the birth of the King of Rome in 1811, Napoleon would never manage to give his Empire true dynastic legitimacy, guarded by a serving aristocracy. His domination over France retained, as its fundamental bases, the guarantee of the new civil law and military glory. It remained dependent on his victories. By making himself emperor, and even by marrying Marie-Louise, he had not gained entry into the family of the kings.

But had he really wanted to? What typifies Napoleon I's history between 1804 and 1814 is not what he did inside the country: the meeting, then the wedding, of the Corsican general with France had already been celebrated, and had already produced their fruits when the young chief of the consular Republic decided to become emperor. What began then – or rather, what had begun in 1803, when war with Britain had resumed – was his affair with Europe. It was perpetual, victorious war, impossible to halt, right up to the point of defeat. The venture of the great conqueror had definitively supplanted the founder of the modern French state; the authoritarian organizer of a nation of property-owners had given way to the emperor who wanted to redesign the history of the civilized world. The two personalities had always coexisted in Bonaparte, but the Carolingian Napoleon of the coronation revealed a sovereign who had become largely independent of the French Revolution. The Brumaire contract had been fulfilled; the emperor's destiny unfolded outside France, like an adventure without end.

Nevertheless, in this series of events, before speaking about him, the Revolution must still have its share. Napoleon had inherited from it a very large army, recruited by conscription, on the terms of Jourdan's law of 1798; as well-off young men could escape the military obligation by paying a replacement, this national army was largely a peasant army: Napoleon would take more than a million men from the French countryside. The fall in the birthrate, which manifested itself in the last decades of the eighteenth century, had not yet affected the age groups which could be called up. Viewed from this angle, the Empire's wars could appear to be supplementary employment offered to the numerous children of old rural France, and an indirect encouragement to wage rises, since there were fewer workers available. But there is less reason to conclude the demographic or economic 'necessity' since many other factors had simultaneously contributed to the reduction of French overpopulation: the drop in the number of children per family and the increase in peasant ownership through the purchase of *biens nationaux* must have led in this directon.

Still more, the economic revival and relative prosperity which marked the end of the Directory, and chiefly the 1800s: good harvests, return to metal coin, then to confidence, industrial and commercial revival, widening of offers of employment, rise in profits and wages. It would therefore seem difficult to think that post-revolutionary France should find itself in the economic impossibility of demobilizing its army and restoring several hundreds of thousands of soldiers to their civilian activities. Certainly, French ascendancy in Europe would not have been possible without the strong demographic growth of the eighteenth century; but the latter is not enough to explain the former.

In truth, reasons of another kind, but perhaps more decisive, contribute to an understanding of the realities and the dreams on which the France of this era fed its soldiers. The reality was social promotion: Napoleon himself was its symbol *par excellence*, the little Corsican officer who had become emperor and yet still remained the *Petit Caporal*, the imaginary brother of all those men whose wounds and battles mapped out their advancement, the abrupt departure from rural life in quest of adventure, the achievement of rank, sometimes even honours. Glory was also a career. Everything had begun with the volunteers of Year I and the *levée en masse*, and the framework of the army remained ensured by the heroes of the threatened Republic, who ten years afterwards had become young veterans. How could they envisage a future other than the very recent glory of the past. Neither 9 Thermidor nor 18 Brumaire nor even the coronation of 2 December had very deeply stirred this republican army, if it is true that the opposition of a Moreau or a Bernadotte to the Empire stemmed more from individual jealousy than from ideology. The soldiery had intervened in public life only on 18 Fructidor, precisely in order to rescue the threatened Republic. The other great internal ruptures in French political life had not put the army's future in doubt.

That future was not confined to an individual promotion, and this army – which was both the seed-bed and the crowning achievement of abilities – was not a professional army; it was the incarnation of the national dream, the great liberating nation struggling against the tyrants of the people. The transfer of French messianism to the army, which was as old as the revolutionary war itself, had become more pronounced in step with the dwindling of popular passions within France: it has been seen that, after Thermidor, the syndicate of regicides governing the Republic were all the more in favour of war since they had disarmed the Parisian faubourgs; they could not wrest the Terror away from the sansculottes unless they preserved for them at least the war with the Europe of the kings.

After Brumaire, in the vast silence of internal political life, the psychological and ideological attachment to the Republic as liberator of the people was invested in the former General-in-Chief of Italy, and it was not by chance that, in the first years of the Empire, there existed this dual designation of the state, 'French Republic. Emperor Napoleon'. Napoleon had not stopped being the great Republic's authorized representative. The hero of the international war was approved by a vast majority for the same reasons as the man of the civil peace; that powerful authority, that glorious dynasty, which together exorcised both the Terror and the return of the kings were, at the same time, conditions and symbols of the French mission in the world. Internally, France had made peace with the past. But it was still combating the *ancien régime* outside its frontiers.

Nevertheless, there is no doubt that French opinion had greeted Lunéville, then Amiens, with satisfaction; but at the cost of a misunderstanding. Because, for France, it was a matter of a victorious peace, that is to say, implicit recognition by Europe and England of the 'great nation' and its universal mission. Now, it looked as if nothing had changed; in December 1802, less than a year after the signing of the peace of Amiens, at the news that the Comte d'Artois, 'wearing an order of a monarchy which England no longer recognizes', had reviewed a regiment, Bonaparte asked Talleyrand to make representations in London

that it is a matter touching our dignity and, we make bold to say it, the honour of the British government that the princes should be expelled from England, or that, if it is desired to give them hospitality, they should not be allowed to wear any order of a monarchy which England no longer recognizes; that it is a permanent insult offered to the French people: that the time of tranquillity has come in Europe.

This 'tranquillity' was so little in evidence that, hardly had the war resumed, when Britain was paying assassins for the Bourbons against the usurper of Paris. This was what made Bonaparte say, on the morning of the Duc d'Enghien's execution: 'I will never consent to peace with England until it expels the Bourbons, as Louis XIV expelled the Stuarts, because their presence in England will always be dangerous for France.' What the First Consul was expressing in terms of dynasty – at bottom, in the same language as his assassins – was merely the translation of the popular conviction according to which there would never be peace between the liberating Republic and the oppressor kings. For peace continued to mean for everyone the return of the kings, and war meant the Republic's victory. In this sense, the Empire, built on a pyramid of notables, remained a peasant and democratic royalty: that would be very clear in the Hundred Days.

Although this war was democratized by a revolutionary ideology which mixed nationalism and universalism, if its ruthless nature arose from its being a conflict of values, the fact remains that it had other sources, from before and after the Revolution. Harking back, the Anglo-French conflict was age-old, marked by French losses at the Treaties of Utrecht (1713) and Paris (1763); economic and colonial rivalries had often roused public opinions against each other, and the sterile egoism of the London plutocracy was a physiocratic theme before becoming a revolutionary aphorism.

The British industrial revolution, which had taken off in the 1780s, had increased London's economic pressure on foreign markets; the political fears which the Revolution of 1789 had swiftly aroused had been reinforced by French expansion in Europe during the Directory years, and by the protectionist and colonial policy of the Consulate: a French Belgium, a 'Protected' Holland, western and Mediterranean Europe tied to French manufactures, the reconquest of Santo Domingo and the short-lived French aspirations in Louisiana – here were a number of factors which were unacceptable to British trade, even in the short term. If the peace of Amiens was broken on account of Malta, it was also because all that had weighed heavily in the side of the scale tipping towards war. The problem of colonial hegemony would quickly be solved, to Britain's advantage; but the stake of the European market would stay at the centre of the Anglo-French struggle, superimposed on the ideological war: a vast stake on the British side, because of its precocious industrial development and its trade structure, and certainly less on the French side, in that territorial domination of Europe did not appear as a necessity written into the still modest turnover of industrial production and national exports. The emperor's neo-Colbertist policy was more a consequence than a cause of his policy, pure and simple.

His policy: this was the great problem, downstream of the revolutionary torrent which had swept him into power. What did he want, this awesome and accidental heir of an exceptional moment in the nation's history? The interminable war against the *ancien régime*, which had brought him to the imperial throne, had also transformed his republican princedom into a royal dictatorship which hung upon his character and his destiny. It was from the time of the coronation in 1804, when his domination over the Revolution became royalty, that it most perceptibly eluded a definition of ends and means; when he was hereditary king he was most independent of revolutionary France, but also the most subjected to what must be termed his 'star'.

His policy: this was the great problem. Internally, it increasingly revealed, day after day, the corruption effected on his domineering nature by the exercise of absolute power, his mania for controlling and deciding everything, his overestimation of his luck and his strength, the development of a police tyranny of which Louis XIV would not have dared to dream. But the French, prisoners of his glory still more than of his police, had no alternative political future: the Bourbons would bring back the nobles; the Republic, the Terror or disorder. The Empire's destiny was being acted out beyond its frontiers, that is to say, in the mystery about Napoleon's intentions and the luck of his wars.

What *did* he want? What had he wanted? Nothing more than his chimera: 'I am destined to change the face of the world; at least, I believe so. Perhaps some ideas of fatalism are mingled with this thought, but I do not reject them; I even believe in them, and this confidence gives me the means of success.'[21] It is easier to define what he had at his command, which explains the wide margin of superiority he enjoyed in comparison with each of his adversaries, taken in isolation. He was master of a modern state, centralized and efficient, and could mobilize all its resources to the best advantage; he was the head of a society founded on civil equality, in which both the administration and the framework of the army were recruited from all strata of the social body. In short, no technological secrets – it was Britain that had those – but a social secret: an eighteenth-century country and army, which had been freed by the revolutionary explosion and rationalized by enlightened despotism.

However, the most important secret was his genius for action and tireless energy, which he threw into dominating the world: for if the Revolution had never clearly defined the objectives of its war – Danton had had his own, as had Carnot and Sieyès – he was even less able to do so. He had learnt war, he had encountered it, had been born of it and had ceaselessly modelled his life on it; doomed not only not to make peace, but also never to lose a battle, he repeatedly laid out on history's table a stake which also continually grew larger.

In this connection, Bonaparte-Charlemagne remained identical with Bonaparte-Consul, obsessed with the unique adventure of his existence. If his army became increasingly a professional one, if he married a daughter of the Habsburgs, if he dreamed of a universal empire, he nevertheless remained at the mercy of fate. The minute he laid down his arms in 1814, his son and heir disappeared with him from the world's stage. Basically, only his administrative reorganization of France had any solidity, born of necessity; that was the bourgeois part of his life. The remainder was the improvisation of an incomparable artist, who drove deep furrows through the history of Europe but in the end reduced France's frontiers to those of the first years of the Revolution.

The fact remains that all those events from which this improvisation was woven formed the history of Europe and of France within Europe: let us now briefly go over the principal features of that history.

TRIUMPH AND DISASTER

In 1803, at the time of the break-up of the Amiens peace, Bonaparte found himself – exceptionally and for a very short while – facing a sole adversary,

[21] Napoléon to Joseph, November 1804, in Miot de Mélito, *Mémoires*.

since he had won a vassal Holland and a weak Spain to his camp. Here, then, was his great plan, which he had already studied in 1798 between Italy and Egypt: to land in England and bring the war to a definitive close in its very heart, in London. During the whole of 1804, at the same time that he was making himself emperor, he continued to press on with preparations for the Boulogne camp, the building of invasion barges, the inventory of necessary equipment. Evidence of his typical style of conducting a war lies in this note to Marshal Soult in April 1805: 'Let me know whether, within a fortnight, horses, provisions, men and everything can be embarked. Do not give me a metaphysical reply to this question, but go and look at the stores and the different warehouses.' But in order to land and get to London quickly without being cut off from the rear, Napoleon needed control of the Channel, at least for several weeks: whence the orders given to French and Spanish squadrons to attract the British fleet – which was superior in numbers and still more in quality – towards the distant Antilles.

The plan overestimated the value of the French fleet, together with that of its crews and its command. Admiral Villeneuve, head of the strongest squadron, refused to confront Nelson in the Caribbean seas and recrossed the Atlantic, only to be ingloriously blockaded at Cadiz. The emperor had never been able to gain the freedom of the Channel. In any case, in the middle of 1805, it was too late: Pitt, having returned to power, had bought a Russian alliance, and Austria, Naples and Sweden joined the Anglo-Russian treaty during the summer, to form a new coalition (the third since 1793) against France. Napoleon, deferring the British plan – which he would never take up again – swung his Boulogne troops towards the Rhine, marching to the aid of Bavaria, his ally: it was the most classic of his campaigns, in which luck – his old partner – completely gave way to his genius.

By means of rapid troop movements, he was able to beat the enemy armies separately – the main one was barring the route to Vienna. Within a month the Grand Army was at the Rhine: it was an admirable instrument of war, the best that Napoleon would ever have, troops with experience and enthusiasm, who were rested and confident; surrounded in Ulm, the Austrian General Mack capitulated on 20 October, and Napoleon was sleeping at Schönbrunn less than a month later. Emperor Francis II had given up the defence of Vienna in order to link up with the Russian army more to the east in Moravia: on 2 December 1805, the anniversary of his coronation, in the presence of the three Emperors, Russians and Austrians were cut to pieces near the village of Austerlitz.

Meanwhile, the triumphs of Ulm and Austerlitz had been offset by Trafalgar (21 October 1805): Villeneuve, lashed by Napoleon's reproaches, had rashly left Cadiz only to be annihilated by Nelson. Temporarily, the imperial publicity services shielded Trafalgar behind Ulm, Vienna and Austerlitz, but the elimination of the French fleet was to be a most important factor of the European conflict: it condemned Napoleon to an inability to attack Britain except in continental Europe. Indeed, an entire reorganization of Europe was already being outlined, with the collapse of Austria: the Treaty of Pressburg, in December 1805, hardened the terms of Campo Formio and Lunéville by doing away with all Austrian influence in Italy; the Habsburgs were similarly ousted from Germany, to the profit of the Electors of Bavaria, Württemberg and Baden.

The end of the Holy Roman Empire gave birth, in July 1806, to a Confederation of the Rhine, of which Napoleon became the 'Protector' and which was entered by the 'vassalized' princes laden with the spoils of Francis II. Thus the Elector of Bavaria took the title of king, and princes were quite simply 'created', like Napoleon's brother-in-law, Murat, who became Grand Duke of Berg. The eldest brother, Joseph, had been 'appointed' to Naples a little earlier, to replace the Bourbons who had been deposed by decree and had taken refuge in Sicily. The family had started acquiring crowns.

Until then, Prussia had not made a move, being content to occupy British Hanover, which had been left to its covetous grasp, while the Tsar had returned home. But the German reorganization upset Berlin all the more because, in the course of unofficial negotiations between France and Britain in the summer of 1806, Napoleon proposed to the British the restitution of Hanover: Frederick William III did a volte-face and turned against France, on the side of the Russians. Since Valmy, France had never confronted this fearsome army, the terror of the eighteenth century, heir of the great Frederick: now, in six days and two battles, Jena and Auerstädt, it had ceased to exist, together with the state whose backbone it had formed; on 27 October 1806 Napoleon entered Berlin.

There remained the Russians, in the strength of their endless plains, who were already posing formidable strategic problems to Napoleon: the emperor was a man for short distances, good roads and lightning concentrations of troops. Now this lover of speed, this Mediterranean man full of nervous energy, dragged out his lines interminably across the great frozen plains of the north. At the end of a terrible campaign, he carried off a dubious and bloody success at Eylau in February 1807, conquered eastern Prussia and freed Poland, and finally beat the Russians at Friedland in June. Neither of the two victories was decisive, even though Napoleon remained in control of the land: but already, on both sides, it had been decided to substitute alliance for war.

Alexander was tired of the British alliance: Britain paid badly and made no attempt to create a diversion in Europe. Napoleon wanted a Russian alliance: he hated this cruel and interminable war which kept him away from the Tuileries for so long, where as usual the great dignitaries of his regime were calculating the opportunities and risks behind his back. He needed the Russians to settle the Prussian dispute which had been left in abeyance, and to put a stop in the east to any possible revenge from Frederick's heirs; but above all, to achieve his great anti-British project and close the whole of Europe to London merchants.

Would he have to venture as far as Moscow to obtain peace? No: in 1807 he succeeded where he would fail five years later; this was the Tilsit meeting, the raft on the Niemen where the two emperors – who were enchanted with each other – made Prussia pay for the new map of Europe, by creating firstly a Grand Duchy of Warsaw, which was given to the loyal king of Saxony, and secondly a kingdom of Westphalia, of which the crown went to Jerome, Napoleon's youngest brother, who became a new member of the Rhine Confederation. Napoleon promised his support against the Sultan, Tsar Alexander his against Britain: the Franco-Russian alliance became the axis and guarantee of the new European equilibrium, which was entirely directed against Britain.

Once more, Britain was the sole adversary: Pitt had died, as had his great rival Fox, but the new authorized representatives of the British oligarchy were more than ever resolved upon a merciless struggle. Since Trafalgar, it was impossible to resume the invasion plan. So Napoleon wanted to change his strategy and turn the weapon of its own industrial and commercial superiority against London.

In the last half of the eighteenth century, the idea was very prevalent that Britain was a giant with feet of clay, because of its credit system and trading structures. In fact, the British economy, whose vast export industries gave a livelihood, through external trade, to a quarter of the population, and depended on massive imports of foodstuffs and raw materials, could be vulnerable to a seriously directed blockade policy: Sieyès had thought about it in 1798, before the setting-up of the expedition to Egypt. But since 1793, thanks to its naval superiority, Britain had been the one to try to ban neutrals from trading with its enemies, and had declared 'blockaded' the ports which it did not control. The aim was not to starve French Europe, the great producer of corn, but to deprive it of the colonial and industrial products necessary to its economy.

In 1803, when war resumed, Napoleon had riposted by banning colonial goods and industrial products of British origin from entering France. In 1806, strengthened by his conquests, he wanted to extend the system of these 'customs posts', as he called them, which were held, for example, by Louis in Holland and Joseph in Naples: this was what lay behind the decrees of Berlin and Milan. The first, signed just after his victory over Prussia (1806), declared 'the British Isles to be in a state of blockade' and forbade all trade with Britain, not only in France, but in all the allied or occupied countries, from Spain to the Vistula. At Tilsit, the following year, Russia gave its backing. It was a matter of asphyxiating British exports and thus of creating industrial overproduction and a generalized crisis in British economy. Britain retaliated by bombarding Copenhagen, opening up the Baltic by cannon fire, and aspiring to control the traffic of neutral countries. The second Napoleonic document, signed in Milan at the end of 1807, held that any neutral vessel 'controlled' by the British should be seized. The Continental System from then on prohibited any neutrality: but the whole of Europe had to be French, peopled with soldiers and customs officers.

Portugal inaugurated the series of 'economic' annexations: in the face of this old British ally's hostility, Napoleon sent Junot to close the port of Lisbon. In a foreseeable sequence of events, the occupation of Portugal brought in its wake that of Spain, arbitration by the emperor over the lamentable quarrels of the reigning family, and finally the appointment of Joseph to the throne of Madrid, while Murat went to Naples. But now Napoleon, accustomed to defeating the mercenary armies of the kings of Europe in open country, found popular guerrilla warfare confronting him: Joseph's throne had to be won back from a people demanding their legitimate kings. Triggered off in May, the insurrection soon gained mastery of the country and, in July at Bailén, forced one demoralized French army to capitulate: this was a thunderbolt for Europe. Shortly afterwards, Junot had to yield Lisbon to the British. What did it matter that Napoleon, who had hastened over at the head of the Grand Army, reinstalled Joseph in December? He left at his heels a Spain that was on its feet, a marvellous parade ground for the invading corps of the future Wellington, who still bore the name Wellesley. In the same year, the logic of the Continental System broadened the emperor's Italian policy: annexation of Tuscany and Parma to the Empire, occupation of Rome, which would be added the following year. Pius VII retaliated with excommunication; he was placed in a guarded residence in Savona, a solitary martyr who was just as dangerous as all the Spanish guerillas.

To these additional costs, to these new adversaries, were added the first tears in the very fabric of Napoleonic Europe: the Franco-Russian alliance and French Germany. Two years afterwards, the spirit of Tilsit no longer reigned in Erfurt; Napoleon, on the point of leading the Grand Army into Spain, would again have liked Alexander's promise. But doubly sensitive to pressure from his boyars and the French failure in Spain, the Tsar resorted to trickery and temporized, secretly encouraged by Talleyrand; he informed Vienna that he would stay neutral should a fresh conflict arise between France and Austria.

In the autumn of 1808, the Viennese court had rebuilt its army and was preparing once again to avenge Campo Formio, Lunéville and the humiliation of the Treaty of Pressburg (1805): as usual, it had received money from London, but this time it could count on the backing of a German population which was weary of French domination. War broke out in the spring of 1809, at the same time as uprisings in the Tyrol and in northern Germany. Napoleon was victorious in three months, after a close shave with defeat; the Archduke Charles had let him enter Vienna by withdrawing his troops towards the east, on the left bank of the Danube; at the end of May, part of the French infantry, which had ventured on to this bank over makeshift bridges, was obliged to beat a hasty retreat before the Austrian counteroffensive. The Grand Army did not manage to cross the river until, a month later, it carried off a decisive victory at Wagram on 6 July. The peace of Vienna, signed in October, took Galicia from Austria and gave it to the Grand Duchy of Warsaw, while all that remained of the Adriatic provinces was directly united to the Empire.

At the end of 1809, Napoleon's construction was at its apogee. Let us take a look at the fantastic and temporary map of French Europe: an Austria excluded from Germany and cut off from the sea, a Prussia almost reduced to its origins, and a French Empire of 131 *départements* stretching from Brest to Hamburg, from Amsterdam to Rome and Trieste – 750,000 square kilometres, plus seventy million inhabitants, of whom thirty million were French. On top of this empire were the satellite states, arranged in a curve: the Rhine Confederation, a 'mediatized' Switzerland, the Italian Republic, with Murat in Naples, Joseph in Madrid. Finally, France's advance guard towards the east, the Grand Duchy of Warsaw, the figure of a Poland being reborn but still frail, trapped by the ambiguities of the Franco-Russian alliance.

This French Europe, built up of bits and pieces during the course of events, corresponded less and less with the aims of its founder and more and more with the hopes of his adversaries. It had been built in order to ruin British trade. In fact, in 1808, the Europe of Tilsit and the beginning of Milan was closed to British products, in the Baltic – despite Sweden – as in the Mediterranean – despite the Maltese entrepôt. At the same time, the retaliatory measures taken by the United States against the attacks of which her vessels had borne the brunt, worsened the deficit in British exports, which went down by more than a quarter; Britain was choked with unsold stocks, and their prices fell dangerously, causing industrial paralysis, unemployment and social unrest.

But after this drop, the curve of exports picked up outstandingly in 1809, reaching a maximum: indeed, British goods were achieving an even better penetration of northern Europe, through the development of Swedish contraband, the self-interested connivance of a certain number of French officials and the reopening of Dutch ports, since Louis had yielded to the pressure of his new subjects; so true was it that the blockade had a boomerang effect, that Napoleon himself had half-opened France's doors to British trade by the granting of special licences. In the same year British trade with the United States slowly picked up, and developed chiefly with Spanish and Portuguese America, facilitated by the exile of the Portuguese dynasty to Brazil and the dislocation of Spanish trade with the South American empire. British prosperity was so dazzling that in 1810 Napoleon tightened the meshes of his net, took Louis's kingdom from him and put under his own direct authority the German shore of the North Sea. But how could he close the American outlet and reservoir?

Paradoxically, the economic crisis which hit Britain in the midst of its prosperity at the end of 1810, did not arise from the Continental System: it represented a cyclical recession, made worse by inflation which financed the costs of war, and the disorganization of the traditional trading structures. It had all begun with the fall of the pound sterling and the catastrophic harvest of 1809, the brutal leap in the price of grain and the threat of famine. At the same time, the tightening of the blockade, saturation of the South American market because its capacity had been overestimated, renewed difficulties and soon war with the United States deeply affected exports: in the long term, the New World countries could pay for British products only with colonial goods – which could not be sold by London except in Europe. The British crisis of 1811–12 was therefore extremely serious, and the people's wretched poverty brought its usual train of workers' riots and savage violence: this was the moment when, as a result of the combination of the economic crisis and the shutting off of the United States, the Napoleonic system struck at the very heart of Britain.

By a piece of good luck for Britain, the Continental System was truly applied for only two years, from the middle of 1810 until Napoleon plunged into the immensity of Russia. Furthermore the great crisis of 1811 spared neither France nor Europe. The trade rupture with Britain aggravated matters in its turn, even though at first it was favourable to the expansion of continental production. If the landowning aristocracy could no longer export its corn or its wood – so be it: it had never liked, and even less upheld, the parvenu soldier of revolutionary France. But now European people and bourgeoisies were rising up in their turn against him, and even in France his rule no longer seemed to be other than a chance venture.

The failure of the Continental System concealed another failure, more long-standing and fundamental: that of a French Europe, rallying to support the ideological and social model born of the Revolution. The imperial and consular conquests had been accompanied by the extension of French social and administrative reforms in the satellite countries: the abolition of serfdom, seigneurial rights and the tithe, civil equality, the Code Napoléon, freedom of worship and conscience, governmental centralization. In Germany, for instance, the states of Baden, Württemberg and Bavaria, which were considerably enlarged, had been profoundly transformed; Napoleonic creations, such as Murat's Grand Duchy of Berg or Jerome's Westphalia, were taken in hand, like model states, by high-quality French personnel who were frequently well received by local society. Thus the young Stendhal, who had himself addressed as 'Monsieur l'Intendant', or even 'Monseigneur', passed delightful youthful years in the small provincial society of Brunswick, which was attached to Westphalia: for French reforms, in Germany, Italy, to say nothing of the Grand Duchy of Warsaw, had won over a good proportion of the elites formed by the eighteenth century. The economic boom had also made its contribution, encouraged by the climate of prosperity, the improvement of roads and the birth of a protected European market.

However, even in these regrouped, rationalized states, liberated from their tiny reactionary oligarchies, the French occupation's fiscal and military inroads formed the basis, in the long run, of general discontent: war nurtured war, and Napoleon's army became ever less French and ever more European, being drawn from the Grand Empire and the satellite states. While the elites were scared by a venture which seemed to have no end in sight, the part of the French Revolution's glorious message which

got through to the people was no longer civil equality or social liberation, but national oppression; thus French revolutionary messianism
would breed throughout Europe a counter-revolutionary and nationalist
messianism, which was an unexpected windfall for the priests, seigneurs
and kings.

In 1807 two significant condemnations of the Napoleonic enterprise
came to light: one from Talleyrand, who believed in a balanced Europe,
and was both a lucid and corrupt interpreter of tradition and of the
future, preparing in advance – at the same time as another career – the
compromise he deemed necessary between French and European elites.
The other came from German millennialists who identified Bonaparte with
the Anti-Christ; they were, so to speak, the foam on the powerful wave
which would sweep European peasants along under the banner of religion
and the kings: a vast and fresh Vendée which rose in Spain to reach as far
as Germany and Italy, and which would have Russian mujiks as its most
redoubtable soldiers.

If this counter-revolutionary crusade was to gain strength, it was
essential that the big European states should get themselves better
organized than in the past. That was exactly what happened. The old
central and eastern European monarchies had preserved their hatred
for the revolutionary ideas which, in their eyes, Napoleon had always
embodied; but, accustomed as they were to measuring an adversary by the
worth of his army, they had inevitably succumbed to the fascination of the
French organization. After Jena (1806), Prussia had relaxed the rigidity
of Frederick's state, integrating peasants and bourgeois in an effort to
resurrect a sense of nation. In Austria, where the aristocracy refused
to surrender anything of its social ascendancy, the army had nevertheless been reorganized, to become an instrument of revenge. The old
eighteenth-century conflicts between aristocracy and monarchic centralization had disappeared, to the advantage of the national priority glorified by
teachers and students, which would unite the masses of the people to the
most traditionalist states in Europe.

This was also the case in Russia, where Alexander and his councillors at
times nursed wild dreams of liberalism without, in the end, doing anything
to modify the traditional balance which would make illiterate peasants into
the most fanatical defenders of orthodox priests and the Tsar. the 'great
nation', turned Empire, saw its own message of liberation turned against
itself and against the values it had claimed to universalize. In short, there
was a terrible anti-Napoleonic reaction, that is to say, national and counter-
revolutionary both together, which gained support from the revival of the
Catholic faith and the philosophies of nationalism and authority.

Around 1810–11, everything contributed to speed up this evolution:
France's increasing fiscal and military pressures in conquered or vassal
countries, the conflict between the emperor and the pope, the Russian
alliance which had been tottering since Erfurt, the deep economic crisis
which was sweeping away business prosperity. Even in France, the imperial

magic was coming undone, conscription had become a very heavy burden, and the war extremely costly. The immense collective passions which go to make great wars had passed over to the adversary.

Napoleon was aware of all that. Once more – and for the last time – on his return from Wagram, he faced the eternal question: how could he make his great venture legitimate, how could he stabilize what had become the Empire? Behind his back, as usual, everyone was talking about a more restful and manageable successor – Joseph, Murat or even Eugène de Beauharnais. He no longer contemplated adoption, since the death of Louis and Hortense's eldest son; after his affair with the Polish Countess Walewska, he knew he was capable of fathering a child; he decided on a divorce and a royal marriage. At the time when Europe was borrowing the Revolution's methods, the soldier of the Revolution went seeking a wife amid the *ancien régime*.

He had in mind a Russian princess, one of the Tsar's sisters, intended to perpetuate the Europe of Tilsit; but Alexander deliberately caused the matter to hang fire, and then sheltered behind her mother's refusal. So then Napoleon leaped at the Habsburg marriage, proposed by the court of Vienna with a view to gaining at least a respite and perhaps a form of insurance; he married Marie-Louise, the daughter of Francis II, at the beginning of April 1810. By taking Europe's first princess into his bed, did he perhaps feel that he had finally gained entry to the select circle of the kings – he who had already been tricked, fifteen years earlier, by Josephine's tales of her 'birth'? By repeating the pattern of Louis XVI's marriage, he believed – just like a Bourbon – that he was ensuring a guarantee for himself with Vienna. But he also thought that he was ensuring for his heir half a true monarchic legitimacy, and that he would reinstate this grandson of the Revolution in the tradition of the kings of France. It was his way of expressing his mother's famous 'Let's hope it lasts!'

The King of Rome, born the following year, was therefore the last and most moving of Napoleon's insurances against the future. But he was also the most illusory: it was vain for the emperor of the French to try to bring the *ancien régime* to life again in forms and customs, to appoint more and more aristocrats to his councils and to increase examples of his absolute power, since for Europe he had never stopped being the crowned incarnation of the Revolution. Could he even have been taken in by words? Though he would write to Francis II 'My dear brother and father-in-law', he knew perfectly well that he was still a usurper. Scarcely more than a year after the birth of his son, the monarch who had everything would once more be the 'Little Corporal'.

To the question, how could Napoleon gamble everything and lose everything at the point when he seemed to dominate everything, there is no other answer than the extraordinary precariousness of his territorial ascendancy in 1811. Napoleon tended to attribute this precariousness – of which he was more than ever aware – to the break-up of what he had always looked on as the axis of his European system: the Franco-Russian agreement. This gave rise to the war of 1812, which was perhaps intended less to break an adversary than to re-establish a partnership.

Relations between Napoleon and Alexander had constantly deteriorated since Erfurt; the growing disagreement concealed both real grievances and assumptions of intent. In their overwhelming numbers, the Russian boyars continued to detest everything connected with the French Revolution, whether from near or far; traditional exporters of corn and wood from their domains to Britain, they were damaged by the Continental System. Sensitive to pressure from them, Alexander's attention to the application of Napoleonic decrees steadily diminished; he had vacillated during the 1809 campaign, used trickery again in the marriage affair before refusing. He feared French expansion towards the east, to which the plan of the Continental System was leading: after Holland, which had been taken from Louis, the Hanseatic towns were 'united' with the Empire, then the Grand Duchy of Oldenburg, on the other side of the Danish peninsula, was seized from a brother-in-law of the Tsar.

In the face of this endless spreading of the French Empire, what was the worth of Russian acquisitions since Tilsit – Galicia, Finland or Bessarabia? Who could say whether Napoleon, in spite of his promises, would not reconstruct a true Poland, a child of France right in the middle of the Slavonic world? For all these reasons, Alexander was ready for the split at the beginning of 1812; he had the secret support of the new regent and crown prince of Sweden, Bernadotte, who had espoused his subjects' hostility to the Napoleonic blockade, and the no less secret assurance of Austrian and Prussian non-intervention.

On his side, Napoleon felt strengthened by the official alliance with Vienna and Berlin. Once more, it was a matter of placing the final stone on his European edifice by a final war, that is to say, of re-establishing the spirit of Tilsit, the condition of the application of the Continental System and victory over Britain: therefore a short war, a great battle, a new raft on the Niemen. This is what he wrote to Alexander, on 1 July, at the time he entered Russia: 'War is therefore declared between us. God himself cannot undo what has been done. But I will always lend an open ear to peace negotiations.' All the drama of 1812 lies in this illusion, in which he was reliving 1807: Napoleon had not realized that the very conditions of the European war had changed.

He himself crossed the Niemen at the head of a cosmopolitan army, nearly half foreign, which had been raised from the Empire and its dependencies; notably 200,000 German soldiers out of 700,000 men. Ahead of them lay the desert, the Russian army which vanished into its retreat, the mujiks burning their crops; and the invasion was already proving difficult: the Russians had altered the rules of the game. In order to attempt to break the national alliance of the Tsar and his people, Napoleon had one weapon at his disposal, and had thought of using it: to re-enact the revolutionary war of his youth and proclaim the emancipation of the mujiks. But, now he was a cousin of kings, and haunted by the imminent agreement with Alexander, as he supposed, he decided not to use it.

Delayed by provisioning difficulties, already depleted by desertions, the immense army entered Smolensk only in the middle of August, and did not reach the Moskva until the beginning of September. The Russian troops, taken in hand by old Marshal Kutuzov, finally gave battle at Borodino, but it was a bloody and uncertain fight: Napoleon entered Moscow on 14 September, at the very end of the summer, with weakened troops and without having seriously worn down those of the enemy. He at least hoped that the capture of the huge exotic city, at the other end of Europe, would provide a pledge of peace: master of the dead metropolis, which had been devastated by fires, he waited in the Kremlin for Alexander's emissaries.

In mid-October, when it had finally dawned upon him that there was to be no new Tilsit, he decided to return home; he had never liked to be absent for long from the Tuileries. But it was already too late. Kutuzov barred a return via the south, so he had to retrace the interminable route to Smolensk, which had already been laid waste by the pillage of the outward journey. Pursued by the enemy, harassed by the Cossacks, decimated by the prematurely cold weather, which swiftly dropped to minus twenty degrees, the Grand Army fell apart into a vast, wretched, frozen column of men who could barely get across the Beresina: at the beginning of December, Napoleon led a mere 100,000 survivors back towards the Niemen. The great Empire was without an army.

It was the signal for the entire system to go into a state of general crisis. The European states saw the arrival of their long-awaited moment of revenge: Prussia turned to Russia and declared war on France in the spring of 1813, while Austria prepared a mediation loaded with menaces. Britain, emerging from the crisis and seeing its trade start to flourish again with the French retreat, had just brought in a government intent on putting an end to the matter. Everywhere public opinion revived the movement which had started to stir in 1809: in Spain, where popular guerrilla activity had resulted in assemblies and a liberal programme, Anglo-Spanish troops drove Joseph from Madrid and soon advanced as far as the Pyrenees. Revolts swept through Italy, their flames fanned by the exile of Pius VII, and Murat quickly left the remains of the Grand Army to look after his own interests in Naples. Popular uprisings broke out on all sides in German territory occupied by the French, while the princes bided their time, one eye on Vienna and the other on Paris.

Immediately on his return, Napoleon had spent the winter raising more soldiers and preparing for war in the spring; but the internal climate was very ominous, and defeat had reawoken a weariness with the endless conflict, together with a growing rejection of the despotism of one man alone. Liberal royalism, which was spreading among the country's notables, showed how far distant were the times of consular unanimity; the whole of affluent France was ready to put an end to the venture, even to take back its former kings, in return for a firm insurance contract on its possessions.

It was clear that in spring 1813 there was no longer any imaginable compromise between Napoleon and Europe: Napoleon could not continue to reign, even in France, unless he had a new victory; outside France, the Europe of both the kings and the people had not risen up for a little territorial readjustment. That is why the Austrian mediation, which proposed a return to Lunéville, had no chance of success on either side: after the French victories over the Russo-Prussians at Lützen and Bautzen in May, the short negotiation which got under way was little more than a general stay of execution. Napoleon insisted on the frontiers of 1812. In August, Austria and Sweden joined the coalition, adding more than a million soldiers. *In extremis*, Napoleon could negotiate only with his prisoners, Pius VII or the Bourbons of Madrid: but what did it matter, since it was all a gamble on the field of battle?

Whether through lack of cavalry, or the youth of his troops, or the fatigue of their leader, Napoleon allowed the junction of three enemy armies, under Bernadotte, Blücher and Schwarzenberg, and the decisive battle was engaged at Leipzig, with two against one, 320,000 members of the coalition army against 160,000 French and allied soldiers; the law of numbers, plus the defection of allied German contingents on the third day of the battle, explain a defeat which quickly became a rout. Napoleon found himself on the Rhine with the debris of his army, and France threatened on its oldest frontiers.

But this time, it was a weary France, broken by despotism and hazardous undertakings, a country of discontented notables, tired marshals and revolutionaries grown old. Napoleon might well be able to get his new conscripts, the 'Marie-Louise', to perform a few strategic feats, but he could no longer mobilize any national force to counterbalance, either in number or will to win, the formidable enemy coalition. His only recourse was the relative moderation of Metternich, who feared Russo-Prussian ambitions; but the iron fist of Britain, handing out grants and orders, was there to impose a war to the finish, and to the French frontiers of 1792. At that time Napoleon's brilliant French campaign, in which he once again displayed against three enemy armies the liveliness and rapidity of the Bonaparte of Italy, could only delay the day of reckoning: Paris, left to the notables by Marie-Louise and Joseph, capitulated on 30 March, and Napoleon resigned himself to abdicating on 6 April, before going to the tiny island of Elba which had been assigned to him by his conquerors.

Deposed by the Senate, abandoned by his Marshals, he had tried to save the throne for his son. But his house, his monarchy, disappeared with him like sandcastles, bringing the Bourbons and the France of the Revolution face to face, after a quarter of a century.

He had realized this beforehand. He had said in 1813, after Leipzig, at the beginning of the shipwreck: 'After me, the Revolution – or, rather, the ideas which formed it – will resume their course. It will be like a book from which the marker is removed, and one starts to read again at the page where one left off.'[22]

[22] Mathieu Molé's speech on receiving Tocqueville into the Académie Française on 21 April 1842, reported in the Marquis de Noailles' *Le Comte Molé*, vol. 1.

PART II

Ending the Revolution

6

The Restoration: 1814–1830

During the months when the Empire was collapsing and when Napoleon was waging war in the Paris basin, the problem of France's government arose yet again. It was an old question, which had been asked since 1789, but this time its solution no longer lay in the hands of the French, since the country was in the throes of being conquered and occupied by the coalition armies. The allies were far from unanimously in favour of restoring the ancient dynasty, divided as they were by their own interests and their views of the future. Austria nursed the idea of a regency for Marie-Louise, a daughter of the family, on behalf of the King of Rome. The Tsar was hostile to the Bourbons and had in mind Marshal Bernadotte, now installed as heir to Sweden's throne; Madame de Staël had toyed with this idea for a time. Prussia had no candidate, and desired above all the lasting enfeeblement of French power. There remained Britain, which favoured the Comte de Provence but was not inclined to impose him: it was still necessary for French opinion to be expressed.

In the event, the decision was made in France. The royal family cleverly played its trump card: its very existence and availability. On 12 March 1814, the Duc d'Angoulême, son of the Comte d'Artois and nephew of the future king, had had the name of the Bourbons acclaimed in Bordeaux, which was filled with a British army. On 29 March, in obedience to an instruction from Napoleon, Marie-Louise withdrew from Paris with her son, leaving the field open to a restoration. The allies were at the gates of the city, which capitulated on 30 March, while Napoleon installed himself at Fontainebleau. Talleyrand, helped and at the same time watched over by the Baron de Vitrolles, the princes' representative, prepared the ground for Louis XVIII, to whom the abdication of the emperor, deserted by his Marshals, left the door wide open. The Comte d'Artois arrived in Paris, 'lieutenant-general of the kingdom' in the name of his brother.

What monarchy, for what kingdom? The imperial Senate was prepared to ensure the continuity of institutions and to make itself the instrument of 'recall' of the monarchy, but on its own conditions, which were those of post-1789 France. On 6 April it adopted the text of a constitution prepared in haste but easy enough to draw up, since it was a matter of making it into a defence for all the men of the Revolution and for all that had been acquired: biens nationaux, titles of nobility, military ranks, political mandates, offices, pensions, annuities. Article 6 went as far as specifying the imprescriptibility of senatorial dignity, together with the generous endowments which were inseparable from it!

The most significant feature, the keystone of the system envisaged by the Senate, the guarantee of these guarantees, was the subordination of the king to the nation: this text which was so clogged with egoisms and personal interests could still let the spirit of the Revolution filter through. 'The French people', it said, 'freely call to the throne', not Louis XVIII, but 'Louis-Stanislas-Xavier, brother of the last king': a way of implying that Louis XVII had never had a legal existence and that the nation had deposed Louis XVI just as freely as it was recalling his brother, as king of the French, or even as king of the Revolution.

To be sure, this concept was not in keeping with the Comte de Provence's idea of his title to the throne of France. He regarded the Senate's constitution as null and void, retaining only its consent to his return. He set off on 19 April, leaving England in easy stages, not letting his intentions be known. He was aware that he had to accept the new France in order to be its king; but he could not agree to repudiate the nature of his title to the throne of France, which was prior to the Revolution and independent of it.

He said as much on 2 May at Saint-Ouen, at the gates of his 'dear town of Paris', in the royal Declaration which Talleyrand had managed to persuade the Senators to accept. In it he undertook to give the kingdom what he termed a 'liberal constitution' in the spirit of the text voted by the Senate; he promised to take for granted, together with civil equality, all the situations and interests which had arisen out of the Revolution. But he did so on his own authority, king of France by the grace of God, and not by the will of the people. The old monarchy would allow circumstances their due, but would not give up its principle.

With Napoleon vanquished, history was offering the Bourbons a last chance: they could take up their copy at the place where Louis XVI had stopped knowing how to write his part, in 1789. Circumstances were dramatic for the nation, but these same circumstances offered Louis XVIII an easier situation than the one which had brought down his unhappy brother. Instead of a France which had suddenly risen in support of its new-found rights and held the king in deep suspicion, he was coming back to a beaten country for which he could be the saviour. War and defeat, the Terror and the Empire had wiped out the Revolution's promises. If he could only clothe it in liberty, tradition might rediscover its roots, and the king of France resume his long family history with the nation.

Louis XVIII would have to tame the Revolution to become the nation's king once more: this was a formidable problem, however, perhaps insoluble. He had therefore refused to let the Senate impose on him, as a condition of his restoration, a text which reaffirmed the priority of the nation's rights. But, in accordance with the Saint-Ouen Declaration, he substituted a constitutional text intended to give the new regime its titles and rules: it was the Charter of 1814, which was largely his own work.

In order to restore the monarchy, more than twenty years after Louis XVI's execution, it was first of all necessary to give it back its continuity: a somewhat extravagant but nevertheless essential exercise, since Louis XVIII had no other claim to reign than the right of hereditary succession to the throne. The preamble to the Charter, dated the nineteenth year of his reign, therefore implied that the monarchy had never ceased to exist. The little Louis XVII being supposed dead in the Temple in 1795, Louis XVI's brother had been king of France since then. 'Recalled' to the throne after a long 'absence', not by the will of the people, but by 'divine Providence', he 'granted' a constitutional Charter to his subjects, according to the needs of the kingdom and following the example of his predecessors.

His ambition was to bridge the gap of the last quarter-century by bringing back with the old monarchy the reference to its 'Constitution': the very one which had foundered so quickly in 1789. With the idea of the current needs of the state, Louis XVIII was opening the way to inevitable concessions to public opinion. With the reference to the works of his ancestors, he was trying to clothe compromises in an imaginary tradition. At once, he was running the risk of losing any advantage to be gained from yielding to the spirit of the times because he was reinventing a language and a past.

Concessions, without doubt, went with the new society, whose rights and acquisitions the French Revolution had established and sanctioned. That was the subject of the Charter's first heading; and 1789 was accepted without any fuss: civil equality, careers open to abilities, freedom of the individual, of worship (although the Catholic religion once more became the state religion) and of the press (within the framework of laws to curb abuses of this freedom, the text prudently adds). Lastly, perhaps chiefly, article 9 guaranteed all property, 'without any exception of those properties which are called national, the law making no difference between them'; and article 11 put forgetfulness under the law's protection, as if it were the most precious of national virtues: 'All research into opinions and votes issued up to the Restoration is prohibited. Courts and citizens are equally commanded to forget.' The French Revolution had wanted to be without a past. The restored monarchy must lose its memory. But in actual fact, it took charge of the Revolution's civil heritage, even up to the Empire's nobility (section IV, article 71).

The most difficult part was not this consent, which was born of necessity. It was, as always since 1789, the organization of a new legitimate political power, capable of governing with the backing of opinion. The Revolution had not been able to constitute it. The monarchy returned with a British-style project (section II of the Charter): a king, two Chambers. 'The king is the supreme head of the state; he commands land and naval forces, declares war, makes peace treaties and treaties of alliance and trade, makes appointments to all posts of public administration, and makes regulations and ordinances necessary to the execution of the law and the safety of the state' (section II, article 14).

He also held part of the legislative power, since he exercised it conjointly with the Chamber of Peers and the Chamber of Deputies. It was he who proposed the law and he who sanctioned it (articles 16 and 22). But the Chambers voting on it (article 18) also received the right to 'entreat the king to propose a law on any matter, and to indicate what they considered suitable that the law should contain' (article 19): thus, in a roundabout way, they regained part of the initiative. At all events, as a major innovation, they had to vote on the budget each year, that is to say, taxation. In case of conflict between the king and the Chambers, the Charter said nothing: ministers were not accountable except in criminal law, and they could not be removed from office by a vote of parliament. Though representative, the regime was not parliamentary.

Moreover, the king appointed the peers, with no limit to their numbers, for life or with right of succession, according to his wish (article 27). In this way, he could find new posts for the great dignitaries of the Empire, reward the most illustrious or the most loyal of his supporters and keep a majority in the Assembly. The true representatives of public opinion were therefore the deputies from the *départements*. They were eligible only on the double condition of having reached forty years of age and paying a contribution of 1,000 francs. As for the electors, they had to be thirty years old and pay at least 300 francs. These tax thresholds excluded 99 per cent of the French from voting; 100,000 citizens would choose the nation's representatives out of 10,000 of them.

Section III organized the legal system, preserving the essence of what had been established under the Consulate and suppressing commissions and special courts, which were symbols of Napoleon's arbitrary rule. Article 68 decreed: 'The Civil Code and those laws at present in existence which are not contrary to this Charter, will remain in force until they are legally repealed.' The entire administrative, legislative and juridical work of the Revolution and the Empire was thus ratified. So that no possible ambiguity should remain regarding any acquired interests, section IV of the Charter, entitled 'Particular rights guaranteed by the state', extended the new regime's guarantee to ranks, pensions, honours and annuities.

It seemed therefore that the new France could sleep peacefully in the shade of the restored monarchy. On 4 June the king publicly let this be understood, by solemnly presenting the Charter to the kingdom's constituted bodies, which were for the most part filled with the heirs of the Revolution and the Empire. Napoleon's Senate had managed to cut itself a large slice of the cake. The king now had to show that he was going to put his doctrine into practice, and wed the tradition which was returning to the throne with him to the spirit of the times which had driven his brother from it a quarter of a century before.

The old king did not have sole responsibility for this. He had his ministry, appointed immediately on his return, in which the Comte de Blacas, his favourite and companion in exile, set the tone, since he was the obligatory intermediary if one wanted to see the king, and the spokesman or the source of his opinions: a symbol of the little court at Hartwell in Buckinghamshire and of the émigrés, the king's liege-man, a man of feudal loyalty, whose other side was an insensitivity to the era and the regained country. Above all, the king had brought back with him to the throne partisans and memories.

This successor to Napoleon was also heir to his brother, the martyr-king. While he had become the head of a centralized state fashioned by the Revolution and the Empire, at the same time, for the former nobility, former clergy, former society, he was the very incarnation of a long-awaited revenge. The contradiction which had made the king of France into a lord of lords and the head of a modern administration, and whose monarchy had died in the eighteenth century, had returned with him into national history, aggravated by the passions of the last quarter-century. The most fervent supporters of the restored king were often the blindest. To those vengeful aristocrats and dowagers, so foreign to modern France in their clothing, their customs and even their language, Louis XVIII could offer only symbolic bonuses which could not give them back their forever vanished supremacy, but which were enough to infuriate public opinion against them.

Positions? He had none to offer them. He had not wanted a massive purge of the emperor's officials, and his Minister of Finance, the Baron Louis, had asked for and obtained cuts in civil posts, in order to get round the critical budget situation. As for the army, peace had rendered useless the hundreds of thousands of ready-for-action soldiers bequeathed by the Empire: over 300,000 men had been sent home, and a good number of their officers put on half-pay; they all formed the formidable propaganda of the imperial myth, but none left a vacant post with which royalist fidelity, a former Vendée fighter or an old courtier from the years of exile might be recompensed. For want of military exploits, the king could distribute only fictitious military ranks, pretexts for fine court uniforms. He grouped about him, in equal measure, in his reconstituted military and civil households, survivors and heirs: what his ancestors had been wont to call 'their' nobility, now reconciled with the throne through misfortune.

These phantoms of the court offices of Versailles did not resuscitate the old world, but they certainly worried the new one, which took fright at the least sign: because private interests in France had eveything to gain from power, they also had everything to fear from it, and the Revolution had aggravated that tradition which had been born under absolutism. The beneficiaries of 1789 thought they could read into the arrogance of the returned nobles a sign of the king's complicity, a threat to the possessions they had acquired: since the Revolution had expropriated the Church and the émigrés, was it not likely that the restored monarchy would expropriate the Revolution?

On 13 September, the Chamber voted for the restitution of all as yet unsold *biens nationaux* – notably, forests – to their returned former owners. Was this a first step towards the annulment of sales effected by the Revolution, in spite of the Charter's formal promises? The Comte Ferrand, Minister of State, clumsily gave this impression when he presented the bill to the deputies:

Gentlemen you will hasten to second the king's wishes: without doubt, he must rejoice in the happiness of those to whom he will restore their property; but you must believe that he has need of such rejoicing in order to soften the regret he feels by not being able to extend this act of justice as far as he most deeply wishes.

An entire property-owning democracy, in both town and country, was upset by this imaginary menace, which had never had any real substance, but which the new regime's style caused to gain ground.

Since it could do so little or nothing about private interests and apportioning posts, the new regime was methodically devoting itself to erasing the Revolution on the symbolic plane. It turned the revolutionary calendar upside down, having expiatory ceremonies held to commemorate the deaths of Louis XVI, Marie-Antoinette, Madame Elisabeth, Louis XVII and the Duc d'Enghien, accompanied by a great number of processions and sermons which restored to the Catholic Church a role magnified by revolutionary persecution. The Concordat of 1801 – which had set the stamp on the alienation of her wealth – remained in force, but was called into question, in the name of the 1516 Concordat. This dream of going back into the past in fact concealed a completely new situation: a persecuted Church and a martyred royalty had been united for ever by Providence; this choice brought about through misfortune provided them with the joint mission of restoring France.

The restored monarchy created out of this union of Throne and Altar – an *ancien régime* image renewed by the Revolution – the supreme symbol of its return, which it tried to impress on French imaginations. This gave rise to a multiplicity of ceremonies and anniversaries, accompanied by much lamentation, in which the monarchy was unwittingly imitating, from the opposite viewpoint, revolutionary democracy's commemorative obsession and pedagogic ambition. On 15 August 1814, the day when Napoleon had wanted to substitute his birthday for Corpus Christi, Louis XVIII re-established the ancient procession celebrating Louis XIII's vow, which had placed France under the Virgin's special protection: candle in hand, the royal family, followed by the state bodies, led the procession through the streets of Paris. On the following 21 January there was the first commemoration of Louis XVI's death. It was the occasion of a solemn national expiation, in the form of a royal funeral which had been delayed for over twenty years: the presumed remains of the last king and Marie-Antoinette were exhumed from the Madeleine cemetery, hastily authenticated and brought with great pomp to Saint-Denis, while the bells of churches throughout the kingdom sounded the hour of national repentance. The old Bourbon obsession with the macabre had found its largest theatre, but it was an artificial spectacle. This forced representation merely intensified the king's death, instead of making royalty live again.

In order to be reborn within public opinion and to erase both the *ancien régime* and Koblenz, this royalty needed not only to reassure interests but also to invent deeds for the future and to embody the new era. Now, that was what the royal family was least capable of doing. Louis XVIII, an infirm old man, essentially lived on the feeling that he had recovered what was due to him. His brother had remained as narrow in his outlook as in the last days of the *ancien régime*, surrounded by a little reactionary court. The impotent king had had no children. Artois had two sons: the first, the Duc d'Angoulême, married to Louis XVI's daughter, his cousin, the little orphan of the Temple, was a rather sickly prince, plagued with nervous tics and impotent like his uncle; the second, the Duc de Berry, was the opposite, a womanizer and the sole genetic hope of his dynasty, though with nothing else to offer but his escapades and his blunders. The family lived in a universe of memories and bitterness, tragedies and little schemes which for all of them perpetuated the world of their childhood (court royalism), and set them apart from the new France. This France would have been able to pardon them its lost glory if they had found the words and gestures of rediscovered liberty. But how could Napoleon be forgotten, if national humiliation put back on the throne mere caricatures of the *ancien régime*?

THE HUNDRED DAYS

As a matter of fact, on 1 March 1815 Napoleon landed at Golfe-Juan. It was the most extraordinary venture of that extraordinary life. The island of Elba was badly guarded, France vaguely uneasy, the great man disconsolate in his tiny kingdom of exile. He had kept intact that power of imagination and action which set him apart from the rest of humanity. He had never stopped putting back on the table the stakes accumulated by his victories, even when those stakes were too awesome to be reasonably gambled again. On the isle of Elba, he had nothing left to play with but his tireless genius and the magic of memories. The historian is astounded that the allies, who had for so long watched him risk everything when he had everything to lose, could not have foreseen more clearly that he would still try to regain everything now that he no longer had anything to lose.

Indeed, his attempt had hardly any chance of lasting in the international context of universal hostility which it would immediately encounter. The astonishing thing is that it should have succeeded in France, and that the Empire – that traditionless regime, linked to victory – could also have been restored, even after his defeat.

Not that the emperor's return was triumphal, as Bonapartist legend would have wished. But it was accepted. The real political temperature in France was a generalized wait-and-see attitude, made up of weariness with civil strife and war, modified at each end by partisans of the rediscovered legitimacy and those humiliated by the Restoration. The former, nobles and notables, relied on the loyal peasantry in the west. The second were to be found among the artisans and ordinary townsfolk who were nostalgic for the Revolution, and sought backing from a spreading anxiety in the country concerning the maintenance of civil equality; they shared with the soldiers who had stayed in the army the treasures of the great national memories. The role of the army would be a decisive one. Landing on French soil with a little troop of loyalists, Napoleon had realized that he would not easily carry off a victory, and that he would have to rally rather than reconquer.

He was not well received in Provence, where the stronghold of Antibes shut its gates to him; he plunged into the Alps, to avoid Marseille and the Rhône valley, old stamping grounds of royalism. This was a clever calculation: the humble people of the Alpine villages fêted his return along the poor roads where his legendary silhouette reappeared as if by a miracle. At Digne, and Sisteron, the royalist authorities withdrew on his arrival, and a first decisive success was won by the returning hero just before Grenoble: Colonel de Labédoyère went over to his side, together with his regiment, and was soon imitated by the town garrison. On 6 March 1815 Napoleon was in command of the capital of the Dauphiné.

Paris had learnt of his landing only the day before: the slowness of communications had given an additional trump card to the enterprise. Louis XVIII reacted with sang-froid. He convened the Chambers, which had been on holiday since the end of December, to display the spectacle of constitutional law in the face of the dizzying influence of memories. He dispatched his brother, the Comte d'Artois, to Lyon to set up, with the help of Marshal Macdonald, a military barricade against the advance of the ex-emperor, who was declared an outlaw. Soon messages of support and proclamations of loyalty were flowing in from all sides, accompanied by oaths of eternal hatred for the usurper. 'Never', wrote one of the best historians of the epoch, Bertier de Sauvigny, 'did honour and loyalty matter so much as at this time, when honour and loyalty were to come under such attack.'[1] While the heart of France waited, official France

---

[1] G. de Bertier de Sauvigny, *La Restauration*, p. 96.

pressed round the throne before deserting it; with this upsurge of loyalty there also came an expression of liberty, through the voice of Benjamin Constant, the old enemy of imperial despotism, who refused in advance to give his services to the new 'Attila': 'I will not go, like a wretched renegade, trailing from one power to another, using sophism to conceal infamy.'

Nevertheless in Lyon everyone decided against the legitimate royalty. Not a shot was fired. The Comte d'Artois and Macdonald harangued the garrison in vain; they met with nothing but a disapproving silence. Everywhere the entire army, officers and men, were leaning towards their old chief. What happened in Lyon on 9 March took place three days later in Bordeaux, where the Duchesse d'Angoulême herself was booed by the troops she was summoning to combat. In Bordeaux, at least the populace was loyal to her cause. In contrast, in Lyon, that old bastion of the class war between weavers and merchants, the working men of the town had taken up the emperor's cause in word and deed, and formed a procession acclaiming his arrival, on the evening of 10 March, to cries of 'Long live the emperor! Down with nobles! Down with priests! Death to the royalists!' Here was a significant reawakening of popular Jacobinism celebrating a Napoleon who had once more become the son of the Revolution for just as long as it took to reconquer his throne: this mixture of revolutionary memory and imperial nostalgia was to have a long career in the nineteenth-century French political theatre.

The last episode in the victorious march took place several days later with the winning over of Marshal Ney. The old comrade-in-arms, at the head of troops gathered in Franche-Comté, had rashly promised to bring back the usurper 'in an iron cage'; but faced with the Little Corporal's emissaries, he yielded to the power of memories and the pressure of his soldiers, thus throwing all his prestige behind a defection for which he would pay with his life on the second return of the kings.

But at that moment, his defection sounded the hour of a new exile for Louis XVIII. Through Louis XVI's brother, royalist France relived the days of October, Varennes and 10 August, royalty humiliated, driven out, vanquished, the oldest crown in the world adorned with a new misfortune. Chateaubriand, the incomparable chronicler of the misfortunes of the Bourbons, would have liked to restore the heroism of the barricades to the monarchy, transforming the Tuileries into an impregnable fortress. This idea of rewriting French annals in reverse and rebuilding the glory of the dynasty on the sites of 10 August 1792, in order to unite royalty and the people again, was no more than an old, farfetched dream; but French history has its trends, and the royal family's fate was for exile. In the middle of the night between 19 and 20 March, at the hour when his brother had left the same palace for the Varennes escapade, Louis XVIII climbed into a coach which set off northwards. Two days later, he was not even able to wait to hear the outcome of events in Lille, in his own kingdom, as he would have wished: the garrison there was no trustier than elsewhere. Crossing the frontier, he finally ensconced himself in Ghent on 30 March, together with his family, his ministers, his household, his court, amid a hurly-burly of rumours and intrigues to which renewed exile gave the comfort of familiarity.

History began once more to revolve around the emperor. The important matter was immediate war with Europe, since the allies at once treated the escapee from the island of Elba as a prisoner who had illegally returned from banishment, despite his protestations of peaceful intent. Having come back to the Tuileries in the evening of 20 March, Napoleon had first of all to give his return the form of a new contract with the French. Even the legitimate dynasty, with the strength of possession dating back nearly a thousand years, had been obliged to go through the same process in the preceding year. Napoleon, now doubly an adventurer because of both his military defeat and his triumphal escape, was even less able to shirk it.

He had never seriously contemplated getting the backing of the neo-Jacobins who had acclaimed him between Antibes and Paris: it would not have been in keeping with either his temperament or his tradition. But neither could he purely and simply re-establish the despotism of a single ruler, which had characterized the Empire. He had to make a gesture towards that bourgeois and property-owning France waiting to see how events would turn out, the France he had kept for nearly fifteen years under his iron rule, in exchange for the protection of its interests, but to which the Bourbons had given the political guarantees of the Charter. How could he do less?

Thus was born the 'Act added to the Constitutions of the Empire' which, under the guise of modifications to the imperial texts, merely went to illustrate the irreversible nature of representative government, which was successively established by the Bourbons and the emperor. It was a sort of reproduction of the Charter, drawn up by Benjamin Constant, who had not been able to resist this poisoned bait. Spiteful gossip said that he had not wanted to leave Paris at the height of his unhappy passion for Madame Récamier; but apart from the pleasure of at last being in the public eye, his palinode also contained a very French scepticism about the nature of the state which was already common among liberals and Jacobins. The monarchy, the Republic and the Empire had taught public opinion to unlearn the virtue of regimes and loyalty to individuals.

Besides, Napoleon attached no importance to this expedient constitution, which the French approved only with extreme wariness. The notables, too, abstained *en masse* when it came to electing the new Chamber, which was finally dominated by the liberals, with the inevitable La Fayette at their head. In short, the new regime had virtually no real support anywhere, even in its executive authority: Napoleon had had great difficulty in finding ministers, and the most conspicuous among them, who had also returned, Fouché, Duc d'Otrante, Minister of Police, was busy preparing for the future rather than serving his chief. The former terrorist of Year II was at the height of his skill and his career, using the usurper's phantom government to get back into the good graces of the legitimate princes, stepping up precautions, advice and overtures in both camps, with a constant eye on the coming restoration, for which he would be the inevitable intercessor.

There was an air of unreality about those Hundred Days. The French, as Fouché had realized, were re-enacting their history without really believing in it. An ageing and uneasy Napoleon, without any firm hold on the country, was no longer that triumphant and adulated First Consul of the days after 18 Brumaire. La Fayette had had the idea of reviving the great memories of revolutionary patriotism by a huge demonstration in the Champ de Mars, but this new Festival of the Federation had lost its impetus.

The only thing missing in this shadow theatre was *chouannerie*, and that erupted in April from northern Brittany to the Vendée – because of conscription, as before: even this civil war was in a minor key, for it had lost the banner of religion, and Paris no longer dispatched fanatical sansculottes against it, but strategists of appeasement. On the day of Waterloo, however, the 20,000 privates stationed in the west would cruelly default on the defeated man. For in the end, everything was settled on the battleground, with the clash of armies, although Napoleon had vainly tried to mollify the allies with protestations of his commitment to peace. In order to try to beat his enemies one at a time, following his usual tactics, he went to Belgium to face Wellington's British and Blücher's Prussians before they were joined by the Russians and Austrians. But after a first success two days before, he was routed on the evening of 18 June at Waterloo, in the wake of a battle which for a long time had hung in the balance.

Paris learned the news on 20 June; then began the three great weeks in the political life of Fouché, the craftsman of the second Restoration, which was completed by the return of the king to Paris. The allies, who had had their fingers burnt by what had happened, were frequently even more sceptical than the year before about Louis XVI's brother, and in Vienna the Tsar had launched the premonitory idea of a monarchy entrusted to the Duc d'Orléans; but it was Wellington who marched on Paris, and Britain wanted to give Louis XVIII a second chance. Fouché, on the spot, neutralized the two dominant groups: the Bonapartists who, after the emperor's second abdication (22 June 1815), would have liked to see the little King of Rome succeed to the throne, to which Napoleon vainly proclaimed his accession, and the liberals, who were already backing the Duc d'Orléans. At the head of an Executive Commission of five members, in which he gave himself total powers of decision, Fouché, the former regicide cleared the way to a second return to the throne for the former leader of the émigrés, expecting a third royal innings after the Revolution and the Empire. He arranged Napoleon's departure for Rochefort, where two British frigates were waiting; still more important, an armistice signed with Wellington and Blücher avoided a battle in Paris and allowed him,

with the complicity of Davout, to send away to the south an overexcited
patriotic army. The road was clear for Louis XVIII who on 28 June had
reaffirmed his undertaking to be faithful to the Charter; he advanced
with measured steps and on 3 July installed himself in Saint-Denis, in
the premises of the Légion d'Honneur. On 6 July he received Fouché,
presented to him by Talleyrand, 'vice leaning on the arm of crime', as
Chateaubriand commented: 'The loyal regicide, on his knees, placed the
hands which caused Louis XVI's head to fall into the hands of the martyred
king's brother; the apostate Bishop witnessed the oath.'[2]

All the former and future Minister of Police now had to do was dissolve
the Executive Commission, which no longer had any purpose. Louis XVIII
entered Paris on 8 July, acclaimed by the royalists and crowds of curious
onlookers.

THE SECOND RESTORATION

The final toll of Napoleon's short reappearance was a heavy one. In 1814,
in order not to clash headlong with national feeling, the allies had been
careful to make a quick withdrawal from French territory; henceforth they
had decided to subjugate France. Up until autumn, more than a million
foreign soldiers occupied sixty-one *départements*, in conditions so harsh that
for a long time they left memories of hatred; for this occupation the allies
had to be paid a heavy indemnity, while they imposed additional rectifica-
tions to the frontiers in the north. Talleyrand's elaborate manoeuvres in
Vienna were broken off, and France's isolation was more complete than
ever. The Revolution's homeland had been relatively well treated the year
before. It was punished in 1815.

This had very important consequences for public opinion and the
internal situation: if the episode of the Hundred Days only temporarily
affected the progress of affairs in Europe, it had lasting effects in France.
For the first time it had revealed a feature which would be characteristic of
French politics in the nineteenth century: the taste, or fatal attraction, for
the repetition of scenes and regimes. The emperor had returned after his
exile on the island of Elba, and Louis XVI's brother – admittedly only
recently a king – reascended the throne of his ancestors for the second
time. This theatrical succession of sovereigns, each garbed in his titles and
tradition, conveys the force of the revolutionary spirit in the nation. But it
also extends it, in that every crisis in the regime weakened the legitimacy
of all the claimants, winners and losers, while it radicalized the fervour of
both sets of supporters. The first Restoration had taken place amid a
consensus by default. The second began with a temptation which would
constantly haunt it: that of revenge. It revived national resentment against
the cause of kings and nobles, like a poisoned gift from the ex-emperor, en
route to St Helena.

[2] Chateaubriand, *Mémoires d'outre-tombe*, book XXIII, 20.

The example had come from the royalists rather than from the king. At the news of Waterloo, in regions of the country where they were organized and strong, the men with the fleur-de-lis emblem took up on their own account, as after 9 Thermidor Year II, the worst of Revolutionary traditions: summary execution. In Provence, in Marseille and Avignon, gangs of fanatics, backed by the ordinary people, massacred those who some months before had celebrated the return from Elba. As during the Revolution, but the other way round, civil struggles also espoused religious quarrels between Catholics and Protestants. The Protestant bourgeoisie of Languedoc paid the price for its loyalty to the Revolution and the Empire: it was the moment for bloody revenge by Catholic nobles and notables, with the support of pro-clerical plebeians, reviving memories of the sixteenth-century League. In Nîmes, an old civil war town, armed bands led by a porter called Trestaillons, had the Protestant churches closed and assassinated several dozen Protestants, to cries of: 'The Bourbons or death!' However, the west remained calm: this was perhaps a sign that the White Terror in the Midi was more of a spectacle than a deep-lying threat to public order.

Louis XVIII, as usual, was more moderate than his family, who demanded examples and victims. The majority of victims of the proscriptions prepared by Fouché were not to be found, since they had been forewarned by the self-same Fouché. Only Colonel Labédoyère in August, and Marshal Ney a little later, were arrested, tried and executed, guilty of having rallied to the usurper in March. But the legislative elections give the best picture of the atmosphere in the summer of 1815. Louis XVIII had appointed a new batch of peers to replace those who had accepted the Hundred Days; he had wanted a new Chamber of Deputies, and some 50,000 voters had fashioned for him an Assembly which he himself called *introuvable*, meaning that he could not have imagined one more favourable to his throne. Of this famous vote in August 1815, so imbued with the feeling of the times, the atmosphere of revenge and the silence of the liberals, the consequences would be paradoxical, because an Assembly that was more royalist than the king would try to test its new-found power in this interval of discord, and to base the liberties of parliament on an overdose of repression.

Neither Fouché nor even Talleyrand was the man of the moment. The first Restoration had kept Bonapartist personnel, who for the most part had emerged from the Revolution. The second inaugurated a political purge, which was a way of regulating state posts and careers destined to enjoy a long national future. Louis summoned as head of the ministry a true aristocrat, a true émigré, a man who had had nothing at all to do with the new France and knew almost nothing about it: the Duc de Richelieu. Having left France after October 1789, this scion of a great family had offered his sword to the Tsar, and Alexander I's favour had brought him in 1803 to administer southern Russia, which had recently been won from the Turks. Louis XVIII, somewhat reluctantly, entrusted him with running the government: 'The Frenchman with the best knowledge of the Crimea', said Talleyrand ironically. He at least had the merit of gracing with his gentlemanly virtues a period when political feelings were scarcely inclined towards magnanimity. Indeed, nearly everywhere, more or less official royalist committees had resumed the revolutionary exercise of denunciation, demanding inquiries, sanctions, causing heads to roll, or at least obtaining posts. The Restoration preserved the structures of the imperial state, but used its own men.

The Chamber was more repressive than the ministry. Not that it was filled with former combatants from the princes' army; but these few hundred provincial nobles and notables, who were often young, elected in a wave of reaction to the Hundred Days and without any political experience other than their loyalty to the throne, pushed their eagerness to serve the king to the point of imitating the language of the Terror in order to threaten other victims. They voted for several repressive exceptional laws in succession, targeting men who had welcomed the adventurer's return; Richelieu, in the king's name, had to oppose the resurrection of the 'suspect' category. Amid these back-to-front debates, the beginnings of the ultra-royalist party took shape.

Two debates in 1816 gave consistency to its extremism. The vote on the budget posed the problem of the debts inherited from the Empire, which were aggravated by the cost of foreign occupation. The Minister of Finance proposed to absorb them by guaranteed bonds on the sale of 400,000 hectares of national forests which had formerly belonged to the Church: this idea was doubly shocking, since it would mean making the legitimate king pay for the usurper's wars with wealth stolen from the clergy by the Revolution. The government had to abandon the idea of selling these forests. There was another lively confrontation on the subject of electoral law, both on the methods of renewing the Chamber and on the tax threshold defining the elector. The majority, who were for the lowering of that threshold, wanted to counterbalance the influence of the rich bourgeoisie by courting more popular votes.

These disagreements were no more than power struggles which surround the very nature of institutions, parliamentary or not. But much that was symbolic also came into it: the *introuvable* Chamber quite simply wanted to uproot the Revolution at long last. With the spectacular brutality of Napoleon's return, the Hundred Days had revealed that revolutionary fire was still smouldering beneath the ashes, and that the first Restoration, while wishing to recognize it had merely succeeded in spreading it. In 1815, therefore, things had to be done differently, and the second Restoration had to be a radically different new beginning: the first act in a head-on combat with the spirit and the men of the French Revolution. Purge the administration, punish the usurper's accomplices, of course, but first of all have a revolution against the Revolution. That was why it was not enough to set up special jurisdictions and exceptional courts (which were not very bloodthirsty): that accursed period which separated the monarchy from its past had to be exorcized.

Therefore the undertakings of the Charter already seemed remote, and that obligation to forget, which totally inspired its first section, was impossible to put into practice. The Chamber voted for the banishment of the regicides, and decided that '21 January each year would be a day of national mourning, and that in expiation of the crime of that unhappy day there should be erected in one of the Paris *Places*, on behalf of and at the expense of the nation, a statue of the martyr-king, bearing the inscription: 'Free France to Louis XVI' (28 December 1815).

Having got under way, the Chamber then took the same measures for Madame Elisabeth, Marie-Antoinette and the Duc d'Enghien. With many invocations and tears, the deputies thus resuscitated not the glory of the monarchy, but its misfortunes; not its tradition, but its downfall. Not only did they offer an involuntary homage to the Terror by, in their turn, giving the White Terror the blessing of the law, but they also placed the restored royalty in the revolutionary calendar, unwittingly subjecting themselves to the tyranny of the memories they were trying to ward off. This funereal procession of dates and ceremonies, which was meant to mark out the rhythm of a collective expiation, revived the memory of the Revolution rather than the tradition of the monarchy.

It was a memory which did not need so much: for it had also been fed by the Hundred Days and the failure of the Hundred Days. The triumphal march from the Golfe-Juan to the Tuileries had revived the Little Corporal defying the monarchs of Europe, and had reanimated revolutionary passions around rediscovered images of primitive Bonapartism. The emperor's last appearance on the world theatre had cost his country dearly, but defeat, invasion and occupation had been entered on the debit side of the monarchy rather than on his. He, on the other hand, had regained some of the magic of his youthful popularity through that hopeless attempt; and the British, who had padlocked him away at the other end of the world, in St Helena, had moreover provided him with a perfect setting, in the imagination of the French, in which to join the cause of liberty to his own misfortune. The Hundred Days had thus favoured the unification of revolutionary memory; the *introuvable* Chamber had done the rest: in the face of the White Terror, there was but one single France of the Revolution, buttressed by its memories and passions which others were trying to take away from it, and where the principles of 1789, the sale of *biens nationaux* and the glory of the tricolour flag were inextricably intertwined.

Louis XVIII had wisely preached forgetfulness in 1814 to try to sew France's two pasts together again, to his own advantage. In 1816, in spite of himself, he had become the king of the counter-revolution. The allies were worried by the sectarianism of the deputies, and the young Minister of Police, Elie Decazes, who had the king's ear, was pushing for the dissolution of the *introuvable* Chamber. As paradoxical as the political situation, the idea was to obtain from the electorate an Assembly less massively loyal to royalism, in order to restore a little more play to the king's powers. The aim, which was risky given the state of opinion, was to find a replacement majority which might be more 'liberal' and less intractable, at the same time less attached to the Bourbons and more willing to submit to Louis XVI's brother. This was what Louis XVIII was gambling on when, on 5 September 1816, he dissolved the Chamber in order to avoid a parliamentary drift in the regime. This was a crucial turning-point, which would thenceforth dominate the history of the Restoration.

RESTORATION LIBERALISM

One may enter the political situation of these years in the wake of two great minds who had been its keenest observers: Chateaubriand and Madame de Staël. While they were both passionately interested in the same things – glory, history, literature, liberty, public life – they came from worlds which were not only different but mutually hostile: precisely those two worlds which had clashed during the French Revolution. Even if they thought in unison about many matters, they would never manage to reduce the distance between them. Their example also makes understandable the chasm which continued to separate their political friends and their backgrounds: the ultra-royalists from the liberals.

Though she had not been a victim of the *ancien régime*, Necker's daughter had never obtained from it the consideration which she thought due to the dazzling success of her father and to her own merits. A Protestant and a commoner, she was snubbed by people of the court: money and marriage did nothing for her. Chateaubriand was the scion of a nobility she hated even more than the Versailles aristocracy: the same 'feudal' hauteur, described at the start of the *Mémoires d'outre-tombe*, without the manners of the *grand monde*. The young Vicomte was not rich, but he was noble and never forgot it.

Madame de Staël welcomed the Revolution with joy, and her enthusiasm – or her ambition – survived the era when her father left the scene; she held a salon, the Egeria of the Feuillants, and still had sufficient influence to push her lover, the Comte de Narbonne, into the Ministry of War at the beginning of the Legislative Assembly. Though she left France during the Terror, she came back with the Thermidorian Convention to become a powerful force in bourgeois republic opinion. The child of Combourg, on the other hand, had fled the Revolution earlier on, to make his American voyage. Then he fought it for several months in the princes' army, before living as an émigré for seven years in England, separated from his homeland by the crimes of the Republic.

The first days of the Consulate were a happy period for both these writers. Madame de Staël, together with her friend Constant, had been involved in the intrigues of the 'Brumairians', and had brought back to the new regime her hope – disappointed under the Directory – of establishing the Revolution within the law. Chateaubriand came back to Paris, his name soon having been erased from the list of émigrés, and would celebrate the religious reconciliation and the Concordat, after his own fashion, with the fanfare of the *Génie du Christianisme* (1802). Nevertheless, they would both get into hot water with the new master of France, who disliked the independence of their writings and their shared taste for political freedom: she in 1802, and he in 1804. For once they were united – morally, of course – in their opposition to imperial despotism.

In consequence, they were two 'liberals', in the political sense, and two supporters of the Charter, when the old royalty returned under the new flag. Chateaubriand welcomed 'his' king more warmly than Madame de Staël, who had for a while plotted in favour of Bernadotte; but in these years both of them had written enough on the regime of the Charter for it to be clear that they attributed to the constitution 'granted' by Louis XVI's brother the same significance, that is to say, representative government. In order to demonstrate its benefits, Chateaubriand devoted firstly his *Réflexions politiques* (1814), then *De la monarchie selon la Charte*, which appeared just at the time when Louis XVIII dissolved the *introuvable* Chamber in September 1816. As for Madame de Staël, who died in 1817 at the age of fifty-one, the analyses which she devoted in the same era and to the same problem form part (the fifth) of a posthumous book published in 1818 by her heirs, the *Considérations sur la Révolution française*.

It was a history book, and not by chance. For both for her and Chateaubriand, the question which the Restoration must resolve as a matter of priority was that of the heritage of the past. It had to mend what the Revolution had torn to pieces and rebuild for the French people one single history spanning both sides of 1789, around a tradition of liberty. In fact, that tradition had not been born in France with the Revolution; as in England, it had for a long time been inseparable from a monarchy controlled by the Estates-General: it was a control which had never managed to be institutionalized within fixed rules and through an English-style parliament, but which bore witness to the antiquity of what the French had tried to do in 1789 and were succeeding in doing with the Charter. Like Chateaubriand, Madame de Staël wanted to restore to the Bourbon dynasty its historic claims to the foundation of a free government. Like him, in order to unify national history she selected from each of its parts. Of the Revolution she preserved only 1789; and of the monarchic heritage, only the part before absolutism, that part which in truth was rather hard to pin down, somewhere between the end of feudalism and the last Valois, when the kings of France had fairly frequently called together their 'Estates'. In this way the two authors rebuilt for France, to the advantage of the Bourbons who had returned to the throne, that liberal tradition in which Burke had seen the condition of liberty.

But they incorporated 1789. In effect, transposed to the beginning of

the nineteenth century, after the agony of the Revolution, the tutelary
monarchy of the fifteenth had to yield to the times, accept civil equality
and modern society, take note of bourgeois advancement, keep pace with
the evolution of minds and customs, instead of enclosing itself in an
attachment to the past: that was the whole sense of the 'representative
government' organized by the Charter. Like Constant, Sieyès before him
and François Guizot after them, Madame de Staël saw in it a necessary end
of European history, following on from the feudal period and the age of the
monarchies. Chateaubriand who, as a writer, cultivated a pessimist view
of the human condition, saw it rather as the indispensable means of
controlling for a while the dizzying evolution of the world in which he had
lived. Both of them, however, were uncompromising about the Charter's
articles: a hereditary king, two Chambers, a ministry; and no absolute or
indivisible sovereignty, but a balance of power which was the guarantee of
citizens' liberty.

But the Baronne and the Vicomte were not breathing the same air. The
spirit of their writings was not only different: it reflected two worlds which
had confronted each other, and continued to hate each other. It was all
very well for Chateaubriand to wax ironical about the huntsmen, the
dowagers, the vengeful aristocrats who were the prime movers in the ranks
and extremism of the ultras; or now and then to acknowledge 1789 and
the Constituent Assembly; he belonged to the ancient nobility out of
which, through the Chamber of Peers, he wanted to form an aristocracy
indispensable to the constitutional monarchy and the dominant circle of
the new regime. Like all his kind, he despised the middle class: a prejudice
which in one sense gave him a freedom, not enjoyed by the bourgeois, to
predict, in his apocalyptic style, the inevitable triumph of equality and
democracy; but which for the moment isolated him from the bulk of the
liberal forces. He loved Christianity, in which he, like Madame de Staël,
saw the origin of modern freedom and the idea of man's universality; but
that Christianity belonged to the Catholic Church, another victim of the
French Revolution, and he ceaselessly saluted its influence, which he
regarded as essential to morality and social order.

He viewed the returned royalty less with a reasoned respect for a
necessary institution than with a filial and aesthetic loyalty. The latter was
nurtured by history, but his history, after being that of France, had
become that of a family's misfortune. An aristocrat and an artist, who
despised the times in which he lived, he constantly wrote the funeral
oration of those kings of France with whom disappeared both his youth
and the future of what he loved. Since he could not make their throne
eternal, he would make the last Bourbons pass into the history of literature. He had loved the royal families only at the tomb, to declaim their
funeral oration. 'Our destiny', he would write on the assassination of the
Duc de Berry, 'is to weep over the tomb of the Bourbons.'

As for Madame de Staël, she had no cause to regret the old world. Her
father, the Protestant minister of the king of France, had suffered from

Catholic intolerance and the rebuffs of the aristocracy. Very early on she had been keenly aware of her own worth, faced with the barrier of 'birth'. Moreover, she had no esteem at all for French nobility. On several occasions, in the *Considérations*, she returns to the servile sycophancy which dominated the court, the haughtiness of the least petty squire, the social parasitism of an order which was defined by privilege alone to the exclusion of any public service: characteristics which, in her eyes, expressed the corruption of French nobility by absolutism, as opposed to what had happened in Britain. What chance was there then to make citizens out of these nobles, and what reason was there to entrust, from choice, the constitutional monarchy to a body of citizen-nobles? Chateaubriand's idea had its moment in Britain; but it had no roots in the history of France. The greatness of French nobility lay in its having constituted a tradition of aristocratic liberty. But that tradition had been lost, or at least dimmed by absolutist domestication, and the banner of liberty had been taken up in 1789 by the Third Estate. Madame de Staël does not claim the merit and all that was acquired by this victory for the middle class alone, as Guizot would do a little later; but it was her wish that an enlightened nobility, of an English-style constitution, should share responsibility with a moderate bourgeoisie.

From the gulf which, in 1816, separated two such distinguished minds – which were at least in agreement as to the goal to be reached – one may infer the feelings and passions which inescapably divided their circles and their supporters. How could they forget the Revolution, which had begun the class hatred between their two worlds? The returned émigrés and *chouans*, given an honoured place, the expiatory festivals, the return of a vocabulary and customs which had been preserved in the close confines of the counter-revolution, continually reawoke the rupture of 1789 at all levels of public life. Memories and passions came before interests, and made them irreconcilable. Chateaubriand and Madame de Staël would have liked to tame the Revolution, linking it up with the national past. But the friends of the former still wanted to destroy it, and those of the latter to begin it again. What their failed dialogue meant was the Restoration's total inability to unite a wide consensus of notables – both nobility and bourgeoisie together – around a representative government. This mistrust and these hatreds were a typically French problem; they had put up walls within the dominant classes and made political agreement so difficult: that, too, was an *ancien régime* legacy, made worse by the Revolution. A monarchy of property-owners: Turgot had already had this ambition. But what he had not succeeded in achieving before the great upheaval, Decazes had even less chance of accomplishing afterwards.

Chateaubriand had just finished *De la monarchie selon la Charte* when Louis XVIII on 5 September dissolved the *introuvable* Chamber. He hastily added a postscript in criticism, not of the king but of his ministers; at the end of a book in which he had chiefly sung the praises of the moderation of opinion, there is this extraordinary sentence:

Even if a bloody daughter of the Convention should emerge from the electoral colleges, the ministers would in no way regret this Chamber, which may have been able to thwart their plans, but which was a meeting-place for the elite of true Frenchmen, men who by sharing the king's exile had retained something of their master's virtues ... they would see whether it is easier to have dealings with an assembly of ambitious revolutionaries than with a Chamber whose deputies the king regarded as *introuvables*, like a blessing from Providence.

It was not a 'bloody daughter of the Convention' which emerged from the voting urns, but a more submissive – or less intractable – Assembly. In effect, the king won the elections against his brother, the Comte d'Artois, who protected the outgoing deputies; he had a new majority of moderate royalists elected, by dint of strong pressure on the electoral colleges: here was the paradox of a 'liberal' victory acquired by a Bourbon by mobilizing the prefects. It was also true that a year had passed since the big swing to the *ultras*, (ultra-royalists), whose rhetoric of revenge annoyed and worried a good many notables. At all events, Louis XVIII had his hands free to resume his 1814 policy, which the Hundred Days had interrupted: to reconcile the French around an English-style compromise, making the monarchy into a strong power, released from aristocratic ascendancy and with no wish to take revenge against what Chateaubriand called 'the party of revolutionary interests'.[3]

There then began the short period during which Louis XVIII tried to make his way along this narrow path, fought by the majority of his own people and incapable of attracting many new friends to the monarchy. What he tried to do in the direction of the France of the Revolution was less attributable to his own credit than to the inevitability of the situation. To tell the truth, his style was not of a kind to impart fresh youth to the institution he embodied. A policy of national reconciliation would have called for a bold, imaginative king, capable of making himself popular. He himself was a twilight monarch, the worst possible symbol of a remarriage of royalty with the nation; anything majestic in his manner and tone, despite his physical infirmities and secretive nature, he had concocted only from Versailles etiquette and from what he had learned from *ancien régime* booklets.

It is true that his princely loftiness had stood him in good stead at the time when he had been a king without a kingdom. But the old man who had come back to the heritage of his ancestors had neither understanding nor any deep intuition about history. More subtle than his two brothers, he resembled them in the narrowness of his political vision, though he was superior to them when it came to intrigue and the manipulation of men. At this epoch, he developed an inordinate interest in the son of a Libourne notary, Decazes, the young 1815 Prefect of Police, who had become one of his intimates and let him into the little secrets and scandalous anecdotes

---

[3] Chateaubriand's political writings of the Restoration are collected in the *Oeuvres complètes* under the title *Mélanges politiques*.

of the secret police office. From these confidential conversations between the old king and the courtier-official arose an unprecedented situation, in which the traditional role of the king's mistress would be played by a minister showered with honours and kindnesses by the sovereign. Opportunist and glib, Decazes had no other horizon than royal favour. But, since he was detested by the ultras, he found himself perforce in the other camp. He had played a key part in the September decision and the new elections; he was the mainspring of all the political measures of the period that followed.

The Duc de Richelieu's ministry, which had been modified to admit men of the constitutional centre, such as Molé and Etienne Pasquier, remained in power until the settlement of the international situation and the end of the country's occupation (December 1818). Decazes then took on the portfolio of the Interior in a new format before becoming, a year later, head of the government for a very short while, since the assassination of the Duc de Berry (see p. 294) ended his ascendancy, despite the regret of the King.

In their constitutional substance, these years produced no concerted effort to organize public authority between the king and the two Chambers in a spirit of sharing and balance. Louis XVIII had broken with the ultras only in order to keep all his power to himself; Decazes went further in the same direction, less on behalf of constitutional principles than because he was merely following the classical characteristics of a favourite. What Royer-Collard and Guizot were developing as an interpretation of the Charter was the product of thinking which was less erudite and more ancient, since it had stemmed from the political situation of royal power and its aim was not to share, but to confirm, that power. In this regard, Louis XVIII was disloyal to neither the letter nor the spirit of the Charter, although he acted mainly according to his own tendencies. Nevertheless, if this period of the Restoration is generally extolled by historians as its liberal age, that is because the constitutional monarchists who dominated the new parliament were getting laws passed which were favourable to modern society, and going against the ultras.

The electoral law, which had formed the subject of impassioned debates in the preceding year, was voted at the beginning of 1817. It granted the right to vote to all Frenchmen aged at least thirty years and paying at least 300 francs in taxes; and the right to be elected to those of forty years and over, paying at least 1,000 francs. Elections were to be held in the *départements*. At last the regime was provided with rules of play in keeping with the Charter (the preceding electoral consultations had been the subject of special decrees), and this worried the ultra-royalist right. Indeed, although these arrangements anticipated a very limited body of electors – about 100,000 individuals – the tax threshold of 300 francs created the risk of peopling the electoral assemblies with citizens who had grown rich in trade and industry, many of whom would be paying trading dues of 300, 400 or even 500 francs, and in addition living in the main town of the *département*, so less inclined to abstain on polling day than the landowner living on his lands. Now, that urban middle class was a hotbed of liberal ideas, one of the centres of opposition to the Bourbons, the face of the other France: that of the Revolution, civil equality and *biens nationaux*. So it could bring to bear on moderate royalism in power – already being challenged by the ultras – a threat which was likely to revive the spectre of 1789: the elections which followed those of 1816 would make this all too apparent.

Another bill which was fiercely debated, and finally voted in 1818, one which for many a long year would be the cornerstone of French military institutions, was the Gouvion Saint-Cyr law. As if naturally, in those years, the army crystallized the political passions of public opinion. During the *ancien régime*, the army had been the exclusive honour of the aristocracy, the noble calling *par excellence*, before becoming, with the Revolution and the Empire, the privileged area of social advancement, and the incarnation of the hope of a Marshal's baton in every soldier's imagination. By his victories, Napoleon had made it the symbol of the nation; and by his defeat, he had given it back the memory of the Revolution. The ultras wanted to regain it as something which had belonged to them, and as if they wanted to exorcize its memories, since they could not share them. Against them, Gouvion Saint-Cyr proposed limited conscription by drawing of lots, adjusted by the possibility of the unlucky conscript's paying a replacement; a system of officer recruitment on merit or by competition, and very carefully regulated promotion; finally, a reserve army after active service of six years. Scandalized by these arrangements which did not offer them a place reserved in advance in the military hierarchy, the old nobility were also afraid of this 'reserve', which would contain all the emperor's *grognards* (soldiers of the Old Guard).

It was against these pretensions that the minister was fighting – a veteran of the Revolution and Empire wars, a soldier of the Moselle army of 1793 right up to the 1812 Russian campaign. There is nothing more revealing of the spirit of the debate than his speech, which was drawn up by Guizot, who had been able to lend his talent to the memories of the Marshal:

We need to know if there are two armies, two nations, among us, one of which is to be anathematized and considered incapable of serving the king and France. And, to confine myself to what concerns me directly, we need to know if we shall still summon to the defence of the homeland soldiers who have been her glory, or if we shall declare them forever a danger to her repose. The latter would be harsh and unjust; for these soldiers were admirable on the day of battle: a tireless ardour drove them on, heroic patience sustained them; they never stopped believing that they were sacrificing their lives for France's honour; and when they had left the flag, they still had immense stores of strength and bravery to offer! Must France no longer ask them for these? Must it, in its adversity, cease to be proud of these men whom Europe has never ceased to admire?[4]

[4] A. de Vaulabelle, *Histoire des deux Restaurations jusqu'à l'avènement de Louis-Philippe*, vol. 4, pp. 465–6.

After winning the battle of what a document of the times called 'the constitutional and citizens' army', the ministry managed to regulate in a liberal sense the liberty of the press: these were the Comte de Serre's laws, in May and June 1819, in which the indefatigable Guizot, in charge of the Ministry of the Interior, had also taken a hand. These texts reaffirmed the principle of liberty of opinion, private and public: it was simply a matter of organizing freedom to publish by defining the abuses which could be repressed; possible offenders could henceforth have the benefit of trial by jury. Here again, the discussion was difficult and the debates stormy, during which Serre the Keeper of the Seals, and a veteran of the Condé army but also a former magistrate under the Empire, tried to implant the monarchy of the Charter in the law and customs of 1789.

This problem formed the obsession of the *Doctrinaires*, who tried to give the Decazes policy a more durable foundation than royal favouritism. The name designated a gathering of like minds which had gradually formed, from a beginning in 1816, in the battle against the domination of the ultras. It united figures who had lived through the great events, like Serre, Royer-Collard and Camille Jordan, but mainly younger men – some of them very young – who had not yet reached the front lines of public life, and were trying to conceive the needs for action in philosophical terms: Prosper de Barante, Charles de Rémusat, the young Duc de Broglie, Madame de Staël's son-in-law who published her *Considérations*, and lastly and chiefly, Guizot, who was thirty in 1817. The master was Pierre-Paul Royer-Collard, whose speeches in the Chamber were speeches of political philosophy. But the soul of the group was Guizot, who had been continually hard at work since his entry into political life in 1814, when he had left his history teaching post at the Sorbonne for the general secretariat of the Ministry of the Interior. He was not yet very conspicuous but was already a great instigator, and no one – friend or enemy – had any doubt about his future. In the various posts of top administration which he took on between 1814 and 1820, he produced many notes, projects and recommendations with exceptional talent and fertility; he was privy to the secret of the royal decision of 5 September 1816, and prepared the electoral and press laws for the Ministers; he even wrote, as has been seen, Marshal Gouvion Saint-Cyr's great speech on the army.

The theme of national reconciliation was, indeed, central for him, as for his friends: it was a question of bringing the Revolution to an end. The old question, the French problem above all others for a quarter of a century, was more than ever on the agenda. Terminating the Revolution meant first of all accepting it, and regarding civil equality and modern society as an unchallengeable historical fact: that was the gulf which divided the Doctrinaires from the ultras. Born a Protestant commoner, Guizot had nothing in his past to make him regret the aristocratic world. On the contrary: 1789 was the great anniversary of the middle class – his own.

But there remained to be found for this new society a free and stable political government, which the Revolution had never been able to ensure

for the French. In this regard, 1789 had not to be carried out again, but to
be recommenced on more assured principles. It was no longer a matter
of basing power on the rights of individuals, as the Enlightenment's
philosophy desired: the course of events had sufficiently demonstrated the
dangers of such an undertaking. Guizot and the Doctrinaires substituted
for the natural individual endowed with rights the authority of reason,
which was also that of history. They thus ceased to make society a product
of human wills, rather to subordinate it to a human nature that could be
rationally known, and unveiled by the course of history. Immediately, the
government of society – that great question mark of the era – lost its
secondary character in relation to civil society, which it had preserved in
the contractualist tradition from Hobbes to Rousseau: just like modern
society, it became one of the ways in which history revealed its function of
fulfilling the nature of man.

The Revolution had illustrated the risks which lay in conceiving of it
as endowed with a sovereignty based on the agreement of contracting
individuals. In fact the Revolution had in the end produced an atomized
society of isolated individuals, united on the political level by a general
will which was deemed to represent what they had in common; but
in reality very quickly subjected to an administrative dictatorship which
alone could avert the anarchy that was inseparable from that radical
individualism. One of the Doctrinaires' problems was therefore that of
rebuilding social powers which, in conjunction with the splitting up of
sovereignty, might form the defences of public liberties. This idea was
admirably expressed by Royer-Collard, in a speech on the freedom of the
press in January 1822, which must be quoted at length:

We have witnessed the death of the old society and, with it, that mass of domestic
institutions and independent offices which it held in its bosom, powerful networks
of private rights, veritable republics within the monarchy. These institutions, these
offices did not, it is true, share sovereignty; but everywhere they set up limits to it
which honour stubbornly defended. Not one of them has survived, and no other
has arisen to take their place. The Revolution left only *individuals* standing. In
this respect, the dictatorship which ended it consummated its work . . . from a
society reduced to dust centralization emerged; there is no need to seek its origin
elsewhere. Centralization did not come on the scene, like other no less pernicious
doctrines, its head held high, with the authority of a principle; it worked its way
in modestly, like a consequence or a necessity. Indeed, where there are only
individuals, all matters which are not theirs are public matters, affairs of the
state. Where there are no independent magistrates, there are only governmental
representatives. That is how we have become an *administered people*, under the
thumb of officials who are not accountable, who are themselves centralized in the
government whose ministers they are. Society was bequeathed to the Restoration
in this condition . . . The Charter therefore had to constitute government and
society at the same time. Society has been, certainly not forgotten or neglected, but
adjourned; the Charter has constituted only government; it has done so by the
division of sovereignty and the multiplicity of authorities . . . in order that a nation
may be free, it is not enough to have it governed by serveral powers . . . Sharing

sovereignty is certainly important, and has very great consequences, in relation to the royal power which it modifies; but the Government which results from it, though divided in its parts, is one in its actions; and if, on the outside, it meets no obstacle which it must respect, it is absolute – no matter what name it is given – and the nation and its laws belong to it . . . It was only by establishing the freedom of the press that the Charter truly established all freedoms, and restored society to itself.[5]

The Doctrinaires' thinking wavered between this theory of shared powers, both in the state and in society, and a more unitarian version of the social and the political. In the first, there was the idea of an equilibrium produced by multiplicity: not only should the state rest on the division of sovereignty but, as with Montesquieu, society should have its own brakes to apply to the actions of the state and the obedience of citizens. But in the second, given more or less emphasis by Guizot according to the times, the accent was less on plurality of powers, since government tends to harmonize the social and political, being based on the reason which can be extracted from the first to form the second.

Within this philosophical framework, representation was no longer a right, but a function. Although they broke with revolutionary tradition, the Doctrinaires recovered this concept from Sieyès, separating it from that of sovereignty: the Charter's Chambers did not 'represent' the nation, they constituted its political reason by the fact that they were constituted through the social superiority of property-ownership and education, which were constantly monitored by an enlightened opinion. As for the king, the precious legacy of national history, the centre of the whole of government, he was the 'representative' *par excellence*, because his person was the incarnation of the authority and power which were spread through all ranks of society. He must still play that role to the full, in unison with that modern society which was the product of the movement of civilization.

This body of ideas would some time later form the platform of the liberal opposition, before attaining power with Louis-Philippe in 1830. As it gradually took shape, between 1817 and 1820, in the speeches of Royer-Collard and Guizot's writings, it immediately ran into the hostility of the ultras, who had no difficulty in reading into it the ambitions of the middle class. They certainly could not recognize any of their memories in this exaltation of civil equality, or any of their history in this almost disembodied movement, in which the monarchy and the Third Estate were abstract figures of civilization. The king himself, whom the Doctrinaires installed in the centre of their representative government, was already no longer theirs: not only because he was no longer inseparable from the nobility, but even more because he had scarcely any past left, being cut off from all that Chateaubriand was extolling in the same epoch as the wedding of a family and a people. The limited monarchy of the

[5] P. P. Royer-Collard, *Opinion sur le projet de loi relatif à la répression des délits de presse*, 22 January 1822, pp. 3–5.

ultras and the representative government of the Doctrinaires were but two interpretations of the same text; but the general agreement on the 1814 Charter masked the divorce between feelings, circles and ideas. The ruling classes in the country were basically very much in agreement about both monarchic and liberal institutions: in either camp, memories of the *ancien régime* and of the Revolution drew minds together on this. However, everything else pushed them apart. The Revolution still lived on.

THE ULTRAS AND THE CHURCH

The turn of events bore witness to this divorce. The liberal coalition centred on Decazes progressively fell apart under the united but antagonistic pressure of the ultras and a left which asserted itself in the by-elections: La Fayette, Benjamin Constant and the barrister Jacques Antoine Manuel had entered the Chamber in 1818. The Comte de Serre was sliding towards the right, and Guizot in the other direction. The problem which was beginning, only five years after the Bourbons' return, was already – or still – the one of legitimacy.

By assassinating the Duc de Berry on 13 February 1820, as he came out of the Opera, the saddler Louis Pierre Louvel gave matters a dramatic turn. The Comte d'Artois's son, recently married, carried the hope of giving the Bourbons some descendants, and his murderer made no mystery about having wanted to extinguish this hope by his action (he was mistaken, because the Duc de Berry had a posthumous son): by causing regicide to re-enter the French political scene, he returned the ultras to power, and legitimate royalty to its most loyal and most dangerous supporters.

As Chateaubriand put it, Decazes 'slipped in the blood'. The minister was unable to survive the hatred of the ultra-royalists, who had regrouped around the Comte d'Artois. It was no longer a time for liberty, but for emergency laws, censorship, repression, regime of a new 'public safety' in reverse, by which the right, through its attachment to the *ancien régime*, displayed a penchant for emergency measures which it shared with the revolutionary tradition. Decazes was replaced by a ministry grouped once more around the Duc de Richelieu, then, at the end of the following year, after elections won by the ultras, by a team whose principal figure was the Comte de Villèle, the Minister of Finance. Villèle remained in power for more than six years, up till 1828; he thus dominated the Restoration's longest and most characteristic political period: royalty's reunion with its memories.

Indeed, the ultras were dominated by nostalgia for the old France, out of sight but so near, just sufficiently present to make them relive each day the enormous toppling fall in which a whole world had disappeared, together with their youth. They could all have signed their name to what Chateaubriand wrote in 1822, which reappeared like an obsession all through the *Mémoires d'outre-tombe* (Memoirs from beyond the grave):

Old men of yesteryear were less unhappy and less isolated than those of today: if, by staying on the earth, they had lost their friends, very little had changed around them; though they were strangers to youth, they were not so to society. Nowadays, one who lingers on in this world has witnessed not only the death of men, but also the death of ideas: principles, customs, tastes, pleasures, pains, feelings – nothing resembles what he used to know. He is of a different race from the human species in whose midst he is ending his days.[6]

Chateaubriand had built his art out of this melancholy. The ultras had to derive a programme of action from it. That was a difficult task in a period which was seeing the beginning of the democratic belief that politics should invent the future, yet less impossible than that modern obsession with the morrow would lead one to believe. For, in the France of those years, though the Revolution had created numerous new interests, attached to 1789 as to a watershed, it had also sharpened – as a pleasure and as a sorrow – a sensitivity towards the past. National history was a major stake, offered to those who could restore it to the country; and the witnesses of the *ancien régime*, clothed in the Charter, were not necessarily the worst placed to do so: between the fourteenth- and fifteenth-century 'monarchy of the Estates' and that of the Restoration, they could hope to reconstitute a royalist tradition in the British style. Moreover, the mood of the time was for worthless trappings of the past, and history – fashionable in literary life, suffused with poetic radiance – surrounded the infirm sovereign with an aureole of the powerful spell of centuries, rallying a crowd of the young around the throne. The ultra-royalist party brought together not only émigrés and lords of the manor: romantic literature also thronged to them. Victor Hugo, Alphonse de Lamartine, Alfred de Vigny and Charles Nodier, in their twenties, contributed the spark of their brilliance before going on to other horizons, when they would have despaired of rediscovering France's history among the party's ranks.

In fact, the tendency of the ultras was not so much to reconstruct the nation's past as to slice off a special share in the name of the particular memories which linked them to the monarchy. But the keenest of those memories were of the shared tragedy: not only because they were the most recent, but also because, from their behaviour before the period of catastrophes which had united them with the king, the nobles had not been able to retain any recollection of great obedience to Louis XIV's descendants. The ultras and Louis XVI's brothers chiefly had memories of misfortune in common, now redoubled by the Duc de Berry's assassination – a new 21 January against legitimacy.

Thence arose that doleful tone which crept into so many ultra-royalist writings of the period, and that image of a melancholy and tearful royalty. The Restoration saw the appearance of the figure of the martyr-king, based on that of Christ, which no longer had anything to do with the *ancien régime* juridico-political construction of the monarchy, without however

[6] *Mémoires d'outre-tombe*, book IX, ch. 10.

contributing to implanting an image of a constitutional king in public opinion. The ultras reinvented a cult of monarchy while they believed they were maintaining or restoring the old one; but the new cult, feeding on the Bourbons' misfortune, drew its substance only from the revolutionary years. It intensified the separation of king and people, instead of averting it.

The best evidences of this political will, or this state of mind, were the funereal celebrations in expiation of the Revolution's crimes, the increase in which has been noted. The monarchy, which had given up burying its kings in public since the seventeenth century, rediscovered the custom only when trying to alter its sense, to its own risk and peril. After the killing of the king, there had to be expiation for the death of Marie-Antoinette, the Dauphin, the Duc d'Enghien . . . Royalty celebrated its return by marking the anniversaries of its sorrows.

Closely linked with these ceremonies, the Catholic Church was the other great mournful figure of the Restoration, as it had been the other victim of the Revolution. It was the Church that gave all its significance to the expiation of the crime of a people, thus renewing its old alliance with the monarchy, which had been sealed in the seventeenth century at the expense of the Protestants. Although the Church had paid dearly for it under the Revolution, it replaced its hand in the hand of the kings, like them a prisoner of the tyranny of memories. In French royalism, the monarchy of the divine right deteriorated into the alliance of Throne and Altar, a fighting phrase, unwittingly inherited from Revolutionary tradition, since it no longer defined an age-old kind of public authority, but the forces of the counter-revolution.

For anyone wishing to understand how this ensemble of feelings, beliefs, memories and passions could become something like a doctrine, it is enough to read the works of the Vicomte de Bonald, who was perhaps the evil genius of the ultras. By that I mean that, in the profusion of ideas and discussions excited by post-revolutionary royalism, Bonald was the most influential thinker, less because he was a philosopher properly speaking than for the certainty he offered to nostalgia. In that sense he was the truth of the ultras, where Chateaubriand represented only their literature.

Nevertheless in 1789 he had espoused ideas of moderate reform. Born in the family château at Le Monna, a little village on the southern edge of the limestone plateau of Larzac, he had been the astute mayor of the neighbouring town of Millau in the summer of 1789, receiving the civic crown in September, re-elected to office in February 1790 and soon president of the departmental assembly. It was the Civil Constitution of the Clergy which plunged this son of the Catholic highlands of Aveyron into radical opposition to the Revolution: Bonald would construct – firstly, among the émigrés, then in the Empire's internal exile, and lastly as the inspiring force of the ultras – a posthumous justification of the *ancien régime*, founded on a theologico-political system of natural order.

His heavy, strong and repetitive prose endlessly fits together, by a chain of deductions, the divine plan, the monarchy, aristocratic society and the family. Everything that has a lasting existence is 'constituted' according to this simple metaphysic, its principle ruled by ontological proof. The Restoration must thus establish France's reunion with the constant order of her existence as a nation; it had no existence if it was nothing but a written contract, a product of the will of men, as the liberals wished. It made sense only if it brought to life again – after the revolutionary anarchy, and according to providential will – the constitution of France.

Madame de Staël had defended it as the finally discovered synthesis of the national past and 1789, made possible by the march of civilization. In opposition to her, and her book of 1818, which he refuted at length in his *Observations sur l'ouvrage de Madame la baronne de Staël*, Bonald established the *ancien régime's* imprescriptible claims over the Restoration: 'France therefore had one constitution; for it is not trade, or academies, or the arts, or the administration or even the army which form a state, but royalty, religion and justice.'[7]

The constitutional royalty of the liberals, for Bonald, either meant nothing or was merely the same old royal constitution as always. Even this contradiction could be masked by a common acceptance of the Charter, which even the most intransigent of the ultras accepted as a matter of obedience. Such a misunderstanding was not possible as far as society was concerned. Bonald's philosophy, in fact, conceived the social element only as organized in bodies linked hierarchically in dependent relationships; it challenged modern individualism, the Rights of Man and civil equality. In this sense, it theorized what most of the ultras thought, or better still, the way they felt; the king might well have accepted civil equality, but the latter had not really entered into their habits or customs. If the spectre of aristocracy hovered over the country, in spite of Louis XVIII's promises, it was because a good number of the nobility continued to keep it alive in their hearts: now that nobility, together with the ultras, was in the process of obtaining something it had never enjoyed under the absolute monarchy – political power.

Certainly, the historian must take care not to overdo it, not to paint this royalism of loyalty according to its most extreme version. There was a whole gamut of opinion between the most moderate constitutionals and the most liberal ultras, Pasquier and Chateaubriand for instance. Moreover, the ultra ministry of 1821 had been formed with the complicity of constitutional political men like the Comte de Serre. And its central figure, Villèle, was the least ultra of ultras: born in 1773 into the petty nobility of the Garonne, a former planter in the West Indies who had returned under the Empire to run the family domain near Toulouse, he had a short period of activism following the Hundred Days, but rapidly became the moderating influence on his friends. In government, he would be that clever and

---

[7] L. de Bonald, *Observations sur l'ouvrage de Madame de Staël ayant pour titre: 'Considérations sur les principaux événements de la Révolution française'*, ch. 3.

prudent man, that top-ranking specialist in finance, so cordially disliked by Chateaubriand; he had a positive, practical mind, little inclined to the historical, theological or mystical speculations which were fashionable among a good number of his friends.

Yet the ultras' political trend was not towards moderation. Rather than Villèle, it was a religious society, the *Congrégation*, that set the tone, proclaiming the alliance of Throne and Altar. Within the Congrégation, the Knights of the Faith manipulated the party's spokesmen and politicians. They had retaliated with emergency laws to the assassination of the Duc de Berry. In 1825, they got the law of the *milliard des émigrés* passed, which was intended to compensate for losses due to the sale of nobles' possessions whose owners had left France under the Revolution: it was a passionately debated bill, which had as its aim to put an end to the threats hanging over new owners by paying off the old ones through the issue of bonds to their profit. But the ultra plan went far beyond this reasonable target: it was a matter of re-establishing, or implanting on a lasting basis, aristocracy's domination in the political life of France.

However, the ultras were in no way trying to dismantle the centralized administrative state they had inherited from Napoleon. Although they were in support of local powers, which ensured the ascendancy of the château over the village, they did not interfere with the all-powerfulness of the prefect; they might well claim to be in favour of electoral rights being extended to a larger number of the French, so as to drown the middle-class vote in popular suffrage, but they made no attempt to free the commune or the *département* from the supervision of the administration by giving them an elected representation.

On the contrary, the path they chose – or borrowed without really choosing it, since it so forced itself upon them – did not belong to their tradition: investing the central state with the power to direct the country's affairs. That was how in 1820, just before getting mastery of the government, they had succeeded in the law of the double vote, which gave two votes to the most highly taxed electors, or a quarter of the electoral body, composed of the great property-owners: they voted a first time with the rest, in the *arrondissement*, to elect three-fifths of the Chamber, and a second time, amongst themselves, in the *département*, to elect the remainder of the deputies. This bill would ensure that the ultras got parliamentary majorities, but it also revealed the weakness of their foundation since, contrary to their declarations, in actual fact they were failing to associate the country with their ambitions.

Two symbolic scenes afford a glimpse of the kind of theatrical unreality of their politics.

The first is the coronation of Charles X. His brother Louis XVIII had died on 16 September 1824 without ever having truly captured the hearts of the ultra-royalists. The side by which he clung to the *ancien régime* – education, etiquette, manners and memories – had not made up for the

Engraving of Charles X, *Robillard Collection.*
(Photo: Lauros-Giraudon)

concessions he had been forced to make to the new society and the new spirit. He had set finances on their feet again, paid for the foreign armies to leave the territory, and restored a little glory to the army by a Spanish expedition, sent to help his cousin Ferdinand VII; but for the ultras he had remained a rather unreliable king, shut away in his infirmities and the tiny circle of his favourites.

On the other hand, his brother, the new king, had been their hope since 1814: for a long time there had been a 'Monsieur's party', and what had been during the emigration period no more than a bunch of henchmen, had with the Restoration become the centre of ultra-royalism. Still dashing, a good horseman, the new king was that ageing young man whose affable nature was a reminder that he had been the Comte d'Artois in the last glorious days of Versailles. People preferred to forget that his youthful conduct had not been very glorious: one of the first to emigrate, he had fled from combat. The Vendéen insurgents had awaited him in vain in 1795, when he was on the Ile d'Yeu, near at hand, but unable to make up his mind to join them, and in the end he had chosen to go back to London, where his creditors were waiting for him.

He was better built for the hunt than for war, and for the ladies than for ideas. With a less secretive and less authoritarian temperament than his brother, he clung to his tradition more through his circle and through symbols than from a liking for power; but because of this, he was less able than his predecessor when it came to effecting a compromise. He was only moderately in favour of the Charter, that innovation. Through him, the French monarchy, instead of adjusting to the times, returned to its daydreams.

Louis XVIII had toyed with the idea of being crowned in Reims after his return to the throne. But the Hundred Days, financial difficulties, the Duc de Berry's assassination and his own poor health had endlessly postponed the ceremony. Besides, for centuries the king of France had become sovereign at the last gasp of his predecessor. Charles X wanted to have the royal pomp of the coronation ceremony revived. The ultras were very much in favour, being passionately interested in history and alert to anything which smacked of tradition; Charles X was crowned in Reims on 29 May 1825.

Half a century before, in 1775, there had been much debate among the entourage of the very young King Louis XVI about any modifications which should be applied to the ceremonial procedures in accordance with the spirit of the times. Turgot had wanted to omit from the solemn oaths pronounced by the monarch the one referring to the extirpation of heresy; and there had been doubts whether it was right to preserve the touching of the scrofulous – with which Louis XVI had finally proceeded. In 1825, the Prince de Croÿ, grand almoner, and the Marquis de Dreux-Brézé, grand master of ceremonies, both entrusted with organizing the coronation, had additional reasons to refuse any innovations: it was a matter of affirming

the everlastingness of the monarchy against the Revolution and obliterating
the imperial mockery of 1804 in Notre-Dame.

However, the ceremony aroused some very bitter arguments: the liberals
were hostile to divine right and the *ancien régime* being brought back on to
the scene: Villèle himself counselled caution. In the end, the phrasing
of the oath was arranged to suit contemporary taste, and included the
'constitutional Charter'; the great royal officers traditionally entrusted with
handing the king the insignia of his authority were replaced by four
Marshals of the Empire, well versed in recantation and repudiation –
Mocey, Soult, Mortier and Jourdan. But the ceremony as a whole bore the
imprint of a traditionalism which was all the more extraordinary because
the taste of the era added a kind of medieval picturesqueness, which has
been well recorded in François Gérard's painting of the coronation.

For the occasion, Reims cathedral was decorated with a neo-gothic
décor; the same architect, Percier, who had transformed Notre-Dame into
a Greek temple for Napoleon I, fell in with the taste of the day – the
Middle Ages instead of Classical antiquity. In the nave, portraits of the
kings were set in line, surmounted by a frieze figuring prelates most
renowned for their virtue. The rood-loft, just after the transept, was
dominated by two statues, of France and of religion, jointly holding the
crown: this signified the Throne and the Altar in union. The iconography
also emphasized French 'worth', the victories of the kings of France: the
image of a military and Christian monarchy sought to dispel the fearful
memories of Robespierre and Napoleon.

On 29 May Charles X, anointed with holy oil (the phial, broken in 1793,
had been miraculously rediscovered), received the ring, the sceptre, the
hand of justice and lastly the crown; he also touched the sores of a few
scrofulous people, but almost secretively, without many witnesses, in
the hospital wards. In the cathedral, its walls draped like a theatre, an
audience of hand-picked guests had flocked to see this unique spectacle,
somewhat flabbergasted to see the king of France stretched out flat on
his face before the altar, during the prayers, before receiving the seven
traditional unctions. The constituted bodies were present but, first and
foremost, the alpha and omega of the Church and the aristocracy, quite
ready to applaud their regained supremacy amid this romantic piece of bad
theatre.

Hugo, who was a guest, was enraptured by it, and even expressed his
thanks in verse, his example followed by Lamartine. Chateaubriand, less
youthful and not looked on very kindly by the royal family, saw nothing in
this pomp but the falsity of what he sought to serve, the performance
of the coronation substituted for the true coronation, and the shade of
Napoleon cruelly superimposed on the ghost from Versailles:

The monarchy perished, and the cathedral was for some years converted into
stables. Seeing it again today, does Charles X remember that he watched Louis

Anne Louis Girodet-Trioson Portrait of Chateaubriand, *Musée d'Art et d'Histoire,
Saint-Malo.*
(*Photo: Lauros-Giraudon*)

XVI receive the unction just where he will receive it in his turn? Can he believe
that a coronation ceremony will keep him safe from all misfortune? There is no
longer any hand virtuous enough to cure scrofula, or any holy phial beneficial
enough to render kings inviolable.[8]

[8] *Mémoires d'outre-tombe*, book XXVIII, ch. 5.

The vicomte, as usual, was well aware of opinion, which remained stonily indifferent. The king's solemn entry into Paris on 6 June was a flop: compared with the enthusiasm in Reims, the capital's coldness gave some idea of the separation between the two Frances. For those who had not been invited to the ceremony, the new king or Reims appeared more ridiculous than sacred, that 'Charles the Simple' prostrate 'at the feet of prelates rolling in money', mocked by the *chansonnier* Béranger in a song which swept the country. The political opposition, for its part, took advantage of the concessions which, even in its moment of triumph, ultra-royalism had been obliged to make to the mood of the times. Thus Guizot, in a letter to Barante:

Such a formal oath to the Charter, the omission of so many ancient phrases, the great timidity on the part of the bishops in the care they took to cut down on anything which had a truly religious nature, so as to reduce religion itself to pure ceremonial; all that has been taken by the public to be a secular victory, and the Congrégation was astounded to have its weakness highlighted in this way in the theatre of its triumph.

The second scene took place at Besançon, in the same year as the coronation, but slightly before, in the depths of winter: this was the great January–February mission, intended to win back souls and minds to religion and royalty. This mission was recounted day by day in the big conservative newspapers *L'Ami de la religion et du roi*, *La Quotidienne* and *La Gazette de France*. It was the subject of a detailed account by a seminarist of the town, the Abbé Clerc, who conscientiously followed the happenings and took notes at the sermons: he is the best guide to be found, and was recently rediscovered by M. Gaston Bordet.[9]

Besançon at this period was a triangular city, comprising aristocracy, bourgeoisie and the common people. The mission covered the entire town. It was preached everywhere simultaneously, in the cathedral of Saint-Jean in the old religious and noble quarter; in the parish of Saint-Pierre in the middle of the commercial part of the town; and at the Madeleine in the working-class suburb to the north of the town, on the other side of the Doubs. It consisted of religious services and exercises in piety which went on almost uninterruptedly for seven weeks, between 9 January and 27 February, in the slack time of the year when manual work is less pressing. It called into action several dozen priests, half of whom had come specially from Paris to spread the good word in a town of 30,000 inhabitants which did not enjoy a very good reputation. The Revolution had chosen the Saint-Pierre quarter as the site for its great festivals, and although the lowly watchmakers and wine-growers crammed around the Madeleine were not Voltairean like the town-centre shopkeepers, they had given their

[9] G. Bordet, 'Une fête contre-révolutionnaire, néo-baroque et ordinaire, la grande mission de Besançon, janvier 1825'.

hearts, during the accursed years, to a juring priest, the Abbé Demandre, a
former Constitutional bishop of the Doubs, who had become curé of the
Madeleine in 1801 at the time of the Concordat, and since his recent death
had been transformed into an object of veneration. Carelessly employing
one of the favourite verbs in the revolutionary vocabulary, the Abbé Clerc
wrote that 'the parish must be entirely regenerated'.

In fact, the mission did not skimp on its means. It enclosed the populace
in a religious use of its time which started at dawn with a two-hour mass,
interspersed with instruction and comment; this was followed by a sermon
at the end of the morning, and ended with an evening exercise, which
began at about half-past five, and was itself divided into four parts: reciting
the rosary; the *glose*, which was a little lesson in piety on an everyday
topic; the sermon, in which eloquence combined with moral theology; and
finally the benediction of the holy sacrament. These exercises took place in
the different parishes, with variations of style according to the diversity
of those attending: fewer preachings and sermons at the Madeleine for
example, where the mission offered to the town's poorer classes, on the
contrary, more sacred theatre and stations of the cross.

These spectacular weeks of piety culminated at the end of February in a
Christian apotheosis intended to relax the tension of souls by re-enacting
the martyrdom of Christ for the whole town: there was to be a solemn
raising of the Cross. It symbolized the nation's Christianity. The populace,
who had been urged to make a retreat for three days, went in procession to
the Place Saint-Jean, where the Cross was elevated on its base. There was a
huge cortège with thousands of participants carefully arranged by sex and
parish, each group under its banner and – behind those who carried the
Cross, themselves surrounded by numerous priests – the clergy and the
constituted bodies, the elites and the uniformed groups, the Church and
the state in hierarchical order: the metropolitan chapter, the Superior of
missions in France, the Vicars General, then the court of justice, the army,
the municipality, the educational body. The comment of our Abbé Clerc,
who made a good observer: 'Contemplating all these spectacles, which
were both religious and military, one was reminded of those happy times
when the glory of arms mingled with that of religion, when the hero of the
Gospel and the hero of battle together blessed the God from whom they
awaited their crown.'

The great Besançon mission had thus wanted to restore to those taking
part the image of a happy *ancien régime* – but at the cost of a long
penitence, trotted out week after week. The chief feature of all those
religious exercises was the exorcizing of revolutionary memories, and even
that philosophy of the Enlightenment which had prepared the ground for
the tragedy, a theme which was particularly hammered home in the church
of Saint-Pierre, which had been the centre of dechristianizing profanation
in 1793. The first solemn ceremony of the mission had taken place there on
27 January: the ceremony of 'making amends'. There also, a little later,
one of the sermons evoked 21 January 1793:

Remember, ye Christians, the contrast presented, on the one hand, by innocence battling misfortune and, on the other, the crime which, amid bursts of furious rage, sacrificed that peaceable victim, on the ill-fated day when Louis XVI was led to the scaffold. The assassins who planned his death could not hide from the turmoil and remorse which pursued them . . . At every moment they feared lest someone should snatch from their sacrilegious hands that unfortunate prince on whom they ceaselessly cast the hideous gaze of the parricide. But the innocent victim slept peacefully while he waited for the hour of his agony; he viewed his approaching death with that serenity and magnanimous courage which can be inspired only by a blameless life.

In this way the Church of that epoch launched into the reconquest of minds through a Catholicism of political repentance which was, like the legitimate monarchy, closely linked to condemnation of the French Revolution. Shared misfortune united the two oldest institutions in national history in a radical rejection which distanced both of them from their traditions, at the very time when they believed they were celebrating them. The cult of the Christ-king was not part of the Bourbons' repertoire. As for the Church, by making a crime of the Revolution, it was going back on the pope's own signature to the Concordat, but it found itself taken over by politics, at risk of being defined by them. Two centuries earlier, confronted with Protestant defiance, it had reacted only by putting its hand in the hand of a triumphant monarchy, by the deplorable revocation of the Edict of Nantes (1685); it had also inspired an awesome effort of discipline, pastoral work and theology.

At the beginning of the nineteenth century, this great body, which had been half-uprooted by the Revolution when it had lost its wealth, many of its faithful and its links with local life, bound its destiny to a fragile royalty. Lacking any capacity for internal revival, without any true theologians, it abandoned itself to the mood of the times, that is, to an accusatory and melancholy cult of grief; without any natural anchor in society, it turned its eyes to the state or, against that state, to Rome, where it found little in the way of succour. Herein lay the birth of clericalism.

With the help of the government, the Church once more began to take a stand, since it was unable to recover its possessions. It made many demands for the suppression of the Imperial University, which it regarded as the road to perdition for the young: this was one of the major themes of that ultra *par excellence* of the clerical reconquest of that epoch – the young Abbé de Lamennais. In the end it merely obtained control of the said University, which was placed under the iron hand of Monseigneur Frayssinous, who purged with might and main, abolishing the *École Normal Supérieure* and suspending the courses of Victor Cousin and Guizot. Another Church victory, but this time more symbolic: the law on sacrilege (1825), with very harsh punishments for theft in churches, and a parricide's penalty for profanation of sacred vessels or the host – the condemned man, his head covered with a black veil, would have his right hand cut off before being executed. Luckily, there were no candidates.

The figures for religious practices under the Restoration mostly show a steady growth in attendance at Mass and Easter communion: a sign that the militant Catholicism of the missions inculcated, or reinculcated, the faith in a proportion of the French. But it was tracing their convictions over the top of their political traditions, superimposing the map of its successes on that of the counter-revolution, powerful in the country regions of the west and in the clerical highlands of the Rouergue and Velay.

On the reverse side of the coin, in the 'other' France, and mainly in the towns, what strong reactions of rejection – even of hatred! Stendhal in that period, so ferociously anti-priest, allows one to gauge how far the Church of the Restoration reactivated the quarrel which the Revolution had opened between religion and democracy. Let us return for a moment to Besançon, just after the great mission, to read what a sixteen-year-old schoolboy, Pierre Joseph Proudhon, scribbled in his notebook about the event: 'Eighteen twenty-five: Besançon Mission, much uproar, much devoutness. From this moment on, nothing is religion any more, it is either hypocrisy or plain stupidity.' There began his first doubts about faith. There was therefore another France.

THE OPPOSITION

What stood across from Charles X, Villèle and the ultras, was the France of the Revolution, and I will try to plumb its feelings by starting with a study of the current political ideas: an old French speciality and, in those years, a real firework.

The entire opposition, from the most moderate liberals to those who had been implacable adversaries of the Restoration from the very first day, was unanimously against the return to power of the nobles and priests, which raised anew the spectre of aristocratic society. Louis XVIII had made it his mission to erase from people's memory both the Revolution and the usurpation. Even before his death, the most pronounced supporters of the throne had reinvented 1789 as the demarcation line of the two Frances, and united the Revolution and usurpation against legitimacy. However, this unity in rejecting the *ancien régime* did not efface the sediments of recent history, the various strata of which can be seen in the range of opinions and parties. The Restoration reveals that tyranny of history over French politics which is so characteristic of the French nineteenth century. Against the ultras, the whole opposition took refuge in the great revolutionary memory; but where would it lead, if this revolution were to be carried out again? Between 1789 and the Empire it had offered as many examples as it presented possible futures to the generation which followed it.

Guizot and his friends remained the men of the Charter and constitutional government. They maintained their confidence in legitimate royalty, at least until Charles X's accession; but they fought bitterly against the ultras. The starting-point of Guizot's political thinking was that 1789 had founded a society, not a government, and that the Restoration's task was to give a firm base to that government, in harmony with the new society. Now, under Villèle's leadership, here was the old society trying to make a comeback; here was the monarchy, instead of drawing support from the wealth and education born of the progress of civilization, trying to build the throne on aristocracy.

In the admirable pamphlets which he wrote from the turn of 1820,[10] Guizot rediscovered the accents of Sieyès in 1789 to celebrate the victory of the Third Estate over the nobility and to underline the dangers lurking in the desire to turn back the clock of history. Yes, he says, the old nobility can, and indeed must, be associated with representative government, but only on condition that it abandons the spirit of revenge and accepts the verdict of history which was pronounced in 1789: failing this, its resistance, which in any case is vain, may moreover revive revolutionary radicalism. There is but one way out for the Charter regime, and that is to root itself in a society born of civil equality and destined for irresistible development:

It is true that part of the new France has not yet unfolded its wings, has not yet risen to the eminence for which its real strength has destined it, has not yet been able to fulfil all the conditions, nor to assume all the habits, all the trappings of superiority. That is a bad thing for it but be careful: it is also a snare . . . The France of the Revolution knows what it is, although it is not yet all it will become.[11]

No reactionary law could lastingly prevail against the movement of history which was characterized by the victory of the middle class over the nobility and by the organization of representative government. Guizot devoted his courses at the Sorbonne (1820–2) to this evolution, until they were suspended. Truly, he and his friends had recaptured the entire past of the nation in this perspective, and transformed it into both a subject of scientific study and a collective heritage. The old theme of the combat between two peoples, which the Comte de Montlosier had used as a vehicle to profit feudal nobility, was taken up and turned round by them to the benefit of a national history formed by the people's exploits.

In 1814, the former 'liberal-feudal' deputy of the Riom nobility in 1789, had brought back from his time as an émigré a hefty treatise on *La Monarchie française*: a whole programme of aristocratic royalty, taken up from the seventeenth-century historian, Boulainvilliers. But Restoration historians considered that the middle class defeat of the aristocracy had been taken for granted since 1789. By restoring to those vanquished in the Frankish conquest the patience and initiative which made ready well in

[10] F. Guizot, *Du gouvernement de la France depuis la Restauration et du ministère actuel*; *Des moyens de gouvernement et d'opposition dans l'état actuel de la France*; *Des conspirations et de la justice politique*; *De la peine de mort en matière politique*.

[11] *Des moyens de gouvernement et d'opposition*, pp. 214–15.

advance for the final emancipation, Augustin Thierry (*Lettres sur l'histoire de France*, 1820) and Guizot (*Essais sur l'histoire de France*, 1823) extolled the people's struggle against the oppressive interests of feudalism as the component fabric of French history; in doing so, they again separated the nation from the king, who since 1820 had realigned with the nobles.

In the same period, Adolphe Thiers and Auguste Mignet wrote histories of the French Revolution which shared the same inspiration, since they honoured the inevitable defeat of the aristocracy and the necessary triumph of the Third Estate. The young Thiers, who had only just 'come up' to Paris from his native Marseille, had a major success in the literary world with the great topic of the times. Mignet, who was more earnest and equally well received by the public, in 1824 established for a long time to come the liberal vulgate concerning the French Revolution: the truth of the event lay in 1789, with the triumph of the Third Estate which founded civil equality and political freedom; 1793 was nothing but a passing episode, due to exceptional circumstances; what he curiously termed 'the government of the multitude', when speaking of the terrorist dictatorship did not belong to the inevitable order of things.

There also returned, in this generation, the comparison with Britain which had been so dear to Madame de Staël. But she had made use of it to preach compromise, during the years in which that had seemed a possibility, and to reconcile the Bourbons with 1789. Starting in 1820, for the liberals British history was useful, by contrast, in criticizing the counter-revolutionary policies of the returned monarchy. There was a comparable conception of liberal individualism, based on property-ownership and private interests, the same mistrust with regard to political democracy, and the desire to borrow from the British the secrets of free institutions: the British tradition offered the liberals of that generation many of the elements of their philosophy and convictions. English history also presented for their contemplation the confrontation of two peoples in the aftermath of a conquest; a triangular struggle between monarchy, aristocracy and Third Estate; and lastly, a revolution and representative government. It was the happy outcome of that revolution, 1688 after 1648, which fascinated them most of all.

Indeed, the English themselves had executed their king, known egalitarian excesses, the dictatorship of one man, then the restoration of the throne and an attempt to return to the old order of things. But forty years later, at the cost of a change of dynasty, they had been able to find a constitutional regime which brought together the king and representative assemblies. The best testimony to the obsession with the British which was so typical of that liberal generation, belongs to Charles de Rémusat, describing a little later, on the eve of 1830, the certainties which some of his friends inferred from it:

Thiers, and Mignet after him, pictured the course of the French Revolution as a graph on which all the points had been predetermined by the progress of the revolution in England. They calculated with almost mathematical precision the direction which events must follow. They therefore unhesitatingly accepted what seemed to them to be inevitable, and even yearned for what they thought must be a necessity – a change of dynasty.[12]

Between this milieu, which would philosophically be the foundation of Orleanism, and the vast camp of all those who, since 1814, had been irreconcilable adversaries of the Bourbons, there was no breach of continuity: the battle against the ultras, the double vote, compensation, the law on sacrilege, temporarily united all the combatants. Having re-entered France through the back door, re-established itself a second time on defeat and foreign occupation, the monarchy had benefited for a while from the weariness of opinion and the caution of the king; but the watershed of 1820 and the victory of the ultra spirit had shattered that precarious reunion. They had again separated the government from the nation and brought about the resurgence of the French Revolution in the face of the Bourbons and nobles.

The great memory united the opposition, but also divided it, since it allowed so many different interpretations of restoring the nation within its rights. For the Revolution had not only formed traditions and loyalties; it had offered to succeeding generations that unheard of example of a re-creation of society through the actions of men, at the same time proposing contradictory methods – reason and will, ownership and virtue, liberty and equality, representative government, Jacobin dictatorship, imperial monarchy. So that even the young generations who believed they had broken away from it, in the name of science or the socialist concept, were still reworking the furrows it had traced.

It was Benjamin Constant who, in the Chamber of Deputies, made the transition between the Doctrinaires and the left. This veteran of the Thermidorian republic, the most profound political thinker of the age, did not enjoy an authority to match his genius. For the theorist of modern liberty was also the man who had applauded 18 Fructidor, prepared 18 Brumaire, and by turns cursed and served the Hundred Days. But in his own way he was true to his ideas, in his relative indifference to regimes. When he was elected to the Chamber in 1818, he did not desire the downfall of the Bourbons, merely confining himself to despising them. He argued for the extension of the liberties promised by the Charter.

The return of the ultras to power gave a more radical turn to his opposition, as it did to the whole of the parliamentary left. His talent thereby reached its full political bloom: he was at his best in the defence of modern France against the ultras, sparkling with ideas, severity and irony, and at last popular, in the twilight of his life, as a hero of republican youth. At the podium of the Chamber, and in the succession of newspapers for which he wrote, he became the great national teacher of liberty, and there

[12] Ch. de Rémusat, *Mémoires de ma vie*, vol. 2, p. 287.

is no better introduction to the debates of that era than his speeches. Here he is, for instance, on 23 February 1825, in the act of fighting the *milliard des émigrés*; he argues that the proposal is rebuilding two distinct Frances, one for the 'compensated' and one for the others, and he examines the claims of the candidates for compensation: the émigrés. Had they been good, law-abiding citizens? Louis XVI had disowned them. Rebellious, had they at least been loyal? They had nearly all returned in 1802, at the time of the consular amnesty:

Was there not an amnesty in 1802? Did not that amnesty impose an oath to make no attempt against the imperial government? Was that amnesty not accepted? Was that oath not sworn? After the amnesty, were not the imperial palaces opened? Who filled them? Who were the people who thronged the *salons de service*? Gentlemen, was loyalty to be found in all that? . . . Ah! if it were only loyalty that were to be recompensed, the charge that it is proposed to lay on France would have been far lighter; we would have no need of a billion for that compensation.

This was an admirable recall of the ups and downs of noble loyalty, by a master of liberal disloyalty: the Chambers of the Restoration buzzed with conflicting memories, just as much as with opinions which clashed.

In the liberty camp there were also bourgeois from the worlds of finance and industry, like Jacques Laffitte or Casimir Périer; ghosts from the French Revolution, like La Fayette, who had almost become as historic a monument in France as in the United States: hardly more intelligent than then, when he had played the leading roles, but still just as symbolic. The extreme left was represented by the barrister, Manuel, an implacable adversary of the Bourbons; this was a transition towards extra-parliamentary republicanism which, since 1814, had been a force of opinion in the towns and among young people. That had been apparent during the Hundred Days, when the emperor's return had been greeted in Grenoble, Lyon and Paris by neo-Jacobin demonstrations. When the Restoration was not quite a year old, the event had early disclosed the resonance of a political feeling which imperfectly distinguished between Jacobinism and Bonapartism, mingling the two traditions round images of the nation, equality and a strong state.

This revolutionary syncretism fed, as if naturally, on the spectacle of defeat and the occupation of the country; against Louis XVIII, it linked up with the patriotic anger of the soldiers of Valmy and Rivoli; it found its confirmation in the fate reserved by the allies for the ex-emperor, relegated to a tiny island at the farthest ends of the earth and persecuted by international reaction: that was what the *Mémorial de Sainte-Hélène* would say when it was brought back from the accursed island by Las Cases and published after Napoleon's death (1821) as the great 'best-seller' of the era.

Former soldiers of the imperial army, seconded by young Republicans, had inspired the first revolutionary secret societies, as a reaction against the White Terror. But the movement grew in scale only in 1821, with the birth of the *Charbonnerie*, modelled on the Neapolitan Carbonaria: a secret society which owed something to both the Masonic model and to Jacobin inspiration, and which developed as a clandestine political party, hierarchically centralized in compartmentalized cells, from the commune right up to the central cell in Paris, following the state model. The aim was insurrectionist and republican, although numerous Bonapartist officers belonged to the movement. And the conspiracy's network, which embraced several tens of thousands of members, extended as far as Parisian deputies – Manuel, La Fayette, Dupont de l'Eure. But the various attempts to seize power – badly prepared and badly executed – were easily put down (1821–2).

The episode is interesting chiefly because, at a time when the modern kind of parties did not exist, it shows the strength of the revolutionary idea and its political ambiguity: the secret preparation for the 'great event' brought together liberals (but not Constant nor, *a fortiori*, Guizot), Bonapartists and Jacobins. A sizeable part of opinion could no longer find relevance in the Charter and took its political action outside the law, following a practice inherited from the Revolution, and in order to recommence the Revolution. This trait moreover was not confined to the left, because the ultra right – which also mistrusted the Charter, though for opposite reasons – equally had its Congrégation and its Knights of the Faith: a sign that revolutionary culture extended even to those who wanted to make it into an instrument against the Revolution. For most of the actors on the scene, it continued to define the stakes and the means of French political life.

However, for the opposition left, a secret society was merely a substitute for the action of the people. The years following the failure of the Charbonnerie show a growing mobilization of opinion against the ultras. As in the eighteenth century, France again produced a formidable political opposition culture; but, convinced of the irresistible movement of history, which the Revolution had made obvious, it had no one left to conquer but the conquered.

This culture owed many of its features to Enlightenment philosophy, while at the same time it tried to rethink that philosophy's basic premises. Dual approach, dual development, which on the one hand allowed a rediscovery of the freshness of criticism of the *ancien régime* and, on the other, the definitive entrenchment of the Revolution in history. The principal theme taken up from the eighteenth century, accompanied by a spate of new editions of Voltaire, was that of anticlericalism: the subject of innumerable pamphlets, caricatures, songs, the vehicles of which were the press, the theatre and café conversation. Against the alliance of the Throne and the Altar, the Voltairean spirit linked up with the old parliamentary Gallican tradition, to make the Jesuits – that Roman militia – into a scapegoat for a regime which was foreign to the interests, and even to the soul, of the nation.

The unity of the ultras could not withstand the debate, and old 'feudals' like the Comte de Montlosier enjoyed great success with pamphlets against the Jesuits and the new clericalism. As for the liberals, they were on familiar ground. By reminding the Chamber of Deputies of the risk of setting up a theocracy in France through the law on sacrilege, Royer-Collard had hit ultra politics and ultra religion with the same condemnation. Not only did the bill 'introduce a new crime into your legislation but, what is far more extraordinary, it creates a new principle of criminality, an order of crimes which are, so to speak, supernatural . . . Thus criminal law calls into question both religion and civil society, and their respective natures, aims and independence . . . Are governments successors to the apostles?'[13] This question, posed by a former Jansenist who had become the augur of representative government, reveals the width of the gap which the Restoration, after the Revolution, had dug between opinion and Catholicism. Briefly ennobled by persecution, the Church had resumed the guise in which the preceding century's philosophy had clothed it: obscurantist, authoritarian, a stranger to the nation, just like the Bourbon monarchy, which had returned in the wagons of the European counter-revolutionary troops.

The 'nation', that collective image of modern citizenry, which had become the subject of the Revolution's great civil and military adventure, was no longer considered in terms of natural law, as it had been in the eighteenth century. It was no longer that indivisibly historical and mystical source, the guardian of the social contract, the general will buried in the mists of time, whose promise had but to be fulfilled anew. Henceforth it was an epic and a heritage, and its survivors jealously guarded its precious memory, which was magnified for following generations by the dual Jacobin and Napoleonic tradition, set in verse by the inexhaustible Béranger.

Above all, it formed the subject matter for a philosophy and science of history which transmuted it into the form chosen by the irresistible movement of time, history's supreme individuality (as German philosophers of the same era saw it), and the product of the new civil society's development within the heart of the old. Augustin Thierry and Guizot, through the action of the communes since the darkness of the Middle Ages, restored to 1789 its title to seniority; and to free institutions – which were slow to appear – their urgent necessity.

But what if the timetable for that necessity were on a vaster scale? In the historicism substituted for natural law, the idea inevitably appeared that the new society and representative government might be only a stage in evolution, themselves destined to be overtaken. Already, even before the Revolution was over, out of the movement for equality Babeuf had raised the project of a communist society, intended to fulfil the promises of 1789.

For the Comte de Saint-Simon, on the other hand, revolutionary reorganization of society found its principle in a criticism of 1789 and the

[13] P. P. Royer-Collard, *Opinion sur le projet de loi relatif au sacrilège*, 12 April 1825, pp. 1–2, 8.

bourgeois individualism of the Rights of Man. This self-taught noble was a peculiar figure, a veteran of the American wars of Independence, a speculator in *biens nationaux* during the French Revolution, and consumed since the beginning of the century by a passion to build the rational society of the future. His mind, however, was quite the opposite of disciplined, although Augustin Thierry and chiefly Auguste Comte (who in their youth had written under his name), had been able, here and there, to instil a little system into his intuitions. This *déclassé* aristocrat had loved the huge upheavals which had provided the framework for his life, and welcomed, in the new society, the future of science and industry working together for the happiness of mankind: but that society would still have to break with the individualistic principles of 1789 in order to rebuild itself as an organic community, liberated from its false elites, and directed by the productive classes and the learned. Then, and only then, Christianity would be restored to its original spirit of fraternity between all men.

Through this tumultuous thought, the nineteenth century both continued and renounced Enlightenment philosophy. It preserved the idea of regenerating man by means of reason, but by organizing his social existence instead of picturing him in the anarchy of individual rights. In the upsurge of abstract principles to form the product of historical development, reason ceased to be the last word in the government of men, which had become both a science and a moral doctrine. Saint-Simon's chief importance as a source of so much political thought in the century was that he founded the scientistic utopia of the end of history, even with the added embellishment of reunion with the spirit of 'true' Christianity.

The 'doctrine', properly speaking, has less importance than the two great currents of thought which it originated – positivism and socialism; chiefly, it reveals many of the characteristics of the intellectual atmosphere in the 1820s by the seductive charm it exerted on a number of young minds: such as those who, after the death of the 'master' in 1825, organized themselves into a politico-religious sect which was a meeting-ground for erstwhile *Carbonari* like Armand Bazard and Philippe Buchez; young *Polytechniciens*, like Olinde Rodrigues and Prosper Enfantin, and future great entrepreneurs, like Eugène Pereire. Their object was to bring about the Saint-Simonian revolution by the overthrow of the aristocrats' and landowners' government, and by setting up the true principles of science and production; it was no longer a matter of recreating 1789, or instituting the Republic, but of reinstituting the community: the revolutionary model of social change was written into a new plan. It thus showed its extraordinary capacity for adaptation, since it fascinated those very people who so harshly judged what 1789 had been able to accomplish.

Had the Revolution failed to fulfil its promises? It needed only to be resumed! The *ancien régime* had left nothing for the Revolution to imitate, so it had considered itself as an original source. But the Revolution itself continued to define everything which followed it. Its example was never more obsessive than for those who wanted radically to modify its aims, such as the socialists. Indeed, it provided at one and the same time the root ideas of equality and fraternity and the condition for their fulfilment: violent seizure of the state. That was what imparted its ambiguous substance to the strange concept of 'revolutionary tradition', so essential to an understanding of French public life in the nineteenth and twentieth centuries, and already omnipresent in the 1820s: the Revolution provided a model, and at the same time a precedent in need of modification.

Another characteristic of French though is that socialist criticism of 1789, as initiated by Saint-Simon, confirmed counter-revolutionary hostility to the Rights of Man. The two rebuttals do not have the same basis, since one looks to the future, the other to the past; one accepts 1789 as the inevitable 'critical period' preceding organic reconstruction; the other sees the destruction of the society of orders as the dissolution of the social link itself. But both share a conviction which is substantially the same, namely that modern individualism is a principle which is powerless to create anything other than anarchy or a jungle. The question dealt with again and again by classic political philosophy, between Hobbes and Rousseau was: What is society if we are free individuals? Both positions reply by substituting a point of departure other than Will for the social contract. This was natural order, or the providential plan, the laws of history, reason or science. But both share a common hostility to the modern world, detesting the bourgeoisie and the rule of money. Politically contradictory, they frequently mingle left and right in shared reactions to a society which was still close to its aristocratic past, and barely developed on the industrial plane.

That ambiguity can be pinpointed nearly everywhere in the political literature of the epoch, and in the context of those years it contributed to the weakening of the ultras rather than of the liberals. The populist tendency of a certain ultra-royalist right could meet the extremism of the left against the middle class the more easily since the fashion was for feelings and emotions, in politics as much as in religion. Chateaubriand was already increasing his attacks, having fallen out with the royal family since he had been dismissed from the Ministry of Foreign Affairs in 1823; he disguised them under the pretext of reconciling with the people a royalty whose corpse he could already scent. But it is Lamennais who offers the classic illustration of this transition. With a prodigious and brilliant mind, and a genius more literary than religious, he had begun with a Catholic exaggeration within ultraism, seeking to replace individual reason with community traditionalism as a basis for belief; then he had slipped imperceptibly from there to immoderate praise of papal authority at first, thence to a conversion from religion to democracy – in such a way as to invest liberty with the spirit of fraternity.

In this manner, romantic philosophy and literature, which had played such an important role in the brilliance of rediscovered royalty, gradually turned against the narrow-minded domination of the ultras; even their conservative aspects found favourable ground on the left. What, then, can be said of their liberal aspects? The Hugo who had celebrated the coronation of Charles X wrote, five years later, the preface to *Hernani*: 'Liberty in art, liberty in society, here is the same goal towards which all rational and logical minds must strive with the same steps. Ultras of every kind, classic or monarchic, will vainly help one another to rebuild the *ancien régime* out of thin air ... each step taken by liberty will make everything they have built crumble away.'[14]

The best account of the role played in Restoration public life by young intellectuals born at the turn of the century is given by the enterprise which began in connection with the newspaper *Le Globe* in 1824. The idea for the publication belonged to a young workman typographer, Pierre Leroux, destined to become well known, a little later, as a socialist thinker. Its strength lay in the wealth of the men and currents of thought which found a meeting place in it: in this respect, *Le Globe* took over from a weekly which disappeared in the same period, the *Tablettes universelles*, where the solidarity of a liberal generation had already begun to take shape. The republican opposition and the admirers of the Doctrinaires had been seen rubbing shoulders there, friends of Manuel and friends of Guizot, Thiers and Mignet on the one hand, and Rémusat on the other; they had been joined by some young professors who had been dismissed by the ultra reaction – Damiron, Jouffroy and Dubois. The disappearance of the *Tablettes* brought the departure of Thiers and the republican left; but it opened the way for a newspaper more specifically turned towards philosophical and literary questions: *Le Globe*.

Two different groups, united by common concerns, had a hand in setting it up. The more active group was made up of graduates of the Ecole Normale (*normaliens*) who had been banned by the University from teaching, men like Dubois, Damiron and Jouffroy. They had been joined by young men from high society, often of aristocratic origin. Jouffroy had brought Ludovic Vitet and Charles Duchâtel, to whom he had given philosophy lessons; Charles de Rémusat and Prosper Duvergier de Hauranne, the bright hopes of the liberal salons, had come to be with them. Jouffroy had also recruited Sainte-Beuve, his former pupil at the Lycée Charlemagne.

The heart of the newspaper was Paul Dubois, a *normalien* and ex-Carbonaro like many of his friends, who had been suspended in 1815 and dismissed again in 1821; he was the archetypal poor young provincial for whom the École Normale Supérieure had opened the gates of success without removing the strength of his resentment against the injustices of life. He was the most militant of the group, a sort of editor-in-chief who had assimilated himself to the paper, pungent, hot-tempered, lively – in short, indispensable.

However, *Le Globe* was a more intellectual than directly political publication, perhaps better typified by men like Jouffroy or Rémusat. The former was also a philosophy teacher, *normalien*, ex-Carbonaro, suspended

---

[14] V. Hugo, Preface to *Hernani*, 1830.

in 1822, but more intellectual than Dubois. After his suspension, he had held in Paris a sort of private seminar in this apartment, where poor *normaliens* and young 'upper-crust' liberals had met. Two of his articles which appeared in 1825 ('La Sorbonne et les philosophes', 'Comment les dogmes finissent') were the *Globe*'s philosophical manifestos, in which he rejected the legacy of the Enlightenment as inappropriate to the century which was beginning, and as killed by 'the force of circumstances'.

Rémusat came from a different milieu and brought other problems; the scion of a liberal aristocracy which had served the Empire – but his father, a prefect under the monarchy, had been dismissed in 1822 – he was more inclined towards political philosophy than metaphysical speculation. He admired the Doctrinaires but he also served as a link between *Le Globe* and Thiers, who had come back to the *Constitutionnel*.

From above, this group of young intellectuals received the friendly blessing of two great elders, to whom they were rather like sons: Guizot and Victor Cousin. Guizot was not yet forty, but already had the beginnings of a political career behind him, plus a great many books. A political leader, historian and philosopher on public liberties, he had taken the lead in the liberal opposition from 1820.

The grand master of the *normaliens* was Victor Cousin, rather older than the rest, since his famous lectures at the Sorbonne, which had entranced all the young people, had taken place between 1815 and 1820. Reading Victor Cousin today, it is impossible to imagine the prodigious success gained by his courses. We miss the rapture brought on by the master's studied eloquence and, more than anything, the mood of the times, which is the only way to account for this fleeting intellectual triumph, since his philosophical work, properly speaking, never recovered from the devastating comments of Taine.[15]

Cousin was an admirable teacher of 'vérités moyennes', more appropriate, according to Taine, to conversation than to science. He reconciled the laws of introspection and those of the external world, reason and the existence of God, the empiric and the certain, science and morality, liberty and ownership. He offered his listeners a sensible way of forming opposition to the alliance of the Throne and the Altar, without in any way renouncing criticism of Enlightenment philosophy or of the Revolution: it was a lay philosophy without being irreligious, rationalist but not materialist, liberal without being revolutionary. Like his disciples, he had been a poor young *normalien*, but a star of the meritocracy of competition; he had a feeling for the times, a team spirit, talent, charm, a taste for intellectual power. He personified in French history, which would offer so many others, the first example of the university guru, who had emerged, as was only proper, from the first years of the École Normale Supérieure.

The young men of the *Globe*, like their master, were both earnest and

---

[15] Hippolyte Taine, *Les Philosophies classiques du XIXe siècle en France*, 3rd edn (1868), p. 85.

trendy. Gravity was fashionable: Royer-Collard, who was both Guizot's inspirer and Cousin's predecessor at the Sorbonne, had put Jansenism in the air. The newspaper's ambition was to be in the forefront of new ideas, while examining them in a truly philosophical spirit – a power too rarely exercised in the history of the press. Among those intellectuals who were for the most part survivors of the Charbonnerie, agreement against the ultras and Bonald's kind of traditionalism almost went without saying. But it was accompanied by an equally radical criticism of the eighteenth century, which was held responsible for the unfortunate course of the Revolution.

One of the *Globe*'s whipping boys was *Le Constitutionnel*, where, carefully maintained, there lived on the old anticlerical spirit of the Enlightenment, the campaign against the Church and the Jesuits, all the old worn-out ideas of the *Encyclopédie* and the vulgarities of revolutionary exaggeration. But this rejection of heritage extended somewhat to all domains: *Le Globe* encouraged romantic literature, while its rival went for the classical conventions; the first loved and discussed foreign literature, while the second stayed strictly French. The same applied to economics, since Duchâtel made Adam Smith, Malthus and Ricardo known in the columns of the *Globe*, while Thiers, the young hopeful of the dinosaurs on the *Constitutionnel*, was already defending, against free trade, 'ideas which nature had given him ready-made'.

To pursue the comparison between the two papers, one can look at Rémusat and Thiers, already friends (and they would stay so through the century) yet so very different. Both were very intelligent and very lively, but the first was curious about everything, open-minded to everything, while the second had formed his ideas about everything very early on – too early. Politically, they would soon have ideas which were very close, but the first was drawn towards things which he wanted to learn, while the second was intellectually conservative, his storehouse of ideas shut once and for all. Thiers's want of curiosity was channelled to the furtherance of his political ambition, while Rémusat was somewhat dilettante; in the years when their careers were just starting, the *Globe*'s young aristocrat wrote more interesting things than the historian-journalist of the French Revolution.

In the matter of politics, the young men of the *Globe* liked neither the *ancien régime* nor the Revolution. This was a difficult situation in France: it was easy to triumph in philosophy, where syntheses cost nothing, but there was not much room in public life, invaded on the right by the ultras and on the left by republican tradition more or less mixed up with Bonapartism. To the *Globe* even Constant seemed too close to the Revolution and the eighteenth century in his philosophy and politics. His book on religion, which appeared in 1824, had not harmed that reputation.

This liberal generation wanted to implant the history it was experiencing in a synthesis of the national past. Some years before, it had applauded Madame de Staël's *Considérations*, which made 1789 into the pinnacle

of French history, but it disliked the revolutionary enthusiasm which
pervaded the books of Mignet and Theirs, and the Empire even more,
since it had been a period of internal despotism and permanent war. In the
end, its plan was nearest to Guizot's: to base liberty on reason, in such a
way as to remove from French revolutionary doctrine all the ideas on
natural law which it had held since 1789, as they had been the point of
departure for the deviation which would follow.

Many different shades of opinion coexisted among the newspaper's
team, chiefly about what chances the returned dynasty might have of
getting rid of its demons. No one shared the ultras' sentimental loyalty to
the kings of France, but neither did anyone share unconditional hatred for
the republican tradition. It seems to me that what united young men so
apparently far apart as Rémusat and Dubois, or Duchâtel and Jouffroy,
was a feeling rather than a theory: the conviction that it was their generation's duty to deliver France from the two nightmares of her past – the
men of the *ancien régime* and those of the Revolution – by founding a new
future.

That sentiment was admirably expressed by Jouffroy in an article
published by the paper in 1825:

A new generation is rising which had its origins in the womb of scepticism . . . and
already these children have outstripped their fathers and sensed the emptiness
of their doctrines. The premonition of a new faith has made itself felt in them;
they cling to this beautiful prospect with enthusiasm, with conviction, with
resolution . . . Superior to everything around them, they could not be dominated,
either by reborn fanaticism, or by the faithless selfishness which blankets
society . . . They understand their mission, and they are aware of their times: they
understand what their fathers have failed to understand, and what the corrupt
tyrants do not realize; they know what a revolution is, and they know this because
they arrived at the right time.

'An awareness of the times': at the same moment, another school had the
same ambition and unfurled the same flag – the adherents of Saint-Simon,
who died in 1825. They came from the same political horizons, since they
too had often been militants of the Charbonnerie. *Their* guru had not been
a charismatic philosophy teacher who had been born with the Restoration,
but an old adventurer of the *ancien régime*'s aristocracy who had finally
gathered around him, with the passing years, a body of disciples, quite a
few of whom had emerged from the École Normale Supérieure, which was
Cousin's kingdom. In 1817 Augustin Thierry had escaped from this band,
then in 1822 Auguste Comte, a Polytechnicien, both of them weary of
the subordination demanded by their master's eccentric genius. But the
school had formed afresh around some newcomers: Bazard, Buchez, young
veterans of the secret societies, and the Polytechniciens Enfantin, Olinde
Rodrigues, who had brought his Jewish friends the Pereires and Léon
Halévy. The problem which united them was the same as that of the
Globe's team: how to produce a synthesis with the elements which formed

the era, the heritage of the Revolution? France and Europe were in ruins: how to set about their reconstruction? Saint-Simon had left a doctrine, and Comte was developing his own.

The Saint-Simonians belonged to the same generation as the young men of the *Globe*. They shared their problem and were looking for the solution in the same direction, common to both Saint-Simon and Cousin: to wrest France from her past in order to give a better foundation to the future. They, too, created a newspaper in 1825, *Le Producteur*, in which they produced serious articles devoted to literary and philosophical subjects, like *Le Globe*, but also to economic and scientific matters. The newspaper was less outstanding than its rival; it was far from having the latter's prestige and circulation, but in it there developed something more lasting and important for French public life: the idea of marrying politics and science with a view to a more rational organization of society following the revolutionary disorder.

In the seventh number an article by Auguste Comte appeared, '*Considérations philosophiques sur les sciences et les savants*'. Comte had disliked the Saint-Simonian coterie since he had left the master, but he was on good terms with the newspaper's editor, Cerclet, yet another ex-Carbonaro, who had associated him with the enterprise on its fringes. And it was on that day, in the pages of *Le Producteur*, that he first made public his law of the three stages of humanity, which was a systematic formulation of an idea of Saint-Simon: the theological age, the metaphysical age, and finally the positive age, when humanity is reconciled with reason.

This was a more systematic construction than Cousin's flabby synthesis. It linked each historical period to a system of thought, thus allowing an account to be rendered in conceptual terms of feudal society and bourgeois society successively. It made possible what the *Globe*'s liberalism was unable to achieve: the capacity to envisage the anarchy of modern society, the risk of disintegration which haunted it, illustrated by the uncontrollable elements of the French Revolution. Seventeen eighty-nine had been merely the manifestation of a critical, 'metaphysical' reason, which destroyed all that had gone before, and was by definition incapable of rebuilding: the modern individual who had emerged from the workings of that reason could offer nothing which might serve as a base for the cohesion of society. The aim and the task of the positive age, on the morrow, would be to reinstitute the spiritual coherence of the theological age through man's reappropriation of himself, which was the work of reason, allowing a synthesis of the two preceding ages.

In this way Comte offered a systematic method of conceiving the post-revolutionary situation as a necessary but temporary stage, which must culminate in the reconciliation of all men with historical reason, in the form of a universally recognized spiritual authority, the embodiment of 'positive politics'. Auguste Comte's is one of the most powerful of the great nineteenth-century historicist machines, incomparably stronger than Cousin's eclecticism; it combines the promise of the socialist concept, turning humanity towards its future, and the certainty which is born when science is substituted for religion. By the criticism it made of the ideas of 1789, notably freedom of conscience, it set the *Producteur*'s Saint-Simonians against the *Globe*'s 'liberals'. But what was most in evidence in the contrasting options of the two teams was the topic already known as the 'social question', in which the Saint-Simonians saw the great problem of the future; their friendly rivals on the *Globe* were not unaware of it, as they commented gravely on Villermé's *Statistiques* on the situation of the workers – but they looked on it with a rather condescending eye as a question to be resolved by the elites. On *Le Producteur*, it was considered to be *the* question for the future.

Nevertheless, the two teams and the two newspapers remained united in the solidarity of their generation: both jeered at the old-fashionedness of the past, the superannuated conventions of classical art, the received idea of French superiority in cultural matters; both were open-minded to England and Germany, and obsessed with the idea of giving some direction to 'modernity'. In a France whose literature and political philosophy were so frequently dominated by rejection of the modern – one has only to look at the ultra party – all these young intellectuals were, on the contrary, busy working away at the question which the philosophy of natural laws had mistakenly believed it had solved. Even in the Saint-Simonian clique, criticism of 1789 was not – not *yet* for some – linked to a rejection of post-revolutionary society. They all made a religion of the future, which was nearer than they thought to what the Revolution itself had founded.

Sometimes they fell out with one another, as can be seen from the amusing quarrel which Stendhal sought to pick with Armand Carrel in a little anti-Saint-Simonian pamphlet published by *Le Globe* in 1825. The two men were not typical of the work they took on temporarily, since Stendhal was older than *Le Globe*'s team, and Armand Carrel passed over fleetingly to the Saint-Simonians before attaining celebrity in republican politics and press. But this is just the point: these dazzling collaborations clearly illustrate the fact that the young intellectual generation had discovered in those newspapers the means of gathering together everyone who was giving serious thought to the future, against the France of the ultras. The aristocratic monarchy of Charles X, like Louis XVI's absolute monarchy, had met its death in public opinion before it foundered in the streets of Paris.

THE END OF THE REGIME

The period between Charles X's coronation and his downfall, 1825 to 1830, recalls the phenomenon which the France of the end of the eighteenth century had already experienced: an isolated monarchy facing a powerful and increasingly unanimous public opinion. If the old nobility, which had learnt by its misfortunes, now stood beside its sovereign, the weight of the past, on the contrary, was working against royalty: this conflict had already taken place and history had cut it short, in a more uncertain epoch when legitimate royalty had seemed to have the strength of eternity. Forty years later, beaten, overthrown, beheaded, re-established, it no longer had any chance of conquering a nation whose history it had not been able to recapture because it had had no share in it. Its downfall was not a thunderbolt – more of a peaceful inevitability.

Following tradition, the king nevertheless contributed his share. In 1826 Villèle had been beaten in the Chamber of Peers over a proposal which sought to maintain large property-ownership by making primogeniture easier. In the same year he attacked the freedom of the press, held to be responsible for the ministry's isolation. Having dissolved the Chamber in an attempt to gain a fresh impetus, he lost the 1827 elections. It was then that Charles X, like his brother Louis XVI between 1787 and 1789, took a step towards a liberal policy without truly adopting its spirit, before identifying the monarchy with the aristocracy more clearly than ever; ruining the first attempt by the weakness of his assent, and the second by the obstinacy of his affection.

The Martignac ministry, patched together at random from among the court coteries, undertook to bring the regime back on centre by extending the control of the University over religious teaching, relaxing legislation over the press and trying to bring to fruition a project for the election of municipal councils. But it did not stand up for long against the combined mistrust of the left and the king. Reading the debates of the period, one is struck by how they are overfilled with symbolic significance borrowed from the Revolution. Do decrees regulate the regime of schools run by the religious congregations? 'The Inquisition's sceptre is broken!' comments *Le Journal des Débats*. And *La Gazette de France*, in the other camp: 'The Revolution triumphs! All that is left to do is consummate the advent of the Republic and the raising of altars to the Goddess of Reason.' The same type of reaction greeted the plan to elect local authorities (on a very restricted property-owning suffrage), even though decentralization was on the ultras' programme: Martignac was accused of resuming 'the principle of popular election hallowed by the Constituent Assembly and the Convention' and of wanting to replace the monarchy with 30,000 republics. To this chorus of memories, Charles added the family note: 'I do not want to ride in a tumbril like my brother.'

He yielded to his inclination, which was to trust those who had shared his destiny; the time had come for the man who had enjoyed the favour of his friendship for a long while, the most faithful of the faithful, the candidate of the Knights of the Faith, Prince Jules de Polignac, ambassador to London. No one better personified loyalty to the *ancien régime* than he: the son of Marie-Antoinette's favourite, who had earlier been vilified by the Revolution's press, he had served the princes while they were émigrés; imprisoned in 1802 following the Cadoudal conspiracy, he had remained a prisoner until 1814; now here he was, an ultra, congregationist, a combatant for the Throne and the Altar, at the forefront of 'Monsieur's party' under Louis XVIII, passionate about politics, though with little aptitude, a royalist visionary, an aristocrat who had passed from the court to life as an émigré, and from that life to captivity.

As if his name alone were not enough to alarm opinion, Charles X flanked him with two particularly dreaded ministers: La Bourdonnaye, the man of the White Terror in 1815, the right's most extreme orator, who had waged war on Villèle's 'moderation'; and Louis de Bourmont, a former leading *chouan* who had backed Bonaparte, an adventurer by nature, who had gone over to the enemy on the eve of Waterloo and had testified against Marshal Ney at the trial of his erstwhile chief. Combined with the temperature of public opinion, the unfettering of the press gave the signal for battle: the nation versus the court . . . just like yesterday!

The succession of events was rapid and as if independent of men's actions; this ministry was a front without any substance, a team without any initiative, abandoned to the unpopularity which it roused. There was one important exception, in foreign policy at the end of January 1830: the decision to intervene in Algeria, after long and fruitless negotiations to call in an old debt. The fleet left in July, too late to win over a little national feeling to royalty, as Charles X had hoped. Meanwhile, in mid-March, the Chamber had sent him an address of no confidence inspired by Royer-Collard, to which he responded by dissolving it on 16 May. New elections were held at the end of June and beginning of July, which resulted in a disaster for Polignac: the 221 supporters of the address became 274. The king continued to make things worse: he thought that concessions had been his eldest brother's great mistake. Making use of article 14 of the Charter, which permitted him to make 'orders and regulations necessary for the execution of laws and for the security of the state', on 25 July he signed the famous four ordinances: the first suspended the freedom of the press; the second dissolved the new Chamber; the third altered, to the benefit of the throne, the number of deputies and the electoral body by restricting it; the fourth fixed the new elections for the month of September.

This attempt to set up a new regime was the signal for revolution. The king had gone outside the Charter, Paris went outside the law. Barricades were the answer to the coup d'état. Everything was over very quickly, in three days of Parisian insurrection, 27, 28 and 29 July. On 30 July Charles withdrew the decrees. But he was too late to save his throne and, on 9 August, his cousin the Duc d'Orléans became king, not of France but 'of the French'.

The 1830 revolution – 'the July flash of lightning', Michelet called it – was thus the most 'successful' in national history, if it is related to its aim, which was to eliminate the ordinances and, at the same stroke, to drive out the Bourbons: both victorious and brief, it achieved its goal within a few days. The will of the people in action, it intensified in spectacular fashion the tradition which had been born on 14 July 1789. If it left many of those taking part with a rather ambiguous memory, that was because it ended with the institution of a new king – as if it had been incapable of asserting itself once it had achieved victory. An analysis of the 'Three Glorious Days' allows a deeper understanding of this dual nature.

July 1830 was the first Parisian uprising since the French Revolution, which had seen so many. In the spring of 1795, the neo-Jacobin riots of Germinal and Prairial – 'for bread and the constitution of Year II' – had been the last revolutionary *journées*, and had ended in the disarming of the faubourg Saint-Antoine. Two generations afterwards, the Parisian insurrectionist tradition resurfaced, like an underground river which had never stopped flowing, and like a great memory rediscovered by grand-children. It was heir to the last popular movements of spring 1795: the technique of building barricades, intended to take advantage of the narrowness of the streets and the huddle of houses round about, the inhabitants of which could shower government troops with a diversity of missiles. Before 1795 the great *journées* of the French Revolution had not known about barricades; the Three Glorious Days reinvented the last legacy of a beaten faubourg Saint-Antoine, turning it into the supreme strategy of nineteenth-century revolutionary Paris.

It was, however, the only resemblance they bore to the last popular battle waged in the twilight of the French Revolution. They achieved a swift victory because they were closer to 14 July 1789 than to Germinal or Prairial Year III. As on 14 July, they mobilized a populace unanimously seeking a clear and simple objective which, in both cases, was identical: to bring the Bourbons to their knees. It is easy to understand what the Paris of July 1830 had been able to offer the historical imagination of the young Michelet, a combatant in those feverish hours: the nation, rediscovered in its support for freedom, in the face of a coup d'état monarchy. Rich and poor, the bourgeoisie and the people, the student and the workman, the shopkeeper and the manual worker, the Institut and the suburbs – all shared in these potent images. The signal for disobedience was given on 26 July by journalists and political notables of the left, but on the 27th it was Paris which led the revolution: that victory was the beginning of a myth.

There was no National Guard: Villèle had made the blunder of disbanding that bourgeois militia, which had too little sympathy for Charles X. Suddenly, the battalions which formed again were no longer on the side of authority. This absence brought the insurgents face to face with soliders of the line, who were reluctant to fight. The three days of street battles saw a rapid decline in discipline among the troops, while barricades continually rose from the pavements, being rebuilt as fast as they were destroyed. There was nothing trivial about this battle, because it produced several hundred dead on the insurgents' side, but it was a fight in which strength very soon lay in numbers, and weakness on the side of arms. From start to finish, the unity of bourgeoisie and people guaranteed the outcome. And what I here term 'bourgeoisie', a world defined by wealth and education, continued to keep control. Money, banking, industry, literature, the university, politics – all the illustrations of the middle classes were part of the combat, if not in the first line of the combatants.

For the rest of the country they were also the guarantee of the revolution. If, as was customary, Paris decided for the nation, those deputies who had won in the recent consultation still knew the heartland of property-owners and petty notables, who were wedded more to their own interests than to revolutionary ideas. This was where the decisive scenario was enacted, which made such a clear distinction between 1830 and 1789. The *ancien régime* bourgeoisie had entered 1789 on the back of the entire Third Estate and Natural Law; the popular risings in July 1789 had not exhausted its store of optimism and it had applauded the October days. What awareness it had of itself continued to draw its strength mainly from what made it hate nobility, not from what led it to fear the people. But the course of the Revolution, 1793 and the Terror had added this latter sentiment to its experience; and the Restoration had revived hatred for the aristocrats without extinguishing fear of the working classes.

July 1830 therefore re-enacted the unity of the people, that great spectacle of 1789, but in a different political context precisely because that spectacle had taken place. This was the first illustration of that lasting character of French public life in the nineteenth century: the French endlessly replayed the Great Revolution, but at the same time tried to adapt their actions according to what they had learnt about it or what they believed they knew. In this regard, the Paris insurrection opened up for the men of the centre-left a situation of which they had not foreseen the exact circumstances, but for which they had constantly prepared the way, each in his own manner, both philosophically and politically. Extolling civil equality while criticizing the sovereignty of the people, Guizot had built the theory of representative government, the only way to end the French Revolution by making that its crowning achievement. Now the right moment had arrived, just a little more than forty years after 1789, as forty years had elapsed in English history between 1648 and 1688. Little Thiers, bustling, talented, omnipresent, swept through the newspaper offices explaining that French history demonstrated the same need as the English revolutionary cycle of the last half of the seventeenth century. The departure of the Bourbons was thus written in accordance with that of the Stuarts, and the Duc d'Orléans was ready to take the role of the Prince of Orange: regicide was a family custom.

The July *journées* thus offered the rare example of a revolution controlled by political calculation, and within a few days turned to a moderate ending. According to a paradox which is to be found in the history of Marxism, but which does not always have such a happy outcome, belief in the inevitability of history had sharpened the victors' eagerness and skilfulness in giving history a helping hand. It is true that everything seemed to prove them right: the resigned support of La Fayette, that monument of the Republicans, to the Orléans solution; still more, the kind of fading away of the legitimate dynasty, offering neither reason nor pretext to a radicalization of the Parisian combatants.

What a fiasco there was on that side! Nothing had been planned and nothing was really defended, not even principles, since Charles X agreed, as if he had the right to do so, to disinherit his son and abdicate in favour of his grandson Henri V, then aged five, to make way for his cousin, the inevitable Duc d'Orléans, who would become lieutenant-general of the kingdom for the period of a new regency. This solution was looked on with favour by Chateaubriand, who never missed an impracticable idea as long as it was literary; but it dishonoured hereditary monarchy without saving it, by renouncing its supreme constituent, the order of succession to the crown. Moreover, Charles X would be king of France in exile, followed, according to the rule, by his elder son, the Duc d'Angoulême, a fleeting Louis XIX whose death alone, in 1844, gave his nephew Henri V the right to the throne.

For the moment, the monarchy was leaving France without the glory of battle. It had even lost that hatred which, a quarter of a century earlier, had still woven a strong bond between it and the France of the Revolution; the July men wanted to frighten it, drive it out and not become burdened with that tragic family again, as in 1792. Having taken refuge at Rambouillet, Charles X still had 10,000 soldiers at his dispoal when, on 3 August, the crowd of volunteers assembled by La Fayette approached. Odilon Barrot, one of the Parisian leaders, the son of a deputy from the Lozère to the Convention, 'a little man with a blue beard' (Stendhal), came to negotiate a withdrawal, brandishing threats of a blood-bath. In the evening, the king gave the signal to leave.

Preceded by Louis-Philippe's commissioners, the procession took almost two weeks to reach Cherbourg, where two ships awaited it, together with 600,000 gold francs sent by the usurper-cousin. This was the monarchy's second funeral cortège, less tragic than Varennes, but definitive for that very reason. The king passed through that western part of France which had been the *chouans*' homeland – Argentan, Vire, Carentan, Valognes; the towns were hung with the tricolour, and only a few old gentlemen turned up along the route to greet their king in his misfortune. There would be no more émigrés than there had been combatants.

Legitimate royalty was dead; Chateaubriand did not miss the funeral oration. Speaking one last time in the Chamber of Peers on 7 August, while Charles X trotted towards exile, he could find in favour of the little Henri V only arguments drawn from the democratic repertoire and the situation as it stood: order must be preserved, together with liberty. Along with the public law of the monarchy, he interred the age-old marriage of France and the Bourbons:

I did not go and bivouac in the past under the old flag of the dead – a flag which is not without glory but which droops along its pole because no breath of life flutters it. Were I to disturb the dust of the thirty-five Capets, I would not raise a single argument that would so much as be listened to. The idolatry of a name is abolished; monarchy is no longer a religion.

7

The July Monarchy: 1830–1848

THE NEW REGIME

A monarchy had succeeded a monarchy, a king had succeeded a king. Louis-Philippe d'Orléans installed himself in the Tuileries palace abandoned by Charles X. What, then, gave the French such a keen feeling of belonging to a different world? A revolution had taken place. July 1830 at once became a great national memory. On 10 August, the day after the enthronement of the new sovereign, there appeared in *Le Journal des Débats*: 'Philippe I has been proclaimed: the Duc d'Orléans is king. This change of dynasty is the accomplishment of the Revolution. Eighteen-thirty has just become the crowning achievement of 1789.' The Three Glorious Days were thus inscribed in the great revolutionary cycle: they had reinaugurated 1789, but in order to 'accomplish' it and to achieve both its course and its purpose. They had once more sealed the fate of the *ancien régime*, this time for ever, by at last instituting representative government.

Which *'ancien régime'*? In this imputation made against the Restoration lay both injustice and inaccuracy. The Bourbons had come back conceding civil equality and the Charter to the new France, and their regime, which had begun in the nostalgia and extremism of their supporters, had made no attempt to re-establish either the society of orders or the absolute monarchy of former France. In many respects it had, on the contrary, presided over the entrenchment of the principles of 1789, the elimination of the difficult problem of *biens nationaux* and the birth of a rich and brilliant parliamentary political life. Nevertheless, that regime also had ended, like Louis XVI's though in a very different manner, by becoming the embodiment of aristocracy and absolutism: the two ingredients of the *ancien régime*.

The old 'absolute' monarchy had not shared power with an aristocracy which it had tamed and divided. The restored monarchy had found itself in a new situation. Reunited with the nobility through the tragedy of memories and so many lost battles, it had found in the nobles not only its most natural social base and its psychological and society milieu, but also its political support, which had become essential since the Charter had provided for two elected Chambers. Its tendency, manifest in 1815, thwarted between 1816 and 1820, and accelerated afterwards, had therefore been towards a completely new regime, unknown to the old France: an aristocratic monarchy, whose more or less mythical point of reference lay the other side of absolutism. For this monarchy had never been 'English': compared with that famous example, so frequently used as a yardstick under the Restoration, it was both more egalitarian – through the form of civil law inherited from the Revolution – and more aristocratic – through the situation of the French nobility, which had emerged from the tragedy more split into 'castes' than ever, with a brand-new tinge of clericalism traceable to its misfortunes.

That contradiction was illustrated in the person of Charles X, and erupted with the July ordinances – a resurrection of royal arbitrariness. Unlike England, France had to choose between an aristocratic and a bourgeois monarchy. Such was the interpretation given to the short three-day civil war by the victors, a mixture of bankers and intelligentsia – Guizot, Thiers, Laffitte, Périer. Besides, the theory had preceded the event: in this respect, July 1830 was the first modern revolution to be written into a science of history controlled by men. The heart of that science lay in a knowledge of the movement of society, the government of which was merely an epiphenomenon. Therefore, whatever resemblances in form there may be between the two constitutional monarchies on either side of the July frontier, a chasm separates them which cannot be expressed in English political vocabulary but is a constituent element of French public life: the war of the two dominant classes, the new and the old, the battle between the bourgeoisie and the nobility. Thiers links up with Sieyès. The rebirth of the Third Estate gives some measure of the failure of the Restoration.

However, the two political regimes are so comparable that quite a few histories of nineteenth-century France place them under the same heading of 'constitutional monarchies'. The 1814 Charter, merely 'revised' by the Chambers between 3 and 7 August while the Hôtel de Ville insurgents were demanding its abolition, had in fact remained the law of the new king, divested of article 14, embellished with liberal measures and, still more, with *promises* of such measures; even the peerage survived, though not in hereditary form, it is true.

Amid all that prudence and all those precautions, one glaring difference separates the 1814 Charter from that of 1830: the second was no longer 'granted' by the king, it was contractually accepted by him as a condition of his accession. There is a symbolic anecdote – the very name of the sovereign was the subject of negotiation with those to whom he owed his crown, La Fayette to the fore: Philippe VII sounded rather too Bourbon; he was for Louis-Philippe I, a royalty which had just been born! Therein lay the other radical break which had occurred in July 1830, concealed in the apparent similarity between the two monarchies laying claim to the Charter: the two regimes were not dependent on the same legitimacy.

The 1814 text was placed both within divine right and the historical election of a dynasty to the throne of France. It was carefully dated so that it legally obliterated the years separating Louis XVIII from the death of Louis XVII, and it was 'granted' by the king by virtue of his full legislative authority, which existed prior to the Charter since it was responsible for constituting that Charter. Certainly, it did not restore absolute monarchy, in that it instituted, on the contrary, a representative system entrusted with the task of controlling the sovereign's actions by voting for or against the laws proposed to it; but this was set up as an addition to the fundamental laws of the kingdom and as a supplementary regulation to the exercise of royal power. Because of that, the Restoration regime was not a constitutional monarchy, if that is taken to mean an ensemble of institutions and powers regulated by a written law, which was prior to and higher than every will. It was a 'limited monarchy', characterized by the unity of the power of the state in the person of the king and the existence of representative authorities in the exercise of that power; it came under the same type of legitimacy as absolute monarchy.

The July regime *was* a constitutional monarchy. Transformed by circumstances, reclothed with a new spirit, draped in the tricolour, the same law took on a new meaning, like the king. With article 14 suppressed, and the initiative of law-making now shared between the Chambers and the sovereign, it was an indication that sovereignty was no longer defined as in the French monarchic tradition: external to the king, it belonged to the nation which partially delegated it to him by constituting him as such. In this respect, the Three Glorious Days had been a sort of lesson; overthrowing Charles X who, by his decrees, had set himself up as the sole origin of sovereignty, they had enthroned a new king, but on conditions. A hereditary king, it is true, but the first person in a dynasty without a past, a sovereign born of the Revolution and subordinate to the July contract. The regimes of 1814 and 1830 might well look alike in their mechanisms and procedures; they were none the less founded on two contradictory legitimacies. There had certainly been a revolution between them.

That was what made Guizot's position difficult from the start; he would become the great man of the new monarchy, having been the philosopher of its accession. During the 1820s, no one more than he had hammered away at the theme of two classes, extolled 1789 as the victory of the middle class, made the need for representative government part of the irresistible strength of the new society. But he was also a critic of the idea of sovereignty, whether popular or personified in a king, being convinced that the political order of the new society could be constructed only on its content of reason, and not on the will of every citizen.

July 1830 demonstrated the historical necessity, but also revived the phantom of the sovereignty of the people. Guizot had kept a watchful eye on the turn of events rather than taking part in them: the Orléans solution was obviously his and, in his view, Louis-Philippe I made an excellent French William III. He still had to be able to allow what had been torn

Daumier Monsieur Guizot: The legislative 'Belly' (*Ventre*): view of the ministerial benches of 1834.
(Photo: Roger-Viollet)

apart to be mended as quickly and as well as possible, in order not to give the people the pride of victory. It was a matter of making him into more than a sort of high official holding his powers by the will of the people: he had to be a true hereditary sovereign, certainly new in his function and office, but called to the throne by reason of his closeness to the former ruling family and of higher needs which had resulted from exceptional circumstances.

Never at a loss for ideas, Guizot unearthed the argument by which Burke, in the wake of others, had justified in his 1790 *Reflections* the 'glorious revolution' of 1688: a short parenthesis which had been essential to the preservation of English liberties. But whereas the history of England bore out the Whig parliamentarian, the French Revolutionary tradition challenged Guizot: all the ideas that he had tried to combat – the clash of the classes, the *tabula rasa*, the king as functionary of the people – had descended in a direct line from 1789, revitalized by 1830 after, of course, being magnificently commented upon by himself in his books and courses. Really, to fit Louis-Philippe easily into Louis XVIII's Charter, he would have needed a revolution that was not at all revolutionary.

There lay the Achilles' heel of Orleanism, already evident in the very first days of this new monarchy which was incapable of thinking about its origins, and forced to take the double risk of accepting and rejecting them. By accepting them, it would create the chasm which divided the upper classes without necessarily obtaining the support of the lower classes, since it would inevitably open the way to revolutionary escalation on the theme of 'Who made you king?' But by rejecting them, it would separate itself from the people without in any way getting the backing of the July losers, and run the risk of exposing itself to the same isolation which had brought about their defeat. Such was the narrow path the new regime had to tread.

Therefore, in the first days of August, it was decided to institute a second monarchy according to the Charter, combining an apparent faithfulness to the text of 1814 with a totally different spirit, which had emerged from the July barricades. The king was not now king of France, but of 'the French'; the Chambers shared with the king the initiative for law-making without being able to be short-circuited by article 14; the peerage was no longer hereditary; Catholicism was merely 'the religion professed by the majority of the French'; a lowering of the electoral property qualification was promised. The revised Charter was enveloped in the tricolour flag, which had re-emerged all over the place as the great emblem of the Three Glorious Days. The regicides returned from Brussels, Sieyès in the forefront.

Louis-Philippe I had picked up his power from the streets, and had then received it more ceremoniously from the Chambers, in this tamed version. He thus settled an old family jealousy regarding the senior branch of the Bourbons. His ancestor, the Regent, had already reigned by proxy over France, between Louis XIV and Louis XV. His father had constantly flirted with liberal philosophy and opposition during the last half of the preceding century, making the Palais Royal into one of the centres of Parisian opinion, which was up in arms against the Versailles court; and the year 1789, from the drawing up of the cahiers to the October *journées*, had been filled with rumour of his intrigues with a view to replacing his cousin, Louis XVI. Going all the way down the road of revolutionary demagogy, he had been elected to the Convention under the name of Philippe-Egalité, had sat with the Montagnards and voted for the death of the king, before being guillotined himself a little later.

His son, who had been brought up 'according to Jean-Jacques', had been an active supporter of 1789; he had fought at Jemappes alongside Dumouriez before leaving France in 1793 by force rather than by choice, as an exile rather than an émigré: he was part of what Madame de Staël had called the 'good emigration' – that of the Terror – to distinguish it from that of the privileged, between 1789 and 1791. Moreover, unlike the émigrés, he had always cultivated the heritage of 1789, and that was the secret of his popularity under the Restoration. A couple of steps away from the Tuileries, in the Palais Royal, a Bourbon shared the same memories as the French. This was both a national and a bourgeois predestination, which Victor Hugo would describe some time later in *Les Misérables*:

He had on his side that great designation for the throne – exile. He had been proscribed, a wanderer, poor. He had lived by his own toil. In Switzerland this privileged holder of the richest princely domains in France had sold an old horse in order to eat. In Reichenau he had given mathematics lessons while his sister Adelaide did tapestry work and sewing. Those memories combined in a king filled the bourgeoisie with enthusiasm. With his own hands he had demolished the last iron cage of the Mont-Saint-Michel, built by Louis XI and used by Louis XV. He was the companion of Dumouriez and the friend of La Fayette; he had been in the Jacobin club; Mirabeau had clapped him on the shoulder; Danton had addressed him as 'Young man!' At the age of twenty-four [he was in fact nineteen], in 1793, as M. de Chartres, from the back of one of the Convention's little loges, he had been present at the trial of Louis XVI, so well named *this poor tyrant* . . . The Revolution had left a tremendous mark on him. The memory of it was like a living imprint of those great years, minute by minute. One day, in front of a witness whom it is impossible for us to doubt, he went through from memory the whole of letter A of the alphabetic list of the Constituent Assembly.[1]

For all that, he was a bourgeois prince, talkative and simple, rather stingy, family-minded and informal, not very 'royal', all of which gave contemporary colour to his throne; but he was also wily and jealous of his authority: 'Louis XI of the philosophical age', Chateaubriand would write.

He cleverly played his initial role of king of the Revolution, hailed by La Fayette on the balcony of the Hôtel de Ville, pleasant with the crowd, shaking the thousands of hands extended to him like a campaigning politician. But he also gathered about him all the shining lights of the '221' who personified continuity with the preceding regime. He summoned them all to join the government: Laffitte, Guizot, Molé, Dupont de l'Eure, not to mention a minor role for little Thiers, who had gone to so much trouble on his behalf during the course of events. But the new ministers were at loggerheads over the attitude to be adopted regarding popular unrest, which was slow to die down: clubs were having open sessions every day, spreading the word – as in the times of their great forerunners – that the revolution had been betrayed (this time it *had* been), demanding the heads of the ministers who had signed the ordinances; Polignac's blood would burst wide open the falsehood of the cobbled-up Charter. Without going as far as that, men such as the banker Laffitte, a jovial financier who was delighted with his popularity, Odilon Barrot, the new prefect of the Seine, and Armand Carrel, who wielded powerful influence over opinion on *Le National*, were fairly ready to yield to the July spirit, turning the new king into a republican high official in favour of democracy and an emancipator of European nations. This was the so-called 'movement' policy, which clashed with an Orleanism of 'resistance', the philosophy and policies of which Guizot had mapped out in advance, and which Casimir Périer would take as a basis for his actions.

---

[1] V. Hugo, *Les Misérables*, part IV, book I, p. 1.

At heart, the king's inclinations were towards them, but it was Laffitte who was chosen to mop up the revolutionary torrent in the first six months, in the hope – soon realized – that he and his friends would quickly wear themselves out. In reality, Laffitte let things slide rather than actually governed, at the risk of worrying Europe, which had rather reluctantly recognized the new regime. Unrest rumbled again during the trial of Charles X's ministers, who were sentenced in December to life imprisonment: the peers dismissed the spectre of the guillotine. The revolution took a further step back, at the end of the month, with La Fayette's resignation from command of the National Guard. But the fire smouldered beneath the ashes, and flared anew in February 1831 in Saint-Germain-l'Auxerrois. The remainder of the ultras had had the idea of holding a religious service there in memory of the Duc de Berry: a mob invaded and sacked the church, in front of battalions of the National Guard, who made no move to intervene. On the following days, it was the turn of the archbishop's palace to be pillaged and ravaged from top to bottom. Crosses were broken or torn away in most of the churches in Paris, and in many provincial towns, where iconoclastic rage was vented preferably on those immense crosses which had been solemnly erected by the great missions of the Restoration. Something which was reminiscent of the dechristianizing wave and vandalism of the end of 1793 was again at work in the July revolution, aggravated by the role which the Catholic Church had played in ultra-royalist politics. French revolutionary democracy was more anticlerical than ever, and that feeling mobilized educated youth perhaps more than the workers in their smocks: at least the former were often to be seen, during those days of February 1831, in the forefront of gangs breaking sacred objects and perpetrating violence against 'Jesuitism', that accomplice of the fleur-de-lis. It was the sign of a virulent anticlericalism, which was certainly stronger among the bourgeoisie than among the working classes, for it was often accompanied by 'philosophical' impiety.

However, Laffitte's inaction in the face of these disorders swiftly brought about his fall and the king, by summoning Casimir Périer to deal with matters (March 1831), now had to face the moment of truth: to indicate on what grounds order must be restored, that is to say, to define his regime. The men who served him were already unveiling an entire programme.

Laffitte was a banker, Casimir Périer came from a long line of Dauphinois industrialists and owned the château which in 1788 had been the cradle of Third Estate revolt. Moneyed bourgeoisie had replaced the aristocracy at the helm of affairs. It had an energetic representative in the person of the new head of government: he cared little for philosophy, and was not particularly sensitive to the sort of problems which tormented a Royer-Collard or a Guizot, with that narrow view of efficiency which may accompany success in business, but nevertheless an active, firm and even rigid leader. 'M. Casimir Périer had one great piece of luck', Royer-Collard said of him a little later. 'He arrived at the moment when his most outstanding defects were transformed into precious qualities: he was ignorant and brutal; those two virtues saved France.'[2] It was spitefulness in the form of homage, or the opposite, with which the old Doctrinaire greeted the re-establishment of order prior to the institution of representative government.

That vaunted regime, the object of so many historical and philosophical speculations, was now within reach. What was it? If one tries now to characterize it, apart from the conditions of its institution and its capacity to stomach its revolutionary origins, how can it be defined? It had not transformed the state, which remained in the hands of a centralized administration, the supreme agents of which were the prefects, and for which recruitment – not yet regulated by competition – lay in the government's hands. In order to replace it, since they could not change it, the July men proceeded in the same way as the men of 1815 after the Hundred Days: they had a massive purge.

The Revolution had been accompanied and followed by a tremendous amount of begging for 'positions': that was a characteristic feature, a truly French way of regulating administrative personnel in the nineteenth century. Besides, a good many high-ranking officials and officers who had served Louis XVIII and Charles X departed of their own accord, having been ordered to take the oath: this left all the more posts free for new ambitions. The majority of prefects appointed by the ultras thus resigned or were dismissed, to be replaced by men with a different loyalty, but who performed the same job – of which preparation for elections was not the least task.

The electoral property qualification had been modified, lowered from 1,000 to 500 francs for eligibility (and one could now be elected at the age of thirty, instead of forty), and from 300 to 200 francs for the right to vote. The concept of suffrage stayed the same as that of the Restoration: voting was a function, not a right. It was intended to extract from the social body whatever it possessed in the way of reason, and could therefore theoretically be extended, in step with the progress of education and the Enlightenment, to far wider categories of the population. The debate on 'entitlements' was concluded in a very restrictive way: holders of university qualifications starting the practice of a liberal profession or teaching post were excluded from the vote if they held no landed property or wealth. The electorate had doubled, but it still did not exceed 200,000 electors.

The one great step forward in the field of political democracy had been accomplished by the law of 21 March 1831, which had made municipal councils elective. Mayors and their deputies continued to be appointed but, chosen from the council, they had to be elected beforehand. Electors were much more numerous than those for the legislative ballot, since they formed between 10 and 14 per cent of all the men in each commune, elected among those in the higher tax brackets: that is to say, a million voters, who reintroduced politics into the villages, where it had been

[2] P. Thureau-Dangin, *Histoire de la monarchie de Juillet*, 1884–92, vol. 1, p. 367.

virtually extinct since 1800, if not 1792. Another law, of June 1833, extended election to members of the general councils: the prefect now had to hold discussions with an elected departmental assembly. He retained a great deal of power over the mayors, through hundreds of ways of applying pressure, chiefly financial; but he had to talk with elected men, through whose intermediary the deputy or deputies could also constitute local authorities for themselves. Apart from Paris and Lyon, the dangerous towns, which remained under direct supervision, France's 40,000 communes were integrated into the modern political system of representation.

Thus the July revolution was fairly quick to institute a regime which, in the end, was quite close to the one it had terminated, yet which was based on a radically opposite spirit: this demonstrated more than ever that typically French contrast between the results of political action and the intellectual activity centred upon it. The Restoration, because of the ultras who had finished by dominating it, had been Catholic and royalist, and even clerical and fideistic. The July monarchy was filled with bourgeois who were hostile to priests and the Bourbons. Nevertheless, it introduced into France that same type of parliamentary public life which the Restoration had sketched out previously: a life dominated by elections, debates in the Chambers, the formation of ministries, the reconciling of the king's wishes, majority votes and the pressures of public opinion. The paradox of the Charter granted by the Bourbons had caused the keenest supporters of the sovereignty of the kings to become the most uncompromising voices for the rights of parliament. That of the July revolution consisted in transforming a victorious uprising into a monarchy of propertied voters: at least in this double movement the two regimes were alike, and the second only very cautiously opened the way to a wider participation by citizens in public life.

However, its spirit remained irreconcilable with that of the first, and the break of July 1830 between legitimism and Orleanism would never be healed: it had renewed the spirit of 1789, once again snapping the threads of the two loyalties which the Restoration had wanted to reinstitute – the Catholic tradition and monarchic sentiment. Uprooted by the Revolution, tamed by Napoleon, the Church had been eager, after 1814, to rediscover the fertile soil of the *ancien régime*; it had increased not only the solemn missions and erection of crosses, but also the building of churches, new congregations, small schools.

The July revolution smashed this attempt to reconquer, not only by bringing to light a very widespread anticlericalism but also by once again putting the Church outside the state. In this regard, the great schools law of 1833 was typical; it was the work of Guizot, who created, under state control, three fundamental obligations: every school teacher – whether congregationist or lay – must obtain a qualification certificate granted by a departmental commission; every commune of more than 500 inhabitants must maintain a primary school and guarantee the teacher's living – at least 200 francs as an annual fixed salary – and his shelter, a building to house his school; every *département* must maintain a primary teacher training school for boys where new masters could be trained and former ones given refresher courses.

This was a crucial law, less for its immediate results – French illiteracy, which was so high in Brittany and to the south of the Loire, would not be eradicated before the end of the century – than for the inspiration which gave rise to it, and which speaks volumes for the driving forces of the new regime. Guizot's Protestant mentality held the conviction that access to books and the lessening of ignorance would influence the mastering of passions and condition reasonable conduct. Having been vaguely suspect under the Restoration, Protestantism made a forceful comeback in the July liberalism. The modernized schools which the 1833 law wanted to set up would therefore liberate young minds and souls from the Church's archaic supervision.

That was not to say they would be in any way antireligious: on the contrary, they must inculcate that minimum of religion which was essential for morality and life in society, but at the same time more substantial subjects than those in the sparse curriculum of the congregationist teachers. The Orleanist notables saw in them an instrument of cultural promotion and also a tool for social preservation; the republicans, in the wake of Condorcet, made popular education the condition of later emancipation. The Church bewailed these two disastrous projects, which were at the expense of its own. Education had become the major stake in French politics, for all parties were investing their contradictory hopes in it, though they started from the shared belief that schools were all-powerful over children's minds.

The other field in which the rupture between the July regime and the one preceding was having an effect was national history. The restored monarchy had wanted to refashion the nation's past into a seamless one based on the annals of the legitimate royalty, but instead of exorcizing the regicide, it had constantly maintained the memory of it; irresistibly drawn to pre-1789, it had aroused something much more universal than the hatred it provoked in its adversaries: a feeling for the times, the movement of minds and morals. The Orléans, on the contrary, had their historical moment, if not their origins, in 1789. Louis-Philippe, since the 'good' emigration to which the Terror had forced him, had cultivated this image of a liberal prince, a descendant not only of a brother of Louis XIV but also of the Rights of Man.

The July monarchy sought to draw its strength from this contradictory heritage. Born out of the Parisian uprising, it could not quite simply hark back to tradition, like the senior branch, and even less to glory, like a Bonaparte; nor did it benefit from a political situation which led the people to obey, like that of 18 Brumaire or spring 1814. To conceal the poverty of its legal standing, it had only the ambiguous claims which it alone could make *simultaneously* on the *ancien régime* and the Revolution. It therefore had to position itself at the exact point where the two traditions of national history were juxtaposed and added together, or rather, at the intersection of the liberal components of both the *ancien régime* and the Revolution: one might say, to re-create 1789 instead of starting it afresh. To reinvent it as a kind of hyphen between the past and the future, whereas the men of the end of the eighteenth century had made it a dividing-line for minds and interests, which had soon become a stake in civil war.

One of the most interesting features of this July Orleanism lies in its desire to effect at long last the synthesis of national history, by reintegrating the Revolution into it as a long epilogue, criss-crossed with swerves and backtrackings, but finally achieved in 1830. Moreover, never had a regime enjoyed the attention of so many historians leaning over its cradle: Thiers, Guizot, Mignet, Thierry, Prosper de Barante, Claude Fauriel, Jules Michelet, Edgar Quinet, to quote only the great names. The nation – that word which was again fluttering like a banner – had never been surrounded by so many professors, all inspired with the same concern to write its annals. They had all had their training in the heated and learned debates of the 1820s, and here they were ready to begin, in power, in decision-making posts.

There again, the crown went to Guizot, the incumbent of a great Ministry of Public Education, created for him in 1832, which gave him supreme control – apart from scholastic establishments and the University – over all the great learned institutions, including the Institut. In 1833, he sponsored the creation of the Société de l'Histoire de France intended to collect and publish documents essential to a knowledge of national history. Shortly afterwards, he set up a committee with the task of directing research into and publishing previously unpublished documents relating to French history, in order to impart a governmental impetus to the under-taking. The national past gained a place of honour also in secondary education: from 1838, Guizot's successor, Salvandy, would make it the sole subject in the first-year history programme, from Clovis to Bonaparte.

In this way the new regime strove relentlessly to entrench itself in a national legitimacy, having finally inherited the entire patrimony, and the guarantee of a sovereignty bought by the efforts of so many generations, the long-awaited moment of achievement of the work of centuries. It made the first systematic attempt, since the Consulate, to bring the Revolution to an end by implanting it both in reason and in history. However, in the very first years, the spectacle of public life reveals the difficulties with which that ambition would collide.

OPPOSITION FROM RIGHT AND LEFT

Firstly: July 1830 had not done away with the split of 1789. Partisans of, or those nostalgic for, the *ancien régime* survived their defeat; the ultras had become legitimists. Counter-revolutionary France, hostile to the principles of the new society, had not – with one or two exceptions – followed its princes into exile. In the heart of the new regime, it formed a circle of insubordination in the name of dynastic loyalty. The refusals started with that of the oath, which was demanded of its officials by the July regime: nearly all Charles X's servitors finished their career here, and many scions of old aristocratic families – such as Lieutenant de Kergorlay, a childhood friend of Tocqueville, and fresh from the capture of Algiers – broke off their career at this point. Most often, there then began for them an existence as rural notables devoted to local influence, where communication was between one château and another, and where the prefect figured as the representative of a usurped authority.

In itself, it was a relatively restricted milieu, but it had the advantage of being regarded favourably by the Church – although Pope Pius VIII had asked the French bishops to accept the new regime loyally – and in the main could obtain support, depending on the province, from a popular royalist feeling which was deeply ingrained in memories of the terrible years. This was the case in the west, particularly in the Vendée, where the recollection of the 1793 uprising had been the subject, since 1815, of so much pedagogic attention. It also happened in the Midi, chiefly where Catholics and Protestants had confronted one another in a latent civil war throughout the whole Revolution: 1830 legitimism, as if naturally, brandished the anti-Protestant banner in the face of Louis-Philippe's men.

The legitimist circle formed a secession, a withdrawal, an exile, a memory, rather than a real force. It is true that it had lived first of all by planning a third restoration by way of an armed insurrection; but that affair, which had been undertaken in 1832 by the Duchesse de Berry on behalf of her son, failed quite pathetically in both the south-east and the Vendée. Because it could not give legitimate monarchy its Hundred Days, it illustrated yet again the ambiguities of royal succession. Charles X had become king once more when he left France, and yet his supporters' feeling was directed prematurely to his grandson, *l'enfant du miracle* (the miracle child), the future Henri V, at the same time short-circuiting his son, the doleful Duc d'Angoulême. It was as if they, too, were unwittingly yielding to the trend of those democratic times, giving their overwhelming approval in advance – at the expense of the very idea which united them – to a king who might one day be crowned by public opinion. The *henriquinquistes* (partisans of Henri V) who invested their candidate with all the magic which still clung to the last Henri – the king who desired that everyone should have a 'chicken in his pot' – showed that even loyalty was not incompatible with a typically modern forgetfulness of tradition.

Nevertheless, this French legitimism, which was more of a residual party than a rising force, was not as weak as the Stuart supporters in the eighteenth-century British monarchy. The Jacobites had had to fight a public opinion widely united over the political, legal and religious heritage of the seventeenth-century English revolution. The French legitimists, on the contrary, placed their action in an entirely different context, which provided them with many more weapons against the compromise regime

which had emerged from the Three Glorious Days. They embodied the
idea of a sovereign hereditary monarchy, linked with a state religion: a
tradition which left small room for shared sovereignty and constitutional
tinkering, and which, beaten but intact, delegitimized in advance any
monarchy organized on other principles. Is it still a monarchy, asks Bonald
after 1830,[3] this government born out of a revolution, without an aristocracy, without a state religion, without any distinction between orders?
Certainly not: it is merely a casual regime, imposed by the passion for
positions and bourgeois cupidity, the meeting of an ambition and a situation, an unstable transition towards the sovereignty of the people and
democracy. On this theme, which drew all its strength from the 1789
precedent, legitimist criticism of July found a powerful political echo in a
public opinion which was more than ever divided over the direction and
scope of the revolutionary heritage.

Indeed, it leant on the spectre of social dissolution, which haunted
nineteenth-century France like an inevitable fate inextricably tied to
bourgeois individualism: July 1830, the second victory of the middle class
over the nobility, opened the way once again to the society of egoisms and
interests; behind equality lay hidden the power of either money or numbers, both equally unsuited to the production of political or social order.
The idea was declined in the mood of radical disapproval, *à la* Bonald: to
overthrow what he called 'the immutable basis of political society', which
was rooted in the natural order willed by God, bourgeois liberalism had no
other support than the fiction of the sovereignty of individuals, that is to
say, the anarchy of wills.

The other version tended rather to envelop the good old times of
legitimate monarchy with the melancholy of regret, without any longer
inspiring the desire to see them again or restore them, since it bewailed their disappearance ás a necessity of evolution. This version was
Chateaubriand's, more than ever the first to weep over the monarchy, but
also announcing the undeniable truth hidden in the July usurpation, which
was nothing other than democracy:

The July movement has nothing to do with politics properly speaking; it has to do
with the social revolution which goes on ceaselessly. Through the sequence of this
general revolution, 28 July 1830 is merely the enforced consequence of 21 January
1793 . . . Let us not think, therefore, that the work of July 1830 is a day's
superfluity; do not let us imagine that legitimacy will forthwith re-establish succession by right of primogeniture; nor must we persuade ourselves that July will
suddenly die a natural death. Without doubt, the Orléans branch will not take
root: it will not be for that outcome that so much blood, calamity and genius have
been expended, so much disaster endured, for half a century! But July, if it does
not bring the final destruction of France by the annihilation of all liberties, July
will come to its natural fruition: and that fruit is democracy.[4]

---

[3] L. de Bonald, *Réflexions sur la Révolution de 1830*.
[4] Chateaubriand, *Mémoires d'outre-tombe*, book XXXIV, ch. 9.

Besides the feeling of inevitability, which was so widespread at the time, something almost like a desire comes across in these lines: all things considered, the legitimist writer preferred the people to the bourgeoisie, and democracy to usurpation. Nostalgia for bygone days could also lead to the hope of regaining, through the advancement of the people, a less selfish society than that of the bourgeois *Louis-Philippards*. It was a feature of this milieu which certainly had great importance in the formative years of the young Tocqueville.

The legitimists thus had a much more far-reaching effect on the Orléans monarchy than their influence, properly speaking, would lead one to believe. Not that that influence was negligible. Where they had the ear of the peasantry, as in many farmlands in the west, the château-dwellers, with the backing of the presbytery, dominated the commune, and often the canton. Cut off in a provincial network of alliances, memories and solidarities, they kept alive the decentralizing idea, since they had hardly even begun to realize it when they were in power: this is evidence of the fascination exerted by the instrument of the centralized state, even on those who had written its demolition into their programme. It was only after being driven from power, and under Louis-Philippe, that the former ultras, who had become internal exiles, finally retrieved the role of tutelary authorities in local life by which – though defeated – they resumed the idea of their erstwhile dominance.

Divided and tamed by the kings, before being quelled by the modern state, French aristocracy remained the joint creation of absolutism and the Revolution. When it escaped from the fascination of Paris, having been beaten there, it found refuge in the provinces and localism: but faced with the prefect and the administration, it was largely removed from any real power. When it came to commanding hearts and souls, the aristocracy had to yield this role to the priesthood, which was infinitely more powerful in that respect.

Nevertheless, it continued to exist at national level through newspapers, books, salons, learned societies and academies. The legitimists thereby wielded a power over opinion which was not merely to do with fashionable society, but which weighed doubly, and strongly, on public life. On the one hand, they continued to render impossible that unity of the ruling classes which had been the major French political problem since the *ancien régime*: the July monarchy would have no more success than the Restoration in bringing together all *propriétaires* under its banner. On the other hand, aristocratic criticism of middle-class royalty often added its effects to those of the opposition left: far from giving weapons to the government in power to neutralize its republican adversaries, on the contrary, it established a political and intellectual meeting-ground with the latter, by denouncing bourgeois individualism.

It was not strong enough to offer the government a good pretext to rally the left under its banner against the extreme right. It was not weak enough not to offer the said left intellectual recognition arising from a common rejection of the rule of money. Chateaubriand bemoaned the misfortunes of the Bourbons, but above all he enjoyed the plaudits of the left and educated young people, for a wink at Béranger or when he visited prison to see his friend Armand Carrel, the brilliant editor of *Le National*, one of the masterminds of the republican party, sentenced in 1834 for violation of press laws.

The real danger, for Louis-Philippe, did not lie with the legitimists. It lay on his left, where the July sleight-of-hand had not succeeded. In fact, the years which followed the institution of the new regime were marked by a general unrest in the country, which on several occasions took the form of revolutionary uprisings, chiefly in Paris. Some share of the blame must be attributed to a social and economic crisis which gave rise to unemployment and poverty, as well as to the famous cholera epidemic of 1832, which lent itself to all kinds of rumours and imputations. But the root of the political situation remained the frustration felt by the revolutionaries of July 1830 in the face of the premature ending of the Three Glorious Days.

By recourse to the Duc d'Orléans's candidature for the throne, Thiers, Mignet, Guizot and their friends had hoped to nip any revolutionary excesses in the bud, to halt the Revolution, so to speak, at 14 July, and to remake a 1789 which would remove any pretext for a 1793. But the events which followed showed them that, despite all their precautions, a little of 1793 must come into any 1789. Evidence of this lies in the insurrection of June 1832, which was linked with the funeral of General Lamarque, a leading figure in the Hundred Days, a great opposition orator under the ultras and, to tell the truth, more Bonapartist than liberal, or even republican, but for that very reason the syncretic idol of revolutionary patriotism.

It was not the only or the last great political riot in Paris during those years; but, in control of the entire east of Paris for a day, between 5 and 6 June, it illustrated how the success of the Three Glorious Days had renewed revolutionary pedagogy. As 14 July 1789 had inaugurated the technique and popularity of the great Parisian 'days' of the French Revolution, the victorious barricades of July 1830 had begun a second cycle of Parisian uprisings, whereby the lowly citizens of the capital forged a link with the epic acts of the heroes.

The root of the matter was more than ever the French Revolution, revived, recalled, recommenced through the popular victory over Louis XVI's brother. Now, hardly had this Revolution been resumed when a plot had replaced it with a new monarch, who was supposed to bring it to an end! Anyone who wants to understand the whole range of passions and ideas for which, during these years, the demand for a Republic was a vehicle, can contrast it, word for word, with the narrowest and most conservative interpretation of July: that of Guizot, which very quickly became Louis-Philippe's, once the inevitable concessions had been made.

All Guizot's efforts went into disengaging the new monarchy from its revolutionary origin and even removing from it that elective character of which bourgeois contemporaries were so proud: Louis-Philippe was not an 'elected' or 'chosen' king, but 'a prince, luckily found near to the broken throne, whom necessity made king' (speech on 21 December 1831), and consequently heir to the historical rights of the senior branch. This denial of the sovereignty of the people, in keeping with Doctrinaire thought, thus made possible the distinction between civil and political rights, another key to 'representative government': only the first were universal, the second were reserved exclusively for those capable of exercising them in accordance with reason.

By contrast, the republican idea was indivisible from that of revolution and sovereignty. The very word 'republic' was sufficient indication that the *res publica* could not be true to its name unless it were the property of all, defined by all, agreed by all and, as far as possible, constantly reaffirmed by all. Now, revolution was the means by which the people had twice seized back this imprescriptible sovereignty usurped by the Bourbons: first, between 1789 and 1792, and then in July 1830.

The example of the French Revolution illustrated just how vain it was to try to reconcile the institution of royalty with the sovereignty of the people: Louis XVI, rechristened a constitutional king, had remained a prince of the *ancien régime*, the man of Varennes and betrayal. For the Republic was also the nation, that collective image of the citizenship of each person, one and indivisible, the bearer of an international right as well, since it was the promise of sovereignty for every people. The July events had seen the reflowering of all the Girondin themes of winter and spring 1792 on the emancipation of nations, rejuvenated, restored to their original freshness by the return of the Bourbons in the baggage-train of the Holy Alliance. The insurgents of the three famous Days did not want a republic only in Paris, but liberty for Belgium, Italy, Poland, and French support for 'nations' in revolt, whereas Louis-Philippe, eager to get himself accepted by Europe, took great care to do nothing. At the news of the capture of Warsaw, in September 1831, which put an end to the Polish revolt, unrest had grumbled anew against the passivity of Casimir Périer's government.

In the days immediately after July, the victors of the street battles had been quickly caught up by Orleanist intrigue, which had the backing of the old La Fayette. Moreover, in the euphoria of the moment, many had not made any distinction between a republic and that monarchy which owed its existence to them. Victor Hugo, who had rapidly passed from one regime to another, dated August 1830 the first sentence of a work he would publish in 1834 under the title *Journal des idées et des opinions d'un révolutionnaire de 1830*: 'What we need is the fact, *republic*, and the word, *monarchy*.' But the development of the said monarchy, in the hands of those who wanted at all costs to forget, and make others forget, their recent allies, made the poet's wish more and more impracticable. Armand Carrel, Thiers's brilliant companion in the *National*'s campaign against the

July ordinances, who had upheld the compromise of August 1830, changed horses in January 1832 and went over to republicanism, bringing it his talent together with the famous newspaper. Did the government, in an effort to discredit him, talk about the 'street press'? 'And what are you, yourselves?' retorted *Le National*.

Where do you come from? Is not your royalty street royalty? . . . Royalty of the streets, ministers of the streets, deputies of the streets; without this nomination from the streets – which freed you from your oaths to three generations of Bourbons – you would be nothing but traitors who had deserted the legitimate monarchy at the very time when it called on you to defend it against the streets.

Substituting a family for a dynasty had certainly allowed the political crisis to be brought swiftly to an end, but it had not prevented the radicalization of minds and revolutionary extremism. On the contrary, it had crystallized their characteristics for a long while, by blocking the Parisian movement from following its natural course, and by so quickly and severely turning on those who had made this substitution possible. The years following Louis-Philippe's accession discredited those who, in the republican camp, had believed in a progressive and open, if not democratic, monarchy; they created a gulf which was soon impassable between royalty – any royalty – and the great principles of the French Revolution.

Any element of conflict which the revolutionary heritage had contained was in that way magnified and given the dignity of an insurmountable political contradiction. Under the Restoration, the entire opposition had claimed its inspiration from the whole of the Revolution. After July, the liberals, with the Doctrinaires to the fore, gave so narrow an interpretation of 1789 as to open the way wide to the maximalism of memories: if those who claimed to have founded 1789 anew denied the sovereignty of the people, then let 1793, and Robespierre, and Jacobinism live again as well.

Far from being a 'glorious revolution' in the French way, a new 1688, July brought back and deepened all the conflicts born of 1789. Instead of founding an institutional consensus, it worsened the revolutionary nature of French political culture. By associating rediscovered liberty with the confiscation of political rights by those who had the most wealth, it abandoned the national democratic tradition to what was least liberal about it: a mixture of Jacobin and Bonapartist. This characteristic is not sufficient to define the entire republican left of that period, which comprised more moderate, or more realistic, elements, such as Armand Carrel, who was little inclined to the romanticism of the barricades. But it gives a fair idea of the dominant tone.

During that era, another passion took a central place in the country's civil struggles, to harden attitudes still further: one which drew its substance not only from the spectacle of social inequality, but also from the idea of social class and a messianic role attributed to the victory of one class over another. This concept also had its source in the French Revolution, but as a result rather than as a cause of the event; it found its full resonance only in those years, forming the cornerstone of socialist doctrines.

In fact, the French Revolution had abhorred the division of civil society according to wealth, and had done its utmost to get rid of the threat and even the idea of it, chiefly through the unity and indivisibility of the nation: nobility was thought of less as a class than as a political obstacle to the formation of a united body of citizens, since it was defined not by its wealth – which, in any case, was very variable – but by privilege, that is to say, inequality.

It was through politics, too, that class feeling made a spectacular re-entry into revolutionary society which had so violently repressed it: first, with the *Enragés* and the whole of the popular movement against the rich, in favour of regulation and the Terror; then, as an indirect consequence, after 9 Thermidor, with the reaction of the well-to-do against the poor and lowly. The suppression of the Babouvist conspiracy began the long history of French bourgeois panics in the face of the poorer classes; the ghost of the Terror thenceforth haunted any popular demands and turned the idea of democracy into a bogeyman; in French history, class consciousness was a legacy of the Revolution before it became the product of industrial development.

Under the Restoration, the resurrection of the counter-revolution by the ultras, in 1815 and again from 1820, had reunited the revolutionary camp. The idea of class was reworked, chiefly to account for the antagonism between the nobility and the bourgeoisie: the latter, guardian of civil equality and political liberty, had conquered in 1789 and was preparing to add the crowning touch to its inevitable dominance by founding representative government. But in granting middle-class rule its historical and philosophical letters patent, Guizot, Mignet, Thiers and their friends had also opened the door to expectations of an 'afterwards', at last achieving the promised equality, this time through the action of the impoverished.

If history is the science of the class struggle, why stop at the bourgeoisie? If the relationship of strength between the classes is the foundation of the law, how could something which was extolled in the past be denied in the present? What justification was there for preventing classes other than the bourgeoisie from desiring an additional levelling-out, this time against the bourgeoisie? The extraordinary revolutionary insistence on equality thus resurfaced in the new garb of the era, having become the science of history and progress, as in the later works of Saint-Simon. It is also to be found in the neo-Robespierrist interpretations of the Revolution, such as that of Buonarroti, the historian of the *Conspiration de l'égalité dite de Babeuf*, which appeared in 1828: if Robespierre had failed to realize the true revolutionary promise, that of equality, if Babeuf's attempt had been ferociously suppressed by Thermidorian bourgeois, the result had been only to prolong its inspiration through the action of an insurrectionist minority of activists, who had decided to effect the equal sharing of property by seizing the state in the name of the people.

July 1830 gave a formidable impetus to this type of exaggeration, for reasons which are easy to understand. The new power which had emerged from the revolution itself affirmed that it was a middle-class government. It thereby gave itself the authority to exclude those who had won the victory from enjoying its fruits, whereas the political situation created by that victory on the contrary reawoke the memory or the legend of a national community united in egalitarian brotherhood. And it thus designated as the new enemy of the Revolution the class which had usurped the people's rebellion for its own advantage: the bourgeoisie. So the idea of class became the epicentre of revolutionary culture, just as the bourgeoisie, in the wake of the nobility, would henceforth be the scapegoat.

There is, however, a major shift in that substitution. As an order, the nobility had been a legally defined social group. the keystone of ancient society conceived as a hierarchized collection of bodies, in keeping with the divine plan. It was in this quality that it had been the privileged victim of the great overthrow of the entire old order effected by the Revolution, which had replaced it with the liberty of individuals who were sovereign in themselves.

The bourgeoisie, for its part, was inseparable from the movement of modernity; it was both the guardian and the offspring of equality, and of money – that great equalizer. Without any legal definition, without any accredited place in the universe, without guarantee of birth or continuity, without any assigned function in government, it formed that uncertain social area, filled with modern society's seething turbulence, consequently so difficult to grasp, to destroy by revolution. The July government itself had already gone a long way by identifying itself as quite plainly bourgeois, thus substituting the fixed target of the state for a mobile and elusive reality.

If the revolutionary politics of those years could thus recover an adversary analogous to the former king of the aristocracy, a 'government of the bourgeoisie' in Montesquieu's sense, it was less able to define what would go to make the equality of the future, and in whose name it would be instituted. That doubtless gave rise to all the borrowing from the old order of things, all those crossing-points which linked it to legitimist nostalgia, in the negation of bourgeois egoism and materialism. The two political families were united by the concept of rebuilding a community going beyond individual interests and class division: it was fairly widespread at the time as, a little later, it would be common to two such distant stars as Tocqueville and Marx.

Furthermore I see as a sign of the times the omnipresence of Catholic thinking in the opposition in principle to the July regime, on both the right and the left. Poor French Catholicism, emerging from the Revolution and the Empire as if wrenched from its age-old breeding-ground and replanted in the inhospitable soil of modern politics; organized into a public service by the Empire, thereafter linking its destiny to a dead royalty; entering the century as an instrument of national repentance; threatened by the people of the barricades; made fragile by the Voltairean bourgeoisie in power; bent, straightened, cast down, hesitating between two refuges, Paris and Rome!

What was most evident, in its recent history, was that it had lost its principle of autonomy and its special relationship with French society. It had been aestheticized by Chateaubriand, sentimentalized by Lamennais and Gallicanized by Montlosier: it had no theologians but was inseparable from literature and politics. Just like the ultras, it tended to be nostalgic and backward-looking; it had no attachment to the July bourgeoisie even though, perforce, it was resigned to it. From 1830 onwards, the great novelty was that Catholic feeling, liberated from its loyalty to the government in power and finding a new, external focus in the 'social question', could also involve itself in socialist thinking.

To demonstrate this, I could take the example of Lamennais,[5] who had begun his literary career as a young *chouan* priest, thundering anathema against the rationalism of the Enlightenment and the French Revolution in the name of a Christianity conceived as the sole principle of authority, the source of every human society, and given material form by tradition: this was the 'romantic' feat of the *Essai sur l'indifférence en matière de religion* (1817). Subsequently, a prisoner of his literature, and inaugurating that taste for excess which so many Catholic pamphleteers of the nineteenth and twentieth centuries would share, the best-selling priest denounced Charles X's France as a 'vast democracy', and argued for the Church's absolute submission to the pope.

Then, just about 1830, that theocratic vision was transferred to become the slogan of his newspaper *L'Avenir*, founded in October 1830: 'God and Liberty'. The defence of religion now switched to that of liberty: less the liberty of individuals than that of communities and peoples, the figureheads of humanity's progress. For Lamennais's conversion to revolution did not affect his rejection of modern individualism; much more, it reinforced it: his God gave the blessing of liberty only to that collective emancipation demanded by the peoples, not for it to be split up among individuals, but so that they should all be joined in a liberated communion. The sympathies of *L'Avenir* in 1830–1 were all the more ardent since they went out to Catholic nations struggling for their national liberation, such as Ireland or, even more, Poland.

An analysis of the libertarian and associative prophetism towards which this second Lamennais evolved after his condemnation by the pope (1832) is less directly relevant to my argument than the case – very different, though comparable – of another contemporary character, who was also of the Catholic persuasion: Buchez. Why Buchez? He was a less outstanding writer, but since adolescence had been wholly engaged in the battle for

---

[5] P. Bénichou, *Le Temps des prophètes*.

social reform, and through him may be deciphered the component elements forming the left of that period: the French Revolution, Christianity, historicism, Saint-Simon, the socialist concept; and one can begin to understand how they shaped the century.

Buchez belonged to the generation which came just after the French Revolution and was constantly obsessed by the revolutionary promise; his intellectual and political development is so typical of the French extreme left in the first half of the nineteenth century that, following its course, one would imagine oneself transported into *Les Illusions perdues* or *L'Éducation sentimentale*, somewhere between d'Arthez, or Michel Chrestien, or Deslauriers. Buchez was a syncretic ideologist; filled, possessed by everything touched by the spirit of the times. Born in 1796 into the middle-ranking civil service bourgeoisie (his father was in tax administration), he was very soon involved in political activism, which would slow down his medical studies so that they were completed only in 1825. In 1818 he was a militant in the secret societies hostile to the Restoration; he was a Freemason but, finding the Grand Orient too moderate, together with his friend Bazard he founded the 'Loge des Amis de la Vérité', which had republican and revolutionary inspiration and was soon engaged in political action. There was a fresh step forward in 1821, with the creation of the French Charbonnerie, a tough version of the Carbonaria or republican movement of Naples so dear to Buonarroti, the survivor of Babouvism.

But the Charbonnerie fell through and Buchez, after some months in prison in 1822, went from rebellious militancy to revolutionary philosophy. The medical student, which he still was, became drawn to a materialist interpretation of man for which the Ideologists – Cabanis and Destutt de Tracy – provided him with the model. But it was by becoming a Saint-Simonian, in 1825, that he discovered both a science of society and positive politics, freed from the naïvetés of the Carbonaro *coup*. In the year of Saint-Simon's death, 1825, just after the publication of the *Nouveau Christianisme*, Buchez was part of the editorial staff of the *Producteur*, together with Enfantin, Rodrigues, Bazard and the master's heirs. He soon took over the column devoted to the philosophy of the sciences abandoned by Auguste Comte, in order to defend the supremacy of physiology over all the sciences, and consequently to place it at the foundation of social science.

However, Buchez, like Comte, would pass from scientism to religious preaching, at the cost of a break with Saint-Simonian tradition. Comte, who had never really been part of the team on the *Producteur*, had tiptoed off. As for Buchez, he shattered the sect's unity at the end of the 1820s by challenging the orthodoxy of the Bazard–Enfantin 'pontificate' on the religious question. One or two years later, here was a Catholic Buchez facing a difficult synthesis: if, for Comte, the new religion would crown the positivist edifice, Buchez must reconcile science with the oldest religion and with the Church itself.

As always in this era, the solution came through a theory of history. Buchez picked out from it the contrast between critical and organic periods, the idea of progress through the 'ages' of humanity, the reinstatement of producers and the popular masses in the management of the human adventure. He made the distinction between a theocratic period, a revolutionary period and a period of 'civil organization', which was the task of his own time: but this long-awaited era was no longer simply 'positive' as it was for Comte. It was inextricably popular and religious, reconciling humanity with divine order through the finally discovered power of the people. For Buchez, history was both scientific and messianic. It obeyed laws which were themselves ordained around a religious finality – the Christian promise of reconciliation and unity. Such is the extraordinary scientifico-Catholic gnosis developed by his *Introduction à la science de l'histoire* (1833) which forms the most general basis of the doctrine.

Meanwhile, Buchez had gathered around him a little group of disciples (the most famous being Vigny, who merely flashed through, and the most productive, Auguste Ott, who would combine studies on Kant and Hegel with Buchezian militancy); he had started a newspaper, *L'Européen*, a 'journal of the moral and economic sciences', founded a historical institute with an annual congress – in short, he was the head of a sect, the leading light of an esoteric knowledge of universal history, just like his master, Saint-Simon, when Buchez was young. *L'Européen*, in the years 1831–2, developed the theme of the separation of the classes as the catastrophe of modern society, and advocated the solution of a morality of equality, rooted in the Christian religion. 'It was through the efforts and the blindness of that egoism', said an anonymous article in no. 14, dated 3 March 1832, probably composed by Buchez,

that this terrible doctrine was proclaimed – that society is divided into two classes: the haves and the have-nots; in a word, the bourgeois and the proletariat . . . Man's whole freedom, in fact, consists of a choice between selfishness and dedication, and as long as there is material inequality between men, the only sentiment which can form the basis of social morality, as of individual morality, must be the trend towards making that inequality disappear . . . The last age of Christianity must be the realization of that equality, the principle of which was proclaimed and dogmatized by earlier ages: equality, fraternity; those were Christianity's first words, and those will still be its last words.

But Buchez does not escape the rule according to which all the political ideas of that time found their source in reflection on the French Revolution. Since the subject was more fashionable than ever in the turmoil following 1830, he plunged into an immense *Histoire parlementaire de la Révolution française*, in forty volumes, which appeared in separate parts between 1834 and 1839 so that it could be read, like cheap books, by a vast public. In the preface to each of these volumes Buchez, some years after Buonarroti, developed a new socialist interpretation of the Revolution, this time interwoven with a Christian reference, and even with a faithfulness to the Catholic Church.

He did this by the device of a teleological vision of history, which was accompanied by a reduction of universal history to the history of France. In the long introduction which opens the *Histoire parlementaire*, devoted to an 'abridged history of the French', both ideas are there: the general direction of world history is given by the realization of the equality of men, in keeping with Jesus' message; and by special election, it is France that provides Christianity's secular arm, the monarchy marching hand in hand with the Church, since the memorable baptism of Clovis, in order to accomplish the divine plan. From that comes the central role of the Revolution, which intensifies the sign of God over France by reaffirming the doctrine of the Gospels with an unequalled brilliance. But the Revolution, like what has gone before it, is divided within itself, because it must overcome the individualist breaking-up of 1789 in order to attain 1793's heralding of the community.

Buchez's work contains an entire repertoire of themes familiar to romantic historiography, such as the idea of a French 'nationality' expressing universal history, or the Christian genealogy of modern democracy, or the continuity between the egalitarian efforts of the kings and those of the Revolution. But they are interwoven in a reconstruction which is more ideological than properly historical, where the entire national past is reorganized according to the huge schism which the Revolution opened between 1789 and 1793, selfish individualism and fraternal equality. Starting from Guizot's idea, for example, that the monarchy had formed the nation by equalizing ranks and uniting society, Buchez nurtured an anti-Protestant passion where Guizot, on the contrary, had extolled Protestantism as a liberation. All he needed to do was to place the sixteenth-century supporters of the Reformation in the camp of what he termed 'aristocratic federalism', battling against the national unity desired by the kings: at once, Protestant individualism seemed as disastrous as would that of the men of 1789 two centuries afterwards!

In fact, in 1789 the Voltairean bourgeoisie, for its own advantage, appropriated the immense upheaval, in order to slow it down and steer it into a road without a future, since it led only to its own bourgeois interests. Here Buchez harks back to the Saint-Simonian theme of 1789 as a 'critical' phase, locked in that pure negation of the social personified by the individual of the Rights of Man. The failure of the Constituent Assembly lay in its inability to perceive the 'right doctrine', the one which allows the historic mission of nationality to be placed before the rights of individuals, by making the sovereignty of the people prevail over the dogma of individual reason.

The price paid for that failure was the almost inevitable rule of violence, the Terror, which began with the September massacres and was a tragic necessity if matters were to be righted: 'French unity, which was on the point of breaking up for want of a common concept and through ignorance of its goal, was maintained by the terror of those executions and of the appalling violence which followed them.'[6] For Buchez, the Terror might be a good or a bad thing, according to the aim it was supposed to achieve: bad when it was exercised under the Roman empire against the Christians, thus running counter to history, but good when it was used to repress the 'antisocial instincts' let loose in 1789, as also between 1792 and 1794. It was all the more necessary because those instincts died hard and re-emerged with the Girondins: their defeat was gained on 31 May through what our author calls 'an act of popular sovereignty produced this time with complete governmental legality; a coup d'état of the people organized in *sections* and backing up their wishes by the deployment of social force itself.'[7] A strange definition if one considers that it concerns the use of force against the law, but coherent if the legality of the violence depends on the historical reason it is deemed to accomplish.

Thus the temporarily victorious Jacobins are seen as the zenith of the Revolution, the point at which its true direction is revealed after being hidden for too long by the intrigues of the bourgeoisie: it is the attempt to rebuild a genuine social community, in keeping with Christian order, in equality and brotherhood. Not that the men of the dictatorship of Year II were all gifted with this just ambition and the means to fulfil it. The Dantonists and Hébertists remained the prisoners of false conceptions, and anyway they were rogues. Buchez's man was Robespierre, who announced the reign of virtue, the soul's immortality and the existence of God. The Incorruptible had placed morality at the centre of politics but had been unable, since he was not a Catholic, to make his morality into a compulsory and undisputed faith. But at least, through him, for a few months the Revolution had attained an 'organic' dimension; at least it had bequeathed to the future the promise of a new fraternal society, intended to be the messianic accomplishment of French 'nationhood'.

Buchez's Catholic socialism therefore contained a nostalgia for the lost community, which explains and is the basis for his hatred of bourgeois individualism: this was a very ancient political tradition in French history, much in evidence, for instance, during the Wars of Religion, when the Catholic crowd, surrounded by their preachers, waged war on Protestants and demanded a Spanish Bourbon rather than a Protestant king. Buchez was heir to those combats and that messianic faithfulness, transforming facts about them by borrowing from modern culture: the revolutionary idea, historicism, social reorganization by the educated for the benefit of producers and the exploited. His prose, neither disciplined nor delicate, possesses the naïve virtue of illustrating better than anyone else's how the archaic mingled with the modern in the socialist understanding of 1789.

This is borne out by the use he makes of Rousseau, his hero of the eighteenth century and yet an author he cannot really follow. In fact, the

---

[6] P. J. B. Buchez, *Histoire parlementaire de la Révolution française*, vol. 19, p. 13.
[7] Ibid., vol. 27, p. 7.

Contrat social, in founding the general will, can get back to the community
only by way of the individual: the latter, by obeying the law, is obeying no
one but himself. For Buchez, it was a matter of preserving the point of
arrival by ridding himself of the point of departure, since that was what
condemned modern society to be no more than anarchy. Our author, who
does not understand the coherence of Rousseau's reasoning, gives the
philosopher half marks, and takes up the idea of general will himself, only
to deduce that it stems from the will of God, as a sort of temporal copy.

This makes him, as has been seen, place Rights of Man and sovereignty
of the people in radical opposition. This restored transcendental reference
allows him to institute the providentialist aim and, in this sense, implanting
the power of the people in divine will takes on a very different meaning,
for him, from the one it had in earlier understanding. In fact, in the
classical Christian doctrine, the sovereignty of the people was merely the
original foundation of the power of the kings, both authorities drawing
their legitimacy from God. For Buchez, that popular sovereignty takes the
form of a divine assignment which it is not free *not* to fulfil: it is inseparable from a 'target of activity' fixed to nationality, the realization of which
is seen in its history. In this way the ex-Saint-Simonian made the transition
from Rousseau to Maistre, without, however, stopping there: if Robespierre
had really been the temporary instrument of the providential mission
assigned to the French nation, the final achievement was unprecedented, as
in Maistre: a socialism for the benefit of the masses, led by those who had
knowledge of the divine plan for France.

Today, it is difficult to imagine the sort of audience enjoyed, under the
July monarchy, by this laboriously packaged gnosis, which has worn so
badly. Part of its success was due to the documentary material which it
brought together for the first time in a form accessible to a vast public.
This haphazard compilation, which became a bookshop best-seller, says a
great deal about contemporary curiosity regarding the French Revolution.
But it does not suffice to explain the response awakened by the way in
which Buchezian socialism reappropriated the revolutionary heritage in the
name of Catholic messianism.

In order to understand that, one must gauge to what extent the French
Revolution, in the first years of Louis-Philippe's reign, no longer divided
the men of the *ancien régime* from those of 1789, no longer the right from
the left, but the left from the left, 1789 from 1793. The preceding decade
had been given over to exalting 1789, the dictatorship of Year II being
merely a necessary but temporary consequence: Mignet (1824) and Thiers
(1823–7) had written the history of the Revolution on those bases, before
re-enacting 1789 in 1830. But for this very reason, opposition to the new
Orléans regime inscribed 1793 on its banner: it was the Republic and the
Montagnard constitution that it needed, and no longer the bastard regime
of the Constituent Assembly. The great memories of Year II, since Babeuf
and chiefly through Buonarroti (1829), had united avant-garde republicans
and socialists.

Buchez dealt with that legacy in an infinitely older style, that of the Catholicism of the League, modernized under a Saint-Simonian veneer. On the learned, or semi-learned side, he brandished the concept of science and of historic necessity. On the popular side, he secularized the image of the priest as leader of the community of believers. In a France where the Revolution had relegated the Church to the *ancien régime* and put a non-believing bourgeoisie into power, he wanted to re-establish the Revolution's Catholic line of descent, which had been artificially masked by the course of events, in order to restore traditional religion to the people under the new flag of socialist ideas. He mobilized both past and future against the individualism of the Rights of Man. Hence, his detestation of 1789, which was the sole claim that the bourgeoisie could invoke to govern the nation; hence his celebration of 1793, the meeting-point of ancient tradition and the heralding of the new day, since the Jacobin dictatorship renewed the alliance of a strong government and the popular masses under the auspices of the Supreme Being, just as kings by divine right had been as one with the people against the high and mighty.

Such is this slightly dishevelled general survey, the symposium of revolutionary history for the following quarter-century, in which it is easy to pick out so clearly the subversive work of the French Revolution in the society which had issued from it and never succeeded in mastering it. Buchez did not have a rich intellect, nor was he a profound thinker, but he was one of the first authors to feel and express with such great force the contradictions bequeathed to French political civilization by the events of the preceding century's last decades: not only the *ancien régime* and 1789, the world of communities and the society of individuals, Christianity and bourgeois democracy; but also 1789 and 1793, the Rights of Man and Jacobinism, liberty and equality. By bringing the Revolution to life again, July 1830 had revived all its conflicts together.

POLITICS IN THE 1830s

Through this long detour by way of the opposition, the reader may see that the essential character of the July regime was the absence of political and moral legitimacy. It was also its principal weakness, which it would never overcome. In a France which had been fascinated for a hundred years by the question of title to power, amid a public opinion obsessed with the great drama of origins which the Revolution had been, the regime was simply a *de facto* authority, deprived of the dignity of legitimacy. Monarchic, it had betrayed the monarchy; revolutionary, it had betrayed the Revolution. A risky compromise between the sovereignty of the kings and that of the people, it was despised from both sides, instead of combining the two traditions to its own advantage, as it would have wished. That contempt was fuelled not a little by cautious foreign policy, which was careful not to create additional difficulties for the new monarchy.

In the general tumult of the year 1830 in Europe, with the Belgian revolution, the uprising in Warsaw, unrest in Ireland and Italy, Louis-Philippe had been careful to present himself to foreign powers as the best guarantee of order against the escalation of revolutionary contagion. By ensuring that his activities abroad followed on from those of the senior branch of the family, he provided his republican and Bonapartist opponents, and even a good many humiliated legitimists, with yet another reason to scorn him. As Chateaubriand bears witness, speaking of the 'king of the French':

If he could ever turn the capital into a city at war with an annual rotation of 60,000 imperial guards, he would believe himself secure. Europe would let him go ahead because he would persuade the sovereigns that he was acting with the intention of smothering the revolution in its cradle, placing the liberties, independence and honour of France as a pledge in the hands of foreigners. Philippe is a policeman: Europe can spit in his face; he would wipe himself, say thank you and show his royal licence.[8]

As a result, the actual authority remaining to him, which he proclaimed to all points of the compass, concerned private interests. Even before the historians, contemporaries had baptized his reign the 'bourgeois monarchy', all in agreement for once, legitimists and Orleanists, not to mention the republican or socialist left; it is true that the term had been allocated beforehand by the Doctrinaires to their French 1688. Nevertheless, the definition is not one that goes without saying, if one considers that the majority of the bourgeoisie continued to be excluded from the regime by the electoral arrangements; and that part of the former nobility – those not wrapped up in their legitimist loyalty – agreed to serve it, even if they could not like it. In reality, it was a government occupied by notables rather than by the bourgeoisie properly speaking, in the modern sense of the word. But traditional terminology, borrowed from the era – when middle class and bourgeoisie were used interchangeably – had a double significance, both political and social. It indicated the existence of an opposition to the regime on the part of those nobles who were loyal to the former king and the old order of things. On the other hand, it referred to a system which had authority to rely overtly on private interests, and consequently to broaden its social base in step with the enrichment of society.

Orleanism was therefore that part of nineteenth-century French politics most in keeping with the liberal doctrine, and it is difficult to imagine today, at a time when democratic reference has swamped the entire language of public life, the almost cynical frankness with which the men of the July monarchy boasted of the bourgeois nature of their government, which seemed to them at last to be in accord with that of the Revolution. In doing so, they gave way to a very French failing, which put them miles apart from those secrets of English empiricism which they believed they

---

[8] Chateaubriand, *Mémoires d'outre-tombe*, book XLIII, ch. 1.

had finally discovered: they yielded to the trend of rational definition at the very moment when their power was supposed to have sprung from nothing other than the movement of society. So that, in their desire to establish both its nature and its necessity, they also made it more fragile as a product of bourgeois advancement. Since Rousseau and the French Revolution, private interests had been excluded from public life in France, and social division had been incompatible with citizenship. The men of July had been most unwise to brandish this banner which had been discredited beforehand.

On top of everything, during the first years of the reign, the contemporary situation was highly unfavourable. Firstly, because the Three Glorious Days, as we have seen, had reactivated revolutionary tradition in its most egalitarian aspects. Then, because France in the 1830s, nearly half a century after the Revolution, had witnessed a developing antagonism between the urban poor and the bourgeoisie. Not that there was a 'proletarian' movement in the sense that the word would acquire with the development of a constituted working class; industrial growth had been very slow under the Restoration, and the idea of a 'proletariat', as it may be defined in Saint-Simon or Buchez, pre-dated the real life of the proletariat: it had its origins in the period of the Parisian poor people's struggles and excesses against the Convention and the Directory. Elaborated as a new category in social and historical analysis by the Saint-Simonians and the Babouvist tradition, it also had a life among craftsmen and tradesmen, and within clandestinely re-formed guilds, like an embryonic working-class consciousness formed in the shelter of the old corporate compartmentalization.

The years which followed the July revolution, which had been largely the work of craftsmen and journeymen, witnessed the explosion of that class feeling in the two workers' uprisings in Lyon, in 1831 and 1834: the silk weavers, the *canuts*, homeworkers exploited by the merchants, had at first rebelled over specific instructions to wage-earners. But the second large-scale revolt, in April 1834, was more linked to political happenings, since it opposed a law extending the prohibition of associations even to groups of fewer than twenty persons: in defending their mutual aid societies, the weavers encountered the struggle of the Parisian neo-Jacobins, orchestrated by the secret society known as the 'Rights of Man and of the Citizen', but which was nearer in spirit to 1793 than to 1789. Radicalizing its slogans, calling for an all-powerful republic capable of changing the society of the wealthy, the republican camp had rebuilt a little of the road leading from Robespierre to Babeuf, and had opened a political outlet for the working-class awareness which was taking shape. If the July monarchy was the reign of the bourgeoisie, 'republic' was an increasingly anti-bourgeois watchword. The opposition of political traditions gradually discovered its *raison d'être* in a battle between the classes which took over from that of the bourgeoisie against the nobility, at the same time borrowing its methods.

In the short term, however, this dialectic of radicalization provided Louis-Philippe's governments with weapons: the two insurrections of April 1834, in Lyon and Paris, were harshly crushed by troops. It would certainly have been more astute of him not to raise the banner of bourgeois interests so high. Certainly it was worse than useless, it was clumsy, to let the ferocity of repression create such vivid memories of hatred, like the massacre in the rue Transnonain. But in post-revolutionary France, filled with Balzacian 'pères Grandet', defence of property and the social order, which had so swiftly become the watchword of the regime, in the end ensured that he would have the backing of country areas and provinces. Having taken power in order to build a kind of government, the July men gained the support of opinion for an imperative need of another sort: the defence of society.

In 1835, they seemed to have won. The republicans had been crushed in the elections of the preceding year, many of their leaders were in prison, and they appeared to be increasingly isolated, the prisoners of an extremist rhetoric which was the counterpart of their temporary defeat. A failed but murderous attempt on the life of Louis-Philippe, on 28 July 1835, the anniversary of the revolution, supplied the opportunity for a trail of repressive laws, voted in September: these modified the conditions and procedures of trial for acts of rebellion, instituted a certain number of precautions against the possible failure of juries, and chiefly increased the severity of rules governing the press, notably raising to the status of 'assassination attempts' incitement to hatred of the king or provocation to revolt. There was a great deal of fuss on the left, and one of their papers wrote, under the heading 'Terror on the agenda': 'The Terror of 1793 was revolutionary and temporary; the terror of 1835 is legal and permanent.'[9] But these laws, which did not manage to break the vitality and virulence of the opposition press, must be considered rather as sealing the final victory of the 'resistance' over the 'movement', a victory dearly bought, not only by the blood that was spilt, but by the reactivation in minds and memories of the revolutionary civil war.

Nevertheless, from 1835 the regime would enjoy its best years, to the point where it appeared, even to those who did not like it, to be ensconced for all time. In the second part of *De la démocratie en Amérique*, published in 1840, Tocqueville devotes a curious chapter to explain why, in democratic times, 'great revolutions will become rare': a truly paradoxical theme in an era when Paris so frequently bristled with barricades, and every French property-owner, whether large or small, was more or less afflicted by panic over social subversion. What Tocqueville meant was equal conditions, that law of the modern world, create so many conservative interests and so many identical ideas among so many individuals, that there is a tendency for minds to be distanced from thoughts of revolution and for society to be rendered more 'stationary' than ever before. But when he

---

[9] Quoted by Thureau-Dangin, *Histoire*, vol. 2, p. 315.

wrote that, he was not thinking only of America; he wanted to criticize chiefly the France in which he was writing, apparently depoliticized through the ardour displayed by politicians, with the help of prosperous times, to enclose each citizen in the sphere of his private interests. This was, in fact, the short period during which Guizot and his Doctrinaire friends could hope that they had won their bet: to have the country governed by the elites of wealth and social standing without those excluded from the electorate feeling frustrated by this reconstitution of a political aristocracy, since civil equality, combined with all the encouragement given to business, allowed the most deserving to gain access to it.

Once the revolution was broken – henceforth dangerous since it had already taken place – the political system revolved round that logic without finding any subjects for serious confrontation. Debates took a technical rather than political turn, linked to problems of economic policy, customs barriers, public works, railways. These had to be grappled with by a relatively stable parliamentary personnel, in that the elections confirmed a political happy medium, also reasonably uniform since, on the one hand, electoral eligibility and, on the other, the sulkiness of many noble property-owners, tended to limit the recruitment of deputies to a bourgeois oligarchy. Top administration and legal men (barristers, notaries, magistrates) formed its essence. The *arrondissement* ballot, too, played its part in a certain atomization of national representation, as it made each deputy the representative of his voters to the government, rather than the elected member of the nation. Institutions and the spirit of the regime thus favoured the constitution of a political class which was socially homogeneous and politically fragmented.

The major political question raised within this tight framework concerned the parliamentary system: should the government be chosen, in the English way, from the majority sifted out by elections? Or was the king free to designate as he wished the president of the Council of Ministers and his principal colleagues? Louis-Philippe was a manipulative and authoritarian king under an outward show of worldly simplicity. Talkative, given to trivial anecdotes, but also a wily tactician, he had all the more desire to govern when he believed the stormclouds had disappeared for good. He had survived several failed attempts on his life (regicide, that old royal curse, had become a republican tradition since that 21 January), and had acquired a brief kind of popularity. The French had welcomed the marriage of his son and heir, the Duc d'Orléans, which was celebrated in a Versailles restored under his auspices. He also handled skilfully and with *savoir-faire* that omnipresent (except in the legitimist camp) store of memories – Bonapartism: in order not to have to try him, he had dispatched to America the pretender Louis-Napoleon (the son of Louis Bonaparte, former king of Holland), who in 1836 had tried to raise the Strasbourg garrison; he was preparing to send one of his sons to St Helena to bring back the emperor's remains. In short, he was at his zenith, and consequently more active in affairs than ever.

Facing him, or at his side, the parliamentary groups or coalitions are not easy to describe, for their personalities have as much importance as their policies, if not more. The Chamber of Peers, decapitated by the suppression of hereditary right of entry, and at the mercy of royal drafts being added should it prove intractable, no longer played the role it had in the preceding regime. In the Chamber of Deputies, three focal points are relatively easy to define. The legitimists, dominated by a very talented barrister, Antoine Berryer: as well as being a born orator, he was a true parliamentarian, skilful in negotiating 'his' votes against the king; the group had lost deputies in the 1837 elections but remained essential as a back-up minority against the Tuileries ministries. At the other end of the semicircle was the dynastic left, the friends of Odilon Barrot, another barrister and survivor of the 'movement' years: his desire was to tame the republican spirit within constitutional royalty, on condition that the latter agreed to confine the monarch to a restricted role and to open itself to a larger electoral body. Barrot criticized Guizot for wanting to replace the nobility of the *ancien régime* with a bourgeois aristocracy of 'representative' politics. Guizot, precisely: he was the guardian of the regime's doctrine, or rather of the interpretation the 'resistance' had given it; and it was he who, over the years, after Casimir Périer's death, had become the head of the conservative party. He had for a long time preserved intellectual ascendancy over the Doctrinaires' group, a real breeding-ground for the political men of July, chiefly over the Duc de Broglie, Madame de Staël's son-in-law and the editor of her *Considérations*, and over Thiers who, under the Restoration, had been on the edges of the group before becoming one of the main instigators of the Orléans candidature on 30 July. But the cohesion of the group did not survive the test of power, and Louis-Philippe had at first made use of Broglie in order to avoid having Guizot as prime minister, as he feared his authoritarianism. However, he had more esteem than liking for this haughty and timid aristocrat, who was given to meditative withdrawal and had taken on this leading role from a sense of duty rather than ambition.

The king had a soft spot for Thiers, a pure product of the reign as well as its inventor. This resourceful little man owed everything to himself and his protean talent. A natural child, a provincial who had started from nothing, he had made a name for himself in Paris by his writing at the same time as his friend Mignet, who had 'come up' from Aix-en-Provence at that period, in 1821. Author of a long-running book on the Revolution, spaced out in volumes between 1823 and 1827, he annoyed Tocqueville by his obvious indulgence towards the Terror, but chiefly he was one of the principal journalists of the liberal opposition, with Armand Carrel one of the pillars of the *National*, an ardent defender of the '221' and the days of July, the one who, with Mignet, drew up the manifesto calling for the accession of Louis-Philippe. That was the start of the first great political period of his life – the other would be the years 1870–3.

At first wavering between the resistance and the movement, he soon rallied behind the resistance and was the ruthless Minister of the Interior during the 1832 riots. Married the following year to a rich heiress whose mother, the ambitious Madame Dosne he had charmed, he had become one of the influential people in Parisian life and an indispensable minister. Already everything contrasted him with Guizot, to whom he was no longer linked by anything but memories: his poor upbringing, his entertainer's charm, his genius for reconciling opposites, little high-mindedness or delicacy of imagination, not to mention that Balzacian core of back-slapping playfulness which astounded political society. Moreover, he had greater feeling than Guizot for republican France, whose history he had recounted and certain of whose passions he shared, such as hatred for the treaties of 1815; that was what made him a potential leader of that parliamentary 'marais' which stretched between the conservatives and the dynastic left, the third party.

Pushed into power in 1836 by one of Talleyrand's last intrigues, who thought he was finally offering Louis-Philippe the long-awaited means of royal government, Thiers was unaware, recounts Rémusat,

how much disdain there was in the hopes that were placed upon him, or, if he did realize it, he made the best of a bad job, being determined to profit some day from the support he was receiving without accepting its conditions. He willingly accepted the blandishments and promises of future greatness from those who, by elevating him, were banking on controlling him. The Duchesse de Dino, looking at him with her lovely velvety eyes, gave his ambition encouragement which his self-conceit interpreted differently. Madame de Lieven did not dare to try the same seductive ways, despite her great propensity for using them, but she showed him kindnesses in keeping with her age and, having snared a good number of European diplomats with the same wiles, so they say, she was not above employing her old ways with this July parvenu. She was successful to the point where Thiers actually told this raddled and peevish old woman that she was charming. Sometimes, when he was holding forth between these two great ladies, Madame de Lieven would exclaim to Madame de Dino: 'Dear Duchesse, how he reminds me of Canning!' Thiers accepted all this flattery. He was not taken in by it, because he would make fun of it when talking about it, but he was still charmed by it.[10]

Talleyrand, however, had got the wrong era if he thought that a nobody who had become prime minister would necessarily be the king's creature. Thiers lost his temper with the king before the end of 1836, because he wanted to intervene in Spain to the advantage of the liberals against the Carlists; he had begun to build his centre-left image. Then began an episode which gives a good illustration of the slightly unreal content of this banter between Louis-Philippe and the Chamber, if one compares it with the splits in public opinion. The king entrusted the formation of the ministry to the Comte Molé, the scion of an old family of the legal nobility, a childhood friend of Chateaubriand, who had already been a minister

---

[10] Ch. de Rémusat, *Mémoires de ma vie*, vol. 3, p. 147.

under the Empire and then the legitimate kings, and was ready to serve
this Crown as he had served the others, with wisdom and distinction,
without Thiers's brio, but with more flexibility than Broglie. In this peer
of France, who was a stranger to the divisions of the lower Chamber, the
deputies scented personal government by the king: and in 1838, one can
observe the regrouping of a parliamentary coalition against him which
united the dynastic left and the legitimist right, Odilon Barrot and Berryer,
flanked by Guizot and Thiers!

At the moment of the decisive battle, that debate on the Address to the
king of January 1839, who defended Molé's ministry? Lamartine, who had
entered the Assembly as a legitimist and had not yet begun to shed those
feathers in a move towards republican lyricism; but who still retained
enough of his former loyalty to prefer the son of a great *ancien régime*
family to the upstarts of bourgeois liberalism, even in the service of Louis-
Philippe. Lamartine loathed Thiers, and Guizot loathed Molé, who loathed
the Doctrinaires, and so on: the keynotes of the parliamentary world of
July, in which Rémusat played Saint-Simon, lay in personal rivalries,
individual ambitions, bands of supporters and coteries rather than in
intellectual opposition. That was the price paid for its narrowness, but it
was a heavy price because it dishonoured political debate in a country
which was only too inclined to regard it as merely a disguising of interests
or a mask for the administration.

The opinion of the country may be gauged from a letter written in 1840
by the Duc de Broglie to Guizot, in which the former president of the
Council, who had just refused to take office again, speaks of

those pallid, indecisive ministries, without any avowed principles, without any
other pretension than to live from day to day, without anything to lean on save
universal weariness and discouragement, reduced to taking a back seat in all
important matters, to being continually accommodating, now to the king, now to
the Chambers and to each group in the Chambers, whether large or small, and
having every morning to fabricate an artificial majority for themselves by either
concessions or compliments, promises or caresses, at the same time weighing on
gossamer scales the number of post offices that have been handed out on the one
hand, and the number of tobacconists' shops on the other.

However, this oligarchic political system, transposed from eighteenth-
century England to nineteenth-century France, would attain a kind of
unity in its last phase, starting from 1840, with the reunion of the king and
Guizot, after the removal of that liability, Thiers.

The crucial year was certainly 1840. Louis-Philippe, who had not won
the elections brought about by Molé in 1839, had reluctantly been forced
to recall Thiers to power, after the Chamber had refused an endowment for
one of his sons: between the bourgeois king and the bourgeois Assembly,
money matters were constantly an occasion for household squabbles to
which both parties contributed, to their common discredit. But the day of
reckoning awaiting the new Thiers cabinet was of quite a different kind: it

was the crisis started in the Near East by the ambitions of the Pasha of Egypt, Mohammed Ali, who compromised the integrity of the ancient Ottoman empire, on which the Tsar of Russia was keeping a watchful eye.

Mohammed Ali, surrounded by the aura of memories of the Egyptian expedition, had become the idol of French opinion, for whom he was a sort of new Alexander, not to say a new Bonaparte. Louis-Philippe and Thiers, both sensitive to the great national memories (they had just obtained the return of Napoleon's remains from the British), would not have been displeased to see Syria officially conceded by the Sultan to the Pasha. But Britain was watching; its imperial interests were no laughing matter and, unknown to the French and against France, in mid-July it organized the co-operation of the four great European powers, (Britain, Russia, Prussia and Austria) in guaranteeing the integrity of the Ottoman empire and forcing Mohammed Ali to yield.

That gave rise to a vast patriotic exploitation of French public opinion, which relived the humiliation of 1815; as usual, the press followed suit, even that of Thiers, in which Europe could read what the minister thought. The republican newspapers were more emphatic. *Le National* evoked 1792 and once more hoisted the flag of a war of propaganda and the universal revolt of the peoples. It used this as a weapon against the king, who was suspected of weakness, as Louis XVI had been in the spring of 1792: 'War is not a possibility for Louis-Philippe, because for him war is suicide'; but Thiers was hardly treated any better: 'If M. Thiers does not want to be mixed up in treason, if he is no other than a muddler who uses events to manipulate public funds [an allusion to an accusation of financial dishonesty which was circulating against the Minister], he will speed up all armament measures, instead of halting them.'

GUIZOT

What strange tyranny of the great scenes of the French Revolution after half a century! But if Louis-Philippe was ready to afford them a place in national memory – at his own risk and peril – he assessed their lack of reality in the international situation of 1840, which was dominated not only by British power but by the bad recollections of French oppression preserved by European peoples themselves: the attack of Anglophobia and Germanophobia provoked in France by the secret agreement of 15 July 1840 had unleashed, as an indirect consequence, anti-French feeling nearly everywhere, but chiefly in the German states. The king did not want war, which Thiers was pretending to prepare for in order to please opinion. The two men went their separate ways in October; at last, Guizot's hour had struck.

The political situation was far from favourable, since Louis-Philippe had lost what consideration he had won on his left during the preceding years, at least until 1839. Thiers had obtained the support of Odilon Barrot at the same time, it is true, as that of the Duc de Broglie, and the assistance in the Ministry of the Interior of the foremost of the Doctrinaires, Rémusat. But it was enough to give his ministry an air of openness to the left which had been consolidated by the 'national' turn of the feigned belligerence of 1840.

Guizot, who had gone to London as ambassador in order to erase the memory of humiliating failure in 1839, had bided his time there negotiating with Palmerston, without much success, over the eastern crisis. He had not so much supported Thiers's ministry as let it take its course. When the king recalled him to Paris in the autumn to be, if not the nominal chief – this would be Marshal Soult – at least the inspirational force of the ministry and its centre of gravity, he was the reincarnation, in opposition to Thiers, of everything he had always symbolized since 1830: the most conservative interpretation of the July institutions. He was the theorist of royal prerogative in representative government, hostile to the sovereignty of the people and the subordination of the throne. But he was also the man of peace and European accord: the man whom his enemies had for years hoped to damn by the reminder of his mission to Ghent, during the Hundred Days, to see Louis XVIII, bearing the vows and advice of the constitutional royalists.

Now, in October 1840, republican opposition had resumed its upsurge at all levels: popular, and even working-class, with strikes and barricades; it was more reformist, with the start of a campaign of banquets and demand for a widening of electoral qualifications; lastly, on a national level, with the external crisis, to the point where the new ministry was hailed in the hostile press as the Ministry of Foreign Interests. Tocqueville, a young deputy elected the year before, wrote on 7 November to his English friend Reeve:

The nation is irritated by the prince who governs it; wrongly or rightly, it believes itself to be deeply humiliated and put down from the rank it should enjoy in Europe, and is on the verge of those desperate resolutions which such impressions give rise to in a proud, uneasy, quick-tempered people like ours. Therein lies the danger, the sole danger. It is not war that the government should fear; it is first of all the overthrow of the government, and then war. Never, since 1830, has the danger been so great. For the moment, radicalism is counting on wounded national pride: that gives it a strength which it has not yet had.

However, it was the Soult–Guizot ministry which would prove to be the safeguard of the regime – at the same time, it is true, as its grave. That eight-year interval was more than a reprieve, since it gave Orleanism its strongest historical image, at last reconciling its philosophy and its politics in the person of its principal minister, though at the risk of that philosophy perishing together with the politics.

If the meeting between Louis-Philippe and Guizot had occurred so late, ten years after the start of the reign, it is because for a long time there had been a gradual build-up between them of small hurts and wounds which had crystallized into sour memories. The king, who owed everything to his supporters, was afraid of finding that there might be superior talents among them, since his advantage was no longer that of birth; what is more, he had nothing which might admit him into Guizot's intellectual world. In many respects, he was a better embodiment than his minister of that bourgeoisie of notables, who straddled landed property, personal wealth and the state, still too aristocratic to be a class of entrepreneurs, but too humiliated by the aristocracy not to be attached to July as to a heritage or an investment.

Guizot himself had constructed a philosophy of the middle class rather than espoused its mores. Isolated by his perception of his own superiority, he passionately loved both ideas and power, revealing an apparently boundless activity in both spheres; saving all his affections and the charm of his conversation for women, he brought only forcefulness into his relations with men: he was honest, indifferent to money for its own sake, and moreover remained relatively poor, but he did not hesitate to corrupt in order to govern. Nevertheless, these two people ended up by meeting each other and governing together in mutual trust, as their correspondence bears witness. The king finally recognized his most organized supporter, and the minister, a sovereign who fitted in with his system.

Through his books and speeches, Guizot had made a great contribution to popularizing the idea that the July monarchy constituted middle-class government; and he constantly affirmed it during those years in which he had become its chief representative. What is intriguing, in his case, is the way he reconciled that central conviction with a regime in which fewer than 60,000 were eligible, and there were 250,000 electors, out of a country of 35,000,000 inhabitants. There was something in his doctrine of representation, which had been formed so early and had remained intangible, which prevented him, if not from understanding the nature of the bourgeoisie, at least from accepting its political consequences. He was well aware of the secrets of its social dominance, the destruction of hierarchies of birth through work and money, by way of ideas about liberty and equality; but when he tried to set up a government from that starting-point, all his effort went into basing that government not on the free and equal consensus of individuals, but on a principle independent of them, above them – reason, justice or divine order.

Amid that permanent mobility which was characteristic of the new dominant class, he looked for an anchor-point in the idea of having the reason of the social body 'represented' by the small number of the wealthiest, who were also the most 'enlightened'. But in doing so, he departed from the 1789 tradition and also from liberal philosophy in general; and he laid himself open to the accusation of wanting to re-establish an aristocracy of wealth in a country which, for the second time, had just driven out the aristocracy of birth.

Basically, his practical aim was the one for which his opponents criticized him: to form a dominant class into a ruling class, to which new entrants would be very sparingly recruited. This is evidenced by the amount of obstinacy with which he rejected any widening of the right to vote and any reform of the representational system. The dynastic left with Barrot, the centre-left with Thiers, and even old friends who had been very close to him like Rémusat, would have liked to see him accept two reforms: the first preventing a certain number of civil servants from having access to elective positions, in order to avoid too easy government pressure on parliamentarians who were, by definition, in its hands; the second broadening the electorate to include the *capacités* (all those qualified for jury service). On both these points, Guizot put up a stubborn and absolute resistance until the last hour of the monarchy. Without any apparent agonizing, he remained the dual character so difficult for today's historian to decipher; both a theorist of representative government and a manipulator of assemblies; yielding to two irreconcilable national traditions, both of which he had criticized: philosophy substituted for politics, and administration for government.

In order to understand how far he had become the most conservative interpreter of his own system, one must listen to him, in the sitting of 14 February 1842, replying to Lamartine, who had taken it upon himself to advocate the second proposal. The poet, disappointed at having obtained nothing from those in power, and in the process of transition from the legitimist pipe dream to democratic lyricism, had brilliantly heckled 'those intimidated men' who formed the government:

To hear them, one would think that the genius of political men lies in one thing only, to land themselves on a situation with which chance or a revolution has presented them and to stay there motionless, inert, implacable . . . [Lively approval on the left.] Yes, implacable in the face of any improvement. And if, indeed, that were all the capability of the statesman with the task of leading a government, there would be no need of a statesman – a block of stone could do the job. [General and prolonged commotion.]

Guizot replied:

I have looked in vain, I have sought in vain; and I cannot find among us today, in the present state of society, a single, real, serious motive for the electoral reform proposed, a single motive worthy of a free and sensible country . . . The movement which has produced the questions we are discussing is superficial, artificial, untruthful and incited by newspapers and committees. [Interruptions on the fringes.]

Guizot thus condemned himself to live in that very narrow political system which he dominated through both his best and worst aspects: his superiority of talent and character, but also all the petty means of power – flattery, money, favours, positions. In the 1842 elections, he had a small, not very obvious majority: he bought the votes he needed from among that welter of personal interests.

There was a reason other than intellectual dogmatism to explain his short-sighted policy, which was so at odds with his puritan vision of morality without the excuse of political intelligence. It is still, and as always, the French Revolution which offers the secret. Guizot loved 1789 as the outstanding date of the social emancipation of his class, which centuries of monarchical authority had prepared for service to the nation. But he hated the interminable train of political disorders to which that famous year had opened the way and which, properly speaking, formed the French Revolution. The July days in 1830, during which he had kept very much in the background, and even more, the years of sporadic uprisings which had followed, had strengthened that feeling.

By contrast, he had become almost obsessed by the need finally to settle French institutions, instead of endlessly modifying them. In a country of revolutionary or counter-revolutionary culture, where the sense of laws and of right had been lost to the point where the state had become the centre of most unreasonable projects – such as re-establishing the *ancien régime* or abolishing property-ownership – for him, restoring order meant using stability to bring to an end what he termed the unsettling of minds. But that unsettling was revolutionary tradition itself or, in other words, the political imagination of the nation: this historian-minister, who wanted to curb it by means of authority, could not understand its strength because he was a stranger to it. In that respect, he was far less representative of the bourgeoisie than a man like Thiers; his rival, for his part, loved the Revolution like a son.

It was the same thing with foreign policy. For national imagination, finding nothing to feed on in the way of reforms, could throw itself into ideas of France's place in the world, which were also heroic or glorious memories. In the republican tradition, Robespierre had erased the memory of the Terror, because he had been the man who cared about public safety. Napoleon had based his legitimacy on war and victory. Now Louis-Philippe, more or less ostracized by European sovereigns, had spent his reign trying to make people forget the revolution which had swept him to power: to such an extent that he had embellished a reasonable foreign policy with a rhetorical discretion in which opinion – legitimist, Bonapartist and republican all combined – constantly sensed a spirit of capitulation.

Guizot was at one with his king for the same reasons, which concerned the objective situation of France in a world now dominated by Britain. But also because, this time as a good liberal, he had no feeling for military glory, propaganda war or the jingoistic mentality. Running counter to public attitudes, following the 1840 crisis, he made an attempt to restore the entente with Britain, but with no very tangible results, as the Pritchard affair showed in 1842, when the two countries were once again in confrontation; the English missionary was expelled from Tahiti, but Guizot found himself accused of weakness in offering compensation. The only lasting great undertaking of the reign would be Algeria, the legacy of the last months of Charles X; it was under Guizot's ministry that Bugeaud really won the country from Abd el-Kader, by counter-guerrilla warfare of savage brutality. But the whole affair, which was conducted in a rather chaotic manner, had never fired national passions.

Guizot, the philosopher of the July monarchy, was therefore the best symbol of the problem the latter had not resolved: its illegitimacy. In his search for a synthesis of national history, Louis-Philippe had not been able to find his origins anywhere. The obsession with public order, which was the dominant political feature of the last ministry, tended to bring the country back to a situation comparable with the one which had preceded 1830, when the government had lost the battle for liberty: there was the same inability to accept the expression of citizens' hostile opinions or political activity, the same will to govern through the police and the administration. Not that opinion was republican, as will be seen: in the nation's deepest memories, the Republic remained associated with the Terror. But it liked 1789, and the 1830 monarchy, which had been born of popular desire to restore 1789 in opposition to the *ancien régime*, was drifting ever farther from the spirit of 1789. A sign of the times: the National Guard, the regime's bourgeois militia, showed signs of hostility.

Providence, for its part, added another: on 13 July 1842 the Duc d'Orléans, heir to the throne, was killed when he leaped from a cabriolet as the horses bolted. He was a likeable and popular prince, who had on several occasions shown evidence of a liberal and national spirit, and had been the hope of the bourgeoisie at all levels, shopkeepers and bankers alike. His premature death created a collective feeling of sympathy for the old king and his family ('How long will this black honeymoon last?' wondered Heinrich Heine in one of his letters), but also enfeebled the monarchy by removing the best image of its future. Following the traditional rules of succession, which Louis-Philippe borrowed from the senior branch, the very young Comte de Paris, aged four, son of the dead prince, became heir to the throne. This of course raised the prospect of a regency, which the Chamber decided to entrust not to his mother, but to the king's second son, the Duc de Nemours: an innovation, this time, which extended the Salic law to the regency, for fear of letting a woman have the safe-keeping of a royalty which was too recent not to be fragile. The opposition had preferred to uphold the rights of the Duchesse d'Orléans, pleaded by Lamartine; the choice of the Duc de Nemours, whose reputation was less liberal, had been made by Louis-Philippe and Guizot, who were supported in this matter by Thiers. By substituting Nemours for Orléans, chance had deprived the regime of one of its trump cards for survival.

Finally, in the political situation of that period, some share must be given to the reappearance of the religious question in public affairs. The July revolution had once again 'disestablished' the Catholic Church, after the unfortunate attempt to unite Throne and Altar and, as has been seen, it had been the occasion of violent anticlerical demonstrations. But the climate had soon improved with the times. Acting on instructions from Rome, even those bishops whose hearts lay with legitimacy had loyally accepted the authority of the new king; and for his part, Louis-Philippe had applied the Concordat with an earnest and open spirit, often replacing old *'ancien régime'* prelates with priests who were less political but better trained for their religious mission. Then two crucial developments occurred which presented in a new way the problems and conflicts involved in the relations between Church and state.

The first concerned the attitude of mind of the ruling classes. The sorrows of exile had brought many nobles back to religious belief – Charles X setting the example. Fear of revolutionary excesses against property began to diminish anticlerical passions among the Voltairean bourgeoisie; the idea – also Voltaire's – began to spread about the need for religion to maintain social order. In its common and most frequent version, this concept saw the Church as a means of obtaining the obedience of the poor; in its philosophical development – for Necker, Staël, Guizot, Tocqueville – it turned Christian faith into a necessary and natural complement of modern democracy. In both cases, it slowly brought bourgeois opinion closer to Catholicism, though causing the Church to run the risk of eventually appearing subordinate to wealth, as it had been to the throne.

That tradition, in any case, gradually died down with the decline of Gallicanism, to the advantage of ultramontanism: if the Church was no longer part of the state, what was the good of remaining Gallican? The intellectual elite among the clergy would seek in Rome the support they had lost from the king of France, and the *curés* hoped to obtain some means of protection from the omnipotence of their bishops; the Church was encouraged thereby to a timid return of the regular orders, which had been destroyed or banished since the Revolution.

But the most interesting phenomenon of the era was the birth of a liberal Catholicism, led by former contributors to *L'Avenir* who had remained in the bosom of the Church when Lamennais had refused to submit to papal condemnation: Henri Lacordaire, the Comte de Montalembert, Frédéric Ozanam. The intention, which had been born in the wake of July 1830 and *L'Avenir* but had stayed Catholic, was to reconcile the Church with modern liberty. It was an enormous programme which soon centred on a demand destined in the century which followed to become a burning cause in national public life: freedom of education, which had been promised in the revised Charter. If, in fact, the Church was a free community *vis-à-vis* the state, in a free society, it could – and should – have its own schools, because the University, which had been endowed since the Empire with the monopoly of education – expanded in 1828 by hostility to the Jesuits – was now dependent on a state without a religion. This was an argument passionately pleaded by Montalembert in the Chamber of Peers, and one which in the 1840s met with agreement from the most ultramontane Catholics, such as Louis Veuillot, who gave it an extraordinary vehemence.

What was at stake was to gain control of secondary education, where the children of the bourgeoisie received their training. Between 1836 and 1840 the problem had given rise to negotiations which had come to nothing. The Church accused the University of having taken teachers, programmes and courses away from religion, under the iron rule of Victor Cousin, who concurrently filled all the positions of authority: the representative of philosophy on the royal Council of Public Education, director of the École Normale, life president of the panel of judges for philosophy in the *agrégation* (competitive qualifying examination for teachers), member of the Académie Française, peer of France. He had imposed a respect for religion on all teachers entrusted with that famous class which was the crowning-point of French secondary education, who formed what he called 'his regiment', but he also personified the superiority of philosophical synthesis over any revealed religion.

Around 1842, certain bishops broke away from the caution they had exercised until then, and gave battle using a vocabulary which, in order to inveigh against the University, brought back the old adjectives used by orthodoxy against heresy. That provoked very violent reaction on the part of the most celebrated professors and anticlerical deputies, Thiers and Cousin in parliament, Michelet and Quinet in the Collège de France, Villemain and Mignet in the Institut, not to mention the opposition press, which was unleashed against the Church. As always, the Jesuits received the lion's share – agents of a permanent conspiracy against liberty, spiritual policemen, servants of a monarchy even more absolute than that of the kings. Quinet in 1843, in his course at the Collège de France which was devoted precisely to the Jesuits, said, 'It is a matter not only of refuting popery, but of dishonouring it and, as the ancient Germanic law against adultery would have it, stifling it at birth.' Like Guizot in 1828–9 at the Sorbonne, the professor of the rue des Ecoles was acclaimed by the students.

As for Guizot, this time he was in power. He had various projects developed which he was forced to withdraw in the face of both camps' intransigence. Trapped between his sincere and deep respect for religion, his desire to uphold one of the Charter's undertakings and his will to maintain the authority and unity of the government, this Protestant academic did not like anticlericalism. But he was equally mistrustful of a certain Catholic intolerance. He had allowed the conflict to develop into two extremes which he found equally distasteful and which, from both sides, diminished his authority. By trying to gather round him a vast anticlerical coalition, Thiers was once again making a bid for power. The suspension by indirect means of Quinet's course at the Collège de France in 1846 added a clumsy blunder to the political impasse.

In the end, the strongest point on the balance sheet was economic policy, where the Soult–Guizot government – which in this field was not the prisoner of a British-style liberal orthodoxy – organized state support for financial and industrial development. The years following 1840 – and up till 1846 – were good ones. Budgets showed a surplus, the mood of the times was for modernization, and the state set an example by making massive investments in public works, with railways coming foremost: the law of 11 June 1842, which planned six great lines radiating from Paris, had given it the task of constructing the railways and compensating the landowners; companies contracting to carry out the work had to lay the rails, supply the equipment and oversee the maintenance of both. This was an advantageous arrangement for private capital and large interests, which were often closely linked with the parliamentary and governmental oligarchy: what a lot of peers of France, generals, top civil servants and deputies were to be found on the boards of concessionary companies! The regime's vision was of an industrial capitalism encouraged by the state, largely financed by loans and indirect taxation, protected by high customs tariffs and linked with major banking. This sector was superimposed without any effects of rapid transformation on the peasant, craftsman and shopkeeper strata of France, who were also sheltered from the chill wind, producing and selling in their small traditional markets. Guizot was in the habit of turning to all these interests, small and large, as if they were the natural supporters of the July regime; it was a strange policy, a curious blindness, in so intelligent a man, to imagine that appealing to the enrichment of private individuals would be sufficient reason for the life of a government, in a country like the France of the Revolution's grandsons.

TOCQUEVILLE, MICHELET, BLANC

Rather than try to describe, in necessarily vague terms, the movements of society faced with the last July government, I have chosen to illustrate them through the reactions of three intellectuals of the era who, furthermore, played an important political role. The heartlands of France did not vote, but intellectual France was more effervescent and more linked with public life than ever; it offered a fresh example of the literary and philosophical nature of the national political debate, at the very moment when Guizot was trying to transform its character by appealing to private interests. The irony of the situation lay in that appeal coming from a professor and writer who was also one of the greatest historians the country had ever possessed; as if renunciation of the abstract tradition of French politics in the name of a shopkeeping bourgeoisie could have been formulated and asked for only by a prince of the intellect. In France, even anti-intellectualism is the concern of intellectuals.

The three selected writers, Tocqueville, Michelet and Louis Blanc, can be placed in this order by virtue of the degree of radicalism in their opposition to the Soult–Guizot ministry. Tocqueville was a supporter of the July institutions, and sat in the Chamber in the centre-left opposition. Michelet had been close to the regime for a long time, and slipped into the republican camp, becoming the figurehead of the secular fight against the Church. Lastly, Louis Blanc was not only republican, but also socialist, an adversary of both the monarchy and bourgeois society. However, one thing united them: all three were historians who were fascinated by the French Revolution, in which they saw the origins of the France of their own times

Théodore Chasseriau Alexis de Tocqueville, *Musée Versailles, Paris.*
(Photo: Lauros-Giraudon)

and of the battles they were waging there. Through them it is possible to spread out a vast range of ideas, and to understand the common roots of the similarities and radical differences of those ideas.

Tocqueville, the scion of an old noble family, came from a legitimist background which had stayed so. His father, a prefect under the Restoration, had refused to take the oath in 1830; his best friend, Louis de Kergorlay, had left the army and been compromised two years later when the Duchesse de Berry tried to raise the Vendée against Louis-Philippe. He himself, as a young magistrate, had made an act of allegiance to Louis-Philippe with rather mixed feelings; he had left shortly afterwards, on the pretext of a mission to study prisons in the United States, in company with his friend Gustave de Beaumont, to make the 1831 American journey from which he would bring back his book and celebrity. The first part of *De la démocratie en Amérique*, more greatly acclaimed by the public, came out in 1835, the second part in 1840. Meanwhile, he had written an essay on 'L'Ancienne et la Nouvelle France', which appeared in 1836 in an English magazine under the title 'The Social and Political State of France before and after 1789'; and after an initial failure in 1837, he had been elected deputy of the Valognes *arrondissement* in 1839, very near the family château to which he was heir. In the Assembly, he sat on the centre-left, but wanted to remain independent; from the outset he was hostile to the Soult–Guizot ministry, but formally joined the dynastic left of Odilon Barrot only in 1842.

This summary omits the main point: his extraordinary originality of thought, which was formed more by constant meditation and observation than through his reading. Born in 1805, Tocqueville was too young to feel still a party to an *ancien régime* which he had not known; but, as a son of the aristocracy, he had nothing to draw him especially to the victorious middle class. Astride both worlds, he perceived and interpreted the time in which he lived as driven by a formidable dynamic of equality, which he termed 'democracy'. Thence arose the American voyage, which was intended to allow him to study that movement on the spot, where it had not encountered any obstacles, since the young republic had emerged from the meeting between a vast empty territory and egalitarian immigrant communities.

One can see everything which separated Tocqueville, a very young man, from the already famous Guizot, whose courses he had keenly followed in 1828 and 1829. Through the French–English comparison, the historian had relentlessly explored the possibilities of a French 1688, that is to say, of a moderation of civil equality by a partial reintroduction of the aristocratic concept into the government of the new society. Through the American example, Tocqueville tried to work out how democracy – the inevitable, unique and all-powerful principle of that society – could be reconciled with liberty. The French example was not very encouraging, since Robespierre and Bonaparte had followed the admirable effort of 1789, and then, from the other direction, the Restoration and the Polignac ministry, against which July 1830 had taken place. The irresistible movement of democracy had for centuries nurtured in France the tentacular development of a centralized administrative state, which was the destroyer of aristocracy but also the natural administrator of citizens' equality.

Tocqueville, as deputy, preserved his philosophical view of the country's affairs (which is one of the clues to his isolation); but he combined it with an examination of current topics to which he thus gave an exceptional depth. Having entered the Assembly following Molé's defeat by the coalition in which Guizot, in his view, had dishonoured himself, he was severely critical of the way in which Thiers's ministry, with Guizot in London, dealt with the international crisis and capitulated without honour to Britain. Internally, he shared the left's hostility to the laws of September 1835, chiefly to the restriction of the right of association, and he upheld Lamartine in the debate on the regency, taking a stand for the Duchesse d'Orléans, the symbol of a more liberal future. He despised Thiers, who had the common talent of an intermediary and was forever manipulating, and he had no love for Guizot, whom he accused of having a naked appetite for power which was poorly concealed in great principles, and whom he blamed for the lack of progress of the government formed in the autumn of 1840.

There is a fascinating document[11] which gives his opinion on the pros and cons of that government: his *Lettres sur la situation intérieure de la France*, written by him for the opposition newspaper *Le Siècle* and published in January 1843. Here is the introduction:

Most of the politicians who have ruled us for the past ten years have changed principles and parties so many times that we are entitled to conclude that they have no principles and are incapable or unworthy of having a party. Witnessing their sterile debates, the people become more and more indifferent; it would seem that the rights which have cost the French most dear have ceased to be precious to them; that they are not worried to see the violation or evasion of those laws which they have had the most difficulty in obtaining, and that they are allowing to slip from their memories everything that their fathers and they themselves have done for liberty. The great liberal cause which triumphed momentarily in 1789 seems compromised once more. Not only is no progress being made, but it is plain to see that we are in decline and that public opinion today shows itself willing to put up with what it would never have endured twelve years ago.

The diagnosis was consequently clear: liberty had once more become as precarious and as threatened as on the eve of 1830, yet the nation seemed passive. Why? Because for the French the spirit of liberty was repressed by a stronger feeling, encouraged by the government: the fear of revolutions.

Tocqueville harks back to the theme already treated in a chapter of the second part of the *Démocratie* which I quoted earlier: namely, that the French Revolution, though increasing property-ownership and creating numerous new interests, had made its renewal all the less desirable because

[11] Alexis de Tocqueville, *Oeuvres complètes*, part III, vol. 2.

it had left such bloody memories. The 'ruling passion' of the citizens had shifted away from liberty to the acquisition of possessions. By blackmailing the country with the danger of revolution, those in power sought in reality to base on an imaginary fear an extension of their prerogatives, accompanied by the reduction of public and individual liberties gained in 1789 and reaffirmed in 1830. The danger was further aggravated by the fact that France was the only country trying to get a representative government and a centralized administrative state to work together: there had never been a power in the world so great as that of the king of the French, supported by that crowd of legally unaccountable civil servants (according to article 75 of the constitution of Year VIII) and that army of 400,000 soldiers.

What was the remedy? It was not to propose to the country – as did the opposition left – reforms of a kind to cause more fear, for example the expansion of the right to vote to a larger electorate; Tocqueville, on the contrary calls on the electorate to defend the conquests of 1830 and restore the liberties that have been won before thinking about obtaining new ones. Preoccupied with not giving any unintentional help to the government by making its blackmail through fear any easier, he makes the distinction between the legacy of the Revolution, the foundation of the nation, and the revolutionary spirit, born of the inescapable struggle against the nobility and the clergy. Now the revolutionary spirit seemed to him to have become at variance with the principles it was claiming to defend: 'This distinction is important and it is essential not to lose sight of it. In my view, the opposition must let it be seen more every day that it preserves none of the revolutionary habits, but never has it been more necessary for it to remain closely faithful to the noble and glorious principles of the Revolution.'

With Michelet, one enters a different world, socially, politically and intellectually. He, too, had ties with the French Revolution – even closer in his case: he, too, was hostile to Guizot's government, and much more vehemently; he was typical of the ideas, feeling and passions which were forming the republican concept in the face of even a constitutional monarchy.

Michelet belonged to the people. In order to understand the Revolution, not simply its heritage, but its course and the passions which had inspired the hordes of its anonymous actors, he did not have to search far back in his memory. He was in touch with that era of great events not only by his date of birth (1798) but through his family saga: through his father, a humble Jacobin printer, through his poverty-stricken childhood and his hard-working youth, the restrictive atmosphere of a worthy but very lowly bourgeoisie – in short, his entire world, both material and moral. Only Hugo, apart from himself, could have had such physical experience of the Paris of the Revolution; he had known it as a child, and still constantly explored it. The Tuileries, the Salle du Manège, the Jacobins, the Cordeliers were not for him those abstract places which they have become for twentieth-century historians; he had spent long hours of meditation in those tiny

Thomas Couture Jules Michelet, *Musée Renan, Paris.*
(*Photo: Lauros-Giraudon*)

theatres of immense happenings, where all the shades of the great generation still roamed. The Revolution had filled his memory.

As a young teacher, however, he had for a long time kept away from the struggles in the city and was regarded with some favour by the Catholic side, since Monseigneur Frayssinous himself had appointed him in 1827 to the Ecole Préparatoire, which had replaced the École Normale Supérieure, counting on him against the more Voltairean of his colleagues; and he had been chosen to teach history to the Duc de Berry's daughter. However, in 1830, he greeted with rapture 'the lightning flash of July', the Latin Quarter uprising, the brief renewal of 1789, the nation's impetus to reconquer liberty.

He had long been loyal to the regime born of the Three Glorious Days, which allowed him to enjoy a brilliant career, head of the Archives Department (1831), professor at the Collège de France (1838); he was even close to the reigning family, and private tutor to Louis-Philippe's children. At the end of the 1830s he gradually drew farther away from all that, while the stabilized monarchy took an increasingly conservative turn; the battle against the Church, in defence of the University's monopoly, was the signal for the break.

Then began the years of the great fight (1843–6), waged in common with his close friend Edgar Quinet from the heights of their professorial chairs in the Collège de France, against the clergy's claims to found a separate teaching body. Like Quinet, Michelet devoted one of his courses to putting the Jesuits on trial – that papal militia in league with monarchies in all the conspiracies against the liberty of individuals and peoples. Through this polemic against the Church, the two professors were posing the whole question of relations between Christianity and modern democracy. From his course Quinet would compile a book, which appeared in 1845, *Le Christianisme et la Révolution française*, in which he contrasts the authoritarian and dogmatic Catholic Church and the true spirit of Christianity, which was identical with that of 1789: freedom of conscience and individuals.

Now Michelet was already challenging that link of filiation between Christianity and the French Revolution; but, engrossed in the writing of his *Histoire de France*, he had not yet touched on the Revolution. Caught up by the urgency, the topicality, the mood of the times, he began to tackle it: in 1843, when he had completed the sixth part of his *Histoire de France*, closed up Louis XI and started on Charles VIII, he set aside the last three centuries of the French monarchy and launched himself into 1789.

His book of 1846, *Le Peuple*, was a kind of warm-up. In it he speaks out against social division, which he hates, in the name of the unity of the people, which is an essential component of the nation. Classes exist, as he describes at length, with an extraordinary sense of their moral history, inasmuch as they are associated with the same history and dominated by the formation of France, which transcends them and must prevent them

from separating or fighting one another. If some measure is to be made of
the gulf which yawned between Michelet and Guizot, in this period, it is
enough to consider how each treated this idea of class. For Guizot, the
necessary advent of bourgeois domination had made sense of history and
allowed combined reflection on the two parent histories of civilization,
Britain and France. On the contrary, Michelet regarded the former as the
country of class division, riddled with the aristocratic spirit; and in the
France of the Revolution he saw the pilot country of humanity, the nation
foretelling universal brotherhood: 'Every other history is mutilated, ours
alone is complete; take the history of Italy – the last centuries are missing;
take the history of Germany, or England – the first are missing. Take
France's – with that, you know the world.'[12]

The republican idea was thus built up, in his mind and in his works,
around the images of the nation and brotherhood. But, in contrast with
what was happening among other socialist authors, for him that idea and
those images were incompatible with the Terror; on the contrary, the
spectre of the Terror needed to be exorcized in order to restore to the
Revolution its radiance and its influence: 'Human blood has a terrible
power against those who have spilt it. It would be too easy for me to
establish that France was saved *in spite of the Terror*. The terrorists have
done us immense and lasting harm. Were you to go into the last cottage in
the farthest country of Europe, you would meet that memory and that
curse.' A little later, he attacked Buchez and Roux, 'those neo-Catholics',
for their eulogy of Marat and the Terror, adding, 'I would not have made
this observation, but for the prevailing fondness for speading these strange
follies, through the medium of cheap newspapers, among ordinary people
and workers who have no time to examine them carefully.'[13]

Just after *Le Peuple*, Michelet's course at the College in 1846 was
on the 'French nationality': France as a model historical individuality,
whose message was conveyed by 1789. Starting from September, he wrote
the first two volumes of his *Histoire de la Révolution française*, which
came out at the end of the summer of 1847, the same year as the books
of the Christian socialist Alphonse Esquiros (*Histoire des Montagnards*), of
Lamartine (*Histoire des Girondins*), and the first part of Louis Blanc's
Histoire de la Révolution. That was the great year for revolutionary history,
preceding the year of the revolution. As for Michelet, he had crystallized
his aims and intentions in a note of 8 February in which he recapitulated
the content of his courses since 1842, ending with: 'lastly, Revolution
and History of the Revolution, part I, with its religious and political
Introduction against Christianity and royalty. Here I have taken sides:
both against royalists (legitimists and Anglophiles), and against terrorist
republicans, and against Christians, and against communists: Louis Blanc.'

[12] J. Michelet, *Le Peuple*, part III, ch. 5.
[13] Ibid., part III, ch. 7, note.

In fact, that great Introduction said it all: that Christianity contained the whole of the *ancien régime*, that the Revolution was the advent of Law, and that the arguments of socialist sects added nothing to that double heritage since it comprised all there was to be known of things ancient and modern. What the men of the Revolution had named the *ancien régime* was a priestly monarchy founded, like the Church before it and using its example, on a mystery of incarnation, according to which the king embodied the people. The Revolution, on the contrary, formed the oneness of the people and the nation through the reappropriation of sovereignty by those to whom it rightfully belonged and who were, in fact, the founders of Law: this was Michelet's interpretation of the famous Declaration of 26 August, and he accused the Constituents of having slightly restricted its sense by stressing the rights of individuals rather than the Law (with a capital L), which was transcendental in relation to subjective rights. To reply to such numerous critics of the philosophy of natural rights, chiefly on the left (Saint-Simon, Comte, Buchez, Leroux, Louis Blanc), he wanted to make the revolutionary foundation absolute and to entrench it in a principle which defined the human essence of man: brotherhood.

Having rid itself on the right of bourgeois individualism, and on the left of the terrorist legacy, the republican concept formed the historic destiny of France, the bearer of the new creed of fraternity on the ruins of the old religion. But also on the necessary overthrow of a king and a minister who had turned social division into a principle of government.

Louis Blanc did not possess a genius like that of Tocqueville or Michelet; he had only talent. But he represented a crossroads of eras and ideas. He offers the best point of entry for anyone wanting to penetrate the extreme militant left of the July monarchy.

He was a son of the *ancien régime* world, persecuted by the Revolution. The family came from the clerical highlands of the Rouergue, and his grandfather, a merchant, had been guillotined during the Terror. His father, of royalist persuasion, married to a daughter of the Corsican nobility, served the imperial administration, and Louis Blanc was born in Madrid in 1811. He was a good student of the classics at Rodez, in a homogeneous Catholic and legitimist family and scholastic ambience. July 1830 dealt the family a blow both in its convictions and in its means, since Louis-Philippe stopped the pension granted to the father by Louis XVIII. The two boys, Louis and his brother Charles, who had just arrived in Paris, had to make do on a small income.

Louis took a post as tutor in Arras, where he read the eighteenth-century authors from whom his education had sheltered him; and in a province so different from that of his childhood, he also discovered working-class wretchedness and pauperism. It was during those years that he constructed, out of family nostalgia for the past, a new prophecy of the future: it was a way of preserving hatred for the bourgeois dynasty of July by reinvesting it in the concept of a fraternal community to be rediscovered in the future, extended to include all working-class people. The *curés'* child found a job in the leftist press; he had gone over to democracy and socialism, but maintained the same enemies – money and the bourgeoisie.

In 1840, he published two works which enable his profile to be outlined. One is a long article transformed into a pamphlet, putting forward his solutions to the social problem: *L'Organisation du travail*. The title reveals its essential point: it is a matter of replacing the capitalist anarchy, which flourishes under a state controlled by the bourgeoisie, with a rational economic order under the authority of a state in the hands of the people's representatives. The plan is related to the socialist utopias of the era in that it leaves plenty of room for the re-education of a new man, who has been freed from the selfishness of interests and passions; once that supposed condition was obtained, the new organization of production could soon receive the agreement of all. It would be guaranteed by an equally renewed state, composed of those elected by universal suffrage, who could be dismissed at any time; the said state would control key industries and exercise a general regulatory role over production through 'social work-shops', intended to demonstrate the superiority of associative work over the competitive sector.

Louis Blanc loved history more than economics. In 1840 he also published a book which met with equally great success: *Histoire de dix ans, 1830–1840*. This was a long chronicle (five volumes) of the past ten years of Louis-Philippe's reign, written with witty eloquence and full of anecdotes and pen-portraits: it is one of the documents which best reflect the intellectual and moral world of the revolutionary left in that period. At the centre of this long account (preceded by a huge introduction on the Restoration) is a collective character which has pulled the strings of French history since 1789: the bourgeoisie. It is defined once and for all in economic terms (the class which possesses the 'instruments of labour'), but followed solely in its supposed political history: that of a class with a single will, which had successively driven out Napoleon in 1814 and 1815, dethroned Charles X to the advantage of the Duc d'Orléans in 1830, and was still battling against Louis-Philippe and his servant Molé to ensure its sole power, through the intermediary of the Chamber of Deputies.

It thus continually undermined the principle of authority, which was essential to any society, to the profit of what it called liberty, which it used as a mask and a lever to exploit the people and dominate the market. The Doctrinaires' central thesis was turned against them; the middle class was well and truly dominant, representative government in place, but they ensured only that interests should reign supreme: 'To seek those who guide the people, the legislators, only among property-owners is to transfer domestic policies to the management of states . . . What can be expected of a system which deliberately makes private interests the source of governments?'[14]

---

[14] Louis Blanc, *Révolution française. Histoire de dix ans*, vol. 5, Conclusion.

In a strong position because of these two best-sellers, Louis Blanc was a personality of the extra-parliamentary opposition. Anti-bourgeois, anti-capitalist, he spoke out for workers' associations; by virtue of that he was linked with the world of all the little socialist and communist sects, which were in permanent conflict, and among which Karl Marx would pass in 1844 before being expelled from France by Guizot. He was a Jacobin, the supporter of a strong state, protector of the poor, and an unconditional defender of 'nationality'; close, for that reason, to the secret societies of Babouvist tradition, to men like Louis Blanqui and Armand Barbès, the leaders of an unsuccessful insurrection, beginning with an attack on police headquarters, in 1839. Through his Catholic turn of mind, he added his note to the Christian gnosis of reconciled humanity, into which Lamennais put more feeling and Pierre Leroux more doctrinal spirit. Lastly, he was also a reformer, pleading for a policy of morality rather than violence; and for the reconciliation of the bourgeoisie and the people through fraternity, the future principle of the social world; that made him an apostle of universal suffrage, and a personality in the Republican party destined to play an important role in the last years of the regime and the first months of the one following. When George Sand met him during those years, after having corresponded with him, she was already an admirer of this short, brilliant and restless man who personified so many of the ideas of the times, including her own: a sort of Thiers of the extreme left.

He, too, right in the midst of all these struggles, began a long *Histoire de la Révolution française*, and published the first volume in February 1847, like Michelet. It was a book which straight away made the main point, with the theme of the two revolutions under the semblance of a single event. In fact, by destroying the principle of authority, both Catholic and royal, 1789 had merely substituted that of individualism, which had made its appearance with Luther, and triumphed, in its secularized form, with the Constituent Assembly. But it soon brought to light, with the Montagne and Year II, a third principle – fraternity, the synthesis of the former two: in the fragmented world of individualism that re-established the lost sense of community, typical of civilizations with authority. That was Rousseau's revolution, foretelling what the morrow would bring, for it had fallen with Robespierre on 9 Thermidor. By secularizing Buchez's history, yet at the same time preserving a Catholic tone derived from his childhood, Louis Blanc turned Jacobinism and Robespierre into the ancestors of his socialist republic. Once again, through him, the French Revolution provided the origin, the inspiration and the model.

Everyone would soon be ready to get down to work.

THE END OF LOUIS-PHILIPPE

Nevertheless, the idea which was most current around 1845 was the one shared with so many of their contemporaries by the three keen observers of the political scene whom I have just described, all determined opponents of the ministry, yet all three convinced that it had the situation well and truly in hand, thanks to the sort of passive backing which it had gained from those with interests. It is true that passivity does not provide a very firm support and that it can reveal its lack of strength precisely when difficulties arise. But for the time being the virulence of the debate on freedom of education had died down a little, although the Catholics were unappeased, and the legislative elections of the summer of 1846 promised to be good for Guizot. They 'are in preparation and will take place', wrote the *Revue des Deux Mondes*, which was badly disposed towards the minister, 'in one of the calmest moments which France has enjoyed for a long time'.

Indeed, they were a very good thing for the government, which had spared neither trouble nor its prefects: 291 victories out of 459. It was the only clear majority in the regime's history, and yet it was the last; a sign that suffrage based on property-ownership did not represent the country, but also that opinion remained in control of the game and could change very rapidly. It was an Assembly of notables, like the others, somewhat rejuvenated by the election of about a hundred 'new boys', composed of property-owners, top civil servants, capitalists and legal men, but this Chamber had no majority of ideas, or any idea of majority: one of the limitations of Guizot's system was to deprive its parliamentary representatives of any means of beguiling public opinion, or indeed of addressing it.

As for the opposition, it was chopped up into little groups, although it sometimes managed to unite on the ocasion of a ballot; a very tiny extreme left, elected in the large towns, a residual legitimist group, a reduced centre-left around Thiers, a large dynastic left led by Odilon Barrot, but without any real homogeneity, and lastly, personalities surrounded by a few faithful supporters and in search of unlikely allies, Lamartine and Tocqueville. Here was the spectacle of a political life without either structure or programme, with the exception of a Catholic lobby of 150 deputies who had pledged themselves to 'religious freedom'. At the start of the 1847 session, Guizot managed to get the Address carried by 248 votes to 84, and believed himself at last to be at the head of a conservative party.

It would prove to be a bad session, however. Guizot once again opposed two projects which had become traditional: one on the extension of the voting qualification, the other on the regulation of the right of civil servants to enter parliament (the latter proposed for the seventeenth time since 1830). Though the electoral reform was set aside by a majority of one hundred votes, the parliamentary reform was only narrowly defeated. Guizot, more doctrinal than ever, treated his colleagues to lectures rather than replies, reciting his books like a schoolmaster for the benefit of the newly elected. To the inflexibility of his nature and the body of his ideas was added the conviction that, in the face of what he called 'political restlessness' – a generic term for everything that went against the government – the only good answer was a fixed and stable power. For his part, the king, now aged seventy-four and weary with having won through so many challenges, had developed a taste for peace and quiet, together with an impatience for any contradiction; the two men gave each other mutual comfort by trying to maintain the status quo, while the Chamber began to attack the ministers.

In the spring of 1847, a nasty affair of corruption exploded, sullying the name of Guizot's entire administration: the ex-Minister of Public Works, who had become a peer of France in exchange for his departure from the ministry, Teste, was convicted of having been 'bought' in 1842 to facilitate a mining concession in Haute-Saône; tried and sentenced in July, together with General Cubières, a hero of Waterloo and former Minister of War under Thiers in 1840, he took part of the regime to prison with him. Immediately afterwards, on 18 August, the Duc de Choiseul-Praslin, also a peer of France and the descendant of an illustrious family, killed his wife, the daughter of Marshal Sébastiani, because he was in love with their children's governess, from whom she had forced him to part. Arrested at his home, while awaiting the warrant from the upper Chamber, he poisoned himself with arsenic, thus avoiding trial by his peers. This was an extraordinarily shocking news item, which brought together a symbolic name and a foul crime – the two ingredients which guaranteed its success with the public; but by poisoning himself, the accused escaped trial and punishment, and that defection provoked so much anger and so many rumours that the chancellor, Pasquier, contrary to the rules of law, issued a report on 30 August on the guilt of the accused dead man, regretting that 'the penalty could not be as devastating as the crime'. It made no difference: the terrible deed of the duke and peer was entered in the liabilities column of the ruling oligarchy. On 27 August Tocqueville wrote to a friend from his Normandy countryside: 'I have found this area in a dreadfully poor state of morale. The effect of the Cubières trial has been immense. Also, the horrible story that has been on everyone's lips for the last eight days is of a kind to cast a vague terror and profound malaise into their souls.'

A grave social and economic crisis then occurred to add its effects, as in 1788–9, to this moral and political discredit, which recalled that of the court in the last years of the *ancien régime*. In fact, the same mechanism was at work: the very bad harvest of 1846 (following a bad one in 1845), the dearness of bread, aggravated by stockpiling and speculation, the poverty of the populace and, here and there, famine – the last in French history. All this saw the reappearance of demands for price-fixing, the seizure of loads of corn by rural or village mobs, looting, intimidation of landowners and violence against the 'fat cats'. These activities took place nearly everywhere, and were particularly acute in the west and the Loire regions, which shows that they had no direct relationship with political life properly speaking, although, as usual, the government took the blame. The most violent revolt occurred in Buzançais at the beginning of the year; in this big Indre township on the Berry borders, dominated by about a hundred property-owners and merchants, the rural lower classes – day labourers, farmhands, weavers, craftsmen – maintained insurrectionary rule for three days, with price-fixing and requisition, after murdering a rich bourgeois. Then came the arrival of the troops, arrests; a few dozen unfortunate wretches taken to the court at Châteauroux before a jury of property-owners; heavy prison sentences and three executions on 16 April, market day, in the main square of the town amid a throng of silent people.

The 1847 harvest was better; it improved the situation in the country areas but brought no end to the industrial depression induced by under-consumption, chiefly in textiles and building, which were the biggest sectors. Bankruptcies increased throughout the year, and unemployment spread. To add to all this bad news came a financial crisis, evidenced by a drop in shares and exaggerated by an attitude of mistrust which followed over-enthusiasm: at once the confidence of the bourgeoisie itself in prosperity broke down and, one thing leading to another, so did the network of interests and expectations which linked propertied people, both large and small.

The signs were unmistakable. One was that the National Guard, the regime's bourgeois militia, was slow or reluctant to re-establish order, and here and there it was necessary to have recourse to the army: the bourgeois and petit-bourgeois who filled the ranks of the Guard, and who had so often defended and rescued their king, were disappointed by a government which was incapable of ensuring order and prosperity and refused any reforms. Those two criticisms combined to break the links which had assured the July monarchy of its most reliable support. Whereas the horizon of the Chambers and the political class stopped at the ministry, public opinion was already talking about the regime itself: this was the French tendency, by which the revolutionary tradition once again spread through people's minds.

The year 1847 was outstandingly lucky for that resurrection. Louis Blanc and Michelet had both published the first volumes of their great histories – one on 6 February and the other on the 13th – with the second due to appear in the autumn. But the real winner of this publishing competition was Lamartine, with his *Histoire des Girondins*, which came out in eight parts, each hard on the heels of the last, between 20 March and 12 June. However, it was a book which did not measure up to the other two, and was very inferior to Louis Blanc's: superficially knowledge-able, written too hastily (Lamartine was also pressed for money), scanty as regards ideas or interpretation. But through that fluent prose, in which everything is subordinate to literary effect, runs a kind of fraternal absolution which is granted to the actors in that great drama, even to its victims, who are haloed by the almost miraculous nature of the event. Lamartine had gone beyond the original framework of the Girondins to embellish the entire Revolution with the poesy of memories. Helped by its very weak-nesses, the book was like a thunderbolt: people fought to get hold of copies. To a France once again in crisis over legitimacy, it offered a sentimental and ecumenical version of her founding event.

There is nothing to indicate that Louis-Philippe and Guizot had sensed the depth of the crisis and the exhaustion of their system. Quite the opposite. In September old Marshal Soult gave up the presidency of the Council and Guizot at last legally occupied the position which had in fact been his since the formation of the government in October 1840. At that time, the opposition launched a campaign of banquets in order to promote the idea of electoral reform in public opinion: this was political propaganda in the form of gastronomic conviviality, which was a national tradition and had already been used by republicans in 1830 and 1840. It had the advantage of flouting both the ban on associations and the obligation to ask the government's permission since, if held on private premises, a meal taken communally did not constitute a political gathering.

This time, the campaign united the centre-left and the dynastic left with the republicans of the central electoral committee of Paris which, for the sake of unity, had agreed to halt its attacks on Thiers. The first banquet took place on 8 July in the public garden of the Château-Rouge, right in the middle of the Teste–Cubières trial, and 1,200 guests attended: eighty-six opposition deputies, with Odilon Barrot at their head, and a host of generally republican personalities, including Armand Marrast, the editor of *Le National*. The weather was glorious, the *Marseillaise* and other songs of the Revolution were played, republican orators moderated their speeches and deputies toughened theirs: for want of a common reference point on the Great Revolution, they found a meeting-ground in the necessity for a re-enactment of 1830, which gave a clear advantage to the former group. For, if the scenario likened Guizot to Polignac, and Louis-Philippe to Charles X, this time there was no alternative dynasty.

The Château-Rouge banquet had given the signal for other meetings of the same kind in the provinces. Odilon Barrot was the most sought-after orator, and the public never tired of seeing the leader of the dynastic left rise to his feet – some time between the fruit and the cheese course – wearing his blue coat and grey trousers, to denounce the scandals of the government and the country's humiliations. He did not attack royalty: he called for *la réforme*. But the alliance which he ended by striking with the republicans, for want of finding sufficient response within the regime, and the backing he sought from the country, for want of being listened to in the Chamber, worked as much against Louis-Philippe as against Guizot. In any case, it was not long before the extreme republicans, the most revolutionary, the secret society men, those who had gathered round the newspaper *La Réforme* in order to distinguish themselves from the moderates of *Le National*, came to join these feasts of rhetoric, to which they imparted quite a different tone: Jacobin memories mingled with the new demand for the 'organization of labour'. The new extreme left deputy, Ledru-Rollin, was the Odilon Barrot of those themes.

During these last months of the monarchy, the king had no shortage of advisers – including some from his own family – recommending that he should part company with Guizot. But Louis-Philippe believed he had the strength of the electorate's vote behind him, as expressed in 1846. Without Guizot, he could see himself in the hands of a Thiers-Odilon Barrot ministry, which would take away his freedom to manoeuvre and launch France into ventures abroad. Together with Guizot, he gave up most of his time to foreign policy; having once again tangled with Britain after the marriage of his youngest son to a Spanish princess, he was patiently rebuilding some room for French intervention in Euopean affairs. At a time when revolutionary unrest was rising almost everywhere, Thiers's disorderly activism would undo all his work. So he kept Guizot, who for his part found additional reasons for remaining in the radicalization of the rhetoric of the banquets.

The minister liked a fight, but he overestimated his forces. This error was shared by opinion, which to some extent explains the pugnacity of the bourgeois opposition. In exile, Louis-Philippe would say later to one of his friends: 'The Parisian bourgeois would not have overthrown me if they had not believed me to be unshakeable.' Tocqueville, in his speech of 27 January 1848, was one of the politicians – not the only one, Montalembert and Emile de Girardin had the same anxieties - to have an intuition of what was about to happen:

Think, gentlemen, of the old monarchy; it was stronger than you, stronger because of its origin; it had better support than you from former practices, old customs, ancient beliefs; it was stronger than you, and yet it fell into the dust . . . Can you not sense, by a sort of intuitive instinct which cannot be analysed, but which is sure, that the earth is again trembling in Europe? [General stir.] Do you not feel – how shall I put it? the wind of revolution in the air?

From the opposite direction. to give some idea of the atmosphere of those days even in the Chamber, here is the summing-up of Thiers's speech on foreign policy, some days later: the Thiers who had prudently refused to associated himself with the campaign of banquets nevertheless concludes:

I am not a radical, gentlemen, as the radicals well know, and you have only to read their newspapers to be convinced of it. But hear my views. I am for revolution, both in France and in Europe; I hope that the government of the revolution stays in the hands of moderate men; I will do all in my power to see that it continues to do so; but, should this government pass into the hands of men who are less moderate than I and my friends, into the hands of impassioned men, whether or not they are radicals, I will not abandon my cause for this reason: I shall always be on the side of revolution.

Thiers also sensed the mood of the times, but in his own way, tactical rather than philosophical: his overstatement stemmed from the same reasons as the revolt of the 'Parisian bourgeois' according to Louis-Philippe. Contrary to Tocqueville, he believed the regime to be invulnerable.

Events would demonstrate the complete reverse – that it had nothing left to hold on to. The crucial fact of the February revolution was, in effect, the desertion of the king by the National Guard; for the second time, as in 1830, it was the unexpected alliance of the bourgeoisie and the people which gave the uprising its success. A popular demonstration had been planned by the republicans for 22 February 1848 to protest against the banning of the great banquet in the twelfth *arrondissement*. The parliamentary opposition had decided the evening before not to be associated with it, but the government was so confident that it cancelled the large-scale military deployment it had arranged, and the summons to the National Guard. However, the demonstrators – manual workers, students, common people – were numerous and determined enough to spread disorder even to the fashionable districts, the Concorde and the Champs-Elysées.

The next day, 23 February, the revolt broke out again in several places, and in the morning rebels were in control chiefly of the area stretching from the quais to the boulevards, on both sides of the rue Saint-Denis – the heart of Parisian revolution. This time the army was ready for action, the National Guard was called to arms; then came the turning-point of the drama: the uniformed bourgeois cried, 'Vive la Réforme!' and placed themselves in the way, to prevent the army or municipal guard from charging the rebels. That was the first big success: Louis-Philippe, going from optimism to depression, dismissed Guizot and sent for Molé. But he combined with this attempt at concession an action which cancelled its value: the appointment of Marshal Bugeaud, who was loathed by the republicans, to command the troops. The rebellion grew and, in the evening, on the boulevard des Capucines in front of the Ministry of Foreign Affairs, it had its baptism of fire: about twenty killed, whose corpses were soon carried in a doleful procession through Paris, where the revolution was rising. Molé made himself scarce and during the night Louis-Philippe summoned Thiers.

The next day saw the rapid failure of a plan to regain control of Paris by Bugeaud's troops, who were surrounded by the crowds and National Guards, the latter ever more reluctant to fire. In any event, this strategy was damned in advance by the call to Thiers, whom the king replaced during the morning with Odilon Barrot: he was the last chance, the man who for eighteen years had been arguing the case for a democratic opening, and who obtained power when it had ceased to exist. The revolution by now controlled the Hôtel de Ville and soon attacked the Tuileries after it had finally found its leaders and its watchwords: the abdication of the king, the Republic. As Charles X had done in favour of the Duc de Bordeaux, Louis-Philippe drew up his deed of abdication, in the middle of the day, in favour of his grandson, the Comte de Paris. The testaments of legitimate royalty have never enjoyed much luck in French history. So what can be said of the last wishes of a sovereign who had found his crown on the streets? In the afternoon the Duchesse d'Orléans made a last attempt on behalf of her young son, in a Chamber soon invaded by a mob of insurgents. The Republic had been proclaimed at the Hôtel de Ville; at the Palais Bourbon, the aged Dupont de l'Eure, followed by Ledru-Rollin, read out the list of a provisional government.

The royal household, who had left in a mad rush for Saint-Cloud after the abdication, slept at Dreux, the Orléans' town, where the queen wanted to gather herself together. Believing the regency established, Louis-Philippe had counted on going to the château d'Eu, as was his wont. But when he learned of the happenings in Paris, on 25 February he went incognito to a small house on the Normandy coast near Honfleur, where he finally boarded an English boat on the evening of 2 March to take him across the Channel. He had followed the same route into exile as Charles X, but minus the twilight majesty of that procession in August 1830. Disguised as a Norman bourgeois, in a farmer's cart, he did not carry with him, as he left France, so many centuries of the country's past.

8

The Second Republic: 1848–1851

The inglorious end of the July monarchy reflected a double abdication: of the king and of the ruling oligarchy. Prolix and changeable, passing from illusion to discouragement, the old king was no longer able to face up to dramatic happenings. But how quickly everything around him went to pieces! 'His' National Guard had already deserted him. But the soldiers of the line and their leaders had hardly done any better: Bugeaud, the outstanding war leader, gave the order to retreat on 24 February. The political class was routed; it had nothing to offer, since it was too restricted to resist the insurrection. In the space of twenty-four hours, Guizot had handed over to Molé, Molé to Thiers and Thiers to Odilon Barrot: even the leader of the dynastic left, although one of those rare politicians who took physical risks during those days at the barricades, had lost all political consistency. A man had vanished into thin air.

To explain this, one could say that on 24 February the regime had paid the bill for its origins: born of a republican insurrection which it had replaced *in extremis*, it was finally overthrown by another insurrection which, this time, instituted a republic. Meanwhile, this bastard monarchy had never really found its national footing: it was too monarchic to be republican, and too republican to be monarchic. This was evidenced by the new dynasty's inability to entrench itself as the founder of a legitimacy, despite all the efforts it had made to reunify national history to its own advantage. The post-revolutionary political synthesis it had wanted to construct around the idea of liberty had been shattered, destroyed by a resurgence of the French Revolution in the name of the very principle the dynasty had taken as its banner.

In fact, the regime had not been able to redeem its initial handicap: that of being a monarchy. Everything its adversaries had to say bore witness to that immediately after July 1830, and more so in the later years. To begin with, the accusation of usurpation was launched by both legitimists and republicans, who managed to agree, albeit negatively, on those bases. In the end, the campaign of banquets continually evoked memories of the ultras, Polignac, Charles X and the ordinances. The last Bourbon had extended to his illegitimate successor, like a belated vengeance, that curse of the *ancien régime* of which he had so clumsily reawakened the memory. Seen from that viewpoint, the July monarchy met its end turning the English example of 1688 upside down: instead of founding a tradition of constitutional royalty which was superior even to the dynastic concept, it had renewed the divorce between the nation and monarchic government. Instead of terminating the French Revolution, as Guizot had wished, it had given it fresh vitality.

The Orléans monarchy did not bear the entire responsibility. In its infancy it had encountered legacies which were infinitely more difficult to reconcile than those of England in 1688. The English monarchy had had a constitutional tradition, so that Stuart absolutism, the regicide, the republican dictatorship and the Restoration had merely been a digression in a long history of liberty, rediscovered in 1688. By contrast, the French monarchy, which had gradually become confused with the absolute sovereignty of the king, had needed to be destroyed in order to establish the sovereignty of the people: the regicide of 21 January 1793 had killed both the king and royalty. The 1830 attempt at compromise had had no roots: constitutional royalty was quite likely to appear to public opinion as merely a bastard monarchy which, though replacing the nobility with the bourgeoisie, was just as authoritarian and oligarchic as that of the Bourbons.

To those risks, or handicaps, Guizot's policies had added their own particular contribution, linked to the dogmatism of their originator. One of the regime's misfortunes, indeed, had been to have its principal theorist as its chief minister, and through him to ascribe too much to ideas and too little to circumstances. Louis-Philippe's reign had not been middle-class government, since it had been based on far too restricted an electorate; nor had it been the accomplishment of national history by the sovereignty of reason and the appeasement of revolutionary passions, to which it had, on the contrary, given a new impetus. But Guizot had only had to think of it in those terms for it to lose the essential part of its capacity to adjust, which was indispensable for its survival: for compromise, not the unveiling of reason, had been inseparable from its coming into being.

Interpreted in terms of historical philosophy, not only had the July monarchy not known how to capitalize on the real progress which had been achieved in public life, but that very progress had boomeranged against it. For example, the law of 1831 on the election of municipal councillors had broadened the electoral qualifications and favoured the development of local political elites; but those elites, which for the most part remained prohibited from access to the position of deputy, had then been tempted more to form an opposition to the regime than to constitute its support.

A further example, culled this time from the narrow confines of parliament: July 1830 had made customary the right of deputies to question ministers; but the manipulation of the Assemblies and ministries by the king and the government had on the contrary greatly reduced parliamentary control of the executive. Of the sixteen ministries which had followed one another from 1830 to 1848, only three had left power on a vote of no confidence. Instead of a true spirit of *juste milieu*, the monarchy had revealed a will to cut back the principle of political citizenship which had nevertheless been an accepted part of its accession. It had not only refused the widening of a restricted electoral body. It had sought to avoid parliamentary control, even of that limited electorate, by filling the Assemblies with civil servants or by increasing administrative pressures on its members. In its desire to found liberal institutions, it had yielded to the temptation to use to its own advantage a centralized state, augmented by a public service as yet unorganized and totally under its thumb.

It might have been able to redeem this deficit of liberalism by a great 'national' policy: French revolutionary tradition was such that Bonapartism was almost omnipresent in the nineteenth century, and more flourishing than ever in Louis-Philippe's reign under all the republican window-dressing. Nostalgia for imperial glory surfaced here and there even in the two royalist families. For without ever having been built up into a constituted doctrine, the memory – or legend – of Napoleon formed the lowest common denominator for the French. The magic of a simple name, universally known, contained both civil equality and the glory of the nation; it was inseparable from the denunciation of the 1815 treaties, after Waterloo, and was a constant reminder that legitimacy can be the prize of war and victory.

Louis-Philippe had not had the means, and even less the taste, for that kind of policy; in a world then dominated by British power, he had conducted his foreign activities with good sense and reason, which was one of the strong points of his reign. But he had enveloped them in that shopkeeper mentality which was part of his nature, exposing himself throughout his reign to neo-Girondin rhetoric about the emancipation of the peoples, and to the tyranny of the great memories left by the emperor. Even the legitimists, forgetting for the nonce the emigration, the Condé army, 1814 and 1815, had often added their voices to this demagogic chorus. The insurgents of February 1848 had wanted to avenge the National Guard by deposing a king who had once again humiliated it.

The time had therefore come for a republic – the second – half a century after the first. The ultra-royalists, and Guizot after them, had successively discredited in public opinion the two solutions to the French political crisis which they had proposed: the restoration of the Bourbons and a British-style monarchy. There remained the concept of a republic, but that too was somewhat shop-soiled. It had its claim to go back a long way with 10 August 1792, the overthrow of royalty and the regicide, and its claim to glory with the Committee of Public Safety and the saving of the patrie. But above all, it recalled the Terror, the hideous period of denunciations and fear, followed by the internal semi-anarchy of the Thermidorian and

Directorial era. Despite Constant's efforts, the old idea of the impossibility
of having a republic in a large country had been confirmed and revived by
the last years of the eighteenth century: the liberals were convinced of
it, which goes a long way to explaining their recourse to Louis-Philippe
in 1830. Eighteen years later, republican qualifications offered nothing
likely to reassure them. For until 2 December 1851, the left, sometimes
so enthusiastic about Robespierre, had never been very harsh about 18
Brumaire. On the second point at least, it expressed the national verdict.

Here, for example, is Rémusat, the farthest left of the liberal Orleanists
– and also one of the most intelligent witnesses of the era – explaining his
reluctance in the face of the triumphant republican concept in February
1848:

The Republic, among other impossibilities, or at least other problems, offered one
which has been unresolved up till now – that is, the constitution of executive
power . . . That difficulty alone justified the reputation it commonly enjoyed for
being impossible.

The revolutionary republics had left the majority of the public with memories
which explained the repugnance, incredulity and disdain which the mere mention
of the word 'republic' aroused. I had neither the thoughts nor the stature to allow
me to combat the antipathy of its adversaries with either confidence or success. On
the contrary, I knew that the bad traditions of the Revolution – toward which I
had never been particularly indulgent – had found favour within the ranks of
democracy, whether by inclination, bravado, logic or corruption. The prejudices
and passions of the February men held no mysteries for me, and I had far less
esteem for republicans than for the Republic. I knew what sort of weaknesses,
with the help of circumstances, could appear in certain hearts for what must be
called Jacobinism, and although I did not believe it must exactly bring back to us
all the horrors of September or the revolutionary Tribunal, I did not think it
impossible that it should have its days, or at least its hours, in the history of the
Republic of 1848.[1]

Nevertheless, Rémusat was not inimical to the idea of the Republic. On
the contrary, he perceived it as having, in its principle, a common feature
with constitutional monarchy: the nation's participation in government,
which is the essence of political liberty. In this respect, both regimes,
Republic and British-style royalty, were together distinct from absolute
monarchy, to the point where the greatest liberal authors, Montesquieu
and Royer-Collard, had likened England to a republic. However, taken to
its logical consequences, the notion of *res publica* or commonwealth implied
the government of the people by themselves, the purest example of which
was offered by the young republic of the United States. That explains the
legend of the old La Fayette under the Restoration, as a living dual symbol
of the American and the French Revolutions. The paradox of that glory lay
in the fact that the veteran of the war of Independence had espoused only
the first part of the course of the French Revolution: precisely the one
which was not republican. But, imprisoned in 1792 by the Austrians while

[1] Ch. de Rémusat, *Mémoires de ma vie*, vol. 4, p. 251.

fleeing from the Jacobin excesses, he had avoided, by this fortuitous captivity, repudiation by the émigrés and also the war in Paris against the Republic – when he would without a doubt have ended on the guillotine. Thus, the former general of the National Guard in 1789 had been able to emerge unscathed from the French civil war, both physically and morally. The Jacobin Republic, which he had not served but in whose name he had suffered from afar, shed no blood through him on the triumphant image of the American republic he had helped to bring into being. Thanks to him, its seductive power was reinforced.

But the national experience was not so easily forgotten that it could be exorcized by the glory of the 'hero of two worlds'. It had its survivors; it had built up its own memories, its own tradition and its idea of the Republic which had appeared with the Restoration: both among the secret societies working for the overthrow of the Bourbons, and in the history books whose authors sought to restore the great hours of 1792 and 1793 to the French people. The 1821 Charbonnerie, to which La Fayette had lent his name, was made up of young militants who were much more radical than the old leader whom they used as a figurehead. It was an adaptation of the Jacobin Club to clandestine activity; its adherents wanted to restore, in opposition to the Bourbons, by the action of an insurrectionist vanguard, a republic which drew its main features from the example of 1793. What they liked above all in 1793 was the reign of civic equality extended to all individuals and dominating all lives, since the Republic presupposed the indivisible nature of the people and the state.

The method of effecting this sovereignty of the people, which had so preoccupied the eighteenth-century *philosophes*, the men of 1789 and the liberals of the 'representative government', was a problem which had been forgotten, or supposed resolved, by the republicans of the first part of the nineteenth century, who were militants rather than minds given to political theory. The solution of the famous impossibility of a republic in a big country was in their eyes to be found in the Montagnard constitution of June 1793, no sooner voted than suspended. Its centre was a single Assembly, elected by direct universal suffrage, embodying the indivisible and imprescriptible sovereignty of the people. Moreover, it offered direct democracy recourse to a referendum, which was compulsory for the ratification or revision of the constitution, and possible for any law what-soever on condition that half the *départements* demanded it within forty days following the deputies' vote.

The executive power was a Council elected at three levels, by both the people and the Assembly, since it was chosen by the latter from lists put forward by electoral assemblies elected by primary assemblies. This mixture of absolute sovereignty in the hands of a single Assembly and direct democracy by referendum had, at the time, illustrated rather than resolved the contradiction of a republican constitution in a large country. But it presented the enormous and double advantage of not having been applied and of being capable of substitution in people's memory for the

Terror, which had replaced it in actual fact. The Revolution rediscovered in it one of its great legacies, the sovereignty of the people, but rid of its trail of blood.

The other key idea of the 'Republican party' – to take up a contemporary expression which was, however, misleading (since there were no parties) – was the 'nation', heroically rescued by the Convention, humiliated by the return of the Bourbons, the Holy Alliance and the 1815 treaties. It was an idea held in common by all in opposition to Charles X before 1830, including the liberals; it became specifically republican from then on, against the foreign policy of compromise and conciliation firmly desired by Louis-Philippe. From the outset it had included nostalgics or admirers of the emperor, who had died on his rocky isle of St Helena in 1821 after dictating to his faithful servitors the *Mémorial de Sainte-Hélène*, which sounded the charge for his posthumous campaigns.

Bonapartism did not form distinct groups, or a party, in the republican opposition. When it did, as at the time of Louis-Napoleon's two attempts at a *coup*, in Strasbourg in 1836 and Boulogne in 1840, it appeared easily isolated and beaten. But its strength derived from its massive diffusion throughout public opinion: peddled through a wide variety of channels, from the twopenny picture to learned literature, the Napoleonic myth fed mostly on national memories. It was the simplest, and thus the most widespread, form in which the spirit of the Revolution continued to haunt the country. It mingled quite naturally with many republican convictions, not only through the idea of the 'great nation' but because the emperor provided a ready-made substitute for the Convention as a symbol of the people's indivisible sovereignty. That was the inevitable price paid by the republicans for their passion to revive the greatness of the dictatorship, counter to political liberty.

To comprehend that this was often their tendency under Louis-Philippe, one has only to bear in mind the reshaping of the Robespierrist tradition by socialist thinking, such as we have seen at work in Buonarroti prior to July 1830, then in Buchez just after, or in Louis Blanc (1847). In their view, the dictatorship of Year II ceased to be an expedient of public safety and foretold the emancipation of the people in relation to the bourgeoisie. It was no longer a necessary and temporary suspension of the Rights of Man in order to save the country, but a negation-cum-overriding of the false principles of 1789, a true instrument of equality. However, the apologia for 1793 had no need of all this philosophical window-dressing in order to please the most politicized elements of the urban lower classes, who made up the guilds, the workers' mutual aid societies and the secret societies. It was fed from the same source as in 1793: that passion for equality which had been the great popular mainspring of the French Revolution and had regained its momentum starting from the ultra-royalist reaction, accompanied here and there – as in the past, but less so – by its punitive complement, the guillotine. The Republic personified the revenge of the poor on the rich; after being the nation's banner against the return of the *ancient régime*, since July 1830 it had been the hope of the people against the bourgeoisie.

The idea of class, unwisely flourished by the Doctrinaires as a means of defining the new monarchy, was used again by the republicans to combat it. It set in motion a dialectic between republican leftism and the panic of property-owners which Marx later interpreted in terms of a struggle between the working class and capitalist bourgeoisie, but which in reality harked back directly to the French Revolution. Victor Hugo had noted in his journal in June 1832, concerning the republican insurgents who had just failed in their bid: 'Those people are a hindrance to the political idea, which would make progress without them. They terrify the honest bourgeois, provoking a fierce backlash. They turn the Republic into a bogeyman. Seventeen ninety-three is a dead duck. Gentlemen, let us speak a little less of Robespierre and a little more of Washington.'

There existed in the political class of the July monarchy another conception of the Republic, invoked by Hugo here and elsewhere as the almost certain future of humanity in its march towards progress: a true government of the people by the people, finally realizing political democracy to the full, after triumphing in society. What was needed was not an insurrectionist vanguard, but the movement of minds and mores as well as the universal education of citizens. Hugo, who was a July supporter, thus viewed Louis-Philippe's monarchy as a long transition; Chateaubriand, who was against it, thought it incapable of that knowledge of history, and too bourgeois ever to let the people have their say; but, like so many intellectuals of that era, they both saw the Republic at the end of the democratic road. A chasm separated them from the republicans who wanted to revive the Convention: the Republic in their eyes was the product of evolution and not insurrection. In order to further its cause, according to Hugo, as with Michelet or Quinet, it must forget the dictatorship and not re-enact it.

Depending on circumstances and individuals, the republican camp therefore occupied a vast area, ranging from the socialists to the fringes of the dynastic opposition, from political activism to social philosophy, from the clandestine militant to the opposition parliamentarian, from the pro-insurrection neo-Robespierrist to the supporter of progressive reforms. From 1840 onwards, Paris had become an amazing crucible of doctrines and conflicts where advanced ideas had their meeting-place. That year, Louis Blanc's *L'Organisation du travail* was published, and also Proudhon's *Mémoire sur la propriété* and Pierre Leroux's *De l'humanité*: this was the signal for the multiplication of socialist sects which tore one another to pieces but at least had in common a hatred for the bourgeois monarchy. It was then, too, that the great debate got under way on the University monopoly, and this mobilized against the Church the other wing of the 'Republican party': that of the bourgeois, students and teachers, who were more drawn to 1789 than to 1793, and all hostile to socialist thinking, which at the time was often mingled with Christianity.

However, there were many crossing-points from one wing to the other, even if it was only through hostility to the regime's bourgeois conservatism, which was soon whipped up by the campaign of banquets. *Le National* held firm to the priority of political revolution in relation to social revolution. Three areas of sensitivity were represented on *La Réforme*: the neo-Jacobinism of the former stenographer, Flocon, a great admirer of 1793, who founded the newspaper in 1843; the more liberal republicanism of its backer, Ledru-Rollin, a young republican deputy from Le Mans, elected in 1841 and leader of the small extreme left parliamentary group; and lastly the state socialism of Louis Blanc, a member of the editorial committee. The other great republican deputy, the astronomer François Arago, had demanded from the rostrum of the Chamber on 16 May 1840 a 'new organization of labour'. The campaign of banquets had shown, mainly towards its end, the growing hold over certain militant sectors of the public of a neo-Jacobin rhetoric which was partly replaced by the theme of social revolution.

Because it is central in the kaleidoscope of the republican philosophy of the time, let us give the concept of fraternity its due. It became part of the national slogan precisely at this point. Fraternity between peoples, fraternity between men: with this third element of revolutionary democracy, the mid-nineteenth-century republicans wanted to avert the confrontation of nations abroad, and social division at home. At the very moment when the idea of class was permeating national political culture, they concocted the antidote to it in the form of a government intended to achieve not only the equality of citizens but also the uniting of hearts. Efforts to get rid of bourgeois individualism, that old French obsession on both right and left, were invested instead in the fraternal Republic of the future. For Louis Blanc the aim of the class struggle was not that the proletariat should crush the bourgeois, but to rally the bourgeois to the superior principle of the fraternity which inspired proletarian action. But for the non-socialist republicans, class struggle was not necessary for the final triumph of brotherly reconciliation: for French society was split only by artificial divisions invented by monarchies to ensure their reigns. By handing power to the citizens, the Republic was restoring to France its nature, the truth about itself and the togetherness of a community.

Michelet, who could well represent the pure republican, made such a cult of civic fraternity that he read into the 1789 Rights of Man not a charter of individualism, as both the bourgeois and socialist interpretation would have it, but the promise of the uniting of citizens, soon to be embodied in the Festival of the Federation (14 July 1790), that most sublime of moments. Freed on the right from the selfishness of individuals, and on the left from the terrorist heritage, Michelet's Republic, as the Revolution had sketched it out without being able to achieve it, gave the historic destiny of France its most beautiful aspect. It foretold what the founders of the Third Republic would later call *laïcité*. That whole collection of ideas which are so specifically French that they have no equivalent in any other culture, harked back to values which were considered incompatible in the liberal tradition and in its socialist criticism, and yet were celebrated together: a cult of civic equality after the fashion of antiquity, joined with a modern love of liberty. Before the educational system became the battleground – although it was already the standard-bearer – Michelet had been the prophet of this almost religious citizenship and this union of hearts in the city, which he identified with France.

Thus, on 24 February 1848 the republicans instituted the Republic of fraternity. It was an ambiguity not destined to last.

THE NEW REPUBLIC

In the evening of the victory, 24 February, the provisional government formed at the Hôtel de Ville, hastily rallied by the republican deputies after the mob invaded the Chamber of Deputies, was the product of a compromise between the men of *Le National* and those of *La Réforme*, in which the former obtained the lion's share. They were the only vestiges of the vanished legality, the bridge between the Assembly which had been elected the preceding summer and the Republic proclaimed by the people of Paris, and must nevertheless offer the country some reference points, and put forward some names. The tiny extreme left of the former Chamber therefore provided the skeleton of the new government, and those republican bourgeois, with the addition of old Dupont de l'Eure, a survivor from the heroic times, were suddenly looked on as moderates by comparison with the men of the secret societies and the uprising. Etienne Garnier-Pagès, Adolphe Crémieux, Marie and Arago were notables who had 'arrived', nurtured on liberal and democratic culture, but with no liking for the situation into which they had been plunged; they would gladly have waited a little longer for this Republic. Ledru-Rollin felt it even more; he was a public orator, with a richer and more gifted nature, but easily drawn to excess and without true political or tactical substance.

The man most in evidence was Lamartine, who had come from legitimism but was naturalized a revolutionary by *L'Histoire des Girondins*. At fifty-eight, he believed the hour had at last come which he had constantly planned for in secret, because for years he had imagined himself chosen by God for a great political destiny, unrecognized by the bourgeois monarchy. In the course of this new Revolution, where Ledru-Rollin already saw himself as the Danton, he would be just the man who had been lacking in the first one: near enough to the revolutionary fire to draw strength from it, and far enough away from it not to get burnt – Mirabeau's old idea.

To this group of well-known deputies the Hôtel de Ville insurgents had added four men who were closer to them and had more or less appointed themselves as members of the government (though hardly more than the preceding ones). After the barristers and literary men came the contingent of journalists and agitators inevitably attached to every revolution: Marrast, editor of *Le National*; Flocon, editor of *La Réforme*; Albert, the only working-class man, a militant of the secret societies; and above all, Louis Blanc, the publicist, historian of the Revolution and theorist of the organization of labour, who brought the socialist concept to the temporary government. For that reason, he was the most important man in this second group. Very short, but all the more anxious to be heard, in any case brilliant in his slightly sententious manner, convinced that he personified a principle and a social class, he would form a focus of opinion. But his colleagues in the government were in no hurry to give him a ministry. While, under the presidency of Dupont de l'Eure, Lamartine undertook Foreign Affairs and Ledru-Rollin the Interior, and portfolios were distributed to other sterling republicans, neither Flocon, nor Albert nor Louis Blanc – the three 'radicals' – obtained any precise appointment. Another oddity of the time, and very characteristic: nobody wanted Finance, which was first of all entrusted to Goudchaux, a Jewish banker and an old faithful of *Le National*, and then to Garnier-Pagès, who was a commercial broker.

For the moment, this government had only the power which the streets allowed it. How can the streets be described? If we read *L'Education sentimentale* again, we see that Paris had passed in a day, in a night, from the ban on the right of meeting and association to absolute liberty; it had entered a kind of collective unrest, let loose by the victory of 24 February, which would last for several months. Everything which had made yesterday's political society had vanished in a trice: the king, the 'château', parliamentary life, the salons and even the questions so passionately stirred up by that world which had been sovereign yesterday, were as if they had never existed. One event had replaced everything, known to everybody because it had already taken place, and one which everybody re-enacted, because the scenario had been distributed beforehand: the French Revolution.

At the bottom of society, meetings, clubs, petitions and delegations – they all began again as people had learned from their forefathers or from propagandists, and as they had read in books or newspapers. At the top end, the force of the storm was already reawakening fear, but it was also spreading a sort of rather servile collusion in the face of the strength of the people, so potent is the French tendency to political sycophancy. As Tocqueville wrote in his *Souvenirs*,

I noticed a universal effort to adapt to the event which chance had sprung on people, and to tame the new master. The great landowners liked to recall that they had always been enemies of the bourgeois class and always in favour of the popular class; the priests had rediscovered the dogma of equality in the Gospels and vowed they had always done so; the bourgeois themselves remembered with a certain pride that their fathers had been working men and, when they were unable, because of the inevitable obscurity of family trees, to go back as far as a worker, properly speaking, who had actually laboured with his hands, they at least tried to trace their ancestry to some lout who had made his fortune by his own efforts.[2]

In fact, Paris in February 1848 had no need of this enforced rallying in order to be fraternal. Arising from the 'massacre' on the boulevard des Capucines, the revolution itself had spilt no blood. Victorious because of the National Guard's support, it had no cause for complaint against the Parisian bourgeoisie; for their part, neither the nobility nor the clergy had ever enjoyed a deep solidarity with the fallen regime. 'Fraternity', which was in tune with the mood of the time, thus met circumstances which were very temporarily favourable and one of the causes of the general rallying. The mob had pillaged the Tuileries and the Palais Royal, the Orléans properties as well as the Rothschild mansion at Suresnes, the symbol of the rule of money. But there was very little violence against individual people, and, in marked difference from July 1830, the Church and religion were respected, sometimes even fêted as allies.

There is no better demonstration of the resonance of ideas among the nineteenth-century urban populace, and consequently the extreme sensitivity of French politics to literature, than this contrast between the two revolutions, with only eighteen years separating them. July 1830 had been accompanied and followed by the destruction of crosses, the breaking of sacred objects, looting and the enforced closure of places of worship; but it had still been the *ancien régime* which was being attacked through the Church. February 1848 put an end to the government of a political oligarchy accused of a Voltairean outlook, in the name of a fraternal equality which many 'popular' authors had recently declared to be also the spirit of the Gospels. That Christian religion, which the French manipulated according to their political sentiments, and which the ultras had wanted to attach to their heritage, was now also a part of the revolutionary panoply and imparted a sort of traditional air even to the revolution: men like Lamartine and Lamennais, who had loved both, had no need to go back on what they believed in order to invoke the 'people' with the enthusiasm they had put into celebrating the old monarchy, or to serve February 1848 with the ardour they had applied to cursing 1789. Concealed in the parody of the French Revolution lay the newest element of the situation: the religion of fraternity eased the task of the government, but it defined only a rejection – of liberal individualism. July 1830 had tried to re-enact 1789; February 1848 wanted to resume 1792.

The deep kinship of the 1848 revolution with the French Revolution, which made it an event belonging to the same family, lay not so much in the one imitating the other; mainly, it was enveloped in the same spirit, which Marx defined in the books written in his youth as 'the illusion of politics'. The men of 1789 had believed that rebuilding the state on the will of the people would be the key to social happiness; the Jacobinism of

[2] A. de Tocqueville, *Souvenirs*, part II, vol. 2.

1793 had represented the apogee of this political voluntarism, since the revolutionary dictatorship had believed itself capable of transforming the whole of civil society by its action, and of re-creating virtuous citizens out of individuals motivated by selfishness. That political overemphasis, which had been characteristic of all French public life since 1789, had its finest flowering in February 1848. Meanwhile the socialist idea had been working on the contradiction, which was inseparable from the proclamation of the Rights of Man, between the promised equality and the actual inequality; and on the left it had reinforced the fight for a republic of true equality. The Robespierrist myth of the dictatorship of virtue had been replaced by the belief in republican fraternity, in which Marx repeatedly and sarcastically denounced the French illustion that the state produces society, whereas it is the opposite which is true. On the morrow, the right's fierce campaign for property-ownership would draw on the same illusion, though in the opposite direction.

Like those of the great epoch, the crowds at the end of the winter of 1848 were manipulated by the ringleaders of the clubs and secret societies, to the accompaniment of much revolutionary overstatement: there is no French-style revolution which does not produce *ad infinitum* the fear of expropriation. In this one there was no lack of appeals for vigilance and violence, fed by the latent resistance of the ruling classes, which the revolutionaries stoked in their turn.

They had their professionals, who had been prepared by long practice in clandestine activities in the numerous neo-Babouvist conspiracies of the July monarchy, so frequently infiltrated by the police. Having just emerged from prison – they had been sentenced to death, the penalty commuted to life imprisonment, following the failed insurrection of 12 May 1839 – Barbès and Blanqui were the Marat and Hébert of February 1848, new representatives of the half-educated bourgeois plebeians among whom Jacobin and post-Jacobin fanaticism so often sought its recruits. They hated each other, and Barbès accused Blanqui of having been an informer in the service of Louis-Philippe's police. Each in his own style – Barbès as a gentleman at the service of the poor and Blanqui as a ragged Robespierre ('a coldly furious man', said Hugo) – both were working on the same public and using the same repertoire of lazy demagogy mingled with the energy of the faithful believer. With them and several others in mind, Hugo noted in his journal in March: 'I prefer 1793 to 1848. I prefer to see Titans wallowing in chaos rather than simpletons in a mess.'

Nevertheless, the call for the guillotine was not echoed; on the contrary, the Republic exorcized the spectre of the Terror by abolishing the death penalty for political matters. But the other theme being handled by the neo-Babouvist demagogues – equality – encountered the socialist concept, which, as has been seen, had made rapid progress among the workers in Paris for ten years, through many interpreters and doctrines. The plan to control the economy by the state, which had about it whiffs of the *ancien régime* at the end of the eighteenth century, was transformed into a vision of the future; moreover, there was a certain urgency about it because of the economic crisis and the large numbers of unemployed. Since it also leaned on the division of society by giving workers the class struggle as the banner of their dignity, it offered the French Revolution a real extension, though conflicting in its very principle with fraternity.

What a lot of effort, and words and debates there were during the months of March and April, in an attempt to resolve the 'social question', to reconcile the 'smock' with the 'frock-coat', to find the philosopher's stone, to devise collective happiness! They would not overcome the idea of class struggle, from which the bourgeoisie of 1830 had already drawn its rights to insurrection, and in which the 'proletariat' found its rights of succession.

Directly after 24 February the latter were knocking at the government's doors, led by the socialist editors of *La Démocratie pacifique*, to demand a guaranteed 'right to work' and a system of sickness and old-age insurance. This was an extraordinary novelty for the time, as out of keeping with republican bourgeois conceptions as with the structures and formulae of the state. But the government had been born the day before, from the rebellion of those men, and the crowds were waiting, in the Place de l'Hôtel de Ville. Louis Blanc, who had only a minor role in the government, saw his opportunity and drew up the famous decree of 25 February: 'The provisional government of the French Republic undertakes to guarantee work for all citizens. It recognizes that workers must form associations among themselves in order to enjoy the legitimate profits of their labour.' Three days later, on 28 February, there was a fresh demonstration by workers demanding a Ministry of Labour (or of Progress) to get state aid going.

Louis Blanc did not obtain a Ministry – his colleagues did not want it – but a government commission for workers, composed of delegates of the various trade bodies and presided over by himself, assisted by Albert. Formed the next day (which shows that it was all ready), this assembly without power had the honour of sitting at the Luxembourg, in the ex-Chamber of Peers. Louis Blanc was enthroned in the high, green velvet chair of Chancellor Pasquier. Artisans and journeymen were seated around him in the armchairs of Louis-Philippe's great dignitaries, to debate working men's conditions and the best forms for workers' associations. The touching aspect of the idea by no means removed its Machiavellian facet: the socialism which was being debated – or defined – within the precinct of the monarchy's High Assembly was a snare in which Louis Blanc trapped himself, without any power except to hoist a scarecrow to the four winds for the edification of property-owners.

In fact, the February revolution rapidly crystallized a feeling or a spreading will to react against the exaggerations of the Parisian extreme left groups, and chiefly against the socialist idea: feeling, or will, which were not solely bourgeois, but also broadly popular, in a country where small property-ownership was widespread. The July regime had found no more defenders in the provinces than in Paris, and the advent of the Republic, which was made known fairly rapidly thanks to the optic telegraph, had aroused only sporadic outbursts of unrest in the country. Commissioners of the Republic, sent from Paris to replace the prefects, were enjoined to give the Republic an aspect of peace and fraternity. But many elements were working in the opposite direction, and came to light in the weeks following February.

Memories, the black legend of the Terror, first of all, were revived both by rumours of social threats and the demagogic predictions of Parisian agitators. The fear of social breakdown, which had always lain just under the surface of opinion since the Revolution, was strengthened by the suspicion of incompetence which hung over this brand-new government, composed of men who had never exercised power, with no firm hold on an administration they had not appointed: the prefects of the preceding regime were at least in agreement on that score with the faithful of the last-but-one monarchy.

To the political risks already contained in the idea of a republic, a note of general subversion of the social order was finally added: the threat to private property, which was inseparable from socialism. In a country where peasant ownership went back a very long way and had been spectacularly increased by the 1789 Revolution at the expense of the Church and noble émigrés, there was certainly no need for a great propaganda effort to weld together the entire bourgeoisie, large and small, and the innumerable masses of the peasantry, against a Paris in the hands of demagogues.

The February government was aware of it, and acted more astutely than its conservative adversaries gave it credit for. Lamartine was no newcomer to politics, and his weakness lay rather in his ideas than in his know-how. He was not really sure what kind of France he wanted to lead, but he detested Orleanism and socialism alike. Between February and May, he was the most constant defender of the democratic Republic in the face of Parisian unrest; he was more energetic and more experienced than Ledru-Rollin, his great rival in popularity. He had saved the tricolour in the face of the red flag demanded by Blanqui. He saw to the reconstitution of the forces of order serving the government, to give a balance to the 'Montagnard' militia initiated by Caussidière, a makeshift and improbable Prefect of Police, the veteran of secret societies and conspiracies, who brought his former world to his new office. To the National Guard, which was still shaken by its passage through the uprising, the government added twenty-four new battalions of Mobile Guards who, unlike the citizens' militia, would be paid, and well paid – 1.50 francs per day, more than the soldiery: there were enough unemployed for this new troop to be recruited rapidly and to form the surest support for the February Republic.

It was precisely to the unemployed – several tens of thousands of men in Paris – that the Republic guaranteed the right to work. It was now or never for Louis Blanc and his assembly in the Luxembourg to put forward the idea of association: all the workers had to do was take over communally the workshops which had been closed following the crisis, to make them not only productive again, but also better than the private sector. But the government was unwilling to undermine the right of property-ownership. It charged the Minister of Public Works, the barrister Marie, a socially conservative republican, with the task of organizing 'National Workshops', replacing the 'social workshops' of Louis Blanc, with the state alone engaging the workers.

In March and April, these workshops enrolled the unemployed, who were all the more numerous because they earned 2 francs per working day, with a minimum of 1.50 francs guaranteed: by mid-March, the numbers reached 20,000, swelled by the inevitable 'fiddlers' who always accompany this kind of operation. What work could be given to this army of toilers, who were increasingly joined by many craftsmen whose employers were paying them lower rates?

All the economic power remained in the hands of the wealthy of all degrees. The bourgeois had not emigrated like the nobility of the *ancien régime*. Here and there they might well give their approbation to republican rhetoric or to such and such a philanthropic project, but they still demanded payment of rents, and were no less unwilling to invest, removing their money from the banks in order to hide it away: plummeting prices on the Bourse were a better indicator than public life of the depths of their political feelings.

Goudchaux was an orthodox banker, who would not dream of going against the advice and interests of the experts in an attempt to solve the cash crisis. He had to get a decree passed stating that the Banque de France was not obliged to exchange its notes against gold, but he successfully combated their depreciation: the price of foodstuffs was low, thanks to abundant harvests, and the demand for capital was weak as a result of the business crisis. The state would set the example – politically costly – of financial stringency by increasing direct taxation by 50 per cent: the famous additional tax of 45 centimes per franc. The ghost of the assignat and compulsory requisitioning explained to a large extent the moderation of the February men.

But everything was put off till the morrow. The Republic had done nothing yet by making a solemn decree of all that comprised its very substance: the imprescriptible liberty of citizens and the abolition of slavery overseas (which had been virtually obtained under the July regime); it now had to accomplish the most difficult feat, to receive a constitution through the votes of the people. It was in that curious situation – rare, yet relatively fortunate, all in all – of having been born of a Parisian uprising, of ensuring liberty and of being unchallenged: accepted at least as an absence of monarchy brought about through force of circumstance. The provisional dictatorship filling this void quite rightly had everything to fear from asking the people for a less vague definition, so enormous was the foreseeable gap between that negative consent and the exaltation of the 'social

Republic' by the small Parisian clubs: the elections flung the arena of class struggle wide open, and offered the conservative parties the opportunity of revenge for February.

However, for the moment there was no hesitation: on 4 March universal suffrage had been established, which swelled the electorate from 250,000 to over 9,000,000. This gigantic, premature political transformation was nevertheless inevitable, following 24 February, and was also irreversible. The French Revolution had not dared so much, since the Constituent Assembly had kept passive citizens and the Convention had instituted universal suffrage only under the tight monopoly of its supporters. The Republic was loyal to democracy, its principle: everyone had become a voter and eligible. The list system was to liberate the elected representatives from the tyranny of local notables. The gates remained firmly closed to women, however, so strong was the common conviction that they belonged to the natural universe of the family, and not to the abstract humanity of the *res publica*.

Nevertheless the approach of elections aroused in Paris the opposition of revolutionary militants and the fears of republicans. George Sand, who was the Egeria of the new Republic, and whom Ledru-Rollin had incautiously asked to compile the unofficial *Bulletin de la République*, wrote in issue no. 16 in March:

If the elections do not bring about the triumph of social truth, if they are the expression of the interests of a caste, snatched from the trustful loyalty of the people, there is no doubt that these elections – which should be the Republic's safeguard – will prove to be its downfall. There would then be but one way to safety for the people, who built the barricades: that would be to demonstrate their will a second time and to postpone decisions of a false national representation. Will France force Paris to resort to such an extreme and deplorable remedy?

That piece of advice was put into practice preventively by the militant revolutionaries who contested the very principle of the election: but a *journée* organized to this end by Blanqui obtained only a short postponement of the elections from 9 to 23 April, Easter Sunday. There was a similar failure on 16 April: National and Mobile Guards put down a new attempt. As for the republicans, they were as divided as the provisional government: Louis Blanc had a leaning towards Blanqui's side, but without wishing to favour him, whereas Lamartine, in the majority, wanted to abide by his undertakings in regard to the country. As he often did, Ledru-Rollin sat on the fence between the two camps. As Minister of the Interior, he finally resumed the practices of his predecessors, trying to 'arrange' the ballot in favour of the republicans with the help of his Commissioners of the Republic; on 8 April, in a circular which has remained famous, he invited them to encourage the election of those he termed 'the republicans of the day before', as opposed to those of the morrow. As Minister of Public Education, Hippolyte Carnot exhorted schoolmasters to follow the same path.

In those early days of spring, almost all France was busy planting trees of liberty, with *curés* and municipal councillors well to the fore. The country lagged behind Paris, where battle raged between clubs and intellectuals, supporters and splinter groups. And it was France that would take decisive action.

THE ELECTIONS AND THE JUNE DAYS

On Easter Day, therefore, the elections took place. The populace had been summoned to the major towns in each district, and had to choose from departmental lists, with the full possibility of electing candidates from different parties. The people often went in procession, walking from the commune to the township, while the women and children stayed at home. Tocqueville recounts how he took his place in the long column going from his village to the Valognes voting station 'in alphabetical order': 'I wanted to walk in the row which my name allotted to me, for I knew that in democratic countries and times one must get oneself put at the head of the people, and not place oneself there.'[3]

At the other end of France, in Haute-Garonne where, like Tocqueville, Rémusat had a château and his July *censitaire* electorate, the area was more disturbed than in the Cotentin. In this *département*, which had belonged to Villèle, little towns like Muret were won over by the February spirit and spread their influence over the countryside round about: 'Our rural communes, while remaining peaceable, were not however completely untouched by the general movement. Without any preparation for, or understanding of, the event which had just occurred, the peasants knew very well that it was of concern to the poor, that they were going to count for something and that their condition was going to be changed.'[4] But there, too, the communes walked in groups to the voting places, behind the mayor and the *curé*.

Can one deduce a local consistency of voting from these collective trips? Tocqueville, who had not had to complain about the votes of his Norman fellow citizens, suggests it may have been so, and in his case he was probably right, since universal suffrage gave a new lease of life to the old domination of the château. But there is a great deal of other evidence to confirm Rémusat's view; it describes how the republican spirit had penetrated the small towns, by way of the schoolmaster or the doctor, and what a struggle there was with the château or the presbytery to influence the rural vote. The polling station had no booths or envelopes, and many of the new citizens were still unable to read the candidates' names, par-

---

[3] Tocqueville, *Souvenirs*, part II, vol. 4.
[4] Rémusat, *Mémoires*, vol. 4, p. 283.

ticularly in the west and south-west of the country, from Brittany to Aquitaine. These were some of the elements which threw the way wide open to intrigue and manipulation, and today still make the first democratic ballot in French history an event which is not fully known.

Be that as it may, that Easter Sunday was a great festival of liberty. There was almost a total vote, and from this very French spate of novelties emerged a national representation which was fairly close to Rémusat's forecast, two months after the revolution, with no surprises in the end: a majority of deputies in tune with the dominant sentiments of the provisional government. In imitation of the Convention and to offer more places open to competition, the electoral law had allowed for 900 deputies; along the entire length of the Palais Bourbon courtyard an enormous wooden building had been improvised. Its 'extraordinary ugliness' shocked Victor Hugo, who thought it resembled a monstrously enlarged small-town theatre. The deputies had to sit on benches more suitable to a public dance hall, with decorations better fitted to a café. But after all, the original Constituent Assembly of 1789 had never had a proper hall.

Out of 900 members, the new Assembly numbered around 500 of the Lamartine or Arago shade of political opinion, supporting a republic and universal suffrage, but hostile alike to social revolution and monarchic reaction. The vote was a triumph for Lamartine, who was elected in ten *départements* with more than a million and a half votes. Having come to power through a history book, the poet-Academician this time received the laurel crown from the people themselves, who had become temporarily Girondin. The big losers were the supporters of a social republic; all the same, about 150 were elected, though all the leaders were defeated – Blanqui, Etienne Cabet, François Raspail. Louis Blanc had only just scraped through, and Ledru-Rollin emerged the weaker from the ballot.

On the right, 250 'republicans of the morrow' completed the national representation: the majority were former legitimists who certainly preferred a conservative republic to the Orléans usurpation. The Catholic Church had also seen to it that its own men were elected, with Montalembert and Frédéric Falloux in the forefront. Of the July political personnel, some members of the opposition of that time had survived, such as Odilon Barrot and Rémusat, but Thiers had been beaten. Indeed, as usual, the change of regime, with the addition this time of an increase in the number of representatives, had brought in a huge wave of new men: filled with barristers, doctors and journalists, this Constituent Assembly was less homogeneous than the Chambers of the two monarchies, and its French was less pure; but through it, the Republic discovered its first democratic expression, and a national legitimacy.

Despite the massive vote of a citizen-people, this legitimacy was tenuous. For it met head-on the contempt of French revolutionary tradition for the law and regular institutions, as this had received a fresh boost from the events of 24 February and had since been feeding on wild exaggerations on the social question. The French idea of the Revolution was characterized by its formidable investment in politics: by its belief in the capacity of the new state to change society. The events of the end of the eighteenth century had certainly created a new state, given responsibility for public happiness, even making that its own ambition, during the Jacobin episode; but the Thermidorian Republic had put an end to that without in any way extinguishing the passions which had given it life. For its part, the February revolution had changed nothing about the state save its form; but it had inherited one hundredfold the hopes which were inseparable from the revolutionary idea.

The democratic promise of equality had in fact been stirring society for more than half a century, from the dual aspect of memories and predictions. It had managed to transform what in 1793 had been the passion of the sansculottes for a just economic order into a historical messianism to the benefit of the workers. By this time it was getting old, and 'warping', as one says of a piece of carpentry, in the fragmented world of individuals produced by 1789: getting what good it could, against that world, from both the past and the future. Because of this, the *exagérés* of spring 1848 caused the appearance of a new type of revolutionary extremism, intellectually more structured than in 1793. They found an unprecedented resistance in their way for the same reasons: in the half-century which separated them from the Revolution, the wealthy too – unable to reach accord over the past and royalty – had nevertheless calculated the perils of equality. February 1848 had wanted to avert social division through fraternity, but the notion of class was really at the heart of what followed it, like the truth hidden within an illusion.

The Assembly had again proclaimed the Republic, but lacked powers over the political and social crisis, which was getting worse. It had brought back the men of the provisional government, with the exception of Louis Blanc and Albert, in the form of an Executive Commission of five members (Arago, Garnier-Pagès, Marie, Lamartine and – just – Ledru-Rollin), the others being returned as ministers. But Paris was worried and becoming restless about the arbitrary power of universal suffrage. The National Workshops, which had comprised 28,000 enrolled men at the end of March, numbered more than 100,100 at the end of April. The inflation in numbers was due to the influx of jobless arriving from the *départements*, which turned Paris into a capital of the wretchedly poor; as can be imagined, this gave rise to thousands of hostile rumours about the army of men who were paid to do nothing, wasting tax money and, moreover, threatening property-ownership with their subversive ideas. This new spectacle of unemployment clumsily subsidized by the state radicalized the political situation. To the manual workers in Paris it gave a guarantee which could not be long maintained, thus exposing the Republic to a dramatic repudiation of the hopes of those who had brought it into being. To the rest of the country, it offered material for a universal and popular theme against Paris: this was 1789 in reverse, property-owners on the side of the counter-revolution.

The contest was unequal and, even in Paris, opinion had crystallized into hostility to the revolutionary agitation of the clubs, as was shown by the attitude of the National Guard on 16 April. The elections had strengthened this current, which the new *journée* of 15 May was intended to halt, but on the contrary accelerated. On that day, a huge popular demonstration organized in support of Poland degenerated into an invasion of the Assembly, in the tradition of 2 June 1793 and 24 February; at least one part of the National Guard seems to have followed the policy of painting things as black as possible. In the Chamber, invaded by an anarchic mob, Buchez, who was presiding, was soon driven from his chair; a few 'Montagnards', Barbès, Albert, who were deputies, joined with the inevitable Blanqui in the great scene of intimidation of the elected members. Aloysius Huber, another Parisian ringleader, declared the Assembly dissolved. But after two hours, National and Mobile Guards who had finally arrived, cleared the hall, which had been abandoned by the deputies and where a new provisional government was in gestation. It was a failure, followed by the beginnings of repression: Albert, Barbès, Blanqui, Raspail and Huber were arrested, at the same time as the chief of the National Guard.

The final test of strength was delayed for a month. Almost inherent in the situation, it was set off by an administrative measure taken on 21 June and intended to deplete the numbers of employees in the National Workshops: this invited young workers between the ages of eighteen and twenty-five to join teams which were being formed to go and work in the provinces, where their presence was more necessary than in Paris; they were also offered the chance of enlisting in the army, on top of the places filled by the regular annual intake. This measure was preparatory to the winding-up of the National Workshops (which was announced several days later, on 28 June) and it lit the powder keg when it was posted up on the evening of the 21st and published in the government newspaper, the *Moniteur*, the next day. The two camps were ready to do battle.

As French civil wars always have their literary side, there is no better indicator of states of mind on the eve of the insurrection than a conversation at table between George Sand and Tocqueville, recorded by the latter in his *Souvenirs*:

Madame Sand gave me a detailed and singularly lively picture of the state of the workers in Paris, their organization, numbers, arms, preparations, thoughts, feelings and their terrifying determination. I thought the picture exaggerated, but it was not; what followed proved it. She seemed to me to be pretty frightened herself of a people's triumph and to evince a rather solemn pity for the fate which awaited us. 'Try to persuade your friends, Monsieur', she said to me, 'not to provoke the common people by worrying or annoying them, as I would like to be able to encourage mine to have patience; for if battle is joined, you may be sure you will all perish.'[5]

---

[5] Tocqueville, *Souvenirs*.

This was an inaccurate prediction, but one which was shared by most contemporaries, so close to the victorious February uprising and at a time when the Republic was still virtually without an army. It at least recognized the merciless nature of the street fighting which broke out on 23 June in the east of Paris, bristling with barricades, and which would end on the morning of the 26th with the capitulation of the faubourg Saint-Antoine, the last refuge of the insurgents, and the round-up of several thousands of prisoners destined to be deported to Algeria. Meanwhile the Executive Commission had handed over to the Minister of War, General Cavaignac, who was given plenary powers. It was the end of Lamartine's political career as he was overwhelmed by a violence he had been striving to avert since February.

The outcome of this short civil war is easier to understand than its ferocity. The determining factor was, as usual in the France of that era, the attitude of the National Guard, who marched as one man against the uprising, whereas in February they had joined it; moreover they were backed by the young Mobile Guards, so recently recruited, who also fought without scruple. One new feature was that thousands of men came from the provinces to fight alongside them. The military situation reflected the inequality of the political forces present. On the side of the rebels, there was no well-known leader, no national point of reference and no other aim save the overthrow of the regime: the men of the clubs had been imprisoned on 15 May; the remainder of the extreme left in the Assembly wavered, like Louis Blanc, or supported Cavaignac, like Flocon. On the other hand, against the insurrection, nearly all the Constituent Assembly formed a solid block, reflecting the feeling of the country. However, this inequality was not perceived until later, at the same time as the military successes of the forces of order, so full were people's minds of the memories of February: that diagnostic error goes some way to explaining the climate of social panic enveloping those days. France had been caught in the trap of its own spectres of social breakdown.

On both sides, passions ran high. Those of the rioters are more obscure because, unlike those of their opponents, and with good cause, they have not received the direct testimony of so many writings. Their origins lay in poverty and unemployment, and their support came from a renewed revolutionary tradition which February had rejuvenated. As in 1793, the Republic was responsible for the well-being of the poor; if it failed to provide it, the cause was its betrayal from within by the rich classes, the bourgeois, who must be made to yield their ill-gotten gains. Revolutionary fanaticism about equality, which was farther than ever from any idea of law, was by now inseparable from class feeling: the 'smocks', as opposed to the 'frock-coats', had become the sansculottes of 1848.

On the other side, this rebellion born of despair was regarded as a threat against property, and therefore against society itself, a return of barbarism against civilization: a feeling which went well beyond the bourgeoisie, and gathered to it many working-class elements, to say nothing of the peasantry. At the time – which was still in touch with 1789 – property was not, as it is today, the symbol of conservatism alone; its value was fresher, cherished like a conquest, and less exhausted by propaganda. Further-more, the social order placed in jeopardy by the insurgents was not that of royalty, but of the Republic, which through universal suffrage had become the legitimate choice of the whole nation.

If the right defended property-ownership first and foremost, the left defended the Republic likewise. Dressed in National Guard uniform, Edgar Quinet did not lead exactly the same fight against the men of the barricades as Thiers; but this unquestioning supporter of republican liberty already had more in common with the former leader of the Orleanist centre-left than with the new sansculottes. The situation would be repeated nearly a quarter of a century later, during and after the Paris Commune.

If one wishes to penetrate more deeply into contemporary reaction to this major episode in nineteenth-century French history, one can read two of the greatest minds of the time, both of whom provided 'on the spot' commentaries, or almost: Marx and Tocqueville. Indeed, both were struck by the strange kind of parodic resurrection of the French Revolution which marked the events of 1848. Marx, in particular, wrestled with this idea of revolutionary parody which had no place in his theory of history. If, in effect, the February revolution no longer accomplished a necessary historical task, if it was merely a reactionary caricature of the great events it was imitating, what was it all about? The bourgeoisie had been in power since 1789; how had it come about that this power had taken on so many successive aspects?

To that question Marx replies in the spirit of his own system, by increasing the number of class divisions in order to be able to account in terms of social interests for the French political kaleidoscope; he arbitrarily rearranges the internal structure of the bourgeoisie according to the succes-sive data revealed by political life. February 1848 had put the whole of the class into power, whereas July 1830 had benefited only a financial oligarchy; but that class soon found itself facing a new day of reckoning: the proletarian revolution. It had its conciliators, such as Ledru-Rollin, representing the 'Montagnard' petite bourgeoisie whom Marx especially loathed: but it was soon united in a 'republican' will for repression, embodied by Cavaignac, which represented the reactionary reversal of the tradition of Year II. Such was the underside of events, hidden in the rhetoric of memories. The true political reality of 1848, and the only movement which was not a parody, was June: the working class was knocking on the gates of history to replace the bourgeoisie and emancipate man.

This résumé disregards the richness of many of Marx's detailed analyses; but in reconstructing the intellectual architecture of 'class struggle' in France, it is perhaps interesting in that it shows how Marx's genius shared

Rue st Antoine during the June days of 1848 (barricade).
(Photo: Photographie Bulloz)

something of the mythology of the era at the same time that it was helping
to erect it. For the June rioters did not form a 'working class' in the
modern sense of the word. A recent study[6] has shown that they belonged
very precisely to the same circles as the young Mobile Guards of the
repression (who for Marx represented the lumpenproletariat): craftsmen,
labourers, journeymen and the unemployed – a world of traditional manual
workers much more than only industrial workers. But Marx saw them as
the class of the future; seeking out the social truth behind the political
illusion, he over-attributed to the June confrontation significances which
were opposite but complementary to those of the well-off; and he gave
the backing of 'science' to the divorce between the rebel workers and
republican democracy, which was reduced to class dictatorship.

As regards 1848, Tocqueville is less complicated than Marx, not only
because he was one of the actors in the play, but also because his intellectual system contained nothing to prevent him from giving its full
amplitude to the concept of the revolutionary phenomenon's long survival
in France. It is true that, like Marx, he had for a short while believed in
the everlastingness of the July regime; but the February revolution had
revealed evidence of the resurgence of the subterranean torrent, which was
immediately recognized: 'Here is the French Revolution beginning once
again, for it is still the same.'[7]

However, through this similarity to itself, the Revolution put forward
an unprecedented idea in 1848: the socialist concept, that threat against
property which 1789 had, by contrast, released, honoured and multiplied.
Socialism, the 'essential nature' of the February revolution, could be
considered as the product of the working of equality in the social body: a
passion consubstantial with democracy, particularly alive and profound in
the French case, which ended by splitting society into two antagonistic
classes. But at the same time, the events of 1848 revealed something
absolutely new, in comparison with 1789 and even 1793; their aim was not
to 'change the form of government but to alter the order of society'. They
targeted property, and no longer political institutions. For Tocqueville, the
June barricades spelled the truth of February, while for Marx they were
the revelation of February's falsehood: thence arose the discredit into
which, for both authors, the republicans of the provisional government
fell, as they literally did not know what they were doing.

But the deputy from Valognes was in the opposing camp to the communist in London. He was on the side of the property-owners, whom he
described as united by a 'universal terror', creating a feeling of 'fraternity'
almost everywhere, and above all in the rural areas, from the owner of the
tiniest plot to the lord of the manor. 'As the French Revolution had spread
the possession of land *ad infinitum*, the entire population seemed to be part

---

[6] Mark Traugott, *Armies of the poor. Determinants of Working-Class Participation in the
Parisian Insurrection of June 1848.*

[7] Tocqueville, *Souvenirs*, part II, vol. 1.

of this vast family. I had never seen anything comparable, and no one had seen its like in France within living memory.'[8]

In this family, he himself encountered plenty of people whom he disapproved of or disliked, Thiers on the one hand and Lamartine on the other; and the reader's surprise stems from how enthusiastically he found himself united with men and ideas he had once fought. Certainly, that brotherhood of property-owners offered him a strong civic bond – he always feared lest the democratic state should be abandoned by its associates; but the bond was one of fear, resulting from threat; and as it was connected precisely with what made democratic individuals indifferent to the public good and wholly concerned with their private interests, it was destined to die a swift death.

But the Tocqueville of the *Souvenirs* was less attentive to that aspect of affairs than anxious to depict for posterity the spirit of the epoch, which combined that panic terror and the keen feeling of class confrontation between property-holders and 'workers'. To describe the opposing camp, even he uses words of bourgeois cruelty surprising in a man who had understood so early and so strongly the irreversible influence of the feeling of equality: the risks it contained, but also the moral nobility which was inseparable from it, since it constituted the universality of men. The *Souvenirs* thus allow us to measure the effect on their author of the violence of the political and social passions aroused by the June revolt.

The smashing of the barricades gave the republican vessel's helm a nudge to the right, marginalizing the extreme left and reinstating the old left of July 1830 in public life. The government was now in the hands of General Cavaignac, the son of a Conventionnel, the brother of a great leader of the republican opposition under Louis-Philippe, a convinced republican, patriotic and loyal to the Assembly, but a republican of *Le National*, a stranger to the social question. He had the support of the Assembly's right wing, where Thiers soon appeared, having won his cause by appeal to the electorate in a by-election.

The National Workshops were closed. As a last symbol, the Assembly gave Odilon Barrot the task of presiding over a commission of inquiry into the June 'days', offering the former chief of the dynastic left his revenge for 24 February: Louis Blanc preferred to go into exile in London before the conclusion was reached. Lamartine eclipsed, Blanqui in prison, Louis Blanc in exile, Thiers rebuilding his influence: the April vote, unwisely defied by the 'smocks' of Paris and worsened by their defeat, had obliterated a large part of February. For the first time since 1789, France was governing Paris.

It is true, there remained the Republic – but it had yet to be defined. The constitutional argument got under way in paradoxical conditions. The right had regained ground in both opinion and the Assembly, but it was republican only by default. At the other end of the political spectrum,

[8] Ibid., part II, vol. 4.

the Republic had just crushed those who had carried it to its baptism in February, the common 'working' people; it had sanctioned a split between socialists and republicans which would have profound consequences for the future. For the present, it had unwillingly contributed to the popularity of a name which had just – on 4 June to be exact – received an overwhelming majority in the by-elections, in Paris, Corsica, the Yonne and Charente-Inférieure: Louis-Napoleon Bonaparte. The workers had voted for him. On a national scale, Bonapartism assumed a social aspect which had been abandoned by the Republic.

The Assembly sitting of 31 July was a fair symbol of the separation and isolation of French socialism. Proudhon mounted the rostrum on that day. He had deliberately kept himself aloof from politics, because for him the solution of the 'social question' lay in popular credit and the organization of workers; moreover, he despised politicians and, above all, socialists. He, too, had been elected on 4 June, in the same batch as Thiers and Louis-Napoleon Bonaparte, and on the day in question he gave his social economy evening-class lecture on free credit to this learned assembly of the people's representatives, who had other things on their mind.

Victor Hugo recounts:

A man of about forty-five made his appearance on the platform; he was fair, with very little hair but abundant side-whiskers. Both his waistcoat and frock-coat were black. He did not speak. He read. He held his hands clenched on the red velvet of the rostrum, his manuscript between them. He had a gravelly, coarse-sounding voice, and his pronunciation was common; and he wore spectacles. The start of his address was listened to anxiously, then the Assembly burst into laughter and murmuring, and finally everyone began chatting. The hall emptied, and the orator concluded, amid lack of attention, the speech which had commenced amid a sort of terror.[9]

Insurrectionist socialism had induced terror; intellectual socialism caused those who were no longer afraid to burst out laughing. It went on its way in an internal exile, building up in advance an autonomous political culture for a working class which was yet to come.

THE CONSTITUTION AND THE PRESIDENCY

The Constitutional Commission given the task of presenting a project to the Assembly had been elected before June. It comprised a small majority of moderate republicans, under the leadership of Louis de Cormenin, its president, who had already drawn up the electoral law, and of Armand Marrast, former owner of *Le National*; but there was also a strong conservative minority, with Odilon Barrot, Thiers, Tocqueville, his friend Beaumont, Dupin, Dufaure. Two disparate 'Montagnards' made up the

[9] V. Hugo, *Choses vues. Le temps présent*, ch. 3.

full complement: Lamennais, who soon resigned, and a follower of Charles Fourier, Victor Considérant, who did not play any outstanding role. Lamennais's resignation deserves particular comment, since it was caused by the commission's refusal to adopt his plan for procedure, which proposed to open the agenda with the question of the powers of the commune.

Tocqueville and Odilon Barrot had backed him, but his proposal had been rejected by a coalition of republicans and conservatives, in which Tocqueville saw yet again evidence of the national consensus on administrative centralization, hidden in the rhetoric of both left and right. In fact, in this respect the Second Republic had no different policy from the preceding regimes, although it had had the idea of creating a School of Administration; but the plan was abandoned in 1849, and in the end it dealt with the problem by a (modest) purge of personnel rather than by changing or reforming structures.

The deliberations of the Constitutional Commission revealed a very strong majority in favour of a single Assembly, that pillar of republican doctrine, which was supported by old Orleanist deputies like Dufaure and Dupin. As for executive power – the traditional stumbling-block for the republicans – the commissioners were in agreement on the American idea of having a president elected every four years by the people: only Marrast, who was after the presidency of the Assembly, held out for election by the Assembly. In his *Souvenirs* Tocqueville tells of his hesitations over the matter; he wrote in the spring of 1851, at a period when he dragged them out as if with regret or remorse; but thoughts of Prince Louis-Napoleon were already present in people's minds in June 1848, since the Bonaparte pretender had been elected on the 4th.

However, Tocqueville and Beaumont backed presidential election by universal suffrage. Like many of their friends, they were receptive to the idea of restoring the state's authority after the revolutionary shake-up of February; faced with an Assembly elected by universal suffrage, the executive power must be enveloped in the same legitimacy, if it were not to become merely a tool. However, a man vested with authority over such a centralized administration could also hold a power that was a danger to liberty. The two friends got the commission to adopt two amendments: the first stipulated that, if an absolute electoral majority were not obtained (i.e. about four and a half million votes), the chief of the executive would be elected by the Assembly; the second declared him not to be re-eligible. Of these two 'safety measures' which were finally retained in the definitive text, the first would prove to be pointless, and the second was the direct origin of the coup of 2 December 1851.

The commission's work had ended just before the June 'days'; before the constitutional debate, the Assembly took care to eliminate the aftermath of the insurrection and to vote for laws once more restricting freedom of association, meetings and the press, in a political atmosphere marked by the growing influence of the conservatives, led by Thiers and Falloux.

The former had begun to weave his web again immediately upon his re-election, his imagination tirelessly at work in parliamentary intrigue. He had passed with ease from his role as leader of the July centre-left to that of the centre-right's *éminence grise* under the Republic, at the cost of modifications to his repertoire which did not basically change it; he rebuilt a popularity and a career for himself in the defence of property and the union of conservatives. At least he no longer had Guizot as a rival. The old anticlerical drew closer to the Church, and the former president of Louis-Philippe's Council of Ministers made contact with the legitimists, who had returned in force in the April elections.

He consulted with Falloux, the deputy for Maine-et-Loire, elected in the last batch of the July Monarchy, and re-elected by universal suffrage; he was loyal to the legitimate dynasty, but was above all a man of the Catholic Church, whose ambassador he was in the political world. He was a social Catholic of conservative hue, substituting organized 'works' of charity for the socialist concept; an influential man, given to intrigue, good at parliamentary manoeuvring, affable and courteous, inflexible in his aims: a 'Jesuit', according to Rémusat, who was little inclined to anticlerical invective. He had played an important role in the campaign against the National Workshops, that 'permanent and organized strike at 170,000 francs per day'. He was one of the augurs of the right-wing deputies, who had acquired the habit of meeting in the rue de Poitiers.

In the Assembly, presided over since July by Armand Marrast, the constitution came under discussion in September. First there was a preamble, which linked up with the 1789 tradition by affirming principles, rights and duties 'prior to and above statutory laws': democracy (by which was meant universal suffrage), liberty, equality, fraternity; among the duties were love of one's country, respect for the bases of society, family, work, property, public order; the text promised free schooling for all, professional training, popular credit and proportional taxation. But as under the French Revolution, this declaration was accompanied by no special guarantee or particular procedure for ensuring its execution. The ways in which these rights could be exercised remained subject to 'conditions which will be fixed by law', that is to say, subject to political power.

The most contested article concerned the 'right to work'; the commission had written this into the plan since it had been one of the great themes of the February mystique and the rallying-flag of June: 'The right to work is that of every man to live by his own labours. Society, by the general and productive means available to it, which will be organized later, is duty-bound to provide work for able-bodied men who have no other way of obtaining it.' There was even, in this first draft, an allusion to the future 'organization' of social work. But the inclusion of the right to work in the Rights of Man guaranteed by the Republic seemed to the majority, after the June days, to be a dangerous concession to socialism. A compromise solution, presented by Mathieu de la Drôme, proposing the 'recognition of the right to work', to distinguish it from the 'guarantee of employment', had similarly been rejected. The Assembly refused to go any farther than the 'fraternal assistance' due to citizens in need: it repudiated February and stayed within the framework of classic economic liberalism inaugurated by the constitution of 1791.

The other great debate had as its topic the methods of electing the president of the Republic: a classic argument, in French politics, between those holding the republican view which recommended an executive power stemming from the legislative, in the name of the indivisibility of sovereignty, as under the Convention, and conservatives who wanted to reinforce the president's authority by giving him the same popular legitimacy as the Assembly. For want of a king, the two monarchist families reached a temporary agreement following the American example; the April vote had reassured them on universal suffrage.

But in the constitutional question everyone was conscious of the specula-tion on personalities: who would stand as a candidate? Who would be elected? The extreme left, in its isolation, hardly had a chance; nor had the republican left, the pieces of which Ledru-Rollin was busy sticking together. But how about the right? Thiers's thoughts certainly turned thither, and his mother-in-law, the indefatigable Madame Dosne, who made a business of his glory, relates too often in her memoirs how much his friends encouraged him for it not to be obvious that her son-in-law entertained high hopes; but while perfect for a property-owning vote, he had no renown among the people, and moreover he had belonged too closely to the monarchy which had fallen in February to hold the Republic's highest office in December. Cavaignac, on the other hand, possessed his republican letters patent, his management of public safety in June, and his role as head of government, which combined in his favour to offer him a possible future as a French Washington.

But Prince Louis-Napoleon, who had stayed in exile in London after his election on 4 June, had just been re-elected at the beginning of September, and took his seat in the Assembly, which refused to avail itself of a law of banishment dating from the time of Louis-Philippe: moreover, two other Bonapartes, elected by Corsica, had been deputies since April. It is true that Louis-Napoleon was a claimant to the succession of his uncle, as he had demonstrated under Louis-Philippe, whence arose the hesitation of a certain number of deputies in the debate on methods of presidential election. Was there not a risk that the people would give a Bonaparte preference over any other candidate? Must this undreamed of chance be offered to this timely deputy, with his rather stupid air, half-simpleton, half-adventurer, more inclined to coups d'état than obedience to the law?

The dispute focused chiefly on the republicans, since the former monarchists passed over the risk in favour of the idea of a strong executive, for fear of an all-powerful Assembly – there was still the obsession with memories and the ghost of the Convention. Among the country's political elites, republican circles were most sensitive to fear of the pretender, because they were the most attached to the form of the regime which had emerged from the February barricades. One of them, Jules Grévy, a moderate republican, but not moderately republican, as the expression goes, acted as their spokesman in the Assembly:

Have you forgotten that it was the elections of Year X which gave Bonaparte the power to raise the throne again and sit upon it? . . . Are you sure that there will never be some ambitious man who will be tempted to perpetuate his line on it? And if that ambitious man is one who has been able to make himself popular; if he is a victorious general surrounded with that prestige of military glory which the French can never resist; if he is the scion of one of those families who have ruled France, and if he has never expressly renounced what he calls his rights, will you reply that this ambitious man will not manage to overthrow the Republic?

Lamartine answered Grévy by saying that no-one could command the votes of the people and that something had to be 'left to Providence'. The article establishing popular election was carried by a huge majority: 627 against 130. The new constitution thus brought face to face two powers elected in the same way, both emodying the sovereignty of the people. The president, when signing a public bill, had to obtain the counter-signature of a minister, but the ministers were under his thumb. There was nothing permitting arbitration of any disagreement between the two powers. In seeking to maintain a balance, the deputies had created all the conditions necessary for a conflict, without planning for any methods of resolving it.

The final vote, on 4 November, was almost unanimous, and opened the electoral campaign for the Presidency, since the ballot was scheduled for 10 December. On the left and extreme left, Ledru-Rollin and Raspail applied, with few illusions as to their chances. Probably Lamartine had more, as his time of glory was so recent. But, in the view of all observers since the start of the autumn, the election would be a duel between Cavaignac and Louis-Napoleon. The former had in his favour his leadership of the government, but he had been its head for too little time to be known to all the French, who were poorly informed and had only recently become voters. In vain did he take a few Orleanists into the ministry, he aroused more than mere reservations among the men of the old regime, being too republican for their taste, once the panic of June was over, and too little amenable to their wishes: that was what he was accused of by Thiers, faithful to his old animosity against the men of *Le National* and feeling, besides, that the general was occupying an office which he himself would have better fulfilled.

The standing of the emperor's nephew went up week by week in public opinion, and the political world was aware of it, for that very reason hastening to offer help where victory was imminent. Molé, a reliable thermometer on the subject, after being firmly decided on Cavaignac's side, at length recalled that he had once served the candidate's uncle. The pretender had friends of longer standing in the party of order, such as

Odilon Barrot, who had been his lawyer in the 1840 trial, and who had no superstitious affection for the republicans of 1848. Thiers, who was stirring things up against Cavaignac, finally rallied to his support and made himself indispensable: since the republican general refused to be his understudy, then this Bonaparte must fill the office. Montalembert and a number of Catholic deputies at last followed suit. The legitimists wavered between the devil and the deep blue sea, but they had not missed the chance of making any mistake since 1815, and most of them made this one – 'the tail of society', wrote Tocqueville, 'dragging along the head'. Even Victor Hugo, who at the time sat on the left of the party of order, fought Cavaignac first and foremost. Between the 'phantom of the Republic and the shade of Napoleon', he plumped for the shade.

Rémusat's memoirs best portray the atmosphere and ambitions of this entire world. One can read in them to what extent recourse to a Bonaparte candidate appeared to the conservative right as a revenge taken against February, and how social fear made that milieu accept the risk of a confiscation of liberties. At its heart lay 'parliamentary idiocy', to quote Marx's expression: those men of the preceding monarchies conceived politics through the narrow prism of groups and assembly intrigues; they had not got the measure of the novelty introduced into the political system by the national nomination of one man. Only a minority of them, following the example of Rémusat, Tocqueville and Falloux, joined the republicans *à la* Grévy in supporting Cavaignac.

Voting was on 10 December; the results were known on the 20th. The country's verdict brooked no appeal, and was surprising in its clarity: Louis-Napoleon, with 5,434,226 votes, wiped out Cavaignac, who had gathered only 1,448,107. Far behind them came the minor candidates, Ledru-Rollin with 370,119 votes, Raspail with 36,920, and poor Lamartine humiliated with a derisory 17,940. The country had voted *en masse*, with 75 per cent of the electorate taking part.

Marx, who was blind to anything unforeseeable or chancy which universal suffrage could introduce into political life, had read into the ballot of 10 December 'the uprising of the peasants', their February, the revenge of the most populous class of society on the working-class Republic, which had threatened property, and on the bourgeois Republic, which had raised taxes. This interpretation in terms of class consciousness is interesting in that it shows the durability of the old rural hostility to the towns which had been at the root of so many *jacqueries*: paradoxically, universal suffrage provided that feeling with a means of triumphing in a France where the Republic evoked so many bad memories in rural districts.

For those peasants owning tiny plots of land, the name of Bonaparte was linked with revolutionary and national tradition; but it was also inseparable from the elimination of the republican shambles and parliamentary nepotism. It guaranteed the property that had been acquired against any return of the lords of the manor, but also against disorder and the socialists of the large towns. And there was one thing that Marx did not add, perhaps because it was too simple or did not come into his system of explanation; namely, that of all the candidates, Louis-Napoleon Bonaparte alone bore a name which was known to every Frenchman, even to the most illiterate. For the first time since 1789, the elections of 23 April had established the will of the people against Parisian dictatorship. The ballot of 10 December marked the entry of the peasantry into the modern political universe by a democratic vote which threatened democracy.

Louis-Napoleon, moreover, had not benefited from rural votes alone. He had taken a very large bite out of the urban lower-class electorate, who were attuned to the Napoleonic legend which he had been able to adapt to suit his own profile, simultaneously 'national' and 'social': the very votes which the June repression had snatched from Cavaignac and the Republic had been transferred to his name rather than to Ledru-Rollin or Raspail. Lastly, the winner of the ballot had gleaned many votes from among all strata of the bourgeoisie, for opposite reasons, because he personified order; but it was also in this sector of opinion that Cavaignac had won the chief number of his votes.

The regional distribution of votes resembled neither that of April nor that of any of the elections which followed. Louis-Napoleon had the majority of voters in all *départements* save four, at opposite ends of the country: Finistère and Morbihan, on the one hand, Bouches-du-Rhône and Var on the other. He received just as overwhelming support in the conservative areas of the west as in the republican ones in the east. The great conquest of the February revolution, universal suffrage, thus transformed the emperor's nephew, the lifelong pretender to the re-establishment of the Empire, into the president of the Republic, chosen by a massive popular vote, and with a majority in nearly every *département*.

LOUIS-NAPOLEON AND THE NEW REGIME

The prince was proclaimed president on 20 December; he took the oath and gave Odilon Barrot the task of forming the ministry. He ensconced himself in the Elysée Palace where, on the next day, he held an initial dinner which smacked somewhat of improvisation. Victor Hugo, who was a guest, relates that the food was poor, the conversation languished, that the president seemed timid and ill at ease, and that everyone left early:

And while I was leaving, I was thinking. I was thinking of this abrupt moving-in; the attempt at etiquette; the mixture of bourgeois, republican and imperial; this surface on something deep, which is today called the president of the Republic; the entourage, the man himself, the whole set-up. It is not one of the least curiosities, or one of the least characteristic facts of the matter, that this should be a man who can be addressed – and *is*, from all sides and simultaneously – as Prince, Highness,

Monsieur, Monseigneur and citizen. Everything that is happening at this moment is randomly leaving its mark on this all-purpose personage.[10]

Indeed, the president was a very mysterious person. Those who were least mistaken about him were the ones caught up in the monomania inspired by his name: his supporters and his adversaries. For he was very precisely the son of the Napoleonic myth. If he was beholden to it for his election, he was also indebted to his uncle for whatever strength lay in his personality, and that was his mystical faith in his destiny as heir to the dynasty. The election of 10 December had crystallized simultaneously the secret passions of the French people and the vague fatalism he carried within him: nothing which might add some clarity to the public life of the nation.

Even his birth did not go unchallenged. He had been born in 1808, the son of Louis, king of Holland, and Hortense de Beauharnais, Josephine's daughter, though his enemies whispered that his mother had had a weakness for Admiral Verhuell and that he was the issue of that liaison. He had spent his youth in adventures and intrigues; having joined the Italian Carbonaria, he had taken part in 1831 in the Romagna uprising, in which his elder brother had perished; as a step towards the reconquest of the French throne, he had nursed the plan of giving the crown of Italy to his cousin the Duke of Reichstadt, the emperor's son.

On the latter's death in the following year, he had himself become the heir, since Napoleon had designated the children of his third brother as his successors, in case of the demise of the direct line. Patronized by Louis-Philippe, he had conspired against him with the republicans; after his expulsion, he had taken refuge with his mother, in a pretty Swiss château on the shores of Lake Constance, dreaming of re-enacting the landing of the Hundred Days and the triumphal march on Paris. From that arose his escapades at Strasbourg in October 1836 and Boulogne in the summer of 1840, which finally brought him to prison. In such time as was left to him by his projects, conspiracies and enterprises, he devoted himself to sport and pleasure, he read and wrote, and was receptive to women and ideas, with little real interest in either apart from their usefulness. He had gathered round him a tiny entourage of devoted supporters, who shared his *idée fixe*, and who were dominated by a former non-commissioned officer, Fialin, who had added 'de Persigny' to his name.

The ideas of this 'chance prince' (Tocqueville) also had a whiff of adventurism about them. Having studied nothing really seriously, he was inclined to let even his reading matter be ruled by his obsession, as if to turn it into a kind of echo of the glory of the Bonapartes. As post-St Helena Bonapartism had tended towards the left, he too was to the left, toying with the sovereignty of peoples and democracy, flirting with

[10] Hugo, *Choses vues*, 24 December 1848.

Armand Carrel and old La Fayette, combining the republican concept with the restoration of the Empire, sharing the revolutionary frustrations which had followed July 1830.

Always alert to the mood of the times, in the 1840s he had added to the family coat of arms the idea of producers' associations, by writing while in prison *L'Extinction du paupérisme*, in a vein which derived from a combination of Saint-Simon, Buchez and Louis Blanc. At that time he had seemed to the bourgeois who were governing France to be a fanciful pedlar of Napoleonic wares. But although he, unlike themselves, had never learnt to argue and write in the classical culture, though he was always ready, as Tocqueville writes in his famous portrait, 'to put an outlandish idea side by side with a good one', he at least had the advantages of eccentricity over them: he spoke several languages, he had an acquaintaince with every kind of milieu (excepting, of course, their own), he was tremendously keen on social politics and he was no respecter of laws; in short, he was driven by one simple idea, which his daydreams embellished without obscuring it. His rather ridiculous *coups* had made people forget that they had taken a man of action beyond the bounds of the law.

As Rémusat, who had put him in gaol in 1840, wrote about him, he was gifted with that exceptional ability to 'put something of himself into human matters': 'Anyone who introduces his imagination into the world's affairs, and produces or modifies events according to his fancy, possesses a certain gift of boldness or strength which elevates him from the crowd and places him on the same level as historical figures.'[11]

Like July 1830, February 1848 had revived the idea of Bonapartism. Louis-Napoleon, struggling along in London after his escape from the Ham prison, had not presented himself at the April elections (in which his cousins had been elected), and had returned to Paris only in September, living in a hotel on borrowed money. In the Assembly, he had appeared intimidated, ill at ease, without any talent. He had known hardly anyone there, two months before becoming the central personality in French politics. That transformation had been the miracle effected by his popularity, combined with the proximity of the presidential election to the advent of universal suffrage. The good parliamentary bourgeoisie thought their power would be assured if they delegated it temporarily to this adventurer who hated parliamentary government and assemblies, using the excuse that he had agreed to muzzle the Parisian clubs and that he seemed to be not overly bright. Now they had to govern with him on the basis of this double supposition.

Molé had envisaged a 'great' ministry, gathering together all the Orleanist grandees of the rue de Poitiers to provide some weight in the face of the new president: Thiers, Barrot, Berryer, Falloux, himself. But neither Thiers nor Berryer was ready for it. At last the moment had come for the former chief of the dynastic left, who had waited for power during

[11] Rémusat, *Mémoires de ma vie*, vol. 4, pp. 359–60.

eighteen years under Louis-Philippe to attain it for only a few hours on 24 February. Here was the Republic, taken back ten months, and with a Bonaparte to boot; Barrot formed an Orleanist ministry, with the original feature of Falloux's presence in Public Education and Religion. Falloux, the ultramontane, the man of the Church and the Vatican, who sealed the union of religion and the liberal right in the name of social order, so soon after the explosion of 'fraternalistic' Catholicism in February. It was a signal which alarmed most of the Assembly, filled with republicans who were linked with the battles led by the University against clericalism: since February, Hippolyte Carnot, the son of the great Lazare Carnot, had been their man in the Ministry of Public Education, inspiring schoolmasters and all the teaching profession in favour of the Republic. Falloux was the bishops' revenge, not only for February, but for Orleanism. To add to everything else, the ministry began to remove the top civil servants who had been in office for ten months, chiefly the prefects.

The situation in the first months of 1849 was thus characterized by a triangular struggle: the parliamentary majority, which had remained republican, where the Cavaignac hue was dominant – the men of *Le National*, Marrast at the head; the party of order, with the ministry under its thumb, and where former Orleanists played the most obvious – and without doubt the most active – role, backed by the Church, which had its own interests, and united with the legitimists, who had another king; lastly, the prince-president, entrenched in the Elysée but already weaving a network with his old henchmen – their numbers swollen by all those who rally round a victor – and hating the Assembly which had voted for Cavaignac, without trusting the Orleanist grandees who wanted to put him under their supervision. With an eye to the future, he demanded from his ministers an amnesty for those sentenced in June, but they refused. Barrot, for his part, did not have a majority in the Assembly, and owed his existence to his appointment by the president, whom he had to handle carefully. The republicans would have liked to prolong the duration of the Constituent Assembly, because they feared that the election of a new Assembly should give a majority to the right. Paris was again in a state of unrest amid – already – rumours of a coup d'état. In the end, it became necessary to take the decision which the Orleanists had desired, because it was part of the logic of the political situation: new elections, which took place on 13 May 1849.

The electoral system had been established by the law of 15 March: as in the preceding year, the features were ballot by list, voting in the main township of the district and incompatibility of an elective mandate with a civil service position. The number of deputies had been slightly reduced (750 members), and they were elected for three years. There were in fact only a little more than 700 deputies, because of candidates being simultaneously elected in several *départements*. The result of the ballot revealed a double development of public opinion which was very marked in comparison with the April vote of the preceding year. The new Chamber inclined very much more to the right, since the party of order accounted for nearly two-thirds of the deputies; the shift in people's minds had been so strong that it had brought back about 140 legitimists as part of that majority, as if the social panic of bourgeois France had temporarily obliterated the frontier between the *ancien régime* and 1789, in the name of the chief danger of the moment: 'There is no small proof of the keenness of the general need to repulse revolutionary parties at all costs, in the facility with which bourgeois France, forgetting its prejudices and bitterness, had allowed the right wing a far greater share than that to which it would normally have laid claim.[12]

The other feature of the election, in the losers' camp, was the collapse of the moderate republicans, who were reduced to fewer than one hundred representatives, to the advantage of the supporters of the democratic and social Republic (the 'democsocs'), who were noticeably more numerous (between 150 and 200, according to the way in which one interprets the votes). These groups were not parties in the modern sense, but political families which were a little fuzzy round the edges, so that counting gives comparative orders of size rather than exact figures.

The right is easier to define than the left; it was, however, just as diverse. Conservatives without any other loyalty than a spirit of social reaction formed the greater part of it. Many were already tending towards moral-order Bonapartism. Those who were royalist through conviction or doctrine are more interesting. In their hostility to the Republic, the Orleanists were contemplating some day bringing back the Duchesse d'Orléans and her son, the Comte de Paris; the legitimists had but one flag to rally to, the Comte de Chambord ('Henri V'), son of the Duc de Berry. The two monarchist groups remained divided by their conceptions of modern society and by the entire width of contemporary history: they shared neither the same memories nor the same vision of 1789, 1815 and 1830. Thiers, Barrot and Broglie harked back to the French Revolution, and detested the *ancien régime*; the left wing of Orleanism – a Rémusat, for example – was infinitely closer to Cavaignac-style republicans than to the émigrés' party. However, several elements temporarily brought together the men, and still more the members of the electorate, who had fought one another so hard since the fall of Napoleon.

Firstly, the spectre of a restoration of the *ancien régime* was dwindling with time. The eighteen years of the July monarchy had exiled most of the nobles in their châteaux; they worked their lands, lived on their farm rents or the shares of produce they received from their tenants, far removed from public affairs – or affairs plain and simple – while the bourgeoisie, on the contrary, prospered. Modern society had taken root, frequently called 'democracy' at the time, to denote that it was founded on the liberty and civil equality of individuals. The February revolution had confirmed its

[12] Ibid., vol. 4, p. 414.

vitality, by extending the benefit of that democracy to the political sphere, through universal suffrage. But while it was still weakening the threat of a return to the *ancien régime*, it had made the phantom of the First Republic reappear, escorted, this time in the front rank, by socialist thinking. That made it doubly easy to bring the two monarchist factions and publics closer together. It further reduced the likelihood of the counter-revolutionary menace, and added relevance to legitimist criticism of modern society, according to which the dynamic of equality must lead to the destruction of the social bond itself: when it was used to defend property, and no longer to combat 1789, this criticism was grist to the mill for the men of 1830.

A political tradition which had emerged from the French Revolution, Orleanism had thus moved during this period into the union of the right-wing groups, in the name of the defence of property. At the end of the twentieth century, it needs an effort of imagination to visualize the force of this subject in public opinion at the time – a force which it has never since regained: the great anti-communist campaigns of the 1920s and 1930s were merely a feeble echo. In order to piece together what could have made that threat against property so credible – since it seems to us today, at a distance of one and a half centuries, to have been so grossly exaggerated by electoral propaganda – it is necessary to go back, as always during the nineteenth century, to the nearness of the French Revolution.

The French were still in touch with it, through their parents or grand-parents; February and June 1848 had re-established it in people's minds, with everything that had been great about it, but also with all the conflicts which its dramatic spectacle had presented. Far from being foreign to the nation, the idea of civil war was quite familiar, and enveloped parties and men in its violence, the victors just as much as the vanquished of June. It had assumed a new strength with the entry of the class struggle as a central theme of political thought and public life; the matter of property, put forward by socialist doctrines and the Parisian clubs, orchestrated with a great many scaremongering tactics by the propaganda of the wealthy, gave it a character of extreme intensity and urgency.

In order to defend what they called quite simply 'society' against the 'socialists', conservatives of every hue, Orleanists and Bonapartists, joined in unison with the traditional violence of legitimist argument, thus borrowing from their old enemies, to combat the socialists, the tone of anathema and excommunication which the ultras had been accustomed to employ against 1789. The right-wing campaign had received a sort of additional vehemence from this rhetorical intensification. To this debate, which was no longer about the Revolution and the *ancien régime*, the French spontaneously brought their revolutionary habits of mind.

Lastly, there was a federating element between the two families of the new right: the Catholic Church. The alliance between it and the legitimists was old and full of memories; it had been born in the *ancien régime*, the misfortunes of the Revolution, the vengeance of the restored monarchy and the difficult years after July 1830. At the time, the Orleanist bourgeois had

made the Church pay a price for that alliance. Some of them had been
Protestant, like Guizot; the majority had been anticlerical, like Thiers. The
bishops and clergy had made the best of the regime, rather than liking it,
and secretly regretted the Bourbons of the senior branch. Deprived of the
state's support and, for far longer, of true autonomy as a political body, the
French Church had drifted towards Rome, breaking with a very ancient
Gallican tradition to which Louis-Philippe's regime had no longer given its
backing. At the end of the July monarchy, the great debate on education
had revealed the fruits of that evolution: a will for political independence
in relation to the state: a Catholic parliamentary lobby; the matter of
schools; new leaders, uncompromising ultramontanes, the liberal aristocrat
Montalembert, who accepted modern society, and the plebeian Veuillot,
who rejected it.

In the light of July 1830, the Catholics had realized that the Church's
future no longer lay in supporting royalty, but in winning over opinion.
The bishops followed the movement only slowly, but were eventually
borne along with it. The Catholic Church gained by dissociating its destiny
from that of legitimism and entering the battle with a new spirit, but by
doing so it also admitted its isolation in relation to civil society: it now
demanded its own schools, its own deputies, its own journalists and even
its own writers.

February 1848 brought no profound modification to the predispositions
of men and forces. It was not, as has been seen, an anti-Catholic revolution. The religious, and even specifically Catholic, spirit blossomed – and
not only in marginal currents, such as the Buchezians. Many were the
priests who accompanied mayors in the village processions to plant the tree
of liberty in the church square. The archbishop of Paris, Monseigneur
Affre, had been killed by a stray bullet, during the June 'days', while
preaching reconciliation to the rioters. However, the post-June situation
revealed that French Catholicism, though not wholly contained in a party,
had nevertheless become a party, which plunged into the movement of
opinion on behalf of order and property, where it met its old Orleanist
adversaries who had come round to better feelings.

In that reunion between Voltairean bourgeois and the Catholic Church,
it is generally only the straightforward recantation of the former that is
emphasized: on meeting Rémusat after February, Victor Cousin had cried:
'Let us hasten to throw ourselves at the bishops' feet; they alone can save
us.' But the idea that the people needed a religion to keep them obedient
was also to be found in Voltaire, and it had enjoyed even more illustrious
backing, for example from Napoleon. The French bourgeoisie had discovered it in its heritage as a means of reconciling the irreligion of the elites
and the spiritual supervision of the poor.

What is most surprising is the enthusiasm with which the Catholic
Church threw itself into this alliance, in which it was used as a political
tool. By doing so, it apparently erased the kind of exclusive preference it
had evinced for legitimism: in fact, it compounded the error which made it

dependent on factional political interests, without even having the excuse of sharing a common history with them. Hardly had it shed its costly loyalty to Louis XVI's brothers, when it was following opinion on the pretext of winning it over: as if, for want of attaining a consciousness of itself in the new society, it had needed to borrow from outside. It thus implicitly endorsed the simple, even vulgar, view that its new friends had of it and of religion. It had voted for Louis-Napoleon in December; it campaigned for the conservatives in May 1849: the priest versus the schoolteacher. The liberal Montalembert had been one of the first Catholic advocates of Bonapartism, which would soon put the Church in the camp of the adversaries of liberty. From that coalition in which it risked everything and its allies almost nothing, it expected to receive the benefits of influence, such as dominance in the educational field, in which Falloux was just starting to get under way. And the Roman question, in which the throne of the Holy Father was involved, certainly constituted a crucial issue for it.

Electoral geography bears witness to the intricate interweaving of religion into the fabric of French politics as brought under the X-ray by universal suffrage. Indeed, the 1849 ballot reveals for the first time that famous correlation, so characteristic of French public life up till recently, between religious practice and right-wing voting. Not that this correlation was present everywhere and always: there is no single cause for electoral behaviour, and many other factors intervene which may frustrate or change it. Rural regions such as Normandy or Saintonge were not areas where religious practice was strong, and yet they voted with the party of order: the former was more subject to its notables, and the latter had a Bonapartist tradition, but in both cases the defence of property had no need of religion.

On the other hand, in the immense farmlands of the west, where clerical control had gained support during the Restoration from memories of the *chouannerie*, the Church of bourgeois order followed in the footsteps of the ultra-royalist Church. And though it is not certain that, in those rural communities of the end of the eighteenth century, the priest had been as powerful as many historians have believed, with Michelet, by a sort of retrospective projection, it *is* certain that he was the key personage in the peasant vote in the middle of the nineteenth century. The same type of analysis can be made of the highlands of Catholic loyalty to the southeast of the Massif Central – Lozère, Rouergue and Velay: very thickly 'clergified' rural areas, where obedience to the *curé* influenced electoral behaviour. That mixture of religion and politics had a name in the other camp: clericalism – which fed its twin opponent, anticlericalism.

The other camp is certainly easier to depict because of the feelings of loathing it bore towards the party of order than because of any political assertions which might give it some sort of unity. The heart of republican thinking was still composed of the pacified heritage of the Convention and hostility to the treaties of 1815; but it had been enriched, and complicated,

by the experience of February and the break-up of June 1848. The great
losers in the ballot were the February republicans who had been in the
forefront of the battle against the June uprising: they had lost on their left
without gaining anything on their right, and their overthrow in May was
the logical sequel to Cavaignac's defeat in December. Lamartine, the
February man *par excellence*, overwhelmingly voted for in April 1848,
humiliated in the presidential ballot, was not re-elected in May 1849. Nor
were Marrast, Marie and Garnier-Pagès.

The wholesale slaughter of that political family which had dominated the
Constituent Assembly with 500 deputies, of whom only eighty returned,
explains the extraordinary rate of replacement of Assembly members: a
cruelty of universal suffrage which had no connection with its novelty,
since there have been many other examples since. The moderate republicans were in reality paying for the torrent of political upsets which had
marked the year 1848 between February and December. Victorious, even
triumphant, in the spring, their Republic had had its moments of greatness
in public opinion only when it had seemed the best shield against social
revolution; after June, it handed over to a timely saviour, still chosen from
among its ranks, and then came the turn of a professional saviour, chosen
by the country at large, but who was working for himself alone. The idea
of a conservative republic or, more precisely, one charged with ending the
Revolution – by which the whole story was to come to a close a little more
than a quarter of a century later – at this period had only circumstantial
support in public opinion. When it came to terminating the Revolution,
the French, as they had fifty years before, from preference still thought of
a Bonaparte.

In effect, the Revolution was still going on, as had been shown not only
by the June barricades but also by the election results of May 1849.
Facing the conservative tide, and almost touching it since the moderate
republicans no longer formed anything but a bloodless centre-left, the
left and extreme left had improved their electoral score compared with
the preceding year, and numbered around 180 deputies. It was an
extraordinarily varied milieu, from every point of view, both as regards
men and ideas, and therefore difficult to describe collectively, although
it had assumed the common title 'Montagne'. As usual, it included a
majority of barristers and journalists, but also some self-taught workers
such as Martin Nadaud, the mason from Bourganeuf, and even two
non-commissioned officers. Ledru-Rollin, who had been elected in four
départements, was their temporary rallying-point, before being – very
swiftly – reduced to exile in London. But this left was anarchic, because it
was full of individuals who had each formed his own vision of it. On the
Montagnard benches were Lamennais and Pierre Leroux, the carpenter
Agricol Perdiguier and the novelist Félix Pyat, Michel de Bourges and
Raspail, not to mention two illustrious names who would soon join them:
Victor Schoelcher, the apostle of the anti-slavery struggle, and Victor

Hugo, who was busy becoming Victor Hugo. How can such a collection be defined, when it was so novel and disparate?

They were called, and called themselves, the 'Montagne': the revolutionary obsession had survived the mishaps of the preceding year and was now spreading its shadow over a parliamentary coalition of democrats and socialists. A gulf separated the two periods and the two situations: in 1849 there existed neither war on the frontiers, nor a threat to public safety, nor dictatorship, nor Terror, and in 1793 there had been neither a party of order nor socialists. Nevertheless, there was more than the compulsion of tradition in the Montagnards' rhetorical imitation. The Legislative left wanted in this way to make itself distinct from the 'Girondins' – the moderate republicans: it was Esquiros's revenge on Lamartine. What separated it from Cavaignac and his friends may be thought of as loyalty to the heritage of the 1793 Montagnards. Firstly, its programme, which was already calling for a revision of the constitution, comprising abolition of the presidential office, a collegial executive which was dismissible and subordinate to the legislative body; that is to say, as in the good old days, an Assembly dictatorship, in keeping with both the Montagnard constitution of 1793 and the 'revolutionary government' which had replaced it. But, even more than this old republican idea, what united them was an anxiety not to be separated from the lower classes and their passions. The Montagnards had allied themselves with the sansculottes. These had not taken part in the June uprising of the year before, but the magnitude of the repression had aroused their indignation and they demanded an amnesty.

Far more than their great ancestors, they were obsessed by the social question. That feature gives some measure of the time which had passed and the distance which had been travelled in half a century by the democratic concept. The problem of the 'abstractness' of the Rights of Man, in contrast with the concrete evidence of inequality between men, was as old as the French Revolution, and had already nourished the egalitarian overstatement of the *Enragés* and the sansculottes. Since then it had been one of the main lines in the development of socialist thought, and was at the heart of the political culture of the left and extreme left.

The democrats' desire was to incorporate social equality into republican citizenship, while the socialists believed it to be inseparable from revolution in relation to capital and labour. In both cases, the republican concept was enriched with social content which might, moreover, take precedence over its purely political dimension – an ambiguity which the prince-president would know how to exploit. The republic demanded by the 'democ-socs' was not the one which had cruelly crushed the common people of Paris, but on the contrary, one which would some day have to give them what it had refused them in the autumn of 1848: the right to work. If it did not, then it, too, was nothing but bourgeois power in disguise.

Republican thinking was thus the repository for a vast range of meanings, the two poles of which were political citizenship on the one hand, and social equality on the other: it was a way of reconciling, amid the confusion, those who gave priority to the one and those who turned the other into the condition of the democratic pact. For the former, the Republic was in itself the representation of the common weal, through the participation of all in the running of the community; it was indivisible from an optimistic anthropology and a history of progress through which man regained sovereignty over himself which for so long had been handed over to the kings.

Through it, men like Victor Hugo, who had rallied to the left of the Legislative Assembly from the summer of 1849, made a meeting-ground with republicans who were clearly hostile to the socialist concept, such as Edgar Quinet. But at the other end, at the extreme left, the most socialist elements, on the contrary, set more value on the social to the detriment of the political, and watched without any particular displeasure the advent of the Bonapartist threat on the bourgeois republic: this was the case, for example, with those whom the repression following June had made most indignant, or with a man like Proudhon, who was wrapped up in his idea of social reorganization and aloof from the purely political debate.

The programme, addressed to the electorate in the name of the 'Montagne' and drawn up by Félix Pyat, mingled the political with the social in such a way as to unite the left and extreme left, which was intellectually divided into numerous factions. It had put alongside the demand for an executive which was both revocable and subordinate to the legislative body, a whole programme of social measures, comprising both democratic reforms – such as recruitment of civil servants by competition and election, the lowering of taxes, reform of military service – and also socialist ideas – such as state management of the railways, mines, canals and insurance, or the affirmation of the 'right to work by credit and association'.

The May 1849 elections had therefore presented the picture of a democratic and socialist bloc: they were united on rather vague ideas, and even more by an anxiety to react against the party of order than by any ambition to govern, but in the end gathered together on a common heritage. That is why this vote offers the first good electoral photograph of the French left, rid of the confusions and illusions which had arisen in the preceding year from the nearness to the February revolution. It reveals that in this very largely pre-industrial mid-century France, when the railways were only just beginning to break into the isolation of the country areas, two great groups of *départements* had massively voted left: the first comprised the north-west of the Massif Central, from the Bourbonnais to the Limousin; the second was the Mediterranean crescent, from the Aude to the Basses-Alpes. This map is just as familiar to specialists in contemporary French electoral behaviour, because it has lasted throughout the twentieth century, being enriched in the years 1880–1900 by a third left-wing electoral bloc, the industrial and working-class north, which did not exist in 1849. The question posed by the distribution of the 'democ-soc' vote in the middle of the nineteenth century is therefore that of a vast rural electorate which had prematurely rallied to the ideas of the left and extreme left, in contrast with the conservative or reactionary vote of the majority of the peasantry – for example in the entire west of the country.

This contrast cannot be explained in terms of economic interests or social structures. In that regard, there is no real distinction between regions, which are fairly close geographically, like the Limousin and Rouergue, and yet the first voted left, the second right. What was at issue, among the countless masses of peasant smallholders, was an attachment to a cultural heritage and a tradition. It becomes understandable when one starts from the religious observance which matches the political cleavage so neatly. The Limousin, abandoned by the priests, did not go to Mass. The Rouergue area, supervised by a large population of clergy, adhered to the Catholic faith. It is not easy to pinpoint the date at which this division began; it remains one of the most interesting mysteries in national history. But though it undoubtedly pre-dated 1789, it was still the Revolution, as has been seen, which had excavated, remoulded and sharpened up this boundary, superimposing new values and memories born of the confrontations which it had provoked. The Church itself from 1814, had slipped into the modern mould, by defining its doctrinal authority in terms of political revenge. For example, to take the case of the west, it is very probable that the mid-nineteenth-century Vendée was even more 'clerical' than at the end of the eighteenth: traditional faith had been remodelled by the strength of the recent memory of the events of 1793, and the support that had been derived from that memory, during the Restoration, by a Catholic Church of counter-revolution.

But there had also been developments in the other direction, as in the Midi of the Rhône and the Var, where Maurice Agulhon[13] has reconstructed the routes by which urban and rural poorer classes, which had been counter-revolutionary at the end of the eighteenth century, had gone over to the side of the social and democratic Republic by the middle of the nineteenth: In these 'red' areas of 1849, the new political culture had developed by way of struggles in the communes between the 'small fry' and the 'fat cats', and through the links of a traditional network of associations: mutual aid, chambers, guilds, co-operatives of all kinds. A part of artisanal and rural France of that period had aligned itself with the left by wedding its customary folklore and its tradition of communal struggles to the co-operative concept drawn from utopian socialism and the republican heritage which had been renewed by 1848.

These 'reds', whom the party of order denounced as a dire threat to order and the very principle of society, were men who were torn between nostalgia for the communities of yesteryear and the modern passion for social equality. Frequently, it needed only a convinced and active leader,

[13] M. Agulhon, *La République au village.*

who had generally emerged from the educated bourgeoisie, to mass them together against the local tyranny of the great dominant families. In Haute-Provence, it was a sheet metal worker of Italian extraction, Langomazino, a disciple of the Robespierrist historian Laponneraye, who created out of almost nothing a powerful socialist republican movement between Manosque and Digne.

In short, the left had learnt lessons from the elections of the preceding year: the 'Montagnards' had launched an assault on the country districts and small townships. The election campaign had provided them with militants, electors and the certainty of winning, on the morrow, in a France more enlightened by the progress of education. But for the moment, they would make use of symbolic stakes in the battle which was beginning between the party of order and the president.

Odilon Barrot remained prime minister. He had to reshuffle his team slightly, at the end of a laborious compromise, as a gesture towards the new parliamentary majority: Dufaure was sent to the Interior, Lanjuinais to Agriculture and Tocqueville to Foreign Affairs. Thus the president had his men in the ministry, as the Assembly had its own. He also took a step in the direction just indicated by universal suffrage, but he chose foreign policy and the Roman question, by which he was able to kill two birds with one stone: pleasing the whole conservative party, but especially the Catholic lobby, which had just demonstrated its electoral influence. He pleased Molé and Thiers, but also Falloux, who remained the Church's eye in Barrot's ministry.

Since the preceding year, Rome had been in the hands of republicans, who had driven out Pope Pius IX, and he had taken refuge with the king of Naples. *Vis-à-vis* Italy, since February the Republic's attitude had been one of sympathy with regard to the various national and democratic movements, but also one of diplomatic and military caution. In 1848, France had joined with Britain to moderate the demands of Austria, which had won a victory over Charles-Albert of Piedmont. In the spring of 1849 the new president followed this line by sending a small French expeditionary force to Italy: it was a question of containing the re-establishment of Austrian influence, while a diplomatic mission strove to come up with the terms of a compromise between the pope and the republicans. But the failure of this mission, at the same time as the party of order's massive victory at the polls in May, led Louis-Napoleon to forget his youth as an insurgent in the Romagna in the cause of his new role as friend of the Church of France: the expeditionary body, commanded by General Oudinot, was instructed to retake Rome in June in order to restore his town and states to the pope.

One must read the letters of Tocqueville, who was the instrument rather than the author of this policy, in order to gauge how much the re-establishment of the *'ancien régime'* in Rome by the French army aroused mixed feelings in the mind of the Minster for Foreign Affairs. The

Tocqueville of this period was, as we have seen, an active member of the party of order; but he remained convinced of what he had understood very early on: the *ancien régime* was forever condemned by the course of history, and the idea of reinstating the ancient papal government made him very uneasy. Then what can be said of the republicans? At the unprecedented sight of the French Republic crushing a sister republic, in contempt of article V of the preamble to the constitution, Ledru-Rollin demanded that the Assembly should indict the ministers, a request which was of course refused. But the Paris of the secret societies was awake once again, heartened by the good voting score of the 'Montagnards', and horrified by the reactionary spirit of the grandees and the president: 'The secret society groups are in permanent session', wrote Hugo in his notes at the end of May, 'plot keeping an eye on plot . . . the parties are weighing one another up, face to face, each with its secret thoughts now out in the open; 10 August is watching 18 Brumaire very closely.'[14]

The conflict was resolved on 13 June by the failure of a large demonstration which was organized, in the name of the constitution, against French intervention in Rome. Some tens of thousands of men, surrounded by unarmed National Guards, filing along the boulevards from the Bastille to the Madeleine, were dispersed by the army at the arrival point of the procession; Ledru-Rollin tried abortively to rouse the east of Paris. It was the time for a new repression, just a year after that of June 1848: less bloody, because it attacked only the remainder of the republican extreme left, but definitive. A state of siege was proclaimed, the democratic legions of the National Guard disbanded, Montagnard press premises devastated – justice was on the march. Ledru-Rollin, who had recently been elected in four *départements*, had to flee to London, where he joined the exile of the year before, Louis Blanc. Through him, the Montagnard tradition accompanied the socialist concept in adversity.

THE COUP D'ETAT

From now on, the only face-to-face encounter was between the president and the parliamentary majority. One year after February 1848, the republic was in the hands of a Bonaparte and a royalist right: two powers which had emerged from universal suffrage, but neither of which intended to be really faithful to its origins. Of the first, the name said it all since, like the Bourbons, even though it was more recent, the Bonapartes had a right over France which came to them from history, before being formally conferred by the people.

As for the legislative power, it was dominated by two groups divided according to their dynastic allegiance, but who at least agreed in preferring the monarchy to the Republic. Legitimists and Orleanists were republican

[14] Hugo, *Choses vues*, ch. 4.

only by default, because they were unable to replace the 1848 constitution with the king of their choice. Even Tocqueville, who was not a party to their disputes and, in a certain fashion, was not inimical to the Republic, which had delivered him from Guizot while simultaneously repulsing the *ancien régime* and the Revolution, could find no merit in it other than that it existed: 'I wanted to maintain it, because I could see nothing either ready or good enough to put in its place.'[15]

This trend of opinion obviously gave the president an advantage. He did not blame the Republic for being a popular power: what did not please him about it was that it had also become a representative government. So he could easily juxtapose a plan to overthrow it with the idea of being faithful to its spirit, whereas the conservative deputies wanted to preserve it in order to misrepresent its inspiration. He could thus combine his contempt for constitutional law with protestations of attachment to the sovereignty of the people, while his adversaries were suspected of invoking respect for the law only in order to perpetuate the government of an oligarchy. Half a century after 18 Brumaire, he found himself in a political situation which was fairly comparable with that of the last years of the Directory: a Republic discredited in its constitution and its men, but national in its principle and its historical legitimacy. The nephew had no rightful claims to receive that heritage, except those which he drew from his uncle; but he had the advantage over the latter of having received in advance the unction of universal suffrage, and of having been put into power by the people before confiscating power in the name of the people. All of which also gave him, against the conservative deputies, unity of decision and the choice of the ground, the date and the means.

He had been elected for four years: his term of office did not expire until 1852, so nothing was really urgent. For a year, from mid-1849 to mid-1850, the conflict did not go beyond the limits of a classic battle for influence between two powers, over men, positions and the interpretation of bills. In October the president appointed a ministry which was more in the palm of his hand than Odilon Barrot's, and in which, under a head of government who was a complete nonentity, his own men dominated – such as Baroche in the Ministry of Justice, or Fould in Finance. His cabinet, led by Persigny, and composed of faithful followers or go-getters who were despised by the Assembly notables, battled on all sides to build up a following and party for him. He himself from time to time, as for example with the Roman expedition, revealed a more 'liberal' note than the men of the party of order. But he did not oppose the parliamentary majority's great idea, which was to legislate at long last on the freedom of education. He had maintained a close relationship with his former minister, Falloux, the chief inspiration behind the new bills, and wanted to associate his name with the spirit of Catholic restoration which had just shown its electoral muscle.

[15] Tocqueville, *Souvenirs*, part III, vol. 1.

In fact Falloux was the man of the hour – the Church's deputy, who had been joined by even the former anticlericals of the party of order, who were by now convinced that in front of the teacher or professor, the priest was the pillar of moral and social order. A first law in January 1850 allowed any congregationist to become a schoolmaster, and gave prefects control over primary schools. A second, adopted in May, known as 'Falloux's law', handed higher education over to the Church. The president had insisted on preserving the University, founded by his uncle, and leaving it the right to confer degrees; but on the one hand, much room was made for bishops in its management and, on the other, the Church was given every liberty to open its own establishments. Here a characteristic conflict in French democracy assumed its classic form. Those laws in effect made clericalism an essential ingredient of conservatism; they turned schools into the centre of an inexpiable political conflict, and secularism into the banner of the republican battle. They conferred upon French political confrontations, which were already over-endowed with intellectualism and philosophy, the additional significance of a war of religion. Through them, the Orleanist bourgeoisie drew closer to legitimist clericalism, making a return to religion; but by repudiating Enlightenment philosophy, it also cut itself off from its own origins and 1789 – its title to govern France.

It was by now too bound up with the counter-revolutionary spirit to envisage a new liberal solution to the French political crisis, after that of 1830; but at the same time, it remained too hostile to the thought of aristocracy to take the risk of a restoration of the senior branch. What sort of a future awaited it, therefore, if not this man Bonaparte, who was both a promise of social and moral order and the least revolutionary of revolutionary guarantees? A letter from the young dramatic author, François Ponsard, to his publisher, the famous Jules Hetzel, puts it all marvellously; written in 1851, it depicted for the benefit of his Parisian recipient the state of opinion in Dauphiné, where Ponsard was temporarily living:

Our bourgeois would like a prorogation, or even an empire; they don't want to hear about the Republic any more, or even constitutional government. They would like Napoleon, but not Henri V. They still feel bitter towards the nobles; but they no longer hate the priests, since religion fits into the same formula as property. Even those who had voted for Cavaignac now ask only for Napoleon.[16]

This bourgeoisie was so afraid of political democracy that its representatives had sought to reconsider the principle of universal suffrage. In May 1850, after several by-elections in which Paris had re-elected 'red' candidates, they had passed a law restricting the conditions for exercising the right to vote, making it subject to a minimum residence of three years, confirmed by inscription on the personal tax register. Since it was not

[16] Quoted in A. Parmenie and C. Bonnier de la Chapelle, *Histoire d'un éditeur et de ses auteurs, P.-J. Hetzel* (Paris, Albin Michel, 1953), p. 146.

possible to re-establish an electoral regime based on property-ownership qualifications, the aim was to rule out from voting, by technical measures, a large proportion of the working-class population, who were obliged to move about the country frequently according to the fluctuations in the job market.

Badly put together, obscure and oblique, the law had caused a violent debate and, for the republicans, had revived the idea of illegal action – since they had abandoned hope of a victory at the ballot-box. But it had also offered the prince-president the chance to dissociate himself from the parliamentary 'reaction' by making known his hostility to the measure and his personal loyalty to universal suffrage. Consequently he had won on all counts. By upholding the clerical drift of conservatism, he had linked himself with what constituted the lowest common denominator of the right's electorate. By keeping himself apart from the attacks made against the universality of electoral rights, he had turned the conservative Republic – which, moreover, had been delegitimized by repudiating its own principles – into the privileged enemy of the republicans: he thus opened up for himself a vast space on the left in which to develop his 'revision' campaign.

His objective was firstly to obtain re-eligibility in 1852, since the constitution authorized only a single mandate, and any revision had to be voted with a majority of three-quarters of the deputies. Louis-Napoleon started campaigning again from the summer of 1850, increasing his tours and styles of address. His adversaries continued to underestimate his political talents. He knew that he held the master cards. His political ambiguities provided him with a formidable electioneering trump card, whereby he could separate the various groups of voters from their appointed representatives to unite them behind his name: he inspired the wealthy with more confidence than Thiers, and was more popular with working men than Louis Blanc; he was more 'national' than anyone else with the army, and no one could rival him in the matter of the feelings which his name aroused among the peasantry.

Now in power, he had the money to buy men and newspapers; at the same time that he was creating his militia of supporters, the loudmouths of the '10 December Society', he was extending his influence in the political class, among the notables who had put him in gaol under Louis-Philippe and despised him under Cavaignac, but who were not too accustomed to resisting success. Among these men, the president had acquired an ambassador in the person of the Duc de Morny, his half-brother, the son of Hortense de Beauharnais and the Comte de Flahaut, a deputy in the last Chamber of the July regime, and in a good position to build a bridge between the Elysée and the Orleanist bourgeoisie.

By comparison, what a division there was on the opposite side! Neither hostility to revision nor the threat of a presidential coup d'état truly brought republican deputies and the conservatives who had remained liberal any closer together: there were too many bad memories and keenly felt passions between the two camps. But the party of order itself was becoming increasingly disunited in the face of the day of reckoning in 1852. Under the leadership of Montalembert and Veuillot, the Catholics, or rather those conservative members who were more Catholic than royalist, gradually sided with the Elysée camp, in the name of the Church's interests. On the contrary, many Orleanists, like Thiers, since Louis-Philippe's death in August 1850, had nursed the idea of the candidature of one of his sons for the presidential election of 1852: they were less worried by the revision of the constitution than by the annulment of the 1848 law which had exiled the Orléans princes.

As for the legitimists, they yielded to the movement of opinion which was bringing the country over to the side of the president, in order to attempt to obtain a good result at the next legislative elections. At all events, they preferred to work for a Bonaparte rather than an Orléans. In this multiplicity of precautions and calculations, there was no majority either to vote for the constitutional revision which would have permitted the legalizing of Louis-Napoleon's ambitions by means of a re-election, or successfully to defend the Constitution and the law against him. Reading the documents of the period, one can see how much the coup d'état of 2 December 1851 was anticipated, discussed and publicly commented upon during the year which preceded it – even in the president's office, in a conversation which he had with Tocqueville on 15 May; and how much, with a few exceptions – like Tocqueville himself – French conservatives were resigned in advance to the inevitable, outflanked as they were by their voters, and divided among themselves internally.

They had lost a first battle, which was waged over General Changarnier, commander of the armed forces and the National Guard, and their man in opposition to the Elysée. At the beginning of 1851 and at the end of a six-month conflict, Changarnier had been dismissed by the president of the Republic. The campaign for revision was going full blast, but it failed. Instead of three-quarters of the votes, on 19 July in the Assembly it obtained only 446 votes against 278. From then on, the Elysée's dilemma was whether to wait until the due date in May 1852 to attempt a second candidature, despite the law (but a new Assembly would have been elected in April), or else to take the initiative by means of a coup d'état, followed by a new constitution to be approved by universal suffrage. Morny and Persigny had been advising the second solution for several months, and that was what Louis-Napoleon decided on in the summer.

The 'technical' preparation was to place the necessary men exactly where they were needed. On the Elysée side, the initiates were Persigny, Morny, Fleury and Rouher. The Prefect of Police, Carlier, was in their confidence. A soldier was required, to command the army on the day: it would be an 'African' general, Saint-Arnaud, an adventurer with no morality but no illusions. It was he, however, who had the first date planned for the coup, in September, postponed because the Assembly was on holiday, and the deputies were not within reach in case of resistance. But in the autumn, he gave every care to preparing the army, chiefly in Paris, for the great day. The political preparation was as follows: the heart of the matter was the law of 31 May 1850, which Louis-Napoleon in October wanted to have repealed, linking it with a fresh demand for revision of the constitution. The Cabinet's resignation was followed by his replacing it with a colourless ministry – except for the War Department, which was entrusted to Saint-Arnaud. The Assembly rejected the abrogation of the law restricting the right to vote, and had a sudden impulse for a counter-offensive: its three *questeurs* (members responsible for administration and finance) tabled a bill which explicitly authorized it to summon armed forces, possibly even against the president. But the republican left refused to associate itself with this proposal, which was similarly opposed by that part of the right, which hoped for the re-election of the prince or even agreed in advance to his coup d'état. The bill was defeated on 17 November by 400 votes to 338. That gave the green light to the Elysée.

Everything happened in the night between 1 and 2 December 1851, and during the day of the 2nd, the anniversary of the 1804 coronation and of Austerlitz in the following year. Bonaparte's nephew was superstitious. Third time lucky: after Strasbourg and Boulogne, Louis-Napoleon succeeded in his third *coup*, which was easier, it is true, than the two previous ones, as he was already in power and it was just a matter of staying there. To tell the truth, success had been almost preordained, rather as in his uncle's case half a century before, if one bears in mind the political conditions surrounding the enterprise, and the imbalance between the forces and resolves confronting each other. Conspiracy was one of the fields in which the nephew's genius surpassed his uncle's, and though 2 December, like 18 Brumaire, was accepted in advance by public opinion, it was executed with much more skill.

The National Guard had not turned out; the army had been the nerve-centre of the coup d'état, helped by the police and prefects who had given their support. It occupied Paris in the small hours of 2 December, at the moment when posters of the decree dissolving the Assembly and re-establishing universal suffrage appeared on the walls, accompanied by proclamations from the president of the Republic to the people and the army. The police had already imprisoned about a hundred of the best-known opponents, for once mingling in its wagons liberal conservatives and 'Montagnards', Thiers and Martin Nadaud, not overlooking soldiers loyal to the law, like Changarnier, Cavaignac or Lamoricière.

There was no other public resistance that day, save that of part of the Assembly – those who had not aquiesced or been won over beforehand to the violation of the constitution: 220 deputies, for the most part conservative, met together at the end of the morning at the town hall of the tenth *arrondissement*, near to the Palais Bourbon which was occupied by troops, and rescued the honour of the people's representation by voting for the deposition of Louis-Napoleon. But they were interrupted after two hours of deliberation by the irruption of troops, and they too were taken off to prison at the beginning of the afternoon. Most of them – Tocqueville, Berryer, Broglie, Odilon Barrot and Falloux, for example – were released in a few days; the police held the few Montagnard deputies and Rémusat, the farthest left of the liberals, for a while longer. But the episode of the tenth *arrondissement*'s town hall and the imprisonment – even temporary – of the great leaders of liberal conservatism had established a profound and lasting rupture between the regime that was being born in violence and the country's traditional political elites.

A sign of the times: most of the republican deputies had acted in isolation, without getting involved in the grandees' resistance. Faced with the coup d'état, they wanted to appeal to the people, but the first reactions in Paris were scarcely encouraging: in the morning of 2 December the large white posters had aroused only disillusioned comments from most people, without too many regrets for the vanished Republic. Throughout the day, the representatives of the republican left took counsel together, to form a resistance committee in the evening, with Hippolyte Carnot, Victor Hugo, Michel de Bourges, Victor Schoelcher and Jules Favre.

The next day, 3 December, they attempted in vain to rouse the faubourg Saint-Antoine: it was here that the representative Baudin got himself killed 'for 25 francs a day', an episode which republican propaganda would use as its rallying flag at the end of the Empire. In the middle of the day, the Parisian militants managed to hold the centre of Paris, from the boulevards to the Seine, the traditional home of the barricades. They were far less numerous than in February 1848, but they were not isolated as in June: the bourgeois evinced to these defenders of the Republic none of the social hostility they had shown to the June rioters. Morny, the Minister of the Interior, adopted Cavaignac's tactics: a temporary withdrawal of the troops, to make a massive clean-up on the following day.

There were more soldiers in Paris on 4 December than there had ever been, and it was an unequal struggle between the thousand to twelve hundred militants and an entire army. But it was bloodier than these figures would lead one to expect, because Louis-Napoleon had over-estimated the resistance, and there were a lot of curious sightseers on the pavements who were fairly hostile to the army. There was a prolonged burst of gunfire on the boulevard des Italiens, which was full of troops, almost on the same spot as the one which, on the boulevard des Capucines on 23 February 1848, had provided the decisive spark which fired the revolution; the one in 1851 claimed many more victims, but it drove the frightened bourgeois back into their homes. To the very end, it would remain one of the reign's taboos – several dozen passers-by mown down by panic-stricken or over-zealous soliders. The destruction of the barricades was then carried out fairly easily. Paris was not in favour of the coup d'état, but neither had Paris risen up against it.

For once, it was in the provinces that revolts occurred which were the most dangerous for the government. It is true that it was not a question of insurrections to overthrow a legal government, but rather of counter-insurrections to re-establish a constitution which had been violated by the Paris coup d'état. That was the major difference from June 1848, and one which, in this respect, brings the popular movements of December 1851 closer to the revolt in the *départements* at the beginning of summer 1793, against the violence done to the Convention of 2 June. It explains why, in these movements, the 'democ-soc' militants saw their ranks swollen by the influx of more moderate republicans, and the bourgeois joined their voice with those of the peasants and lower classes. Whereas June 1848 had deeply divided the republican camp, as the May elections showed, the coup d'état tended to reunite it by superimposing on the social question the prerequisite of the defence of the constitution. Nevertheless, the majority of the risings and revolts were provided by the socialist democrats' popular supporters, peasants, craftsmen, marshalled by the militants of the secret societies. The big cities, Marseille, Bordeaux, even Lyon, made no move – or hardly any – since they were kept as tightly under police and army control as Paris. It was the country areas and the small towns which rebelled, where there were very few or no troops. The danger zones for the government for a few days, from 3 to 10 December, were situated in those regions which had voted 'red' in 1849, and where a political framework had been set up to prepare for the 1852 elections: the coup d'état had brought that day forward by a few months, but it allowed the Republic to regain an impetus which could stir the people to action. The areas of unrest present a roughly triangular map: that is to say, in increasing order of gravity, the south-west (Gers and Lot-et-Garonne), the north of the Massif Central (Yonne, Nièvre, Cher, Allier, Saône-et-Loire), and lastly the Rhône and Languedoc Midi, along an arc from Perpignan to Digne. The insurgents had been in control for three days, from 6 to 9 December, of the Basses-Alpes *département*, where they numbered about 15,000, half of whom were peasants.

What is known today of these movements gives the impression that they oscillated between two extremes, egalitarian violence and revolt in defence of the Republic; and that, in varying degree, they all contained a mixture of those two characteristics. From this fact, they could be interpreted and used in opposing ways, both by the victims of the Parisian coup d'état and by those who had profited from it. For the former, Victor Hugo in the lead, they had saved the country's honour, behind the banner of the law. For the second, they had been no more than a premeditated *jacquerie*, a new June rising which had been planned for 1852 and forced to show its colours prematurely. For the time being, the propaganda theme provided by what had happened gave the men of the coup d'état, after the event, a new justification for their action. On the morning of 2 December, the bills prepared by the accomplices had as their principal aim the neutralization of the left: they proclaimed the re-establishment of universal suffrage, evoked the sovereignty of the people and the glory of the nation. Some days later Paris was buzzing only with rumours of social panic, which were revived by the happenings in the provinces and orchestrated by thousands of horrific stories. And it was on that theme that the brand-new government organized its propaganda in order to get 2 December approved by the country as a whole. In a circular of 10 December, Morny set the tone:

Monsieur le Préfet, you have just undergone several testing days; you have just withstood in 1851 the social war which would have broken out in 1852. You must have recognized it by its incendiary and murderous nature. If you have triumphed over the enemies of society, it is because they have been taken by surprise and because you have been aided by decent people.

Thus, the coup d'état had been nothing more than a provident action to forestall a plot which had long been planned against social order. Thus rallying behind the prince-president had been a social duty which took precedence over any constitutional scruple. Besides, he himself was not lacking in conservative overstatement: he ordered the systematic arrest in every *département* of the principal republican chiefs and militants. His reign opened with more than 25,000 imprisonments. The Bourse took an upward leap; confidence was restored. Giving massive applause to this entry of a second Bonapartism on the scene, the conservatives, royalists and the Church ensconced themselves once again in revolutionary tradition, through fear of the Revolution. But by the same token, they abandoned reference to the law to those republicans who wished to grasp it.

The vote took place on 21 and 22 December, on the following proposition: 'The French people wish Louis-Napoleon to maintain authority and delegate to him the necessary powers for the establishment of a constitution on the bases announced in the proclamation of 2 December.' There were 7,145,000 ayes and 592,000 noes – such an impressive majority that it was, quite wrongly, suspected of having been rigged.

9

The Second Empire: 1851–1870

In the nineteenth century, French political regimes tended to disappear rather than be overthrown, and the Second Republic was no exception to the rule. It had expired before it received its death certificate in right and due form; it had died on 10 December 1848, and again on 13 May 1849. Having passed the first time into the hands of Louis Bonaparte, and then into those of the royalists, it had survived merely as a temporary pawn between the factions, poorly supported, besides, by the socialist republicans, who blamed it for June 1848. Obsessed by the memory of the First Republic, it had wanted to imitate and follow its path, and had managed only to shorten its own duration, passing in less than a year from Lamartine to Bonaparte, in the twinkling of an eye burying February's promises under the vengeance which had followed June.

The old refrain about the impossibility of having a republic in a large country like France had thus very swiftly regained its freshness intact. The French had continually skirted around that impasse, without ever being able to escape from it – in 1789 by a royal republic; in 1793 by a republican dictatorship; in 1799 by a consular republic, and in 1830 by a republican monarchy – but when it was tackled head on, without trying any trickery with the force of principles and circumstances, in short, founding a republican Republic on the franchise for all, the results proved even less durable: after six months, the Second Republic was nothing more than a meeting-ground for a confrontation between the ghosts of the past three monarchies. When all was said and done, it met the same fate as the first, without even having the excuse of yielding to an incomparable hero: merely to the prosaicness of a sad inevitability. That was what deprived 2 December 1851 of the potent magic of 18 Brumaire.

Indeed, although the men of 1848 had always thought of their revolution in comparison with the Great Revolution, to make way in the end for a second Bonaparte, the history of the two Republics is comparable less for their respective courses than for the sheer weight brought to bear by memories of the first on the behaviour of those taking part in the second.

The circumstances were totally different, and yet men reacted to them with the feeling that they belonged to the same familiar pattern. The most salient contrast was that the nation was not at war, and that there was no public safety crisis. But civil passions and fears were just as strong as in the period of the Terror, because men imagined they were reliving what was at stake. The left of the secret societies was ceaselessly making preparations for the great 'day', and the right of the party of order brandished public safety in the name of property. Once again, revolution and counter-revolution confronted each other under the watchful eye of a Bonaparte. What had made the Second Republic such a short experience was the heritage of identity of which it had never been able to gain mastery. Bonaparte had been the inevitable arbitrator in that bogus civil war which it had started up again in the national imagination, and he had been chosen beforehand since this story had already taken place.

This Bonaparte had not been singled out by a campaign in Italy, but by universal suffrage: in any case, his name alone caused the evocation of his uncle's victories. But the main point lay elsewhere: the triumphal election of 10 December had clearly shown that the Second Republic, like the first, had continually run up against the insoluble problem of executive power. The Convention had concocted an assembly regime balanced by the dictatorship of the Committees – an exceptional government which had dishonoured the Republic. Next, the Directory had provided only a divided and erratic executive, tossed between royalism and republican coups d'état. The men of 1848 had believed they could resolve the problem by envisaging a president who would be elected by all citizens, like the Assembly. But out of that universal suffrage – and they had underestimated the power of this means – no Washington had emerged, but Louis-Napoleon Bonaparte. The last heir to the history of the French Revolution, but also heir to a family and a throne. Without any foreign war, without the guillotine, the Republic had irresistibly brought back together on to its stage the great actors of its past: an insurrectionist Montagne, clerical royalism and the phantom of the emperor.

In that sense, the second Bonapartism resembled the first, from which it drew its principle and strength. It was a version of the French Revolution at once conservative and popular; the first trait set it against the Montagne, the second against the coalition of royalisms. Now, the French in the mid-nineteenth century were pretty conservative, but they were also attached to the rights of man; of the heritage of 1789 they retained, indivisibly, property and democracy. The Restoration had threatened property and ignored democracy. The July monarchy had sanctified property and refuted democracy in the name of representative government. The president of the Second Republic, who also stood for property-ownership, had broken representative government in the name of democracy.

Thus, in the very middle of the nineteenth century, there again arose the dilemma of representation which had bedevilled the French Revolution, and which the free exercise of universal suffrage had not resolved, but merely posed once more with even greater clarity than a half-century before. By electing Napoleon's nephew, the people had chosen a man who shared and personified their history, and through whom they could again be a constituent part of the nation and the state. Unlike Orleanism, Bonapartism had no theorists; but it is not hard to understand that it owed its principal strength to the concept of the sovereignty of the people: an absolute sovereignty, above the law, since the latter derived its *raison d'être* from it, precisely where Guizot had seen the dangerous error of revolutionary tradition. The election of 10 December had in its own way sanctioned the victory of this revolutionary principle over the oligarchies of royalism.

There is another way of looking at the same idea: that is to see in Bonapartism – and even more in the second than in the first – the expression of the state's autonomy and permanency, rising above society and its political vicissitudes. The first Bonaparte had founded the modern democratic state on the principles of 1789, while resuming the centralizing tradition of the former monarchy. The second discovered in that state constituted by his uncle the means of his dominance over society. This can be understood in the technical sense of the term, since no one let him down on 2 December: neither the army, nor the police, nor the prefects nor the administration. State centralization, which is one of the conditions of successful revolutions, similarly favours coups d'état. But Louis-Napoleon, in his total seizure of the apparatus of state, which the election of 10 December had in any case largely handed over to him, found a way of personifying the general interest in the name of the people and over the heads of the ruling classes who had preceded him in power – nobility and bourgeoisie together. His image of the adventurer who had appeared out of the blue, scorned and combated by the elites, bound to France by the faithfulness of his feelings and intellect alone, made a fine symbol of that state which was the guarantor of equality, independent of class and an impartial arbiter between citizens.

Besides, a good number of the political class had looked on 2 December as the victory of the state over society. The most profound observers of the time had also interpreted it in that light. Marx, who continually traced class interests as the bedrock of the bourgeois democratic state, for once forms a different hypothesis: the break between the bourgeoisie and the country's government, as demonstrated by 2 December, was a necessary part of the age-long growth of a centralized state, which was perfected by the first Napoleon on the ruins of aristocratic society, and had become, under the second, an immense body independent of society; this phenomenon forms the background to the bourgeois abdication in the face of the adventurer and his clan. Marx had never been so close to Tocqueville as in the lines of *Le Dix-huit Brumaire* in which he puts forward this interpretation. For the former minister of the prince-president, who had been one of the protesters at the tenth *arrondissement* town hall, had witnessed before his very eyes a second showing of the film which led from revolution to the despotic state. From that he derived the first germ of what was to become *L'Ancien Régime*, which started with the decision to work on the Empire: it was a way of understanding what he had just lived through in the light of a precedent which served him as example and excuse – those first years of the century when the paradoxical consequences of the Revolution were revealed, an all-powerful state constructed on the equality of citizens and on the servitude of society.

The traitor president of the Second Republic had realized that his name allowed him to embody legitimacy against the law of that state, national sovereignty against representative government, and the responsibility of the social question against the power of wealth. The first two points were part of the profoundest beliefs of his life, and had led him into the crazy Strasbourg and Boulogne expeditions before they finally encountered the expectations of a public opinion grown disenchanted with the Republic. As for the third, his entire person confirmed it, and his political behaviour had gradually built up its component elements. The emperor's nephew had never had a bourgeois imagination; his obsession, comparable in this respect with that of the republicans, was to reach the 'will of the people' and to give it life; and in any case, it was the bourgeois of the July monarchy who had put him in prison.

In his Ham gaol he had read and discussed socialist writers, received Louis Blanc and corresponded with George Sand. No sooner had he been elected president than he had busied himself over those sentenced in June. After the law of 31 May 1850, he had let his commitment to universal suffrage be known before actually proclaiming it. He had deliberately cultivated his habit of keeping his own counsel, and nearly all his various interlocutors inferred from his silence that he shared their opinion, socialists and reactionaries alike. In his immediate circle, each person had his role and his personal language: his cousin, Prince Napoleon, the son of Jerome, speaking to the republican left, Morny to the wealthy, Persigny to the faithful. So, on 2 December, the strength of the coup d'état had lain less in its ability to gain support from all the machinery of the state than in appearing to re-establish state arbitration, six months away from the electoral eventuality of a civil war. That collective feeling, adding the weight of circumstance to the images of imperial tradition, is the best explanation of the electoral triumph of the vote of ratification.

Nevertheless 2 December has not preserved a good reputation in French history, as can be seen if it is compared with the precedent it merely imitated, 18 Brumaire. The second Napoleon's coup d'état has remained darkened by moral condemnation, whereas the first Napoleon's is most often absolved. The difference in treatment, the paradoxical indulgence which is afforded to the model the better to condemn the copy, certainly convey the disparity in genius and glory between uncle and nephew. But they are also connected with the special ensemble of circumstances and feelings surrounding the success of the 1851 conspiracy, which tarnished its image right from the start.

Although badly executed, the 18 Brumaire coup had not aroused resistance, and had not had to cause bloodshed. Acting with the greatest sang-froid, the conspirators of 2 December had found it necessary to have the crowds fired on in Paris, here and there to recapture villages and small towns from rebels who had remained loyal to the constitution, to imprison 28,000 republicans and exile illustrious people. At no time did these shows of resistance in any way jeopardize the success of the undertaking, which had the massive approval of public opinion. But in a France which remained under the almost exclusive spell of revolutionary culture, on the left they brought out a new respect for the constitution and the law; this heritage from the great shipwreck of the Republic would be one of the powerful weapons of the future. From condemnation of 2 December, the Second Empire republicans would go on to that of 18 Brumaire, whereas their predecessors, between 1815 and 1851, had not sufficiently followed the opposite route, *a priori* more natural, to oppose Bonapartism, or simply to be distinct from it.

The time had come, but too late. As in 1799, but along other paths, public opinion – breaking with all the groups in the political class – gave total power to Louis-Napoleon Bonaparte.

The plebiscite of 20 December 1851 had given Louis-Napoleon the task of promulgating a new constitution, based on what had been announced in the proclamations of 2 December: a president elected for ten years, vested with full executive powers and the initiative for law-making, sovereignly choosing his ministers, who were answerable to him alone, and three Assemblies, of which only one would be elected, the Legislative Body, with the responsibility for debating and voting on laws; the other two would be appointed – the Council of State to prepare legislative plans, and the Senate to safeguard institutions as a whole. Everything had been drawn up at full speed; the constitutional bill, prepared by Rouher, was ready on 14 January 1852. The central idea consisted of returning to consular institutions, which had allowed the creation of the modern state:

The proclamation reads: 'Since France has for the last fifty years kept going only by virtue of the administrative, military, judicial, religious and financial organization of the Consulate and the Empire, why should not we also adopt the political institutions of that era?' Immediately afterwards, the spirit of the new constitution was defined thus: 'In this country of centralization, public opinion has constantly laid everything, both good and bad, at the door of the head of government. So to write at the head of a charter that this chief is not accountable . . . would be to try to establish a fiction which has vanished three times in the noise of revolutions.'

This sentence says everything about the simplicity, and also the strength, of Louis-Napoleon's political conceptions: a head, elected by the nation, who governs it through a centralized administration which has the task of transmitting his directives and ensuring that they are carried out to the very ends of the Republic. He alone is enveloped in the supreme

François Flameng Literary History.
(*Photo: Roger-Viollet*)

legitimacy of the sovereignty of the people. The members of the Legislative Body, elected like himself (but every six years), cease however to be like him 'representatives' of the nation: by breaking with this fundamental principle of revolutionary public law, affirmed in 1789, the constitution of January 1852 regards those elected by the people as nothing more than mere 'delegates' from their part of the territory, and consequently incapable of legally constituting – as in the system envisaged in 1848 – a body invested, like the president, with the national will. Furthermore, the president convenes, adjourns, prorogues and dissolves the Legislative Body; each year, he appoints its president and vice-presidents.

Thus there came to an end the long ambiguity which, since the Restoration, had so often united Bonapartist and republican tradition around the concept of the sovereignty of the people. By using the principle of dynastic legitimacy against the 'usurper', the Bourbons had erased the memory that this principle had also belonged to the Empire. In 1815, after the Hundred Days, they had regained the Tuileries less from a hereditary sovereign than from a national head to whom the people had again given an overwhelming vote. The Napoleonic legend had thus shared with republican ideology, against the granted Charter, the cult of the sovereignty of the nation.

July 1830 had not modified that situation for long, since the revolution had been followed, in republican eyes, by a monarchic usurpation of the people's will, and a deliberate repudiation of revolutionary tradition: in those years, moreover, the young Louis-Napoleon had been on the best of terms with the republicans. By organizing two governments which were directly vested with the sovereignty of the people, the men of 1848 would demonstrate the incompatibility, in the French exercise of representation, of two sovereign powers in a single and indivisible Republic. By placing together the heirs of the Convention and the heir of the Consulate, they had started a conflict in which the former had not had time to play their cards, since they had been swiftly replaced by conservatives who were hostile to the very principle which formed their strength; but the latter, by contrast, would play with conviction his main trump card, that dogma from which he had derived everything – universal suffrage. But though the republicans had been powerless to prevent his victory, they concluded from 2 December and the 1852 constitution that never again would they assist in the investiture of the head of executive power by popular election.

The regime which was installed was truly a Caesarean democracy, in which the famous sovereignty of the people was entirely absorbed by one man, as on 18 Brumaire. The prince-president appointed a new Council of State (the preceding one had been dissolved on 2 December) and began on the batches of senators. The army gave unconditional support, and the prefects had nearly all followed the coup d'état, so that the purge remained very limited. On the other hand, the University had to be brought to heel, since it was largely liberal or republican; the Minister of Public Education now had total power of appointment and dismissal over teaching personnel, from the primary school teacher to the faculty professor. Victor Cousin, Michelet, Quinet and Jules Simon were excluded from the University. A decree of 17 February strictly regulated the operations of the press, returning to the practices of the Empire and the Restoration: prior authorization for every new publication, a raised guarantee rate and increased stamp duty, control by the Ministry of the Interior and Prefects by way of 'cautions' which, if repeated, would bring about the newspaper's suspension.

The most important matter in those transitional months was to eliminate republican opposition. Some 28,000 people had been arrested in the week after 2 December. In Paris, their fate had been summarily, and arbitrarily, decided by the administration or the police, and deportation to Algeria had been the most frequent decision. In the provinces their number was too great for some sort of procedure not to be instituted. The prisoners were tried, on the basis of their files and without appeal, by mixed commissions, formed in each *département*, comprising the general, the prefect and the state prosecutor. Almost 10,000 of them were deported to Algeria, and some hundreds to Cayenne. Several thousand were interned in France. That left the exiles, numbering nearly 2,000, among whom there were famous names, the proscribed members of the Legislative Assembly, the great witnesses to the shame of 2 December – Jean-Baptiste Charras, Quinet, Emile de Girardin, Schoelcher and Hugo; all those who, between December and the end of January, had arrived in Brussels; not all republicans, moreover, since the two great Orleanist generals, Changarnier and Lamoricière, were there too, paying for their past conflicts with the prince-president. The latter, in Paris, made a pretence of considering that repression had been carried too far by overzealous servitors, and was full of promises when seeing George Sand, who came to intercede for her proscribed friends. Be that as it may: never had a regime since 1815 proceeded with such intimidation of its adversaries, and with such arbitrariness. The thousands of poor wretches who were deported without a hearing, simply on administrative judgement, gave this dictatorship which was clothed in popular election its other aspect: that of social fear.

For that was still the fundamental psychological impetus among the entire bourgeoisie and the greater numbers of the peasantry. It had been visible at work so often since the spring of 1848 that no one was any longer surprised at its reappearance after the violent revolts which had followed 2 December; but what distinguished the situation in 1852 was that this feeling completely obliterated all sense of public liberty. Heaven knows that the February Republic had not been bloody, and that it had increased appeals to fraternity and constitutional scruples! But it had needed only to make its appearance to reawaken the phantom of the Terror, to which the June insurrection had given consistency: from now on, the fear of a 1793 dictatorship against property united all owners around the maintenance of order, even at the cost of contempt for the law. Tocqueville, who had rejoiced prematurely over this rediscovered unity, sadly gauged its true nature on 2 December: it was not a matter of a resurgence of public-spiritedness centred on the public good, but the return of the old fear of the Revolution in national life. In its own way, the bourgeoisie was practising what the socialists preached, the priority of the 'social question' over constitutional texts. France was more than ever a prisoner of the Revolution, where it had learned about politics.

This was a time when interests were more important than laws. The *rente* had not stopped climbing since 2 December, the repressive decrees had been welcomed with as much favour as they would have aroused indignation four years previously. Only one caused protest, in January, but precisely because it affected interests still more than liberties: that was the one quashing the endowments made by Louis-Philippe (with reserve of usufruct) to his children, on the eve of his accession to the throne in 1830, and confiscating the assets to the benefit of the state, allocating their use to social works. The Orleanists, those who had rallied to the dictatorship, Rouher, Fould and Louis-Napoleon's half brother, Morny, had resigned from the government, amid a row which would be too short for the statement of principle to be really firm. Louis-Napoleon was in control of everything; he held all the positions to be distributed. He had appointed the Senate, mingling in it nobility and notables from the three regimes – Empire, Restoration and July monarchy – flanked by cardinals and generals, and under the presidency of Jerome, the last surviving brother of the emperor. These men, who had seen the passing of so many regimes without losing the thread of their careers, were now entrusted with the country's laws; the holders of powers both vast and vague, guardians of the constitution, they were appointed for life and were irremovable, therefore theoretically independent; but their origin did not constitute a reliable guarantee of their liberty.

THE IDEA OF EMPIRE

The election of the Legislative Body took place at the end of February, by a two-round vote for a single name; the mood of the times was enough to designate the victors, to whom the prefects lent the authority of the state in advance, by indicating 'good' candidates. The Assembly was completely in the hands of the president, save for three legitimists who won in the faithful west, and a few republicans who had survived 1848, among whom were General Cavaignac and Carnot, elected in Paris. But they would resign rather than take the oath demanded in the new institutions.

In reality, the interest of this first legislative election lies less in its overall result, which was predetermined by the balance of the political forces, than in the way Persigny, the Minister of the Interior, conducted it, and in the new men he got elected. He used as his instruments not the electoral committees of Bonapartism, which had been working since the presidential ballot of 1848, but the prefects and sub-prefects; the object was to replace, as far as possible, the great families who had dominated the constituencies since the Restoration with new notables who were closely bound to the administration, and would form government networks across the whole of the country. This was a conception which was quite opposite to the theory of representative government, and yet the Restoration, and still more the July regime, had borrowed certain features from it which were more or less imposed by the logic of the centralized state. With the dictatorship of the second Bonaparte, that logic discovered – or rediscovered – its philosophy.

Simultaneously head of state and elected chief of the people, the prince-president superimposed on the pyramid of the administrative hierarchy a network of supporters, elected in his wake, who were to be his spokesmen in town and village. By doing so, he gave the second the benefit of efficiency in intervention, and the first the backing of universal suffrage. Through these two chains of public authority, from the bottom upwards, the people recognized in the absolute power of the elected president the image of their own power, and the means of their emancipation in relation to the local dominance of the great property-owners – legitimists and Orleanists alike. In that sense, the democratic aspect of the 1852 legislative election was indivisible from its plebiscitary and administrative aspects: a truly French paradox, the origins of which Tocqueville was just at that time beginning to seek in the Revolution, before being drawn to go back even farther, to the *ancien régime*.

The election of the deputies had seemed a triumph for the government, but it was simply a good result. More than five million votes for the official candidates, 850,000 for the opposition; massive solidarity amongst the peasantry, but strong reluctance in the big towns, which was apparent chiefly in the rates of abstention. Regions such as the south-east, very 'democ-soc' in 1849, or the Breton and Vendéen west, with a legitimist majority, continued to keep aloof. But Persigny had succeeded to a large extent in bringing in new parliamentary personnel, aided in this by the abstention instructions finally issued by the Bourbon pretender, and by the voluntary withdrawal of the majority of Orleanists.

From then on, a new Empire was almost a matter of course. Louis-Napoleon, however, hesitated a little and, as was his wont, let the movement of opinion in favour of the Empire simply happen, with the help of some secret remote control by Persigny and his prefects. By becoming hereditary, his power was cut off from universal suffrage, from which he had up till then drawn his republican legitimacy and his all-powerful authority, on both his right and his left. Moreover, in the matter of heredity, who would be his successor? To a government which was barely installed, the Empire would already be posing the question of its duration; for Prince Jerome, his uncle, was of neither the temperament nor the age to present the embodiment of its future, and Jerome's son, Prince Napoleon, spent his time lampooning his cousin with little groups of republicans. Nevertheless, logic and history soon won the day over these reservations, and the decisive step was taken in October, during a trip to the Midi during which the prince-president had gone to sound out the mood of the country in those regions which had proved the most recalcitrant. Persigny, the prefects, local authorities, the Church, the army, every body of some standing in France, all tried to outdo one another in sycophancy in the campaign to re-establish the Empire; but throngs of the populace were also present, and the tour progressively turned into a triumph: Louis-Napoleon was crowned king of France, through that coronation by public opinion special to the Bonapartes and known as the Empire.

The famous speech on 15 October in Bordeaux was his speech of acceptance of the throne, in which he lifted the last shackle weighing on the tradition to which he was heir, before going on to define his coming reign, after his own fashion. That shackle was war with Europe, the cradle of his dynasty; he proclaimed: 'The Empire means peace.' And he went on, playing on the idea and the word 'conquests':

I admit that, as emperor, I have a good many conquests to make. In that role, I want to win over dissident parties to reconciliation and to bring back into the flow of the great popular river those hostile currents which are lost without benefiting anyone.

I want to win over to religion, to morality and to comfortable circumstances that still numerous part of the population who, in the midst of a country of faith and belief, are barely aware of the precepts of Christ; who, in the bosom of the most fertile land in the world, can scarcely enjoy the bare necessities of life.

We have immense tracts of uncultivated land to clear, roads to open, ports to create, rivers to make navigable, canals to finish and our railway network to complete. Facing Marseille, we have a vast kingdom to assimilate to France. We have all our great western ports to bring closer to the American continent by the speed of those communications which we still lack. Everywhere we have ruins to restore, false gods to cast down and truths to bring to triumph.

That is how I would see the Empire, if the Empire is to be re-established. These are the conquests I am contemplating, and all of you, surrounding me now, who desire, as I do, the good of our nation – you are my soldiers.

Through this remarkable speech, the nephew revealed, in regard to his uncle's legendary heritage, a freedom and inventiveness which were infinitely superior to the Bourbons' confusion in the face of the *ancien régime*, or the fideism of the republicans *vis-à-vis* Year II. From the Napoleon of 18 Brumaire he once more took up the theme of national reconciliation in its classically bourgeois and peasant version, combining the return of faith with that of prosperity. But he invented a new goal for the national glory which was part and parcel of his inheritance, and one that was unprecedented in French public life: technical progress and the expansion of the economy. In doing so, he also rediscovered one of the Revolution's powerful images – that of the legislator-hero. Through him, Saint-Simonism made its entry into government vocabulary to encourage the idea of an Empire built on the productive works of peacetime.

From a juridical point of view, institutional transformation was swift. The Senate proposed it, the people voted for it on 21 November, by 7,800,000 votes against 250,000 – with over 2,000,000 abstentions, it is true, particularly numerous in those *départements* which had been reluctant or hostile in the preceding ballots. But the result was even more favourable than in December 1851, and appeared to be an additional and definitive recognition of the coup d'état. After all, the new emperor was in a strong position with three successive electoral triumphs – December 1848, December 1851 and November 1852. In the rural areas, the peasants had been astounded that anyone should have taken the trouble to consult them so often on the matter of the head of state, but their response had merely become more emphatic over the years. A little later, in 1863, Jules Ferry gives us the lucid appraisal of a republican: 'One day, the agricultural masses demonstrated that they were capable of having a will. The peasants wanted to put the crowning touch to the legend and, with one word, created the Empire. That word was passionate, free and sincere. They repeated it three times. And with more enthusiasm in 1852 than in 1848 and 1851.'

The Empire was re-established on 2 December 1852. Louis-Napoleon took the title of Napoleon III, out of respect for the very short reign of Napoleon's son, the King of Rome, who had been proclaimed emperor by his father's declaration of 22 June 1815. He had obtained the inclusion, in the *senatus consultum* of 7 November re-establishing the Empire, of his right to settle the order of succession to the throne within the Bonaparte family, should there be no direct heir.

Some months later, the new emperor married a young girl of the Spanish nobility, Eugénie de Montijo, who would give him a son, thus rendering pointless the precautions taken against the succession of his cousin, Prince Napoleon. Faced with the reluctance of European courts to offer him their daughters, he had chosen a marriage of inclination, in which the inclination was less lasting than the influence thus offered to the new empress, who was narrow in outlook and more conservative and more Catholic than if she had been born to the throne. The emperor broke with his English mistress, the beautiful Miss Howard, who had also been one of the financial backers of the coup d'état of 2 December, and whom he had had to compensate; but he did not entirely close the door on the short-term amorous adventures to which his tastes led him and for which his power allowed him to increase the opportunities.

So there he was, at the age of forty-four, Europe's most despotic sovereign in the name of democracy. It was a fact that no other monarch of the time possessed, as he did, the magic of a heritage combined with all the administrative means of domination, and adorned with the seal of the sovereignty of the people. Therein lay his secret, which he had understood very early on, and so profoundly that he had not truly gauged the weight of circumstances on his enterprise. In 1836 in Strasbourg, and in Boulogne in 1840, he had had no other idea in mind than the one he would cause to triumph in 1851: to replace an oligarchy of disloyal 'representatives' with an elected head. But at that period, bourgeois France had not yet exhausted the virtues of the Orleanist solution, which continued to fulfil the function inscribed on its birth certificate: a political formula which consolidated modern society, and which was neither the Bourbons nor the Republic.

In 1848, on the other hand, circumstances smiled on the ideas of one who passed for an adventurer: within a few months, the Republic was dying because it had established universal suffrage. What needed to

Hippolyte Jean Flandrin, Portrait of Napoleon III, *1861*, *Musée Versailles, Paris.*
(Photo: Lauros-Giraudon)

be found then was a regime which was neither the Bourbons, nor representative monarchy, nor parliamentary republic, and which could be democratic. What linked Napoleon III to the bourgeoisie and all the country's property-owners, including the peasants, was what had created the first Bonaparte: the inability of representative governments, monarchic or republican, to maintain social order in post-revolutionary France.

Among the emperor's intellectual luggage he still carried his uncle's military and national heritage, the great memories of a France extended to European scale, and the denunciation of the 1815 treaties. It was a heritage which gave his rhetoric a turn that was closer to the republicans than the Orleanists, but which Napoleon III handled cautiously, for though public opinion was glad to have its history restored, it could not forget that this history had ended badly and was afraid of re-enacting it. Therein lay the seed of an element of discord which was all the keener since the time was ripe for a reworking of the map of Europe; the day had been postponed by the repression of the 1848 revolutions, but its inevitability had not been dispelled.

In the first years of the Empire, however, national pride was cleverly invested in rediscovered order and prosperity. Napoleon III offered the unique spectacle of a Saint-Simonian who had attained absolute power, through which in the silence of the Assemblies he fulfilled something for which the physiocrats had drafted the doctrine: a state attempting to embody economic reason and the harmonious development of wealth, leaning for support on entrepreneurs. In this image of a 'managerial' Empire, much was circumstantial: the rapid economic growth of the 1850s had reasons which were independent of politics, and the structures of the state remained in essence unchanged between 1852 and 1870. Nevertheless Napoleon III had the advantage over the French bourgeoisie of the period, if not of understanding the economy, at least of grasping its importance in the government of a modern nation, and of making himself both its reflection and instrument. Through him, and thanks to his support, those second-generation Saint-Simonians who were the first technocrats of economic growth entered into the national elites.

The regime thus offered the spectacle of an entirely personal government, in the hands of a single man, yet which derived neither its origins nor its *raison d'être* from circumstances of national danger. Unlike the monarchies which had preceded it, this dictatorship appealed to the nation's imagination, but it was firmly anchored, like the July monarchy, in the prose of interests and not in the poesy of glory. For that reason, the second Bonapartism is easier to fathom than the first, since it owes more to the dominant passions of the era and of society, and less to the unpredictable genius of the leader.

Napoleon III governed alone. He had no Council of Ministers; he had ministers whom he appointed and called together, but in the manner of the erstwhile king of France: in order to consult them, without being tied by any of their counsels, either individual or collegial. They were the heads of their administrations, not the guardians of the public will. So no prime minister; a Minister of State had the task of co-ordinating interministerial affairs and acting as intermediary between the government and the Assemblies; but it was the emperor who had the last word on everything. In fact, the limits to his power did not arise from the constitution, but from state tradition and the nature of things. He was not as ubiquitous as his uncle; he had less tendency to see to everything himself, and all his life he would be unaware of the mechanisms and procedures of French administration, which formed the filters through which his decisions must necessarily pass. The administrative nature of his dictatorship, which explains its extent, also limited its arbitrariness by causing him at least to respect the rules of administrative law and the famous institutions of the Consulate.

One can understand the spirit of the system through one of its pillars, the prefectoral administration, whose powers were increased by the decree of 25 March 1852 (completed later by the one of 13 April 1861): the prefects were from now on, within their *départements*, representatives of the Ministries of the Interior, Agriculture, Finance and Public Works; they therefore had extraordinarily wide-ranging powers, designated very many categories of local officials, appointed the mayors in communes of fewer than 3,000 inhabitants (they could if necessary choose them from outside the municipal council), schoolteachers and police superintendents in towns of fewer than 6,000 inhabitants; lastly, they kept a kind of control over the general council through the appointment of its bureau, which was effected in Paris on their suggestions.

Thus every matter of any importance depended upon the prefectoral administration, in both villages and towns. But the extension of the prefects' prerogatives, although it added to the weight of state supervision over local life, was also a way of adjusting the administration's decisions to fit the variety of situations and circumstances. Tocqueville and Marx had taken a clear view of the nature of the Second Empire when they had diagnosed the triumph of the centralized state, concealed in the electoral victory of a political tradition. That was also what gave this dictatorship, alongside the arbitrariness which it employed against its adversaries, its regulated and institutional nature.

The strength of the Napoleonic legend would not have sufficed to entrench this second edition of the Empire so strongly – born like the first from a coup d'état – if it had not been accompanied by that kind of traditional security which the French saw in the state's omnipotence. Those years at the beginning of the Second Empire make it easiest to understand to what extent there existed in nineteenth-century France, behind the permanent civil war about the form of the state, a national consensus about its functions and its nature. Neither the Restoration, nor the July monarchy nor the Second Republic had touched that centralized administration which Napoleon III made the tool of his dictatorship; it was part of the revolutionary heritage which united legitimists, Orleanists and republicans, without their being aware of it, because its roots lay in the *ancien régime*, and in the new regime it had become a condition of social order as well as a guarantee of equality. In this regard, the second Bonapartism once again radically averted the two great panics of post-revolutionary France; on the right, it protected against the disintegration of society, and on the left against the return of privilege.

This explains the ease with which Napoleon III rallied or neutralized even the political figures of preceding regimes, who had been 'dropped' by the electorate. His feeling of dynastic loyalty kept him aloof from legitimism, his contempt for assemblies from Orleanism; and the violation of the law and the deaths of 2 December distanced him from the republican leaders. Nevertheless, how many great *ancien régime* families, how many former Orleanists, how many former deputies of the Constituent Assembly were to be found filling his councils! It was not a question of the leaders, who were loyal to their ideas and their past; but of what might be termed the political elites, who had rallied in support more frequently than they had shown hostility. Morny is not a good example: a former conservative deputy in Guizot's parliament, he was Louis-Napoleon's half-brother, and had very early on been associated with his activities, a leading actor in the coup d'état, but too much of a crook to be truly representative.

But an Orleanist bourgeois and a bourgeois favourable to the Second Empire had enough in common for the transition from one regime to the other not to be a rarity; the same type of political profile was to be found, dominated by the priority of social order, the fragility of which had been revealed once again by the republican experience of 1848. The man to whom Napoleon III had entrusted the presidency of the Council of State was a notable of the July monarchy, Baroche, former president of the Bar, former Public Prosecutor at the Court of Appeal, ex-deputy of the dynastic opposition; this liberal had enthusiastically greeted February and the Republic, before winning renown for his zeal in the service of the party of order; elected to the two Assemblies, Minister of the Interior in 1850 and, in that capacity, one of the authors of the law of 31 May, Minister of Foreign Affairs in 1851, he had welcomed 2 December. A good lawyer, clever, well versed in business matters, with a physique ideally made for caricature by Daumier, this liberal and Gallican Catholic is a good illustration of how the Empire picked its servants from preceding regimes, even though it was challenged by the most striking personalities among them.

More or less the same path had been trodden by Billault, the first president of the Legislative Body, before he yielded his place to Morny in order to become Minister of the Interior in 1854: he came of a good bourgeois family in Nantes, his grandfathers were barristers, his father a top civil servant during the Empire, himself a barrister linked through his marriage with the local oligarchy of shipowners, and deputy at a very early age. He had sat with Odilon Barrot's group, then in the centre-left with Thiers before founding, at the beginning of the 1840s, the little group of left-wing independents with Tocqueville, Lanjuinais, Abbatucci, Drouyn de l'Huis – all of whom would be Napoleon's ministers, but some before and some after 2 December. He himself, under the July monarchy, had had the original idea of trying to interest the state in the 'social question', and for that reason had been popular with the left in the spring of 1848, without afterwards falling into the atmosphere of White Terror which followed the June insurrection. Apart from family tradition, his Bonapartism had had its roots in a liking for both the ideas and the person of the prince-president.

Other, more specifically Bonapartist, supporters had come to the emperor from the republican ranks. For example, Joachim Petri, the Prefect of Police during those years, who centralized the army of policemen and informers, also inherited from preceding regimes but more powerful than ever. He was a former member of the Society of the Rights of Man, close to Ledru-Rollin, a commissioner of the Republic in his native Corsica in 1848; then Montagnard deputy in the Legislative Assembly, and very soon in the personal service of the prince-president, who appointed him prefect of the Ariège *département* after 2 December.

Upheld by public opinion as a new and strong government, the Second Empire thus derived part of its success, as the First had done, from the synthesis it effected in the name of the state between earlier political traditions. It posthumously reconciled Odilon Barrot's supporters with those of Guizot, moderate republicans with socialist-democrats. And time played its part, bringing into political life men who were born to it with the Empire, who were often more concerned with economic modernization than with the political rows of the past: the Legislative Body contained a contingent of entrepreneurs quite unknown to the Chambers of the two monarchies. As in 1800, the Bonapartism of the 1850s is better defined as a political state of affairs than as a party: it was the meeting of a situation and a man. Unlike the first, the second Bonaparte enjoyed the bonus of finding the administrative state ready constituted to be at his service. Why should he need the addition of a Bonapartist party? In a droll yet profound joke, which emerged from the conversation of the era, he himself had ridiculed the notion: 'The empress is legitimist, Morny is Orléanist, Prince Napoleon-Jerome is republican and I am socialist. There is only one Bonapartist, Persigny – and he's mad.'

Lastly, let us add to the kaleidoscope of forces summoned up to offer him absolute power that of the Church, which was by no means the least. The alliance had started up in 1848 around the party of order, and afterwards, in the conflict between the president and the Assembly. The Church had little to regret about the July monarchy, which had never clearly denied its Voltairean origins, and towards the Republic which had followed it had shared the same sentiments as the upper classes: little disposed to prolong its existence if a more firmly conservative solution could be found.

Its memories and its heart belonged in the legitimist camp, which itself had preferred a new Bonaparte to the risk of the candidacy of a son of Louis-Philippe in the presidential election of 1852. It had witnessed the return to religious faith of a mass of bourgeois in search of a divine guarantee of social order. In 1851 Montalembert, whose roots lay in liberal Catholicism, and Veuillot, never behindhand when it came to insulting modern society, had both accepted the coup d'état in advance; and on 3 December, Louis-Napoleon had not done Montalembert the honour of arresting him with the band of deputies resisting in the name of the law, among whom had been his friend Falloux.

Thereafter, he had stepped up his good behaviour and friendly attitude in regard to the Church, prompted by personal faith but also by the old family belief (which his uncle had made a principle of government) that the obedience of the populace increases by having its source in religion. He had allowed the setting up of numerous congregations, associated the Church with the authority of the state, looked after the upkeep and restoration of places of worship, and created a whole atmosphere: 'The Decembrists, in return for the devotion of the pontiffs, are flocking to Mass left, right and centre', wrote Schoelcher sarcastically from his exile in London, in *Le Gouvernement du deux décembre*.[1] On the other hand, the majority of the bishops praised the emperor with that extravagant homage which was one of the features of their style, if not of their nature; the Church was a party to the elections, and the prefects had recourse to it, especially where it was most useful to them: either to combat legitimist influence, or to come to terms with it in the west or the Midi.

Lastly, in the most sensitive area of relations between Church and state – education – the law of 15 March 1850 had effected the essential part of what the clerical party wanted: the University as an institution had not been abolished, but it had lost its powers to departmental councils, crowned by a higher council in which the clergy had carved out a dominant influence for themselves. In 1854 Napoleon III strengthened the authority of the state by creating sixteen academies headed by a *recteur*. But he excused himself in advance for this loyalty to an institution created by his uncle by imposing a strict intellectual, moral and religious conformism at all levels of education. The philosophy class was withdrawn in 1854, to be replaced by a year of what was called logic. Mass was compulsory in state schools on Thursdays and Sundays, and confession each term. Reading the memories of Taine about those years gives a measure of the half-police, half-clerical atmosphere which the minister, Hippolyte Fortoul, caused to hold sway in these establishments.

In such a system, both popular in public opinion and under the firm control of public authority, where did the opposition stand? It had practically no legal existence: the Legislative Body was the only elected assembly, and it was resigned to its minor role; Montalembert alone, by a few bursts of independence, sought to make amends for the support he had

[1] V. Schoelcher, *Le Gouvernement du deux décembre*, 1853, p. 334.

at first given to the institutions. The great parliamentary leaders of the July monarchy and the conservative party under the Republic lived in an internal exile, cut off from public affairs. The misfortunes of the era had not reconciled them, but had brought them together, legitimists and Orleanists, men of the movement and men of the resistance, centre-left and centre-right: Berryer, Falloux, Thiers, Guizot, Tocqueville, Rémusat, Salvandy, Broglie, Villemain, Cousin.

The principal disaccord continued to bear on dynastic loyalty. But the compromise which they all yearned for, between the Comte de Chambord and Louis-Philippe's sons, did not come about: through the princes, there were still two Frances in confrontation, and 'Henri V', who had no other claim to the future but his past, could not desert his flag. Since they were unable to embody the hopes of a single monarchy, the notables of representative government wore mourning for public liberties. Henceforward, they would mainly live in their country estates, Guizot in Val-Richer, near Lisieux; Tocqueville in his family château in Cotentin; Falloux in Bourg-d'Iré, in Anjou: they would visit one another to talk about the past and comment sadly on the present. The liberals of the Catholic party, Falloux, Montalembert and Monseigneur Dupanloup, liked to inveigh against Veuillot and the Church's headlong rush into servitude. The old adversaries of 1830, Thiers and Berryer, told each other about their Three Glorious Days, as seen from each side of the barricades, like a melancholy commentary on the vulgarity of despotism.

All of them were writing books on politics and history, as was their wont; they now had plenty of leisure time in which to do so. Guizot finished his *Histoire de la Révolution d'Angleterre* which he had begun under the Restoration, Tocqueville worked on his *Ancien Régime*, which came out in 1856, Thiers went on with his *Histoire de l'Empire*, Montalembert published *L'Avenir politique de l'Angleterre* and Rémusat wrote admirable articles on the heritage of the Revolution in French politics. The French–English comparison had remained in everyone's mind, but it was now treated in a pessimistic manner, since the English model had to be contrasted with the French failure to found power on liberty.

The French Revolution carried on, never-ending, giving the lie to the hopes and prognostications of all these old liberals. Contemporary woes did not serve to reconcile their analyses of the past, as may be seen in Guizot and Tocqueville, but at least united them in their condemnation of Napoleonic despotism. Deprived of the parliamentary rostrum, without any influence on opinion, these notables had found the natural refuge befitting their social status and their propensity for scribbling: the Académie Française. Many had already been elected to it before 1852: Tocqueville, Thiers, Molé, Vitet, Rémusat, Villemain, Cousin. They co-opted their friends on to it in a spirit of opposition to the regime: Montalembert, elected in 1851, Berryer in 1852, Falloux in 1856, Lacordaire in 1860, not forgetting M. de Sacy, the descendant of an illustrious Jansenist family and editor of the *Journal des débats*, the organ of this anti-authority oligarchy.

One of their aims was to mock those intellectuals who were in favour of the regime, who thronged to the salons of Princess Mathilde, the daughter of Jerome: Sainte-Beuve, Mérimée, Théophile Gautier, sometimes Flaubert. Thus the Académie Française became a kind of shadow of the parliament of the great years, where all these beaten political men seemed to forget their old quarrels and to unite at last in pleading a common cause, though to a very restricted audience. It became a symbol – that illustrious yet confined place, the refuge for those who had been vanquished by universal suffrage. The dome of the Académie Française had gathered in both the brilliance and the collapse of French liberalism.

On the republican side, the collapse was more obvious than the brilliance. The trees of liberty which had been planted on all sides in 1848 had been felled, and the republican device scratched off the façades of public buildings. Napoleon III had tempered the cruelty of the arrests and deportations following 2 December by pardons granted upon the proclamation of the Empire and on the occasion of his marriage: at the beginning of 1853, about 6,000 prisoners were left, some of whom had been transferred to Algeria (and the more unfortunate ones to Cayenne), the rest being assigned forced residence in France or in exile. In 1852 Brussels had temporarily been the home of that enforced emigration, the first of such size since the French Revolution. But the majority of exiles finally settled in Switzerland and Britain when, their first illusions dispelled, they realized that the exile would be lengthy if, as many of them did, they refused the amnesty proposed by 'Badinguet' (Napoleon III) in return for their recognition of the regime. Those long years outside France as always added their weight of bitterness and unreality to the vision of men for whom realism had never been a strong point.

The Second Republic's extreme left was as divided in London as it had been in Paris: furthermore, those outlawed on 2 December had met up there with exiles from May–June 1848, like Louis Blanc, and from June 1849, like Ledru-Rollin, which implied a hierarchy of exile and disagreement as to its reasons. Ledru-Rollin had his Revolution Society, chiefly devoted to the struggle of European nationalities. As for the socialists, they had transferred their shops and their methods to London, a revolutionary commune which brought together Félix Pyat and the Blanquists, the heirs of rebellious Babouvism, and the supporters of Louis Blanc, those of Cabet and those of Pierre Leroux.

Lastly, on his rocky isle, there was Victor Hugo, who had already published *Napoléon le Petit* in Brussels before leaving for Jersey in 1852, whence he would be expelled by the British government in 1855 to the neighbouring island of Guernsey. Strangely enough, until the summer of 1849, he had figured among the members of the party of order who remained on good terms with the prince-president. Breaking with the conservatives over the Rome affair, at that period, he had become one of the great orators of the republican left, but more hostile to his former friends than to Louis-Napoleon, being more fearful, he wrote, of 'Pichegru, that is to say, Changarnier, than of Bonaparte'. On 2 December he made

one of the great choices of his life: he would be the Republic in the face
of the 'usurper', liberty in the face of dictatorship. He was the most
formidable power to rise up against the Empire, but only he was aware of
it, and had never had any doubts about his own genius, wanting to be the
king of his century. The future would be the judge. During the first years
of the regime, the bombshell of the *Châtiments* (1853) did not reach outside
the small circles of implacable enemies of the Empire, who secretly slipped
the book to one another.

If republican opposition was so weak internally – although its latent
existence was suspected at the 1852 elections because of the hostile votes
and high percentage of abstention in the big towns – it was not only
because it had been bludgeoned by repression, the suppression of its
newspapers and the exile of its leaders. There were older reasons, connected
with its having been divided in the spring of 1848, and being on the
defensive since the elections of December 1848 and May 1849. The
wounds of June 1848 continued to cause a profound split between socialists
and republicans, who accused each other of having killed the Republic, the
first group denouncing the second for having backed bourgeois repression,
and the second criticizing the first for wanting to justify a rebellion against
the government elected by the people.

Louis-Napoleon had cleverly played on that division since the summer
of 1848, and it had been evident on the evening of 3 December that many
of the elements of the Parisian extreme left had been all the less inclined to
budge in favour of the conservative Republic because the author of the
coup d'état had enjoyed the reputation of being the workers' friend. Why
defend Thiers or Falloux against the author of *L'Extinction du paupérisme*,
who was, moreover, the restorer of universal suffrage? At least he could be
no worse than the regime which he had just brought to an end. 'We were
going along the worst possible road', wrote George Sand to her friend, the
publisher Hetzel, exiled in Brussels; 'now here we are on a different road.'[2]

Proudhon held the same attitude, having published, barely six months
before the coup d'état, a caustic criticism of all the political dogmas of the
extreme left, under the title *Idée générale de la Révolution au XIXe siècle*. In
his view, the nineteenth-century revolution ought to establish society,
by restoring its autonomy through association, on the ruins of political
authority, whether monarchic or democratic. After 2 December he considered the dictatorship more favourable to that revolution than the
bourgeois Republic; in Louis-Napoleon he saw socialism's man; he
condemned exile and recommended participation in the 1852 elections,
even finding some virtue in universal suffrage.

So the imperial dictatorship had nothing to go against it but the remants
of the Republic's two great opposing parties, who were still hostile and
even foreign to each other, and, on top of that, cut off from their electorate
and more divided than ever internally, without any practicable plan for the

[2] Letter of 21 December 1851, *Correspondance*, vol. 10, p. 592.

future of the nation. The liberals had no monarchy, and the republicans shed no tears for the Republic.

The Second Empire had had some elbow room, and had taken advantage of it. These were its happy years, both at home and abroad. The Crimean War (1854–6), which had arisen from European rivalry over protection of the Holy Places of Jerusalem, gave the emperor – at a high price, it is true – the lustre of military victory, which he had not needed to embody a 'national' regime, but which confirmed that he belonged to the Bonaparte family. It also brought him a benefit which was not part of his tradition: that of conducting a foreign policy favourable to Catholic interests. The uncle had treated the pope as an enemy; the nephew made himself the defender of St Peter's throne in the Holy Places. Increasingly ultramontane, the Church of France bathed the Holy See and Napoleon III in the same veneration: it was the most intense moment of this unforeseen idyll between the former Carbonaro insurgent in papal territory and a Church whose bishops had hailed 1815 as religion's great revenge on the 'usurper'.

In the shelter of this spiritual benediction, the Second Empire was also helped by the economic situation, for which the French gave it the credit and which it at least knew how to profit by – in both senses of the word. The regime presented a scene of political racketeering and easy money; it treated itself to the first and only truly bourgeois court in French history: entertainments, waltzes, a style, an Opera.

But it was also the period of a rapid economic transformation of the country, in which the state played its part: in that field, the emperor was ahead of the France of property-owners and *rentiers* who voted for him, and as an ex-Saint-Simonian he understood better than they the spirit of enterprise. France built its railway network, freed its countryside from its rural enclaves by constructing local roads; the new prefect of the Seine, Haussmann, was busy remodelling the map of Paris from top to bottom, starting with the ancient centre, that tangle of medieval streets between the rue Saint-Denis and the rue Saint-Martin, the supreme abode of popular insurrection. This was an admirable symbol of the fact that the Empire did not separate the modernization of the country from the strengthening of social order. It inscribed its dual vocation in the very stone of Parisian houses, with the overwhelming support of its dual electorate, both bourgeois and peasant.

The 1857 elections brought no important change to that political and social balance. Instigated by the government, with the object of taking advantage of the favourable climate of public opinion, and carefully organized by Billault, Minister of the Interior, they returned a very strong majority for those in power, comparable with 1852. There was, however, one difference, which was important because it marked the limits of the Empire's popularity in the large towns: twenty republican deputies were elected in Paris, where their total votes equalled those gained by the official candidates. Three of them were ghosts from 1848 – Cavaignac, Carnot and the banker Goudchaux who, after February, had briefly been in charge of the Republic's finances; the two others were free of this past, Emile Ollivier because he was too young, and Louis Darimon because he was a Proudhonian. Cavaignac died before he could take his seat, and Carnot and Goudchaux refused to take the oath, according to the precedent of 1852. In the three by-elections which followed, there were two republican victories, Jules Favre and Ernest Picard. With another elected member from Lyon, the parliamentary opposition was now five republican deputies strong. The Empire was not seriously threatened by them, but both the emperor and the political class were struck by the persistence of Parisian hostlity, which was rejuvenated by the appearance of a new, brilliant and pugnacious republican generation.

For the moment, the first disturbances in the regime's social strata would come from another quarter, both more unexpected and yet traditional: the emperor himself, through his foreign policy. In a word, Napoleon III took it into his head to have an Italian policy which favoured national unification, and this would of necessity alienate him from the pope and, in consequence, the Church and the Catholic electorate. The unexpected nature of the affair stemmed from his having just played the opposite role in the Crimea, where the imperial army had been the sword of Roman Catholicism in the quarrel over the Holy Places. But in other respects the enterprise had been entirely in keeping with the spirit of Bonapartism, hostile to the treaties of 1815 and favourable to European nationalities.

In his youth, the Emperor had fought to liberate the Romagna from papal control and had retained a keen memory of it, not being at all repentant. What is most enthralling for the historian about his Italian initiative is that it illustrates the weight of a tradition and a state of mind which the second Napoleon resolutely upheld even to the detriment of his own political interests. Nephew of the great emperor, Napoleon III felt obliged to follow in his footsteps: not only did he have to cover the flag with glory, but also to rebuild a Europe in keeping with the march of history, to bring to an ordered close the underground work of the Revolution. Italy was both the family cradle and the scene of his youthful adventures, after providing his uncle with the theatre for his earliest exploits. It therefore formed a favoured ground where he could pursue his dreams as well as his memories, and finally win his laurels in an Italian campaign in order to obliterate the rather miserable failure of that uprising in Romagna which had left his brother dead.

It was not only literature, Hugo in the forefront, which laid the unkindest stress on the parallel between the two Napoleons; for far longer than his adversaries, the nephew had been drawing on it for the material of his psychological and political life, since it was the secret of his perseverance. He knew its cruelty just as well as they. But at last events had yielded to his will between 1848 and 1852; and in a sense he had reached such a pinnacle on the world stage – he who had risen from so low – only to prove continually, to himself and the public, that he was not unworthy of the hero whose name he bore. Italy was the first scene of that failed demonstration.

The rapprochement with Piedmont had a strange origin: in January 1858, a bomb exploded in the path of the imperial carriage, in the forecourt of the Opera, leaving eight dead and one hundred and fifty injured, but without touching Napoleon III. The culprits were immediately arrested; the plot was Italian, organized by activists from the peninsula who had taken refuge in London; the mastermind was Felice Orsini, a former member of the Constituent Assembly of the Roman Republic, famous for his exacting demands in 1849 at Ancona and Ascoli, a tireless conspirator since then, imprisoned by the Austrians in 1855 and escaping death by fleeing.

The aim of the assassination attempt was not so much to punish Napoleon III for the part played by France in the ending of the Roman Republic as to provoke, through his death, a new European wave of revolutions comparable with that of 1848. The result of its failure was to arouse anew the public sense of the frailty of the dynasty, panic among the courtiers and anxiety among politicians, the reappearance of the spectre of the Terror and its train of revolutionary measures intended to exorcize it: a new firm-handed Minister of the Interior, a general security law which revived the 'suspect' category, the resumption of arrests and the sad convoys bound for Algeria.

Nevertheless the emperor had grasped something of the message of his would-be assassin, who went to the scaffold in March. Orsini had clothed his criminal act in the cause of Italian liberty: Napoleon III had not been able to save the murderer, but he had heard his voice.

His idea was to help Cavour, the prime minister of the kingdom of Piedmont, to liberate the north of Italy from Austrian domination in such a way as not to leave the monopoly of the Italian cause to Mazzini and the Italian republicans. In return, France would receive Savoy and Nice from Piedmont. But this plan, conceived in July 1858 at Plombières between Cavour and Napoleon III, presupposed war with Austria and a break with Pope Pius IX: that carried a double risk internally – both in relation to the promises made in the Bordeaux speech and in regard to the support of Catholic opinion.

The bourgeoisie had not retained the same memories of the First Empire as had its heir; it remembered less about the Italian campaign than about the last years of the reign, forced conscription and the ultimate catastrophe. It had given overwhelming support to the nephew so that he should rebuild the order enjoyed under the Consulate, not so that he should start the imperial adventure all over again. It liked a strong state, but it did not have a Bonapartist imagination. The rural world was indifferent; but if war brought in its wake the hostility of the pope and the Catholic Church, there was a risk that country folk would follow their *curés* and bishops. There was but one sector of the population that liked the idea of a war on Italy's behalf: the inhabitants of the large towns, who for so long had been indistinguishably republican and Bonapartist, before the two traditions had been separated by 2 December. The Italian affair once more mobilized them jointly, illustrating what continued at bottom to bind the second Bonaparte to the Revolution in spite of 2 December.

When the emperor departed to take command of his troops in Italy on 10 May 1859, his barouche did not get as far as the Bastille Station, where he was to take the train, before it was unharnessed and pulled by the people, who formed a triumphal procession for the new missionary of the Great Nation, a combination of 1792 and 1804. Without a doubt, the man of the Tuileries had the same image, the same memory, in his mind on that day: for the first time since 1815, France was going to involve its flag in the liberty of the peoples, thereby reviving what the Revolution shared with the Bonapartes.

There was no 'Italian campaign' comparable to that of 1796. There were two difficult and bloody battles in June, Magenta and Solferino, French victories which did not destroy the Austrian army. The emperor, in fact, had neither the eye nor the temperament for military matters, and even less a taste for war. The beginning of July saw him negotiating with Franz-Joseph, having only half-fulfilled the secret Plombières contract, with Piedmont receiving Lombardy but not the Veneto. Like the commencement of the conflict, this midway halt was a decision which he took on his own, withdrawing at the prospect of either a long siege, or the possible intervention of Prussia, or the beginnings of a revolutionary movement in the Papal States, or the hostile reactions of the Church in France. Those reasons were not incompatible, but the difficulties were all foreseeable. The Villafranca armistice with Austria set Napoleon at odds with Cavour; although Piedmont had received Lombardy from French hands, France had succeeded in alienating Italian patriots when coming to their aid. On the other hand, in Paris the Church and bourgeoisie breathed again, while the faubourg Saint-Antoine wept for abandoned Venice. On his return, Napoleon III celebrated victory and granted amnesty to the remainder of the exiles.

The strange feature of imperial foreign policy was the constant to-ing and fro-ing between contradictory positions. After Villafranca it would have been logical to capitalize on the fruits of that semi-victory, externally by acquiring Savoy and Nice, and internally by reassuring conservative forces after the Italian escapade. But no. The Italian problem, reopened by Napoleon III, was not closed when he withdrew. Tuscany, Parma and Modena, which had been in a state of revolt since April, were demanding to be united with the Piedmont, and the Romagna, which was papal territory, was in a state of rebellion. At the beginning of autumn 1859, it became increasingly clear that the emperor was again leaning towards the Italian revolution, to the detriment of Pius IX: this position was all the more acrobatic because, since 1849, a small French expeditionary force had been in Rome, keeping watch over the pope's temporal kingdom.

In the latter months of 1859 and the first few of 1860, battle recommenced between the Catholics and the government in France. Now was the moment for the liberal Catholics, Falloux, Montalembert, Broglie and Augustin Cochin, who gained the Church's ear since they had the longest-standing claims to opposing the Empire. They were joined by Veuillot, who brought a wealth of supporters, his country *curés* and the old reactionary hard core of the faithful. More strangely, the great names of Orleanism climbed on this train, which was not really theirs, in order not to miss the chance of reunion with the electorate and a large section of public opinion: Guizot, Thiers, Villemain and Cousin abruptly took the papal cause to heart (though not Rémusat, who was most deeply liberal). Lacordaire was elected to the Académie Française on 2 February 1860, and Cousin had declared: 'I vote for the holy Pius IX.'

Napoleon III counter-attacked, took on a new Minister of Foreign Affairs, Edouard Thouvenel, who was completely under his thumb, banned *L'Univers*, and got a Gallican strategy under way. Here was an old scene from French politics, borrowed from the repertoire of the former monarchy and Bonapartism, by which a Catholic government did battle with Rome in the name of its authority over the Church of France, after having so widely facilitated the creation of new congregations: now the Empire was back-pedalling, trying to limit their number and control their activities.

In March 1860 the Piedmont annexed the territories of central Italy, including the Romagna, with France's consent. Napoleon asked for, and received, in return Savoy and Nice, which voted massively in favour of being united with France. The epilogue to this story took place at the end of the summer, when Lamoricière's Franco-papal troops were defeated at Castelfidardo by the Piedmontese army, which was trying to forestall Garibaldi, with the tacit assent of the emperor. The territory of the Holy See was reduced to Rome and the surrounding lands. Napoleon III had lost the hearts of French Catholics, and had gained a province and a town: such was the balance sheet of an affair which he had conducted so strangely, and which was dangerous less for its consequences at home than for what it revealed of a personal and foreign policy ruled by memories. For the emperor could more easily regain the bulk of Catholic conservatism than give up being what he was, which was also what had brought him to power.

A LIBERAL EMPIRE?

During the same year, two decisions on internal policy – these, too, very personal – reorientated the nature of the regime and showed the direction which its leader intended it to take.

The first, in January, instituted free trade through a commercial treaty with Britain. Industrial circles were hostile to the idea, being convinced that opening up the frontiers would give the signal for the ruin of French industry, which was incapable of competing with British products; in a country where protectionism had such a long tradition, it was like a dogma of French political and economic conservatism, and a guarantee of the country's stability. Napoleon had not needed to force his lifelong convictions in order to listen to Michel Chevalier, an old Saint-Simonian like himself and a great advocate of free trade. Moreover, he was making a gesture towards Britain, which had not been too keen on his Italian policy. But above all, he believed in the virtues of opening the frontiers for the economic development of the country, and for improving the lot of the working classes. In this battle, too, his adversaries were among those that had previously upheld the regime, while his support came from those who had always fought against him, liberals and republicans.

Was that why he decided to modify the way the institutions functioned, in a liberal direction? For such was really the significance of the decree made at the end of the same year (1860) on 24 November: from now on, the government would have to give account of itself each year before the Legislative Body and the Senate at the opening of the session, which would give rise to a general policy discussion. Further innovations included unabridged shorthand records of debates, easier execution of the right of amendment of laws and ministers without portfolio given the special task of maintaining contact with the Assemblies. These arrangements, without changing the 1852 constitution, greatly altered its spirit, since the most important one brought back into practice that right of Address which the two monarchies in succession had made parliament's essential prerogative.

Historians are still arguing about the causes of this shift in position, which redirected the entire development of the regime: the Second Empire presents the exceptional example of a dictatorship which was liberalized by the will of the dictator. It was precisely at the moment when he was once more taking up his uncle's message in Italy that Napoleon III began an unprecedented internal policy which was very far removed from the spirit of Bonapartism. The emperor had not suddenly shed his contempt for the Assemblies, since he governed more than ever in secrecy and all alone; but his regime had lasted ten years: the French, and above all the younger generation, had forgotten the rigours which had accompanied its birth as well as the civil disorders of the Second Republic.

In a large modern and democratic country, how was it possible to perpetuate a dictatorship born of circumstance? Napoleon I had done it, but he had never emerged from a war with Europe which had ended badly. His nephew, on the contrary, brought back from a war which he halted before he had completely won it the idea that one day the French would have to be drawn closer to that liberty whose cause he had gone to uphold in Italy. At bottom, dictatorship compromised the opportunities of his son by making everything subordinate to him personally; on the other hand, the representative principle would strengthen the hereditary principle; liberty would crown a dynastic foundation.

So thought Morny, who also was worried by the hostility between the empress, who was officially regent in Napoleon III's absence, and his cousin Napoleon, Jerome's son, who was frustrated by the birth of an heir to the throne to which he believed he had some right. The decree of 24 November 1860 therefore seems to me to be a document offering an almost perfect contrast with the adventurism which distinguishes the Italian policy; it begins to depersonalize the Empire, as far as it possibly can, in order to entrench it in representative institutions, adding to the rich panoply of the images of Bonapartism that of a liberal-national monarchy.

The emperor had invited parliamentary France to have its say. It accepted at once, at the opening of the 1861 session, in the general debate on the Address. The Italian policy was at the forefront of minds and passions: Italy still and always meant revolution. Prince Napoleon, the republican of the family, declaimed for several hours in the Senate a harangue against the Catholic and legitimist right and the conquered sovereigns of the Italian wars, glorifying the cause of unity in the peninsula: 'We are not', he said, 'representatives of reaction, but of modern society. Napoleon III represents popular right opposed to divine right . . . We keep our sympathy for the glorious Italian cause. For the ex-king of the Two Sicilies we have nothing but pity.' Some days later, on 13 March, a Catholic deputy from Alsace, Emile Keller, answered him from the rostrum of the Legislative Body, in the Palais Bourbon, in what was the speech of his lifetime. He first challenged the government: 'France was plainly revolutionary in 1793, plainly a conqueror under the First Empire, plainly conservative in 1848 and 1849. But you, who have been imprudent enough to reopen this arena without judging its extent, who are you and what do you want to become?' There followed this profession of faith, which was heartily applauded: 'You have asked us to make known all our thoughts, and I will certainly tell you mine. It is time to look the Revolution in the face and say to it: You will go no further!' Thus, those first public liberties caused the reappearance of the great phantom of French politics.

Napoleon III was not as republican as his cousin, but Keller had fully understood where his regime was heading the instant that the question of the revolutionary heritage arose: it was on the side of the Revolution. That was socially obvious before becoming a political lesson, either at home or abroad. In fact, the Second Empire deep down was bound to the modern society which had emerged from 1789. Of all the nineteenth-century French political regimes, this was the one which wanted to be, and was, the most involved in the capitalist economy, the most interested in the growth of production and the modernization of the country – whether it concerned rail or road networks, urban infrastructures, the alterations to Paris or the promotion of trade, both internal and international.

The nature of the state's functions was not greatly changed as a result, for the administration remained aloof from direct intervention in the economy, to say nothing of the idea of redistributing revenues. Nevertheless, there existed a central impetus to the movement of the economy, a recognition of the worth of the world of production and wealth, which had so often been overlooked or misused by a bourgeoisie tugged between democratic universalism and counter-revolution, and generally lacking in economic culture. Moreover, because it did not have at its disposal a good bourgeois philosophy of market society, the Second Empire had fitted the Saint-Simonian philosophy of planned economy into a bourgeois mould: an intellectual telescoping which once again revealed the French propensity for intellectually anticipating the way things would develop. For, whatever the role played by Saint-Simonians in the corridors of the imperial regime, no economic planning, no technocracy was yet on the agenda. If 2 December had truly had a political economy, it had been contained, apart from expenditure invested in public works, in a systematic will to give the market its head, and society its dynamism, for the creation of prosperity.

Now, this movement of society had a name in the nineteenth century – democracy. Its origin can be located in the civil equality of 1789. It belonged wholly to what had begun in that era, on the ruins of aristocratic society: a world in which there were only individuals, equal before the law, competing for the appropriation of wealth and self-realization. That democracy triumphed under the Second Empire, far more than under any of the preceding regimes: it was a natural effect of the passage of time, but it was also the express will of Napoleon III, at the very moment when he deprived the French of political liberty. But at the same stroke he had also created, in the long term, conditions which were favourable to the ending of the dictatorship. Whereas Napoleon I had constantly fed his despotism on war, his nephew ceaselessly jeopardized the future by his peacetime operations.

In step with the affirmation of modern society's vitality, fear of a restoration of the *ancien régime* receded – a fear which had still been very strong in the first half of the century. If the peasants were less afraid of the return of the nobles, they would be less fearful of liberty, and the extreme left socialist-democrats would have less need of the revolutionary repertoire: the dictatorship of 2 December had been based on those panic fears. One last, even more unavoidable thing threatened it: how to deny for any length of time participation in public affairs to a society which was daily becoming more active, more urban, more educated and more wealthy? The Empire had two legitimacies: one fragile, the right of inheritance; the other essential, universal suffrage. It clung to monarchy only by the weakest link, but its best claim drew it closer to the Republic.

From that arose the force of what the decree of 24 November had begun to outline: a regime which was taking a step towards the idea of representation, in a form no longer based on eligibility through property, but democratic, and thenceforth enveloped in universal suffrage. It was a matter of putting together elements which had not coexisted in any other regime or any other country: a hereditary head (but of plebiscitary origin), a centralized administration and a parliamentary representation elected by universal suffrage. Such a heterogeneous system tends of its own accord towards simplification, by returning to its origins or by creating an executive accountable to the legislative power. The political history of the latter half of the Second Empire is the history of that simplification, in the sense of the 1860 bill. That is to say that, in the main, it is also the history of its opening up to the left, on the side of the Republic.

One political family on that left, where they were so numerous, had no need to be convinced or won over: the socialists who loathed the bourgeois of the Second Republic even more than the adventurist of 2 December. Some among them were inspired mainly by circumstances, but those circumstances had been the June uprising, the cruelty of the repression, the obsessive anti-socialist fear which had marked the men of the party of order. Others had made a kind of doctrine of the workers' indifference towards the nature of bourgeois government. The rupture on that point between socialists and republicans was of long standing; we have seen that it went back to the first years of the July monarchy. Speaking of her long familiarity with the Parisian extreme left in *L'Histoire de ma vie*, George Sand wrote that in 1835 'the time was beginning to dawn when purely political ideas and purely socialist ideas would dig chasms between the supporters of democracy.'[3]

The entire history of the Second Republic had thus reinforced passions and doctrines which were part of the precociousness and strength of the idea of class struggle. It is true that, at the time when the left was on the defensive, a wide fringe of extremists had been allowed to survive and go on demanding Republic and socialism together; but nevertheless, the two philosophies had been distinct and even contradictory, because the Republic, even though accompanied by the right to work, had not had the same historical or intellectual foundations as the social revolution, even in a republican form.

Now, on top of everything else, the new master of France, detested by the grandees of the Republic, was displaying 'socialist' ideas. It was indeed bizarre to see Louis-Napoleon combining with the violent anti-republican repression which followed the coup d'état a loyalty to his plans on behalf of the working classes. He disbanded what remained of the workers' associations which had flourished in 1848, for fear that they might harbour a political opposition, but entertained the idea of replacing indirect taxes, which weighed so heavily on the poor, with a tax on income, which was socially more just. The entire bourgeoisie cried out against 'governmental socialism', and Proudhon, at that time close to the Elysée, wrote on 6 March 1852: 'L.-Napoleon has come to a dead halt with his socialist plans . . . The bankers are keeping out of it, and the bourgeoisie are siding with Cavaignac.'[4]

In reality, nothing had gone very far in that direction. The most

---

[3] G. Sand, *Histoire de ma vie*, vol. 5, ch. 8.
[4] P.-J. Proudhon, *Correspondance* (1875), vol. 4, p. 232.

important and most symbolic act had been a programme of social expenditure, financed at the outset by the confiscation of Orléans wealth, and devoted to workers' housing, property loan institutions and friendly societies. It was on this last point that the new regime's social policy achieved the most rapid results. The idea was common to both Proudhon and social Catholicism: mutual aid, whereby workers took out insurance amongst themselves against the hazards of existence. It was an ancient practice, although not recognized by the state, which had arisen from the traditional solidarity of the guilds. But a decree of March 1852 had elevated friendly societies almost to the dignity of public institutions. They could be freely constituted – an inordinate privilege in a legislation which was still subject to Le Chapelier's law banning associations – and certain of them, known as 'approved', received public assistance, with the reservation that their president should be appointed by the head of state. In all this legislation at the beginning of the reign, there appeared the dual concern with easing the conditions of the working man's life and also the control exercised over it by the state.

Proudhon's influence is perceptible as well, at least on the first point. Today almost forgotten, and in any case seldom read, Proudhon was at that period the most influential author in the French working-class elite when it was trying to formulate its autonomy. He belonged to those socialist writers who wanted at all costs to shift the Revolution from political abstractness to social reality; who believed that 1789 had been unable to create a lasting society, merely substituting a centralized state and bourgeois government for absolutism and the aristocracy. In the book which he published in 1852, which bears a significant title, *La Révolution sociale démontrée par le coup d'état du 2 décembre*, he took up in his own fashion the obsessive comparison between the two revolutions, the Great Revolution and that of 1848, in order to demonstrate that their two failures had much in common.

The French Revolution had believed it was substituting a people's government for that of the king, Rousseau for Bossuet; it is true, it had enjoyed an initial period, which lasted up to the Montagnards, when society had gained control of power and local freedoms had flourished. But centralization started again from the events of 31 May–2 June, with the almost superstitious belief in the state and the negation of the people's powers in the name of the people. February 1848 had seen the reappearance of the revolutionary idea, but that was once again betrayed by the bourgeoisie and the Church, which had joined forces in May and June to crush it; all at once, Louis-Napoleon Bonaparte became its herald on 10 December 1848. He was an ambiguous herald, because he was also the man of the party of order and of anti-socialist reaction; but his opposition to the law of 31 May 1850 put him back entirely on the side of universal suffrage, in which the people saw the means of their emancipation.

Thenceforward, the fate of social revolution lay in his hands, through 'the inevitability of things', provided that he had the will:

Let 2 December, therefore – and what I now say for the outgoing government, I address equally to all those who are to come – let 2 December openly embrace its *raison d'être*; let it affirm, unequivocally and without restriction, the social revolution; let it speak out loud to France, let it make known abroad the terms of its mandate; let it summon to itself, instead of a body of mutes, a true representation of the middle class and the proletariat; let it prove the sincerity of its sympathies by acts of explicit liberalism; let it purge itself of all clerical, monarchic and Malthusian influence.[5]

However naïve or even incongruous this appeal may seem, in the political situation of 1852, it is interesting in that it reveals the strength that the concept of social revolution retained in the French political repertoire, as a way of finally succeeding where 1789 had failed. Of working-class origins and self-taught, Proudhon is probably the French political writer with the keenest understanding of working-class small communities and solidarity, who, for that reason, felt the most instinctive rejection of the legal individualism and democratic abstractness forming the basis of modern society. What constitutes his system, strictly speaking – that clockwork organization between micro-societies whose mutual exchanges ensure harmony – is rooted in the idea of association, the natural form of man's existence, which must be extended by the exercise of will to embrace all social mechanisms.

In order to come up with an alternative solution to the failure of the socialisms of 1848, Proudhon did not even need the emperor's collaboration. All he required was his backing to extend the network of workers' associations and thus to inspire an original and strong working-class culture: simultaneously separated from political republicanism and characterized by an almost corporate reformism, quite apart from the struggles of public life. The breach between the republican tradition and the socialist tradition, so important in French political history, had found its doctrinaire in Proudhon.

Napoleon III would not be his disciple, as he had hoped. But neither would he be indifferent to the progress in working-class consciousness and demands. Other men around him would act as spokesmen – the journalist Armand Lévy, and Arlès-Dufour, an industrialist of Saint-Simonian origins. Their influence was noticeable at the beginning of the 1860s, at the time when the emperor was shifting the regime towards the left, for the reasons we have seen. In autumn 1861, he gave his backing to sending a delegation of 200 workers to the International Exhibition in London the following year; the organizer of this venture was a Proudhonian bronze engraver, Henri Tolain, and the delegates were genuinely chosen by their peers in the friendly societies to represent the various professions. They would return from a long stay in London even more resolutely in support of the right to unite and the right to strike.

---

[5] P.-J. Proudhon, *La Révolution sociale démontrée par le coup d'Etat du 2 décembre*, p. 236.

In the legislative elections of 1863, the workers as such played only a symbolic part, rather as in the government of February 1848. But the next year, at the by-elections, Tolain stood in Paris against one of the leading lights of the republican party, a veteran of 1848, Garnier-Pagès. He had no chance of being elected, but used the occasion as the pretext for a manifesto, signed by sixty workers, and mostly written by himself. It was a document of major importance because, for the first time within democratic politics, it revealed the demand for specific working-class representation – rather as Sieyès had asked in 1789 that all deputies to the Third Estate should come from the Third Estate. Inspired by Proudhon, the *Manifeste des soixante* did not hark back to the class war or the Republic. Silent on the subject of the regime, by contrast it raised very forcibly the question of the exclusion of working men from democratic public life; they had no representatives, either at the political level, since the deputies all belonged to the rich or educated classes, or at the professional level, since the right to form associations and trade unions was denied. In this moving document, there is a long-deferred response from the working world to the social harshness of the country's elites, which were enclosed in the panic fear of revolution. There is also a question put to the new generation, liberal and republican, on the place of the workers in a future democracy.

The reply came first from the emperor, in a decision which marked a milestone: a law authorizing workers' 'coalitions', at the same stroke quashing Le Chapelier's law of 1791, which had been maintained ever since in French legislation, chiefly in articles 414 to 416 of the Penal Code. It meant the right to strike, the first step towards freedom to meet and form associations, which would come later: the former in 1868, the latter only in 1884. The industrialists fought it, and the republican left refused to accept it from a hated regime. But the emperor imposed the bill on his majority. To strike was no longer illegal; the right to do so now formed part of the workers' liberties. One of the chief defenders of this liberal law had been Emile Ollivier, breaking for the nonce with his republican colleagues. On that side, too, the Empire was busy 'rallying' support.

Of the group of five republican deputies who had been elected in 1857 and 1858, the most brilliant and the most in evidence was Emile Ollivier. The son of a republican militant known under the July monarchy, he had been sent at a very early age (twenty-two) to Marseille by the February revolution as a commissioner of the Republic, and had succeeded in bringing a difficult local situation under control. Restored to his profession of barrister by the conservative drift of the Republic, he had devoted his talent for oratory to the Bar during the years of the anti-republican depression, without changing his political views. From 1857, he had then been the most outstanding of the republicans elected to the Legislative Body, a brilliant orator, cultured, sincere, his political thinking rather unstructured, quite soon torn between memories and realism.

He belonged to that generation of young republicans who wanted to shake off the 1848-style rhetoric, which still flourished among so many survivors and among the exiles, while France was changing so rapidly. But he had not tried to build a doctrine out of the new conditions in which the fight against the Empire was being waged; his political thinking remained as marked by sentimentalism as that of 1848, and almost equally hazy in regard to the outlines and content of republican concepts. Its slightly ingenuous and at the same time moderate qualities made it vulnerable to the liberal evolution of the regime, which was looking to its left for areas of support. In fact Emile Ollivier that year had greatly welcomed the bill of 24 November. In a famous reply to Morny, who was president of the Legislative Body and the man in favour of opening up the political spectrum, he had improvised an outline of republican rallying which had committed his political life before he himself had completely made the decision.

Faced with the 1863 elections, the republican camp found itself once more pulled between the old guard of 1848 and the new generation, among whom Emile Ollivier and Ernest Picard were the most outstanding. The matter of the oath – now demanded not only from the elected members but also from the candidates – hardly counted any more, except for the exiles; having either stayed abroad or returned to France after the amnesty, they were set fast in a radical refusal. On the other hand, in the various republican committees a very lively battle was going on over the candidacies, in which contemporaries perceived the revival of public life. The 'five' found themselves in rivalry for influence with the men of 1848, and the liberal newspapers also had their candidates: *Le Siècle* run by Havin, a moderate republican; *Le Journal des débats*, which was more Orleanist; *La Presse* of Emile de Girardin, the great press chief of the epoch; *L'Opinion nationale* of Adolphe Guéroult, who had come from Saint-Simonism and was a firm supporter of 'nationalities', and lastly Auguste Nefftzer's *Le Temps*, preaching the alliance of men of liberty.

There were tentative approaches between moderate republicans and Orleanist liberals, which were made easier by the assumption of responsible posts by new men, too young to have been mixed up in 1848. The rising star of Orleanism, Lucien Prévost-Paradol, had still been a student at the time of the February revolution, and had joined the École Normale Supérieure only in 1849, a year after Taine. Having become a fashionable journalist, he applied for candidature with one of the republican committees which included the 'five' and several newspaper editors; finally turned down through Girardin's hostility, he nevertheless benefited in his Parisian campaign from the militant support of a young republican, who was none other than Léon Gambetta.

However, the elections also showed up the permanence of the traditional oppositions. On the right, the legitimists were semi-paralysed by the Comte de Chambord's abstention instruction, when he reacted like the exiled republicans: no compromise at all with the imperial regime was acceptable. The troops only half-followed this negative slogan: even Berryer, a veteran of the great battles for legitimacy, finished by coming forward as a candidate, since he had been unable to persuade his prince.

In this sector of opinion, the interests of the Church, which were threatened in Rome, did most to mobilize the royalists. Falloux had set off again to conquer his stronghold of Anjou. But not all the Catholic party candidates were legitimists, it is true, since half were nostalgic for the idyll of the 1850s between the bishops and Napoleon III. As for the Orleanists, they were less sensitive to the Roman question since hope of a representative government had reappeared; side by side with the new men, like Prévost-Paradol, all the great names of the July monarchy answered the call, Thiers at the head, but also Dufaure, Odilon Barrot and Rémusat. Memories and passions continued to keep them apart from the bulk of republican militants. It was the newspapers and the group of 'five' which drew them nearer.

At long last a liberal union could be formed around a common liberal demand, the minimum programme which Nefftzer had mapped out in advance in *Le Temps*: 'Legally, there are neither legitimists, nor Orleanists nor republicans, and these party qualifications of which no one can take advantage must not be turned against anyone . . . Legally, there is the party of resistance and the party of progress, the party of restriction and the party of liberty.' By its attacks, the Second Empire made it easier for those it termed the 'old parties' to unite temporarily; by its policies, it offered them, at least for a while, the meeting-ground of a shared hostility towards the power of the army and administrative centralization; by its electoral law, it obliged them to unite in order to beat the official candidate in the second round.

The liberal union had formed an alliance which was very unequally applied according to electoral districts, but on traditional divisions, which had frequently been revived by the Catholic question or the policy of nationalities, it had superimposed a liberal logic going from Thiers to the republicans, even flanked on their right by Berryer and Falloux. Against the London exiles and the 1849 'democ-soc' tradition, the new republican generation had brought to bear a logic which was more reformist than revolutionary, borrowed from the repertoire of parliamentary action, the success of which had been made easier by the concentration of the workers' movement on managing its class interests. One can discern the scope of that development in the ideas presented to the electorate in 1863 by the majority of republican candidates, all more or less inspired by the re-establishment of a true legislative power and public liberties: debate and voting on laws by the Assembly, repeal of the general security law, freedom of the press, free exercise of universal suffrage, municipal autonomy (including Paris and Lyon, the two cities under the exceptional control of the state). To political families which had been divided by their heritages, the Second Empire thus gave the opportunity for a common battle for liberty.

As in 1853 and 1857, the government leant on the administration. But it had itself given the signal for the thaw, and the electorate returned it a less tractable Legislative Body. Out of slightly fewer than 7,500,000 'sound' votes (having deducted the abstentions, which were less numerous than in 1857), the government candidates gained 5,300,000, that is, somewhat fewer than in 1857, but the opposition trebled its total vote, going from 665,000 to just under 2,000,000. It was not a triumph, but a semi-success, shared unequally because it comprised an Orleanist failure and a republican victory.

In fact, rural France had in the main stayed loyal to the Empire, while the large towns had most frequently gone over towards the republicans: the Orleanists remained more than ever that headquarters of notables cut off in the Académie or in narrow strongholds, paying dearly, each time the electorate was consulted, for their denial of the people's sovereignty. On the other hand, the republicans had made steady progress in universal suffrage, and were now dominant in Paris, Lyon, Lille, Bordeaux, Nantes, Toulouse, Nancy, Saint-Etienne and Le Havre. They had obtained seventeen seats and their leaders were deputies: not only the re-elected 'five' – Emile Ollivier, Picard, Jules Favre, Darimon and Jacques-Louis Hénon – but also Jules Simon, Marie, the man of the February 1848 government, soon joined (in the 1864 by-elections) by Carnot and Garnier-Pagès. Thiers had been elected in Paris as the liberal union candidate; there then began that delicate navigation between republicanism and Orleanism which gave his political countenance its originality.

For the time being, the liberal union had not received enough votes truly to exist as a parliamentary force. What formed the centre of the new Legislative Body, between the republicans and the regime's 'official' deputies, was what was known from 1864 as the third party: a collection of sincere but independent Bonapartists and moderate members of the opposition – Catholics, liberals or protectionists who had found themselves in a rather delicate situation as regards imperial policies – that often had an orator in Thiers: the common hope was for a liberal evolution of the Empire, in which the Assembly could enlarge on the power it had recovered in November 1860.

Thus the 1863 election had restored a little parliamentary room for manoeuvre to the institutions. When the republicans voted with the third party, the opposition mobilized about sixty votes in favour of the re-establishment of public liberties, in the name of an increasing control of the executive power by the legislative: a policy which Morny encouraged and to which Emile Ollivier's public support for the Empire could add the crowning touch. Both men, Morny the roué and Ollivier the sentimental, had understood and accepted, each in his own way, what was probably the basis of imperial wisdom in internal politics: if the Empire could not be separated from what the century called 'democracy', and if it did not rely (like the preceding one) on military glory, it must inevitably meet up with liberty.

Morny died in 1865, and his disappearance from the scene put off the day, leaving the field open to a less subtle version of the regime, though temporarily more in keeping with the habits it had acquired. The emperor had not back-pedalled, at least in any lasting fashion, since in the end he would return to the parliamentary idea, in order to take the credit for it in the people's eyes; but he was ill, suffering from an old malady, a stone in the bladder, which was getting worse and causing him much pain. Moreover, he had taken it into his head to write a life of Caesar, which gave him a great deal of trouble and took up a lot of his time. He remained the sole head, but without being as attentive to affairs as formerly. In a strong position because of that spasmodic attention, the Minister of State, Rouher, was in full control of all the state's work.

For French politics, what was most important in those years did not take place in the corridors of power but in the thinking of the Republican opposition.

JULES FERRY

In this era was born a government republicanism which the younger generation wanted to set against the condemned conceptions of their elders, the men of 1848. The best way to understand it is to begin with the example of Jules Ferry.

His generation had given much thought to failures. In fact, of the waves of republican militants who had launched attacks on the nineteenth century, the first, of Carbonarism and July 1830, had been trapped without any opposition by the Orleanist bourgeoisie. That of 1848, fed on ideas of socialism and brotherhood, had been torn apart between the working-class populace, crushed on the June barricades, conservative notables, obsessed with maintaining a proprietorial order, and Bonaparte's nephew, crowned king by the votes of the people when two monarchist families had been left clutching their respective rights to the national heritage. In 1848 Jules Ferry was sixteen. He was born into a good bourgeois family in the Vosges, which had links with local politics: his grandfather had been mayor of Saint-Dié under the Directory and the Empire; his father, a barrister with liberal opinions, had been a general councillor for the Vosges under the July regime, and an opponent of Guizot's ministry. The family tradition, favourable to the republican concept, was dealt a blow by the June uprising; nor did it like the socialist and revolutionary spirit which persisted in the ideology of the 'Montagnards' in May 1849. According to an expression of that era, which Marx would not have disowned, the Ferrys were 'unconditional republicans', sticklers for legality and the law, hostile to the criticism of the political by the social which formed the basis of socialist doctrines. That was why they also hated the December coup d'état. At that time, the family had been in Paris since the preceding year; a brilliant student, the young Jules Ferry, who wanted to make his career in public office, fell back on the profession of barrister.

During those first years of the Empire, which were the gloomiest and most restrictive for a young republican, he learned his trade and worked relentlessly. By studying his case, the historian can best understand how new ideas were penetrating French politics amid the silence of despotism. The February revolution continued to feed on the quarrels of those in exile, but Jules Ferry rejected its spirit as being responsible for the final disaster. He condemned, in the 1848 revolution, both its socialist systems and its sentimental rhetoric and religious messianism, whether latent or blatant. Against the more or less hare-brained doctrines of the 'Forty-eighters', the surest refuge was to follow the route of science, and that could be understood in two ways which were not incompatible. It was necessary to serve an almost professional apprenticeship and then to apply what had been learnt to the field of political action, which was now enlightened by knowledge instead of being filled by the disorder of passions and interests. What is striking about the young lawyer's programme of studies under the Empire is its earnestness, together with the quality of his historical curiosity and the extent of his reading: German philosophy, utilitarianism and English economics, the history of France. A typical characteristic of Jules Ferry was his particular enthusiasm for industrial development; he studied the economic history of England and France from the sixteenth century and noted, in the French instance, the role played by the monarchic state, and in passing reproved the Revolution for having unwisely abandoned that absolutist tradition. All his papers of that era bear the imprint of the almost dogmatic will which is also to be found in Renan and Taine, his seniors by some years: to turn a knowledge of the past into a science, an area of learning as certain as the discovery of the laws of nature.

But science was not merely an essential acquisition of reason, it was equally a prefiguration: for it also represented the 'positive' age of humanity which must replace both the clergy's preaching of the theological spirit and the revolutionary utopias of the metaphysical age. In the middle of the century, the men of Jules Ferry's generation rediscovered the preachings of Saint-Simon, rationalized by Auguste Comte. Like Saint-Simon and Comte, they were more than ever sensitive to the disorder of the era and of revolutionary thinking: how could they be otherwise after the spectacle presented by the Second Republic?

But for the same reasons they also challenged the sort of generalized affectivity in which the later Comtism had gone astray, positive religion after the manner of Clotilde de Vaux. They held on to Emile Littré's version of August Comte's positivism, which was the least incompatible with the democratic heritage. For the difficulty still lay in holding together the Rights of Man and liberty on the one hand and, on the other, a historicist vision of the march of reason, in which there was no place for the sovereignty of individuals. The synthesis, epistemologically lame but politically fertile, consisted in soft-pedalling on the idea of the natural rights of individuals – the source of insoluble conflicts – in order to accentuate, by contrast, the value of educating citizens, whereby each member of the social contract would, in the long run, find his universality: a pedagogy of reason.

Here one meets the birth of a new republican creed, a syncretic philosophy of will and reason, the posthumous reconciliation of Rousseau and Condorcet. The part of Comtism which Jules Ferry chose to keep was the idea of humanity's material and spiritual progress, which allowed the concept of the subjective rights of individuals in the form of social acts accepted and organized in the movement of history: republicanism was no longer deduced from abstract natural law, but was to be based on a science of evolution. The spiritual power which Auguste Comte had deemed indispensable to any society worthy of the name could be realized only through the republican education of the citizens: that is to say, in democracy.

Here was a new event in French history: in that optimism of historical reason combined with the heritage of 1789, an unprecedented strength was imparted to both the republican and the liberal way of thinking. For the Doctrinaires, historical necessity had been mobilized only in the service of the bourgeoisie and representative government. As a consequence, it had been turned by their opponents to the benefit of the working class and the social revolution. Caught in the middle of this philosophical battle of the classes, the Republic had never been able to find its political balance. Here it was in its turn, clad in the dignity of history's eldest daughter, an image of reconciliation between men and within themselves. It was identified with the most powerful concept in the imagination of nineteenth-century men, the only one which would counterbalance religion: science. In short, it offered to the enlightened elites, faced with the clericalism of the nobles and notables, a realistic solution to the famous question posed by Rousseau, which had been discredited by the Terror yet was still ever-present: how can a man of modern society be transformed into a citizen? That regeneration would be effected by the school of the Republic. At last, democracy and liberty would be united.

This was one of the lessons learned not only from the election of 10 December 1848, but also from the exercise of universal suffrage under the Empire. In 1857, Jules Ferry had witnessed the election of the 'five' and he was one of those close to Emile Ollivier; but he was chiefly an observer of the rural electorate's loyalty to the regime, and was sufficiently clear-sighted not to attribute it entirely to intimidation by the prefects. Though he drew up, for the 1863 elections, a *Manuel electoral* intended to inform voters of their rights, he was convinced that in the long term the peasants' political independence would come about through school and education, the condition for an enlightened vote. He would have liked to be a candidate in these elections, as his friend Ollivier had encouraged him to be; but he still had to bow before the coalition of the 'ancients' of 1848, and finally wage Garnier-Pagès's campaign: even then, such was party life.

At that period, he was one of the most liberal republicans, notably a supporter of the idea of decentralization, which was more liberal than republican, since it was opposed by the majority of republicans in the name of revolutionary tradition, for fear of what remained to the local oligarchies in the way of prestige and power. Now Ferry was a decentralizer, who preached the Anglo-Saxon example, both British and American – a new point of reference in his political family. For this was an idea widely shared on the right, in the legitimist and Orleanist camp: the administrative nature of imperial despotism had spread the conviction, often expressed by Tocqueville, that it was virtually impossible to graft parliamentary freedom on to centralization. A decentralization campaign had been launched by liberal conservatives, organized by the Comte d'Haussonville, in 1859; Odilon Barrot had devoted a book to it in 1861. The subject united royalists and republicans: Montalembert, Falloux, Berryer and Guizot, with Carnot, Garnier-Pagès, Jules Simon, Etienne Vacherot and Eugène Pelletan. The idea was taken up again in 1865 by the Nancy faction of decentralizers, to whom Jules Ferry gave this piece of advice:

If you want to be an industrious, peaceful and free people, you have no business with a strong power. Split it up, therefore, in order to weaken it . . . France needs a weak government . . . To break up prefectorial authority, to cause the disappearance of even the name of this institution, which has descended in direct line from the Caesars in their decadence, would be truly . . . to set the pyramid back on its base.[6]

Those lines were written right in the middle of the battle against the Empire, when the prefect – a departmental, swaggering, *comédie italienne* Captain Fracasse – carried a great deal of clout, arm in arm with the bishop. The later Jules Ferry, he of the Republic, would forget this state reform when he had need of good republican prefects. But he would retain and apply the idea of balancing departmental authority with municipal democracy: a close fabric of municipal councils and mayors, elected by their citizens, bringing the benefits of representative government to the level of local life. That was the only way in which the existence of a national government, with the strength of indispensable unity, could be reconciled with the sharing of power with an enormous municipal democracy, the bastion against local oligarchies.

Jules Ferry had another way of putting it: historical, as was the rule in nineteenth-century French politics. In the French Revolution, he would be a man of the Constituent Assembly, against the Convention. Or, in the Convention, he would be a Girondin, against the Montagnards.

A great book made its appearance in 1865, precisely on this topic, written by a celebrated exile, a republican writer of the preceding generation, a man of 1848 if ever there was one, Edgar Quinet. This exile,

[6] J. Ferry, 'Lettre aux auteurs du programme de Nancy', *Discours et opinions*, vol. 1, pp. 558, 562–3.

too, had been engaged since 2 December in a long reflection on the downfall of the Second Republic, conducted through the history of the first. Like all his contemporaries, he had believed he was reliving the French Revolution in its nineteenth-century version: the rebirth of democracy in February, compromised by the neo-Jacobin extremism of June, jeopardized by the election of a Bonaparte in December, beaten and usurped three years later by a new 18 Brumaire. His problem therefore was not to celebrate the Revolution, nor once more to turn it into the great annunciation scene of national history, but to try to understand and explain its failure. By doing so, he found eager listeners among the young republican generation, who were still indignant about the collapse which had followed, and which they had encountered in their cradles.

Two ideas formed the basis of his book. The first was that the Revolution, the sublime promise of a new political and moral order, had been unable to fulfil its mission because it had lacked the daring to conceive and found a new religion, following the example of Protestantism in the sixteenth century. This idea held no interest for Jules Ferry, who was too anticlerical, or too positivist, to want to base democracy on even a renewed Christianity. On the other hand, Ferry was fascinated by Quinet's second thesis. Quinet had turned, to the advantage of 1789, the opposition put forward by socialist historiography between 1789 and 1793 – in Buchez, Esquiros and Louis Blanc. He saw the true spirit of the Revolution, the emancipation of the free individual, in the work of the constituent Assembly, which had left nothing standing of the old monarchy except its ghost.

The Convention, on the contrary, brought about the spectacle of its destruction only to revive its spirit: after the fall of the Gironde, indeed, the Jacobin dictatorship, under the old pretext of public safety, linked up again with the ancient 'reason of state' and the worst traditions of absolutism (Roman and monarchic both together). By reincarnating Richelieu, Robespierre foretold Bonaparte. In the Revolution he was the first to create national servitude; Napoleon would be the second. Like Tocqueville, but in a different way, Quinet was seeking the secrets of Bonapartism in the tyrannies which had preceded it: in his view, every struggle against the Second Empire proceeded from a criticism of Jacobinism and the Terror. His book thus opened up a vast Parisian polemic within the republican party, which found itself obliged to abandon part of the sacred heritage.

It was the Jacobins who opened fire, on 17 November 1865 (the very day when the book made its appearance), with the first of a series of twelve articles published in *L'Avenir national* – a Republican paper – by its editor Alphonse Peyrat, which continued until the end of January 1866. Jules Ferry would reply to these articles, starting at the beginning of January, in *Le Temps*, to which he regularly contributed. The debate deserves to be quoted at length, by virtue of what it reveals of the passions and matters at stake which still made up the history of the Revolution, and because of what it discloses about the developments taking place inside republican ideology.

Peyrat's tone had been controversial. Political interests of the greatest importance were under discussion: Quinet was accused of undermining or even 'breaking up' the 'democratic party', the heart of opposition to the imperial regime. To challenge his book was consequently a duty:

Some people have claimed that, in criticizing it, I could have expressed myself with less sharpness. On the contrary, I thought, and I still think, that the purer the author's intentions, and the more honourable his character, the more potentially dangerous his errors and, in consequence, the more severely they should be refuted. I have had to forget the author and concentrate only on the truth.

And here, to concentrate on the truth meant to concentrate on the most serious interests of the democratic party. Just like a human being, a great political party stays true to itself only through memories of what it has undergone and what it has achieved. The permanent identity of the democratic party therefore implies not only a knowledge of the events by which it was formed, but also a respect for the men who have accomplished the greatest things which make up its history. To slander these illustrious men, to misrepresent their actions, to shatter the solidarity which links us to them and which policy and morality impose upon us, is to break up the democratic party, to misjudge the conditions of its existence, its true *raison d'être*. In such an instance, indifference would be a desertion, silence an ingratitude.

To this political argument, Jules Ferry replied on the political score. He dealt with the relations between Jacobinism and democracy, which had been the central theme of republican philosophy since the Restoration: is what is at stake, he asked, as important today as it was then? Does it merit the abdication of critical consideration in the name of loyalty to the republican fight? No. The Jacobin religion, just like the Bonapartist legend, came about as necessary reactions against the return of the kings and the Holy Alliance. But half a century later, when the French Revolution has conclusively triumphed, they no longer have a *raison d'être*: the success of the second Bonapartism itself bears witness to this:

Today, everything has completely changed. Modern society is not disputed by a living soul: the *ancien régime* no longer exists except for those old newspapers which are unwilling to give up the habit of assailing it. In the bosom of an exuberant democracy which, instead of enemies has nothing but sycophants, Jacobinism is no longer a weapon of war, but a peril, for it represents in our midst something sadder than the memory of the scaffolds: the prejudice of the dictatorship.

This is an important document, which resumes in a new form a vital distinction of French liberal thought since the Directory and Benjamin Constant: the Revolution has founded a society, not a government. This society, democracy, is so deeply rooted that its enemies no longer have any strength: the aristocracy is dead. But, in its triumph, it also has its flatterers who lack a *raison d'être*: by this Jules Ferry means those who adhere to Bonapartism, profiting from a tradition which belongs to an outmoded part of the revolutionary repertoire.

The dictatorship no longer had the excuse of the counter-revolution. Ferry's problem remained the same as that of Guizot in the 1820s: the founding of free institutions on the society which had emerged from 1789; but two generations separated him from Louis-Philippe's minister, and society had continued to march forward. He was seeking ways of democratizing the Orleanist party and basing public liberties on a republic of universal suffrage. What was it that still divided French society from the government of democracy, that is to say, the Republic? Precisely that 'Jacobin religion', the adversary and yet the accomplice of the Bonapartist religion which had been built and cultivated around the two ideas of public safety and dictatorship. The course of the Second Republic had demonstrated it once again: Parisian neo-Jacobinism, composed of great memories which no longer had any substance, scared the country without managing to govern it and, at the end of the day, brought back the anachronistic despotism of an adventurist Bonaparte.

During those years when he expected the fall of the Empire without being able to predict it, what Ferry wanted to give to the republican left for the future was governmental credibility. He therefore, at all costs, had to exorcize the spectre of the Terror from the opinion which the country held of that left, and most of all from within itself:

Whoever will demonstrate that the Terror was not necessary, whoever will rid democracy of that dream of dictatorship which sometimes stirs it like a temptation, and sometimes obsesses it like a nightmare, will deserve much from the future: he will be able to stand up to the harsh voices of those ghosts of 1793, who are so enamoured of their memories, so blinded by their own methods, as to imagine that in France the government could ever be based on a spirit of cliques or intolerance.

There followed, all through those articles in January 1866, a theoretical discussion on the dictatorship and the Terror, in which Ferry, arguing against Peyrat, wanted to demonstrate that the two phenomena, born of a spontaneous reaction by the mass of the people to invasion, had very soon constituted a system of absolute power, independent of the circumstances which had facilitated its formation, and propelled by its logic of domination, not by national safety. Seen in this perspective, the drama of the Revolution really started at the point Quinet had visualized: 31 May–2 June, when the new France of liberty yielded to the armed threat of the Parisian *sections* against the Convention, when they forcibly expelled the Girondin deputies. A show of strength which foretold and exonerated in advance 18 Brumaire – which itself served as a model and a justification for 2 December.

Thus, between Edgar Quinet and Jules Ferry, the old exile and the young militant, was formed a common interpretation of the Revolution which united the two generations around a tradition that was both republican and liberal. Many things separated the two men, in philosophical matters for example: Quinet believed in democracy as a daughter of the Christian concept, while Ferry saw in it the advent of the 'positive age'. But what united them was the sense of liberty and law. On those two points, the moderate republican who admired the 'five' was as uncompromising as the isolated preacher in exile. It explains why he refused to follow his friend Emile Ollivier in his acceptance of the imperial regime.

At the moment when the men of 2 December were seeking help to transform the Empire into a republican monarchy, thereby reducing the political space of the moderate republicans, his intransigent refusal preserved intact the future chances of a republic which would be both democratic and liberal. In this respect, he is a good symbol of what had changed in French politics during the Second Empire, under the appearance of a similarity of opinions and the fidelity of political families to their traditions.

IMPERIAL DECLINE

However, the period between the 1863 elections and those of 1869 showed more of that similarity and that fidelity than of elements of transformation. The situation had altered more quickly than the actors. The emperor could no longer govern as in the first years of his reign. He himself had yielded much to revolutionary tradition in his foreign policy, had given the beginnings of liberty to the Legislative Body and had established the workers' right to strike. Then the years had passed, bringing with them a new 'mood of the times', the characteristics of which were enhanced by the volatile and lively nature of national political passions: public opinion had rushed headlong into servitude, but was now regaining a taste for liberty.

As has been seen, the emperor himself had made that evolution easier, but he did not force the pace – quite the contrary. Many historians blame his illness, without perhaps affording sufficient importance to the fact that 'slowness' is the inevitable ingredient of the liberal evolution of a dictatorship: a 'subjective' slowness, due to the impatience of a public opinion whose expectations have been aroused; and an objective slowness, on the part of the dictator, who seeks to gauge the real effect of first measures in order to space out or cancel others. There is nothing to indicate that Napoleon III had changed direction since 1860; but he measured out the doses of liberty according to a calendar for which the reasons are not clearly apparent.

Thanks to Morny, he had Emile Ollivier in his game since 1864. But Morny had died and the leader of the 'five' had been deserted by his republican friends; there was scarcely anyone else who could be brought into the possible service of a policy which cost a great deal, since the regime was parliamentary. As things stood, the true beneficiaries of a development of this kind would be more likely to be the third party, which had no real leader, unless it was Thiers, who had once again become the tireless politician attacking the government. In the time it took the emperor to cover the ground which lay between him and the decisive leap, the regime slipped a little farther along its own path, momentarily thwarted by its chief, but at least regaining on its right the support of the good old days, the Church and the men of order, who wanted to forget the Italian escapades.

The time had come for Rouher to have his moment – a good specimen of Bonapartist bourgeoisie, a jurist from the Auvergne, with a strong character and realistic mind little inclined to liberty. An unsuccessful candidate of the conservatives in 1846, under Guizot's banner, he had been a deputy to the Constituent Assembly in 1848 and had, unemotionally and with no particularly strong feeling, joined the camp of the president of the Republic in the name of social order. There was nothing about him which could make him understand, far less like, Emile Ollivier's hesitancy. Minister of State since 1863, he was Number Two in a despotic regime from which the despot had slightly withdrawn, which gave his authority the stamp of authoritarianism.

The conditions in which power was exercised had changed not only in the Legislative Body, but in the country itself. The Church and the clerical party were still regarded as pillars of what was called 'society', but they were all the less able to put the final full stop to the Italian affair because the Roman question was still pending, reactivated by the evacuation of French troops from Rome at the end of 1866. For its part, the Empire had difficulty in adjusting to the ultramontane trend of the majority of the clergy. Rome's publication in 1864 of the encyclical *Quanta Cura*, accompanied by a systematic inventory of all the 'modern' errors, made matters even more difficult, for the good 'Roman' Catholic was now enjoined to reject the whole of the modern political world – liberalism, the individual, liberty of conscience, progress, the sovereignty of the people, the secularism of the State: Veuillot authenticated by Pius IX.

It was no use for Monseigneur Dupanloup, the last bastion of Gallicanism, to intervene in an attempt to remove the character of in- tellectual ultimatum from the document; the trend of French Catholicism towards counter-revolutionary extremism found comfort in it. By taking it up, the regime might well try to repair the damage caused by its Roman policy; but it ran the risk of alienating enlightened public opinion by linking the authority of the state with clerical obscurantism. For example, by suspending Renan's course at the Collège de France on the pretext of that famous phrase: 'Jesus, that incomparable man', it reawoke the suspicion of its complicity with the Jesuit party which, since the monarchy, had been a prime target for accusations in France.

Times had changed since the last years of the July monarchy, when the University had done battle with the Church in the name of monopoly. The conservative bourgeoisie had largely returned to religion for reasons of social reaction; but while it thus weighed down with utilitarian pre-occupations a Catholicism already predisposed to political obsession, it left the purely intellectual ground open to criticism of religion, and more especially of the Roman religion: the model of authoritarianism, the incarnation of a bygone age.

It was about the year 1860 that the concept of the advent of science on the ruins of a theocratic age became a kind of collective belief of the new educated generations: as if the iron grasp of the clergy on education, brought about by the 1850 law and the measures taken by Fortoul at the start of the regime, had resulted in the exact opposite of the goal sought. In that dichotomy between science and faith lay a simplification of the philosophies of history which the century had proliferated, a sort of popularized positivism, in which Auguste Comte's admiration for the coherence of the theological age and Renan's affection for the history of the Church no longer had any existence.

In this narrow culture, the rejection of religion more easily assumed the colours of the destruction of the *ancien régime* since the Church, together with Rome, was more definitively entrenched in radical condemnation of the modern world. Veuillot and *Quanta Cura* were among the great purveyors of militant anticlericalism; in the face of the Masonic lodges, they recommenced the great fight of the Revolution. Since the aristocracy was dead, and the monarchy dying, it was the Church that had inherited the banner of the *ancien régime*; and it was science that had replaced the Rights of Man. The formidable impact of positivism on French republican thought was thus made evident by two opposite results.

The Comtist legacy, on the one hand, had moderated revolutionary passions by subordinating them to the production of a new order, which itself had gradually emerged from the march of time and the education of men: there was no longer any 'great event' in this concept of progress. But, on the other hand, it had radicalized the break between the democratic universe and Catholic tradition, firmly placing in the philosophy of history the antagonistic passions born of the circumstances of the French Revolution. Therefore the political moderation of the young positivist generation was accompanied by a radical hostility to Catholicism in which a longer-term revolutionary ambition had been reinvested.

The Catholic Church had remained the absolute monarchy of modern times, after being the model for it in the past: that was an image which haunted not only the young Republicans, but also the libertarian of 1848, Edgar Quinet, the elderly Proudhon of *De la justice dans la Révolution et dans l'Eglise*, those close to Princess Mathilde, such as Mérimée or Sainte-Beuve, and Prince Napoleon, one of the most dyed-in-the-wool anticlericals.

The emperor himself would not recapture with the Catholics the erstwhile understanding they had enjoyed. He had never truly repudiated his Italian policy and was officially Gallican. In 1863, to general surprise, he imposed on the Ministry of Public Education a history professor, who specialized in Roman antiquity and who had helped him to write his biography of Julius Caesar: Victor Duruy. This was a sovereign's whim which turned out to be a good choice, but which placed in a post that was closely scrutinized by Catholics a man of liberal and rather anticlerical tradition, who was respectful of the Church's rights but also punctilious about the prerogatives of the state.

The new minister was neither a political man nor an official in the service of the emperor. Unassuming but zealous, isolated yet enthusiastic, he proved to be a missionary in the cause of education, ceaselessly stirring up administrations (chiefly financial) in the service of a great educational policy. Everywhere he found himself the target for the animosity of Catholics, ultramontanes and Gallicans combined against the widening of the state's role in schooling: In primary education, he would ask for it to be free and compulsory, which he did not achieve; but he enriched the curriculum and extended the range of free schooling. In secondary education, he created a special organization for girls (1867). In higher education, he re-established the *agrégation* in philosophy, created law faculties in the provinces and introduced the *École Pratique des Hautes Etudes*, in order to develop in France university research comparable with that provided by German universities. A single quotation is enough to let us understand the enmity which his work aroused in Catholic circles; it is taken from Veuillot's *L'Univers*: 'The idea of entrusting, in a general way, in a great empire, the literary and scientific education of young girls to men is simply unheard of, without parallel in the history of any society.'

The other absorbing problem of those years was military reform, which could not be divorced from foreign policy. Through his Italian campaign Napoleon III had fully realized that military genius is not hereditary; for all that, he had not escaped from the family superego. He had said, 'The Empire means peace', but the Empire was still inseparable from a France that was more active in Europe and the world. He had launched into a rather absurd adventure in Mexico, sending a French expeditionary corps to give an exotic throne to an Austrian archduke (1861): in doing so, he had at least regained some of the Catholic approval which had been lost in Italy. An inglorious evacuation closed the affair in 1867.

His German policy concealed quite different dangers, which revived the hazards of the intervention in Italy, but with the redoubtable Prussia instead of peaceable Piedmont. The emperor had taken it into his head to initiate with Bismarck the bargaining which had so nearly failed with Cavour: French diplomatic support against Austria in exchange for territorial rewards, this time on the north-east frontier – Luxembourg for instance. But he had underestimated his partner, who played the game very well on his own: when Prussian smashed Austria at Sadowa (1866), it seemed to many that France, by encouraging its action in Germany in the name of the principle of nationalities, was helping to build a new and formidable enemy for itself in Europe. That sentiment was to be found particularly among the Orleanist opposition, Thiers for example, or

Prévost-Paradol, who since Italy had been a tireless critic of the regime's foreign policy; but it was to be encountered also among the Bonapartists of the third party, and the republican opposition (Edgar Quinet and Jules Favre among others). In those sectors of opinion, however, many people rejoiced instead over the double victory of the national idea, formed by the birth of the Germanic Confederation and the uniting of the Veneto with the new kingdom of Italy.

Napoleon III maintained his course. He had long wanted to put greater means at his disposal by a reform of the army. A poor commander-in-chief in the field, the author of *Etudes sur le passé et l'avenir de l'artillerie*, written at Ham during his years of captivity, had always been keenly interested in military problems. As emperor, he had imposed on his military staff some useful technical adjuncts, such as the new 'hunter's' rifle. His main idea was to have done with Gouvion Saint-Cyr's law and bourgeois examption from military service by setting up compulsory service on the Prussian model, the value of which had been shown in the Sadowa victory. This plan ran into opposition from the military, who were committed to the idea of a professional army; from the bourgeoisie, who set great store by the privilege accorded to their sons; and lastly from the republicans, who were divided between the memory of a *levée en masse* should the need arise, and the dawning illusion of an exemplary disarmament.

Reading the different elements of this interminable debate, which ended in January 1868 with a vote for a compromise which largely left the status quo, the historian gets the feeling of a France which is very busy with peacetime works, and as far as can be from any great external undertaking: loyal, at last, to the spirit of the second Bonapartism, which was more bourgeois than 'national', more economic than military. This feature was noted by the more intelligent observers, such as Prévost-Paradol in his book of 1868: his 'new France' was increasing the signs of its 'democratic' decadence at a time when the hour of a decisive conflict with Germany was approaching. The emperor ran the risk of being trapped between legend and truth. A victim of the constraints arising from his tradition and the alterations imputable to his reign, which produced contradictory incitements and effects: an idea of national grandeur for which the French no longer wished to pay the price.

The weakened despotism into which the regime had settled since the 1863 elections no longer had the strength to force upon opinion anything other than layers of different policies, which pleased successive and fragmented sections of the public. Lacking consistency, it had not succeeded in really opening out to the left. It had compromised Emile Ollivier enough to distance him from his moderate republican colleagues, but it had never offered him enough power or means of influence to provide him with means of proving himself. It had isolated the man before putting him to the test, emptied his magazine before allowing him to fire, dangerously exposed his policy before putting it into effect. The clearest result of this waiting game had been to strengthen the more radical elements in the republican camp, at the expense of the more moderate. At the very time when the dictatorship had become more liberal, it provoked the most cries of hatred.

Not that contacts ceased between the liberals of the Académie Française and the decentralizing republicans, since the Nancy programme was drafted in 1865. But, as has been seen, part of the republican rhetoric had shifted to the field of the struggle against the Church, where the notables could not fall into step with the slogan launched by Alphonse Peyrat in his newspaper: 'Clericalism is the enemy!' Even if certain of them, like Thiers, could find an echo of it back in their youth, the positivist-republican watchword, unfurled like a battle-flag, did not belong to their culture. The anticlericalism of the Orleanists in 1830 had merely been a temporary outcome of circumstances, their revenge on the alliance of Throne and Altar. That of the republicans in the 1860s was a vision of the world, the declaration that democracy was also the reign of reason, at last reconciling man with himself, substituting the politics of science for the ministry of God.

At the same time, there reappeared in the republican opposition of the big towns the revolutionary extremism of happier days, freed from the fraternal and religious elements of February 1848. The romantic illusion had vanished, but the great revolutionary memories could still – for the last time – mobilize a generation of the Parisian extreme left, influenced by 1793 and the idea of seizing possession of the state in order to change man and society. The militants redistributed the classic roles among themselves. Longuet was a Robespierrist, Tridon had written a book on Hébert, Rogeard was an admirer of Marat, and Fouquier-Tinville was Raoul Rigault's hero.

Above this world of secret societies there again hovered the shadow of one of the nineteenth century's evil geniuses of French democracy: Blanqui, the veteran of the Charbonnerie and all the conspiracies which had shaken the two monarchies and the Republic, the prisoner of 15 May 1848, amnestied with everyone else in 1859, sentenced once more in 1861 and managing to escape in 1864. Life had woven a legend around him, composed of militant obstinacy and simple ideas. Blanquism was that body of convictions, fanatically held, through which the Jacobin heritage passed into the nineteenth century in its Babouvist version. It comprised a conception of revolution based on violent seizure of power, a cult of dictatorship as regenerator, and absolute contempt for opinion and suffrage, accompanied by the spirit of exclusivenesses which comes naturally to influential minorities; social revolution was its aim, but that would come after seizure of the state, and was conditional upon it. Blanquism was the purest product of the dual revolutionary belief that the state can do everything, and that it is easy to take control of the state. Its rebirth at the end of the Empire showed that neither prosperity nor urban renewal had yet broken down the old Paris of the barricades. The Commune would show good evidence of that.

Even the workers' movement, so hesitant with regard to the 'politics first' of Jacobin tradition, gradually radicalized its position against the imperial regime, despite additional gestures from the latter's leader in favour of the workers, such as the abolition of the article in the Civil Code which sanctioned the inequality of master and workman before the court. The International Working Men's Association, which had developed from meetings at the Exhibition in London and had been founded in 1864, expanded in France, where its adherents were at first under the influence of the Proudhonians: Tolain and his comrades preached the development of mutual credit banks and co-operative associations. But in Paris as in London the Association soon became the seat of a very keen struggle for influence between the different currents of socialism.

In London, Marx fought to impose his thinking, chiefly against the French, whom he dismissed without distinction, whether Proudhonians or Blanquists; but in France, Proudhon's theories of workers' mutual insurance lost ground to Blanquism and the return of the 1793 tradition. Although the International Association remained somewhat suspect in the eyes of republicans until the end of the Empire, the extreme left of the opposition would tend to bring together once more – as between February and June 1848 – the ideas of social revolution and political revolution.

Was it in order to nip this development in the bud that the emperor gave a little push in the liberal direction? Was it in order to regain among the bourgeoisie of the towns what he had lost among the conservatives and Catholics? His intentions are easier to decipher than his timetable. Since 1860 he had wanted to set the seal on his dynasty by creating free institutions, but he had left the field open to Rouher for such a long time, yet without discouraging Emile Ollivier, that it is difficult to grasp his use of time. In 1867, he widened the deputies' right of Address into a right of interpellation; the following year, he did away with pre-censorship and the system of warnings for the press, relaxed restrictions on the right to hold meetings and granted freedom for electoral gatherings.

The 1869 elections therefore took place in a new situation, which turned this ballot into an unprecedented day of reckoning, beyond the control of the prefects. The climate had changed so much that there was no crowding round the Minister of the Interior to obtain the designation 'official candidate'. In many of the large towns, Paris at their head, the government was tactful, for fear that its official recommendation might handicap the candidates it favoured. Meetings were numerous and lively, newspapers proliferated: it was like a return to the early days of the Second Republic.

Paris was still under the influence of Gambetta's plea on behalf of the newspaper editors who had opened a subscription for a statue of Baudin, the deputy killed in the coup d'état of 1851. Recollections of 2 December, the barricades and the joint commissions returned like so many memories of civil war, uniting liberals and republicans. It was the latter who had the wind in their sails, revealing once again the wealth and confusion of their political range: the young against the old, 'workers' against the 'bourgeois', the men of the class struggle against those of democracy, republicans who were pro-insurrection against republicans who were pro-universal suffrage, and so on. Out of this vast resurrection, in which everyone mingled his memories with his ideas to form an uncompromising passion, the young generation of republican bourgeois, democrats and anticlericals, most frequently emerged victorious from an electoral combat in which they had generally beaten a liberal on their right and an insurrectionist on their left. In Paris, for instance, those elected were Léon Gambetta, Bancel (who beat Emile Ollivier), Picard, Raspail, Jules Ferry, Jules Favre, Jules Simon (who beat Jules Vallès) and Pelletan.

In the country as a whole, government candidates obtained barely 4,500,000 votes (compared with 5,300,000 in 1863), and those of the opposition 3,000,000. Among them, the old Orleanist and legitimist leaders such as Hippolyte Passy, Falloux, Rémusat, Duchâtel and even young liberals, like Prévost-Paradol and the Duc de Broglie (the son of Louis-Philippe's minister) had been beaten; the most obvious success was therefore shared among moderate and extreme republicans, both opposed to the Empire. But between them and the deputies who supported the emperor extended a political zone which is difficult to define, composed of independent representatives who were ready to give their backing to the liberal development of the regime and thus, should that be the case, to form an alliance with Bonapartist members who were also tending in this direction (that is, almost half of them). So the 1869 elections allowed the creation in the new Chamber of an unprecedented majority, around a form itself without precedent - that of a liberal Bonapartism.

Apparently the decision had come from the Assembly: at the opening of the session, at the beginning of July 1869, a group of 116 deputies, who had emerged from the former third party and Bonapartism properly speaking, asked for 'the constitution of a government responsible to the emperor and the Chamber'. Napoleon III seized the opportunity: several days later Rouher read out to the Chamber a message announcing the head of state's agreement to the reform, thereby bringing about his resignation. A transitional government was formed to prepare the *senatus consultum* in September, which was to be completed by that of April 1870: these Acts transformed the Senate into an upper Chamber which, with the Legislative Body, was able to initiate and vote on laws. The Ministry of State disappeared. Ministers were declared accountable to deputies, whereas they had been 'answerable only to the emperor': in other words, the latter both reigned and governed, but it was difficult for him to have a government which did not enjoy the confidence of the Assembly. The situation recalled the ambiguity of the July regime, with two great differences: suffrage was universal and, in case of conflict, the head of state possessed, over and above the right of dissolution, that of consulting the country directly by plebiscite.

The *senatus consultum* did not therefore set up a parliamentary regime, thereby disappointing the supporters of the old Orleanist centre-left watch-word – 'the king reigns, and does not govern' – such as Thiers and Prévost-Paradol. By restoring rights to parliament, Bonapartism had not intended to renounce its nature, which linked the dynasty directly to the sovereign people. In this original compromise, which combined three principles – representative government, democracy and the hereditary power – the liberal Empire offered one more solution to the problem which had haunted every French constitution since 1789: that of a monarchic republic.

One man was still missing from this plan of action, but he was already found since he had been awaiting the role for five years: Emile Ollivier. He was officially designated as head of the future ministry after a long secret negotiation with Napoleon III, at the end of the year, with the new prerogative of proposing ministers' names. Straddled across centre-left and centre-right, uniting 'pure' Bonapartists and ex-Orleanists, the team was a good representation of the reconciliation of all notables, old and new, with the man of 2 December and the plebiscitary dictatorship. Even on the left, not all were uniformly hostile. George Sand, who had come round, it is true, from her ideas of 1848, welcomed the news; Ernest Picard, a veteran of the 'five' and re-elected in 1869 on a republican programme, was not hostile. On the Orleanist side, Prévost-Paradol was won over in January, and Thiers weighed the hazards of the operation for what he represented and what he fully intended to personify before he died. Rémusat had said it for him in his memoirs: 'I could not be unaware that the attempt at a liberal Empire was the most painful experience for the Orléans, since it might well take away from them at one fell swoop their friends, their rallying cry and their sole claim to power, that monopoly of liberalism in the monarchy which seemed linked with their name.'[7]

The opposition of authoritarian Bonapartists to the new course was not dangerous; it was made up of people who were condemned willy-nilly to follow the emperor. That of the republicans was the only one which counted, proclaimed on 10 January in the Chamber by Gambetta:

If you wish to give a foundation to liberty together with the Empire, and you wish to do so with our help, you had better give up the idea and never expect to obtain it. What we want . . . is to be given, without a revolution, peacefully, that form of government whose name you all know: the Republic . . . You are nothing but a bridge between the Republic of 1848 and the Republic that is to come, and we shall cross that bridge!

On the same day Prince Pierre Bonaparte, the son of Lucien, a violent adventurer and dangerous bearer of that name, fired a revolver at a republican journalist, Victor Noir, in the course of a quarrel and killed him; the funeral two days later produced an atmosphere of unrest not seen since 1848. While Emile Ollivier was putting the finishing touches to the

[7] Ch. de Rémusat, *Mémoires de ma vie*, vol. 5, pp. 257–8.

constitutional bill which I analysed earlier, and setting afoot plans for administrative decentralization and the re-establishment of protectionism, street republicanism and insurrectionist socialism had regained a little of their old fraternity in the face of the compromise which had been effected between the old notables and the Empire.

It is an interesting feature of the political situation that the imperial regime had never aroused so much enmity on the part of the Parisian street mobs as when it was coming to terms with its old foe, the Orleanist bourgeoisie. Passion for equality and the idea of class resumed all their rights against the emperor, if his dictatorship was declining only to allow the reappearance of those moneyed oligarchies which had been shattered by the people in February 1848. The wave of feeling in Paris was so strong that it worried republican deputies as well.

Louis-Napoleon was better armed against it than Louis-Philippe, and he had kept a weapon for himself that the citizen-king had not possessed in his armoury – the plebiscite. It was Rouher's idea to submit the *senatus consultum* of 20 April to the people, as he was intent on getting his revenge on the Orleanists. In fact, the centre-left ministers, Louis Buffet and the Comte Daru, resigned, realizing the dual nature of the new regime, of which they accepted only the aspect they liked. The ballot was fixed for 8 May, the text drawn up as follows: 'The people approve the liberal reforms which have been effected in the constitution since 1860 by the emperor, with the assistance of the great bodies of the state, and ratify the *senatus consultum* of 20 April 1870.' Napoleon III himself, in his proclamation to the French, had steered them in the direction of a 'yes': 'You will avert the threat of revolution, you will set liberty and order on a solid footing, and you will make it easier for the crown to be passed on to my son.'

Everything had been astutely calculated by the ageing dictator, and forms a strange contrast with the absurdity of his foreign policy, which would lead him to his downfall shortly afterwards. His main aim was, in effect, to take advantage of circumstances in order to remarry that unlikely pair, heredity and universal suffrage. The new constitution brought the liberal bourgeoisie back to him while embarrassing the republicans; it would above all be the opportunity to give his son the people's baptism. Where Napoleon I had failed, Napoleon III would succeed.

When he saw the results, he said: 'I have regained my target figure.' Indeed, he had 7,350,000 'yes' votes, nearly as many as in 1851 and 1852, and 1,500,000 'noes'. Paris remained hostile, but much less clearly than in the legislative elections of the preceding year. The Second Empire seemed to have been founded anew.

Nevertheless, it would crumble away, like the First, in military defeat. At the moment when the nephew could believe himself ready to succeed where his uncle had failed, when he had carried off an internal political operation which was infinitely better planned than the improvisation of the Hundred Days, he was overthrown by military defeat. It was as if the fatal destiny of Bonapartism had overtaken even him *in extremis*, a man who had neither the passion nor the talent nor the kind of obsession for war possessed by the founder of the dynasty.

In fact, the matter of the Hohenzollern candidacy for the throne of Spain had been settled to France's satisfaction, when he himself started the conflict afresh, exposing himself to the humiliation of the Ems telegram from which war with Bismarck's Prussia arose. However, neither he nor Emile Ollivier had wanted it. The enthusiasm for war, which was as always widespread in Parisian opinion, found its political support in the Bonapartist right, those nostalgic for dictatorship, closely grouped round the empress, and keeping an eye open for revenge on the liberal ministry.

It was to them and to her that the emperor yielded, at the beginning of July, when he asked Bismarck for additional guarantees, even though he had received satisfaction on the main points. Perhaps he was in too much pain, the prey to a grave inflammation of the bladder, to retain the full capacity for decision. Perhaps he wanted to increase still further the surge of popularity which the plebiscite had recently renewed, by flattering the chauvinism of the large towns, which had still been reluctant in the May vote. What is certain is that in the fatal summer of 1870 he reverted to a pattern familiar to the house of Bonaparte: staking everything on the next victory. His son was in the end in the same boat as the King of Rome. Their fathers had gambled everything, even the right of inheritance of the throne.

Disaster awaited him, and defeat followed defeat. In vain the empress formed a new ministry of 'hard-line' Bonapartists to replace Ollivier. The emperor, surrounded in Sedan, capitulated on 1 September. On 4 September the Republic was proclaimed in Paris.

10

The Republic: 1870–1880

The emperor was not deposed by a Parisian mob, he was taken prisoner by the Prussians. In Paris his regime had left the stage under the same conditions as the two preceding monarchies: overthrown on 4 September by an insurrection, while the Legislative Body was deliberating, after having its hand forced by the proclamation of the Republic at the Hôtel de Ville. Like Louis-Philippe, the empress-regent had to leave the Tuileries in some haste in a cab in order, like him, to get to England, the classic country for exile. The constitutional arrangements so meticulously prepared to ensure the continuity of the dynasty had evaporated with the capture of the emperor. In the hearts of nineteenth-century French people, the house of Bonaparte probably had deeper roots than those of the Bourbons, which had been torn out forever in the preceding century, to say nothing of the Orléans' roots, which had never found any soil between the *ancien régime* and the Revolution. Nevertheless, it too had disappeared without anyone to defend it.

The explanation lies partly in Bonapartism's special vulnerability to defeat. The Empire had been built on a declaration of peaceful intent, which had reassured the conservatives. But the hearts of those faithful to imperial tradition had continued to beat for another France, active and glorious beyond her frontiers, hostile to the 1815 treaties, once more bringing emancipation to European nations: the triumphal send-off given to the emperor by the Parisian crowds in 1859 on his departure for Italy had demonstrated the strength and the enduring quality of this feeling in urban lower classes that were otherwise reluctant or plainly hostile in regard to the property-owners' Empire.

Now, with this military defeat, the emperor lost on two scores. On the conservative side, he paid dearly for a policy which the notables and the bourgeoisie in general had never liked, chiefly in its Italian form. And their man, 'Monsieur Thiers', had solemnly expressed to the Legislative Body, on 15 July, his reservations with regard to the imperial government's warmongering exaggerations. In so far as it had formed a stake in the game at home, the war had been a marked success for the imperialist party; defeat was therefore their own defeat. This dynastic war had been recommended and undertaken by the ultras of Bonapartism in order to restore to the Empire, over and above the ambiguous crowning by the May plebiscite, the true legitimacy of the Bonapartes – victory. Once it was lost, so was the dynasty. The empress, the rallying-point of those ultras, foundered with them.

On the left the situation was exactly the same: once beaten, the Empire had ceased to exist. Not only beaten but captive, Napoleon III had received from history the famous punishment for 2 December. Taken up by the wealthy as a defender of property, he had been elected by the French on the magic of a name; the bourgeois could have seen him only as the inevitable instrument of their dominance, for the people he had been a banner to rally to. The conquered emperor, a prisoner, was no longer a banner – so he was no longer a sovereign. Moreover, everything goes to show that the liberal development of the regime had not gained him any additional support among the working classes in the big towns: the 1869 elections, and even the referendum of May 1870, revealed that Paris was still broadly hostile.

Similarly, it is very likely that any ground gained among the moderate Orleanist and republican voters had been lost again in Bonapartist left circles, which had no taste for parliamentary liberties. It is indeed clear that extreme left republicanism was on the offensive during the latter years of the Second Empire, keeping republican deputies from any tendency to rally to the regime. The end of the Second Empire is in this respect entirely different from that of the first. In 1814 Napoleon's defeat had for a while revived the idea of resorting to the Bourbons. In 1870 Napoleon III's caused the reappearance of a Republic of Public Safety. The first had buried the Revolution, the second brought it back to life.

There is another, less circumstantial, way in which the collapse of 1870 was seen by the two opposing camps of the monarchist right and the republican left: when it came to the test, the Empire found no defenders anywhere, because the Bonaparte dynasty had no true supporters. It had not put down deep enough roots in the country to benefit from that mysterious force known as tradition which, in France, no longer belonged to anyone. In 1848, the memories it summoned up had been enough to let it triumph through the fear aroused by the Republic, but had not conferred on it that privilege of true royalty – to command obedience by right of birth. The power of kings had no origin, whereas Napoleon III had remained the man of 2 December. He himself had understood that better than anyone, since he had turned for support, first of all to universal suffrage and then, in addition, to the idea of representation: now the first was a republican element, and the second belonged to constitutional monarchy. Not only were they not easily compatible, but they belonged to political legitimacies which, in France, had other traditions than the Empire.

Renan had clearly expressed this in 1869, in an article in the *Revue des Deux Mondes*, devoted to the constitutional monarchy in France, in which he commented on the reforms: 'Can the sovereign who is vested by plebiscite with the full rights of the people be parliamentary? Is not the plebiscite the negation of constitutional monarchy? Has such a government ever emerged from a coup d'état? Can it exist with universal suffrage?' The respect due to the sovereign, added Renan, prevented him from examining these questions. The reply was delivered less than a year later not simply by the defeat, but by the disappearance of a regime with no defenders, which, as before, caused the reappearance of the republicans at the Hôtel de Ville, and two monarchist groups in the country.

In this apparently permanent recommencement, there were however some things which had altered profoundly during the two decades of the Empire. Under the pressure of economic progress France had become modernized. It was still a rural country, but railways, local roads, trade improvements, education and universal suffrage were all elements which had contributed to the opening up of rural areas more rapidly than at any other time in the nineteenth century. The towns were still dominated by craft industries and small traders, but modern industry had made great leaps forward; almost everywhere, first of all in Paris, a policy of major works had redistributed the population, giving the signal for workers and the poor to be exiled to the outskirts. In the medium term, the latter factor would have a fundamental importance in national political life, transforming Paris into a conservative city around the years 1880–1900. But in the short term, the most obvious consequence of imperial modernization on French politics had more to do with country areas; the entire population had undergone the apprenticeship of universal suffrage.

The world in which we live at the end of the twentieth century offers too many examples of the difficulties and failures which are part and parcel of that apprenticeship for the historian not to credit the Second Empire with having been its craftsman and instrument in France. Republican rhetoric against the practice of 'official candidacies' should not conceal the main point from us: French peasants had become accustomed to voting at regular intervals in order to designate, according to the law, representatives to the Legislative Body.

In fact, universal suffrage had been inaugurated in 1848 with the suddenness typical of French political life; it had been premature both in relation to opinions and in relation to reality. In the first place, it had not been one of the watchwords of the banquets campaign; secondly, it had presupposed a level of political education – or education plain and simple – which was far from being achieved in mid-century French rural areas, notably in the west and south-west of the country. Furthermore, the result of the vote of 10 December had sanctioned the situation. In February 1848 Paris had overthrown the constitutional monarchy amid the indifference of the country as a whole, but the election on 10 December had shown that the country was not much more in favour of the Republic.

Now the imperial regime had originated from universal suffrage. The abolition of the law of 31 May 1850 had been the first measure taken by the coup of 2 December, and the people had twice been invited to confirm that transformation of institutions. From its bastard birth certificate, composed of the coup d'état and the vote of the French people, the regime had not relaxed its efforts to expunge the first by means of the second. Side by side with the plebiscite, it had made room for periodic legislative elections. Not in a big way, to be sure, in the minds of both the emperor and the opposition. The former detested the representative concept, and the latter – legitimists and republicans in union – boycotted a ballot organized by an illegal government. Nevertheless, it was this ballot which, over the years, became the major political decision-maker, as in a representative regime or a parliamentary monarchy.

The administration's pressures on the electorate did not radically alter its nature, for those pressures were almost inbuilt in the character of the state in France. They were particularly obvious under the Second Empire, but they were generally applied just as much by the Republic which followed. It can also be argued that, in the middle of the nineteenth century, the prefects' supervision of elections freed the peasantry, in many places, from the influence of the notables. Reading the famous pages of the *Souvenirs* in which Tocqueville recounts how, in the spring of 1848, he led the population of his village in procession to the main town of the district to vote for him, it is easier to understand how the administration's intervention in elections also had a liberating effect. In many regions, voting for the official candidates had been the opportunity to renew the alliance between the peasantry and the imperial state, in the person of the prefect or sub-prefect, thus giving a true direction to a solicited vote, and democratic roots to a practice which had long been reserved for the upper classes. In order to gauge how much the Bonapartist practice of universal suffrage had loosened the aristocratic grip on rural areas between 1850 and 1870, one need only observe the evolution of *départements* in the west, legitimist in 1849 and Bonapartist in 1869.

The principle of universal suffrage had been established by the First Republic but had never been applied. After the Empire, the Restoration and the July monarchy had based parliamentary representation on a very restricted electoral body. The Second Republic had truly given the French the rights promised by the First, but had died as a result. The Second Empire had introduced universal suffrage into national customs. Furthermore, although the Comte de Chambord had insisted on a boycott of the elections, imitated in this by some intractable exiles from 2 December, the legitimists had given him no more lasting attention than the Republicans had to their great predecessors of 1848.

In 1857, and even more after 1863, elections to the Legislative Body formed the regime's great political battle; what is more, the regime itself helped to raise the stakes by restoring rights and powers to the elected Assembly. When one considers the way in which both those in power and those in opposition prepared for the 1863 elections, not to mention those of 1869, it is evident that one of the unexpected results of the Second Empire was to have created a very broad consensus concerning the legitimacy of universal suffrage, combined with a general acceptance of a piece of parliamentary logic: legislative elections must be won in order to govern.

Matters did not really have quite such clear-cut simplicity, but they were heading in that direction. On the right, many legitimist politicians, for example Berryer and Falloux, were also taking that path despite the pretender. The Orleanists, in spite of Guizot, but following Thiers's example, were perforce in the throes of accepting universal suffrage. On the republican side, the old insurrectionist spirit was still alive among the Blanquists and many other socialist sects, but the Ferry–Gambetta generation was fighting to win the elections one day on a platform of democratic reforms which would give the new Republic its direction. That is what Gambetta told his Belleville voters in 1869. In other words, the Second Empire, at the moment of its disappearance, had carried out a vast transformation in the conditions of French public life. In its social sense, there was no going back on the 'democracy' which had been gained. In its political sense, it had imposed its rule in nearly all minds – that was, universal suffrage and a government responsible to its elected members.

Nevertheless, the Second Empire finished badly, just as it had started badly. And the circumstances of its downfall, very different from 1830 and 1848, would reconstruct, one last time, the whole theatre of the French Revolution, played in reverse: public safety and the Commune, ahead of the phantom of the Bourbons and the *ancien régime*. It was as if this last exorcism was essential to the entry on the scene of those who would finally ring down the curtain on the French Revolution, nearly one hundred years later: 'Monsieur Thiers' and Gambetta.

In August 1870, the imperial regime swiftly disintegrated, under the onslaught of defeats: those of August 6 (Frœschwiller, Woerth, Forbach) had swept away Ollivier's ministry, and he had been replaced by an old 'Algerian' general, Cousin-Montauban. The atmosphere of 'public safety' took the republicans back to the great era, and already, on 14 August the Blanquists had attempted a raid on the fire station at La Villette; as for the bourgeoisie, they were already looking to Thiers, who was credited with the prestige of Cassandra. On 4 September, when the news of the military surrender was made known in Paris, the Legislative Body was seeking a 'legal' solution to the deposition of the empress when it was invaded by a mob demanding a Republic.

This was a classic scene from the French repertoire, known and re-enacted as such by the players, on the side of the rioters just as much as the deputies: Jules Favre took charge and went off with Gambetta to proclaim the Republic at the Hôtel de Ville. The Blanquists would have liked to impose a revolutionary government, but the deputies substitued the list of the Parisian elected members of 1869. Thus continuity was safe, in the silence of the Assembly which was dissolved the following day, 5 September; universal suffrage extended its legitimacy from the last vote to the new provisional government, known as the government of National Defence. Jules Favre had Foreign Affairs, Gambetta the Interior, and the presidency was given to General Trochu, for it had been necessary to find a soldier – but a popular one – to head a wartime government.

The originality of the political situation, compared with 1830 and 1848, was that the new regime, which had emerged from the Parisian revolution, owed its birth to the defeat of the troops, and that civil struggles, which were part and parcel of its beginnings, spread in relation to the war: this was the central stake of the political battle, just as in 1793. It was one of the moments in nineteenth-century France when images of the Revolution came back most obviously to contemporaries: foreign invasion added its dramatic touch to the train of memories and traditions. Everyone knew how it had accelerated the course of the French Revolution in 1792, and the role it had played in the dictatorship and the Terror.

The republican deputies, at least the most moderate among them – Jules Favre, Jules Simon and Jules Grévy for example – wanted to negotiate with Bismarck, both because they judged the military situation to be hopeless and also because they feared the development of Jacobin, dictatorial, Blanquist excess on their left. Thiers, who had for a while become the arbiter of conservative opinion, supported them with all his might. But Jules Favre failed in his negotiations of 19 and 20 September with Bismarck (who demanded surrender pure and simple), and Thiers had no luck in his round of European capitals to try to obtain favourable mediation.

So the war went on, and continued also to be the field of Parisian battles for power. In fact, for the first time since 1793, Paris had rediscovered the major ingredient of political radicalism: the idea of public safety, which allowed opinions to be turned into crimes; and its opposite, conservative defeatism, which was unable to see anything other than social subversion in patriotic passion. I deliberately say Paris, for the country as a whole – if Lyon, Marseille and some large towns are excluded – remained aloof from these struggles. It wanted an armistice and elections, as did the moderates of the National Defence government. But in the situation created by the war, Paris ruled France: those months from autumn 1870 to spring 1871 were the last in French history when Parisian revolution governed France, returning by chance to a situation existing prior to universal suffrage. The crushing of the Commune by the Assembly would bring that survival to an end.

Universal suffrage: in September 1870, this was certainly the hope of the conservatives and also of the Jules Favre school of republicans, both to give a legitimate foundation to the Republic of 4 September and to vanquish the Parisian mobs. But war, on the contrary, preserved this Republic's revolutionary character: in September a Central Committee for the twenty *arrondissements* had been set up at the instigation of the militants of Marx's Socialist International, heading a network of local committees.

In the decisions of this Committee is to be found all the traditional luggage of 'public safety': requisitioning, the *levée en masse*, arming the people, plus an unprecedented idea – communal self-management, bizarrely associated with military victory: 'The sovereign commune', said the Manifesto of 22 October, 'revolutionarily carrying out the defeat of the enemy' would thereafter open the way to 'government of the citizens by themselves'. The demand for municipal autonomy had been fed by hostility to the exceptional regime which had been put into effect for Paris and Lyon throughout the whole period of the Empire; it allowed an escape not only from state oppression but from the national tyranny of universal suffrage. It at last gave a radical form to the decentralizing political trend, which had been so active almost everywhere in the last years of the Empire: it was the Proudhonian vision of municipal liberty.

However, in the situation in autumn 1870, it was inextricably mixed up with direct democracy and the *levée en masse* of the sansculottes of the French Revolution: the Blanquists, too, those plebeian Jacobins, made it their own. There thus took shape a completely heterogeneous revolutionary movement – which would constantly annoy Marx – because in it were to be found ex-pacifists from the Socialist International and patriotic fanatics, Proudhonian communalists and neo-Babouvists, and the old insurrectionist republicanism combined with all the socialist doctrines. Social revolution and political revolution, so often divided since the 1830s, now joined hands to let off a last firework which united the eighteenth and nineteenth centuries: a republic of public safety and social fraternity.

Even in Paris, however, the populace was far from unanimously following the activists in the clubs and committees: armed and formed into National Guards, the majority remained loyal to the government. That was very evident on 31 October, when a mini-uprising temporarily gained control of the Hôtel de Ville at the news of the surrender of Bazaine in Metz on the 27th, which coincided with the failure of a *sortie* intended to loosen the stranglehold of the Prussian blockade round Paris. While the rebels were divided between communalists and Blanquists, the National Guards of the moderate *arrondissements* had no difficulty in recapturing the Hôtel de Ville on behalf of the government. The latter had promised municipal elections. Deeply split over this issue, it ended by agreeing on a vote to confirm its powers by the population of Paris on 3 November, a ballot to be followed two days later by the election of the mayors of the twenty *arrondissements* and their deputies. There were a good many abstentions, but a very large majority of the successes went to the authorities born of 4 September. Only the most 'working-class' *arrondissements* voted against the National Defence government by choosing mayors who supported an elected Commune of Paris.

Paris under siege, however, was no longer the centre of national politics. From Tours Gambetta organized defence policy, after Thiers, during the first days of November, had vainly tried to wrest from Bismarck honourable conditions for the cessation of hostilities. This policy had little real chance of checking the enemy advance, and Gambetta – wrongly, as it turned out – clung to the plan of liberating Paris, for which he lacked the military means. But the interesting feature is that it shifted the political conflict a notch or so in relation to the Parisian situation. Itself clad in great memories of *la patrie en danger* and the *levée en masse*, the policy aroused a major war effort in the name of a Jacobin Republic which was not revolutionary.

Gambetta cleverly regained control of the communalist uprisings in Marseille and Lyon, with a mixture of concessions and repression, between September and November. His tireless words mapped out a strategy which aimed at enveloping the extreme left in the effort for national safety, in the name of the republican tradition, but under the direction of his prefects and within the framework of the civil and military institutions of the state.

The Gambetta of autumn 1870 was no longer Robespierre, but Danton, the future hero of the Third Republic. But the road he sought to follow was too narrow to be really practicable in the conditions of a war which had been irreparably lost after the defeats at Sedan and Metz. On his left he had Parisian activism, isolated from the rest of the nation. But chiefly, on his right, what a host of enemies! His republican rhetoric evoked the French Revolution far too much, and he had appointed too many of his political friends as prefects, not to alarm the entire right, and even more than the right. In that autumn of 1870, the heartland of France was reliving memories too: like Paris, but in opposition to it.

The disappearance of the Empire had liberated not only revolutionary energies. By the same token, it had also reawakened the social panics of the conservatives, the class violence of the wealthy and the fears of the peasants, who rather liked the fallen emperor. Beaten, the country was not heroic; it wanted peace, even on Bismarck's conditions, because that was the only way to get back to normal. The elites, the bourgeoisie and politicians often added to this mass feeling the violence of reactionary passions inseparable from the French political heritage.

Marshal Bazaine had provided a sorry illustration when he had capitulated with his entire army at Metz on 27 October: obsessed by the idea of keeping his troops intact in order to re-establish order in Paris, he had first plotted with the empress in exile before negotiating with the enemy. The conservatives did not go that far, but they hastened to obtain an armistice in order to base their government on elections, against Gambetta. Thiers was the idol of the bourgeoisie, the indispensable man. He had won over many moderate republicans to his camp, such as Jules Grévy, who were anxious about the hard-line Jacobin nature of Gambetta's politics.

In January 1871 the military situation was hopeless after the failure of the so-called 'Loire' armies. Siege fever grew in Paris. On the 19th, a vast 'mass sortie', organized by Trochu under pressure from the Central Committee, which had become the Delegation of the Twenty

Arrondissements, was smashed by the Prussians at Buzenval. It was Jules Favre who conducted the armistice negotiations between 24 and 28 January 1871. In return for the surrender of Paris, Bismarck granted a three-week armistice: enough time for France to elect a national Assembly which would work out peace terms.

The elections took place on 8 February on a list ballot and with a relative majority; a reaction against the electoral law of the Empire and dictated by the desire to have only a single round, this type of ballot worsened the republicans' defeat: scarcely 150 were elected, of whom only about forty were 'radicals', that is to say, close to Gambetta. There were 400 monarchists, shared equally between the two pretenders. An *'introuvable'* Assembly, as Tolain put it, which at once entrusted executive power to Thiers. Jules Favre stayed as Minister of Foreign Affairs. The matter which took precedence over all others was the peace negotiation, which had been given overwhelming support in advance by the whole country. Under the Treaty of Frankfurt, signed at the beginning of May, France was to cede Alsace (with the exception of Belfort) and part of Lorraine to Germany, and promise to pay compensation of five billion francs, which was the condition for a staggered evacuation of German occupying troops.

THE COMMUNE

At the very moment when the treaty was signed, Thiers had to confront the Paris Commune. No event in modern French history, or perhaps in all French history, has been the subject of such a surfeit of interest in relation to its brevity. It lasted less than three months, from March to May 1871, and did not weigh heavily on the events which followed, since it ended in defeat and repression. If, however, it has since then continued to live on so strongly in national memory and historiography, it is first of all because it was the last armed confrontation in French civil war; the last scene in the Revolution when, together with the Tuileries and the Hôtel de Ville, Paris burned the monuments to so many *journées* which had taken place since 1793. The Commune wiped out February and June 1848, the week which had followed 2 December 1851, and 4 September 1870, replacing the great days of French revolutionary annals with the capital city's most spectacular revolt, which was also the funeral of the Paris of *Les Misérables*.

The fires bore witness in their own way to the extreme violence of passions in both camps; but as always, it is the blood shed on either side which takes the longest to forget: the Commune was a murderous civil war, with a particularly bloody aftermath of repression. What excuse could there be for such ferocity, unless it was a great cause on the one side, and an immense danger on the other? Thus the *Communards* and the Versaillais re-enacted one last time in France the roles of the revolutionary and counter-revolutionary regeneration of society: on both sides the event was thereby magnified, surcharged with the admiration it inspired in socialist thought and the fear it engendered in the bourgeois tradition.

Furthermore, the memory of the Commune had the luck to find itself transfigured by a great event which came afterwards: the Russian revolution of 1917 integrated it with its own genealogy, by way of the book which Marx had devoted to the event in 1871. As a result, communist historiography in the twentieth century followed the Marxist line and, instead of being the last of the nineteenth-century revolutions, the Commune was promoted to the rank of herald of the twentieth-century socialist revolutions. To the Russian Bolsheviks, obsessed by the Jacobin line of descent, it offered an intermediate link; and it enriched the tradition of French working-class memory by firmly implanting Soviet communism in it. Thus a history of memory was replenished through ideological loyalty.

However, the Commune owed much more to the circumstances of the winter of 1871 and the breeding-ground of French politics than to Marxist socialism, with which it had no ties. It was the outcome, both logical and tragic, of the political exasperation of Parisian activists, in the besieged and starving capital, against the indecision of Trochu and the government of National Defence. The armistice concluded by Jules Favre at the end of January aroused accusations of betrayal; on 8 February, Paris voted left and extreme left: it was revenge for Louis Blanc, the old exile of 15 May 1848, who obtained the maximum votes. Also elected were Victor Hugo, Gambetta and Garibaldi, the republican hero of Italian unity. Not all-out 'reds' – they would keep aloof from the Commune – but confirmed Republicans and patriots: this was the dominant colour in Paris. It was enough to make the capital an exception in this election in which the 'rurals', as they were already being dubbed, and their conservative elected members triumphed.

What, then, can be said of the state of mind of the militants in the *arrondissement* committees or the National Guards? In their eyes, Gambetta was most frequently nothing but a defeatist, like Trochu, disguised in false rhetoric. What reappeared in the Paris of that era was the obsessive fear of treason and the idea of direct democracy, breeding a scorn for politicians and representatives – even though elected by universal suffrage: the passion of Year II regained its former accents, though the course of time had slightly shifted the objects of popular condemnation. The sansculottes had found socialist leaders.

But what a host of socialisms! The political background was still provided by the French Revolution, Jacobins and Blanquists, nostalgic for both the constitution of 1793 and the dictatorship, supporters of Robespierre, Hébert or Babeuf, at the same time rivals, yet combined in a common admiration for the great era. But the nineteenth century had added its layers to this heritage, and Parisian activism, since the last years of the Second Empire, had joined militants of the social revolution with those of the political revolution: Proudhonians, communalists who had little liking for Jacobin dictatorship; the men of the International – themselves divided; anarchists, followers of Mikhail Bakunin, and all the varied advocates of the co-operative organization of labour. 'Learned'

The men of the Commune, *1871*.
(Photo: Roger-Viollet)

socialism supplied the leaders of the Commune, but it was good old-fashioned sansculotte passion which provided its troops.

The events are well known, and do not offer the dramatic suspense of Year II: the war was over, Thiers massed his troops at Versailles and what was happening in Paris was no longer universal history. The uprising broke out on 18 March, when Parisian militants had refused for two weeks to give up their arms and cannon to the government. Thiers wanted to disarm Paris forcibly, and suddenly the great city slid into revolution between 18 and 28 March. The mayors of the *arrondissements*, Georges Clemenceau at their head, failed to find a compromise between Versailles and the Central Committee of the National Guards. At the end of March, the Committee had gained control of the town halls and had caused a municipal assembly to be elected which took the name 'Commune'.

It contained old Jacobins from 1848, like Charles Delescluze and Félix Pyat, who had been elected deputies in February; Blanquists who were also Hébertists, like Tridon; Blanquists plain and simple, like Théophile Ferré – the leader himself was once again in prison; Proudhonians (Beslay, Lefrançais); supporters of the International (Varlin, Malon and Frankel, the only 'Marxist'); even the patriotic officer was not missing, the romantic *condottiere* of the Commune, Louis Rossel; and the painter Gustave Courbet, a little out of his depth among such colleagues; Jules Vallès, who would write a novel about it; and Gustave Flourens, the son of a well-off family, a great enthusiast for the Committee of Public Safety.

The Commune would have no leaders, singular or plural, not only because it found such an idea repugnant on principle, but because none of these men had either the temperament or the means. They formed a group in which no one was notably outstanding, constantly involved in their petty squabbles, unable to measure up to the circumstances through which they were living or the ideas they represented. The communalist idea, more or less borrowed from Proudhon, served them as a banner, but did not survive the situation for long: it was soon necessary to replace the dream of the people's self-management with the Blanquist idea of revolutionary dictatorship, which alienated the Proudhonians without really improving the Communards' military capacity.

Thus there was a Commune which was Proudhonian, democratic and socialist in tone, instituting a moratorium on rents, seeking to found free and compulsory state education, and to reorganize production based on the association of producers, both men and women together, for the idea of women's equality made its first serious appearance among the extreme left. And there was a Commune of public safety, linking up again with dictatorship and the law of hostages, the persecution of the clergy and summary executions. The two pictures followed each other in time, but were not strictly superimposed on the rivalry between Proudhonians and Jacobins.

In the venture of the Commune, which was complex and failed to come off, circumstances guided men rather than the other way round. Socialist ideas had encountered the egalitarian and patriotic passion of the Parisian

lower classes, which had been aroused by the siege and defeat; having
become, rather by chance, the rallying-point of a revolt against universal
suffrage, and during the peace negotiations, these ideas had embellished
the funeral dirge of revolutions in Paris, which Thiers had always dreamed
of conquering.

For Thiers applied a strategy which he had contemplated since those
famous days of February 1848 when, as prime minister for a few hours, he
had featured among the vanquished: to recapture Paris from outside, if
necessary with support from the provinces. For this reason, he would
dawdle over attempts at mediation between Versailles and Paris which
would be sketched out in April and May by republican groups or the
Freemasons. He had the advantage of a Paris transformed by Haussmann,
where the quarters which lent themselves to barricades had disappeared;
he had been elected by universal suffrage, only recently empowered by the
country's vote. The situation resembled that of June 1848 rather than
February. It was as if the story had been written in advance, and it ended
as in June, but with an extra degree of ferocity.

The military recapture of Paris took place between 21 and 27 May, and
was both easy, from the army standpoint, and appallingly bloody. Thiers
could have cut the matter short: there was something implacable about the
methodical slowness of overrunning Paris. The Communards, retreating
from west to east, set fire to the Tuileries, and then burned the Conseil
d'État, the Cour des Comptes and finally the old Hôtel de Ville; they shot
hostages, including the archbishop, Monseigneur Darboy. The Versailles
troops, for their part, gave no quarter: from the 26th, Paris was the theatre
of a real manhunt, in which several thousand 'suspects', including women
and children, were killed without trial: the grisly tally is not statistically
exact, but the figure of 20,000 dead is probable. Furthermore 40,000
prisoners were dumped in mostly primitive conditions. In the end, half of
them were released, provided with a police dossier for future reference;
among the remainder, there were 10,000 hastily contrived sentences, a
great number of which were of deportation to New Caledonia.

The historian remains dumbfounded by the unleashing of passion
which, in public opinion, surrounded this kind of terror in reverse, the
bloodiest in French history since the Revolution. In fact, the Commune
renewed the violence of class feelings which had been seen so often in
nineteenth-century France, but it carried them to a degree of white heat
never reached before. The rebellion of spring 1871 was a June 1848 which
had succeeded, at least for the time being.

It had united the same elements of society as twenty-three years previously: the world of traditional occupations linked with that of budding
industry, a little more of the latter, a little less of the former – something
nearer to what could be termed the urban lower orders than to a class. It
had placed at its head not well-known leaders, since Ferry, Gambetta,
Clemenceau and even Louis Blanc had kept away after the failure of the
mid-March negotiations, but top men who were less anonymous and more

Barricade in the Faubourg Saint-Antoine during the Commune, *1871*, *Bibliothèque Nationale, Paris.*
(Photo: Lauros-Giraudon)

doctrinaire than those of June 1848; socialists unfurling their flag in the revolutionary heritage.

Taking over power against the Republic, governing Paris for a few months, executing hostages and burning the centre of the capital, the Commune had provided a concrete object of loathing not only to the fear of the wealthy, as has often been written, but also to public opinion as a whole, which never looked leniently on the losers in a civil war. The massacres carried out by the Versailles troops between 25 and 30 May received general approval. Zola, who was not exactly a reactionary author, wrote on the 29th:

The slaughter was atrocious. Our soldiers . . . meted out implacable justice in the streets. Any man caught with a weapon in his hand was shot. So corpses lay scattered everywhere, thrown into corners, decomposing with astonishing rapidity, which was doubtless due to the drunken state of these men when they were hit. For six days Paris has been nothing but a huge cemetery.[1]

---

[1] Extract from an article published in *Le Sémaphore de Marseille*, for which Zola was the Parisian correspondent from February 1871 to May 1877.

Thus, the last great uprising in the French revolutionary tradition was also the one which created the most fear and shed the most blood, as if it formed the ultimate exorcism of a violence which had been an inseparable part of French public life since the end of the eighteenth century. In this Paris in flames, the French Revolution bade farewell to history. The bourgeoisie, however, took the opposite view: it was proof of the terrifying threat which increasingly hung over their destiny, and over the future of civilization. In that sense, the memory of the Commune renewed and prolonged the feelings of social hatred which had arisen from the Revolution, crystallizing them on working-class socialism, which replaced the phantom of Year II.

But the brutal crushing of the rebellion at least averted danger for a good while, by the deportation of those among its most active participants who had not been killed. It also rendered less fearsome those republicans who had condemned the Commune right from the start, such as Ferry and Gambetta: their Republic was explicitly cleansed of the suspicion of insurrection and memories of the Terror. By separating them once again from socialist tradition, the Commune had opened up a place on the centre-left for them. In the short term, its dead had thus facilitated the coming together of the centres, Republican and Orleanist, which would be the basis of the Third Republic.

In the long term, they had once more – and more deeply than in June 1848 – dug the chasm which divided the working-class left from bourgeois republicanism. The Commune represents a major date in the history of the exile of the working-class movement in French democracy; only Jaurès, at the end of the century, would try to bring it to a close, but without success, because after the First World War the communists would, on the contrary, turn it into the principle of their influence.

LIVING WITH DEFEAT

The crushing of the Commune did not suppress the national drama which had been the source of the uprising: France was having to face up to its defeat. The country was living through it in a different way from the Parisian workers, but just as profoundly, and certainly in a greater national communion than in 1814 or even 1815. At that time, the French campaign and Waterloo had put an end to the interminable wars in which the nation had become intoxicated with military glory: defeat and the end of the Empire, at the hands of the whole of Europe, had been received by at least part of opinion as the end of an endless adventure, and the opportunity to have a fresh attempt at reworking the idea of post-Revolutionary France. It is true that the Hundred Days, Waterloo and the Holy Alliance had reactivated feelings of national humiliation, but the defeat had remained swathed in the glorious flag of the Revolution.

There was nothing like that in 1871: the war had been the confrontation of two national wills constituted on the modern model. It no longer consisted of an *ancien régime* to be vanquished or a revolution to be defended. It was two peoples face to face, their identities in relation to each other having been forged over a long period, and one of them just achieving its unity against France. Throughout this history, which had been going on for centuries, the French had become accustomed, if not to being always the conquerors – there had been Rossbach and Leipzig – at least to figuring as the dominant power. Now the roles were reversed, and the modern national idea, the heart of the French Revolution, indicated a Europe where the new Germany, enlarged by Alsace-Lorraine, laid down the law to the France of the Treaties of Westphalia and Tilsit.

Only the Parisian workers, lingering in the tradition of Year II and 1815, had made a revolutionary pretext out of this historic reversal. The nation itself now looked beyond these memories: the policy of nationalities which had for so long intoxicated it revealed the unexpected sight of a beaten France and a victorious Germany. The entire French political and intellectual world, from legitimists to Republicans, reflected on this unprecedented result of a history the national principle of which no one any longer sought to challenge or fight, as if it had become obvious to everyone. Thenceforth, a common patriotism tended to unite political families which remained divided over their internal political aims.

Of this 'German crisis in French thought', to quote the pithy title of C. Digeon's book,[2] there is no better witness than Renan, who published in February 1871 his little book *La Réforme intellectuelle et morale de la France*. Renan knew Germany, and had admired it more than any other French author of his generation: like so many nineteenth-century savants, he had seen in German universities the model to be imitated in order to implant in France a scientific spirit, and especially modern historical research. The war, desired by the Empire, had appeared to him to be an aberration, an anachronistic, almost absurd, rebirth of military temptation in a country grown sluggish with democratic prosperity. Renan interpreted in his own way the rapid transformations which had occurred in French society under the Empire. France had lost what it had in the way of Germanic and military spirit, to draw ever closer to the calculating and utilitarian mentality of the Anglo-Saxons: a second America, but lacking in everything which made the United States an exceptional case, that is to say, 'a second-class America, mean and mediocre, perhaps more similar to Mexico or South America than to the United States'. Now it was that democracy obsessed by the pursuit of wealth which the emperor had hurled against a Germany which still had all the strength of its aristocratic and military traditions: this was a major error of judgement, immediately punished by defeat.

Critical of the money mania and civic laziness which went hand in hand with democratic pacifism, Renan also accused universal suffrage, the idea

[2] C. Digeon, *La Crise allemande de la pensée française*.

that popular assent is the condition of the legitimacy of power: with the social fragmentation they produced, he contrasted the image of a 'historic' royalty, the guardian of the nation's right and prerogatives. He borrowed this part of his demonstration from Germany: 'M. de Savigny has shown that a society needs a government coming from outside, beyond and before it, that social power does not emanate entirely from society and that there is a philosophical and historical law (divine, if you will) which is vital to the nation.'

Which royalty, which dynasty? Renan knew very well that the oldest one, the 'historical' one, to be precise, had become almost 'impossible' (he uses this word); and that the other, which had disappeared without a fight in February 1848, had no 'royal rights in the strictest term'. He inclined towards an Orleanism which, more than under Louis-Philippe, would give their rightful place to virtues other than bourgeois virtues. But, like the French elites of the era, he deferred the question of the regime to delineate only the reforms which were most necessary for the rebirth of the nation. The end of his essay is perhaps most interesting for the historian of opinion, for it gives an inkling of a 'spirit of the times' which is half-way between liberalism and conservatism.

Renan was not a counter-revolutionary. He accepted modern society as inevitable but, like all French liberals, he came up against the problem of the good use of democracy; and like all the men of post-1870, he had to think of the nation in terms which were different from both revolutionary tradition and aristocratic loyalty to the fallen dynasty. In order to contain universal suffrage, which he considered another inevitability, he put forward the idea (like Taine, in the same period) of a two-degree vote, in such a way as to form a tissue of little local aristocracies, and the need for an upper Chamber, with several dozen hereditary seats, in the British fashion, but mainly appointed for life, recruited from all the bodies and sectors of national activity, to be the custodian of rights and liberties.

As a liberal, Renan argued also for administrative decentralization, which at the time was on everyone's lips, from the Communards to the legitimists; as an anticlerical, for the separation of Church and state. But, in his view, the essence of national rebirth lay in educational reform, the veritable keystone of the future. For France's defeat at German hands was above all an intellectual defeat, due to the superiority of German education, which was earnest, open and scientific, over French, which was too concerned with training orators and wits. Protestant descent against Catholic heritage: as a good son of positivism, Renan was reworking there a theme dear to moderate republicans like Jules Ferry, also a positivist. He was not as anticlerical as they, since he remained attached to a religion which never ceased to be the basis of his emotional life and his whole being; but, like them, against the decadence of the nation he set the remedy of education, and against the uncertainties of history, the sovereignty of science.

Thus, though his attempt may well have presented ideas which were too reactionary for the republicans, such as the resurrection of an aristocracy of officialdom, extolling the monarchy, or recommending an upper Chamber, he nevertheless created around the national crisis fresh space for common discussion between conservatives and republicans. He no longer used revolutionary tradition as his principal frame of reference; he did not set out expressly to achieve the ending of the Revolution; he did not give a verdict on institutions. His aim was to combine modern society, with its tendency towards hedonistic individualism, with the need for a nation which was strong both intellectually and militarily; thence arose the question of training citizens in democracy, whereby the conservative which Renan had become united with the preoccupations of republicans of positivist persuasion. His vision of education was not wholly theirs, as he desired full and complete freedom of minds with regard to Catholicism only at the higher level, with the reform of universities. But at the heart of his programme for national recovery through the rational training of elites lay something which was not unconnected with the idea of republican civic virtue enlightened by science right from primary school. The future would in any case show that Renan was not irreconcilable with the Republic.

However, during the course of 1871, the most obvious results of national defeat were not to be found in those intellectual developments which were causing France to enter another political age. The Commune had revived the terrorist patriotism of Year II. After its destruction, it was the turn of counter-revolution to pay its funereal visit to blameworthy France. It added a third motive for an examination of conscience to defeat and the Commune: the abandonment of Rome to the kingdom of Italy, the disappearance of the pope's temporal power. The three tragedies had been connected: the first two were divine punishment deserved by the nation which was responsible for the third.

The Catholic Church, that great specialist in public repentance, rediscovered the tones it had used under the Restoration for the expiation of the Revolution's crimes. In 1871, exercises of redemptive piety were organized around the cult of the Sacred Heart – to which the basilica of Montmartre was to be dedicated; this occasion witnessed the rebirth of a missionary Catholicism, both popular and populist, largely inspired by Veuillot and inseparable, as under the last Bourbons, from the idea of monarchism. What would come to be called 'moral order' renewed the alliance of the Throne and the Altar.

What throne? The Assembly of February 1871, thanks to exceptional circumstances, had seen the return of a sizeable majority of royalists but, as always, at odds over the name of their king. At bottom, this Chamber resembled that of May 1849, as if the Empire had been merely a long digression. The years ahead would destroy that illusion of a time rediscovered but, for the moment, what a temptation it was! The Assembly was swamped with the great families which had for so long been in internal exile, the La Rochefoucaulds, the Noailles, the Broglies, the Harcourts and the Haussonvilles, not to mention the great bourgeois names, Guizot and

Casimir-Périer. The Orleanists had had their princes elected, two sons of Louis-Philippe, Aumale and Joinville. Two hundred legitimists, two hundred Orleanists, elected by a rural France which wanted peace. Once peace was secure, and the Commune crushed, the grand plan was still to have a king. The law of exile was repealed on 8 June, and the Orleanists let it be known that they were prepared to forget their more recent rights, to benefit the legitimate dynasty. It was now up to the Comte de Chambord to speak, from his retreat in his Austrian château.

He had grown up in the circle and atmosphere decribed by Chateaubriand at the time of his visit to the dethroned Charles X at Hradschin. Since 1830, the French nobles had taken it in turns to attend on their prince, exiled at the age of nine, far from his homeland, to try to give him the traditional life of his ancestors, the kings of France; they had rebuilt for him the daily routine, the Masses, the audiences, the hunts and the boredom. He had nothing but unhappy memories of France, his father assassinated before his birth, and his grandfather driven out by rebellion; another good reason to settle into that imaginary royalty to which he was confined by the conviction of his rights, his scanty interest in politics and the paucity of his knowledge.

He had married a princess from a little Italian court which, like himself, had been abandoned by the century, and he had not been too unhappy to reign over France in the divine order of things, temporarily thwarted by an intractable people. Under the Empire, he had recommended electoral abstention, greatly to the cost of his loyal followers: the most illustrious of them, as we have seen, disobeyed. In 1871, the wheel of Fortune gave him a little more chance to play; truly by chance, as if Louis XIV's last descendant could find in the debris of a dead royalty only enough to try a lucky throw.

A Bonaparte would have seized the opportunity. So would a Henri IV, a political king, on the look-out for a situation in which the dynasty could be re-created. But he refused. He came to France in July, and at Chambord received a small delegation of his supporters, who urged him to advance towards modern France. The symbol of his refusal was the flag. He wanted to retain the fleur-de-lis. This is what he wrote in his message published by *L'Union* on 5 July: 'Henri V cannot abandon the white flag of Henri IV. I received it as a sacred trust from the old king, my grandfather, as he died in exile; for me it has always been inseparable from the absent homeland; it fluttered over my cradle, I want it to shade my tomb.'

These lines form the testament of the old monarchy, and yet their spirit is foreign to everything which had made the grandeur of the dynasty. They were written by a prince who had read too much Veuillot and not enough Richelieu: uprooted by the French Revolution, royalty had never retrieved its place and its past, of which the Church, also uprooted, constantly offered it the illusion. French monarchy in the nineteenth century had lived in the myth of its own tradition, just like other powers since 1789. Daniel Halévy wrote some admirable lines on its fall, which deserve to be quoted in full:

Chambord does not belong to old France, his action is in no way linked to the completely realist tradition of our kings. Chambord is a child of the émigrés, a reader of Chateaubriand. His letter is the last, and not the least beautiful, of the great Romantic odes. Romantic, therefore, revolutionary. The Comte de Chambord's decision is, in fact, by its nature a revolutionary act: because of it, one of the firmest supports of the old ruling classes was broken, and their definitive downfall, which would fill the next ten years, was precipitated. Because of it, the French monarchy left the world, became legend and myth. In that form it would have remarkable and passionate reawakenings.[3]

So there was no restoration. But those royalist deputies would have none of the Republic. In the interval, there was 'Monsieur Thiers'.

THIERS

At the age of seventy-three, Thiers was at the pinnacle of his career. He had been elected to the Assembly of Bordeaux by twenty-six *départements*, at last reaping the benefits of that truly national popularity which he had lacked in 1848, at the time of the presidential election. He had intelligently opposed the excessive belligerence of the Empire in July 1870, and capitalized on it after the defeat. An indispensable personage, overwhelmingly voted for by the nation – universal suffrage had become the only rule in this country without rules – he had also, for much longer, been the man who stood for parliamentary liberties.

The Assembly had entrusted him with authority as the 'Chief of Executive Power of the French Republic'. He had concluded the peace treaty, broken the Commune. On 31 August, Rivet's law conferred upon him the most prestigious title, which he had asked for, of 'president of the Republic'. He was at the peak of his talent, in the centre of political life, which had finally absorbed his whole existence: talkative, amusing, intelligent, wily, filling a role which was in reality only slightly lower than his national renown, a successful Louis-Philippe, a quasi-monarch who was at last bourgeois. Here he was at the summit of power, and of a regime which had yet to be defined.

What a life he had had! Totally bourgeois, punctuated by the most classic successes, fame, a rich marriage, the ministry, the Académie, influence – yet pursued like a Romantic adventure, successful by dint of talent and energy, criss-crossed with setbacks and recantations. There was in that existence something which resembled the anxiety and instability of the bourgeoisie itself, caught between the volcanic event from which it drew its claims to govern the country and its inability to control the effects of that event. When little Thiers had arrived in Paris in 1821, at the age of twenty-four, in the footsteps of his friend Mignet, who was Provençal like himself, he had immediately revealed an extraordinary *savoir-faire* in everything to which he turned his hand; he had done wonders in

[3] Daniel Halévy, *La Fin des notables*, 2, p. 29.

Restoration Paris – that bourgeois version of court civilization – rather like Diderot's *neveu de Rameau* heading for success. He had read everything, written about everything, explained everything; he had a knack, a flair, cynicism, cheerfulness. Everything had attracted this illegitimate son to the republican opposition; he was pro-1789, he made excuses for 1793, he had a soft spot for Napoleon; he was anticlerical, liberal and a patriot: his *Histoire de la Revolution*, which he had never repudiated, had been his entry into the world.

After that he had become a true bourgeois, married, rich, settled, a minister, largely because of the July revolution, in which he had played a decisive role at the right moment. He had been one of the inventors of the bourgeois monarchy; he had served it, while at the same time pursuing his career, and had not been responsible for its downfall, since he had for so long been Guizot's adversary in the name of the 'national' spirit and parliamentary liberties. February 1848 had proved him right, but more than he would have wished; like the men of July, he had believed he was ending the revolution of 1830. It was then that his liberal bourgeois tune was enriched with right-wing tones which brought him nearer to what he had detested: religion and the aristocracy. But the future showed that he had still more to fear from drawing nearer to what he had loved: one of the leaders of the party of order, he advocated the vote for Bonaparte against Cavaignac in December 1848, before becoming one of the rallying-points of the notables against the president in 1850–1, and one of those temporarily proscribed on 2 December.

Then began a long crossing of the desert, where he found himself divided from his political supporters, who were in favour of the coup d'état. He wrote the continuation of his *Révolution*, the *Histoire du Consulat et de l'Empire*. United in common defeat with his former legitimist opponents of the party of order, whom he saw in social circles and at the Académie, he kept in touch with the more liberal of the republicans, since it was from a liberal union list which also contained the 'five' that he was elected in Paris in 1863. Indefatigable, he then resumed the centre-left tones of the July Chambers, and orchestrated the same opposition against Rouher that he had used against Guizot, in the name of parliamentary liberties.

However, history thumbed its nose at him one last time in 1870: for the warmonger of 1840, the man who had fought Guizot's policy of appeasement in the eastern crisis, was in July 1870 the deputy who warned the government of the Empire against war. In clear-sighted old age, he had forgotten his young man's weakness for the Napoleonic legend and the jingoistic spirit of the prime minister of 1840. His career sprang back into new life from the national disaster which he had feared and predicted, preaching the exact opposite of his youthful convictions. Twice he would ward off the spectre of revolutionary patriotism: firstly, by beating Gambetta and his supporters in the February elections, and then by crushing the Commune in the streets of Paris.

Not that he had deliberately preferred Bismarck to his own country for reasons of social conservatism, thus repeating the treason of the émigrés: that partisan thesis, itself borrowed from sansculotte imagery, had fabricated a made-to-measure defendant in order to re-enact the trials of the revolutionary Tribunal. The France of 1871, unlike that of Year II, had been militarily outclassed by the enemy and conquered. It had no external allies, and at home offered nothing which might allow hope, even in the long run, of a counteroffensive likely to be victorious. Peace was therefore entirely compatible with patriotism. What was true, however, was that it had become a stake in the gamble of internal politics: the conservatives desired it as passionately as the Jacobin republicans – soon superseded by the Communards – rejected it. In his hour of triumph, Thiers had become inextricably the man of peace and of reaction – a fate which the young author of the *Histoire de la Révolution* would have neither foreseen nor desired.

His life had embraced all the vicissitudes of the nineteenth-century French political crisis; he had followed all its twists and turns and had even tried to steer some of them. It had never contained either great views of the future or generosity of spirit or imagination. If Thiers was so representative of France's bourgeoisie of that era, it was because, having started off from the Revolution, he had followed and betrayed its cause according to circumstance, in order to salvage the possibility of a free and conservative, or even parliamentary and bourgeois, government. A Voltairean, he had become clerical; a revolutionary, he had been a pillar of the party of order; a jingoist, now here he was, a man of peace; an Orleanist – no one knew any longer whether he still was.

There was a naïve side to his opportunism which revealed glimpses of the superficial character of his philosophical ideas, without imbuing him with the Machiavellianism of great politicians. But he had a real talent for compromise. It is easy to understand why men like Guizot and Tocqueville looked down on him somewhat, as they were so superior to him on the intellectual and moral plane. In French politics, Tocqueville had never had his moment, and Guizot had wasted his. Thiers on the other hand, in a century when the French Revolution had continued to wear all men out so quickly, had finished by wearing out the Revolution. In 1871 he attained that quality of national recognition compatible with the characteristics of French public life and the political narrowness of the ruling classes.

His talent may be measured if he is compared with his great British contemporaries, Disraeli or Gladstone. Such a comparison crushes him. With Disraeli he shared only a youth spent on the sidelines and a battle to make an entry into public life; but he had nothing of Disraeli's immense charm, and his sense of the national venture smacked of Bonapartist or bourgeois kitsch, according to the period, if compared with the ties which the Jewish leader of the Tories wove in his heart with the Roman greatness of Britain. France had had the Empire, but not an imperial middle class. As for Gladstone, they were as unlike as chalk and cheese: they were

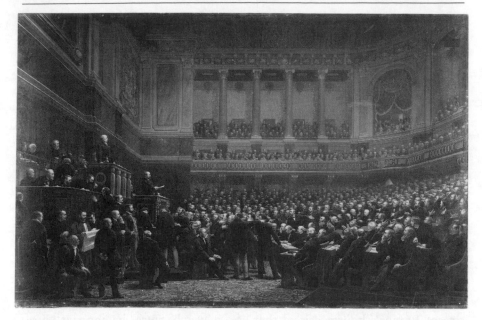

Benjamin Ulmann Thiers applauded by the deputies during the sitting of 16 June
1877, *Musée Versailles, Paris.*
(Photo: Lauros-Giraudon)

separated not only by birth and social milieu, but above all by religious
sources of political action and the moral concept of society. The leader of
British liberalism had imposed his will on the era, rather than grasping
at circumstances. But his history had been very different; he had not
had to overcome the French Revolution. Thiers was the greatest French
statesman of the nineteenth century because *he* had managed to do so; but
on the day of his victory, he had to number among his claims to the
country's gratitude a peace based on surrender and the massacre of 20,000
working men.

What did this indispensable old man want? That was the question
all were asking, since the nature of institutions was largely dependent
upon the answer. But no one knew the answer. He was president of the
Republic, which gave the Republic the advantage of being the *de facto*
government, and of enjoying day after day the benefit of simply existing.
Thiers talked, pontificated and flew into rages against the Assembly: as
long as the Germans occupied the country he was irreplaceable. Loyal to
the laws which all his life had ruled the organization of the country, he
refused to allow the deputies to consider administrative decentralization, or
the reform of taxes or military service. He strove to speed up payment of
the compensation due to Germany, in order to bring forward the time
when the troops would evacuate the country.

On the matter of institutions, by contrast, he played a waiting game. As head of the government, he was in no hurry to set up a king above himself. Understanding the country well, he had to a certain extent grasped the scale of the transformation which had taken place under the Empire, the irreversibility of universal suffrage which had once again demonstrated, in the 1871 elections, that it could be a guarantee of order: as an elected representative of the nation had he not broken the Commune? Lastly, the republicans were more than ever cut off from revolutionary extremism: Gambetta himself, whom he had beaten in the February ballot, had definitively rallied the moderate republican camp, which was gaining votes at each election.

Fundamentally, Thiers's republicanism was the product of a development already in evidence in Orleanist thought during the last years of the Second Empire, and hastened by the events of 1870 and 1871. In *La France nouvelle*, published in 1868, his young friend Prévost-Paradol had already shown that a democratic and liberal government (that is to say, one based on universal suffrage and a parliamentary regime comprising two chambers) could take a republican just as well as a monarchist form. Another great liberal notable, Edouard-René de Laboulaye, had worked and reworked the idea. At the end of 1872, Thiers no longer made a secret of his rallying to the Republic, 'the regime which least divides us'. He said as much to the Assembly, at the opening of the autumn session, in his message of 13 November: 'The Republic exists; it is the legal government of the country', to which he immediately added: 'The Republic will be conservative or nothing.'

This commitment was not enough. The right of the Assembly did not want the Republic. It was worried about the way the electorate was heading: in Paris, in April 1873, an obscure radical, Barodet, beat the most liberal of the Orleanists, Rémusat. Thiers had just obtained the early evacuation of the territory by the Germans; he was forced into a minority by the Assembly on 24 May and left in a huff, faithful to his parliamentary convictions. But already, with the complicity of the republicans, he had made impossible what those on the right would attempt one last time. This was the ultimate metamorphosis of this Protean politician. The Minister of the Interior who, in 1834, had massacred the rebels on the rue Transnonain; the man who had presided over the bloody destruction of the Commune, when he finally left the stage, became one of the fathers of the Republic.

Then began the last battle around the cradle of the Third Republic, between 1873 and 1877. It would comprise two stages, on either side of the caesura represented by the 1875 vote on the principal founding bills of the new regime. They can be described by studying the players in the two leading roles, Broglie and Gambetta.

BROGLIE

The man who had masterminded Thiers's defeat was Albert de Broglie, the son of Victor, Louis-Philippe's prime minister, and grandson, on his mother's side, of Madame de Staël: great-grandson, therefore, of Necker. An admirable dynasty of intellectuals and politicians, to whom must be added Benjamin Constant, the father of Albertine de Staël. Duc Albert inherited from all of them a taste for public affairs, accompanied by great intellectual curiosity and a philosophical turn of mind. Through them, too, he was a monarchist and a liberal, that is, Orleanist. What caused him to stand out was a particular interest given to religious questions and the future of the Catholic religion in the modern world.

Not that this anxiety was anything new in the family heritage, but having emerged from Protestant circles, it was more Christian than Catholic. Necker had been one of the first to consider the necessity of religion in society; his daughter had looked on the French Revolution's rupture with the Church as a disaster, and Constant had made an examination of religious ideas his life's work. But the marriage of Albertine de Staël and Duc Victor made the matter become more specifically one of liberal Catholicism: by marrying a son of the old French nobility, the daughter of Benjamin Constant and Madame de Staël had also wedded one of the biggest problems of French liberalism – the Catholic Church.

Her son, born early in the Restoration, would thus meet it in his cradle and make it the centre of his moral existence. More gifted than his father in the field of public relations, less timid, less melancholy but just as narrow in his vision of the social world, he had had the misfortune, in his prime, to encounter the Second Empire. Leaving the diplomatic service which would have brought him into Napoleon III's service, he had devoted those long years to the liberal opposition, as one of the pillars of the *Correspondant* group, who wanted to reconcile the Catholic Church with the society which had emerged from the Revolution.

He had created a little collection of friends who shared the same concerns, Monseigneur Dupanloup, Augustin Cochin and Albert de Meaux, and had devoted a large part of his time to study. Between 1856 and 1863, he had published the six volumes of a *Histoire de l'Église et de l'Empire au IVe siècle*, which still holds an honourable place in the revival of works on religious history of which Renan is the symbol. As often happens, the thesis he was defending was not unconnected with the circumstances in which he was writing. The fourth-century Catholic Church had, in his view, built an essential bridge between Rome and the society which would be born from the Germanic invasions, preserving, while taking over the future, all that had been gained from pagan civilization; would the nineteenth-century Church be capable of playing the same role in relation to modern society, and not remain like a stranger in the midst of the liberal evolution which was sweeping the world along?

The fall of the Empire had brought back political deadlines. Albert de

Broglie was well acquainted with Thiers, although belonging to the next generation: Thiers, together with Broglie's father, had been one of the political stars of the July monarchy. Family memories were mixed about the new great man. They had many ideas in common: social conservatism and support for parliamentary liberties, but also old rivalries which had left their mark, and Broglie's mistrust, both moral and political, of the talent for intrigue possessed by the man who had just risen again to power. Elected to the Assembly in February 1871, then immediately made ambassador to London, Broglie was not at first displeased with Thiers's policies. He had never nurtured either hopes or illusions about the restoration of the senior branch of the Bourbons; that of the Orléans was not on the agenda, since it could be so only after the death of the Duc de Chambord. Thiers occupied a place which was empty, to the benefit of social order which, in Broglie's view, ranked higher than dynastic order.

Things went wrong when the chief of the Executive clashed with the Assembly – over administrative decentralization, for example: the notables held fast to this reform, which was as old as they were and had never been put into effect, and was their revenge on the Empire. Then, as the months went by, it appeared that Thiers, while seeming to play for time, was hand in glove with Gambetta, who no longer attacked him, but whose campaign was growing throughout the country on the strength of by-election successes. Respect for the man who had crushed the Commune changed into worry about the republican intrigue he was suspected of conducting. The suspicion, as has been seen, was well founded, even if the plot did not take the organized form ascribed to it; furthermore, at the end of 1872, there was no longer any mystery: Thiers was ready to look for support on the left in order to found the Republic. It was for that reason that Broglie, who had returned to his position of deputy in spring 1872, waged the parliamentary offensive against him which toppled him. It was now his turn to play.

His plan was simple. It consisted of gathering together all those on the right – legitimists, Orleanists, plus, if possible, the small group of Bonapartists which was forming again with some success in the by-elections – around a common conservative project. The insoluble problem of the monarchy would be put to one side, and agreement would be reached on measures to ensure the continuance of the majority elected in 1871. On Thiers's downfall, the Assembly had already dissociated the offices of president of the Republic and head of the government, electing to the former Marshal Mac-Mahon, a reactionary soldier devoid of political skill, who at least kept the place of the absent sovereign; Broglie presided only over the Council of Ministers. What remained to be done was to keep the Assembly functioning as long as necessary, against the republicans who were demanding new elections, so that it could vote on laws which would be fundamental to the future.

The most urgent of these concerned the Senate. It was an old Orleanist idea, which was older than Orleanism, to temper the democratic passions of the Commons by means of an aristocratic Chamber. This was an English recipe which Necker had not succeeded in slipping into Louis XVI's programme on 23 June 1789, and which the Revolution had rejected that September. It had had its finest days under the Restoration and the July monarchy but, by the same token, some bad moments as well: for it was precisely a part of what the nineteenth-century notables, both noble and bourgeois, wanted to salvage of aristocracy in democracy. The notables of these years were no different from those of the July monarchy, even if they were too young to have played any role in it: they were slightly more docile towards the concept of universal suffrage, which had already carried them to power twice, in 1849 and 1871, but which was in danger of dislodging them in 1873. At all events, if universal suffrage had become inevitable, it was necessary to erect against it the dam of an Assembly chosen in a different manner, in which the socially superior could have the upper hand.

Broglie thus mapped out the lines of a great conservative party, that old project of which his grandmother, Madame de Staël, had already put forward the idea at the beginning of the Restoration in her *Considérations sur la Révolution française*. It had then been a matter of uniting with the ancient nobility the elites that had emerged from 1789 around an English-style monarchy. A little more than half a century later, her grandson was still taking his example from England, but he no longer had a king, since he was still unable to persuade the dynasty conquered by the Revolution to accept the Revolution's flag.

Lacking a political solution, he was at least better placed than Madame de Staël to be the symbol of a shared conservatism on the social plane: 1789 was in the distant past, even 1830 was distant, and the old aristocracy had discovered in modern democracy opponents who were more to be feared than Orleanists. But the argument also backfired on the Duc de Broglie's attempt: in a France which was already approaching the end of the century, leaving behind the long trail of the Revolution, the Second Republic and the Second Empire, what did the old nobility represent, apart from the unpopular shadow of the past? How could it be forgotten, fused into a unified oligarchy, if it was still demanding its king? How history had marched on, between grandmother and grandson! From being a necessary part of the alliance, the nobility had become the guarantee of its defeat. Broglie's blindness in not understanding that gives some measure of the aristocratic drift of the second Orleanism.

Thus, late in the century, the problem posed by the Comte de Chambord remained an insurmountable obstacle to the unity of the conservatives. Thanks to the fall of Thiers, the legitimists, insensitive to the irony of the situation, had made another approach to the pretender: in order to become their king he would have to agree to abandon his flag. There was a new negotiation, a new psychodrama – the last – between the *ancien régime* and the Revolution; it ended like the previous one, to the relief of most of the Orleanists, who preferred to wait in Mac-Mahon's shadow for their own pretender's right moment, since Chambord had no offspring.

They had other reasons for anxiety about the Restoration atmosphere which had followed Broglie's ministry, apart from simply the dynastic question: the royalist idea was more than ever enveloped in a formidable religious orchestration, conducted by the Church as a body. What was recommencing was not the *ancien régime*, but the Restoration, the alliance between Throne and Altar being sought once again, this time with the difference that the Church had since swung to the side of ultramontanism, finding it all the easier to combine the king of France and the pope, the two symmetrical figures in its repudiation of the modern world, the two exiled sovereigns who were symbolic of its own exile, Henri V outside France and Pius IX a prisoner in Rome. Veuillot had been the supreme chronicler of that double woe, with the old theme of France as the eldest daughter of the Church leaning on the necessity for a double deliverance.

The monarchic and Catholic dolorism of the Restoration found its true popular basis in this period, cloaking the unhappy king in the misfortune of the pope; the extraordinary picture of an ultramontane king of France had its origin in the passionate rejection of the two usurpations in which modern society revealed its wicked nature. As in the years between 1815 and 1820, mission campaigns, solemn processions, public prayers, pilgrimages were organized on all sides to ask God for the double miracle of Paris and Rome; they mingled the old theme of national expiation with the new devotion to the Sacred Heart and the cult of the Virgin. The counter-revolutionary idea developed by romanticism had, in these years, found its most eloquent interpreter in a Church that had become ultramontane. The republican part of the country was plunged into sarcastic rage.

In fact, the idea contained everything which could bring back bad memories to the Orleanists as well. On principle, they were hostile to anything which might remind them of the Restoration ultras: they had been won over late to Catholicism, many by simple social conservatism. They hated that clerical extremism which moreover fuelled republican anticlericalism and abetted its progress under the guise of combating it. Broglie himself was a Catholic from the other end of the spectrum, a friend of Dupanloup and the sworn enemy of Veuillot: he was liberal and Gallican. But the country priests and the peasants in the west listened to Veuillot.

Because of that, Orleanist politicians were isolated: since they shared none of the royalist camp's passions, either religious or political, deepseated agreement between the right-wingers was never achieved; since they had not followed Thiers in opening out towards the Republic of the republicans, they had no room for manoeuvre on the left. They had nothing to say on the matter of institutions. To define themselves, they had only the least popular of programmes: to consolidate the power of the notables. The entire weakness of Broglie lay in his embodying nothing

other than his *fin-de-siècle* version of aristocratic egoism. The only card left
to play had been the social solidarity of the notables, as after June 1848;
but since the destruction of the Commune no one had threatened order or
property. I will again leave the last word to Daniel Halévy, who put it
marvellously:

The Duc de Broglie was never in personal contact with any of the diverse families
of the French people. There was a republican people, whom Broglie regarded
with reprobation. There was a Bonapartist people, whom Broglie regarded with
contempt. In the rural areas of the west and in Provence, there was a legitimist
people, but Broglie was not a legitimist. Nowhere was there anything which could
be called an Orleanist people, and Broglie was an Orleanist.[4]

Now, in the face of this void, a great force had risen: republican France.
In fact, almost all the by-elections between 1872 and 1875 – sixty-five in
all – were republican victories. These consultations took place within the
framework of the 1848 electoral law, which had been slightly modified in
1849: a two-stage ballot on a departmental list, to which, in 1872, was
added the requirement of an absolute majority of votes for success in the
first round. No system more clearly revealed the political significance
of the votes; now, during those years the republican lists carried off
the majority of vacant seats, at the expense of the monarchists; and in
these successes, the most confirmed republicans who, like Gambetta for
example, were old adversaries of Thiers in February 1871, carved out an
increasing place for themselves. France was becoming republican. The
large towns had been so for a long time. The rural areas had mapped out
the first geography of a republican vote in May 1849; next they had voted
massively Bonapartist, even in 1869 and 1870, and in 1871 the monarchists
had made great personal capital of a rural vote for peace. But circumstances had changed, and were revealing a general development of opinion
in favour of the Republic.

What circumstances? Peace had been made, the Parisian socialists had
been eliminated with scant ceremony, proving that the Republic knew how
to be conservative. In June 1848, it is true, that proof had not sufficed
to erase memories of the Terror and socialist threats. At that period,
however, it had been possible to resort to a Bonaparte, who had since
exhausted his virtues. In the 1870s, that possibility was no longer there. If
the country areas did not wish to vote for the notables and the monarchy,
for the list of the château and the presbytery, they no longer had any
solution other than to vote republican, so long as the Republic promised
them order and property, together with equality. Just like the notables,
republicans too had the advantage of having Bonapartism behind them.

In that development of attitudes of mind disclosed by electoral sociology, time must be allotted its share. Universal suffrage was an institution
which had been working for a quarter of a century; it had become a right

[4] Halévy, *La Fin des notables*.

which people valued, which they exercised in public peace and which could not be taken away from them. In many respects, as has been seen, administrative intervention had in the long term created conditions for a greater peasant autonomy with regard to local notables. Let us give the Empire its due: in many cases it had represented public interest for country people, allowing them to isolate those great property-owners, the legitimists, and those rich bourgeois represented by Orleanism. When it vanished, public interest was left without a strong embodiment. The Repubic could fill its place, if it could only gain a significance which would be both egalitarian and conservative.

GAMBETTA

The republicans had already realized this under the Second Empire – certain among them, at least, such as Jules Ferry. It was Léon Gambetta who would be their spokesman and leader during the crucial years: the man who had been the Jacobin republican in the National Defence government, the figurehead of rediscovered revolutionary patriotism, would be the founder of government republicanism. The quick-wittedness of this turn-round, and the talent with which he had taken on the two roles, made him the central politician of those years, after Thiers, who had opened the way for him, and before Jules Ferry, who would put the finishing touches to what he had begun.

Gambetta was the grandson of a poor Italian fisherman, who had come in 1818 from a village on the Ligurian coast and set himself up as a shopkeeper in Cahors. His father, a partner in the family grocery, Le Bazar Génois, had married a girl from Tarn-et-Garonne in 1837. Léon was born the following year. After studying in religious schools, then at the Cahors *lycée*, he had come up to Paris in 1857 to study law. He had settled there in 1861, despite paternal opposition, already enjoying a modest celebrity in the Latin Quarter. He had a doubly southern temperament, both Italian and Gascon, which would today be called extrovert, much given to eloquence and theatricals, adoring the great tradition of oratorical art, reciting Demosthenes by heart, as well as Cicero and Mirabeau. He was a Parisian bohemian who felt at home in the French Revolution, as if he were the personification of its blessings. In short, a young man whom everything contrasted with his future comrade in arms and rival, Jules Ferry, who was a little older: everything – starting with temperament, the one austere, the other exuberant – with the exception of their ideas.

Ferry came from the old legal provincial bourgeoisie, whereas Gambetta was born in the shop of an Italian father who dreamed of having a barrister son in Cahors. Ferry had reacted very strongly against the men of 1848; Gambetta was too young to maintain such hostility towards them. Ferry had a better-trained mind, formed by systematic study and reading; Gambetta's talent was for improvisation and instinct, embellished by a literary memory. Nevertheless, the ideas of the two young barristers were comparable: the tradition of 1789, the repudiation of socialism, anticlericalism, the concept of a positive science to set against religion, the Republic reconciling equality and liberty in the modern citizen. Their hostility to the Empire, which would not weaken, and their anticlericalism, which would deepen, gave their republicanism a polemical force which concealed its basic moderation.

Gambetta served his apprenticeship in the shadow of the 'five', elected in 1857, defending the republican militants brought to trial by the regime. But he did not belong to the extreme left. In 1863, he was one of the most ardent supporters of the campaign of the young Orleanist, Prévost-Paradol, in the sixth *arrondissement*, against three other candidates: a Bonapartist of the left, the ex-Saint-Simonian Adolphe Guéroult (who was elected), a man of the regime, and the liberal Catholic Augustin Cochin. Perhaps he had felt in sympathy with the denunciation of Napoleon III's foreign policy, which was one of Prévost-Paradol's specialities: this would be a further indication of the moderate nature of his uncompromising republicanism.

In the last years of the Empire, he began to be one of the opposition's celebrated figures: his renown in Paris began in 1868 with his plea in favour of the journalists who had opened a subscription to raise a monument to the deputy Baudin. The following year saw him as candidate for both Marseille (where he was received in one of the Grand Orient lodges, La Réforme) and in Belleville, in the heart of working-class Paris. Elected in both places, he chose Marseille, but it was his candidacy in Belleville that remained famous, because of the programme he developed there as a contract agreed with his electorate, which would stay as a key reference of radical republicanism. Its ideas were not truly new, and he shared them with the 'intransigent' republicans of the end of the Second Empire; but he made them fly like a banner: suppression of permanent armies, separation of Church and state, freedom of the press, of meetings and associations, free education for all.

We have already met the Gambetta of the National Defence government. He was a man whom circumstances transported, in the space of a few weeks, at the age of thirty-two, not only to a national role but also to major influence on public opinion, combined with civil and military dictatorship, since he was both the political authority of a still free France, and Minister of War and the Interior. It was a hopeless war, but a famous episode, from which he emerged beaten by Thiers, but not eliminated: for he had played the part of Danton and not Robespierre; he had not shed French blood, he had not gone outside the law and he had resigned on the eve of the February elections, hated by the monarchist right, but carrying away with him for better days the idea of national resistance to Germany.

Elected to the Assembly by ten *départements* (while Thiers had been chosen by twenty-six), he had symbolically picked the Bas-Rhin, only to resign when Alsace became German the following month – a gesture of patriotic protest. The main action was going on between Versailles and

Paris, and he had no desire to be trapped in a pincer movement: he left Paris to visit his parents in Cahors and get some rest in Spain, where he held his peace during the Commune.

His enemies, and sometimes his friends, reproached him for this absence and this silence; but what more or better could he have done than Ferry or Clemenceau or Louis Blanc, who had intervened in vain? It is not too difficult to reconstruct how he must have felt, and the impasse in which he found himself. He could not approve of Thiers and the ferocity of Versailles, but he could not encourage the Communards, still less figure among their ranks. He had defended Delescluze, he had given Rossel a command, he knew the chief insurgents (though far from liking all of them), but his concept of the Republic did not allow for the right of insurrection against the law.

Now was the time for the decisive choice of his political career: he had been defeated, isolated, slandered, but he did not despair. Many 'historic' republicans threw in their hand. Hugo was the first, that great addict of exile, leaving the Versailles Assembly after the vote for peace; he had gone back to Guernsey where he had opened his house to fugitive Communards. Michelet had been equally unwilling to watch this series of disasters in Paris; he had taken himself off to the provinces to write his *Origines du XIXe siècle*, the sequel to his *Révolution*, a sad commentary on that dawn without a morning. Louis Blanc, who had no liking for uprisings, was at least accustomed to sharing and paying for moral responsibility for them. At Versailles, far from his vanquished friends, close to the victors whom he detested, with all that blood shed, the old man would never regain a political footing. Gambetta's situation was different. At the end of June, while the vindictive Assembly was deciding on a commission of inquiry into the actions of the government based at Tours during the siege of Paris, he made his political comeback in a major speech in Bordeaux.

Then began the greatest period of his life, the battle to found the Republic. He had immediately set the tone, in Bordeaux, by a surprising show of moderation. The Republic was the government of the country, and must remain so, *de facto* and *de jure*, in the face of the factions of all colours that might threaten it. Thiers had said: 'The future belongs to the wisest.' One month after the Commune, Gambetta was already proffering him his hand without actually naming him: 'We must therefore be the wisest, it will cost us nothing.' The man whom the whole of conservative France had denounced as red was sounding the end of the civil war: but he was subtly attributing the credit for it to the Republic. He also moved into the orbit of that reconciliation of the French around legal government, in which Thiers was the popular figure, if not exactly to manipulate its hero, at least to get him on to the right side. The great memories of Year II, the dictatorship of Paris, were all over. Denunciation of the 'rurals', glorification of republican towns versus backward country districts, were finished: it was France in its entirety that would create the Republic. 'For my part', he said in Bordeaux, 'I believe in the republican future of the provinces and the rural areas. All it takes is a little time and the wider spread of education.'

Time: all those young men who had grown up under the Empire had seen France changing before their very eyes. The same phenomenon would be reproduced exactly one hundred years later, and we are in a good position to understand it. Between 1850 and 1870, not only had the country been caught up in the first wave of modernity, it had also been generally conscious of the fact, and the ex-Saint-Simonian emperor had set the example to turn the idea of progress into the banner of the regime. One has only to read the correspondence of the great republican exiles (Quinet, for instance) to see how difficult they found it to understand the reality; they suspected brainwashing of public opinion by the government. On the contrary, the growing republican or liberal generation in the country sought to extend its blessings to the political domain: prosperity, railways, roads and schools were, in the long term, means of liberty.

When Prévost-Paradol had published his book in 1868 on the political future of the country, he had entitled it: *La France nouvelle*. When Renan wrote his *Réforme intellectuelle et morale* some years later, it was pointless for him to dislike the materialistic and bourgeois France emerging from the imperial years, for he too spoke of a new country, transformed by prosperity, even in the rural areas: in 1869, in the article from the *Revue des Deux Mondes* which I have already quoted, he was already mournfully observing:

France daily sees the growth in its bosom of a mass of the people who are devoid of religious ideals, and who reject any social principle higher than the will of the individual. The other mass of the people, who have not yet been penetrated by this selfish notion, are daily diminished by primary education and the adoption of universal suffrage.

Renan's regrets were Gambetta's optimism. The republican leader loved the new France which he sensed emerging from the progress of social wealth and enlightenment. He saw the country through his own eyes, and understood its feelings and aspirations all the better because he could relate them to his life, from the shop in Cahors to the Palais Bourbon. Not industrial France, both capitalist and proletarian, whose inevitable conflicts so many socialists predicted and orchestrated in advance: Gambetta had no intuition about that France. The one he evisaged and wanted to make the basis of the Republic belonged to the bourgeoisie and petite-bourgeoisie, combining interests and talents, trade, artisans, rural landowners, liberal professions. A proud and industrious country, standing on 1789 as the origin of its independence, but for which 1789 was merely a starting-point: for it had gradually grown rich through hard work, and education allowed its sons to have the highest ambitions. In the face of the great notables who were still so wrapped up in the matter of their birth, as if they were still nobles and the Revolution had never happened, Gambetta's Republic was a meritocracy of talents. It finally managed to speak with one tongue the two languages which the country waited to hear, and to reconcile its two deepest aspirations: passion for equality and fear of revolution.

That was the gist of the famous speech made by Gambetta in Grenoble in September 1872: since democratic society increases new talents, let us democratize politics so that they may have the role that is due to them.

Have we not seen, throughout the length and breadth of the country – and I must emphasize this – the new generation of democracy, new politicians, a new electorate, new people involved in universal suffrage? . . . Yes, I foresee, I feel, I predict the arrival and presence in the field of politics of a new social stratum which has been engaged in affairs sometimes for eighteen months and which, without any doubt, is far from being inferior to its precursors.

Gambetta had said 'social stratum' because he did not want to use the word 'class', which belonged to socialist vocabulary. In fact, he was expressing a completely different idea: not that of a social conflict rooted in the economy, to which 1789 would merely have formed a preface and which a new revolution must inevitably cut short, but instead democracy as an irresistible integrating force on the march.

In this republican version of the old Orleanist dilemma about 'capacités', treated this time in the democratic mode, schooling played a major role: it ensured the equality of rights and the promotion of talents. But it was much more besides: it formed individuals by reason, freeing them from the Church's obscurantist tyranny. Like Ferry, Gambetta was a positivist, an admirer of Auguste Comte. He had less philosophical culture than Ferry, and a more erratic acquaintance with books, he was more intuitive, and in any case the two men were not too fond of each other. They were nevertheless very similar, both in their successive activities (since Ferry would play the leading role after Gambetta's death) and for the body of ideas which they held in common.

Their common inspiration was Littré, the popularizer of Comte's *Politique positive* in the 1840s, whose relations with the Master had become strained towards the end, when Comtism became a religion. For that reason he had been pushed aside from succeeding Comte. But the great grammarian, an inflexible republican with a very fine mind, remained the principal craftsman of the intellectual marriage between republicanism and positivism,[5] so characteristic of that period. He had been the first to imagine it, after the failure of the Second Republic, in a little book which had come out just at the moment of the coup d'état, *Conservation, révolution, positivisme*, the last concept supplying the synthesis of the first two, which had constantly stirred French civil disorder since 1789.

After the Empire, the situation was no different. Littré had loathed the Commune, the latest evidence, and this time against the Republic, of

[5] There is a good recent analysis of this intellectual marriage in C. Nicolet, *L'Idée républicaine en France*, vol. 1, chs 6 and 7.

that retrograde revolutionary violence so often condemned by Comte. A Paris deputy at the age of seventy, from February 1870 the old savant devoted his belated political life to reconciling what his master had deemed incompatible, a Republic of the sovereignty of the people and the 'positive' age. He got out of it neatly by way of historicist optimism: whatever 'metaphysical' part the Republic preserved would be gradually transformed by the passing of time. But what was necessary about it was that it alone was capable of creating order in a France torn between revolution and conservatism.

For Gambetta (as indeed for Ferry), the synthesis was still more acrobatic. It was not merely a matter of putting together the idea of the dictatorship of a rational power and that of two elected Chambers in their turn electing a President – a spate of 'metaphysical' illusions according to good Comtist doctrine. Above all, it was necessary to base political action on both 1789 and the criticism of 1789, on the philosophy of the subjective rights of individuals and on the forward march of historic reason towards the positive age.

Gambetta was a sufficiently eclectic Comtist never to have attempted the impossible synthesis. He had seen it in an alternative light, inclining sometimes towards the tradition of 1789 when he wanted to speed things up on the left, sometimes towards a conservative positivism when he wanted to reassure a rural public, or justify the institution of a Senate, following Littré's example. His talent made it a very popular doctrine, in which the revolutionary heritage found its moderating element in a marriage with the philosophy which had radically called it into question: the final reconciliation of Rousseau's republic with that of Condorcet, which proved to be an infinitely more powerful means of national synthesis than the Orleanists' English monarchy which, too, had already disappeared in the irreversible march of history. Gambettism clothed and fed the anti-aristocratic passion of the French, together with their dread of disorder, whereas Orleanism had eyes only for their fear of revolution.

One last feature is essential to define this republicanism: the battle against clericalism. The conflict which had begun in 1790 between the Church and democracy had its outcome here. The Concordat had been merely a truce, maintained by the emperor's iron hand after it had been welcomed by opinion. The Restoration had seen the resurgence of the two adversaries, a counter-revolutionary Church united with an aristo-cratic monarchy facing a violently anticlerical republican camp. Half a century later, confrontation had never been more intense: Catholics and Republicans were divided by two incompatible philosophies, and they threw themselves into a war which was literally a war of religion. The Church had become ultramontane, enfolded in the *Syllabus Errorum* of 1864, and tending towards the excommunication of the modern; it con-demned without differentiation liberals and socialists, the freedom of the press and atheism, Renan and the Commune. On the republican side, the main concern was science, thought of as contradictory to religion and needing to replace it, with the development of republican education. There lay the great popular legacy of positivism, announcing a new religion which was the opposite of religion, yet which in its own way adopted the latter's promise: to reconcile man with the order of things. It had filled France with a multitude of 'Messieurs Homais', who spread the good word. In the Yonville pharmacist, Flaubert had mainly seen the semi-educated, simplifying mind, everything which left this scientistic culture somewhat lacking; but those petty notables in the main towns of the cantons, waging the republican battle against the *curé*, also tamed the democratic concept in the form of the progress of reason.

The centre of political combat, apart from the institutions, was education: an old theme, an old combat, waged by Michelet and Quinet in the last years of the July regime. It was no longer a matter of the University. What was now at stake was elementary education, that indispensable instrument of democracy and democratic culture, since it was there that all French children must learn to become citizens, under the guidance of reason. Though it was true that the old idea of the virtuous citizen essential to republics had given way to that of the reasonable citizen, school was the main ingredient of this apprenticeship. It had to be compulsory and free, but *laïque*; this difficult word defined everything which divided it from the obscurantist education offered by the Church: modern citizenship, conceived as inseparably reasonable and participative, uniting civic virtue and rational consideration.

In this the Republic rediscovered the inspiration of Michelet; it at last represented the post-revolutionary state, freed from both superstition and private interests, capable of uniting all its children in civic brotherhood; through this peaceful version of revolutionary regeneration, education gained its full sense. The idea of the secularization of the state and of non-clerical, free and compulsory education formed the cement of republican ideology; through it, revolutionary tradition and positivist philosophy were reconciled. Its great manifesto had been the speech made by Jules Ferry on 10 April 1870, in the Salle Molière. The League of Education made it its banner; Freemasonry rediscovered in it the ideals of Enlightenment philosophy and Voltairean deism against the Church. A network of militant societies was thus set up in the country, through which the republican party affirmed its unity.

Gambetta's Marxist historians (mostly Anglo-Saxon), are very willing to see in the republican ideology of that period a hoax intended to anaesthetize the class struggle, in order to make sure of bourgeois dominance in the left's rediscovered unity. Gambetta himself provided material for this accusation by the passion he put into averting the idea of social division which served as a foundation for socialist doctrines. The bourgeoisie he loved was indefinitely open to the rising talents which replenished it. His refusal to base republican action on class conflict had more to do with reflection on the most recent history of France than with political calculation. The tragedy of the Commune, which was so near, had once again illustrated the isolation into which the socialist version of the fight for democracy had led its followers. There remained the republican version: Gambetta's greatness lay in his being able to personify a Republic that was loyal to the Revolution, yet capable of presenting an image of it which finally exorcized the phantom of civil war.

THE THIRD REPUBLIC

I will not pursue the ins and outs of the struggle between republicans and conservatives after the election of Marshal Mac-Mahon to the presidency and the formation of Broglie's cabinet (May 1873). The fresh failure of the Comte de Chambord in the autumn, at the same time as the republicans' progress against 'moral order', rapidly broke up the political contrivance envisaged by Broglie. A year later the legitimists went over to the opposition and, returning to what they had so often practised under Louis-Philippe, they added their votes to those of the republicans in order to overthrow the liberal duke. Mac-Mahon had been elected for seven years, thus giving time for the constitutional impasse to ripen, or for the Comte de Chambord to die. But Broglie's fall hastened matters. The Assembly, in trouble since 1871, had exhausted its stock of devices: it had sheltered behind Thiers, it had sent Thiers packing, it had caused the downfall of his successor. It was at the end of its tether: it must either throw in its hand – which the Republicans had been demanding for a long time – or find a new *raison d'être* by at last becoming Constituent, in order to keep *in extremis* the advantage of a conservative majority, which had been increasingly nibbled away by republican victories in the by-elections.

This state of mind was making progress among the Orleanists, whom Thiers had anticipated by several years but whom he still encouraged. The triumphal election of a Bonapartist in the Nièvre, just after Broglie's fall, made conservatives ruminate on the risks of a situation they had already been through. The Republic existed; the Assembly, the president and the government formed a regime whose rules were accepted; why not try to vote for constitutional bills inspired by what was actually working?

Gambetta and his friends, who had been relatively silent during Broglie's ministry, then found room for manoeuvre which they occupied at the price of a tactical volte-face: those who had always demanded dissolution were now quite prepared to found the Republic together with part of the conservatives. They too had registered the signal coming from the Nièvre. They were anxious to halt an opposition developing on their left: Ledru-Rollin, Madier de Montjau, veterans of 1848, had made their political comeback and were criticizing Gambetta's moderation. They easily gained the ear of the guardians of revolutionary tradition in order to oppose the resurrection of an upper Chamber, which was one of the Orleanists' chief demands. Louis Blanc, Peyrat and Edgar Quinet, for example, forgot their quarrel of 1865 to combat in unison that old idea, simultaneously conservative and liberal, which had disappeared from the French Revolution in the summer of 1789.

Now Gambetta had for several years ceased his opposition to the setting up of a Senate in the Republic. He was ready to compromise on the matter too. In an interview given to an American newspaper in January 1873, he had put forward the idea of a 'Grand Council of State', similar to the American Senate in its functions, though not elected by universal suffrage, appointed half by the Assembly, half by the president; he spoke of it in almost Anglo-Saxon terms, as a power having to counterbalance both the despotic impulses of a president and the risks of unreasonable turbulence on the part of the Assembly.

At that period, the republicans as a whole had not come together under his authority, but his influence was dominant. With his friends Spuller, Ranc, Challemel-Lacour, he directed the Republican Union, which was even farther to the left than the republican left of the three Jules: Simon, Grévy and Ferry. Between the two groups lay the bad memories of 1870, when Jules Simon and Thiers together had fought Gambetta's Jacobinism. But at the time of the Commune, the hero of the National Defence had been no more favourable than they towards the revolution. He retained more regrets about it than they did, and was more ready to fight over the amnesty for those sentenced in 1871. His *alter ego*, Ranc, had sat for a short while with the Communards. That heritage linked him with the republican extreme left, grouped around Louis Blanc: they were very militant over the amnesty, but hostile to the constitutional rapprochement which was being sketched out with the chief Versaillais, Thiers. Gambetta thus found himself in the centre of the republicans. Hated by many of them, mainly on the extreme left, he was none the less their centre of gravity; on the left he shared the rhetoric of memories and, on the right, institutional realism.

Thanks to him, the elements of a constitutional compromise were in place by 1873: the Orleanist centre-right was closer to the republican centre-left than to the legitimists. Universal suffrage was no longer truly contested; since 1871 the Assembly elected by the people had proved to be the supreme embodiment of sovereignty delegated by common assent. Its power was not incompatible with that of a strong president and chief of the executive: that was the reasoning behind the seven-year term of office given to Mac-Mahon. The notorious problem of executive power in a republic was therefore not as insoluble as the deplorable precedents of 1793 and 1848, each in its own way, had led people to believe.

Gambetta, once more opposed on this point to the conceptions of the surviving republicans of 1848, desired a strong government just as much as Casimir-Périer. For the first time since 1789, French legislators looked at what existed, rather than what should exist: an English trend of mind, so strongly recommended by Taine and Renan in the same era, which suggested a combined republican, parliamentary and monarchic system, uniting the sovereignty of the Assembly and an accountable government with a head of state independent of it and forming the keystone of all the institutions. All that remained to be discussed was the Senate, on the matter of which agreement was reached without much difficulty. Broglie had envisaged an Upper Assembly, gathering together France's socially illustrious, modelled on the July Chamber of Peers. This was an aristocratic phantom unacceptable to the more moderate republicans, while Gambetta, Ferry and their friends were receptive to the idea of an Assembly as a counterweight to the driving forces of universal suffrage, elected in another way, but still elected: on that basis, centre-right and centre-left could reach an understanding.

They did so. The first signal was given by the famous vote on Wallon's amendment on 30 January 1875, with a majority vote of one (353 to 352). Agreement at that period rested on a regime with three ruling parts: Senate, Assembly and president. But no one had yet named this regime; this was done by Henri Wallon, a member of the Institut, man of the centre-right, in his bill: 'The president of the Republic is elected on a majority vote by the Senate and the Chamber of Deputies joined in a National Assembly. He is re-eligible.' Not that the title 'president of the Republic' was unknown: Thiers had had it, and Mac-Mahon bore it. The novelty lay in the impersonality of the office, thenceforth built into a constitutional Act and no longer conferred *ad hominem*. It is thus very true that the vote on that day possessed a particular value, because it decided the designation of the regime, thus opening the way to less tense votes on the organization of public authorities. Wallon had brought with him enough centre-right and centre votes to scrape through a majority with all the republicans. Gambetta had finally won over to his camp the diehards of the republican doctrine, hostile to both Senate and president – Louis Blanc, Quinet, Peyrat, Madier de Montjau.

After that, things followed on swiftly and more easily, since the terms of a compromise had already been widely debated. The discussion on the Senate, however, met a significant snag: the amendment of a radical republican, Duprat, proposing the election of the Senate by universal suffrage, was adopted by a majority comprising republicans, Bonapartists and legitimists. Gambetta saved the situation, and used it to put pressure on Mac-Mahon and the Orleanists, and to obtain a 'deal', as he called it, in his favour on the Upper Assembly: this was done on 24 February 1875, with the vote by a regained majority for a Senate of 300 members, of whom seventy-five would be appointed for life by the Assembly, and the rest elected by a method of voting which ensured the preponderance of country areas over towns. The number of senators envisaged for each *département* was not proportional to population (Paris had five seats, the Lozère two), and each was elected on a second-degree departmental list ballot by a college comprising deputies, general and *arrondissement* councillors and delegates from communes, at the rate of one per commune, regardless of its size, chosen by municipal councillors. The age of eligibility was fixed at forty years, and the Upper Assembly was renewable by a third every three years. Mac-Mahon had abandoned his claim to appoint senators, like Louis-Philippe, in return for guarantees obtained on the rural bias given to universal suffrage.

The next day the Assembly voted for a law on the organization of public authorities. Gambetta did not manage to get all his people together, but the majority had grown sufficiently large (435 votes against 254) for him to allow himself a little 'loss of blood' on his left; eleven radical republicans abstained, among them Louis Blanc and Quinet, the veterans, but also Barodet, elected in 1873, who had solemnly promised his electors a single Assembly. On 16 July it was by a majority of five to one that the Assembly voted on the last of the constitutional laws on the relations between the authorities. The strategy of uniting the centres had increased its victory. Mac-Mahon had had to call on the Orleanist, Buffet, to form the ministry; he took with him two centre-left deputies. Gambetta was the real victor, but memories of 1870, and the fighting rhetoric with which he embellished his moderation horrified the conservatives; the Marshal-President disliked his slovenliness, which still smacked of the Latin Quarter cafés.

The Republic now had regular institutions. For the first time since the Revolution, these were not fitted into a constitution (or a Charter) properly speaking, but were embodied in three constitutional laws, of 24 and 25 February and 16 July 1875. What was republican about this Third Republic was clearly the single source from which it drew its legitimacy, the sovereignty of the people: all the powers owed their existence to universal suffrage, which was thenceforth accepted by all as the only way of appointing a public authority. Assent had not been given with any enthusiasm by those on the right, but it was no less strong for having been the result rather of resignation in the face of the inevitable, perhaps mingled with hope: after all, the law of 31 May 1850 was not among the best memories of the party of order, and the Assembly of February 1871, by contrast, had allowed its survivors and descendants to govern France after the Empire. That Assembly, moreover, was still placed at the centre of the entire mechanism of the new authorities; it would choose from within its bosom seventy-five senators, and had elected, and was to elect, a president, who would be re-eligible and therefore dependent upon it. In those constitutional arrangements of 1875, there was in effect something of the collective spirit of an Assembly which had held all the power in its hands for four years.

However, the Orleanists were poles apart from this republican doctrine, and against it had imposed a head of state and the Senate. A president elected for seven years by the two Chambers, sharing with them the initiative for making laws, possessing the right of dissolution, making appointments to all civil and military authorities, and lastly armed with the right of reprieve, had many features in common with the king of the French in 1830. The office, occupied by Mac-Mahon and renewable, could furthermore be transformed in the future to the advantage of one of Louis-Philippe's grandsons, should circumstances lend themselves to it; so the

Orleanists left the future open. By making a distinction between the presidential function and that of the head of government, they opened the way to a parliamentary government – the ministers accountable before the Chambers – which had proved impossible under the July monarchy; but they were also taking the risk of giving irresistible power to universal suffrage.

Against this risk, the Senate was seen as providing a rampart: lacking an appointed upper Chamber, they had obtained only a method of election which would supposedly have a moderating influence, because it gave special weight to the rural areas against the towns. After being the backbone of the Empire, the French peasants had become the last hope of the notables. But they were not certain allies in this new role. Legitimism still held solid rural positions in the west, but Orleanism had never had comparable strongholds. The Chamber of Peers dreamed of by Broglie had become what Gambetta would call the 'Grand Council of the Communes of France'; by giving this democratic baptismal name to an Assembly for which the legislators had gone to such lengths to ensure its conservative nature, Gambetta was wagering that these precautions would not hold out against universal suffrage; and that the principle of the Senate's recruitment would quickly sweep away the fragile dams erected as a bastion against the will of the people.

It is therefore inexact to write, as has often been the case, that the presence of the Senate in the institutions of 1875 was plainly an Orleanist victory and a republican concession. The protests of radical republicans – Quinet among the seniors and Clemenceau among the juniors – would lead one to believe it. But Gambetta had understood better than they that his apparent concession had been a victory. For in reality, the Senate of 1875 no longer had any trace of an aristocratic chamber, either hereditary or appointed. Like the other authorities, it was enveloped in universal suffrage, the unique principle of the institutions; it also had something of the nature of what was called in classical Europe 'popular government'. A century after the United States, France had found the means of reconciling the division of powers with the existence of a single source of public authority: the will of the people.

Finally Daniel Halévy quite rightly emphasized an essential feature of the 1875 arrangements, which is frequently passed over without a word: that the law of 25 February includes in article 4 the re-establishment of the appointment of members of the Council of State by the president. The Council of State, since Year VIII (1800–1), had figured as the keystone of French administration, of which it was the pinnacle, the guarantor and the protector; French civil servants, as regards anything connected with public service, were exempt from any legal action against them, and came under its aegis alone. The Council of State of the Second Empire had been suspended by the National Defence government on 15 September 1870, and replaced by a temporary commission; in 1872, at Thiers's request, the Assembly had re-established it, but reserved to itself the right to elect the members; it was that arrangement that it repealed in February 1875, by restoring the right of appointment by the executive, both in order to avoid 'republicanization' of that great body, and to pay Mac-Mahon the price of his giving up a Senate appointed by himself.

The circumstances of that restoration were less important than its spirit: the Orleanists re-established in full the royal arrangements which placed in the hands of the chief of the executive the Council of State, which had once more become the keystone of that centralized state they professed to hate; the Republicans permitted the restoration of the institution they had abolished in 1870, and did so without uttering a protest. Both groups were acting in the name of opposite political hopes, since one relied on Mac-Mahon and the other counted on winning the presidency. But by their different reckonings, the two camps perfectly expressed the French consensus on administrative centralization which had persisted through the century, despite so many contrary professions of faith.

Once the institutions were settled, they had to be fleshed out. Mac-Mahon alone was not part of the game, having been elected for seven years in 1873. But the two Chambers still had to be elected. The Senate came first, in January 1876. In order to choose the seventy-five irremovable members, Gambetta secretly negotiated an alliance with the legitimists, those eternal losers in the competitive prediction of disaster. He obtained fifty-seven seats, while those loyal to the Comte de Chambord had a dozen; the remainder – virtually nothing – went to the Orleanists, who were unable even to obtain the election of their chief, the Duc de Broglie. An old revolutionary heritage, the question of legitimacy would divide French conservatives even longer than the republicans. At the end of the same month of January 1876, the senatorial elections gave a slight victory to the right, who obtained 133 seats (of which thirty-nine were Bonapartist) against ninety-two to the republicans. This finally gave the conservatives a too pathetically feeble majority (151 against 149) to make the Senate into the notables' defence against the Republic. Many of the great figures of the 'historic' left had their seats, Victor Hugo to the fore, elected in Paris, and also Esquiros, Schoelcher and Peyrat. But on both the right and the left, the moderates had won the day in each camp.

The legislative elections took place on 20 February and 6 March 1876, on a two-round departmental list ballot. The parliamentary alliance of the centres which had formed the institutions was over and done with. The battle brought face to face the right (including Bonapartists) and the left, moral order and progress, religion and science, clericals and anticlericals. Gambetta had refused to make the theme of constitutional revision one of the subjects of the republican campaign, though it had already been demanded by Alfred Naquet, one of his extreme left opponents. The results were excellent for him: on the evening of the second round there were 340 republican seats against 155 conservative (of which ninety-four were Bonapartist) and a few dozen without clear designation. The type of ballot had offered a prize in seats to the victors, who were in any case better organized in the second round; but France had well and truly given a clear majority to the Republic, 4,000,000 votes against 3,200,000. The relative success of the Bonapartists removed still more political credibility from the votes obtained by the conservatives: it would have been difficult to put the votes carried off by the house of Bonaparte in the same bag as those of moral order, properly speaking. The right kept no really predominant influence except in the north and west. Elsewhere France disclosed strong republican majorities.

The period separating the elections of March 1876 and the crisis of May 1877 confirmed the victory of the republican principle of the institutions, universal suffrage, over their Orleanist interpretation. The three powers were constituted, but two at least were in confrontation, rivals for entry to the game: the Assembly and the president, the new republican majority and the seven-year man, Gambetta and Mac-Mahon. The Senate, a new-comer to the political arena, brought no decisive weight to either of them. Mac-Mahon had successively summoned to the government the elderly Dufaure, of the centre-left, then the most moderate of republicans, Jules Simon. But they were both caught up in the political battle which was immediately engaged over the religious question. On 16 May 1877 Mac-Mahon broke away from Jules Simon, repudiating the weakness of the head of the government in the face of the anticlericals. He called Broglie to the government, the symbol of moral order, thus setting up the conflict between the presidency and the Assembly. There followed dissolution and elections. The interpretation of the constitutional laws was at stake. And this was the last great battle of that Republic which Daniel Halévy called 'the Republic of the dukes'.

Broglie prepared for the elections as under the Second Empire, against which he had fought so hard; he changed nearly all the prefects. But what did he have to say, except that he wanted a new majority in the name of order and religion, thus endorsing republican logic? Facing him, Gambetta had set the tone: 'A cry has rung through France, it is a priests' govern-ment, a *curés'* ministry. You call yourselves the counter-revolution, we have facing us nobles who are unwilling to accept democracy, a *congrégation* that wants to enslave France.' The decisive ballot thus took place, once more and for the last time, around the *ancien régime* and the Revolution, in their *fin-de-siècle* versions, both enveloped in religion. This made the conflict between aristocracy and democracy more acute than ever before. But if the aristocracy had rediscovered God, it no longer had a king; it was fighting to uphold a president of the Republic.

Thiers died in September, and the funeral procession of the Commune's executioner was a republican triumph. In October the conservatives regained a little ground in the elections, but not enough to win; they gained sixty seats, and the republicans lost about forty. They had been 363 against Mac-Mahon, and 321 of them returned. But they held a broad majority in seats and votes: 4,200,000 against 3,600,000. Broglie resigned in November, and Mac-Mahon 'submitted', as Gambetta had requested beforehand, by recalling Dufaure; in a message in which he stressed that 'the 1875 Constitution founded a parliamentary Republic, establishing my unaccountability, while it instituted the accountability, both joint and individual, of ministers', he unwittingly established a fundamental interpretation of the institutions.

He could have resigned, but he had his heart set on overseeing army appointments. He did so a little more than a year later, at the beginning of 1879, after the renewing of the first third of the Senate had given a republican majority to the Upper Assembly as well. Instructed by Dufaure and pressed by the deputies to accept a republican purge of the administration and the army, be preferred to tender his resignation. Jules Grévy was then elected to the supreme office, which Gambetta had wanted to hand over to Thiers. The Republic belonged to the republicans. The Republic *was* republican: two points which were linked and yet distinct from each other.

First of all, the republicans: the most spectacular aspect of their victory was their capture of offices, which was done indiscriminately. But confrontation had carried that risk, and democratic politics is an unsubtle art. The nobles and wealthy bourgeois who had governed France by family right watched in horror as the badly-cut republican frock-coats invaded the ministerial palaces in the heart of the faubourg Saint-Germain, without realizing that this talented bourgeoisie installing itself in the state buildings had been paying its way, and even paying very dearly, for the past fifty years. In any case, had they been able to take an unprejudiced look at the country, the outgoing people would have seen what republican victory was bringing in its wake: not a threat to order, and even less to property but, on the contrary, a municipal democracy of small property-owners and minor notables, backed up by 1789 against 1793. An immeasurable society, at last bound together by a strong civic spirit which combined equality and liberty.

The religious question had imparted the very French tone of civil war to the electoral struggle; but in reality, the republicans' success was the first great anti-aristocratic victory to be won by the French without a revolution. Because of that, it founded much more than a Parisian regime, liable to all the hazards of its origin. The republicans took over control of the state only by the express will of all the citizens, which was strengthened by a legitimacy no longer challenged by anyone. That state offered them, as it had to all who had taken possession of it since 1789, the facilities for government afforded by a centralized administration; but its greatest strength lay in what had been the weakness of all previous regimes: the conditions of its birth. Republican France in its own way had just found a sort of Burkean solution to the crisis which had begun in 1789. For want of any political tradition other than that of the Revolution, it had had to dissociate democracy and revolution; it had succeeded in turning the democracy it had found in its cradle into an intellectually and morally accepted order, before setting it up at the summit of the state.

For that reason the regime instituted in 1875 had changed its nature in a few years: the brevity of this trial period still kept something of a revolutionary rhythm, although for the first time it was a matter of adapting institutions to the times and mores. The Senate was never that aristocratic upper Chamber which those on the right had desired, since it too was republican; it would have a moderating effect on the Assembly, not by acting against it, as Broglie had envisaged, but within the Republic, as Gambetta had wanted.

The principal change affected the presidency of the Republic. The republicans' doctrine contained the idea of a collegial government issuing from a single Assembly; they had never liked the 'monarchic' presidential office, which had worked out so badly in 1848. It is true that, since 1871, the president had been elected by the deputies alone, but he had still had the right of dissolution, and therefore the possibility of an appeal to the people. As it happened, Mac-Mahon's defeat saw the disappearance of that prerogative. It opened the way to a president of the Republic confined to a ceremonial office and, in the periodic appointment of the man entrusted with the task of forming the ministry, with no choice but to follow the indications of the Chambers.

Thus in 1879, in institutions largely developed by the Orleanists, a regime was set up which, with the exception of the Senate, was almost totally in conformity with republican tradition: a government stemming from the representatives of the people, and dismissible by them. The sole, omnipotent sovereignty resided in universal suffrage and therefore in its elected members. That 'therefore' contained many problems for the future, for neither institutions nor events had magically dispersed the difficulties which French public life had been multiplying for a hundred years over the problem of political representation: the crises of anti-parliamentary government would bear witness to this, one after the other. But the nation was united at least about universal suffrage, which had become the peaceful master of its destiny, and founder of the Republic.

One last feature characterized the institutions which emerged from the laws of 1875; it was illuminatingly commented upon by the great jurist Carré de Malberg,[6] in his classic book in 1931: that was the omnipotence given to the legislative power. In fact, none of the Acts which founded the Third Republic bore any mention of the principles – the Rights of Man, for example – which might be invoked as higher than written law; nor did any of them foresee an instance of monitoring the constitutionality of laws; there was no provision for consulting the people by way of a referendum. The two Assemblies were sovereign in the full monarchic sense of the term. It was the triumph of representation of the people over the will of the people, the successful outcome of a development which had started in 1789 in the September debate on the veto, full of potential conflicts, among a people who for a century had found it so very difficult to envisage the

---

[6] R. Carré de Malberg, *La Loi, expression de la volonté générale*.

concepts of sovereignty and representation at the same time. On that plane, France would completely modify the omnipotence of the legislative power and written law in the constitutional Acts that came after the Second World War. Those of 1875 were still organizing the Republic according to a tradition which was faithful to the French Revolution, the Constituent Assembly and Convention together: the supremacy of the law over rights, and handing the will of the nation over to legislators.

Three symbolic decisions illustrate the reunion of the republican country and its tradition, which had almost been tamed. The national festival was established on 14 July, not so much to celebrate 1789 directly, since it had been tragically overshadowed by so many murders, as the first anniversary of 1789, that first unanimous commemoration of the Revolution on the Champ de Mars. The national hymn became 'La Marseillaise', to enfold the orphans of Alsace-Lorraine, in the patriotism of their great ancestors, the victors of 1789. Lastly, the Chambers returned to Paris. When the old monarchy had left Versailles for Paris, in October 1789, it was under pressure from a threatenining crowd. Royalty had left its deliberate exile only to pass into the custody of the people of Paris. When the deputies and senators followed the same route, ninety years afterwards, it was as representatives of the people, reconciling the nation with its capital. The French Revolution was coming into port.

Appendix 1: Chronological Table

1770

The Dauphin marries the Archduchess Marie-Antoinette.

June–December Conflict of the government with the parlement regarding the Duc d'Aiguillon.

December Disgrace of Choiseul.

1771

20 January One hundred and thirty magistrates of the parlement of Paris are exiled.

23 February Chancellor Maupeou reorganizes the legal system: magistrates are appointed by the government and the Paris parlement split up.

1774

10 May Death of Louis XV.

24 August Maupeou and Terray leave the government which Maurepas, Vergennes and Turgot had joined shortly before; the latter becomes Controller-General of Finance.

13 September Turgot establishes free trade in grain.

12 November Louis XVI recalls the parlements.

1775

Coronation of Louis XVI.

Malesherbes and the Comte de Saint-Germain join the government.

Edict of the Comte de Saint-Germain.

Du Pont de Nemours writes up for Turgot his *Mémoire sur les municipalités à établir en France*.

April–May The Flour War.

1776

January–February Turgot abolishes the guilds and replaces the *corvée* with a money tax.

12 May Disgrace of Turgot.

4 July American Declaration of Independence.

1777

June   Necker becomes Director General of Finance.

1778

Birth of Madame Royale.
Death of Voltaire and Rousseau.
6 February   Treaty of alliance between France and the United States of America.
12 July   Creation of a provincial assembly in the Berry.

1779

Abolition of serfdom in the royal domains.

1781

Birth of the Dauphin.
Ségur's edict.
February   Necker publishes his *Compte rendu au roi.*
May   Dismissal of Necker.

1783

3 September   Peace treaty with Britain.
10 November   Calonne becomes Controller-General of Finance.

1785

Birth of the future 'Louis XVII'.
Affair of the Diamond Necklace.

1786

Franco-British trade treaty lowering customs duties in both countries.
20 August   Calonne proposes his plan for reform.
29 December   Louis XVI announces the impending convocation of an Assembly of
   Notables.

1787

22 February   Meeting of the Assembly of Notables.
8 April   Dismissal of Calonne; ministry of Loménie de Brienne.
25 May   Dissolution of Assembly of Notables.
June–August   The parlement of Paris refuses to register Loménie de Brienne's
   edicts and calls for an Estates-General; the *parlementaires* are exiled.
September   Negotiation between Loménie de Brienne and the parlement of Paris.
17 September   The American Constitution is adopted by the Congress.
November   Edict of toleration.
19 November   Royal session of the Paris parlement; Louis XVI orders the registration of the financial edicts and exiles Philippe d'Orléans to Villers-Cotterêts.

1788

3 May   The Paris parlement publishes a *Déclaration des lois fondamentales du
   royaume.*

5 May   Arrest of parlement counsellors Duval d'Eprémesnil and Goislard de Monsabert.

8 May   Lamoignon's judicial reform reducing the powers of parlements.

May   Resistance of provincial parlements.

7 June   'Day of the tiles' in Grenoble.

5 July   The King's Council orders research to be made into earlier Estates-General.

21 July   Vizille assembly.

8 August   The Estates-General are convened for 1 May 1789.

24–6 August   Dismissal of Loménie de Brienne and recall of Necker.

September   Re-establishment of parlements; the Paris parlement demands that the Estates-General be convened in the 1614 form.

5 October   Convocation of a second Assembly of Notables.

6 November   Meeting of the Assembly of Notables.

November   Sieyès publishes the *Essai sur les privilèges*.

27 December   The King's Council declares itself in favour of doubling the Third Estate's representation.

1789

January   Sieyès publishes *Qu'est-ce que le Tiers Etat?*

24 January   Electoral regulation for the Estates-General.

March   Beginning of elections to the Estates General.

26–8 April   'Réveillon' riot in Paris.

4 May   Procession for the opening of the Estates-General at Versailles.

5 May   Opening of the Estates-General.

6 May   The deputies of the Third Estate demand common verification of the powers of the three orders.

4 June   Death of the Dauphin.

10 June   The Third Estate decides to commence the verification of powers on its own.

13 June   Three Poitevin *curés* leave the Chamber of the Clergy to join the Third Estate.

17 June   The Third Estate constitutes itself a National Assembly.

19 June   The clergy decide to join the Third Estate after a close ballot.

20 June   The Tennis Court Oath.

23 June   Royal session when Louis XVI sets out his programme and commands the orders to hold separate sittings; when the session is over, the Third Estate's deputies and part of the clergy refuse to leave the hall, contrary to the king's orders.

25 June   Forty-seven deputies from the nobles join the Third Estate.

27 June   The king enjoins the clergy and nobility to meet with the Third Estate.

End of June–beginning of July   Movement of troops towards Paris and Versailles.

11 July   Dismissal of Necker.

14 July   Taking of the Bastille; its governor, de Launay, and the *prévôt des marchands*, Flesselles, are assassinated.

16 July   Recall of Necker.

17 July   Louis XVI wears the cockade at the Paris Hôtel de Ville, where he is received by Bailly, the new mayor.

End of July–August   Peasant revolts and the Great Fear in the provinces.

22 July   Murders of Foulon de Doué and Bertier de Sauvigny in Paris.

4 August   Destruction of the feudal regime formulated between 5 and 11 August.

26 August   Declaration of the Rights of Man and of the Citizen.

10 September   The Assembly rejects the institution of a second chamber.

11 September   The king is accorded a suspensive veto (the right to refuse the promulgation of laws during two legislatures).

5 October   Women of Paris march on Versailles.

6 October   The king is brought back to Paris; the Assembly installs itself in Paris shortly afterwards.

29 October   Decree of the 'silver mark'.

2 November   The clergy's possessions are put at the nation's disposal.

7 November   The Assembly decides that ministers may not be chosen from its ranks.

December   New territorial organization: *départements* and *municipalités*.

19 December   Creation of assignats.

1790

13 February   Abolition of monastic vows.

13 April   The Assembly refuses to declare the Catholic religion to be the state religion.

17 April   Assignats become legal currency.

April–June   Confrontations between Catholics and Protestants in southern France.

12 July   Vote on the Civil Constitution of the Clergy.

14 July   Festival of the Federation in Paris.

31 August   Mutiny of the Swiss garrison at Nancy put down by Bouillé.

4 September   Necker's resignation.

November   Publication of Burke's *Reflections on the French Revolution*.

27 November   Ecclesiastical public officials have to take the oath of the constitution.

1791

2 March   Allarde's law: suppression of the guilds.

10 March and 13 April   Papal briefs condemning the Civil Constitution of the Clergy.

2 April   Death of Mirabeau; on 4 April his body is placed in the church of Sainte-Geneviève, transformed into the Panthéon on 3 April.

18 April   Louis XVI forbidden to leave Paris to celebrate Easter at Saint-Cloud.

16 May   Vote on the ineligibility of Constituents to the next Legislative Assembly.

14 June   Le Chapelier's law banning workers' coalitions.

20 June   Louis XVI and Marie-Antoinette flee from Paris.

21 June   Arrest of the royal family at Varennes.

25 June   The king is brought back to Paris.

17 July   The National Guard puts down a demonstration at the Champ de Mars.

August–September   Revision of the constitution.

27 August   Suppression of the 'silver mark' for eligibility to the Assembly, but increase in electoral property qualification.

14 September   Louis XVI takes the oath to the constitution; Avignon and the Comtat Venaissin are united with France.

30 September   Last session of the Constituent Assembly.

1 October   First sitting of the Legislative Assembly.

29 November   Ecclesiastics refusing to take the oath are declared suspect.

1792

9 February   Decree confiscating émigrés' possessions.

3 March   Rising at Etampes during which the mayor, Simoneau, who opposed the fixing of grain prices, is killed.

20 April   War is declared on the 'king of Bohemia and Hungary'.

27 May   Decree on the deportation of refractory priests.

8 June   Decree on the formation of a camp of *fédérés* in Paris.

11 June   Louis XVI places his veto on the decrees of 27 May and 8 June.

12 June   Dismissal of the ministers, Roland, Clavière and Servan, by Louis XVI; the Assembly renews its confidence in them.

20 June   The mob invades the Tuileries to compel the king to lift his veto; Louis XVI refuses to yield but has to don the red bonnet.

11 July   The Assembly declares 'the country in danger'.

3 August   Publication of Brunswick's manifesto.

10 August   The Tuileries stormed; Louis XVI, taking refuge within the Assembly, is suspended.

11 August   Constitution of an Executive Council in which Danton is Minister of Justice, Roland Minister of the Interior, Clavière Minister of Finance and Servan Minister of War.

13 August   The royal family is incarcerated in the Temple under the supervision of the Paris Commune.

19 August   La Fayette, unable to persuade his army to march on Paris, joins the Austrians, who intern him.

23 August   Fall of Longwy.

30 August   Capture of Verdun.

2–5 September   Massacre of prisoners in the Paris prisons.

20 September   Victory at Valmy; last sitting of the Legislative Assembly: it decrees divorce and the secularization of births, marriages and deaths.

21 September   The Convention meets and abolishes royalty.

27 September   The Convention renews the incompatibility of the offices of minister and deputy; Roland chooses to be a minister and Danton a deputy.

9 October   Returned émigrés are liable to the death penalty within twenty-four hours.

6 November   Dumouriez beats the Austrians at Jemappes.

7 November   Mailhe's report concluding that the king should be tried by the Convention.

13 November   Saint-Just declares that the king should be fought rather than tried.

14 November   French troops enter Brussels.

20 November   Discovery of the 'iron cupboard' containing the royal family's papers in the Tuileries.

27 November   Savoy is united with France.

3 December   Robespierre demands the death of the king.

11 December   First appearance of Louis XVI before the Convention.

26 December   Louis XVI's second appearance.

27 December   Salle moves an appeal to the people regarding the king's sentence.

1793

4 January Barère rejects the proposal of appeal to the people, which Buzot and Vergniaud supported in the case of Louis XVI's trial.

16–18 January The Convention votes for the death of the king.

21 January Execution of Louis XVI.

22 January Roland resigns from the Ministry of the Interior.

1 February Declaration of war on Britain and Holland.

24 February The Convention decrees the levy of 300,000 men.

Beginning of March Austrian counteroffensive in Belgium while Dumouriez pursues his plans in Holland.

7 March Declaration of war on Spain.

9 March The Convention decrees the dispatch of representatives on mission to the *départements*.

10 March Creation of the extraordinary criminal Tribunal (the revolutionary Tribunal).

10–11 March Machecoul massacres (start of the Vendée insurrection).

18 March Defeat of Dumouriez at Neerwinden.

19 March A republican army is defeated by the Vendéens at Pont-Charrault.

21 March Institution of local revolutionary watch committees.

4 April Dumouriez goes over to the Austrians, taking with him the Duc de Chartres (the future Louis-Philippe).

6 April First Committee of Public Safety, whose most important members are Danton and Barère.

24 April Marat, decreed under indictment by the Convention on 13 April, is acquitted by the revolutionary Tribunal and taken in triumph to the Convention.

4 May The Convention decrees the Maximum for grain prices.

10 May The Convention leaves the Salle du Manège to sit in the Tuileries.

18 May Creation of the Commission of Twelve, whose members are Girondins, given the task of inquiring into the Paris Commune.

24 May The Commission of Twelve has Hébert, deputy prosecutor of the Paris Commune, and Varlet, one of the leaders of the *Enragés*, arrested.

25 May Isnard threatens the representatives of the Commune who have come to demand the release of Hébert.

29 May In Lyon, the municipality is in the hands of Girondins and royalists.

31 May The Paris *sections* invade the Convention.

2 June Bid for power by the Paris *sections* against the Convention: fall of the Girondins.

June Fewer than sixty departmental administrations protest against the Parisian bid for power.

9 June Capture of Saumur by the Vendéens.

18 June Capture of Angers by the Vendéens.

24 June The Convention votes for a constitution (which does not come into force).

25 June Jacques Roux presents a petition to the Convention on behalf of the Cordeliers (the *Enragés*' manifesto).

29 June Nantes repulses the Vendéens.

July Publication of the *Contributions destinées à rectifier le jugement du public sur la Révolution française* by Fichte.

10 July   Renewal of the Committee of Public Safety; at this date it comprises Barère, Couthon, Gasparin, Hérault de Séchelles, R. Lindet, Prieur de la Marne, Jean Bon Saint-André, Saint-Just and Thuriot.

13 July   Assassination of Marat.

17 July   Execution of Chalier in Lyon.

23 July   Capitulation of Mainz; the French garrison assigned to the west.

27 July   Robespierre enters the Committee of Public Safety (replacing Gasparin).

28 July   Capitulation of Valenciennes.

1 August   The Convention decides on the destruction of the Vendée.

14 August   Entry of Carnot and Prieur de la Côte-d'Or to the Committee of Public Safety.

23 August   The Convention decrees a *levée en masse*.

24 August   Creation of the Great Ledger of the public debt.

27 August   Toulon gives itself up to the British.

5 September   The Terror is put on the agenda by the Convention, invaded by sansculottes; arrest of Jacques Roux.

6 September   Entry of Collot d'Herbois and Billaud-Varenne to the Committee of Public Safety.

8 September   Victory of Houchard at Hondschoote.

9 September   Organization of the revolutionary army.

11 September   The Maximum for grain and fodder is decreed.

17 September   Vote on the law on suspects.

19 September   Kléber and the Mainz army are beaten by the Vendéens at Torfou.

29 September   Vote on the general Maximum.

9 October   Capture of Lyon by the Convention's army.

10 October   The Convention proclaims revolutionary government until the advent of peace.

16 October   Jourdan beats the Austrians at Wattignies; Marie-Antoinette is executed.

17 October   The Vendéens are beaten at Cholet by Kléber and Marceau; following this defeat they cross the Loire.

31 October   Execution of the Girondins.

7 November   Convention sitting regarding dechristianization.

8 November   Execution of Mme Roland.

10 November   Festival of Reason at Notre-Dame de Paris.

11 November   Execution of Bailly.

14 November   The Vendéens fail to take Granville.

17 November   Arrest of Basire, Chabot and Delaunay, compromised in the Indies Company scandal.

21–2 November   Robespierre and Danton tackle the antireligious masquerades.

24 November   Adoption of the republican calendar.

29 November (9 Frimaire Year II)   Execution of Barnave.

4 December (14 Frimaire)   Organization of the revolutionary government.

5 December (15 Frimaire)   Appearance of the first number of Camille Desmoulins's *Vieux Cordelier*.

12 December (22 Frimaire)   The republican army crushes the Vendéens at Le Mans.

19 December (29 Frimaire)   Recapture of Toulon.

23 December (3 Nivôse)   Republican victory at Savenay over the Vendéens; the war in the west peters out in guerrilla warfare.

1794

12 January (23 Nivôse) In the night of 12–13 January, arrest of Fabre d'Eglantine, compromised in the Indies Company affair.

26 February–3 March (8–13 Ventôse) Vote on the sequestration of suspects' goods and their distribution to the needy.

4 March (14 Ventôse) The Cordeliers call for an insurrection.

13 March (23 Ventôse) In the night of 13–14 March, arrest of the Hébertists.

24 March (4 Germinal) Execution of the Hébertists.

28 March (8 Germinal) Suicide of Condorcet.

30 March (10 Germinal) In the night of 30–1 March, arrest of Danton and Camille Desmoulins.

6 April (16 Germinal) Execution of the Dantonists.

7 May (18 Floréal) The Convention recognizes the existence of the Supreme Being.

8 June (20 Prairial) Festival of the Supreme Being in Paris.

10 June (22 Prairial) Law on the revolutionary Tribunal which inaugurates the Great Terror.

26 June (8 Messidor) Victory of Jourdan at Fleurus.

27 July (9 Thermidor) Fall of Robespierre.

31 July (13 Thermidor) Renewal of the Committees.

1 August (14 Thermidor) Repeal of the law of 22 Prairial.

18 September (2nd complementary day) The Republic pays no salary to any religious cult.

11 October (20 Vendémiaire Year III) Transfer of Rousseau's remains to the Panthéon.

23 October (2 Brumaire) Capture of Koblenz; meeting of the armies of the Sambre et Meuse and the Rhin et Moselle.

1 November (11 Brumaire) Hoche is appointed Commander-in-Chief of the western army.

12 November (22 Brumaire) Closure of the Jacobin Club in Paris.

8 December (18 Frimaire) Reintegration of the '73' (Girondins excluded from the Convention).

24 December (4 Nivôse) Abolition of the Maximum.

1795

21 January (2 Pluviôse) Celebration of Louis XVI's execution.

3 February (15 Pluviôse) Formation of the Batavian Republic.

8 February (20 Pluviôse) Marat 'depantheonized'.

15 February (27 Pluviôse) La Jaunaye agreements: pacification of the west.

21 February (3 Ventôse) Decree proclaiming the freedom of worship.

2 March (12 Ventôse) Arrest of Barère, Collot d'Herbois and Billaud-Varenne.

1 April (12 Germinal) The Convention is invaded by a sansculotte demonstration.

5 April (16 Germinal) Treaty of Basle; Prussia recognizes the French Republic.

April–May Development of the White Terror in the Rhône valley and the Midi.

7 May (18 Floréal) Execution of Fouquier-Tinville.

20 May (1 Prairial) The Convention is invaded by demonstrators demanding 'bread and the 1793 constitution'; they kill the deputy Féraud.

24 May (5 Prairial) Disarmament of the Parisian *sections*.

30 May (11 Prairial) Unsold churches are restored to the faithful.

8 June (20 Prairial)   Death of Louis XVII.

17 June (29 Prairial)   Death sentence on six Montagnard deputies, who commit suicide.

23 June (5 Messidor)   Boissy d'Anglas's report on the constitution.

24 June (6 Messidor)   Proclamation of Louis XVIII in Verona.

21 July (3 Thermidor)   At Quiberon, Hoche crushes the émigré landing.

27 July (9 Thermidor)   Celebration of the fall of Robespierre.

18 August (1 Fructidor)   Decree on the 'two-thirds'.

22 August (5 Fructidor)   The Convention adopts the new constitution.

1 October (9 Vendémiaire Year IV)   Annexation of Belgium.

5 October (13 Vendémiaire)   Barras and Bonaparte crush a royalist rising in Paris.

12–21 October (20–9 Vendémiaire)   Elections.

25 October (3 Brumaire)   Reapplication of terrorist legislation against priests.

26 October (4 Brumaire)   Separation of the Convention.

3 November (12 Brumaire)   Entry into office of the Directory, composed of Barras, Reubell, La Révellière-Lépeaux, Letourneur and Carnot (who replaces Sieyès, who had refused though elected).

1796

19 February (30 Pluviôse)   The issue of assignats is halted.

2 March (12 Ventôse)   Bonaparte is appointed General-in-Chief of the Italian army.

9 March (19 Ventôse)   Bonaparte marries Joséphine Beauharnais.

14 March (24 Ventôse)   Pichegru, suspected of royalism, is replaced by Moreau at the head of the Rhin et Moselle army.

27 March (7 Germinal)   Bonaparte joins his headquarters in Nice.

12 April (23 Germinal)   Victory of Bonaparte over the Austrians at Montenotte.

13 April (24 Germinal)   Victory over the Piedmontese at Millesimo.

15 April (26 Germinal)   Victory over the Austrians at Dego.

21 April (2 Floréal)   Bonaparte's victory over the Piedmontese at Mondovi.

27 April (8 Floréal)   Bonjamin Constant publishes *De la force du gouvernement actuel de la France et de la nécessité de s'y rallier.*

28 April (9 Floréal)   Armistice of Cherasco between Bonaparte and the king of Piedmont-Sardinia.

10 May (21 Floréal)   Bonaparte's victory over the Austrians at Lodi; the Directory arrests the leaders of the Conspiracy of the Equals.

15 May (26 Floréal)   Bonaparte enters Milan.

20 May (1 Prairial)   Resumption of the Rhine campaign.

3 June (15 Prairial)   Withdrawal of the Austrians to the Tyrol, but they leave a garrison in Mantua.

12 June (24 Prairial)   The French army penetrates into papal territories.

23 June (5 Messidor)   Armistice of Bologna between Bonaparte and Pius VI.

16 July (28 Messidor)   Capture of Frankfurt by Jourdan.

5 August (18 Thermidor)   Bonaparte beats the Austrians at Castiglione.

24 August (7 Fructidor)   Jourdan is beaten at Amberg; the French armies of the Rhine have to retreat.

4 September (18 Fructidor)   Bonaparte beats the Austrians at Roverdo.

8 September (22 Fructidor)   Bonaparte beats the Austrians at Bassano.

9 September (23 Fructidor)   Failure of the 'camp de Grenelle' conspiracy in Paris.

16 October (25 Vendémiaire Year V)   Proclamation of the Cispadane Republic.

15–17 November (25–7 Brumaire)   Victory of Bonaparte at Arcola.
December   Failure of Hoche's expedition against England (the Irish expedition).

1797

14 January (25 Nivôse)   Bonaparte beats the Austrians at Rivoli.
2 February (14 Pluviôse)   Surrender of the Austrian garrison in Mantua.
19 February (1 Ventôse)   Peace treaty of Tolentino between the pope and France: Pius VI recognizes the annexation of Avignon and the Comtat Venaissin and has to pay a heavy indemnity.
March–April   Legislative elections; royalist success.
18 April (29 Germinal)   Signature of peace preliminaries between Bonaparte and Austria at Leoben.
22 April (3 Floréal)   Hoche and Moreau learn of the Leoben preliminaries and suspend their offensive manoeuvres in Germany.
26 May (7 Floréal)   Babeuf sentenced to death; Barthélémy is elected Director in place of Letourneur.
June   Barras, Reubell and La Révellière-Lépeaux, having learnt of Pichegru's negotiations with Louis XVIII, decide to appeal to Hoche and his troops.
9 July (21 Messidor)   Proclamation in Milan of the Cisalpine Republic.
8 August (21 Thermidor)   Augereau, sent by Bonaparte to support the republican Directors, is appointed local commandant in Paris.
15 August (28 Thermidor)   Opening in Paris of the first national council of the constitutional Church.
4 September (18 Fructidor)   Coup d'état.
8 September (22 Fructidor)   Merlin de Douai and François de Neufchâteau are elected Directors.
19 September (3rd complementary day)   Death of Hoche.
17 October (26 Vendémiaire Year VI)   Peace of Campo Formio between Bonaparte and Austria; ratified by the Directory, 26 October.
28 November (8 Frimaire)   Opening of the Congress of Rastatt.
25 December (5 Nivôse)   Bonaparte is elected a member of the Institut.

1798

January   French intervention in Switzerland.
11 February (23 Pluviôse)   French troops enter Rome.
11 May (22 Floréal)   Numerous Jacobins and royalists elected in April are removed from office.
15 May (26 Floréal)   Treilhard is elected Director to replace François de Neufchâteau.
19 May (30 Floréal)   Departure of the expedition to Egypt.
11 June (23 Prairial)   Capture of Malta by Bonaparte.
1 July (13 Messidor)   Bonaparte disembarks at Alexandria.
21 July (3 Thermidor)   Bonaparte wins the battle of the Pyramids.
1 August (14 Thermidor)   Nelson destroys the French fleet at Aboukir.
5 September (19 Fructidor)   Vote on Jourdan's law instituting compulsory military service.
November (Brumaire Year VII)   Mme de Staël works on *Des circonstances actuelles qui peuvent terminer la Révolution*.

December Championnet beats the Neapolitan army which had driven him out of Rome.

29 December (9 Nivôse) Treaty of alliance between Russia, Britain and Naples.

1799

26 January (7 Pluviôse) Proclamation of the Parthenopean (Neapolitan) Republic.

February Uprising of the Calabrian peasants against the French and their partisans; Bonaparte marches towards Syria.

2 March (12 Ventôse) Jourdan and Bernadotte resume their offensive on the Rhine.

12 March (22 Ventôse) France declares war on Austria.

25 March (5 Germinal) Jourdan, beaten, retreats to the Rhine.

March Defeats of the Italian army commanded by Scherer.

28 March (8 Germinal) Pius VI is arrested by French troops.

April Legislative elections favourable to the Jacobins.

27 April (8 Floréal) Defeat of Moreau at Cassano; the French evacuate Milan.

28 April (9 Floréal) Assassination attempt on the French plenipotentiaries at the Congress of Rastatt.

16 May (27 Floréal) Sieyès is elected Director to replace Reubell.

17 May (28 Floréal) Bonaparte lifts the siege of Saint-Jean d'Acre and retreats towards Egypt.

4 June (16 Prairial) Masséna resists the Austrian offensive in Switzerland.

17 June (29 Prairial) Treilhard, removed from office, is replaced by Gohier on the Directory.

18 June (30 Prairial) Merlin de Douai and La Révellière-Lépeaux are forced by the Councils to resign; Moulin replaces the second on the 20th.

12 July (24 Messidor) Law on hostages.

14 July (26 Messidor) Pius VI is interned at Valence.

13 August (26 Thermidor) Sieyès has the Jacobin Club closed after it had opened at the beginning of July.

15 August (28 Thermidor) Joubert, commander of the Italian army, is killed at the battle of Novi.

23 August (6 Fructidor) Bonaparte embarks for France.

29 August (12 Fructidor) Death of Pius VI.

19 September (3rd complementary day) Victory of Brune at Bergen.

25–6 September (3–4 Vendémiaire Year VIII) Victory of Masséna at Zurich against the Russians and Austrians, who evacuate Switzerland.

6 October (14 Vendémiaire) Victory of Brune at Castricum against the British and the Russians.

9 October (17 Vendémiaire) Bonaparte disembarks in France.

17 October (25 Vendémiaire) Bonaparte is received by the Directory.

1 November (10 Brumaire) Interview between Sieyès and Bonaparte.

9–10 November (18–19 Brumaire) Coup d'état.

15 December (24 Frimaire Year VIII) Proclamation of the constitution.

25 December (4 Nivôse) Establishment of the Council of State.

27 December (6 Nivôse) Establishment of the Senate.

28 December (7 Nivôse) Reopening of churches on Sundays.

1800

1 January (11 Nivôse)   Establishment of the Tribunate and the Legislative Body.

13 February (24 Pluviôse)   Creation of the Bank of France.

17 February (28 Pluviôse)   Law on the administrative organization of France.

19 February (30 Pluviôse)   Bonaparte installed in the Tuileries.

3 March (12 Ventôse)   Closure of the list of émigrés.

14 March (23 Ventôse)   Election of Pius VII.

18 March (27 Ventôse)   Law on judicial organization.

May–June   Recapture of Italy.

14 June (23 Prairial)   Battle of Marengo; assassination of Kléber in Egypt.

18 June (27 Prairial)   Bonaparte attends a *Te Deum* in Milan cathedral.

2 July (13 Messidor)   Bonaparte returns to Paris.

12 August (24 Thermidor)   Appointment of the preparatory commission for the Civil Code.

3 September (16 Fructidor)   The British retake Malta.

7 September (20 Fructidor)   Bonaparte replies in the negative to approaches from Louis XVIII.

20 October (28 Vendémiaire Year IX)   Striking off from the list of émigrés of 48,000 émigrés.

5 November (14 Brumaire)   Beginning of Concordat negotiations.

3 December (12 Frimaire)   Victory of Moreau over the Austrians at Hohenlinden.

24 December (3 Nivôse)   Attempt on Bonaparte's life in the rue Saint-Nicaise.

1801

5 January (15 Nivôse)   *Senatus consultum* orders the deportation of 130 Jacobins as a consequence of the attempted coup of 24 December.

7 February (18 Pluviôse)   Law on the special courts.

9 February (20 Pluviôse)   Peace of Lunéville: the main points of the Treaty of Campo Formio are confirmed and France obtains the left bank of the Rhine.

29 June (10 Messidor)   Opening of a national council organized by the constitutional clergy in Paris.

June–August   The British gain control of Egypt.

15 July (26 Messidor)   Signing of the Concordat.

23 July (4 Thermidor)   Beginning of the discussion on the Civil Code in the Council of State.

1802

26 January (6 Pluviôse Year X)   Bonaparte becomes president of the Italian Republic.

6 February (17 Pluviôse)   Leclerc, sent to quell Toussaint-L'Ouverture's revolt, lands in Santo Domingo.

18 March (27 Ventôse)   Purge of the Tribunate and the Legislative Body.

25 March (4 Germinal)   Peace of Amiens.

3 April (13 Germinal)   *Articles organiques* concerning the Catholic and Protestant religions.

14 April (24 Germinal)   Chateaubriand publishes *Le Génie du Christianisme*.

18 April (28 Germinal)   Promulgation of the Concordat.

26 April (6 Floréal)   Amnesty for émigrés still figuring on the list of émigrés (if they return and swear loyalty to the regime), with the exception of about a thousand.

1 May (11 Floréal)   Law on public education: creation of the *lycées*.
19 May (29 Floréal)   Creation of the Légion d'Honneur.
2 August (14 Thermidor)   Consulate for life granted to Napoleon.
4 August (16 Thermidor)   Constitution of Year X.
11 September (24 Fructidor)   Piedmont joined to France.

1803

23 January (3 Pluviôse Year XI)   Reorganization of the Institut.
24 March (3 Germinal)   Empire ordinance adopting the French plan of 23 February for the reorganization of Germany.
28 March (7 Germinal)   The value of the franc is fixed at 5 g of silver.
9 April (19 Germinal)   Creation of junior officials of the Council of State.
14 April (24 Germinal)   The Bank of France receives the privilege of issuing notes.
3 May (13 Floréal)   Sale of Louisiana to the United States.
12 May (22 Floréal)   Breaking of the peace of Amiens.
20 June (1 Messidor)   Bonaparte prohibits goods of British origin.
1 December (9 Frimaire Year XII)   Institution of the worker's identity card.
2 December (10 Frimaire)   The army of the Boulogne camp takes the title of the army of England.

1804

February–March   Arrest of Cadoudal and his accomplices: compromised, Pichegru commits suicide and Moreau is banished.
21 March (30 Ventôse)   Execution of the Duc d'Enghien at Vincennes; promulgation of the Civil Code.
18 May (28 Floréal)   Bonaparte becomes hereditary emperor of the French.
June   Execution of Cadoudal and his accomplices.
2 December (11 Frimaire Year XIII)   Coronation of Napoleon.

1805

9 March (18 Ventôse)   Creation of a Press Bureau to supervise publications.
26 May (6 Prairial)   Napoleon is crowned king of Italy in Milan.
26 August (8 Fructidor)   Napoleon abandons the conquest of England and plans the Austrian campaign.
September–October   Bavarian campaign.
20 October (28 Vendémiaire Year XIV)   Mack's Austrian army surrenders at Ulm.
21 October (29 Vendémiaire)   Nelson crushes Villeneuve's fleet at Trafalgar.
14 November (23 Brumaire)   Napoleon enters Vienna.
2 December (11 Frimaire)   Napoleon beats the Russians and the Austrians at Austerlitz.
26 December (5 Nivôse)   Treaty of Pressburg.
31 December   End of the republican calendar.

1806

18 March   Creation of industrial tribunals.
30 March   Joseph Bonaparte becomes king of Naples.

4 April   Publication of the imperial catechism by Bernier and d'Astros.
10 May   Foundation of the University.
5 June   Louis Bonaparte becomes king of Holland.
12 July   Creation of the Confederation of the Rhine.
6 August   Dissolution of the Holy Roman Empire.
14 August   Creation of the *majorats* (hereditary fiefs of the Empire).
October   Prussian campaign.
14 October   Battles of Jena and Auerstädt.
27 October   Napoleon enters Berlin.
21 November   Continental System: prohibition of all trade, even for neutral countries, with Britain.

1807

January–June   Prussian campaign.
7–8 February   Battle of Eylau against the Prussians and the Russians.
14 June   Napoleon beats the Russians at Friedland.
8 July   Peace of Tilsit; Franco-Russian alliance.
9 August   Talleyrand leaves the Ministry of Foreign Affairs.
16 August   Jerome Bonaparte becomes king of Westphalia.
19 August   Suppression of the Tribunate.
11 September   Commercial Code.
16 September   Creation of the Revenue Court.
November–December   French intervention in Spain and Portugal.
17 December   Worsening of the Continental System: neutral ships permitting British boarding parties will be treated as hostile.

1808

2 February   Occupation of Rome.
1 March   Organization of the imperial nobility.
23 March   Murat enters Madrid.
May   Beginning of the Spanish rebellion.
15 July   Murat becomes king of Naples.
20 July   Joseph, appointed king of Spain, enters Madrid.
22 July   Capitulation of General Dupont at Bailén in Spain.
August   British landing in Portugal.
30 August   Capitulation of Junot at Cintra in Portugal.
17 September   Monopoly of teaching granted to the University.
27 September   Interview at Erfurt between Napoleon and Tsar Alexander: France evacuates Prussia.

1809

10 April   Austrian offensive.
12–13 May   Capture of Vienna.
17 May   Annexation of Papal States.
22 May   The Austrians halt the French at Aspern-Essling.
5–6 July   Battle of Wagram; arrest of Pius VII.
14 October   Peace of Vienna.
15 December   Divorce of Napoleon.

1810

6 January Franco-Swedish alliance.

17 February The city of Rome is united with France.

2 April Marriage of Napoleon with Marie-Louise, daughter of Francis II, emperor of Austria.

6 June Creation of the Council for trade and manufacture.

9 July Annexation of Holland to the Empire.

21 August Election of Bernadotte as heir to the throne of Sweden.

31 December Breaking of the Franco-Russian alliance.

1811

20 March Birth of the King of Rome.

17 June–20 October National synod in Paris.

1812

23 February Breaking of the Concordat.

5 March Franco-Prussian alliance.

9 April Russo-Swedish alliance.

8 May Fixing of grain prices.

June Beginning of the Russian campaign.

19 June Pius VII is brought to Fontainebleau.

5–7 September Battle of the Moskva.

14 September Napoleon enters Moscow.

19 October The French army abandons Moscow.

26–8 November Crossing of the Beresina.

5 December Napoleon leaves the Grand Army.

18 December Napoleon arrives in Paris.

1813

25 January Concordat of Fontainebleau.

January–February Prussia breaks its alliance with France and joins Russia.

March Uprising of northern Germany; Bernadotte reinforces the coalition.

30 March Organization of a Regency Council.

14 April Austria breaks the French alliance but remains neutral.

May The French evacuate Madrid.

May–June French offensive in Germany.

12 August Austria joins the coalition.

September–October German campaign.

16–19 October Battle of Leipzig.

November Murat turns to the allies.

29 December The Legislative Body declares itself against pursuing the war.

1814

January–April French campaign.

24 January Joseph is appointed Lieutenant-General of the Empire.

25 January Fall of Lerida, last French post in Spain.

12 March The Duc d'Angoulême is enthusiastically welcomed in Bordeaux.

30 March Capitulation of Paris.

1 April Formation of a provisional government presided over by Talleyrand.

2 April Senate declares deposition of Napoleon.

6 April Abdication of Napoleon at Fontainebleau; vote on the senatorial constitution.

24 April Louis XVIII lands at Calais.

2 May Royal Declaration of Saint-Ouen.

30 May First Treaty of Paris: France is reduced to its 1792 frontiers.

4 June Proclamation of the Charter.

27 November Publication of Chateaubriand's *Réflexions politiques*.

November 1814–June 1815 Congress of Vienna where Talleyrand represents France.

1815

3 January Signing of a secret treaty of alliance between France, Austria and Britain.

21 January Celebration of the anniversary of Louis XVI's death.

1 March Having left Elba on 26 February, Napoleon lands at Golfe-Juan.

13 March At the Congress of Vienna the allies banish Napoleon from the Empire.

20 March Napoleon at the Tuileries. Benjamin Constant assists in drawing up the Additional Act to the Constitutions of the Empire.

18 June Waterloo.

22 June Napoleon's second abdication. Fouché forms a provisional government.

24 June Start of the White Terror in the Midi.

3 July Capitulation of Paris.

7 July Talleyrand–Fouché Ministry.

8 July Louis XVIII returns to Paris.

15 July Napoleon surrenders to the British.

14–22 August Legislative elections: the *Chambre introuvable*. Fouché resigns from the government.

20 September Talleyrand's resignation.

24 September Formation of the Richelieu ministry; he takes the Foreign Affairs portfolio.

26 September The Holy Alliance between Russia, Prussia and Austria is concluded.

29 October Law on general security.

9 November Law against seditious writings.

20 November Second Treaty of Paris: France is reduced to its 1790 frontiers.

27 December Law establishing special courts (exceptional courts of law).

1816

12 January Law excluding from amnesty the regicides who had rallied to Napoleon in the Hundred Days.

5 September Dissolution of the *Chambre introuvable*.

17 September Chateaubriand publishes *De la monarchie selon la Charte*.

25 October Elections favourable to the Constitutionnels.

1817

February Laîné's law fixes the electoral property qualification and conditions for eligibility.

14 July   Death of Madame de Staël.

20 September   The left progresses in the elections. In the Chamber, formation of the Independent group.

1818

12 March   Gouvion Saint-Cyr's law.

April   Publication of Madame de Staël's *Considérations sur la Révolution française*, which provokes replies notably from the ex-Conventionnel Bailleul and from Bonald.

September–November   Congress of Aix-la-Chapelle, where France is openly admitted to deliberate with the great powers and obtains agreement on war indemnity liquidation and the withdrawal of foreign troops from her soil.

October   By-elections in which the left makes progress; among the newly elected: Benjamin Constant, La Fayette, Manuel.

December   End of the occupation of France by the allied armies.

29 December   Formation of Decazes's ministry.

1819

March   Creation of peers to ensure the ministry's majority.

May–June   Serre's law on the press.

September   Victory of the left in the by-elections; the Abbé Grégoire, elected, is invalidated.

1820

A. Thierry begins to publish his *Lettres sur l'histoire de France*.

13 February   Assassination of the Duc de Berry by Louvel.

20 February   Decazes resigns. Formation of the second Richelieu ministry.

12 June   Law on the double vote.

29 September   Birth of the Duc de Bordeaux.

November   Elections won by the right.

1821

March   Birth of the *Charbonnerie*.

5 May   Death of Napoleon.

15 December   Formation of Villèle's ministry.

1822

March   Laws on the press re-establishing preliminary censorship.

21 September   Execution of the four sergeants of La Rochelle.

September–December   Congress of Verona where Chateaubriand represents France; against opposition from Britain and Villèle, the principle of intervention in Spain is decided upon.

28 December   Chateaubriand appointed Minister of Foreign Affairs.

1823

Publication of Las Cases' *Mémorial de Sainte-Hélène*, Guizot's *Essais sur l'histoire de France* and the first volume of Thiers's *Histoire de la Révolution*.

4 March   Expulsion of Manuel from the Chamber.
April   French intervention in Spain.
24 December   Dissolution of the Chamber of Deputies.

1824

Publication of Mignet's *Histoire de la Révolution française*.
February–March   Legislative elections: the 'Chambre retrouvée'.
16 September   Death of Louis XVIII.

1825

Death of Saint-Simon.
January–February   Great mission to Besançon.
20 April   Law on sacrilege.
27 April   Law on compensation for the émigrés.
29 May   Coronation of Charles X in Reims.

1826

7 April   Rejection of the law on primogeniture.

1827

April   Dissolution of the Parisian National Guard.
June   Re-establishment of censorship.
July   Russia, Britain and France decide to intervene against Turkey.
November   Dissolution of the Chamber and new elections unfavourable to Villèle.

1828

Guizot starts to publish *Histoire de la civilisation en France* and *Histoire de la civilisation en Europe*.
5 January   Villèle's resignation. Formation of the Martignac ministry.
June   Legislation on the press (abolition of preliminary censorship) and exclusion from teaching of members of unauthorized congregations.

1829

8 August   Formation of the Polignac ministry.

1830

31 January   Decision to intervene in Algeria.
18 March   Address expressing no confidence in the ministry supported by the so-called '221', largely inspired by Royer-Collard.
16 May   Dissolution of the Chamber.
23 June–19 July   New elections which reinforce the '221'.
5 July   Capture of Algiers by French troops.
25 July   The four ordinances: suspension of the freedom of the press, re-establishment of preliminary censorship and prior authorization; only land taxes will be taken into account in calculating taxable rating; dissolution of the Chamber and date of the next elections.

26 July　Mobilization of the Parisian press.

27, 28, 29 July　The Three Glorious Days:

　27 July: First barricade in rue Saint-Honoré. The demonstrators arm themselves overnight.

　28 July: Rioting in the east of Paris. The centre of Paris is invaded by demonstrators who have been joined by National Guards. Marmont, incapable of re-establishing order, assembles his troops between the Louvre, the Tuileries and Place Vendôme.

　29 July: Defection of the troops. The Louvre is taken by force and Marmont retreats towards Saint-Cloud. On Guizot's proposal, La Fayette is appointed Commander-in-Chief of the National Guard. A municipal commission of five deputies is formed. The final toll is heavy: nearly 800 dead and 4,000 wounded on the insurgents' side; 200 dead and 800 wounded on the side of the forces of order.

30 July　Charles X rescinds the four ordinances. Thiers and Laffitte put forward the candidature of the Duc d'Orléans.

31 July　Louis-Philippe accepts the post of lieutenant-general of the kingdom.

2 August　Charles X abdicates in favour of the Duc de Bordeaux, Henri V.

3 August　Vote on revision of the Charter. Departure of Charles X for exile.

9 August　Louis-Philippe, king of the French, swears loyalty to the revised Charter.

25 August　Belgian rebellion.

2 November　Laffitte ministry.

21 December　Charles X's ministers sentenced to imprisonment.

1831

20 January　Belgian neutrality.

14 February　Risings in Paris on the occasion of a funeral service to the memory of the Duc de Berry at Saint-Germain-l'Auxerrois.

13 March　Casimir Périer Ministry.

March　Law on municipal organization.

April　Law lowering the electoral and eligibility qualifications: the electorate is thereby doubled.

July　Legislative elections.

November　Silk workers' revolt in Lyon.

December　Abolition of hereditary peerage.

1832

April　Landing of the Duchesse de Berry.

16 May　Death of Casimir Périer, victim of the cholera epidemic.

5–6 June　On the occasion of the burial of General Lamarque, a rising gains control of the east of Paris.

12 October　Soult ministry (Thiers at the Interior, Broglie at Foreign Affairs, Guizot at Public Education).

1833

Buchez publishes his *Introduction à la science de l'histoire*.

March　Occupation of Oran.

June　Law on the general councils and law on primary education.

1834

Victor Hugo publishes *Journal des idées et des opinions d'un révolutionnaire de 1830*.
Buchez and Roux begin to publish, in parts, *L'Histoire parlementaire de la Révolution française*.
9–12 April Workers' rising in Lyon after the dissolution of a mutual aid society, in accordance with law extending the banning of associations.
13 April Rebellion and massacre in the rue Transnonain in Paris.
21 June Legislative elections: large-scale defeat of the Republicans.

1835

Tocqueville publishes the first part of *De la démocratie en Amérique*.
28 July Fieschi's assassination attempt on Louis-Philippe.
September Repressive laws.

1836

Tocqueville publishes *l'État social et politique de la France avant et depuis 1789*.
22 February Thiers ministry.
6 September Molé ministry.
30 October Louis-Napoleon Bonaparte tries to win over the garrison in Strasbourg.

1837

November Legislative elections.

1838

December Parliamentary coalition against Molé.

1839

2 March Legislative elections (Tocqueville is elected).
8 March Resignation of Molé.
12 May Soult ministry. Failure of an attempted sedition in which Blanqui and Barbès take part.

1840

Tocqueville publishes the second part of *De la démocratie en Amérique*.
Louis Blanc publishes *L'Organisation du travail* and *L'Histoire de dix ans*.
1 March Thiers ministry (with Rémusat at the Interior and Cousin at Public Education).
July Campaign of banquets.
15 July Treaty of London between Britain, Russia, Prussia and Austria, which isolates France over the Eastern Question.
6 August Attempt by Louis-Napoleon Bonaparte at Boulogne.
15 October Darmès's attempt on Louis-Philippe's life.
29 October Soult–Guizot Ministry.
December Return of Napoleon's remains.

1841

July Dardanelles Convention.

1842

11 June Law on the railways.
9 July Legislative elections.
13 July Accidental death of the Duc d'Orléans.

1843

August The visit of Queen Victoria breaks the isolation in which European monarchs were keeping Louis-Philippe.

1844

August Battle of the Isly won by Bugeaud in Algeria.

1845

Quinet publishes *Le Christianisme et la Révolution française.*
Thiers begins to publish *L'Histoire du Consulat et de l'Empire.*

1846

Michelet publishes *Le Peuple.*
August Legislative elections.

1847

Publication of *L'Histoire de la Révolution française* by Michelet, of the first book of *L'Histoire de la Révolution française* by Louis Blanc, of *L'Histoire des Montagnards* by Esquiros and of *L'Histoire des Girondins* by Lamartine.
April–May Teste–Cubières scandal.
9 July Beginning of the 'banquets campaign' in Paris.
August The Choiseul-Praslin affair.
September Soult leaves the presidency of the Council. Still keeping his portfolio, Guizot succeeds him on 11 October.
December Surrender of Abd el-Kader.

1848

22 February Popular demonstrations against the banning of the banquet in the twelfth *arrondissement.*
23 February Rising in Paris. Dismissal of Guizot and recall of Molé. Shooting in the boulevard des Capucines. During the night the king sends for Thiers.
24 February Abdication of Louis-Philippe in favour of the Comte de Paris; proclamation of the Republic at the Hôtel de Ville and formation of a provisional government.
25 February The provisional government undertakes to guarantee employment. Departure of Louis-Philippe.
26 February Abolition of the death penalty for political matters.
29 February Following a demonstration which, on the preceding day, demanded the creation of a Ministry of Labour, a government commission for workers is constituted.
2 March The working day is limited to ten hours in Paris and eleven hours in

the provinces. The principle of universal suffrage is affirmed. Louis-Philippe embarks for England.

4 March Agreement on the freedom of the press and the freedom to hold meetings.

5 March Elections are decided for 9 April.

6 March Michelet returns to his Chair in the Collège de France.

16 March Demonstration of the 'bearskins' organised by the right.

17 March Failure of a *journée* organised by Blanqui, which however achieved the postponement of the elections from 9 to 23 April.

8 April Ledru-Rollin, Minister of the Interior, urges electors to uphold 'yesterday's' republicans against those of 'the day after'.

16 April Failure of a demonstration against the government.

23 April Election of the Constituent Assembly.

4 May Meeting of the Assembly and official proclamation of the Republic.

15 May The Assembly is invaded by a demonstration, provoking a reaction which allows the elimination of the leaders of the left.

17 May Cavaignac appointed Minister of War.

4 June Louis-Napoleon Bonaparte is elected to the Constituent Assembly, but prefers to stay in England where he has been in exile; among the others elected are: Thiers, Changarnier, Victor Hugo, Caussidière, Pierre Leroux and Proudhon.

21 June Decree on the National Workshops.

23–6 June Barricades and street fighting in the east of Paris. On the 24th a state of siege is decreed in Paris. On the 25th the forces of order begin their offensive; death of Monseigneur Affre.

28 June Dissolution of the National Workshops. Cavaignac has the task of forming the new ministry to replace the Executive Commission.

End of August Louis Blanc leaves for exile.

4 September The Assembly begins to discuss the constitution.

17 September Louis-Napoleon Bonaparte, re-elected, takes his place in the Assembly.

4 November Vote on the constitution by the Assembly: the presidential campaign is opened.

10 December Presidential elections.

20 December Louis-Napoleon Bonaparte, proclaimed elected, gives Odilon Barrot the task of forming the ministry.

26 December Changarnier is appointed commander of the army of Paris.

1849

15 March Law organizing the elections.

30 April Oudinot's attack on Rome.

13 May Legislative elections: success for the party of order despite the election of about 200 'Montagnards'.

3 June Oudinot's second expedition to give Rome back to the Pope.

13 June Repression of a demonstration opposed to the French expedition to Rome and proclamation of a state of siege in Paris; departure of Ledru-Rollin into exile.

30 June–3 July Capture of Rome.

31 October Hautpoul ministry.

1850

11 January   Parieu's law which allows any congregationist to become a primary school teacher and entrusts the supervision of primary teaching to the administrative authorities.

10 March   Legislative by-elections.

15 March   Falloux's law on higher education.

31 May   Law restricting the right of suffrage.

July   Louis-Napoleon Bonaparte's tour of the provinces.

26 August   Death of Louis-Philippe.

1851

3 January   Dismissal of Changarnier.

24 January   New ministry composed of men dedicated to the president.

19 July   The Assembly rejects the revision of the Constitution which would have permitted presidential re-election.

27 October   New ministry in which Saint-Arnaud is the strong man.

4 November   Message from the president to the Assembly demanding the repeal of the law of 31 May 1850; the Assembly rejects its urgency.

6 November   Proposal of the *questeurs* (right of the president of the Assembly to request armed force).

17 November   The *questeurs'* proposal is rejected by the Assembly.

2 December   Coup d'état by Louis-Napoleon Bonaparte. At dawn there is an announcement in Paris of the dissolution of the Assembly, the preparation of a new constitution, the organization of a plebiscite and the re-establishment of universal suffrage; the principal opponents, chiefly the republicans, are arrested. During the morning, the deputies meet at the town hall of the tenth *arrondissement* and vote for the deposition of Louis-Napoleon Bonaparte; troops intervene and 220 deputies, including Berryer, Tocqueville, Rémusat, Odilon Barrot and Falloux, are arrested. At the end of the day, the republicans form a resistance committee.

3 December   Attempt by the republican left to rouse the Parisian suburbs. The deputy Baudin is killed on a barricade. Saint-Arnaud proclaims a state of siege.

4 December   The army regains control of Paris and the opposition is muzzled.

3–10 December   Demonstrations of resistance to the coup d'état in the provinces.

21–2 December   Plebiscite which gives an overwhelming majority in favour of Louis-Napoleon Bonaparte.

1852

Proudhon publishes *La Révolution sociale démontrée par le coup d'état du 2 décembre*.

14 January   Promulgation of the constitution.

23 January   Nationalization of the Orléans' possessions.

29 February   Election of the Legislative Body.

25 March   Decree on prefectorial administration.

26 March   Decree on mutual aid societies.

15 October   Louis-Napoleon Bonaparte's speech at Bordeaux.

7 November   *Senatus consultum* modifying the constitution: re-establishment of the Empire.

21 November   Second plebiscite ratifying the *senatus consultum*.

2 December   Proclamation of the Empire.

1853

Victor Hugo's *Les Châtiments*.
30 January   Marriage of Napoleon III.
1 July   Haussmann Prefect of the Seine (until January 1870).

1854

27 March   France and Britain declare war on Russia.

1855

10 September   The Allies enter Sebastopol.
May–November   Universal Exhibition in Paris.

1856

Publication of Tocqueville's *L'Ancien Régime et la Révolution* and Guizot's *Histoire de la Révolution de l'Angleterre*.
18 January   End of the Crimean War.
February–April   Congress of Paris between the combatants.
26 July   Legislation on commercial companies.

1857

29 April   Dissolution of the Legislative Body.
21 June   Legislative elections.

1858

Proudhon publishes *La Justice dans la Révolution et l'Église*.
14 January   Orsini's attempt on Napoleon III's life outside the Opera.
27 February   Law on general security (but, from March, it was applied only in exceptional instances).
21 July   Napoleon III and Cavour meet at Plombières.
10 December   Conclusion of a defence treaty between France and Piedmont.

1859

18 February   Occupation of Saigon.
29 April   Austria attacks Piedmont.
10 May   Departure of the emperor for the army of Italy.
4 June   Battle of Magenta.
24 June   Battle of Solferino.
12 July   Armistice of Villafranca.
16 August   Law granting amnesty to political prisoners.

1860

1 January   Extension of the boundaries of Paris.
23 January   Trade treaty with England.
24 March   Piedmont annexes central Italy. France obtains Savoy and Nice.
24 November   The Chambers are granted the right of Address and the ministers will have to defend government policy before the Assemblies. Emile Ollivier outlines a reconciliation with the regime.

1861

31 December   No supplementary or extraordinary funds without the vote of the Legislative body.

1862

29 March   Trade treaty with Prussia.

1863

23 May   Law on limited liability companies.
30 May   Legislative elections.
June   Victor Duruy Minister of Public Instruction.
October   Rouher Minister of State.

1864

Founding of the International Working Men's Association in London.
17 February   Publication of the *Manifeste des soixante* drawn up by Tolain.
25 May   Law on the right of coalition; the right to strike is granted.
8 December   Pope Pius IX publishes the encyclical *Quanta Cura*.

1865

Edgar Quinet publishes *La Révolution*.
Nancy programme.
10 March   Death of Morny.
October   Napoleon III and Bismarck meet at Biarritz.

1866

3 July   Victory of Prussia over Austria at Sadowa.
December   French troops evacuate Rome (under the convention of 15 September 1864).

1867

February   Repatriation of the French expeditionary force from Mexico.
April–November   Universal Exhibition.
4 November   French troops have to return to protect the Papal State against Garibaldi.

1868

Prévost-Paradol publishes *La France nouvelle*.
14 January   Niel's law.

1869

23 May   Legislative elections.
12 July   The emperor announces reforms; resignation of Rouher.
8 September   *Senatus consultum*: the Legislative body shares the law-making initiative with the emperor and votes on the budget by items.

16 November　Inauguration of the Suez Canal.
8 December　Opening of the Vatican Council.

1870

2 January　Emile Ollivier forms a government.
12 January　Funeral of the republican journalist Victor Noir.
20 April　*Senatus consultum*: reaffirmation of the principles of 1789, transformation of the Senate, double responsibility of ministers to the deputies and the emperor.
8 May　Referendum-plebiscite on the *Senatus consultum* of 20 April; massive 'yes' in favour of Napoleon III.
13 July　The Ems telegram.
19 July　France declares war on Prussia.
1 September　Capitulation of Napoleon III at Sedan.
4 September　Proclamation of the Republic in Paris.
5 September　Dissolution of the Legislative Body.
19 September　Beginning of the siege of Paris.
20 September　Breakdown of negotiations between Jules Favre and Bismarck.
28 October　Paris learns of Bazaine's surrender at Metz.
31 October　A rising gains control over the Hôtel de Ville in Paris.
November　Talks between Thiers and Bismarck to try to halt the fighting.

1871

Renan publishes *La Réforme intellectuelle et morale de la France*.
19 January　Failure of Parisian *sortie* against the Prussians.
24 January　Negotiations between Jules Favre and Bismarck.
28 January　Armistice and capitulation of Paris.
8 February　Elections: royalist but divided majority.
17 February　Thiers appointed 'Chief of the Executive Power of the French Republic'.
3 March　Formation of the Central Committee of the National Guard in Paris.
18 March　Failure of an attempt by Thiers to retrieve the cannon of the National Guard in Montmartre; the two generals charged with this mission are executed. The government takes refuge at Versailles and the Central Committee of the National Guard seizes power in Paris.
26 March　Municipal elections in Paris.
28 March　Proclamation of the Commune.
19 April　The Commune votes a 'Declaration to the French People'.
10 May　Treaty of Frankfurt: France cedes Alsace and part of Lorraine and has to pay five billion francs in indemnity.
21–7 May　Recapture of Paris.
5 July　The Comte de Chambord (Henri V), back in France, refuses to abandon the white flag.
9 July　Following Falloux, the majority of royalist deputies affirm their loyalty to the tricolour flag.
31 August　Rivet's law: Thiers president of the Republic.
13 November　Thiers declares that the Republic exists and that it will be conservative.

1872

26 September   Gambetta's speech in Grenoble.

1873

7 January   Death of Napoleon III.
January   Gambetta declares himself ready to accept a second Chamber.
24 May   Thiers, placed in a minority, resigns. Mac-Mahon is president of the Republic and summons Broglie to form the ministry.
July   Germany evacuates the last of the occupied *départements*.
16 November   Law of the seven-year term of office, extending Mac-Mahon's powers.

1874

16 May   The Broglie government is overthrown; the Cissey ministry succeeds it.

1875

30 January   Vote for Wallon's amendment: the president of the Republic to be elected by the Chambers.
24 February   Law organizing the Senate.
25 February   Law organizing the public authorities.
16 July   Law organizing the relations between public authorities.

1876

30 January   Senate elections.
20 February, 6 March   Legislative elections.
9 March   Dufaure's ministry.
2 December   Dufaure's resignation. Mac-Mahon summons Jules Simon.

1877

4 May   Gambetta designates clericalism as the enemy.
15 May   The republicans propose the abrogation of the 1875 law on press offences.
16 May   Mac-Mahon asks Jules Simon to resign.
17 May   Formation of Broglie's ministry.
22 June   Dissolution of the Chamber.
8 September   Funeral of Thiers.
14 October   Elections: the republicans continue to hold the majority. Mac-Mahon recalls Dufaure.
13 December   Dufaure's ministry.

1879

5 January   Elections to replace one-third of the Senate: victory of the republicans.
30 January   Mac-Mahon's resignation. Election of Jules Grévy to the presidency of the Republic.
4 February   Waddington's ministry.
21 June   The Chambers leave Versailles and take their seats in Paris.
28 December   Freycinet's ministry.

1880

6 July   The Republic adopts 14 July as the annual national festival.
11 July   Amnesty for the Communards.
14 July   First celebration of the national festival.

Appendix 2: The Republican Calendar for Year II (1793–1794)

Vendémiaire, An II. Sept.–Oct. 1793		Brumaire Oct.–Nov.		Frimaire Nov.–Dec.		Nivôse Dec. 1793–Jan. 1794		Pluviôse Jan.–Feb.		Ventôse Feb.–March		Germinal March–April		Floréal April–May		Prairial May–June		Messidor June–July		Thermidor July–Aug.		Fructidor Aug.–Sept.	
1	22	1	22	1	21	1	21	1	20	1	19	1	21	1	20	1	20	1	19	1	19	1	18
2	23	2	23	2	22	2	22	2	21	2	20	2	22	2	21	2	21	2	20	2	20	2	19
3	24	3	24	3	23	3	23	3	22	3	21	3	23	3	22	3	22	3	21	3	21	3	20
4	25	4	25	4	24	4	24	4	23	4	22	4	24	4	23	4	23	4	22	4	22	4	21
5	26	5	26	5	25	5	25	5	24	5	23	5	25	5	24	5	24	5	23	5	23	5	22
6	27	6	27	6	26	6	26	6	25	6	24	6	26	6	25	6	25	6	24	6	24	6	23
7	28	7	28	7	27	7	27	7	26	7	25	7	27	7	26	7	26	7	25	7	25	7	24
8	29	8	29	8	28	8	28	8	27	8	26	8	28	8	27	8	27	8	26	8	26	8	25
9	30	9	30	9	29	9	29	9	28	9	27	9	29	9	28	9	28	9	27	9	27	9	26
10	1	10	31	10	30	10	30	10	29	10	28	10	30	10	29	10	29	10	28	10	28	10	27
11	2	11	1	11	1	11	31	11	30	11	1	11	31	11	30	11	30	11	29	11	29	11	28
12	3	12	2	12	2	12	1	12	31	12	2	12	1	12	1	12	31	12	1	12	30	12	29
13	4	13	3	13	3	13	2	13	1	13	3	13	2	13	2	13	1	13	1	13	31	13	30
14	5	14	4	14	4	14	3	14	2	14	4	14	3	14	3	14	2	14	2	14	1	14	31
15	6	15	5	15	5	15	4	15	3	15	5	15	4	15	4	15	3	15	3	15	2	15	1
16	7	16	6	16	6	16	5	16	4	16	6	16	5	16	5	16	4	16	4	16	3	16	2
17	8	17	7	17	7	17	6	17	5	17	7	17	6	17	6	17	5	17	5	17	4	17	3
18	9	18	8	18	8	18	7	18	6	18	8	18	7	18	7	18	6	18	6	18	5	18	4
19	10	19	9	19	9	19	8	19	7	19	9	19	8	19	8	19	7	19	7	19	6	19	5
20	11	20	10	20	10	20	9	20	8	20	10	20	9	20	9	20	8	20	8	20	7	20	6
21	12	21	11	21	11	21	10	21	9	21	11	21	10	21	10	21	9	21	9	21	8	21	7
22	13	22	12	22	12	22	11	22	10	22	12	22	11	22	11	22	10	22	10	22	9	22	8
23	14	23	13	23	13	23	12	23	11	23	13	23	12	23	12	23	11	23	11	23	10	23	9
24	15	24	14	24	14	24	13	24	12	24	14	24	13	24	13	24	12	24	12	24	11	24	10
25	16	25	15	25	15	25	14	25	13	25	15	25	14	25	14	25	13	25	13	25	12	25	11
26	17	26	16	26	16	26	15	26	14	26	16	26	15	26	15	26	14	26	14	26	13	26	12
27	18	27	17	27	17	27	16	27	15	27	17	27	16	27	16	27	15	27	15	27	14	27	13
28	19	28	18	28	18	28	17	28	16	28	18	28	17	28	17	28	16	28	16	28	15	28	14
29	20	29	19	29	19	29	18	29	17	29	19	29	18	29	18	29	17	29	17	29	16	29	15
30	21	30	20	30	20	30	19	30	18	30	20	30	19	30	19	30	18	30	18	30	17	30	16

Note: Five 'complementary days' (equivalent to 17–21 September) were set aside for republican festivals. As a result of leap years, correspondence with the Gregorian calendar varies in some years after 1793–4.

Bibliography

The following pages are not intended to be an exhaustive bibliography of the French Revolution – an undertaking which in any case becomes increasingly problematical as the years pass. Nevertheless I wished to provide the reader with a carefully thought-out list of articles and books which have furthered my own work, chapter by chapter, and I hope that this acknowledgement of my debt of gratitude may also serve as a guide to students.

I THE ANCIEN RÉGIME

This chapter is an introduction to the revolutionary crisis. Rather than attempting to provide a complete description of old French society and the old monarchy, I have sought to explain the factors in their radical negation by the *tabula rasa* of 1789.

On the concept of the *ancien régime*, as developed by the Revolution to designate a past that it totally rejected:

VENTURINO, Diego, 'La Naissance de l'Ancien Régime', in *The French Revolution and the Creation of Modern Political Culture*, vol. 2: *The Political Culture of the French Revolution*, ed. Colin Lucas, Oxford, Pergamon Press, 1988.

FURET, François, 'L'Ancien Régime' in *Dictionnaire critique de la Révolution française*, Paris, Flammarion, 1988 (English translation, François Furet and Mona Ozouf (eds), *Critical Dictionary of the French Revolution*, Cambridge, Mass., Harvard University Press, 1990).

On the *ancien régime*, and the relationship of continuity-discontinuity that links it to the French Revolution, the decisive work, to which this book owes much of its intellectual structure, remains that of:

TOCQUEVILLE, Alexis de, *L'Ancien Régime et la Révolution française* (1856), in *Oeuvres complètes* (18 vols, part II, vols 1 and 2 (for de Tocqueville's fragments and unpublished notes on the Revolution), Paris, Gallimard, 1952, 1953 (reissued in coll. 'Folio Histoire', 1987) (English translation, *Old Régime and the French Revolution*, Doubleday, 1955).

See also:

TAINE, Hippolyte, *Les Origines de la France contemporaine* (1876–96), reissued Paris, Robert Laffont, coll. 'Bouquins' (part I: *L'Ancien Régime–La Révolution*;

part II: *La Révolution–Le Régime moderne*) (English translation, *The Origins of Contempory France*, University of Chicago Press, 1978.

GOUBERT, Pierre, *L'Ancien Régime*, 2 vols (vol. 1, *La Société*; vol. 2, *Les Pouvoirs*. The second volume is more particularly concerned with the cohesion between society and the state), Paris, Armand Colin, coll. 'U', 1969–73.

FURET, François, *Penser la Révolution française*, Paris, Gallimard, coll. 'Folio Histoire', 1978 (English transl. *Interpreting the French Revolution*, Cambridge University Press, 1981).

On the spirit that presided over the formation of the absolute monarchy, the two most important philosophical works seem to me to be:

BODIN, Jean, *Les Six Livres de la République (1576)*, 6 vols, Paris, Fayard (Corpus des oeuvres de philosophie en langue française), 1986.

BOSSUET, Jacques-Bénigne, *Politique tirée des propres paroles de l'Ecriture Sainte (1709)*; reissued Geneva, Droz, 1967.

On institutions:

LEMAIRE, André, *Les Lois fondamentales de la monarchie française d'après les théoriciens de l'Ancien Régime*, Paris, 1907; reissued Geneva, Slatkine, 1975.

MOUSNIER, Roland, *Les Institutions de la France sous la monarchie absolue, 1598–1689*, Paris, PUF, 1974–80.

ANTOINE, Michel, 'La Monarchie absolue', in *The French Revolution and the Creation of Modern Political Culture*, vol. 1, *The Political Culture of the Old Regime*, ed. Keith Michael Baker, Oxford, Pergamon Press, 1987.

On the functioning of those institutions in the eighteenth century:

ANTOINE, Michel, *Le Conseil du Roi sous le règne de Louis XV*, Paris and Geneva, Librairie Droz, 1970.

On the constant reworking of aristocratic society by the absolute monarchy's sale of offices and titles, the best author is an American historian, David Bien: 'Offices, Corps and a System of State Credit: The Uses of Privilege under the Ancien Régime', in *The French Revolution and the Creation of the Old Regime*. This article is essential for an understanding of *ancien régime* society. See also 'La Réaction aristocratique avant 1789: l'exemple de l'armée', *Annales ESC* (1974). See also:

BOSSENGA, Gail, 'From "Corps" to Citizenship: the "Bureaux des Finances" before the French Revolution', *Journal of Modern History* (September 1986).

On the nobility and its relations with the rest of society:

MEYER, Jean, *La Noblesse bretonne au XVIIIe siècle*, 2 vols, Paris, 1966; reissued Flammarion, 1972.

FORSTER, Robert, *The Nobility of Toulouse in the Eighteenth Century*, Baltimore, 1960.

TAYLOR, George, 'Non-Capitalist Wealth and the Origins of the French Revolution', *American Historical Review*, (1967).

COBBAN, Alfred, *The Social Interpretation of the French Revolution*, Cambridge University Press, 1968.

LUCAS, Colin, 'Nobles, Bourgeois and the Origins of the French Revolution', *Past and Present*, 60 (1973).

CHAUSSINAND-NOGARET, Guy, *La Noblesse française au XVIIIe siècle, de la Féodalité aux Lumières*, Paris, Hachette, 1976; reissued Brussels, Ed. Complexe, 1984.

On the parlements and their conflicts with the monarchy in the eighteenth century, see:

FLAMMERMONT, Jules, *Remontrances du Parlement de Paris au XVIIIe siècle*, 3 vols, Paris, Imprimerie Nationale, 1888–9; reissued in facsimile, Geneva, Megariotis, 1974.

On institutions:

DOYLE, William, *The Parlement of Bordeaux and the End of the Old Regime, 1771–1790*, New York, St Martin's Press, 1974.

BLUCHE, François, *Les Magistrats du Parlement de Paris, 1715–1771*, Paris, Economica, 1986.

On the conflict:

EGRET, Jean, *Louis XV et l'opposition parlementaire*, Paris, Armand Colin, 1970.

DOYLE, William, 'The Parlements of France and the Breakdown of the Old Regime, 1771–1788', *French Historical Studies* (1970).

On the ideas for which the conflict served as a vehicle, the principal work, absurdly unrecognized today, is:

CARCASSONNE, Elie, *Montesquieu et le problème de la Constitution française au XVIIIe siècle*, Paris, 1927; reissued in facsimile, Geneva, Slatkine, 1970.

See also:

BICKART, R., *Les Parlements et la notion de souveraineté nationale au XVIIIe siècle*, Paris, F. Alcan, 1934.

RICHET, Denis 'Autour des origines idéologiques lointaines de la Révolution française: élites et despotisme', *Annales ESC* (1969).

VAN KLEY, Dale, *The Jansenists and the Expulsion of the Jesuits from France, 1757–1785*, New Haven and London, Yale University Press, 1975.

On the financial crisis of the French monarchy in the eighteenth century, the best introduction is still Necker's *L'Administration des finances de la France*, which came out in 1784 vols 4 and 5 of the *Oeuvres Complètes*, 15 vols, Darmstadt, Scientia Verlag Aalen, 1970 reprinted from the Paris edn, 1820).

Two recent important articles:

MORINEAU, Michel, 'Budgets de l'Etat et gestion des finances royales au XVIIIe siècle', *Revue Historique* (1980).

GUERY, Alain, 'Le Roi dépensier: le don, la contrainte, et l'origine du système financier de la monarchie française d'Ancien Régime', *Annales ESC* (1984).

Lastly, an excellent book:

BOSHER, John Francis, *French Finances, 1770–1795, from Business to Bureaucracy*, Cambridge University Press, 1970.

On the philosophy of the Enlightenment and its influence on the mores and minds of the French in the eighteenth century, there can be no substitute for turning to the authors themselves, both major and minor, in every genre: treatises, essays, history, economics, novels and correspondence. I will not even attempt here to broach the vast literature engendered by the movement of ideas and the great authors over the last two centuries, but I would like to mention that the best synthesis remains:

CASSIRER Ernst, *The Philosophy of the Enlightenment*, Princeton University Press, 1951 (published in 1932 in Tübingen as *Die Philosophie der Aufklärung*).

For half a century, historians have paid particular attention to the circulation of ideas in society. See, for example:

MORNET, Daniel, *Les Origines intellectuelles de la Révolution française, 1715–1789*, Paris, Armand Colin, 1933, 6th edn 1967.

GROETHUYSEN, Bernard, *Les Origines de l'esprit bourgeois en France*, Paris, Gallimard, coll. 'Tel', 1977.

ROCHE, Daniel, *Le Siècle des Lumières en province, académies et académiciens provinciaux, 1680–1789*, 2 vols, Paris and The Hague, Mouton, and École des Hautes Etudes en Sciences Sociales, *Civilisation et Sociétés*, 62 (1978).

TUCOO-CHALA, Suzanne, *Charles-Joseph Panckoucke et la librairie française, 1736–1798*, Paris, Pau Marrimpouey Jeune, 1977.

DARNTON, Robert, *The Business of Enlightenment, A Publishing History of the Encyclopedie, 1775–1800*, Cambridge, Mass., Harvard University Press, 1979.

DARNTON, Robert, *The Literary Underground of the Old Regime Enlightenment*, Cambridge, Mass., Harvard University Press 1982.

For a grasp of the general elements of the relationship between the ideas of the Enlightenment and the French Revolution, two very old works, almost contemporaneous with the event, remain useful:

MOUNIER, Jean-Joseph, *De l'influence attribuée aux philosophes, aux francs-maçons et aux illuminés sur la Révolution de France*; Tübingen, J. G. Cotta, 1801.

PORTALIS, Jean-Étienne Marie, *De l'usage et de l'abus de l'esprit philosophique durant le XVIIIe siècle*, 2 vols, Paris, A. Egron, 1820. The second edition contains also an *Essai sur l'origine, l'histoire et le progrès de la littérature française et de la philosophie* (Paris, Moutardier, 1827, 3rd edn 1834). (Tocqueville, in dealing with this problem, borrows part of his analysis from Portalis.)

A recent collection of articles from the last ten years focuses on the penetration of the Enlightenment's ideas into the political culture of the Ancien Régime:

BAKER, Keith, *Inventing the French Revolution. Essays on French Political Culture in the Eighteenth Century*, Cambridge University Press, 1990.

A more recent study can be found in Furet and Ozouf, *Critical Dictionary*. See the articles 'Montesquieu' and 'Rousseau' (by Bernard Manin), 'Voltaire' (by Mona Ozouf), 'Physiocrats' (by Pierre Rosanvallon), 'Enlightenment' (by Bronislaw Baczko).

Below are some of the most useful works on the different political episodes discussed in this chapter.

On Maupeou's reform, see:
ANTOINE, Michel, *Louis XV*, Paris, Fayard, 1989.

On Turgot's ministry:
FAURE, Edgar, *La Disgrâce de Turgot, 12 mai 1776*, Paris, Gallimard, coll. 'Trente journées qui ont fait la France', 1961.

On Necker:
EGRET, Jean, *Necker, ministre de Louis XV (1776–1790)*, Paris, Champion, 1975.

Lastly, on Louis XVI and Marie-Antoinette:
GIRAULT DE COURSAC, Pierrette, *L'Education d'un roi: Louis XVI*, Paris, Gallimard, 1972.

BLUCHE, François, *La Vie quotidienne au temps de Louis XVI*, Paris, Hachette, 1980.

MADAME DE CAMPAN, Jeanne Louise Henriette, *Mémoires sur la vie de Marie-*

Antoinette, Paris, Firmin-Didot, 1879.

Madame de Campan: première femme de chambre de Marie-Antoinette, Paris, Mercure de France, coll. 'Le Temps retrouvé', 1988.

THOMAS, Chantal, 'L'Héroïne du crime: Marie-Antoinette dans les pamphlets', in Jean-Claude Bonnet, *La Carmagnole des muses. L'homme de lettres et l'artiste dans la Révolution*, Paris, Armand Colin, 1988.

2 THE REVOLUTION OF 1789

General histories of the Revolution

MICHELET, Jules, *Histoire de la Révolution*, 7 vols, Paris, Chamerot, 1847–53; ed. Gérard Walter, 2 vols, Paris, Gallimard, La Pléiade, 1976–7. (This work remains the cornerstone of all revolutionary historiography and is also a literary monument.) Also available in Éditions Robert Laffont, coll. 'Bouquins', vol. 1, books I–VII; vol. 2, books VIII–XXI, 1979 (English translation, *History of the French Relovution*, University of Chicago Press, 1967).

TAINE, Hippolyte, *Les Origines de la France contemporaine*. (This is the greatest counter-revolutionary historical work. English translation, *The Origins of Contempory France*, University of Chicago Press, 1978).

JAURÈS, Jean, *Histoire socialiste de la Révolution française*, (1901–4); ed. J. Rouff, 10 vols, Paris, n.d.; ed. A. Mathiez, 8 vols, Paris, Librairie de l'Humanité, 1922–4; ed. A. Soboul and E. Labrousse, 7 vols, Paris, Messidor/Ed. Sociales, 1968–73. (A classic social history of the Revolution, combined with an assiduous political and parliamentary history.)

LEFEBVRE, Georges, *La Révolution française*, Paris, PUF, coll. 'Peuples et Civilisations', 1951, reissued 1980. (A historian of Jacobin inspiration, Georges Lefebvre, is the great twentieth-century specialist in the history of the French Revolution, and the man with the most complete and reliable information on the subject. English translation, *The French Revolution*, New York, Columbia University Press, 1970).

PALMER, Robert R., *The Age of the Democratic Revolution. A Political History of Europe and America, 1760–1800*, 2 vols, Princeton University Press, 1959–64. (An excellent setting of the French Revolution in an international perspective, intelligent and informed.)

Apart from these general works, the reader who is interested in more recent debate on the interpretation of the French Revolution may like to consult:

COBBAN, Alfred, *The Social Interpretation of the French Revolution*.

FURET, François, *Penser la Révolution française*, Paris, Gallimard, coll. 'Folio Histoire', 1978 (English translation, *Interpreting the French Revolution*, Cambridge University Press, 1981).

On the pre-Revolutionary years 1787–9, sometimes called the 'pre-Revolution', the best available synthesis is that of

DOYLE, William, *Origins of the French Revolution*, Oxford University Press, 1980.

See also:

COCHIN, Augustin, *Les Sociétés de pensée et la Révolution en Bretagne (1788–1789)*, 2 vols, Paris, Plon, 1928.

EGRET, Jean, *La Pré-Révolution française, 1787–1789*, Paris, PUF, 1969; reissued Geneva, Slatkine reprints, 1978.

EGRET, J. *La Révolution des notables. Mounier et les Monarchiens 1789*, Paris, Armand Colin, 1950.

GRUDER, Vivian, *Class and Politics in the Revolution: the Assembly of French Notables of 1787*, in Ernst Hinrichs, Eberhard Schmitt and Rudolf Vierhaus, *Vom Ancien Regime zur Französischen Revolution Forschungen und Perspektiven*, Vandenhoeck and Ruprecht, 1978.

On the convocation and meeting of the Estates General, the fundamental documentary work is by

BRETTE, Armand, *Recueil de documents relatifs à la Convocation des Etats généraux de 1789*, 4 vols, Paris, Imprimerie nationale, 1894–1915.

See also:

COCHIN, Augustin, *La Campagne électorale de 1789 en Bourgogne*, Paris, Champion, 1904.

HALÉVI, Ran, 'Etats généraux' in Furet and Ozouf, *Critical Dictionary*.

FURET François, 'La monarchie et le règlement électoral de 1789', and Ran Halévi, 'La Monarchie et les élections: position des problèmes', in *The French Revolution and the Creation of Modern Political Culture*, vol. 2, *The Political Culture of the Old Regime*, ed. K. M. Baker; and Furet and Ozouf, *Critical Dictionary*.

The great events of the year 1789 may be approached by way of a vast contempory literature, in which there are two categories of works. The first is composed of accounts by witnesses and participants of what took place at Versailles and in Paris. Among the most interesting are:

YOUNG, Arthur, *Travels during the Years 1787, 1788 and 1789*, New York, AMS Press (reprint of 1794 edn).

MORRIS, Gouverneur, *Diary and Letters of Governeur Morris*, Jersey City, Da Capo (reprint of 1888 edn, American Public Figures Series).

LAMETH, Alexandre, Comte de, *Histoire de l'Assemblée Constituante*, 2 vols, Paris, Moutardier, 1828–9.

DUQUESNOY, Adrien-Cyprien, *Journal d'Adrien Dusquesnoy, député du Tiers-Etat de Bar-le-Duc, sur l'Assemblée Constituante, 3 mai 1789–3 avril 1790*, ed. Robert de Crèvecoeur, 2 vols, Paris, Picard et fils, 1894.

FERRIÈRES, Charles Elie, Marquis de, *Mémoires du marquis de Ferrières, avec une notice sur sa vie*, 3 vols, Paris, Baudouin fils, 1821.

BAILLY, Jean Sylvain, *Mémoires*, 3 vols, Paris, Baudouin fils, 1821–2.

Lastly, particular mention must be made of the memoirs of the Swiss

DUMONT, Etienne, *Souvenirs sur Mirabeau et sur les deux premières assemblées législatives*, a posthumous work, ed. J. L. Duval, Paris, C. Gosselin, 1832. (This is a fundamental work for knowledge of the debates in the Constituent Assembly.)

The second category contains works which are more directly linked with the debates and new political matters at stake: newspapers, pamphlets, speeches. The various political writings of Emmanuel-Joseph Sieyès have recently been edited, unfortunately without critical apparatus, by Dorigny Marcel (EDHIS): the reader will find there Sieyès's three fundamental pamphlets of autumn–winter 1788–9: the 'Essay on privilege', 'Views on the means of action available to the representatives of France in 1789', and the famous 'What is the Third Estate?' (the last is also published by Droz, 1970, and PUF, coll. 'Quadrige', 1982). There is no better introduction to the events of 1789 than these three pieces of writing.

On Sieyès:

BASTIDE, Pierre, *Sieyès et sa pensée*, Paris, Hachette, 1970; Geneva, Slatkine, 1978.
BREDIN, Jean-Denis, *Sieyès, la clef de la Révolution française*, Paris, Ed. de Fallois, 1988.

Two articles specifically devoted to Sieyès's political thinking:

CLAVREUIL, Colette, 'Qu'est-ce que le Tiers-Etat?', in François Chatelet, Olivier Duhamel and Evelyne Pisier, *Dictionnaire des Oeuvres politiques*, Paris, PUF, 1986.
BAKER, Keith, 'Sieyès', in Furet and Ozouf, *Critical Dictionary*.

An anthology of speeches and supporting memoirs of the other great leaders of opinion in 1789:

FURET, François, and Ran Halévi, *Orateurs de la Révolution française*, vol. 1, *Les Constituants*, Paris, Gallimard, La Pléiade, 1989. (My recommendation would be to give priority to reading Mounier and Lally-Tollendal for the *Monarchiens*, Mirabeau and Sieyès for the Patriots.)

Lastly, as essential reading, two great witnesses of the era on the year 1789: the celebrated *Reflections on the Revolution in France* by Edmund Burke, published at the end of 1790 (available in Penguin Classics), and a *Histoire de la Révolution française*, written in 1795 by Jacques Necker during his Coppet exile, in *Oeuvres complètes* repr. from the Paris edn of 1820 (Darmstadt, Scientia Verlag Aalen, 1970; *De la Révolution française*, vols 9 and 10). The first is the great source from which all criticisms of the great French event drew sustenance. The second offers a detailed account and a profound analysis of the chain of circumstances which wove together the year 1789, by one of the principal actors in the drama.

On the main stages in the development of the Revolution, in 1789, the following books and articles are important.

On the composition of the Constituent Assembly:

LEMAY, Edna-Hindie, 'La composition de l'Assemblée Nationale Constituante: les hommes de la continuité?', *Revue d'histoire moderne et contemporaine*, 16 (July–September 1977).

On 14 July 1789:

GODECHOT, Jacques, *La Prise de la Bastille: 14 juillet 1789*, Paris, Gallimard, coll. 'Trente journées qui ont fait la France', 1965.

On the rural uprising:

LEFEBVRE Georges, *La Grande Peur de 1789*, Paris, Armand Colin, 1932; reissued (with *Les Foules révolutionnaires*) 1988 (English translation, *The Great Fear of 1789*, New York, Schocken, 1989).

On the night of 4 August, the best analysis is to be found in:

JAURÈS, Jean, *Histoire socialiste de la Révolution française*, vol. 1, ch. 3, 'Journées révolutionnaires', pp. 393ff. in the Messidor/Ed. Sociales edition, 1968–73.

Also read

FURET, François, 'The Night of 4 August', in Furet and Ozouf, *Critical Dictionary*.

The Declaration of the Rights of Man: the subject has recently been freshly dealt with by

GAUCHET, Marcel, *La Révolution des Droits de l'homme*, Paris, Gallimard, 1989.

On the decisive constitutional debates of August–September 1789, the two great Chambers and the right of veto, see the following articles:

'Sieyès', 'Constitution', 'Sovereignty' by Keith Baker. 'Monarchiens' by Ran Halévi and 'Mirabeau' by François Furet, in Furet and Ozouf, *Critical Dictionary*.

On the colonial question:

JAURÈS, Jean, *Histoire socialiste de la Révolution française*, vol. 2, ch. 4, 'Le mouvement économique et social en 1792 – la question coloniale'.

The central political question which dominated the entire history of the Constituent Assembly was that of the monarchy, the keystone of the *ancien régime*, destroyed and yet preserved as a power subordinate to the new Assembly. The *Monarchiens* were unable, in August–September 1789, to win a more active role for it, and the *journées* in October 1789 confirm *de facto* the purely theoretical nature of the suspensive right of veto granted to the king in September. Mirabeau afterwards vainly devoted his efforts to the reinstatement of the principle of monarchic authority within the Revolution. The most interesting work on this period is Mirabeau's secret correspondence with the Comte de la Marck:

MIRABEAU, *Correspondance entre le Comte de Mirabeau et le Comte de la Marck*, ed. A. de Bacourt, 3 vols, Paris, Librairie Vve Le Normant, 1831; ed. Chaussinand-Nogaret, *Mirabeau entre le roi et la Révolution: notes à la Cour et discours*, Paris, Hachette, coll. 'Pluriel', 1986.

On religious matters and the Civil Constitution of the Clergy, one may begin with a study of how Church possessions and property were placed at the nation's disposal, with the articles 'Biens nationaux' by Louis Bergeron and 'Assignats' by Michel Bruguière, in Furet and Ozouf, *Critical Dictionary*.

On the religious question: the book which best enables one to understand to what extent it formed the philosophical and political heart of the revolutionary enigma, is that of

QUINET, Edgar, *Le Christianisme et la Révolution française* (1846), reissued Paris, Fayard, 1984.

See also:

MATHIEZ, Albert, *Rome et le clergé français sous la Constituante*, Paris, Armand Colin, 1911.

LA GORCE, Pierre de, *Histoire religieuse de la Révolution française*, 2 vols, Paris, Hachette, 1946–50.

TACKETT, Timothy, *Religion, Revolution and Regional Culture in Eighteenth-Century France: The Ecclesiastical Wrath of 1791*, Princeton University Press, 1985.

VAN KLEY, Dale, 'The Jansenist. Constitutional Legacy in the French Pre-Revolution', *Historical Reflections*, 13 (1986).

Varennes and the revision of the constitution: a good introduction to the period of the Constituent Assembly is given by the speeches and posthumously collected writings of Barnave, who was both its politician and philosopher. For Barnave the politician, see Furet and Halévi, *Orateurs de la Révolution française*. For Barnave the philosopher, see Barnave, *Oeuvres*, ed. Bérenger de la Drôme, 4 vols (1843), chiefly the first two sections. See the reissue, arranged and annotated by Patrice

Gueniffey, entitled *La Révolution et de la Constituante* (Presses Universitaires de Grenoble, 1983). Another work essential to an understanding of this period:
MICHON, Georges, *Essai sur l'histoire du parti feuillant, Adrien Duport*, Paris, Payot, 1924.

On Barnave and Duport, see Furet and Ozouf, *Critical Dictionary*, the articles 'Barnave' by François Furet and 'Feuillants' by Ran Halévi.

On the activities of the Constituent Assembly in general and the Constitution of 1791, the most important work for an understanding of the constitutional thinking of the Constituent and the absolute sovereignty of the law, the principle established by the representatives of the people, is that of the great lawyer:
CARRÉ DE MALBERG, Raymond, *Contribution à la théorie générale de l'Etat*, 2 vols, Paris, Sirey, 1920–2; reissued Paris, CNRS, 1962.
CARRÉ DE MALBERG, Raymond, *La Loi, expression de la volonté générale*, Paris, Sirey, 1931; reissued Economica, 1984.

Another legal contribution to the study of the same matter, from a different angle, belongs to:
DUCLOS, Pierre, *La Notion de Constitution dans l'oeuvre de l'Assemblée Constituante de 1789*, Paris, Dalloz, 1934.

See also:
TROPER, Michel, *La Séparation des pouvoirs et l'histoire constitutionnelle française*, Paris, LGDJ, Bibliothèque Constitutionnelle et de Science Politique, 1973, reissued 1980.

Among all the Constituent Assembly's measures which might be called indivisibly social, economic and financial, the sale of the Church's possessions, followed by the creation of the assignat and its rapid transformation into paper money, had the most far-reaching consequences.

Michelet is the most constant commentator on the transfer of property which was effected to the benefit of the bourgeois and peasant through the alienation of the Church's estates. He continually underlines its primary role in the marriage between the Revolution and the new landowners (books III–X of *Histoire de la Révolution française*).

On the financial policies in which the Constituent Assembly became engulfed in 1790, the conscious choice of inflation as a means of financing public expenditure and the social and political consequences it brought about, there is a good general clarification in a recent book:
AFTALION, Florin, *L'Economie de la Révolution française*, Paris, Hachette, coll. 'Pluriel', 1987.

On the management of public finances in general during the Revolution there is very little, but recently an excellent work has appeared by:
BRUGUIÈRE, Michel, *Gestionnaires et profiteurs de la Révolution. L'administration des finances françaises de Louis XVI à Bonaparte*, Paris, Olivier Orban, 1986.

3 THE JACOBIN REPUBLIC

Perhaps the best way to approach this 'heroic' period of the Revolution, which has fed so many passions and debates, is through works that evoke the atmosphere of the times either directly, through contemporaneous writings and speeches, or indirectly through memoirs published later, chiefly under the Restoration, by active participants. In the first category, I would recommend above all the speeches of Brissot and Vergniaud on the war in autumn and winter 1791–2, those concerning the trial of the king between November 1792 and January 1793, the presentation by Condorcet of his democratic constitution (February 1793), and of course Robespierre's great interventions in the Convention, mainly in autumn and winter 1793–4. References are given below. As for the second group of sources, the authenticity of which must always be verified instance by instance (certain so-called 'memoirs' having been largely rewritten), I would give priority to the following authors:

THIBAUDEAU, Antoine Claire, Comte de, *Mémoires, 1799–1815*, Paris, Plon, Nourrit, 1913.

MADAME ROLAND, *Mémoires de Madame Roland*, Paris, Mercure de France, coll. 'Le Temps retrouvé', 1966 (English translation, *The Private Memoirs of Madame Roland*, New York, AMS Press, repr. of 1901 edn, Women of Letters Series). A shortened version appeared in 1795 under the title *Appel à l'impartiale portérité*; ed. Champagneux in 1800 under the title *Oeuvres de M. J. Ph. Roland*; ed. Berville and Barrière in 1820 in the *Collection des mémoires relatifs à la Révolution française*. Madame Roland's manuscripts were properly studied in 1864 for the edition by Dauban and Faugère. In 1905 Claude Perrous published the *Mémoires de Madame Roland* in a critical edition.

BUZOT, François, *Mémoires sur la Révolution*, Paris, Béchet aîné, 1923; reissued Pichon and Didier, 1928.

PÉTION, Jérôme, François BUZOT and Charles-Dauban BARBAROUX, *Mémoires inédits de Pétion*, followed by memoirs of Buzot and Barbaroux and previously unpublished notes by Buzot, Paris, Plon, 1866.

LA RÉVELLIÈRE-LÉPEAUX, Louis-Marie, *Mémoires*, 3 vols, Paris, Plon, Nourrit, 1895.

NODIER, Charles, *Souvenirs, épisodes et portraits pour servir à l'histoire de la Révolution française et de l'Empire*, Paris, A. Levassour, 1831; reissued as *Souvenirs de la Révolution et de l'Empire*, 2 vols, Paris, Charpentier, 1850; reissued as *Souvenirs et portraits de la Révolution et de l'Empire*, 2 vols, Paris, Tallandier, coll. 'Intexte', 1988. (These volumes by Nodier are perhaps the most valuable item in the immense literature of French Revolution memoirs.)

Of all the revolutionary Assemblies, the Legislative is the poor relation. It sat for one short year, driven out by the popular rising which brought down the throne and took away both its *raison d'être* and its authority. Wedged between the two formidable bodies of the Constituent Assembly and the Convention, it had no chance of competing with either its predecessor or its successor. Nevertheless, it played a major role in the march towards war and the radicalization of the Revolution. To understand that one need only compare the last two months of the Constituent Assembly, which were marked by Feuillant stabilization, and the first two of the Legislative (October and November 1791), when the spirit of revolutionary excess, flourished by Brissot and his friends, broke out again in full force. I tried to make sense of that contrast in a talk given to a Symposium on the Girondins held at Saint-Emilion (April 1990). The secret lies broadly in the elections of summer 1791: on this subject see the major contribution made by Patrick Gueniffey's thesis devoted to the 1791 and 1792 elections, and defended in 1989 at the Ecole des Hautes Etudes en Sciences Sociales (to appear in 1991).

On the war which began in April 1792 between the Revolution and the Habsburgs, to be extended to much of Europe in the following year, there is the admirable work of

SOREL, Albert, *L'Europe et la Révolution française*, 9 vols, Paris, Plon, Nourrit, 1903–6 (which highlights the continuity of the Revolution's foreign policy and that of the Bourbons).

An old book by the German historian Henri von Sybel should also be consulted (4 vols, Düsseldorf, 1853–1870; French translation, *Histoire de l'Europe pendant la Révolution française*, 3 vols, Paris, Germer Baillière, 1869–1875). This work is more quoted than read by French historians, but remains a monument of erudition and intelligence comparable to Sorel's, but more sensitive to the novelty of the revolutionary phenomenon.

On the declaration of war of 20 April 1792, and the Girondins' political responsibilities in it, the best analysis is that of Jaurès, in vol. 2 of *Histoire socialiste de la Révolution française*, ch. 2, 'La Guerre ou la paix'. The socialist historian explains how the war, for Brissot and his friends, was a manoeuvre of internal politics, intended to bring them to power against the Feuillants, taking the risk that the throne might fall.

On 10 August 1792, the temporary dictatorship of the Paris Commune, the first Terror and the threats of September, the meeting of the Convention, the most detailed account of the circumstances of 10 August remains

MATHIEZ, Albert, *Le 10 Août, 1792*, Paris, 1931; reissued Montreuil, Ed. de la Passion, 1989.

A work may be added with a general bearing on the sociology of the great Parisian *journées* during the Revolution:

RUDÉ, Georges, *The Crowd in the French Revolution*, Oxford University Press, 1959.

On the Paris commune, a very old book still speaks with authority:

BRAESCH, Frédéric, *La Commune du 10 Août 1792. Étude sur l'histoire de Paris du 20 juin au 2 décembre 1792*, Paris 1911; reissued Geneva, Mégariotis Reprints, 1978.

On the massacres of September 1792 in the Paris prisons, the classic work is:

CARON, Pierre, *Les Massacres de Septembre*, Paris, Maison du Livre Français, 1935.

As a complement, in the evaluation of responsibility and complicity:

Bluche, Frédéric, *Septembre 1792: les logiques d'un massacre*, Paris, Robert Laffont, 1986.

The Convention elected in August met in September 1792. There is a *Dictionnaire des Conventionnels* by Auguste Kuscinski (Paris, Rieder, 1916), a work posthumously published under the aegis of Aulard (reissued Breuil-en-Vexin, Éd. du Vexin Français, 1973).

On the political composition of the new assembly, the best work available is that of

PATRICK, Alison, *The Men of the French First Republic: Political Alignments in the National Convention of 1792*, Baltimore, Johns Hopkins University Press, 1972.

In fact, the Convention immediately became the arena of conflict between the Girondins and Montagnards: the main body of the Assembly, its centre, which was known as the Plaine, was the arbiter between the two groups.

Nineteenth-century historiography, which was still linked to events by oral history, never really closely examined the social and political reality of the Girondin/Montagnard dichotomy. Twentieth-century historiography, when written under the influence of Marxism as in France, desperately tried to trace a line of class, or sub-class, between the two groups, but was never convincing; there is testimony to these vain efforts is the 1975 Symposium, *Girondins and Montagnards*, the Proceedings of which were edited by Albert Soboul (Paris, Société des Etudes Robespierristes, 1980).

For its part, English-language historiography has for a quarter of a century been questioning the validity of the very idea of 'Girondin' and 'Montagnard' groups. Doubt was cast by Michael J. Sydenham, *The Girondins*, (1961; reissued, London, Greenwood, 1973). Alison Patrick, in the book cited above, measured the growing coherence of the group from the six roll-calls which took place in the Convention between the king's trial and the re-establishment of the Commission of the Twelve: she concluded that there was an evident distinction between a fairly amorphous 'Plaine' and a 'Girondin' minority.

A recent article, the work of three American historians, slightly modifies Alison Patrick's conclusions, showing that a true coherence of Girondin votes cannot be spoken of before spring 1793, that is to say, on the eve of defeat: 'Was There a Girondist Faction in the National Convention (1792–1793)?', *French Historical Studies*, 15 (Spring 1988), no. 3, by Michael S. Lewis, Anne Hildreth and Alan B. Spitzer.

As for the problems and positions which separated Girondins and Montagnards, the best synthesis is provided by two articles by Mona Ozouf, in Furet and Ozouf, *Critical Dictionary*.

On the king's trial, the central event of the Revolution but little studied by twentieth-century historians, the two essential authors who explore the implications of the head-on confrontation between the monarchy and the Convention are:

MICHELET, Jules, *Histoire de la Révolution française*, book X.

JAURÈS, Jean, *Histoire socialiste de la Révolution française*, vol. 5, *La Mort du roi et la chute de la Gironde*, ch. 2, 'Le Procès du roi'.

On the progress of the trial itself and the difficulty in counting the different votes at the moment of judgement, see:

JORDAN, David, *The King's Trial: Louis XVI vs the French Revolution*, Berkeley, University of California Press, 1979.

PATRICK, Alison, *Men of the First Republic*.

WALZER, Michael, *Regicide and Revolution: Speeches at the Trial of Louis XVI*, Cambridge, 1974 (French translation by J. Debouzy, under the title *Régicide et Révolution: le procès de Louis XVI*, followed by *Discours au procès de Louis XVI*, translated by A. Kupiec, Paris, Payot, 1989).

This work contains the main speeches given in the Convention concerning the king's trial, preceded by a long introduction. In the French edition, the book's epilogue is a discussion between M. Walzer and F. Feher; the American political scientist defends the idea that the trial was conducted with the maximum legality compatible with the political situation, whereas the Hungarian philosopher who took refuge in the US sees in it a precursor of the Terror.

On the crisis of summer 1793, the best overall picture can be found in Georges Lefebvre's course on 'Le Gouvernement revolutionnaire', duplicated copies from

Centre de Documentation Universitaire, Paris, 1947.

There is only one scholarly work devoted to the *journées* of 31 May and 2 June 1793:

SLAVIN, Morris, *The Making of an Insurrection. Parisian Sections and the Gironde*, Cambridge, Mass. Harvard University Press, 1986.

But it is in Michelet (*Histoire de la Révolution française*, book X) and Jaurès (*Histoire socialiste de la Révolution française*, vol. 5, ch. 10, 'La Révolution de 31 mai et 2 juin 1793') that the most detailed account and the most profound analysis of the purge of the Convention are to be found.

On the origins of the war in the Vendée a vast literature exists, both old and recent, caught up for many years in the long survival of memories of the civil war into the nineteenth and twentieth centuries. The reader may begin with one of the latest books on the matter, by Jean Clément Martin, *La Vendée et la France* (Paris, Le Seuil, coll. 'L'Univers historique', 1987), and also the synthesis which I have tried to make of the question in the article 'Vendée' in Furet and Ozouf, *Critical Dictionary*. The 'white' and 'blue' historiographies of the Vendée have long been as divided as the two sides whose incompatible glories they celebrated. Now, at the end of the twentieth century, such confrontations have lost a little of their intensity and the ideas which fed them have altered; Jean Clément Martin's work is one of the signs of this, as is Alain Gerard's *Pourquoi la Vendée* (Paris, Armand Colin, 1990).

On the counter-revolutionary episode in Lyon beginning in May 1793, see the excellent book by

HERRIOT, Edouard, *Lyon n'est plus*, 4 vols, Paris, Hachette, 1937–8.

On what has been called the 'federalist' crisis following the expulsion of the Girondins, the Montagnard dictatorship and the revolutionary government, much study has been devoted to the schism between Girondins and Montagnards from the angle of social conditions: the temporary alliance between Montagnards and sansculottes was sealed by the exclusion of the Girondins. The Montagne was not without an ulterior motive in forming this alliance with the militants of the Parisian sections.

Since the Second World War this has been one of the most exhaustively researched subjects, with a profusion of works and articles. I will limit myself to three principal authors who are all, each in his own way, very significant:

GUÉRIN, Daniel, *La Lutte des classes sous la Première République: bourgeois et bras nus (1793–1797)*, Paris, Gallimard, 1946; reissued, 2 vols, 1968; abridged version under the title *Bourgeois et bras nus (1793–1797)*, Gallimard, coll. 'Idées', 1973. Left-wing interpretation of the French Revolution, with Robespierre as a 'bourgeois' centrist.

SOBOUL, Albert, *Les sans-culottes parisiens en l'an II: mouvement populaire et gouvernement révolutionnaire, 2 juin 1793–9 thermidor an II*, Paris, Clavreuil, 1958 (English translation, *The Parisian Sans-Culottes and the French Revolution*, London, Greenwood, 1979, repr. of 1964 edn). Social and political interpretation of the alliance between Montagnard bourgeoisie and Parisian lower classes, under Robespierre's leadership.

COBB, Richard, The *Police and the People: French Popular Protest 1789–1820*, Oxford University Press, 1970. This work contains a critism of the concept of a sansculotte 'movement' in favour of a more individualistic conception of social marginality.

We must not forget the work that made the above ones possible by raising the question of the relationship between economic regulation and popular movement:
MATHIEZ, Albert, *La Vie chère et le mouvement social sous la Terreur*, 2 vols, Paris, Payot, 1927, reissued 1973.

The institution of the revolutionary government: the substitution of a *de facto* government for the Montagnard constitution hastily assembled by Hérault de Séchelles in June was effected in two major stages (March–April, and July/September 1793), from the creation of the Committee of Public Safety to putting the Terror on the agenda.
PALMER, Robert R., *Twelve who Ruled: The Committee of Public Safety During the Terror*, Princeton University Press, 1941, a work which gives a good account of the largely improvised nature of the revolutionary government.

For the chronology of the process, see Georges Lefebvre's duplicated course, quoted above, and my article 'Gouvernement révolutionnaire', in Furet and Ozouf, *Critical Dictionary*. Finally read Robespierre's great speech to the Convention on 25 December 1793; it is the philosophic manifesto of the revolutionary government. The speech is reproduced notably in
ROBESPIERRE, Maximilien de, *Discours*, Paris, UGE, 10/18, reissued 1988.

Jacobinism and the Terror: the dictatorial nature of the revolutionary government was not merely or exclusively the product of a defensive reaction in the face of danger, but also the manifestation of a potentiality of the French Revolution's political culture. Not that the Terror was a necessity built into the principles of 1789; but the undeniably exceptional circumstances of 1793 inflamed ideas and passions that were not compatible with the establishment of political liberty. For a general discussion of this interpretation, the reader may refer to my articles 'Jacobinism' and 'Terror', in Furet and Ozouf, *Critical Dictionary*.

The first line of analysis consists of looking behind the revolutionary dictatorship to the authority of orthodoxy wielded on a national scale by the Jacobin Club. On this point, the two major authors are:
MICHELET, Jules, *Histoire de la Révolution française*, book X.
COCHIN, Augustin, *Les Sociétés de pensée et la démocratie*, Études d'histoire révolutionnaire, Paris, Plon, 1931.

One may add:
BRINTON, Crane, *The Jacobins: An Essay in the New History*, New York, Macmillan, 1930.
JAUME, Lucien, *Le Discours jacobin et la démocratie*, Paris, Fayard, 1989.

On the Terror properly speaking, there is a lack of case studies, for instance on the revolutionary Tribunal in Paris, or the punitive action of particular representatives on mission, or the massive executions without trial, as in Lyon or the Vendée. We must also distinguish between the period before and the period after the centralization of the Terror in Paris, from April 1794. One of the best analyses of the revolutionary Terror is to be found in
QUINET, Edgar, *La Révolution*, Paris, 1865 (books XVI and XVII); reissued Paris, Belin, 1987.

In modern scholarship, a classic work:
COBB, Richard, *Les Armées révolutionnaires, instrument de Terreur dans les départements: avril 1793–floréal an II*, 2 vols, Paris, EHESS, and Mouton de

Gruyter, 1961 (English translation, *The People's Armies*, New Haven, Yale University Press, 1987).

A good recent monograph:

LUCAS, Colin, *The Structure of the Terror: The Example of Javogues and the Loire*, London, Oxford University Press, 1973.

A study, also recent, of the mass repression in the Vendée between January and May 1794:

SECHER, Reynald, *Le Génocide franco-français: La Vendée-vengé*, Paris, PUF, 1986.

A statistical study of those sentenced to death under the Terror:

GREER, Donald, *The Incidence of the Terror During the French Revolution: A Statistical Interpretation*, Cambridge, Mass., Harvard University Press, 1935.

Robespierre's dictatorship: in order to understand Robespierre's domination over the course of the Revolution which, between April and July 1794, he exercised alone, it is essential to read his great speeches.

Robespierre's works have been the subject of several editions: Laponneraye (3 vols, 1840), Vellay (1910) and, after the departure of Vellay, the edition continued by the Société des Etudes Robespierristes.

Robespierre's great speeches may be found either in vol. 10 of his *Oeuvres complètes*, (ed. Bouloiseau and Soboul, 1967), containing the speeches from 27 July 1793 to 27 July 1794; or, more easily, in the three volumes of *Textes choisis*, (ed. Jean Poperen, Paris, Éditions Sociales, coll. 'Les Classiques du peuple', 1974).

French biographies of Robespierre are spoilt by hagiography, such as *Robespierre* by Ernest Hamel (Ledrappier, 1987); *Robespierre* by Jean Massin (Paris, Livre Club Diderot, 1956; reissued Aix-en-Provence, Alinéa, 1988); and *Robespierre* by Gérard Walter, 2 vols (1936–40; reissued Paris, Gallimard, 1961).

I would suggest:

THOMPSON, J. M., *Robespierre*, 2 vols, Oxford, Basil Blackwell, 1935.

JORDAN, David P., *The Revolutionary Career of Maximilien Robespierre*, New York, Free Press, 1985.

See also the article 'Robespierre' by Patrice Gueniffey, in Furet and Ozouf, *Critical Dictionary*.

On the battle of the factions, the elimination of the Hébertists and the Dantonists by Robespierre, there is a vast scholarly twentieth-century century literature, frequently polemical, since the subject revives the old Aulard–Mathiez debate between Dantonists and Robespierrists. Georges Lefebvre acted as arbiter, in his courses and his work on *La Révolution française*, (PUF, coll. 'Peuples et Civilisations', 1951, reissued 1980). There is no doubt that Danton was not the model of patriotic virtue described by Aulard, but his execution, quite unconnected with the passion for morality in Robespierre celebrated by Mathiez, was motivated by Robespierre's hunger for power.

On the problems of the dechristianization advocated by the sansculottes in autumn 1793, the sharp check given by Robespierre and the revolutionary cults that were to replace Catholicism, the reader may begin with Michelet *Histoire de la Révolution française*, book V (*La Religion*) and book XVI (*La Religion sous la Terreur*), which blame the Revolution for its timidity in the affair. See also Aulard and Mathiez:

AULARD, Alphonse, *Le Culte de la Raison et de l'Etre suprême, 1793–1794*, Paris, F. Alcan, 1892.

MATHIEZ, Albert, *La Révolution et l'Eglise*, Paris, Colin, 1910.

MATHIEZ, A., *Origines des cultes révolutionnaires: 1789–1792*, Paris, Société Nouvelle de Librairie et d'Edition, 1904.

One of the mysteries of this period is the worsening of the Terror by the law of 22 prairial (10 June), two days after the Festival of the Supreme Being. There is no convincing work or article on this mystery. The epoch of the Great Terror has not yet found its historian.

On 9 Thermidor, and the growing isolation of Robespierre since the last fortnight in June, there is an evocative book:

Ollivier, Albert, *Le Dix-huit Brumaire, 9 novembre 1799*, Paris, Gallimard, 1959.

4 THE THERMIDORIAN REPUBLIC

With the downfall of Robespierre began the period when the despotic and egalitarian Revolution stopped its rush forward, and the movements of civil society became visible again. The ideas of 1789 spawned a simultaneous system of private interests and a fund of contradictory memories and passions: all this was almost impossible to manage, and was supplemented by the logic of war and conquest, personified from 1796 in the glory of a young general.

It was in this era that the most profound commentators and the best observers of the French Revolution made their appearance.

In the first group, I would pick out two intellectual families: firstly that of the inaugurators of the liberals' great debate on the mixed nature of revolutionary events, the contrast between the principles of 1789 and the terrorist drift of 1793: foremost, Benjamin Constant and Madame de Staël, whose detailed works written between 1795 and 1799 are still fundamental.

CONSTANT DE REBECQUE, Benjamin de, *Lettres à un député de la Convention*, published in *Nouvelles politiques, nationales et étrangères, juin 1795 (Messidor an III)*, collected in *Recueil d'articles 1795–1817*, Geneva, Droz, 1972, 1978, 1980.

CONSTANT, B., *De la force du gouvernement actuel de la France et de la nécessité de s'y rallier*, no place, 1796.

CONSTANT, B., *Des réactions politiques*, n.p., Year V (1797); 2nd edn with *L'Examen des effets de la Terreur added*, n.p., Year V.

Certain of Benjamin Constant's writings under the Directory were first published by Olivier Pozzo di Borgo under the title *Ecrits et discours politiques*, (2 vols, Paris, Pauvert, 1964) (English translation, *Political Writings*, Cambridge University Press, 1988).

Recently reissued writings: *De la force du gouvernement actuel de la France with Des réactions politiques*, and *Des effets de la Terreur*, (Paris, Flammarion, coll. 'Champs', 1988), preface and notes by Philippe Raynaud.

STAËL, Germaine de, *Réflexions sur la paix adressées à M. Pitt et aux Français*, no place or publisher, 1795.

STAËL, G. de, *Réflexions sur la paix intérieure*, published anonymously.

STAËL, G. de, *De l'influence des passions sur le bonheur des individus et des nations*, Lausanne, Mourer, Hignon, 1796; 2nd edn, Paris, Dufart, 1797, Desenne, 1797.

STAËL, G. de, *Des circonstances actuelles qui peuvent terminer la Révolution et des principes qui doivent fonder la République en France* (written in 1798 but unpublished at the time), Paris, Fishbacher, 1906; reissued Geneva and Paris, Droz, 1979.

Roederer (notably his contributions to the *Journal d'Économie Publique*) and Lezay-Marnesia, may also be added:

ROEDERER, Pierre-Louis, *De l'usage à faire de l'autorité publique dans les circonstances présentes*, with a *Traité de l'émigration*, Paris, Desenne, Year V.

ROEDERER, P.-L. DE *Mémoires sur quelques points d'économie publique*, read at the Lycée in 1800 and 1801, Paris, Firmin-Didot, 1840. See also his *Oeuvres*, 8 vols, Paris, Firmin-Didot, 1853–9.

LEZAY-MARNESIA, Adrien, *Des Causes de la Révolution et de ses résultats*, Paris, Desenne, 1797.

LEZAY-MARNESIA, A., *De la faiblesse d'un gouvernement qui commence, et de la nécessité òu il est de se rallier à la majorité nationale*, Paris, B. Mathey, Year VI.

There is a German book on Adrien Lezay-Marnesia:

WESTERHOLT, Egon Graf von, *Lezay-Marnesia, Sohn der Aufklärung und Präfekt Napoléons (1769–1814)*, Meisenheim am Glan, Hain, 1958.

Lastly, on all the debates between liberals under the Directory, the reader may refer to the articles 'Constant' and 'Staël' by Marcel Gauchet in Furet and Ozouf, *Critical Dictionary*.

The second intellectual family embraces the first great French counter-revolutionary authors:

MALLET DU PAN, Jacques, *Considérations sur la nature de la Révolution française et sur les causes qui en prolongent la durée*, Brussels, Plon, 1793.

MALLET DU PAN, J., *Correspondance inédite de Mallet du Pan avec la cour de Vienne (1794–1798)*, 2 vols, Paris, Plon, Nourrit, 1884.

MALLET DU PAN, J., *Correspondance politique pour servir à l'histoire du républicanisme française*, Hamburg, P. F. Fauche, 1796.

MALLET DU PAN, J., *Mémoires et Correspondance pour servir à l'histoire de la Révolution française*, 2 vols, Paris, Amyot and Cherbuliez, 1851.

MALLET DU PAN, J., *Mémoires* (extracts), Paris, M. Gautier, 1894.

MAISTRE, Joseph de, *Considérations sur la France*, Neuchâtel, 1796, and London, Fauche-Borel, 1797. See *Oeuvres complètes*, 7 vols (14 parts), part I, Geneva, Slatkine Reprints, 1979, repr. from the edn of Vitte and Perrussel, Lyon, Librairie Générale Catholique et Classique, 1884–6. *Considérations sur la France*, followed by *Essai sur le principe générateur des constitutions politiques*, reissued Brussels, Ed. Complexe, 1988.

BONALD, Louis de, *Théorie du pouvoir politique et religieux dans la société civile, démontrée par le raisonnement et par l'histoire, par M. de B., gentilhomme français*, published anonymously, 3 vols, Konstanz, 1796. See vols 12–15 of *Oeuvres complètes*, 15 vols-in-9, Geneva, Slatkine, 1982, repr. from the Paris edn, Librairie d'Adrien Le Clerc 1817–43.

BONALD, Louis de, *Essai analytique sur la loi naturelle de l'ordre social*, published in 1797; reissued 1801 under the title *Essai analytique sur la loi naturelle ou Du pouvoir, du ministre et du sujet*. See *Oeuvres complètes*, vols 1 and 2.

Lastly, a look at memoirs of the period is essential, especially

MOLÉ, Comte, *Souvenirs d'un témoin de la Révolution et de l'Empire: Mathieu, comte Molé 1791–1803*, ed. Marquise de Noailles, Geneva, Ed. Milieu du monde,

1943; see also Marquis de Noailles, *Le Comte Molé, 1781–1855, sa vie, ses mémoires*, 6 vols, Paris, Champion, 1922–30.

PASQUIER, Etienne-Denis, Chancellor, *Histoire de mon temps. Mémoires du chancelier Pasquier*, ed. Duc d'Audiffret Pasquier, 6 vols, Paris, Plon, 1893–5. (Vols 1–3 are concerned with the Revolution, the Consulate and the Empire, vols 4–6 with the Restoration.)

BARRAS, Paul, *Mémoires de Barras, membre du Directoire*, ed. G. Duruy, 4 vols, Paris, Hachette, 1895–6.

CHASTENAY, Comtesse Victorine de (or Madame de), *Mémoires 1771–1815*, ed. A. Roserot, 2 vols, Paris, Plon, Nourrit, 1896.

LA TOUR DU PIN, Henriette-Lucie, Marquise de, *Journal d'une femme de cinquante ans (1778–1815)*, edited by her great-grandson, Colonel Comte Aymar de Liederkerke-Beaufort, 4 vols, Paris, Imprimerie de R Chapelot, 1907–11.

LA RÉVELLIÉRE-LÉPEAUX, Louis-Marie, *Mémoires*.

DELÉCLUZE, Étienne-Jean, *Louis David et son temps*, Paris, Didier, 1855; reissued Macula, 1983.

SAND, George, *Histoire de ma vie*, 20 vols, Paris, V. Lecou, 1854–5 (English translation, *Story of My Life: The Autobiography of George Sand*, State University of New York Press, 1991, Woman Writers in Translation Series); reissued Michel-Lévy frères, 1856; recent reissues: Paris Stock, 1985; and Gallimard, La Pléiade, 1970–1: *Oeuvres autobiographiques*, 2 vols (vol. 1, *Histoire d'une famille, de Fontenoy à Marengo – Mes premières années, 1800–1819 – De l'enfance à la jeunesse, 1810–1819*; vol. 2, *Du mysticisme à l'indépendance, 1810–1822 – Vie littéraire et intime, 1832–1850*).

Memoirs by émigrés:

FRENILLY, Auguste-Francois, *Mémoires: 1768–1848. Souvenirs d'un ultra-royaliste*, reissued Paris, Librairie Académique Perrin, 1987.

MONTLOSIER, Comte de, *Souvenirs d'un émigré, 1791–1798*, ed. Comte de Montlosier-Larouzière and Ernest d'Hauterive, Paris, Hachette, 1951.

ESPINCHAL, Comte d', *Journal d'Emigration*, ed. Ernest d'Hauterive, Paris, Perrin, 1912.

FABBRY, Abbé de, *Mémoires de mon émigration*, Paris, Champion, 1933.

BLONDIN DE SAINT-HILAIRE, *Onze Ans d'émigration. Mémoires du chevalier Blondin d'Abaucourt, adjutant major des gardes-suisses*, Paris, 1897.

General Histories of the period:

LEFEBVRE, Georges, *Les Thermidoriens*, Paris, Armand Colin, 1937.

LEFEBVRE, Georges, *Le Directoire*, Paris, Armand Colin, 1946.

SCIOUT, Ludovic, *Le Directoire*, 4 vols, Paris, Firmin-Didot, 1895–7.

MATHIEZ, Albert, *Le Directoire du II Brumaire an IV au 18 Fructidor an V*, Paris, Armand Colin, 1934.

FURET, François and Denis Richet, *La Révolution française*, vol. 2, Paris, Hachette, 1966; reissued Fayard, 1973, Hachette-Pluriel, 1986.

One may read more specifically on the crises that punctuated the entire political history of the period:

MEYNIER, Albert, *Les coups d'État du Directoire*, 3 vols, Paris, Presses Universitaires de France, 1927–8 (vol. 1, *Le Dix-huit Fructidor an V*; vol. 2, *Le Vingt-deux Floréal an VI (11 mai 1798) et le Trente Prairial an VII (18 juin 1799)*; vol. 3, *Le Dix-huit Brumaire an VIII (9 novembre 1799) et la fin de la République*).

SURATTEAU, Jean-René, 'Les Opérations de l'assemblée électorale de France (4 Brumaire an IV–octobre 1795)', *AHRF* (*Annales historiques de la Révolution française*) (1955).

SURATTEAU, J.-R., 'Les elections de l'an V aux Conseils du Directoire', *AHRF* (1955).

On 13 Vendémiaire Year IV:

ZIVY, H., *Le 13 Vendemiaire an IV*, Paris, 1898, fasc. 6 de la Bibliothèque de la Facultédes Lettres de l'Université de Paris.

On Babeuf and Babvouvism, there is an immense communist-inspired literature, very repetitive and already very dated. It is preferable to refer to the book that founded the Babouvist tradition:

BUONARROTI, Philippe, *Conspiration de l'Égalité dite de Babeuf*, followed by the trial to which it gave rise and its written evidence, etc., 2 vols, Paris, 1828; reissued Paris, Editions Sociales, 1957.

There is also a recent interesting article by an American historian on the Parisian sociology of Babouvism:

ANDREWS, Richard M., 'Réflexions sur la conjuration des Egaux', *Annales ESC* (1974).

On 18 Fructidor, Year V:

BALLOT, Charles, *Le coup d'État du 18 Fructidor: rapports de police et documents divers*, Paris, Société de l'Histoire de la Révolution Française, 1900.

MATHIEZ, Albert. 'Saint-Simon, Lauraguais, Barras, Benjamin Constant et la réforme de la constitution de l'an III après le coup d'État du 18 Fructidor an V', *AHRF* (1929).

On the coups d'état of 22 Floréal Year VI and 30 Prairial Year VII, see:

MEYNIER, Albert, *Les Coups d'Etat*, vol. 2.

On 18 Brumaire Year VIII:

VANDAL, Albert, *L'Avènement de Bonaparte*, vol. 1, *La Genèse du Consulat. Brumaire. La Constitution de l'an VIII*, Paris, Plon, Nourrit, 1902.

BAINVILLE, Jacques, *Le 18 Brumaire*, Paris, Hachette, 1925.

I would also advise a reading of several recent works on the political culture of the era, notably on the tyranny exercised over men's minds by memories of the Convention and the Terror:

OZOUF, Mona, 'Thermidor ou le travail de l'oubli', in *L'Ecole de la France, essais sur la Révolution, l'utopie et l'enseignement*, Paris, Gallimard, coll. 'Bibliothèque des distoires', 1984.

BACZKO, Bronislaw, *Comment sortir de la Terreur: Thermidor et la Rèvolution*, Paris, Gallimard, coll. 'Essais', 1989.

WOLLOCK, Isser, *Jacobin Legacy, The Democratic Movement under the Directory*, Princeton University Press, 1970.

An old but important book on the emigration:

DAUDET, Ernest, *Histoire de l'émigration pendant la Révolution française*, vol. 3, *Les Emigrés et la seconde coalition, 1797–1800*, Paris, Librairie Illustrée, 1886–90.

A collection of documents necessary for a feel for the state of public opinion:

AULARD, Alphonse, *Paris pendant la réaction thermidorienne et sous le Directoire*, 5 vols, Paris, Le Cerf, 1898–1902.

On the Italian campaign:

GUYOT, Raymond, *Le Directoire et la paix de l'Europe des traités de Bâle à la deuxième coalition (1795–1799)*, Paris, F. Alcan, 1911.

FERRERO, Guglielmo, *Aventure, Bonaparte en Italie* (1796–1797), Paris, Plon, 1936.

REINHARD, Marcel, *Avec Bonaparte en Italie, d'après les lettres inédites de son aide de camp, Joseph Sulkowski*, Paris, Hachette, 1946.

GODECHOT, Jacques, *Les Commissaires aux armées sous le Directoire. Contribution à l'étude des rapports entre les pouvoirs civils et militaires*, 2 vols, Paris, Fustier, 1938.

BONAPARTE, Napoléon, *Lettres à Joséphine, pendant la première campagne d'Italie, le Consulat et l'Empire*, Paris, Firmin-Didot, 1833.

BONAPARTE, Napoléon, *Lettres de Napoléon à Joséphine et lettres de Joséphine à Napoléon*, Paris, Le Livre Club du Libraire, 1959.

BONAPARTE, Napoléon, *Napoléon et Joséphine, leur roman*, complete edn. Numerous unpublished letters from Napoleon to Josephine, collected by Jean Savant, Paris, Fayard, 1960.

BONAPARTE, Napoléon, *Lettres de Napoléon à Joséphine et de Joséphine à Napoléon*, complete edn, ed. J. Haumont, Paris, J. de Bonnot, 1968.

5 NAPOLEON BONAPARTE

The best approach to this period of history, dominated and even personified by one man alone, is to begin by reading Napoleon's own writings which portray him far better than any commentary. These are mostly military or government papers, or things recorded by his close associates; for example, they may be found in:

Vie de Napoléon par lui-même, d'après les textes, lettres, proclamations, écrits, Paris, Gallimard, 1930.

NAPOLÉON BONAPARTE, *Proclamations, ordres du jour, bulletins de la Grande Armée*, Paris, UGE, 10/18, 1964. Also consult Napoleon's *Correspondance*, published at the instigation of Napoleon III, 32 vols, Paris, Imprimerie Impériale 1858–69.

The second category of sources is formed by contemporary witnesses, quite numerous, as it happens. I would cite:

ABRANTÈS, Joséphine Amet, Duchesse d', *Mémoires ou souvenirs historiques sur Napoléon*, 18 vols, Paris, Ladvocat, 1831–5; reissued, 10 vols, Garnier frères, 1893.

BARANTE, Amable, Baron de, *Souvenirs*, 8 vols, Paris, 1890–1901 (see vols 1 and 2).

BOURRIENNE, Louis Antoine Fauvelet de, *Mémoires sur Napoléon, le Directoire, le Consulat et la Restauration*, 10 vols, Paris, 1829–31; reissued, 4 vols, Garnier frères, 1899.

BEUGNOT, Jacques Claude, Comte de, *Mémoires du comte Beugnot, ancien ministre (1783–1815)*, 2 vols, Paris, E. Dentu, 1866.

CHASTENAY, Comtesse Victorine de (or Madame de), *Mémoires, 1771–1815*, ed. A. Roserot, 2 vols, Paris, Plon, Nourrit, 1896.

HYDE DE NEUVILLE, Jean Guillaume, Baron, *Mémoires et souvenirs*, ed. Madame de Sardonnet, 3 vols, Paris, 1888–92.

MIOT DE MELITO, André François, Comte de, *Mémoires du Comte Miot de Melito, ancien ministre, ambassadeur, conseiller d'Etat et membre de l'Institut (1788–1815)*, 3 vols, Paris, Michel-Lévy frères, 1858.

PASQUIER, Etienne-Denis, Chancelier, *Histoire de mon temps. Mémoires du chancelier Pasquier*, ed. Duc d'Audiffret-Pasquier, 6 vols, Paris, Plon, 1893–5.

PELET DE LA LOZÈRE, Comte Privat Joseph, *Opinions de Napoléon sur divers sujets de politique et d'administration, recueillies par un membre de son conseil d'État*, Paris, Firmin-Didot frères, 1833.

SAVARY, René, Duc de Rovigo, *Mémoires pour servir a l'histoire de Napoléon*, 8 vols, Paris, A. Bossangre, 1828; reissued 4 vols, Garnier frères, 1900.

TALLEYRAND-PÈRIGORD, Charles-Maurice, Duc de, *Mémoires du prince de Talleyrand*, ed. Duc de Broglie, 5 vols, Paris, Calmann-Lévy, 1891–2; ed. Paul-Louis Couchoud, 2 vols, Paris, Plon, 1957 (English translation, *Memoirs of the Prince de Tallyrand*, New York, AMS Press, repr. of 1892 edn).

SÈGUR, Philippe, Comte de, *Histoire et mémoires*, 7 vols, Paris Firmin-Didot, 1873.

The third category of written documents to which priority should be given is the vast literature of portraits of Napoleon. Here is one very selective list in chronological order:

STAËL, Madame de, *Mémoires de Mme de Stael, Dix années d'exil*, ed. Duc de Broglie and Baron de Staël, Paris, 1818; reissued Charpentier, 1861; Plon, Nourrit, 1904.

STENDHAL (Henri Beyle), *Vie de Napoléon*, Paris, Calmann-Lévy, 1876; reissued Payot, 'Petite Bibliothèque Payot', 1969 (English translation, *Napoleon*, ed. Ernest Abravanel and Victor Del Litto, 2 vols, New York, French and European, 1970).

CHATEAUBRIAND, François-René, Vicomte de, *Mémoires d'outre-tombe, La Presse* (Paris), 1848–50; 12 vols, Paris, Penaud frères, 1849; reissued, 6 vols, Paris, Dufour, Mulat and Boulanger, 1860; Paris, Garnier frères, 1895; ed. Edmond Bire, 1899–1900; ed. Levaillant in the Flammarion centenary edn. Recent editions include: Gallimard, La Pléiade, 1947, 1951 (vol. 1, books I–XXIV; vol. 2, books XXV–XLIV). Also in paperback, 3 vols, Livre de poche.

TAINE, Hippolyte, *Les Origines de la France contemporaine (1876–1896)*, reissued Paris, Robert Laffont, coll. 'Bouquins' 2 vols (vol. 1, *L'Ancien Régime–La Révolution*; vol. 2, *La Révolution–Le Régime moderne*. See *Le Régime moderne*, ch. 1 devoted to Napoléon Bonaparte.)

FAURE, Elie, *Napoléon*, Paris, CRES, 1921.

Finally, though of lower literary quality, there is the fundamental work:

MASSON, Frédéric, *Napoléon et sa famille*, 13 vols, Paris, Ollendorf, 1897–1919.

General works:

BAINVILLE, Jacques, *Napoléon*, Paris, Fayard, 1931.

This is still the most brilliant synthesis on the man and his deeds.

LEFEBVRE, Georges, *Napoléon*, Paris, PUF., coll. 'Peuples et Civilisations', 1935; reissued 1947, 1965 (English translation Napoleon, 2 vols, New York, Columbia University Press, 1990).

MARKHAM, Felix, *Napoleon*, London, Weidenfeld and Nicolson, 1963.

TULARD, Jean, *Napoléon ou le mythe de sauveur*, Paris, Fayard, 1977; reissued Hachette, 'Pluriel', 1988.

TULARD, J., *Napoléon à Sainte-Hélène*, Paris, R. Laffont, coll. 'Bouquins', 1981.

TULARD, J., *Napoléon et la noblesse d'Empire*, with a list of members of the imperial nobility (1808–15), Paris, Tallendier, 1986.

MISTLER, Jean, *Napoléon et l'Empire*, 2 vols, Paris, Hachette, 1968.

Imperial France. On the ideas used as a basis for the legitimacy of the regime, the most significant author is:

FIÉVÉE, Joseph, *Correspondance et relations de J. Fiévée avec Bonaparte (1802 à 1813)*, 3 vols, Paris, A. Desrez, 1836.

On the civil legislation:

FENET, P. Antoine, *Recueil complet des travaux préparatoires du Code civil*, 15 vols, Paris, 1827; reissued Paris, Videcoq. 1836.

SAGNAC, Philippe, *La Législation civile de la Révolution française (1784–1840), essai d'histoire sociale*, Paris, Hachette, 1898.

GOY, J., 'Code civil', in Furet and Ozouf, *Critical Dictionary*, which may be used as an introduction to these studies.

On the government and administration:

PONTEIL, Félix, *Napoléon Ier et l'organisation autoritaire de la France*, Paris, Armand Colin, 1956.

DURAND, Charles, *L'exercice de la fonction législative de 1800 à 1814, Annales de la Faculté de Droit d'Aix-en-Provence* (1958).

THUILLIER, G., 'L'administration vue par un préfet de l'Empire', *La Revue administrative* (1955).

TULARD, Jean, *Paris et son administration (1800–1830)*, Paris, Ville de Paris, Commission des Travaux Historiques, 1976.

On the coronation, an excellent work:

CABANIS, José, *Le Sacre de Napoléon (2 décembre 1804)*, Paris, Gallimard, 1970.

On the Concordat and the temporary settling of relations between the Catholic Church and post-revolutionary society:

DANSETTE, Adrien, *Histoire religieuse de la France contemporaine*, Paris, Flammarion, 1948, vol. I.

LEFLON, Jean, *E. A. Bernier, évêque d'Orléans, et l'application du Concordat*, 2 vols, Paris, Plon, 1938.

DELACROIX, Simon, *La réorganisation de l'Église de France après le Concordat (1801–1809)*, Paris, Ed. du Vitrail, 1962.

GODEL, Jean, *Histoire religieuse du départment de l'Isère. La reconstruction concordataire dans le diocèse de Grenoble après la Révolution (1802–1809)*, La Tronche, the author, 1968.

LANGLOIS, Claude, *Le diocèse de Vannes (1800–1830)*, Rennes Université, Klincksieck, 1974.

On the social foundations of the imperial regime:

BERGERON, Louis and Guy CHAUSSINAND-NOGARET, *Les Collèges électoraux du Premier Empire*, Paris, CNRS, 1978.

TULARD, Jean, 'Les composantes d'une fortune: le cas de la noblesse d'Empire', *Revue historique* (1975).

VALYNSEELE, Joseph, *Les maréchaux du Premier Empire, leur famille et leur descendance*, Paris, the author, 1957.

VALYNSEELE, J., *Les Princes et ducs du Premier Empire, non-maréchaux, leur famille et leur descendance*, Paris, the author, 1959.

France's foreign policy and dominance in Europe: because I wished to concentrate on France's domestic policy, I have left this major aspect of Napoleonic history aside. The pages devoted to it draw their principal inspiration from the following works:

SOREL, Albert, *L'Europe et la Révolution française*, vols 5–8.

LEFEBVRE, Georges, *La Révolution française*.

The reader will find a systematic bibliography in

GODECHOT, Jacques, *L'Europe et l'Amérique à l'époque napoléonienne*, Paris, PUF., coll. 'Nouvelle Clio', 1967.

6 THE RESTORATION

Twenty-five years after the Revolution, twenty-one years after the execution of Louis XVI, the return of the Bourbons to the throne of their ancestors proved to be a risk-ridden undertaking, from Napoleon's Hundred Days to the Three Glorious Days in 1830. However, the monarchy which had come back was not a form of absolutism, but both a more reactionary and a more liberal regime, in which France underwent its long-delayed apprenticeship in parliamentary government. It was then that the groupings of intellect and opinion arose which would dominate the century and even beyond.

Literary and politico-literary sources

France in 1814, or rather 1815, suddenly deprived of the awesome role of scout-soldier of universal history, once more became a supremely literary country, obsessed with reinvesting its glory in fathoming its past and the future in store. Thence arose the importance of romantic literature in understanding this period. Nobody conveys that spirit better than Stendhal, notably in what are called his *Oeuvres intimes*, Chateaubriand in the *Mémoires d'outre-tombe* (from book XXV) or Musset in the *Confession d'un enfant du siècle*:

STENDHAL (Henri Beyle), *Oeuvres intimes*, 2 vols, Paris, Gallimard, La Pléiade, 1982 (including the *Journal: 1801–1817*, *Souvenirs d'égotisme* and *Vie de Henri Bruland: 1818–1842*). *Souvenirs d'égotisme*, Charpentier and Fasquelle, 1892; *Journal: 1801–1817*, Garnier, 1888; *Vie de Henri Brulard*, Carpentier, 1890 (English translation, *The Life of Henry Brulard*, University of Chicage Press, 1986).

CHATEAUBRIAND, Francois René, *Mémoires d'outre-tombe*, Paris, Gallimard, La Pléiade, 1947, 1951.

MUSSET, Alfred de, *Confession d'un enfant du siècle*, 2 vols, Paris, F. Bonnaire, 1836 (English transl. *The Confession of a Child of the Century*, New York, Fertig, 1977).

The Revolution of 1789 continued to be at the centre of all debates, as is witnessed by a posthumous work (published one year after her death), of Madame de Staël, *Considérations sur les principaux événements de la Révolution française*, (3 vols, Paris, Delaunay, 1818; reissued as *Considérations sur la Révolution française*, Paris, Tallandier, 1983, 1987).

This work is the subject of two criticisms that converge, but from opposite directions. The one on the right:

BONALD, Louis de, *Observations sur l'ouvrage de Madame la baronne de Staël, ayant pour titre: 'Considérations sur les principaux événements de la Révolution française'*, Paris, A. Le Clère, 1818 (see *Oeuvres complètes*, vol. 11).

The other, on the left, written by a former Conventionnel of Girondin tendency:

BAILLEUL, Jacques-Charles, *Examen critique de l'ouvrage posthume de Madame la baronne de Staël, ayant pour titre: 'Considérations sur les principaux événements de la Révolution française'*, 2 vols, Paris, A. Bailleul, 1818.

Apart from that polemic, two classic works signal the appearance of the history, properly speaking, of the French Revolution:

THIERS, Adolphe, *Histoire de la Révolution française, accompagnée d'une histoire de la Révolution de 1355 ou des États généraux sous le roi Jean*, 10 vols, Paris, Lecointe and Durey, 1823–27.

MIGNET, François-Auguste, *Histoire de la Révolution française depuis 1789 jusqu'en 1814*, 2 vols, Paris, Firmin-Didot. 1824.

I have already noted (ch. 3, bibliography) the proliferation, under the Restoration, of memoirs of men of the French Revolution. This can be explained by the extraordinary curiosity of public opinion regarding the event, a curiosity which the return of Louis XVI's brother to the throne heightened rather than extinguished.

On the great intellectual debates of this period, the three essential authors are Bonald, Lamennais and Chateaubriand.

Louis de Bonald, a somewhat forgotten writer, yet fundamental to an understanding of the ultra-royalist party of which he was the principal inspiration (and which, it is too often overlooked, gathered together around 1820–5 the greatest names in romantic literature: Balzac, Hugo, Lamartine, Vigny, etc.)

BONALD, Louis de, *Réflexions sur l'intérêt général de l'Europe, suivies de quelques considérations sur la noblesse*, Paris, Le Normant, 1815.

BONALD, L. de, *Pensées sur divers sujets et discours politiques*, 2 vols, Paris, A. Le Clère, 1817.

BONALD, L. de, *De la Chrétienté et du Christianisme*, Paris, Imprimerie de Lachevardière fils, 1825.

BONALD L. de, *Sur la liberté de la presse*, Paris, Imprimerie de Beaucé-Rusand, 1826.

BONALD, L. de, *De la famille argicole, de la famille industrielle et du droit d'aînesse*, Paris, A. Le Clère, 1827.

There is a good edition of the *Oeuvres complètes de Bonald*, by the Abbé Migne, 3 vols, Paris, 1864.

Félicité Robert de LAMENNAIS is probably the key author for an understanding of the strength of the religious reaction under the Restoration, and also the political ambiguity of that counter-revolutionary Christianity. See his *Essai sur l'indifférence en matière de religion* (Paris, Tournachon-Molin and H. Seguin, 1817), *De la religion considérée dans ses rapports avec l'ordre politique et civil*, part I (Paris, Bureau du 'Mémorial Catholique', 1825); part II (Paris, Bureau du 'Mémorial Catholique', 1826) and *Des Progrès de la Révolution et de la guerre contre l'Église* (Paris, Belin-Mandar and Devaux, 1829).

François René de CHATEAUBRIAND, the greatest writer of the era, and celebrated as such by his contemporaries, was also a profound political thinker, and the uncontrollable maverick of the ultra party. His political writings of the end of the Empire and the Restoration were collected under the title *Mélanges politiques*; they form two volumes (parts XXIV–XXV in the Ladvocat edition of *Oeuvres complètes*, 18 vols, 1826–31). But in existence prior to that were *Mélanges de politique (et opinions et discours)* (2 vols, Paris, Le Normant, 1816).

There is an anthology, in selected extracts, of Chateaubriand's political writings in the book by Jean-Paul Clément, *Chateaubriand politique* (Paris, Hachette, coll. 'Pluriel', 1987).

At the centre of the political and intellectual chessboard are two men and their works: Francois Guizot and Victor Cousin. The second is scarcely readable these days; he did not survive the damning criticism of Taine in *Les Philosophes classiques du XIXe siècle en France* (Paris, Hachette, 1857; reissued Slatkine, 1979), but he enjoyed considerable influence on the young students of the day. Engrossed in the same task, which consisted of reflecting on the post-French Revolution era, Guizot possessed gigantic emergy and multiple talents, being simultaneously a publicist, historian and politician. A good approach to his work is three essays which he wrote at the political turning point of 1820.

GUIZOT, François, *Du gouvernement de la France depuis la Restauration et du ministère actuel*, Paris, Ladvocat, 1820.

GUIZOT, F., *Des moyens de gouvernement et d'opposition dans l'état actuel de la France*, Paris, Ladvocat, 1821.

GUIZOT, F., *De la peine de mort en matière politique*, Paris, Béchet aîné, 1822; reissued (with *Des conspirations et de la justice politique*) Paris, Fayard, coll. 'Corpus des oeuvres de philosophie en langue française', 1984.

From these one might turn to his books on history, which often resulted from his courses at the Sorbonne, for example:

GUIZOT, F., *De l'histoire des origines du gouvernement représentatif en Europe (Cours d'histoire moderne 1820–1822)*, 2 vols, Paris, Didier, 1851.

GUIZOT, F., *Essais sur l'histoire de France . . . pour servir de complément aux 'Observations sur l'histoire de France' de l'abbé de Mably*, Paris, 1823; reissued Ladrange, 1836.

GUIZOT, F., *Histoire générale de la civilisation en Europe depuis la chute de l'Empire romain jusqu'à la Révolution française*, in *Cours d'histoire moderne*, 6 vols, Paris, Pichon et Didier, 1829–32 (including *L'Histoire de la civilisation en France depuis la chute de l'Empire romain jusqu'en 1789*); ed. Pierre Rosanvallon, Paris, Librairie Générale Française, Livre de poche, coll. 'Pluriel', 1985.

Besides Guizot, two other theorists of representative government are of importance. The first is Pierre-Paul Royer-Collard, whose principal speeches are to be found in Prosper de Barante, *La Vie politique de M. Royer-Collard, ses discours et ses écrits* (Paris, Didier, 1851).

The second is Benjamin Constant, whose genius finally found its full political use in the Chamber of Deputies. His main speeches were published under the Restoration (*Discours de M. Benjamin Constant à la Chambre des Députés* 2 vols, Paris, A. Dupont, 1827–8; reissued in the Pléiade edition of Constant's works, Paris, Gallimard, 1957). His *Cours de politique constitutionnelle* can be most easily consulted in the Laboulaye edition (*Cours de politique constitutionnelle ou collection des ouvrages publiés sur le gouvernement représentatif*, 2 vols, Paris, Guillaumin, 1861; reissued Slatkine, 1982); and *De la liberté des Anciens comparée à celle des Modernes*, ed. Marcel Gauchet with an important preface, under the title *De la liberté chez les modernes, écrits politiques de Benjamin Constant* (Paris, Librairie Générale Française, Livre de poche, coll. 'Pluriel', 1980).

Lastly, a special place must be given to the work of the Comte de Saint-Simon and of his disciple and temporary ghost-writer August Comte; socialism and positivism were to fill the twentieth century, in France and abroad, with their powerful echoes.

Claude-Henri de SAINT-SIMON's *Oeuvres*, published in six volumes by Anthropos in 1966, taken from the 47-volume edition of the writings of Saint-Simon and Enfantin (Paris, E. Dentu, 1865–78), were reissued, 6 vols, Slatkine, Geneva, 1978. Note especially: *De la réorganisation de la société européenne*, written in 1814 in collaboration with Augustin Thierry, Anthropos edn, vol. 1; *Du système industriel* (1820–2, Anthropos edn, vol. 3); *Catéchisme des industriels* (1823–4, Anthropos edn, vols 4–5, also containing the *Système de philosophie positive* written by Auguste Comte) (English translation, *Positive Philosophy*, New York, AMS Press, repr. of 1855 edn).

Besides Saint-Simon and the young Auguste Comte, the reader may also take a less philosophical approach to the social question. The Restoration witnessed the development of statistical analysis. Two essential works:

CHAPTAL, Jean Antoine, *De l'industrie française par M. Le Cte Chaptal*, 2 vols, Paris, A. A. Renouard, 1819.

DUPIN, Charles, Baron, *Forces productives et commerciales* de la France, Paris, Bachelier, 1827.

Baron Dupin introduced the comparison between the two Frances (north and south) in regard to social and economic development.

The press

The Restoration newspapers were often of a high political and literary standard. I had recourse to:

Les Archives philosophiques, politiques et littéraires (1817–18), run by Royer-Collard and Guizot.

Le Conservateur (1818–20), Chateaubriand's paper.

La Minerve française (1818–20), inspired by Benjamin Constant.

Le Globe (from 1824), newspaper-manifesto of the young generation, in which Guizot and Cousin, the two intellectual leaders, played a dominant role.

Le Producteur (from 1825), the organ of the Saint-Simonians.

Literary and intellectual history

The following are the works of criticism that I most often consulted on the intellectual movements at the beginning of the nineteenth century:

SAINTE-BEUVE, Charles-Augustin, *Portraits contemporains*, 3 vols, Paris, Didier, 1846.

GOUHIER, Henri, *La Jeunesse d'Auguste Comte et la formation du positivisme*, 3 vols, Paris, Vrin, 1936–41, reissued 1964–70 (vol. 2, *Saint-Simon jusqu'à la Restauration*; vol. 3, *Auguste Comte et Saint-Simon*). An essential work on Saint-Simon as well as on Comte.

BÉNICHOU, Paul, *Le Temps des prophètes, doctrines et l'âge romantique*, Paris, Gallimard, coll. 'Bibliothèque des idées', 1988.

BÉNICHOU, P., *Le Sacre de l'écrivain*, Paris, Jose Corti, 1985.

BÉNICHOU, P., *Les Mages romantiques*, Paris, Gallimard, coll. 'Bibliothèque des idées', 1988. (Bénichou's three books can be regarded as destined to become classics).

POUTHAS, Charles H., *Guizot pendant la Restauration, préparation de l'homme d'État (1814–1830)*, Paris, Plon, 1923.

ROSANVALLON, Pierre, *Le Moment Guizot*, Paris, Gallimard, 'Bibliothèque des sciences humaines', 1985 (the most profound analysis of 'representative government').

GAUCHET, Marcel (ed.), *Philosophie des sciences historiques*, Presses Universitaires de Lille, 1988. This is a collection of writings by Barante, Cousin, Guizot, Michelet, Quinet, Thierry, concerning the birth of history as a science. Also by Marcel Gauchet, on the same subject, is the remarkable commentary on the *Lettres sur l'histoire de France* by Augustin Thierry, in Pierre Nora, *Les Lieux de mémoire*, vol. 2, part I, *La Nation*, (3 vols, Paris, Gallimard, 'Bibliothéque illustrée des histoires', 1986).

MANENT, Pierre, *Les Libéraux*, 2 vols, Pluriel, 1986 (a work essential for comparison of French and British liberal thinking).

Journals and memoirs

Let us begin with the most famous, which was destined to have universal repercussions in French politics and among the French population:

NAPOLEON, I., *Mémorial de Sainte-Hélène*, issued in numerous editions, e.g. *Mémorial de Sainté-Hélène, ou Journal où se trouve consigné, jour par jour, ce qu'a dit et fait Napoléon durant dix-huit mois*, by the comte de Las Cases, 8 vols, Paris, the author, 1823; *Mémorial de Sainte-Hélène*, Paris, dépôt du Mémorial, 1823–4; Lecointe, 1828; 26 vols, Barbezat, 1830–2; 2 vols, Lequien fils, 1835; 2 vols, Bourdin, 1842; Garnier frères, 1851, and others. See also Napoleon's *Correspondance*, vol. 32, *Oeuvres de Napoléon à Sainte-Hélène*.

On the period covering the setting up of the Charter regime, the *Mémoires* of Eugène, Baron de Vitrolles, ed. Pierre Farel (2 vols, Paris, Gallimard, 1950–2) are a fascinating source.

On the Restoration in general, one may enter the epoch's fashionable society through the *Mémoires* of the Comtesse de BOIGNE, née d'Osmond (4 vols, Paris, Plon, 1907). Read also:

FERRAND, Antoine, Comte, *Mémoires*, Paris, Picart et fils, 1897.

VILLELE, Jean-Baptiste, Comte de, *Mémoires et correspondance*, 5 vols, Paris, Perrin, 1888–90.

MOLÉ, Mathieu, Comte, *Mémoires de Mathieu Molé*, ed. A. Champollion-Figeac, 4 vols, Paris, J. Renouard, 1855–7.

BROGLIE, Jacques Victor Albert, Duc de, *Souvenirs: 1785–1870*, 4 vols, Paris, Broglie, 1886.

The last two books also give insight into the following regime, the July Monarchy, in which Broglie and Molé played central roles.

The memoirs of two key characters of the era (and the one which followed) are also very useful:

GUIZOT, François, *Mémoires pour servir à l'histoire de mon temps*, 8 vols, Paris, Michel-Lévy frères, 1858–67.

RÉMUSAT, Charles de, *Mémoires de ma vie*, ed. Charles Pouthas, 5 vols, Paris, Plon, 1958. (This memoir is perhaps the most intelligent account of the vicissitudes of the intellectual and political history of these years, and has the added advantage of going right up to the Third Republic.)

Needless to say, I must complete my list with Chateaubriand's *Mémoires d'outre-tombe*, that incomparable introduction to the variations in the history of France, by the greatest writer of the age.

Political history

General works:

DUVERGIER de HAURANNE, Prosper, *Histoire du gouvernement parlementaire en France, 1814–1848*, 10 vols, Paris, Michel-Lévy frères, 1857–71. Essential for following parliamentary debates.

VAULABELLE, Achille de, *Histoire des deux Restaurations jusqu'à la chute de Charles X en 1830*, preceded by a *Précis historique sur les Bourbons et le parti Royaliste depuis la mort de Louis XVI*, 7 vols, Paris, Perrotin, 1844–54 (or *Histoire des deux Restaurations jusqu'à l'avènement de Louis-Philippe, de janvier 1813 à octobre 1830*, 8 vols, Paris, Perrotin, 1855–6).

POUTHAS, Charles, *Histoire politique de la Restauration*, typed course, Paris, 1947.

BERTIER DE SAUVIGNY, G. de, *La Restauration*, Paris, Flammarion, 1955; completed and reissued 1974 as *Au soir de la monarchie, histoire de la Restauration*.

LA GORCE, Pierre de, *La Restauration, Louis XVIII*, 2 vols, Paris, Plon, 1926.

Works on particular subjects:

BORDET, Gaston, 'Une fête contre-révolutionnaire néo-baroque et ordinaire, la grande mission de Besançon, janvier 1825', in *La Fête: pratique et discours*, *Annales litteraires de l'Université de Besançon*, no. 262 (1982), Paris, Les Belles Lettres.

BORY, Jean-Louis, *La Révolution de Juillet, 29 juillet 1830*, Paris, Gallimard, coll. 'Trente journées qui ont fait la France', 1972.

BRUGIÉRE, Michel, *La Première Restauration et son budget*, Paris, Droz, 1969.

PINKNEY David Henry, *The French Revolution of 1830*, Princeton University Press, 1972.

RÉMOND, René, *La Droite en France de 1815 à nos jours: continuité et diversité d'une tradition politique*, Paris, Aubier, 1954; reissued as *La Droite en France de la Première Restauration à la Ve Republique*, 2 vols, Paris, Aubier, 1963, 1977.

RESNICK, D. P. *The White Terror and the Political Reaction After Waterloo*, Cambridge, Mass., Harvard University Press, 1966.

SEVRIN, E. *Les Missions religieuses en France sous la Restauration: 1815–1830*, 2 vols, Paris, Vrin, 1948–59.

SPITZER, Alan B., *The French Carbonari Against the Bourbon* Restauration, Cambridge, Mass., Harvard University Press, 1971.

SPITZER, A. B., *The French Generation of Eighteen-Twenty*, Princeton University Press, 1987.

7   THE JULY MONARCHY

Often studied as a second version of the constitutional monarchy in France, the July regime was rather a second attempt at post-revolutionary political synthesis, after the failure in 1814–15 of hereditary Bonapartism. To understand what was at stake in the *journées* of 1830, when the *ancien régime* and the Revolution had their final confrontation, it is enough to read Stendhal or Balzac. Among the history books that have recently appeared on this subject one is particularly useful:

RIALS, Stéphane, *Révolution et Contre-Révolution au XIXe siècle*, Paris, Albatros and DUC, 1987.

Literary and politico-literary sources

On the atmosphere of the time in Louis-Philippe's France:

STENDHAL (Henri Beyle), *Mémoires d'un touriste*, Paris, A. Dupont, 1838; reissued, 2 vols, Paris, Michel-Lévy frères, 1854 (English transl. *Memoirs of a Tourist*, Evanston, Northwestern University Press, 1985).

MÉRIMÉE, Prosper, *Correspondance générale*, vols 1–5, Toulouse, Privat, 1941–7 (starting from vol. 7, the remaining 11 vols were published in Paris, Le Divan, to 1964) (English transl. *Correspondence*, New York, French and European, 1941–64).

SAND, George, *Correspondance*, 6 vols, Paris, C. Lévy, 1882–4 (vol. 1, 1812–36; vol. 2, 1836–47; vol. 3, 1840–53; vol. 4, 1854–63; vol. 5, 1864–70; vol. 6, 1870–76); ed. Georges Lubin, Paris, Garnier frères, from 1964 in coll. 'Prestige hors série' and 'Classiques Garnier' (vol. 1, 1812–31 (1964); vol. 2, 1832–June 1835 (1966); vol. 3, July 1835–April 1837 (1967); vol. 4, May 1837–March 1840 (1968); vol. 5, April 1840–December 1842 (1971); vol. 6, 1843–June 1845 (1969); vol. 7, July 1845–June 1847 (1970); vol. 8, July 1847–December 1848 (1971); vol. 9, January 1849–December 1850 (1972); vol. 10, January 1851–March 1852 (1974); vol. 11, April 1852–June 1853 (1976); vol. 12, July 1853–June 1854 (1976); vol. 13, January 1855–June 1856 (1978); vol. 14, July 1856-June 1856 (1979); vol. 15, June 1858–June 1860 (1981); vol. 16, July 1860–March 1862 (1982); vol. 17, April 1862–July 1863 (1983); vol. 18, August 1863–December 1864 (1984); vol. 19, January 1865–May 1866 (1985); vol. 20, June 1866–May 1868 (1985); vol. 21, June 1868–March 1870 (1986); vol. 22, April 1870–March 1872 (1987)).

BLANC, Louis, *Révolution Française. Histoire de dix ans*, 5 vols, Paris, Pagnerre, 1830–40.

The debates over the French Revolution, which I have discussed at length, continued to mount under the July monarchy. Centring upon the Three Glorious Days, they naturally regained a special passion at the beginning of the regime and at its end, when the revolutionary idea reappeared with renewed strength.

BUONARROTI, Filippo or Philippe, *Conspiration pour l'égalité dite de Babeuf, suivie du procès auquel elle donna lieu et des pièces justificatives . . .*, Brussels, Librairie, Romantique, 1828; reissued, 2 vols, Paris, Baudouin frères, 1830. (Although this book dates from before 1830, I quote it here because it inaugurates the long series of works in which the communists or socialists passed beyond the limiting ideas of the Revolution of 1789).

BUCHEZ, Philippe and Pierre Célestin Roux-Lavergne, *Histoire parlementaire de la Révolution française ou Journal des assemblées nationales, depuis 1789 jusqu'en 1815*, 40 vols, Paris, Paulin 1834–38. (This is a fundamental work, because it is both a historiographical crossroad and a testimony to the birth of a Jacobin-Catholic culture in French politics. On Buchez, one can read the book of François-André Isambert, *De la charbonnerie au saint-simonisme* (Paris, Ed. de Minuit, 1966), and also the article I recently devoted to him in Furet and Ozouf, *Critical Dictionary*.)

HUGO, Victor, *Etude sur Mirabeau*, Paris, A. Guyot, 1834.

TOCQUEVILLE, Alexis de, *Etat social et politique de la France avant et depuis 1789*. This is a first version of *L'Ancien Régime*, written in 1836 and intended for an English public, *Oeuvres complètes*, Paris, Gallimard, vol. 2, part II, 1953.

CABET, Etienne, *Histoire populaire de la Révolution française de 1789 à 1830*, 4 vols, Paris, Pagnerre, 1839–40.

BLANC, Louis, *Histoire de la Révolution française*, 12 vols, Paris, Langlois and Leclercq, 1847–62. The first volume of this work, like the first two of Michelet's appeared the year preceding the February revolution.

ESQUIROS, Alphonse, *Histoire des Montagnards*, 2 vols, Paris, V. Lecou, 1847.

LAMARTINE, Alphonse de, *Histoire des Girondins*, 8 vols, Paris, Furne, Coquebert, 1847.

MICHELET Jules, *Du prêtre, de la femme et de la famille*, Paris, Hachette, 1845.

MICHELET, J., *Le Peuple*, Paris, Hachette et Paulin, 1846; ed. Paul Viallaneix, Flammarion, coll. 'Champ', 1979. (These two works are essential to an understanding of how Michelet approached his study of the French Revolution. See also Michelet's *Histoire de la Révolution française*, vol. 1, ch. 2, bibliography).

Below are authors and books which though not directly concerned with the Revolution, have been essential to this work:

CHATEAUBRIAND, Francois-René, *Mémoires d'outre-tombe*, part III.

HUGO, Victor, *Choses vues*, Paris, E. Hugues, n.d., reissued in *Oeuvres inédites*, 9 vols, Paris, Hetzel, Quantin, 1886–93, (*Choses vues*, vol. 3, 1887); reissued, 4 vols, Paris, Gallimard, 1972 (vol. 1, 1830–46; vol. 2, 1847–48; vol. 3, 1849–69; vol. 4, 1870–85); reissued Laffont, coll. 'Bouquins', 1988. The best chronicle of the era.

HUGO, V., *Les Misérables*, Paris, Pagnerre, 1862; numerous reissues, e.g. Gallimard, La Pléiade, Folio, 1973 (English translation, *Les Misérables*, Viking Penguin, 1982. An extraordinary account of Paris in the last years of its age of revolutions, with Orleanist society viewed by the poet and peer of France. Compare Hugo's portrait of Louis-Philippe with that depicted by Chateaubriand.)

TOCQUEVILLE, Alexis de, *Oeuvres complètes*, part III, vols 1 and 2 (1962 and 1985): *Ecrits et discours politiques*; part VIII (1967): *Correspondance d'Alexis de Tocqueville et de Gustave de Beaumont*, 3 vols; part XI (1959): *Correspondance d'Alexis de Tocqueville avec Pierre-Paul Royer-Collard et avec Jean-Jacques Ampère*.

BONALD, Louis de, Vicomte de, *Réflexions sur la Révolution de 1830*, reissued Presses de l'Institut d'Etudes Politiques de Toulouse, 1984.

MICHELET, Jules, *Mon Journal*, Paris, Marpon et Flammarion, 1888; reissued, 4 vols, Paris, Gallimard, 1959–76 (vol. 1, 1828–48; vol. 2, 1849–60; vol. 3, 1861–7; vol. 4, 1868–74).

COMTE, Auguste, *Cours de philosophie positive*, Paris, Société Positiviste, 1830–42; reissued, 2 vols, as *Philosophie première et physique sociale*, Paris, Hermann, 1975 (English translation, *Introduction to Positive Philosophy*, Indianapolis, Hackett, 1988).

The great polemic of the 1840s over freedom of education may be approached via Michelet and Quinet, on the anticlerical side, for instance:

MICHELET, Jules and Edgar Quinet, *Des Jésuites*, Paris, Hachette et Paulin, 1843.

QUINET, Edgar, *Le Christianisme et la Révolution française*, Paris, Comon, 1845; reissued, Paris, Fayard, 'Corpus des oeuvres de philosophie en langue française', 1984.

On the side of the Church, see three authors who loathed one another (the priest who had broken with Rome, the Gallican liberal, the ultramontane), representing the three paths taken by post-revolutionary catholicism:

LAMENNAIS, Félicité Robert de, *Des Progrès de la Révolution et de la guerre contre l'Eglise*, Paris, Belin, Mandar and Devaux, 1929.

LAMENNAIS, F. R. de, *Mélanges catholiques* (extracts from *L'Avenir*), 2 vols, Paris, Agence Générale pour la Défense de la Liberté Religieuse, 1831.

LAMENNAIS, F. R. de, *Paroles d'un croyant*, 1833, Paris, E. Renduel, 1834.

LAMENNAIS, F. R. de, *Le Livre du peuple*, Paris, Delloye, 1838.

DUPANLOUP, Félix, bishop of Orléans, *Lettre à M. le duc de Broglie, rapporteur du projet de loi relatif à l'instruction secondaire*, Paris, Poussielgue-Rusand, 1844.

DUPANLOUP, F., *Des Associations religieuses, véritable état de la question*, Paris, Lecoffre, 1845.

DUPANLOUP, F., *De la liberté d'enseignement, état actuel de la question*, Paris, A. René, 1847.

VEUILLOT, Louis, *De l'action des laïques dans la question religieuse (réponse à La Presse)*, Paris, Bureau de 'L'Univers', 1843.

VEUILLOT, L., *Lettre à M. Villemain, ministre de l'Instruction publique, sur la liberté d'enseignement*, Paris, Bureau de 'L'Univers', 1843.

Lastly, the 'social question', the centre of so many anxieties, hopes and fears in the France of that period, fed both a vast literature of inquiry and reform, and the upsurge of socialist thinking. The first area can be approached by:

VILLENEUVE-BARGEMONT, Jean-Paul (Vicomte d'Alban), *Economie politique chrétienne ou recherches sur la nature et les causes du paupérisme en France et en Europe et sur les moyens de le soulager et de le prévenir*, 4 vols, Paris, Paulin, 1834.

GÉRANDO, Gustave, Baron de, *Traité de la bienfaisance publique*, 4 vols, Paris, Renouard, 1839.

VILLERMÉ, Dr Louis-René, *Tableau physique et moral des ouvriers employés dans les manufactures de coton, de laine et de soie*, 2 vols, Paris, Renouard, 1840.

As regards socialist thought, one may begin with George Sand, *Histoire de ma vie*, (vol. 1, ch. 4 and bibliography) where the circles of the socialist left are depicted by someone who shared their aspirations.

Also read:

FOURIER, Charles, *Pièges et charlatanisme des deux sectes: Saint-Simon et Owen, qui promettent l'association et le progrès . . .*, Paris, Bossange père, 1831.

FOURIER, C., *La Fausse industrie morcelée, répugnante, mensongère, et l'antidote: l'industrie naturelle, combinée, attrayante, vérifique, donnant quadruple produit*, 2 vols, Paris, Bossange père, 1835–6.

FOURIER, C., *Oeuvres complétes*, (vol. 1, *Théorie des quatre mouvements et des destinées générales*; vols 2–5, *Théorie de l'unité universelle*; vol. 6, *Le Nouveau Monde industriel et sociétaire*), Paris, 'La Phalange', 1841–5.

LEROUX, Pierre, *De l'Humanité, de son principe et de son avenir*, 2 vols, Paris, Perrotin, 1840; reissued Paris, Fayard, 'Corpus des oeuvres de philosophie en langue française', 1985.

PROUDHON, Pierre-Joseph, *Qu'est-ce que la propriété? ou recherches sur le principe du droit et du gouvernement. Premier Mémoire (1840): Qu'est-ce que la propriété? . . . Deuxime Mémoire (1841): Qu'est-ce que la propriété? . . . Troisieme Mémoire (1842)*, vol. 10 of *Oeuvres complètes*, Geneva, Slatkine, 1982, 19 vols-in-15 (facsimile of

Paris edn, 1923–59) (English translation, *What is Property?* New York, Gordon Press).

PROUDHON, P. -J., *De la création de l'ordre dans l'humanité ou principe d'organisation politique* (1843), *Oeuvres complètes*, vol. 5.

PROUDHON, P. -J., *Système des contradictions économiques ou Philosophie de la misère* (1846), *Oeuvres complètes*, vol. 1 (English translation, *System of Economic Contradictions, or, The Philosophy of Misery*, Salem, Ayer, 1972, repr. of 1888 edn). Also published in paperback, with the reply by Marx, *Misère de la philosophie*, UGE, 10/18, 1964).

BONAPARTE, Louis-Napoléon (Napoléon III), *L'Extinction du paupérisme*, Paris, Pagnerre, 1844.

Memoirs

Most of the basic works in this category are cited under chapter 6 above. The most important memoir-writers under the July monarchy were Chateaubriand, Rémusat, Guizot, Molé and Broglie. I would add another work of Guizot's, the *Lettres de Fançois Guizot à la princesse de Lieven*, with a preface by Jean Schlumberger, (3 vols, Paris, Mercure de France, 1963–4). On another intellectual level, and regarding quite another social world, there are two great memoirs by men of humble origins:

NADAUD, Martin, *Mémoires de Léonard, ancien garçon-maçon*, Bourganeuf, Duboueix, 1895; reissued Paris, Hachette, with a preface by Maurice Agulhon, 1976.

GUILLAUMIN, Émile, *La Vie d'un simple (mémoires d'un métayer)*, Paris, Stock, 1905.

The press

The four main Parisian newspapers of the era are useful for understanding the state of opinion; *La Presse, Le Siècle, Le Constitutionnel* and the *Journal des Débats*. I have made particular use of *Le National*, founded in 1830, both because of the talent of Armand Carrel, and also because it is perhaps the paper in which one can best get a sense of the tension between the 'resistance' and the 'movement'. Similarly useful is *L'Atelier* (from 1840) for Buchez, and *La Réforme* (from 1843), the supreme organ for the 'social question'.

General history

THUREAU-DANGIN, Paul, *Histoire de la monarchie de Juillet*, 7 vols, Paris, Plon, Nourrit, 1884–92. (This remains the outstanding reference work on the political history of the regime, as is Vaulabelle on the Restoration.)

DUVERGIER DE HAURANNE, Prosper, *Histoire du gouvernement parlementaire en France, 1814–1848*, 10 vols, Paris, Michel-Lévy frères, 1857–71.

CHARLETY, Sebastien, *La Monarchie de Juillet*, Paris, 1921, vol. 5 of Ernest Lavisse (ed.), of *Histoire de France contemporaine, depuis la Revolution jusqu'à la paix de 1919*, 10 vols, Paris, Hachette, 1921–2.

COLLINGHAM, H. A. C., *The July Monarchay, A Political History of France, 1830–1848*, London and New York, Longman, 1988.

TUDESQ, André-Jean, *Les Grands Notables en France, 1840–1849*, 2 vols, Paris, PUF, 1964.

Works dealing with particular points

On the Catholic Church:

DUROSELLE, Jean-Baptiste, *Les Débuts du catholicisme social en France (1822–1870)*, Paris, PUF, 1951.

MARCILHACY, Christianne, *Le Diocèse d'Orléans au milieu du XIXe siécle, les hommes et leurs mentalités*, Paris, Sirey, 1964.

DROULERS, Paul, *Action pastorale et problèmes sociaux sous la monarchie de Juillet chez Mgr d'Astros, archevêque de Toulouse, censeur de Lamennais*, Paris, Société d'Histoire Ecclésiastique de la France, Vrin, 1953.

On political life at the local, provincial level:

AGULHON, Maurice, *La République au village, Les populations du Var de la Révolution à la Seconde République*, Paris, Plon, 1970 (English translation, *The Republic in the Village: The People of the Var from the French Revolution to the Second Republic*, Cambridge University Press, 1982).

LEVÊQUE, Pierre, *Une société provinciale: la Bourgogne sous la monarchie de Fuillet*, Paris, EHESS, 1983.

On economic life:

LEVY-LEBOYER, Maurice, 'La croissance économique en France au XIXe siècle', *Annales, ESC* (July–August 1968).

GILLE, Bertrand, *La Banque et le Crédit en France de 1815 à 1848*, Paris, PUF, 1959.

On the social question:

CHEVALIER, Louis, *Classes laborieuses, classes dangereuses à Paris pendant la première moitié du XIXe siècle*, Paris, Plon, 1958; resissued Hachette, coll. 'Pluriel', 1984.

8   THE SECOND REPUBLIC

Modern historians of the Second Republic have the good fortune to come after the two greatest observer/commentators of the event: Tocqueville and Marx. Although these two authors staunchly embraced different and opposing political agendas, they did share the same query: why did the Second Republic in France end, like the First, in a Bonaparte? Their responses to this enigma differ widely, but their accounts and analyses have offered a wealth of material for the present work.

MARX, Karl, *Les luttes de classes en France (1848–1850)*, and *Le Dix-huit Brumaire de Louis Bonaparte*, Paris, Scheicher frères, 1900; both works reissued by Messidor, Editions Sociales, 1984 (English translations, *Class Struggles in France*, and *The 18th Brumaire of Louis Bonaparte*, New York, International Publishing, 1964 and 1963).

TOCQUEVILLE, Alexis de, *Souvenirs*, Paris, C. Levy, 1893, in *Oeuvres complètes*, vol. 12 (English translation, *Recollections*, New York, Anchor Books, Doubleday, 1971).

Literary and politico-literary sources

SAND George, *Correspondance*, vol. 2.

FLAUBERT Gustave, *L'Education sentimentale*, 2 vols, Paris, Michel Lévy, 1870; numerous recent reissues: Le Seuil, coll. 'L'Intégrale', 1970; (an antidote to

George Sand's enthusiasm. Garnier Flammarion, 1980 English translation, *Sentimental Education*, Oxford University Press).

LAMARTINE, Alphonse de, *Histoire de la révolution de Février 48*, 2 vols, Paris, Perrotin, 1849 (English translation, *History of the French Révolution of 1848*, New York, AMS Press (reprint of 1854 edn).

STERN, Daniel (pseudonym of Marie de Flavigny, Comtesse d'Agoult), *Histoire de la révolution de 1848*, 3 vols, Paris, Sandre, 1850–3.

TOCQUEVILLE, Alexis de, *Ecrits et discours politiques*, in *Oeuvres complètes*, part III, vol. 2.

GUIZOT, François, *De la démocratie en France*, Paris, Masson, 1849 (analysis by the loser in February 1848. English translation, *Democracy in France*, New York, Fertig, 1974, repr. of 1849 edn).

THIERS, Adolphe, *De la propriété*, Paris, Paulin, Lheureux, 1848.

PROUDHON Pierre-Joseph, *Actes de la révolution. Résistance: Louis Blanc et Pierre Leroux, précédé de: Qu'est-ce que le gouvernement? Qu'est-ce que Dieu?*, Paris, Bureau de la 'Voix du peuple', 1849.

PROUDHON, P. -J., *Les Confessions d'un révolutionnaire, pour servir d'instruction aux souscripteurs et adhérents à la Banque du peuple*, Paris, Boule, 1849.

PROUDHON, P. -J., *Idées révolutionnaires*, Paris, Garnier frères, 1849.

PROUDHON, P. -J., *Au président de la République, le socialisme reconnaissant*, Paris, Quai des Grands Augustins, 1850.

PROUDHON, P. -J., *Idée générale de la révolution au XIXe siècle* (selected studies on revolutionary and industrial practice), Paris, Garnier frères, 1851.

During this period, discussion about the French Revolution remained lively, to say the least; in fact it provided the entire political repertoire of the regime, from start to finish. From Lamartine to Louis-Napoleon Bonaparte, by way of Thiers, Tocqueville, Louis Blanc, Hugo, Michelet and Quinet, the actors of 1848 relived the great revolutionary drama which they all knew by heart, even if through contradictory interpretations. Marx was the ironical witness to this parody which had become general. No systematic study of the matter exists, but the reader may approach it via a comparison of Michelet's and Louis Blanc's histories of the French Revolution. The former was largely written, first euphorically then with sadness, under the Second Republic; the latter was written in premature exile (Louis Blanc left for England after the *journées* of June 1848) as a socialist riposte to Michelet's republican tableau.

Memoirs

Aside from Tocqueville's *Souvenirs*, no memoir equals Victor Hugo's *Choses vues* as a chronicle of the Second Republic. See also:

MICHELET, Jules, *Mon Journal* (vol. 2, ch. 7, bibliography).

RÉMUSAT, Charles de, *Mémoires de ma vie*, part IV.

FALLOUX, Alfred, Comte de, *Mémoires d'un royaliste*, 2 vols, Paris, Perrin, 1888.

NADAUD, Martin, *Mémoires de Léonard* (an original contribution to the history of the republican and socialist left in the legislative Assembly).

General history

GARNIER-PAGÈS, Louis-Antoine, *Histoire de la Révolution de 1848*, To vols, Paris, Pagnerre, 1861–72.

RENARD, Georges, *La République de 1848*, part IX of Jaurès's *Histoire socialiste*.

LA GORCE, Pierre, *Histoire de la Seconde République française*, 2 vols, Paris, Plon, 1887.

SEIGNOBOS, Charles, *La Révolution de 1843 et le Second Empire (1848–1859)*, vol. 4 of Ernest Lavisse, *Histoire de France*.

AGULHON, Maurice, *1848 ou l'apprentissage de la République, 1848–1852*, Paris, Le Seuil, coll. 'Points', 1973 (English translation, *The Republican Experiment, 1848–1852*, Cambridge University Press, 1983).

MAÎTRON, Jean, *Dictionnaire biographique du mouvement ouvrier français, 1789–1864*, 3 vols, Paris, ed. Ouvrières, 1964–6 (an extremely valuable work, in which are to be found very many militants of 1848).

Actes du Congrès du centenaire de la Révolution de 1848, Paris, PUF, 1948.

Works dealing with particular points

VIALLANEIX, Paul, *La Voie royale. Essai sur l'idée de temps dans l'oeuvre de Michelet*, Paris, Delagrave, 1959. (This is an important work because it gives, through Michelet, a collective image of the men of 1848.)

On June 1848:

SCHMIDT, Charles, *Des ateliers nationaux aux barricades de Juin*, Paris, PUF, 1984.

TRAUGOTT, Mark, *Armies of the Poor: Determinants of Working-Class Participation in the Parisian Insurrection of June 1848*, Princeton University Press, 1985.

On the 'republican party', an old work but one which has not been superseded:

WEILL, Georges, *Histoire du parti républicain en France: 1814–1870*, Paris, F. Alcan, 1900, reissued 1928.

On the working-class and socialist left:

SEWELL, William H., *Work and Revolution in France*, Cambridge University Press, 1980.

On the 1849 elections, an important article:

BOUILLON, J., 'Les démocrates socialistes aux élections de 1849', *Revue Française de Science Politique* (1956).

On the Church and freedom of education:

MICHEL, Henri, *La Loi Falloux*, Paris, Hachette, 1906.

PROST, Antoine, *L'Enseignement en France 1800–1967*, Paris, A. Colin, coll. 'U', 1968, reissued 1986.

On the Catholicism of 1848:

PIERRARD Pierre, *Mille huit cent quarante-huit, les Pauvres, l'Evangile et la Révolution*, Paris, Desclée, 1977.

BERENSON, Edward, *Populist Religion and Left-Wing Politics in France 1830–1852*, Princeton University Press, 1984.

Two great provincial monographs:

VIGIER, Philippe, *La Seconde République dans la région alpine. Études politiques et sociales*, 2 vols, Paris, PUF, 1963.

CORBIN, Alain, *Archaïsme et modernité en Limousin au XIXe siècle (1845–1880)*, 2 vols, Paris, Rivière, 1975.

On the end of the Republic:

DANSETTE, Adrien, *LOUIS NAPOLÉON A LA CONQUÊTE DU POUVOIR*, Paris, Hachette, 1961.

9   THE SECOND EMPIRE

Of all the French regimes in the nineteenth century, the Second Empire is the one which has given rise to the most hostile historiography; it was born of a coup d'état, and died of a national disaster; because of the circumstances of its birth and death we have tended to forget the role it played in the enrichment of the country and even, when all is said and done, in the progress of universal suffrage and democracy. In fact, it was first condemned in 1851 before the eyes of republican opinion, which would write its history between twenty-five and fifty years later. For the last half-century, history has liberated itself from Victor Hugo in order to understand what constituted the staying-power and the brilliance of the 'little' Napoleon.

Literary and politico-literary sources

In the literature of radical animosity towards the Second Empire, I quote the two most celebrated émigrés, who remained outside France to the very end:

HUGO, Victor, *Histoire d'un crime*, 2 vols, Paris, C. Lévy, 1877–8.

HUGO, V., *Les Châtiments*, Brussels, H. Samuel, 1853; also published the same year in Geneva, New York and St Helier, Imprimerie Universelle; reissued Paris, J. Hetzel, 1870.

QUINET, Edgar, *Lettres d'exil à Michelet et à divers amis*, followed by *Lettres après l'exil*, 4 vols, Paris, C. Lévy, 1885–6.

In order to give some qualification to this picture of an intelligentsia totally up in arms against 2 December 1851, see:

PROUDHON, Pierre-Joseph, *La Révolution sociale démontrée par le coup d'Etat du 2 décembre*, Paris, Garnier frères, 1852.

PROUDHON, P. -J., *Mélanges d'articles de journaux, 1848–1852*, vols 17–19 of *Oeuvres complètes*, 26 vols, Paris, Lacroix, Verboeckhoven.

SAND, George, *Correspondance*, vol. 3: 1848–53.

On the era:

TOCQUEVILLE, Alexis de, *Correspondance d'Alexis de Tocqueville et de Gustave de Beaumont*, part VIII (1967), vol. 3 in *Oeuvres complètes*; *Correspondance d'Alexis de Tocqueville et de Louis de Kergolay*, part XIII (1977); *Correspondance d'Alexis de Tocqueville avec Pierre-Paul Royer-Collard et avec Jean-Jacques Ampère*, part XI (1959).

SAND, George and Gustave Flaubert, *Correspondance entre George Sand et Gustave Flaubert*, Paris, C. Lévy, 1904; ed. Alphonse Jacobs, Paris, Flammarion, 1981.

ZOLA, Emile, *Les Rougon-Macquart. Histoire naturelle et sociale d'une famille sous le Second Empire*, ed. Henri Mitterand, 5 vols, Paris, Jean-Jacques Pauvert, 1972.

TAINE, Hippolyte, *Correspondance, in Oeuvres complètes*, 4 vols, Paris, Hachette, 1902.

FERRY, Jules, *Discours et opinions*, vol. 1, ed. Robiquet, Paris, Armand Colin, 1893.

OLLIVIER, Emile, *L'Empire libéral*, 14 vols, Paris, Garnier, 1895–1915.

DU CAMP, Maxime, *Souvenirs d'un demi-siècle*, Paris, Hachette, 1949.

PRÉVOST-PARADOL, Lucien, *La France Nouvelle*, Paris, Michel-Lévy frères, 1868.

RENAN, Ernest, 'Monarchie constitutionnelle en France', *Revue des Deux Mondes* (November 1869).

JAURÈS, Jean, *La Guerre franco-allemande de 1870–1871*, Paris, G. Rouff, 1908; reissued Flammarion, 1970.

The debate on the French Revolution was fuelled more than ever during the Second Empire, notably within the liberal and republican opposition: the coup d'état of 2 December and the revival of the Bonapartist despotism reawakened the problem of the relationship between democracy and liberalism in the revolutionary tradition.

The question was dominated by de Tocqueville's *L'Ancien Régime*, which came out in 1856. But the author died in 1859 before being able to write the second volume, which was to be devoted to the Revolution.

See, on the Revolution, from the liberal side:

PIERRE, Lanfrey, *Essai sur la Révolution* (Paris, Chamerot, 1858) and, from the 'Robespierrist' side, the biography of Robespierre by Ernest Hamel, *Histoire de Robespierre* (3 vols, Paris, Lacroix Verboeckhoven, 1865–7).

In addition, Louis Blanc published from London his great *Histoire de la Revolution française*, (12 vols, Paris, Langlois et Leclercq, 1847–62).

The most significant and important work on the subject appeared in autumn 1865. This was Edgar Quinet's *La Révolution*, the crowning achievement of his *Philosophie de l'histoire de France*, which appeared in 1854 (see vol. 3 in *Oeuvres complètes*, 10 vols, Paris, Pagnerre, 1857–8). Exiled in Veytaux on the shores of Lake Geneva, he was trying, in his own way – which was not Tocqueville's – to make sense of why state despotism returned in the revolutionary tradition of 1789. His work caused a huge polemic with many participants, notably Alphonse Peyrat, Louis Blanc, Emile Ollivier, Jules Ferry and Michelet himself. On this topic see:

FURET François, *La Gauche et la Révolution au milieu du XIXe siècle. Edgar Quinet et la question du jacobinisme, 1865–1870*, Paris, Hachette, 1986.

Lastly, I should like to cite the following memoirs:

MICHELET, Jules, *Mon Journal*.

RÉMUSAT, Charles de, *Mémoires de ma vie*, vols 4 and 5.

GONCOURT, Edmond and Jules, *Journal. Mémoires de la vie littéraire*, Imprimerie Nationale de Monaco, 1956–7; reissued Paris, Laffont, coll. 'Bouquins', 1990.

OLLIVIER, Emile, *Journal (1844–1869)*, Paris, Julliard, 1961.

DARIMON, Alfred, memoirs published between 1883 and 1887 under various titles, notably *Histoire d'un parti. Le Tiers Parti sous l'Empire (1863–1866)*, Paris, Le Dentu, 1887.

See also the very useful *Dictionnaire universel des contemporains* by Louis-Gustave Vapereau (2 vols, Paris, Hachette, 1858; numerous reissues under the Second Empire and after, 1861, 1865, 1870, 1880, 1893 etc.).

The Press

The press is of course more interesting to look at in the second part of the regime, under the so-called 'liberal Empire'. I found useful *La Presse* of Emile de Girardin, Auguste Nefftzer's *Le Temps*, Adolphe Guéroult's *L'Opinion Nationale*, and lastly Alphonse Peyrat's *l'Avenir National*.

General history

The best portrait of Napoleon III can be found in Tocqueville's *Souvenirs*. See also Dansette, *Louis Napoléon à la conquête du pouvoir*.

On the political system of the second Napoleon, the essential works are:
ZELDIN, Theodore, *The Political System of Napoleon III*, London, Macmillan, 1958.
PRELOT, Marcel, 'La signification constitutionnelle du Second Empire', *Revue Française de Science Politique* (January–March 1953).

Works on the period as a whole

LA GORCE, Pierre de, *Histoire du Second Empire*, 7 vols, Paris, Plon, 1894–1904.
POUTHAS, Charles, *Histoire politique du Second Empire*, Paris, CDU, 1954.
SEIGNOBOS, Charles, vol. 6 (*La Révolution de 1848. Le Second Empire*) and vol. 7 (*Le déclin de l'Empire et l'éstablissement de la ILLe République*) of *Lavisse, Histoire de la France contemporaine*.
DANSETTE, Adrien, *Du 2 décembre au 4 septembre*, Paris, Hachette, 1972.
PLESSIS, Alain, *De la fête impériale au mur des fédérés, 1852–1871*, Paris, Le Seuil, coll. 'Points', 1973.
GIRARD, Louis, *La Politique extérieure du Second Empire*, Paris, Gallimard, 1946.

Works on particular topics

On the social and economic take-off see:
BRAUDEL, Fernand and Ernest Labrousse, *Histoire économique et sociale de la France*, 4 parts in 8 vols Paris, PUF, 1976–9; see the two vols of part III, *De 1789 a 1880: L'Avènement de l'ère industrielle*.
GIRARD Louis, *La Politique des travaux publics du Second Empire*, Paris, Armand Colin, 1952.
CARON, François, *Histoire d'un grand réseau francais: la Compagnie des Chemins de fer du Nord de 1846 à 1936*, Paris and The Hague, Mouton, 1972.
PINKNEY, David Henry, *Napoleon III and the Rebuilding of Paris*, Princeton University Press, 1958.

On politics:
ZELDIN, Theodore, *Emile Ollivier and the Liberal Empire of Napoleon III*, Oxford, Clarendon Press, 1963.
GIRARD, Louis et al. *Les Elections de 1869*, Paris, Rivière, 1960.

On the relations between Church and state:
LATREILLE, André, Jean-Rémy Palanque, Etienne Delaruelle and René Rémond, *Histoire du catholicisme français*, vol. 3, Paris, Spes, 1962.
MARCILHACY, Christianne, *Le Diocèse d'Orléans sous l'épiscopat de Mgr Dupanloup, 1849–1878*, Paris, Plon, 1962.
MAURIAN, Jean, *La Politique ecclésiastique du Second Empire*, Paris, Alcan, 1930.

Regional or local monographs

ARMENGAUD, André, *Les populations de l'Est aquitain au début de l'époque contemporaine. Recherches sur une région moins développée (vers 1845–vers 1871)*, Paris and The Hague, Mouton, 1961.

CORBIN, Alain, *Archaïsme et modernité en Limousin au XIXe siècle.*
THABAULT, Roger, *Mon village. Ses hommes. Ses routes. Son école . . . (1845–1914. L'ascension d'un peuple)*, Paris, Delagrave, 1944.

Biographies

GUIRAL, Pierre, *Prévost-Paradol, 1829–1870. Pensées et action d'un libéral sous le Second Empire*, Paris, PUF, 1955.
ROHR, Jean, *Victor Duruy, ministre de Napoléon III. Essai sur la politique de l'Instruction publique au temps de l'Empire libéral*, Paris, Librairie Générale de Jurisprudence, 1967.

10 THE REPUBLIC

The period separating the collapse of the Second Empire and the defeat of General Mac-Mahon, between 1870 and 1877, finally saw the institution of a lasting regime in post-revolutionary France, thanks to the passing of the three 'constitutional' laws of 1875, and the republicans' victory in the 1877 elections. On this dual development, both institutional and socio-political, there is an incomparable historian, the author of two works which are masterpieces:

HALÉVY, Daniel, *La Fin des notables*, Paris, Grasset, 1930 (English translation, *The End of the Notables*, Middletown, Conn., Wesleyan University Press, 1974).
HALÉVY, D., *La République des ducs*, Paris, Grasset, 1937.

Literary and politico-literary sources

MARX, Karl, *La Guerre civile en France*, Paris, 1871, reissued Paris, Editions Sociales, 1953, (English translation, *The Civil War in France*, New York, International Publishers, 1988).
FLAUBERT, Gustave, *Correspondance*, 4 vols, Paris, G. Charpentier, 1887–93; reissued Paris, Bibliothèque Charpentier, Eugène Fasquelle, 1913 (vol. 4 covers the period from 1870); reissued, 2 vols, Paris, Gallimard, La Pléiade, 1973, 1980) (vol. 1, January 1830–June 1851; vol. 2, July 1851–December 1858).
SAND, George, *Correspondance*, vol. 7 (1870–6).
TAINE, Hippolyte, *Correspondance*, vols 3 and 4.
RENAN, Ernest, *La Réforme intellectuelle et morale de la* France, Paris, Michel-Lévy frères, 1871; reissued Paris, UGE, 1967.
RENAN, E., *Caliban, suite de 'La Tempête', drame philosophique*, Paris, C. Lévy, 1878; reissued 1907.
LITTRÉ, Emile, *Conservation, révolution et positivisme*, Paris, Ladrance, 1852; reissued Paris, Bureaux de 'La Philosophie positive', 1879. (A fundamental book as regards the positivist origins of the victorious republican ideology in the 1870s. In the reissue of 1879 Littré adds vital commentaries.)
RENOUVIER, Charles-Bernard Joseph, *Science de la Morale*, 2 vols, Paris, Ladrange, 1869; reissued Paris, Alcan, 1908.
REVOUVIER, C. -B. J., *Uchronie (l'utopie de l'histoire), esquisse historique apocryphe du développement de la civilisation européenne tel qu'il n'a pas été, tel qu'il aurait pu être . . .*, Paris, Bureau de la 'Critique Philosophique', 1876.
LABOULAYE, Edouard de, *Questions constitutionnelles*, Paris, Charpentier, 1872.
LABOULAYE, E., *La République constitutionnelle*, Paris, Charpentier, 1871.

FERRY, Jules, *Discours et opinions*, ed. J. Robiquet, 7 vols, Paris, Armand Colin, 1893–7.

GAMBETTA, Léon, *Lettres*, ed. D. Halévy and E. Pillias, Paris, Grasset, 1938.

MEMOIRS

RÉMUSAT, Charles de, *Mémoires*, vol. 5.

BROGLIE, Jacques Victor Albert, Duc de, *Mémoires*, Paris, Calmann-Lévy, 1938.

FAVRE, Jules, *Le Gouvernement de défense nationale* (vol. 1, *Du 30 juin au 31 octobre 1870*; vol. 2, *Du 31 octobre 1870 au 28 janvier 1871; vol. 3, Du 29 janvier au 22 juillet 1871*), Paris, Plon, 1871–5.

MEAUX Vicomte de, *Souvenirs politiques, 1871–1877*, Paris, Plon, 1905.

ADAM, Madame Vve Edmond, née Juliette Lamber, *Nos angoisses et nos luttes, 1871–1873*, Paris, Lemerre, 1907.

PELLETAN, Camille, *La Semaine de mai*, Paris, Dreyfus, 1880. (Account of the massacres which accompanied the recapture of Paris by the Versailles troops. Its reissue in 1889 provoked a scandal.)

RANC, Arthur, *Souvenirs. Correspondance. 1831–1908*, Paris, Cornély, 1913.

THIERS, Adolphe, *Thiers au pouvoir (1871–1873)* (his letters, annotated by G. Bouniols), Paris, Delagrave, 1921.

NADAUD, Martin, *Mémoires de Léonard, ancien garçon-maçon.*

The Press

As under the Second Empire, the *Journal des Débats* and the *Revue des Deux Mondes* were the principal organs of intellectual society, discreetly nostalgic for Orleanism, hostile to Catholic ultramontanism, and gradually inclining towards a conservative Republic. Veuillot's *L'Univers* remained the popular newspaper of ultramontane reaction, a symbol of the clerical principle within French monarchism. For legitimism, properly speaking, the preserve of the aristocracy, see *L'Union* and the *Gazette de France*. On the left, my chief sources were Gambetta and J. Reinach's *La République Française*.

General Works

HANOTAUX, Gabriel, *Histoire de la foundation de la IIIe République*, 4 vols, Paris, Plon, 1925–6 (Équal to Vaulabelle on the Restoration, Thureau-Dangin on the July Monarchy or La Gorce on the Second Empire; informed, reliable, detailed).

SEIGNOBOS, Charles, *Le Déclin de l'Empire et l'établissement de la IIIe République, 1859–1875*, Paris, Hachette, 1921.

GOGUEL, François, *La Politique des partis sous la IIIe République*, Paris, Le Seuil, 1958.

MAYEUR, Jean-Marie, *Les Débuts de la IIIe République, 1871–1898*, Paris, Le Seuil, coll. 'Points', 1973.

RUDELLE, Odile, *La République absolue: aux origines de l'instabilité constitutionnelle de la France républicaine, 1870–1889*, Paris, Publications de l'Université de Panthéon-Sorbonne, 1982.

RÉMOND, René et al., *Atlas historique de la France contemporaine*, Paris, Armand Colin, 1966 (excellent documentary aid on the far-ranging demographic, economic, social and political variables from the start of the Third Republic).

GOGUEL, Francois (ed.), *Géographie des élections françaises sous la IIIe et la IVe République*, Paris, Armand Colin; new edn, 1970.

Works on particular topics

On the Commune:

LISSAGARAY, Prosper-Olivier, *Histoire de la Commune de 1871*, 3 vols, Paris, Maspéro, 1969, 1976 (still fundamental reading).

ROUGERIE, Jacques, *Procès des Communards*, Paris, Julliard, coll. 'Archives', 1964.

On the founding of the Third Republic:

GOUAULT, Jacques, *Comment la France est devenue républicaine*, Paris, Armand Colin, 1954.

BURY, John Patrick, *GAMBETTA and the Making of the Third Republic*, London, Longman, 1973 (remarkably well-documented study; in my opinion, the best on the subject).

On men:

CHASTENET, Jacques, *Gambetta*, Paris, Fayard, 1968.

KRAKOWSKI, Edouard, *La Naissance de la IIIe République*, and (with Challemel-Lacour) *Le Philosophe et l'homme d'Etat*, Paris, Plon, 1932.

HANOTAUX, Gabriel, *Mon temps*, vol. 2, *Gambetta et Ferry*, Paris, Plon, 1938.

RECLUS, Maurice, *Jules Favre, 1809–1880, essai de biographie historique et morale*, Paris, Hachette, 1912.

On economic and social history, two books by American historians sensitive to the relative 'backwardness' of France:

CAMERON, Rondo, *France and the Economic Development of Europe, 1800–1914. Conquests of Peace and Needs of War*, Princeton University Press, 1961.

WEBER, Eugen, *Peasants into Frenchmen. The Modernization of Rural France: 1870–1914*, Stanford University Press, 1976.

On the history of relations between Church and state:

GADILLE, Jacques, *La Pensée et l'action des évêques français au début de la IIIe République: 1870–1883*, Paris, Hachette, 1967.

OZOUF, Mona, *L'Ecole, l'Eglise et la République, 1871–1914*, Paris, Armand Colin, 1963.

On intellectual history:

DIGEON, Claude, *La Crise allemande de la pensée française*, Paris, PUF, 1959 (an excellent book full of ideas and new references).

NICOLET, Claude, *L'Idée républicaine en France 1789–1924, essai d'histoire critique*, Paris, Gallimard, 1982. (The second half of the book centres on an interesting analysis of the ideological origins of the Third Republic.)

On the constitutional inspiration:

CARRÉ DE MALBERG, *La Loi, expression de la volonté générale*, Paris, Sirey, 1932.

Glossary

Commune The revolutionary government of Paris formed in 1789; taken over by an insurrectionary committee in August 1792. The name was revived in March 1871 when a left-wing municipality defied the French (Versailles) government.

Constituent Assembly The body formed by representatives of the Third Estate and their allies in the Estates-General. It drafted France's monarchical constitution and acted as a provisional legislature from 1789 to 1791.

Convention The revolutionary single-chamber parliament, 1792–5.

Cordeliers Paris revolutionary club on the left bank of the Seine with a large working-class membership.

Corvée Unpaid feudal work on land or roads.

Cour des Aides The court of law supervising taxation.

Dévots Catholics emphasizing state support for the Church as their main policy.

Estates-General The consultative assembly summoned by Louis XVI in 1789 to consider taxation and expenditure.

Farmers General Officially appointed syndicate contracting to collect taxes.

Feuillants Constitutional monarchists who broke away from the Jacobins in protest at moves to depose Louis XVI.

Gallicanism The doctrine of the French Church's national independence (and freedom from papal control).

Generalité Tax district under the supervision of an *intendant*.

Girondins Revolutionary members of the Legislative Assembly and Convention (their nucleus was a group from the Gironde in south-western France), largely eliminated by the Jacobins in 1793.

Jacobins Paris revolutionary club of 'Friends of the Constitution' meeting in a former Jacobin (Dominican) monastery; the main centre of revolutionary, and increasingly left-wing, discussion, influential nationally through a network of Jacobin Clubs in the provinces.

Jansenists Sect believing in predestination, influential in the seventeenth century but persecuted by Louis XIV to make its members submit to state and Church authority.

Legislative Assembly The single-chamber parliament elected under the constitutional monarchy, 1791–2.

Lit de Justice Royal session of the Paris parlement at which the king presided and enforced registration (i.e. acceptance) of his edicts.

Marais See *Plaine*.

Mercantilists Advocates of protection of industry, state regulation of trade, and intervention to ensure food supplies and control prices.

Montagnards Jacobin members of the Convention occupying the highest seats (the *Montagne*), and generally supporting extreme revolutionary policies.

National Guard Civil militia formed in 1789 to maintain order and guard against counter-revolution.

Parlement High court of law in charge of regional justice, and with the right of remonstrance at royal legislation.

Perpetuels Members of the Convention automatically appointed to serve in the new assembly (1795) under the Law of the Two-Thirds.

Philosophes The rationalist and sceptical writers of the eighteenth century (e.g. Voltaire, Montesquieu, d'Alembert, Diderot) who called for the use of reason (as opposed to custom, tradition, faith or superstition) in the organization of society and the state.

Physiocrats Advocates of a free economy based primarily on agriculture, with a minimum of state regulation and internal restriction.

Plaine (or Marais) The middle group of members of the Convention, uncommitted either to the Girondins or the *Montagne*.

Provincial Estates Local assemblies of the three orders (clergy, nobility and commons).

Sansculottes Revolutionaries who made a virtue of plain dress (*culottes*, breeches, being regarded as a mark of privilege).

Sections The forty-eight areas into which Paris was divided by the Commune, each run by a revolutionary watch committee and able to organize armed *sectionnaires* to intimidate the government.

Thermidorians The politicians who took power after the fall of Robespierre on 9 Thermidor (27 July 1794).

Third Estate The commons (i.e. not clergy or nobility) in the Estates-General.

Ultramontanism Acceptance of papal authority over the French Catholic Church (as opposed to Gallican advocacy of national independence).

Index of Names

Index of Subjects

(